Pro Spring Batch

Michael T. Minella

Apress®

Pro Spring Batch

ISBN-13 (pbk): 978-1-4302-3452-4

ISBN-13 (electronic): 978-1-4302-3453-1

President and Publisher: Paul Manning
Lead Editor: Steve Anglin
Technical Reviewer: Manuel Jordan
Editorial Board: Steve Anglin, Mark Beckner, Ewan Buckingham, Gary Cornell, Jonathan Gennick, Jonathan Hassell, Michelle Lowman, James Markham, Matthew Moodie, Jeff Olson, Jeffrey Pepper, Frank Pohlmann, Douglas Pundick, Ben Renow-Clarke, Dominic Shakeshaft, Matt Wade, Tom Welsh
Coordinating Editor: Anita Castro
Copy Editor: Tiffany Taylor and Mary Behr
Compositor: Bytheway Publishing Services
Indexer: BIM Indexing & Proofreading Services
Artist: SPI Global
Cover Designer: Anna Ishchenko

To my best friend and wife, Erica.

Contents at a Glance

Contents

About the Author

■ **Michael T. Minella** is a software engineer, teacher, and author with over a decade of enterprise development experience using commercial and open source technologies. He is a software engineer for Trustwave and an instructor at DePaul University. He wrote the popular Refcard JUnit and EasyMock, was the technical reviewer for Struts 2 Web Application Development by Dave Newton, and maintains a popular blog on open source technologies.

Michael's technical background runs the gambit. From the first programming language he learned (mainframe Assembler) to the languages he uses and teaches now (Java, JavaScript, Flex/ActionScript, and so on) he has been all over the map. His passions include quality software development, learning new things, and sharing knowledge with others through both mentoring and formal teaching. When he's not in front of a computer, Michael enjoys spending time with his family and friends as well as pursuing other hobbies including woodworking and reading.

You can follow Michael on Twitter at www.twitter.com/michaelminella or read his blog at www.michaelminella.com.

About the Technical Reviewer

 **Manuel Jordan Elera** is a freelance Java developer. He designs and develops personal systems for his customers using powerful frameworks based in Java such as Spring and Hibernate, among others. Manuel is now an autodidact developer and enjoys learning new frameworks to get better results in his projects.

Manuel received a degree in systems engineering with honors, and he won the 2010 Springy Award – Community Champion. In his little free time, he likes reading the Bible and composing music with his guitar. Manuel is a senior member of the Spring Community Forums, where his username is dr_pompeii.

Manuel has been the technical reviewer for the follows books: *Pro SpringSource dm Server*, *Spring Enterprise Recipes*, *Spring Recipes* (Second Edition), and *Pro Spring Integration*.

You can contact him through his blog at http://manueljordan.wordpress.com/.

Acknowledgments

In the space of a page or so, I can't hope to convey my appreciation to everyone who helped me along the way to making this, my first book, a reality. However, I would like to call out a few specific people who have made extraordinary contributions to the process.

First, anyone who has written a book knows that although there is one name on the cover, it takes one heck of a team to write a book. Thank you to everyone at Apress for giving me the opportunity. Thanks to Steve Anglin for believing in the concept and allowing me the chance to write as a first-time author. Thank you to Anita Castro and Douglas Pundick for your relentless drive to help me finish this book. I'd also like to thank all of the editorial staff who worked on the book; your efforts made me look like I actually knew how to spell and construct an intelligent sentence.

A special thank you to Manuel Jordan, my technical reviewer. Without his thorough feedback on the text and testing of every example, this book would not be nearly what it is now.

Within my professional life, a number of people have helped me along the way to this milestone. First I'd like to thank Peter Costa and the Fees team for giving me the opportunity to work with Spring Batch in such a demanding environment. Thanks to Joel Tosi for his encouragement and for pushing me to expand who I am professionally beyond what happens in a cubicle. I'd also like to thank my manager at Trustwave, Matt Konda: his ongoing support and encouragement is more than I ever expected or could have asked for.

Thanks to David Sayer and the people on the Spring Batch team. You have not only put together a great framework but also built an amazing community around it.

Writing a book takes a toll not only on the author but on everyone in the author's life. Their support allows me to do what I do. I'd like to offer a special thank you to my family and friends who have put time with me on hold to allow me to make this dream come true. Thank you to my parents, my sister, my extended family, my wife's family, and all my friends. All of you sacrificed over the course of the eight months it took me to write this book. I love you all very much.

I conclude with the one person who has supported me without question during this entire process. While she put things on hold for us and made things happen when I couldn't, I wrote my book. My most heartfelt thank you goes to my best friend and wife, Erica. Without you, neither this book nor who I am today would be possible. I love you and thank you.

CHAPTER 1

Batch and Spring

When I graduated from Northern Illinois University back in 2001 after spending most of the previous two years working on COBOL, mainframe Assembler, and Job Control Language (JCL), I took a job as a consultant to learn Java. I specifically took that position because of the opportunity to learn Java when it was the hot new thing. Never in my wildest dreams did I think I'd be back writing about batch processing. I'm sure most Java developers don't think about batch, either. They think about the latest web framework or JVM language. They think about service-oriented architectures and things like REST versus SOAP or whatever alphabet soup is hot at the time.

But the fact is, the business world runs on batch. Your bank and 401k statements are all generated via batch processes. The e-mails you receive from your favorite stores with coupons in them? Probably sent via batch processes. Even the order in which the repair guy comes to your house to fix your laundry machine is determined by batch processing. In a time when we get our news from Twitter, Google thinks that waiting for a page refresh takes too long to provide search results, and YouTube can make someone a household name overnight, why do we need batch processing at all?

There are a few good reasons:

- You don't always have all the required information immediately. Batch processing allows you to collect information required for a given process before starting the required processing. Take your monthly bank statement as an example. Does it make sense to generate the file format for your printed statement after every transaction? It makes more sense to wait until the end of the month and look back at a vetted list of transactions from which to build the statement.

- Sometimes it makes good business sense. Although most people would love to have what they buy online put on a delivery truck the second they click Buy, that may not be the best course of action for the retailer. If a customer changes their mind and wants to cancel an order, it's much cheaper to cancel if it hasn't shipped yet. Giving the customer a few extra hours and batching the shipping together can save the retailer large amounts of money

- It can be a better use of resources. Having a lot of processing power sitting idle is expensive. It's more cost effective to have a collection of scheduled processes that run one after the other using the machine's full potential at a constant, predictable rate.

This book is about batch processing with the framework Spring Batch. This chapter looks at the history of batch processing, calls out the challenges in developing batch jobs, makes a case for developing batch using Java and Spring Batch, and finally provides a high-level overview of the framework and its features.

A History of Batch Processing

To look at the history of batch processing, you really need to look at the history of computing itself.

The time was 1951. The UNIVAC became the first commercially produced computer. Prior to this point, computers were each unique, custom-built machines designed for a specific function (for example, in 1946 the military commissioned a computer to calculate the trajectories of artillery shells). The UNIVAC consisted of 5,200 vacuum tubes, weighed in at over 14 tons, had a blazing speed of 2.25MHz (compared to the iPhone 4, which has a 1GHz processor) and ran programs that were loaded from tape drives. Pretty fast for its day, the UNIVAC was considered the first commercially available batch processor.

Before going any further into history, I should define what, exactly, batch processing is. Most of the applications you develop have an aspect of user interaction, whether it's a user clicking a link in a web app, typing information into a form on a thick client, or tapping around on phone and tablet apps. Batch processing is the exact opposite of those types of applications. *Batch processing*, for this book's purposes, is defined as the processing of data without interaction or interruption. Once started, a batch process runs to some form of completion without any intervention.

Four years passed in the evolution of computers and data processing before the next big change: high-level languages. They were first introduced with Lisp and Fortran on the IBM 704, but it was the Common Business Oriented Language (COBOL) that has since become the 800-pound gorilla in the batch-processing world. Developed in 1959 and revised in 1968, 1974, and 1985, COBOL still runs batch processing in modern business. A Gartner study[1] estimated that 60% of all global code and 85% of global business data is housed in the language. To put this in perspective, if you printed out all that code and stacked the printout, you'd have a stack 227 miles high. But that's where the innovation stalled.

COBOL hasn't seen a significant revision in a quarter of a century.[2] The number of schools that teach COBOL and its related technologies has declined significantly in favor of newer technologies like Java and .NET. The hardware is expensive, and resources are becoming scarce.

Mainframe computers aren't the only places that batch processing occurs. Those e-mails I mentioned previously are sent via batch processes that probably aren't run on mainframes. And the download of data from the point-of-sale terminal at your favorite fast food chain is batch, too. But there is a significant difference between the batch processes you find on a mainframe and those typically written for other environments (C++ and UNIX, for example). Each of those batch processes is custom developed, and they have very little in common. Since the takeover by COBOL, there has been very little in the way of new tools or techniques. Yes, cron jobs have kicked off custom-developed processes on UNIX servers and scheduled tasks on Microsoft Windows servers, but there have been no new industry-accepted tools for doing batch processes.

Until now. In 2007, Accenture announced that it was partnering with Interface21 (the original authors of the Spring framework, and now SpringSource) to develop an open source framework that would be used to create enterprise batch processes. As Accenture's first formal foray into the open source world, it chose to combine its expertise in batch processing with Spring's popularity and feature set to create a robust, easy-to-use framework. At the end of March 2008, the Spring Batch 1.0.0 release was made available to the public; it represented the first standards-based approach to batch processing in the Java world. Slightly more than a year later, in April 2009, Spring Batch went 2.0.0, adding features like replacing support for JDK 1.4 with JDK 1.5+, chunk-based processing, improved configuration options, and significant additions to the scalability options within the framework.

---

[1] http://www.gartner.com/webletter/merant/article1/article1.html

[2] There have been revisions in COBOL 2002 and Object Oriented COBOL, but their adoption has been significantly less than for previous versions.

Batch Challenges

You're undoubtedly familiar with the challenges of GUI-based programming (thick clients and web apps alike). Security issues. Data validation. User-friendly error handling. Unpredictable usage patterns causing spikes in resource utilization (have a blog post of yours show up on the front page of Slashdot to see what I mean here). All of these are byproducts of the same thing: the ability for users to interact with your software.

However, batch is different. I said earlier that a batch process is a process that can run without additional interaction to some form of completion. Because of that, most of the issues with GUI applications are no longer valid. Yes, there are security concerns, and data validation is required, but spikes in usage and friendly error handling either are predictable or may not even apply to your batch processes. You can predict the load during a process and design accordingly. You can fail quickly and loudly with only solid logging and notifications as feedback, because technical resources address any issues.

So everything in the batch world is a piece of cake and there are no challenges, right? Sorry to burst your bubble, but batch processing presents its own unique twist on many common software development challenges. Software architecture commonly includes a number of *ilities*. Maintainability. Usability. Scalability. These and other ilities are all relevant to batch processes, just in different ways.

The first three ilities—usability, maintainability, and extensibility—are related. With batch, you don't have a user interface to worry about, so usability isn't about pretty GUIs and cool animations. No, in a batch process, usability is about the code: both its error handling and its maintainability. Can you extend common components easily to add new features? Is it covered well in unit tests so that when you change an existing component, you know the effects across the system? When the job fails, do you know when, where, and why without having to spend a long time debugging? These are all aspects of usability that have an impact on batch processes.

Next is scalability. Time for a reality check: when was the last time you worked on a web site that truly had a million visitors a day? How about 100,000? Let's be honest: most web sites developed in large corporations aren't viewed nearly that many times. However, it's not a stretch to have a batch process that needs to process 100,000 to 500,000 transactions in a night. Let's consider 4 seconds to load a web page to be a solid average. If it takes that long to process a transaction via batch, then processing 100,000 transactions will take more than four days (and a month and a half for 1 million). That isn't practical for any system in today's corporate environment. The bottom line is that the scale that batch processes need to be able to handle is often one or more orders of magnitude larger than that of the web or thick-client applications you've developed in the past.

Third is availability. Again, this is different from the web or thick-client applications you may be used to. Batch processes typically aren't 24/7. In fact, they typically have an appointment. Most enterprises schedule a job to run at a given time when they know the required resources (hardware, data, and so on) are available. For example, take the need to build statements for retirement accounts. Although you can run the job at any point in the day, it's probably best to run it some time after the market has closed so you can use the closing fund prices to calculate balances. Can you run when you need to? Can you get the job done in the time allotted so you don't impact other systems? These and other questions affect the availability of your batch system.

Finally you must consider security. Typically, in the batch world, security doesn't revolve around people hacking into the system and breaking things. The role a batch process plays in security is in keeping data secure. Are sensitive database fields encrypted? Are you logging personal information by accident? How about access to external systems—do they need credentials, and are you securing those in the appropriate manner? Data validation is also part of security. Generally, the data being processed has already been vetted, but you still should be sure that rules are followed.

As you can see, plenty of technological challenges are involved in developing batch processes. From the large scale of most systems to security, batch has it all. That's part of the fun of developing batch processes: you get to focus more on solving technical issues than on moving form fields three pixels to the right on a web application. The question is, with existing infrastructures on mainframes and all the risks of adopting a new platform, why do batch in Java?

Why Do Batch Processing in Java?

With all the challenges just listed, why choose Java and an open source tool like Spring Batch to develop batch processes? I can think of six reasons to use Java and open source for your batch processes: maintainability, flexibility, scalability, development resources, support, and cost.

Maintainability is first. When you think about batch processing, you have to consider maintenance. This code typically has a much longer life than your other applications. There's a reason for that: no one sees batch code. Unlike a web or client application that has to stay up with the current trends and styles, a batch process exists to crunch numbers and build static output. As long as it does its job, most people just get to enjoy the output of their work. Because of this, you need to build the code in such a way that it can be easily modified without incurring large risks.

Enter the Spring framework. Spring was designed for a couple of things you can take advantage of: testability and abstraction. The decoupling of objects that the Spring framework encourages with dependency injection and the extra testing tools Spring provides allow you to build a robust test suite to minimize the risk of maintenance down the line. And without yet digging into the way Spring and Spring Batch work, Spring provides facilities to do things like file and database I/O declaratively. You don't have to write JDBC code or manage the nightmare that is the file I/O API in Java. Things like transactions and commit counts are all handled by the framework, so you don't have to manage where you are in the process and what to do when something fails. These are just some of the maintainability advantages that Spring Batch and Java provide for you.

The flexibility of Java and Spring Batch is another reason to use them. In the mainframe world, you have one option: run COBOL on a mainframe. That's it. Another common platform for batch processing is C++ on UNIX. This ends up being a very custom solution because there are no industry-accepted batch-processing frameworks. Neither the mainframe nor the C++/UNIX approach provides the flexibility of the JVM for deployments and the feature set of Spring Batch. Want to run your batch process on a server, desktop, or mainframe with *nix or Windows? It doesn't matter. Need to scale your process to multiple servers? With most Java running on inexpensive commodity hardware anyway, adding a server to a rack isn't the capital expenditure that buying a new mainframe is. In fact, why own servers at all? The cloud is a great place to run batch processes. You can scale out as much as you want and only pay for the CPU cycles you use. I can't think of a better use of cloud resources than batch processing.

However, the "write once, run anywhere" nature of Java isn't the only flexibility that comes with the Spring Batch approach. Another aspect of flexibility is the ability to share code from system to system. You can use the same services that already are tested and debugged in your web applications right in your batch processes. In fact, the ability to access business logic that was once locked up on some other platform is one of the greatest wins of moving to this platform. By using POJOs to implement your business logic, you can use them in your web applications, in your batch processes—literally anywhere you use Java for development.

Spring Batch's flexibility also goes toward the ability to scale a batch process written in Java. Let's look at the options for scaling batch processes:

- *Mainframe:* The mainframe has limited additional capacity for scalability. The only true way to accomplish things in parallel is to run full programs in parallel on the single piece of hardware. This approach is limited by the fact that you need to write and maintain code to manage the parallel processing and the difficulties associated with it, such as error handling and state management across programs. In addition, you're limited by the resources of a single machine.

- *Custom processing:* Starting from scratch, even in Java, is a daunting task. Getting scalability and reliability correct for large amounts of data is very difficult. Once again, you have the same issue of coding for load balancing. You also have large infrastructure complexities when you begin to distribute across physical devices or virtual machines. You must be concerned with how communication works between pieces. And you have issues of data reliability. What happens when one of your custom-written workers goes down? The list goes on. I'm not saying it can't be done; I'm saying that your time is probably better spent writing business logic instead of reinventing the wheel.

- *Java and Spring Batch:* Although Java by itself has the facilities to handle most of the elements in the previous item, putting the pieces together in a maintainable way is very difficult. Spring Batch has taken care of that for you. Want to run the batch process in a single JVM on a single server? No problem. Your business is growing and now needs to divide the work of bill calculation across five different servers to get it all done overnight? You're covered. Data reliability? With little more than some configuration and keeping some key principals in mind, you can have transaction rollback and commit counts completely handled.

As you see as you dig into the Spring Batch framework, the issues that plague the previous options for batch processing can be mitigated with well-designed and tested solutions. Up to now, this chapter has talked about technical reasons for choosing Java and open source for your batch processing. However, technical issues aren't the only reasons for a decision like this. The ability to find qualified development resources to code and maintain a system is important. As mentioned earlier, the code in batch processes tends to have a significantly longer lifespan than the web apps you may be developing right now. Because of this, finding people who understand the technologies involved is just as important as the abilities of the technologies themselves. Spring Batch is based on the extremely popular Spring framework. It follows Spring's conventions and uses Spring's tools as well as any other Spring-based application. So, any developer who has Spring experience will be able to pick up Spring Batch with a minimal learning curve. But will you be able to find Java and, specifically, Spring resources?

One of the arguments for doing many things in Java is the community support available. The Spring family of frameworks enjoy a large and very active community online through their forums. The Spring Batch project in that family has had one of the fastest-growing forums of any Spring project to date. Couple that with the strong advantages associated with having access to the source code and the ability to purchase support if required, and all support bases are covered with this option.

Finally you come to cost. Many costs are associated with any software project: hardware, software licenses, salaries, consulting fees, support contracts, and more. However, not only is a Spring Batch solution the most bang for your buck, but it's also the cheapest overall. Using commodity hardware and open source operating systems and frameworks (Linux, Java, Spring Batch, and so on), the only recurring costs are for development salaries, support contracts, and infrastructure—much less than the recurring licensing costs and hardware support contracts related to other options.

I think the evidence is clear. Not only is using Spring Batch the most sound route technically, but it's also the most cost-effective approach. Enough with the sales pitch: let's start to understand exactly what Spring Batch is.

Other Uses for Spring Batch

I bet by now you're wondering if replacing the mainframe is all Spring Batch is good for. When you think about the projects you face on an ongoing basis, it isn't every day that you're ripping out COBOL code. If that was all this framework was good for, it wouldn't be a very helpful framework. However, this framework can help you with many other use cases.

The most common use case is data migration. As you rewrite systems, you typically end up migrating data from one form to another. The risk is that you may write one-off solutions that are poorly tested and don't have the data-integrity controls that your regular development has. However, when you think about the features of Spring Batch, it seems like a natural fit. You don't have to do a lot of coding to get a simple batch job up and running, yet Spring Batch provides things like commit counts and rollback functionality that most data migrations should include but rarely do.

A second common use case for Spring Batch is any process that requires parallelized processing. As chipmakers approach the limits of Moore's Law, developers realize that the only way to continue to increase the performance of apps is not to process single transactions faster, but to process more transactions in parallel. Many frameworks have recently been released that assist in parallel processing. Apache Hadoop's MapReduce implementation, GridGain, and others have come out in recent years to attempt to take advantage of both multicore processors and the numerous servers available via the cloud. However, frameworks like Hadoop require you to alter your code and data to fit their algorithms or data structures. Spring Batch provides the ability to scale your process across multiple cores or servers (as shown in Figure 1-1 with master/slave step configurations) and still be able to use the same objects and datasources that your web applications use.

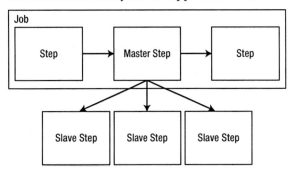

Figure 1-1. *Simplifying parallel processing*

Finally you come to constant or 24/7 processing. In many use cases, systems receive a constant or near-constant feed of data. Although accepting this data at the rate it comes in is necessary for preventing backlogs, when you look at the processing of that data, it may be more performant to batch the data into chunks to be processed at once (as shown in Figure 1-2). Spring Batch provides tools that let you do this type of processing in a reliable, scalable way. Using the framework's features, you can do things like read messages from a queue, batch them into chunks, and process them together in a never-ending loop. Thus you can increase throughput in high-volume situations without having to understand the complex nuances of developing such a solution from scratch.

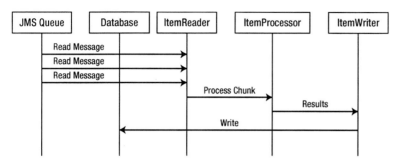

Figure 1-2. Batching JMS processing to increase throughput

As you can see, Spring Batch is a framework that, although designed for mainframe-like processing, can be used to simplify a variety of development problems. With everything in mind about what batch is and why you should use Spring Batch, let's finally begin looking at the framework itself.

The Spring Batch Framework

The Spring Batch framework (Spring Batch) was developed as a collaboration between Accenture and SpringSource as a standards-based way to implement common batch patterns and paradigms.

Features implemented by Spring Batch include data validation, formatting of output, the ability to implement complex business rules in a reusable way, and the ability to handle large data sets. You'll find as you dig through the examples in this book that if you're familiar at all with Spring, Spring Batch just makes sense.

Let's start at the 30,000-foot view of the framework, as shown in Figure 1-3.

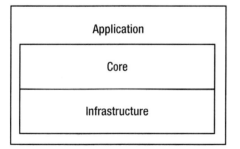

Figure 1-3. The Spring Batch architecture

Spring Batch consists of three tiers assembled in a layered configuration. At the top is the *application layer,* which consists of all the custom code and configuration used to build out your batch processes. Your business logic, services, and so on, as well as the configuration of how you structure your jobs, are all considered the application. Notice that the application layer doesn't sit on top of but instead wraps the other two layers, core and infrastructure. The reason is that although most of what you develop consists of the application layer working with the core layer, sometimes you write custom infrastructure pieces such as custom readers and writers.

The application layer spends most of its time interacting with the next layer, the core. The *core layer* contains all the pieces that define the batch domain. Elements of the core component include the Job and Step interfaces as well as the interfaces used to execute a Job: JobLauncher and JobParameters.

Below all this is the *infrastructure layer*. In order to do any processing, you need to read and write from files, databases, and so on. You must be able to handle what to do when a job is retried after a failure. These pieces are considered common infrastructure and live in the infrastructure component of the framework.

■**Note** A common misconception is that Spring Batch is or has a scheduler. It doesn't. There is no way within the framework to schedule a job to run at a given time or based on a given event. There are a number of ways to launch a job, from a simple cron script to Quartz or even an enterprise scheduler like UC4, but none within the framework itself. Chapter 6 covers launching a job.

Let's walk through some features of Spring Batch.

Defining Jobs with Spring

Batch processes have a number of different domain-specific concepts. A *job* is a process that consists of a number of steps. There maybe input and output related to each step. When a step fails, it may or may not be repeatable. The flow of a job may be conditional (for example, execute the bonus calculation step only if the revenue calculation step returns revenue over $1,000,000). Spring Batch provides classes, interfaces, and XML schemas that define these concepts using POJOs and XML to divide concerns appropriately and wire them together in a way familiar to those who have used Spring. Listing 1-1, for example, shows a basic Spring Batch job configured in XML. The result is a framework for batch processing that you can pick up very quickly with only a basic understanding of Spring as a prerequisite.

Listing 1-1. Sample Spring Batch Job Definition

```
<bean id="accountTasklet"
  class="com.michaelminella.springbatch.chapter1.AccountTasklet"/>

<job id="accountJob">
  <step id="accountStep">
    <tasklet ref="accountTasklet"/>
  </step>
</job>
```

Managing Jobs

It's one thing to be able to write a Java program that processes some data once and never runs again. But mission-critical processes require a more robust approach. The ability to keep the state of a job for reexecution, maintaining data integrity when a job fails through transaction management and saving performance metrics of past job executions for trending, are features that you expect in an enterprise batch system. These features are included in Spring Batch, and most of them are turned on by default; they require only minimal tweaking for performance and requirements as you develop your process.

Local and Remote Parallelization

As discussed earlier, the scale of batch jobs and the need to be able to scale them is vital to any enterprise batch solution. Spring Batch provides the ability to approach this in a number of different ways. From a simple thread-based implementation, where each commit interval is processed in its own thread of a thread pool; to running full steps in parallel; to configuring a grid of workers that are fed units of work from a remote master via partitioning; Spring Batch provides a collection of different options, including parallel chunk/step processing, remote chunk processing, and partitioning.

Standardizing I/O

Reading in from flat files with complex formats, XML files (XML is streamed, never loaded as a whole), or even a database, or writing to files or XML, can be done with only XML configuration. The ability to abstract things like file and database input and output from your code is an attribute of the maintainability of jobs written in Spring Batch.

The Spring Batch Admin Project

Writing your own batch-processing framework doesn't just mean having to redevelop the performance, scalability, and reliability features you get out of the box with Spring Batch. You also need to develop some form of administration toolset to do things like start and stop processes and view the statistics of previous job runs. However, if you use Spring Batch, it includes all that functionality as well as a newer addition: the Spring Batch Admin project. The Spring Batch Admin project provides a web-based control center that provides controls for your batch process (like launching a job, as shown in Figure 1-4) as well as the ability to monitor the performance your process over time.

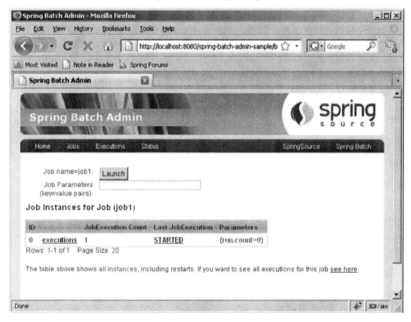

Figure 1-4. The Spring Batch Admin project user interface

And All the Features of Spring

Even with the impressive list of features that Spring Batch includes, the greatest thing is that it's built on Spring. With the exhaustive list of features that Spring provides for any Java application, including dependency injection, aspect-oriented programming (AOP), transaction management, and templates/helpers for most common tasks (JDBC, JMS, e-mail, and so on), building an enterprise batch process on a Spring framework offers virtually everything a developer needs.

As you can see, Spring Batch brings a lot to the table for developers. The proven development model of the Spring framework, scalability, and reliability features as well as an administration application are all available for you to get a batch process running quickly with Spring Batch.

How This Book Works

After going over the what and why of batch processing and Spring Batch, I'm sure you're chomping at the bit to dig into some code and learn what building batch processes with this framework is all about. Chapter 2 goes over the domain of a batch job, defines some of the terms I've already begun to use (*job*, *step*, and so on), and walks you through setting up your first Spring Batch project. You honor the gods by writing a "Hello, World!" batch job and see what happens when you run it.

One of my main goals for this book is to not only provide an in-depth look at how the Spring Batch framework works, but also show you how to apply those tools in a realistic example. Chapter 3 provides the requirements and technical architecture for a project that you implement in Chapter 10.

Summary

This chapter walked through a history of batch processing. It covered some of the challenges a developer of a batch process faces as well as justified the use of Java and open source technologies to conquer those challenges. Finally, you began an overview of the Spring Batch framework by examining its high-level components and features. By now, you should have a good view of what you're up against and understand that the tools to meet the challenges exist in Spring Batch. Now, all you need to do is learn how. Let's get started.

## CHAPTER 2

Spring Batch 101

The Java world is full of open source frameworks. Each has its own learning curve, but when you pick up most new frameworks, you at least understand the domain. For example, when you learned Struts or Spring MVC, you had probably developed a web-based application before. With that previous experience, converting your custom request-handling to the way a given framework handles it is really just a matter of learning a new syntax.

However, learning a framework where the domain is completely new is a bit harder. You run across jargon like *job*, *step*, and *item processor* as if it made sense in the context you're coming from. The fact is, it probably doesn't. So, I chose this chapter to serve as batch processing 101. The chapter covers the following topics:

- *The architecture of batch:* This section begins to dig a bit deeper into what makes up a batch process and defines terms that you'll see throughout the rest of the book.

- *Project setup:* I learn by doing. This book is assembled in a way that shows you examples of how the Spring Batch framework functions, explains why it works the way it does, and gives you the opportunity to code along. This section covers the basic setup for a Maven-based Spring Batch project.

- *Hello, World!* The first law of thermodynamics talks about conserving energy. The first law of motion deals with how objects at rest tend to stay at rest unless acted upon by an outside force. Unfortunately, the first law of computer science seems to be that whatever new technology you learn, you must write a "Hello, World!" program using said technology. Here you obey the law.

- *Running a job:* How to execute your first job may not be immediately apparent, so I'll walk you through how jobs are executed as well as how to pass in basic parameters.

- *The job results:* You finish by seeing how jobs complete. This section covers what the statuses are and how they impact what Spring Batch does.

With all of that in mind, what is a job, anyway?

The Architecture of Batch

The last chapter spent some time talking about the three layers of the Spring Batch framework: the application layer, the core layer, and the infrastructure layer. The application layer represents the code you develop, which for the most part interfaces with the core layer. The core layer consists of the actual components that make up the batch domain. Finally, the infrastructure layer includes item readers and writers as well as the required classes and interfaces to address things like restartability.

This section goes deeper into the architecture of Spring Batch and defines some of the concepts referred to in the last chapter. You then learn about some of the scalability options that are key to batch processing and what makes Spring Batch so powerful. Finally, the chapter discusses outline administration options as well as where to find answers to your questions about Spring Batch in the documentation. You start with at the architecture of batch processes, looking at the components of the core layer.

Examining Jobs and Steps

Figure 2-1 shows the essence of a job. Configured via XML, a batch *job* is a collection of steps in a specific order to be executed as part of a predefined process. Let's take for example the nightly processing of a user's bank account. Step 1 could be to load in a file of transactions received from another system. Step 2 would all credits to the account. Finally, step 3 would apply all debits to the account. The job represents the overall process of applying transactions to the user's account.

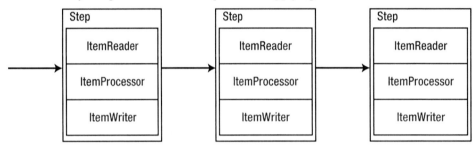

Figure 2-1. A batch job

When you look deeper, at an individual step, you see a self-contained unit of work that is the main building block of a job. Each step has up to three parts: an ItemReader, an ItemProcessor, and an ItemWriter. Notice that the names for each of these elements (ItemReader, ItemProcessor, and ItemWriter) are singular. That's by intent. Each of these pieces of code is executed on each record to be processed. A reader reads in a single record and passes it to the item processor for processing before it's sent to the item writer to be persisted in some way.

I stated a step has up to three parts. A step isn't required to have an ItemProcessor. .It's ok to have a step that consists of just an ItemReader and an ItemWriter (common in data-migration jobs) or just a tasklet (the equivalent of an ItemProcessor when you don't have any data to read or write). Table 2-1 walks through the interfaces that Spring Batch provides to represent these concepts.

Table 2-1. The Interfaces that Make Up a Batch Job

Interface	Description
`org.springframework.batch.core.Job`	The object representing the job, as configured in the job's XML file. Also provides the ability to execute the job.

• `org.springframework.batch.core.Step`	Like the job, represents the step as configured in the XML as well as provides the ability to execute a step.
• `org.springframework.batch.item.ItemReader<T>`	A strategy interface that provides the ability to input items.
• `org.springframework.batch.item.ItemProcessor<T>`	A facility to apply business logic to an individual item as provided.
• `org.springframework.batch.item.ItemWriter<T>`	A strategy interface that provides the ability to output a list of items.

One of the advantages of the way Spring has structured a job is that it decouples each step into its own independent processor. Each step is responsible for obtaining its own data, applying the required business logic to it, and then writing the data to the appropriate location. This decoupling provides a number of features:

- *Flexibility:* The ability to alter the order of processing with nothing more than an XML change is something many frameworks talk about yet very few deliver. Spring Batch is one that does deliver. Thinking about the earlier bank account example., If you wanted to apply the debits before the credits, the only change required would be to reorder the steps in the job XML (Chapter 4 shows an example). You can also skip a step, execute a step conditionally based on the results of a previous step, or even run multiple steps in parallel by doing nothing more than tweaking the XML.

- *Maintainability:* With the code for each step decoupled from the steps before and after it, steps are easy to unit-test, debug, and update with virtually no impact on other steps. Decoupled steps also make it possible to reuse steps in multiple jobs. As you'll see in upcoming chapters, steps are nothing more than Spring beans and can be reused just like any other bean in Spring.

- *Scalability:* Decoupling steps in a job provides a number of options to scale your jobs. You can execute steps in parallel. You can divide the work within a step across threads and execute the code of a single step in parallel (you see a bit more about this later in the chapter). Any of these abilities lets you meet the scalability needs of your business with minimum direct impact on your code.

- *Reliability:* By decoupling each step and each piece within a step, you can structure jobs such that they can be restarted at a given point in the process. If a job fails after processing 50,000 records out of 10 million in step 3 out of 7, you can restart it right where it left off.

Job Execution

Let's look at what happens with the components and their relationships when a job is run. Notice in Figure 2-2 that the piece most of the components share is JobRepository. This is a datastore (in memory or a database) that is used to persist information about the job and step executions. A *JobExecution* or

StepExecution is information about a single run of the job or step. You see more detail about what is in the executions and the repository later in this chapter and in Chapter 5.

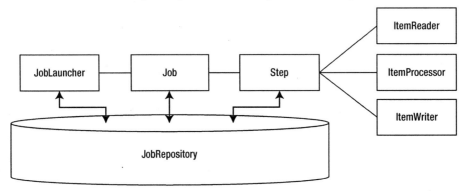

Figure 2-2. *The job components and their relationships*

Running a job begins with the JobLauncher. The JobLauncher verifies whether the job has been run before by checking the JobRepository, validates the parameters being passed into the job, and, finally, executes the job.

The processing of a job and a step are very similar. A job goes through the list of steps it has been configured to run, executing each one. As a chunk of items completes, Spring Batch updates the JobExecution or StepExecution in the repository with the results of the execution. A step goes through a list of items as read in by the ItemReader. As the step processes each chunk of items, the StepExecution in the repository is updated with where it is in the step. Things like current commit count, start and end times, and other information are stored in the repository. When a job or step is complete, the related execution is updated in the repository with the final status.

One of the things that changed in Spring Batch from version 1 to 2 was the addition of chunked processing. In version 1, records were read in, processed, and written out one at a time. The issue with this is that it doesn't take advantage of the ability to batch-write that Java's file and database I/O provides (buffered writing and batch updates). In version 2 and beyond of Spring Batch, the framework has been updated. Reading and processing is still a singular operation; there is no reason to load a large amount of data into memory if it can't be processed. But now, the write only occurs once a commit count interval occurs. This allows for more performant writing of records as well as a more capable rollback mechanism.

Parallelization

A simple batch process's architecture consists of a single-threaded process that executes a job's steps in order from start to finish. However, Spring Batch provides a number of parallelization options that you should be aware of as you move forward. (Chapter 11 covers these options in detail.) There are four different ways to parallelize your work: dividing work via multithreaded steps, parallel execution of full steps, remote chunking, and partitioning.

Multithreaded Steps

The first approach to achieving parallelization is the division of work via multithreaded steps. In Spring Batch, a job is configured to process work in blocks called *chunks*, with a commit after each block. Normally, each chunk is processed in series. If you have 10,000 records, and the commit count is set at 50 records, your job will process records 1 to 50 and then commit, process 51 to 100 and commit, and so on, until all 10,000 records have been processed. Spring Batch allows you to execute chunks of work in parallel to improve performance. With three threads, you can increase your throughput threefold, as shown in Figure 2-3.[1]

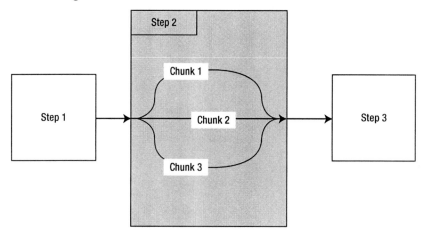

Figure 2-3. Multithreaded steps

Parallel Steps

The next approach you have available for parallelization is the ability to execute steps in parallel, as shown in Figure 2-4. Let's say you have two steps, each of which loads an input file into your database; but there is no relationship between the steps. Does it make sense to have to wait until one file has been loaded before the next one is loaded? Of course not, which is why this is a classic example of when to use the ability to process steps in parallel.

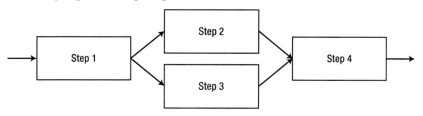

Figure 2-4. Parallel step processing

---

1 This is a theoretical throughput increase. Many factors can prevent the ability of a process to achieve linear parallelization like this.

Remote Chunking

The last two approaches to parallelization allow you to spread processing across multiple JVMs. In all cases previously, the processing was performed in a single JVM, which can seriously hinder the scalability options. When you can scale any part of your process horizontally across multiple JVMs, the ability to keep up with large demands increases.

The first remote-processing option is *remote chunking*. In this approach, input is performed using a standard ItemReader in a master node; the input is then sent via a form of durable communication (JMS for example) to a remote slave ItemProcessor that is configured as a message driven POJO. When the processing is complete, the slave sends the updated item back to the master for writing. Because this approach reads the data at the master, processes it at the slave, and then sends it back, it's important to note that it can be very network intensive. This approach is good for scenarios where the cost of I/O is small compared to the actual processing.

Partitioning

The final method for parallelization within Spring Batch is partitioning, shown in Figure 2-5. Again, you use a master/slave configuration; but this time you don't need a durable method of communication, and the master serves only as a controller for a collection of slave steps. In this case, each of your slave steps is self-contained and configured the same as if it was locally deployed. The only difference is that the slave steps receive their work from the master node instead of the job itself. When all the slaves have completed their work, the master step is considered complete. This configuration doesn't require durable communication with guaranteed delivery because the JobRepository guarantees that no work is duplicated and all work is completed—unlike the remote-chunking approach, in which the JobRepository has no knowledge of the state of the distributed work.

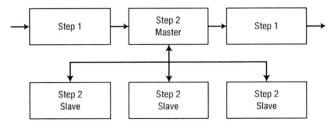

Figure 2-5. *Partitioning work*

Batch Administration

Any enterprise system must be able to start and stop processes, monitor their current state, and even view results. With web applications, this is easy: in the web application, you see the results of each action you request, and tools like Google Analytics provide various metrics on how your application is being used and is performing.

However, in the batch world, you may have a single Java process running on a server for eight hours with no output other than log files and the database the process is working on. This is hardly a manageable situation. For this reason, Spring has developed a web application called Spring Batch Admin that lets you start and stop jobs and also provides details about each job execution.

Documentation

One of the strengths of Spring Batch is that real developers wrote it who have experience developing batch processes in various enterprises. From this experience comes not only a comprehensive framework but also a wealth of documentation to boot. The Spring Batch web site contains one of the best collections of documentation for an open source project I've ever worked with. Along with the formal documentation, the JavaDoc is also useful for API specifics. Finally, Spring Batch provides 19 different sample jobs for you to reference as you develop your own batch applications (see Table 2-2).

Table 2-2. Sample Batch Jobs

Batch Job	Description
adhocLoopJob	An infinite loop used to demonstrate the exposing of elements via JMX and the running of the job in a background thread (instead of the main JobLauncher thread).
beanWrapperMapperSampleJob	A job with two steps that is used to demonstrate the mapping of file fields to domain objects as well as validation of file-based input.
compositeItemWriterSampleJob	A step can have only one reader and writer. The CompositeWriter is the way around this. This sample job demonstrates how.
customerFilterJob	Uses an ItemProcessor to filter out customers that aren't valid. This job also updates the filter count field of the step execution.
delegatingJob	Using the ItemReaderAdapter, delegates the reading of input to a configured method of a POJO.
footballJob	A football statistics job. After loading two input files, one with player data and one with game data, the job generates a selection of summary statistics for the players and games and writes them to the log file.
groovyJob	Uses Groovy (a dynamic JVM language) to script the unzipping and zipping of a file.
headerFooterSample	Using callbacks, adds the ability to render a header and footer on the output.
hibernateJob	Spring Batch readers and writers don't use Hibernate by default. This job shows how to integrate Hibernate into your job.
infiniteLoopJob	Just a job with an infinite loop, used to demonstrate stop and restart scenarios

ioSampleJob	Provides examples of a number of different I/O options including delimited and fix-width files, multiline records, XML, JDBC, and iBATIS integration.
jobSampleJob	Demonstrates the execution of a job from another job.
loopFlowSample	Using the decision tag, demonstrates how to control execution flow programmatically.
mailJob	Uses the SimpleMailMessageItemWriter to send e-mails as the form of output for each item.
multilineJob	Treats groups of file records as a list that represents a single item.
multilineOrder	As an expansion of the multiline input concept, reads in a file with multiline nested records using a custom reader. The output is also multiline, using standard writers.
parallelJob	Reads records into a staging table, where a multithreaded step processes them.
partitionFileJob	Uses the MultiResourcePartitioner to process a collection of files in parallel.
partitionJdbcJob	Instead of looking for multiple files and processing each one in parallel, divides the number of records in the database for parallel processing.
restartSampleJob	Throws a fake exception when processing has begun, to demonstrate the ability to restart a job that has errored and have it begin again where it left off.
retrySample	Using some interesting logic, shows how Spring Batch can attempt to process an item multiple times before giving up and throwing an error.
skipSampleJob	Based on the tradeJob example. In this job, however, one of the records fails validation and is skipped.
taskletJob	The most basic use of Spring Batch is the tasklet. This example shows how any existing method can be used as tasklets via the MethodInvokingTaskletAdapter.
tradeJob	Models a real-world scenario. This three-step job imports trade information into a database, updates customer accounts, and generates reports.

Project Setup

Up to this point, you've looked at why you'd use Spring Batch and examined the components of the framework. However, looking at diagrams and learning new lingo will only take you so far. At some point, you need to dig into the code: so, grab an editor, and let's start digging.

In this section, you build your first batch job. You walk through the setup of a Spring Batch project, including obtaining the required files from Spring. You then configure a job and code the "Hello, World!" version of Spring Batch. Finally, you learn how to launch a batch job from the command line.

Obtaining Spring Batch

Before you begin writing batch processes, you need to obtain the Spring Batch framework. There are three options for doing this: using the SpringSource Tool Suite (STS), downloading the zip distribution, or using Maven and Git.

Using the SpringSource Tool Suite

SpringSource (the maintainers of the Spring Framework and all of its derivatives) has put together an Eclipse distribution with a collection of plug-ins designed specifically for Spring development. Features include wizards for creating Spring projects, XML files and beans, the ability to deploy applications remotely, and OSGi management. You can download this from the SpringSource web site.

Downloading the Zip Distribution

The Spring Batch framework is also available via download from the SpringSource web site as a zip file with two options: all dependencies or no dependencies (as indicated by *-no-dependencies* in the file name). Given that the project is set up for Maven use (although a build.xml file is included for those who use Ant), the no-dependencies option is a better bet to download.

The zip file contains two directories: dist and samples. dist contains the release jar files: two for core, two for infrastructure, and two for test (a source and compiled for each). In the samples directory, you find a samples project (spring-batch-samples) that contains all the sample batch jobs you saw earlier in this chapter, a project shell (spring-batch-simple-cli) that can be used to as a starting point for any Spring Batch project, and a Maven parent project for the two. This template project is the easiest way for you to get started with Spring Batch and will be the way you build our projects going forward.

Checking Out from Git

The final way to obtain the code for Spring Batch is to obtain it from the source code repository SpringSource uses, Github. The Git version control system is a distributed version control system that allows you to work with a full copy of the repository locally..

Listing 2-1. Checking Out the Project from Github

```
$ git clone git://github.com/SpringSource/spring-batch.git
```

This command exports the source code for the Spring Batch project including a shell for a project, sample applications and all of the Spring Batch framework's source code. The command in Listing 2-1 will obtain the entire Spring Batch Git repository. In order to get a particular version execute the command in Listing 2-2 from within your checked out repository.

Listing 2-2. *Getting a particular version of Spring Batch*

```
$ git checkout 2.1.7.RELEASE
```

Configuring Maven

In order to use Maven for your builds, you need to tweak your local Maven installation slightly. The Project Object Model (POM) files that are provided as part of the downloaded distributions for Spring projects don't have the Spring Maven repositories configured in them. Because of that, you should add them to your settings.xml file. Listing 2-3 shows the added configuration you need.

Listing 2-3. *Getting the Repository DDL from SVN*

```
<pluginRepositories>
    <pluginRepository>
        <id>com.springsource.repository.bundles.release</id>
        <name>SpringSource Enterprise Bundle Repository</name>
        <url>http://repository.springsource.com/maven/bundles/release</url>
    </pluginRepository>
</pluginRepositories>
```

With the project shell created and Maven configured, you can test the configuration by running a quick `mvn clean install`. With a successful build, you can move on to your first batch job.

It's the Law: Hello, World!

The laws of computer science are clear. Any time you learn a new technology, you must create a "Hello, World!" program using said technology, so let's get started. Don't feel like you need to understand all the moving parts of this example. Future chapters go into each piece in greater detail.

Before you get too far into the new code, you should do some clean up of files and references to them that are not needed. These files, while being provided for examples, are not kept in a typical Spring Batch project. To start, we can delete all of the java source code and tests. These are located in the src/main/java and src/test/java directories. Once those are removed we can remove the module-context.xml file. This is a sample job configuration that you will not need in your project. Finally, since you removed a few java files that were referenced in the project's configuration, that needs to be updated as well. In the file src/main/resources/launch-context.xml you will want to remove the import at the top for the module-context.xml as well as the dataSourceInitializer bean at the bottom of the file. The dataSourceIntializer will be looked at further in Chapter 12.

As discussed earlier, a job is configured in XML. To create your "Hello, World!" job, create a new directory in src/main/resources called jobs; in the new directory, create an XML file called helloWorld.xml, as shown in Listing 2-4.

Listing 2-4. *The "Hello, World!" Job*

```
<?xml version="1.0" encoding="UTF-8"?>
<beans:beans xmlns ="http://www.springframework.org/schema/batch"
        xmlns:beans="http://www.springframework.org/schema/beans"
```

```
        xmlns:xsi="http://www.w3.org/2001/XMLSchema-instance"
        xsi:schemaLocation="http://www.springframework.org/schema/beans
                http://www.springframework.org/schema/beans/spring-beans-3.0.xsd
                http://www.springframework.org/schema/batch
                http://www.springframework.org/schema/batch/spring-batch-2.1.xsd">

    <beans:import resource="../launch-context.xml"/>

    <beans:bean id="helloWorld"
                    class="com.apress.springbatch.chapter2.HelloWorld"/>

    <step id="helloWorldStep">
        <tasklet ref="helloWorld"/>
    </step>

    <job id="helloWorldJob">
        <step id="step1" parent="helloWorldStep"/>
    </job>
</beans:beans>
```

If that looks kind of familiar, it should. It's the high-level breakdown discussed previously, only in XML form.

▨**Note** Although most of Spring has added annotation equivalents to the XML configuration options, Spring Batch doesn't. As part of the 2.0 release, Spring did add a namespace to assist with managing the XML.

If you walk through this, there are four main pieces: the import of launch-context.xml, the bean declaration, the step definition, and the job definition. Launch-context.xml is a file that is included in your shell project that contains a number of infrastructure pieces configured for your jobs. Things like the datasource, the JobLauncher, and other elements universal to all the jobs in the project are found here. Chapter 3 covers this file in more detail. For now, the default settings work.

The bean declaration should look like any other Spring bean, for a good reason: it's just like any other Spring bean. The HelloWorld bean is a tasklet that does the work in this job. A *tasklet* is a special type of step that is used to perform a function without a reader or writer. Typically, a tasklet is used for a single function, say performing some initialization, calling a stored procedure, or sending an e-mail to alert you that the job has finished. Chapter 4 goes into semantic specifics about tasklets along with the other step types.

The next piece is the step. Jobs are made up of one or more steps, as noted earlier. In the HelloWorld job, you start with a single step that executes your tasklet. Spring Batch provides an easy way to configure a step using the batch XSD. You create a tasklet using the tasklet tag and reference the tasklet you defined previously. You then wrap that in a step tag with just an id. This defines a reusable step that you can reference in your job as many times as you need.

Finally, you define your job. The job is really nothing more than an ordered list of steps to be executed. In this case, you have only one step. If you're wondering if the step tag in the job definition is the same type of tag that you used in the job definition, it is. You can declare the steps inline if you want. However, in this example I created a step outside of the job and made it the parent of the step within the job.[2] I did this for two reasons: to keep the XML cleaner and to allow for easy extraction of steps into other XML files if needed. You'll see in future chapters that the XML for steps can get quite verbose; the approach shown here helps to keep the job readable.

Your job is configured, but you have a class in that configuration that doesn't exist: the HelloWorld tasklet. Create the tasklet in the src/main/java/com/apress/springbatch/chapter2 directory. As you can guess, the code is pretty simple; see Listing 2-5.

Listing 2-5. *HelloWorld Tasklet*

```
package com.apress.springbatch.chapter2;

import org.springframework.batch.core.StepContribution;
import org.springframework.batch.core.scope.context.ChunkContext;
import org.springframework.batch.core.step.tasklet.Tasklet;
import org.springframework.batch.repeat.RepeatStatus;

public class HelloWorld implements Tasklet {

    private static final String HELLO_WORLD = "Hello, world!";

    public RepeatStatus execute( StepContribution arg0, ChunkContext arg1 ) throws Exception
{
        System.out.println( HELLO_WORLD );
        return RepeatStatus.FINISHED;
    }
}
```

To create the HelloWorld tasklet, you implement the Tasklet interface's single method: execute. StepContribution and ChunkContext represent the context of the step (commit count, skip count, and so on) in which this tasklet is being executed. Future chapters get into those in more detail.

Running Your Job

That's really it. Let's try building and running the job. To compile it, run mvn clean compile from the root of the project. When the build is successful, run the job. Spring Batch comes with its own job runner called CommandLineJobRunner. As you can guess, it's intended to be run from … a command line! In this book, you will execute your jobs from your project's target directory so that you won't need to go through setting up the classpath. The CommandLineJobRunner takes two or more parameters: the path to the XML file that contains the job configuration, the name of the job to be executed, and a list of job parameters. In the case of HelloWorldJob, you only need to pass the first two parameters. To execute the job, run the command shown in Listing 2-6.

Listing 2-6. *Execute the HelloWorld Job*

```
java -jar hello-world-0.0.1-SNAPSHOT.jar jobs/helloWorld.xml helloWorldJob
```

---

[2] Chapter 4 covers the parent attribute of a step in detail.

After you've run the job, notice that in traditional Spring style, there is quite a bit of output for a simple "Hello, World!" But if you look closely (around line 33 of the output), there it is:

```
2010-12-01 23:15:42,442 DEBUG
org.springframework.batch.core.launch.support.CommandLineJobRunner.main()
[org.springframework.batch.core.scope.context.StepContextRepeatCallback] - <Chunk execution
starting: queue size=0>

Hello, world!

2010-12-01 23:15:42,443 DEBUG
org.springframework.batch.core.launch.support.CommandLineJobRunner.main()
[org.springframework.batch.core.step.tasklet.TaskletStep] - <Applying contribution:
[StepContribution: read=0, written=0, filtered=0, readSkips=0, writeSkips=0, processSkips=0,
exitStatus=EXECUTING]>
```

Congratulations! You just ran your first Spring Batch job. So, what actually happened? As discussed earlier in the chapter, when Spring Batch runs a job, the job runner (in this case, the CommandLineJobRunner) loads the application context and configuration of the job to be run (as specified by the first two parameters passed in). From there, the job runner passes the JobInstance to a JobLauncher that executes the job. In this case, the job's single step is executed, and the JobRepository is updated accordingly.

Exploring the JobRepository

Wait. JobRepository? That wasn't specified in your XML. Where did all that information go? It went into the job repository, as it should. The problem is that Spring Batch is configured to use HSQLDB by default, so all that metadata, although stored in memory during the execution of the job, is now gone. Let's fix that by switching to MySQL instead so you can do a better job managing the metadata and look at what happens when you run your job. In this section, you look at how to configure your JobRepository to use MySQL, and you explore what Spring Batch logs to the database with a run of HelloWorldJob.

Job Repository Configuration

To change where Spring Batch stores the data, you need to do three things: update the batch.properties file, update your pom, and create the batch schema in your database.[3] Let's start by modifying the batch.properties file found in your project's /src/main/resources directory. The properties should be pretty straightforward. Listing 2-7 shows what I have in mine.

Listing 2-7. batch.properties File

```
batch.jdbc.driver=com.mysql.jdbc.Driver
batch.jdbc.url=jdbc:mysql://localhost:3306/spring_batch_test
```

---

3 I'm going to assume you already have MySQL installed. If you don't, go to www.mysql.com to download it and get installation instructions.

```
# use this one for a separate server process so you can inspect the results
# (or add it to system properties with -D to override at run time).
batch.jdbc.user=root
batch.jdbc.password=p@ssw0rd
batch.schema=spring_batch_test
#batch.schema.script=schema-mysql.sql
```

Note that I commented out the batch.schema.script line. When you run your job, the dataSourceIntializer executes the script specified. This is helpful when you're working in development, but if you want to persist the data, it's a bit less useful.

With the properties file now pointing to your local instance of MySQL, you need to update your POM file so that you include the MySQL driver in your classpath. To do that, find the HSQLDB dependency, and update it as shown in Listing 2-8.

***Listing 2-8.** Maven MySQL Dependency*

```
<dependency>
    <groupId>mysql</groupId>
    <artifactId>mysql-connector-java</artifactId>
    <version>5.1.3</version>
</dependency>
```

In this dependency, 5.1.3 is the version of MySQL running locally.

With your database connection configured, Spring Batch needs you to create the schema. Using MySQL, you can create the schema as shown in Listing 2-9.

***Listing 2-9.** Creating the Database Schema*

```
mysql> create database spring_batch_test;
Query OK, 1 row affected (0.00 sec)
mysql> use spring_batch_test;
Database changed
mysql> source ~/spring_batch/src/main/resources/org/springframework/batch/core/schema-
mysql.sql
```

That's it. Let's run the job again (be sure to do a mvn clean compile first, to copy your updated batch.properties file to the target). Using the same command as earlier, you should see the same output. The difference is that this time, Spring Batch left something behind. Let's look at the database.

The Job Repository Tables

Spring Batch uses the database to maintain state both during a single execution and from execution to execution. Information is recorded about the job instance, the parameters passed in, the results of the execution, and the results of each step. Here are the six tables in the job repository; the following sections describe their relationships:[4]

---

[4] Those using MySQL and some other databases may see three additional "tables": batch_job_execution_seq, batch_job_seq, and batch_step_execution_seq. These are used to maintain a database sequence and aren't discussed here.

- BATCH_JOB_INSTANCE

- BATCH_JOB_PARAMS

- BATCH_JOB_EXECUTION

- BATCH_JOB_EXECUTION_CONTEXT

- BATCH_STEP_EXECUTION

- BATCH_STEP_EXECUTION_CONTEXT

BATCH_JOB_INSTANCE

Let's start with the BATCH_JOB_INSTANCE table. As you saw earlier, a job instance is created when the job is created. It's like calling a new on a job. However, a job instance is really the combination of the job instance itself and the job parameters (as stored in the BATCH_JOB_PARAMS table). This combination can only be executed once to success. Let me say that again: a job can only be run once with the same parameters. I won't pull out the soapbox on why I don't like this feature, but I will say that it's common to pass in the date and time of the run as job parameters to get around this. After running your HelloWorld job, the BATCH_JOB_INSTANCE table looks like what is shown in Table 2-3.

Table 2-3. *BATCH_JOB_INSTANCE Table*

Field	Description	Value
JOB_INSTANCE_ID	Primary key of the table	1
VERSION	The version[5] for the record	0
JOB_NAME	The name of the job executed	helloWorldJob
JOB_KEY	A hash of the job name and parameters used to uniquely identify a job instance	d41d8cd98f00b204e980098ecf8427e

BATCH_JOB_PARAMS

It should come as no surprise that the BATCH_JOB_PARAMS table contains all the parameters passed to the job. As mentioned in the previous section, the parameters are part of what Spring Batch uses to identify the run of a job. In this case, the BATCH_JOB_PARAMS table is empty because you didn't pass any parameters to your job. However, the fields in the BATCH_JOB_PARAMS table are shown in Table 2-4.

---

[5] To learn more about the versions and entities in domain-driven design, read *Domain Driven Design* by Eric Evans (Addison-Wesley, 2003).

Table 2-4. BATCH_JOB_PARAMS Table

Field	Description
JOB_INSTANCE_ID	Foreign key to the BATCH_JOB_INSTANCE table
TYPE_CD	The type of value being stored (string, date, long, or double)
KEY_NAME	The parameter key (job parameters are passed in as key/value pairs)
STRING_VAL	The value, if the type of parameter was a string
DATE_VAL	Date parameters
LONG_VAL	Long parameters
DOUBLE_VAL	Double or float parameters

BATCH_JOB_EXECUTION and BATCH_STEP_EXECUTION

After a job instance is created, it's executed. The state of the job execution is maintained in—you guessed it—the BATCH_JOB_EXECUTION table. Start time, end time, and results of the last execution are stored here. I know what you're thinking: if a job with the same parameters can be run only once, what's the point of the BATCH_JOB_EXECUTION table? The combination of job and parameters can only be run once to success. If a job runs and *fails* (assuming it's configured to be able to be rerun), it can be run again as many times as needed to get it to succeed. This is a common occurrence in the batch world when dealing with data that's out of your control. As the job processes data, it can find bad data that causes the process to throw an error. Someone fixes the data and restarts the job.

The BATCH_STEP_EXECUTION table serves the same purpose as the BATCH_JOB_EXECUTION table. Start time, end time, number of commits, and other parameters related to the state of the step are maintained in BATCH_STEP_EXECUTION.

After the execution of the HelloWorld job, you have a single record in the BATCH_JOB_EXECUTION table. Notice in Table 2-5 that the times are all the same: it's because `System.out.println(HELLO_WORLD);` doesn't take long.

Table 2-5. BATCH_JOB_EXECUTION Table

Field	Description	Value
JOB_EXECUTION_ID	Primary key of the table	1
VERSION	The version of the record	2
JOB_INSTANCE_ID	Foreign key to the BATCH_JOB_INSTANCE table	1
CREATE_TIME	The time the job execution was created	2010-10-25 18:08:30
START_TIME	The start time for the job execution	2010-10-25 18:08:30
END_TIME	The end time for the execution, regardless of success	2010-10-25 18:08:30
STATUS	The status as returned to the job	COMPLETED
EXIT_CODE	The exit code as returned to the job	COMPLETED
EXIT_MESSAGE	Any exit message that was returned to the job	
LAST_UPDATED	The last time this record was updated	2010-10-25 18:08:30

Your BATCH_STEP_EXECUTION table also contains only one record because your job had only one step. Table 2-6 outlines the columns and values that the table has after your execution.

Table 2-6. BATCH_STEP_EXECUTION Table

• Field	• Description	• Value
STEP_EXECUTION_ID	Primary key for the table	1
VERSION	The version of the record	2
STEP_NAME	The name of the step as it's configured in the job's XML	step1
JOB_EXECUTION_ID	Foreign key back to the BATCH_JOB_EXECUTION table	1
START_TIME	The time the step was started	2010-10-25 18:08:30
END_TIME	The time the step completed, regardless of result	2010-10-25 18:08:30
STATUS	The current status of the step	COMPLETED
COMMIT_COUNT	The commit count the step is currently on	1
READ_COUNT	The read count the step is currently on	0
FILTER_COUNT	The number of items that have been filtered	0
WRITE_COUNT	The number of items that have been written	0
READ_SKIP_COUNT	The number of items that have been skipped being read	0
WRITE_SKIP_COUNT	The number of items that have been skipped being written	0
PROCESS_SKIP_COUNT	The number of items that haven't gone through the ItemProcessor (straight from ItemReader to ItemWriter)	0
ROLLBACK_COUNT	The total number of rollbacks during the execution, including each rollback for a given item skip or retry	0
EXIT_CODE	The exit code that was returned a the step completed	COMPLETE
EXIT_MESSAGE	Any message returned by the step	
LAST_UPDATED	The last time the record was updated	2010-10-25 18:08:30

Job and Step Execution Context Tables

That leaves the two context tables, BATCH_JOB_EXECUTION_CONTEXT and BATCH_STEP_EXECUTION_CONTEXT. These tables are the persisted versions of the ExecutionContext related to either the job or the step. The ExecutionContext is the Spring Batch similar to the servlet context or session in a web application in that it's a global place to store information. It's essentially a map of key/value pairs that are scoped to either the job or the step. The job or step execution context is used to pass information around within the given scope; for jobs, it's used to pass information from step to step, and for steps, it's used to pass information across the processing of multiple records.

The tables BATCH_JOB_EXECUTION_CONTEXT and BATCH_STEP_EXECUTION_CONTEXT are the serialized version of these maps. In this case, they both contain the same data, with only the foreign key (which is the primary key of the table) being different (BATCH_STEP_EXECUTION_CONTEXT refers to the BATCH_STEP_EXECUTION table, and BATCH_JOB_EXECUTION_CONTEXT refers to the BATCH_JOB_EXECUTION table). Table 2-7 shows what the tables contain.

Table 2-7. *BATCH_JOB_EXECUTION_CONTEXT and BATCH_STEP_EXECUTION_CONTEXT Tables*

Field	Description	Value
JOB_EXECUTION_ID / STEP_EXECUTION_ID	Foreign key to the BATCH_JOB_EXECUTION / BATCH_STEP_EXECUTION table	1
SHORT_CONTEXT	A string representation of the context	{"map":""}
SERIALIZED_CONTEXT	The serialized execution context for future use on retries, and so on	NULL

Summary

In this chapter, you got your feet wet with Spring Batch. You walked through the batch domain covering what a job and step are and how they interact through the job repository. You learned about the different features of the framework, including the ability to map batch concepts in XML, robust parallelization options, the formal documentation (including a list of the available sample jobs), and the administration application Spring Batch Admin.

From there, you wrote the Spring Batch version of "Hello, World!". You learned the different methods of obtaining the Spring Batch framework, including checking it out from Git, using the SpringSource Tool Suite, and downloading the zip distribution. When you had your project set up, you created your job in XML, coded a tasklet, and executed your job. Finally, you explored the job repository that Spring Batch uses to maintain information about the jobs it runs.

I want to point out that you've barely taken a peek into what Spring Batch can do. The next chapter walks through the design of a sample application that you'll build later in this book and outlines how Spring Batch addresses issues that you'd have to deal with yourself without it.

CHAPTER 3

Sample Job

This book is designed to not only explain how the many features of Spring Batch work but also demonstrate them in detail. Each chapter includes a number of examples that show how each feature works. However, examples designed to communicate individual concepts and techniques may not be the best for demonstrating how those techniques work together in a real-world example. So, in Chapter 10 you create a sample application that is intended to emulate a real-world scenario.

The scenario I chose is simplified: a domain you can easily understand but that provides sufficient complexity so that using Spring Batch makes sense. Bank statements are an example of common batch processing. Run nightly, these processes generate statements based on the previous month's transactions. The example is a derivative of the standard bank statement: a brokerage statement. The brokerage statement batch process shows how you can use the following features of Spring Batch together to accomplish the result:

> *Various input and output options:* Among the most significant features of Spring Batch are the well-abstracted options for reading and writing from a variety of sources. The brokerage statements obtains input from flat files, a database, and a web service. On the output side, you write to databases as well as flat files. A variety of readers and writers are utilized.

> *Error handling:* The worst part about maintaining batch processes is that when they break, it's typically at 2:00 a.m., and you're the one getting the phone call to fix the problem. Because of this, robust error handling is a must. The example statement process covers a number of different scenarios including logging, skipping records with errors, and retry logic.

> *Scalability:* In the real world, batch processes need to be able to accommodate large amounts of data. Later in this book, you use the scalability features of Spring Batch to tune the batch process so it can process literally millions of customers.

In order to build our batch job we will want a set of requirements to work from. Since we will be using user stories to define our requirements, we will take a look at the agile development process as a whole in the next section.

Understanding Agile Development

Before this chapter digs into the individual requirements of the batch process you develop in Chapter 10, let's spend a little time going over the approach you use to do so. A lot has been said in our industry about various agile processes; so instead of banking on any previous knowledge you may have of the subject, let's start by establishing a base of what *agile* and the development process will mean for this book.

The agile process has 12 tenets that virtually all of its variants prescribe. They are as follows:

- Customer satisfaction comes from quick delivery of working software.

- Change is welcome regardless of the stage of development.

- Deliver working software frequently.

- Business and development must work hand in hand daily.

- Build projects with motivated teams. Give them the tools and trust them to get the job done.

- Face-to-face communication is the most effective form.

- Working software is the number-one measure of success.

- Strive for sustainable development. All members of the team should be able to maintain the pace of development indefinitely.

- Continue to strive for technical excellence and good design.

- Minimizing waste by eliminating unnecessary work.

- Self-organizing teams generate the best requirements, architectures, and designs.

- At regular intervals, have the team reflect to determine how to improve.

It doesn't matter if you're using Extreme Programming (XP), Scrum, or any other currently hip variant. The point is that these dozen tenets still apply.

Notice that not all of them will necessarily apply in your case. It's pretty hard to work face to face with a book. You'll probably be working by yourself through the examples, so the aspects of team motivation don't exactly apply either. However, there are pieces that do apply. An example is quick delivery of working software. This will drive you through out the book. You'll accomplish it by building small pieces of the application, validating that they work with unit tests, and then adding onto them.

Even with the exceptions, the tenets of agile provide a solid framework for any development project, and this book applies as many of them as possible. Let's get started looking at how they're applied by examining the way you document the requirements for the sample job: user stories.

Capturing Requirements with User Stories

User stories are the agile method for documenting requirements. Written as a customer's take on what the application should do, a story's goal is to communicate the how a user will interact with the system and document testable results of that interaction. A user story has three main parts:

- *The title:* The title should be a simple and concise statement of what the story is about. *Load transaction file. Calculate fee tier. Generate print file.* All of these are good examples of story titles. You notice that these titles aren't GUI specific. Just because you don't have a GUI doesn't mean you can't have interactions between users. In this case, the user is the batch process you're documenting or any external system you interface with.

- *The narrative:* This is a short description of the interaction you're documenting, written from the perspective of the user. Typically, the format is something like "Given the situation Y, X does something, and something else happens." You see in the upcoming sections how to approach stories for batch processes (given that they're purely technical in nature).

- *Acceptance criteria:* The acceptance criteria are testable requirements that can be used to identify when a story is complete. The important word in the previous statement is *testable*. In order for an acceptance criterion to be useful, it must be able to be verified in some way. These aren't subjective requirements but hard items that the developer can use to say "Yes it does do that" that or "No it doesn't."

Let's look at a user story for a universal remote control as an example:

- *Title:* Turn on Television

- *Narrative:* As a user, with the television, receiver, and cable box off, I will be able to press the power button on my universal remote. The remote will then power on the television, receiver, and cable box and configure them to view a television show.

- *Acceptance criteria:*

  - Have a power button on the universal remote.

  - When the user presses the power button, the following will occur:

    a. The television will power on.

    b. The AV receiver will power on.

    c. The cable box will power on.

    d. The cable box will be set to channel 187.

    e. The AV receiver will be set to the SAT input.

    f. The television will be set to the Video 1 input.

The Turn on Television user story begins with a title—Turn on Television—that is short and descriptive. It continues with a narrative. In this case, the narrative provides a description of what happens when the user presses the power button. Finally, the acceptance criteria list the testable requirements for the developers and QA. Notice that each criterion is something the developers can easily check: they can look at their developed product and say yes or no, what they wrote does or doesn't do what the criteria state.

USER STORIES VS USE CASES

Use cases are another familiar form of requirements documentation. Similar to user stories, they're actor centric. Use cases were the documentation form of choice for the Rational Unified Process (RUP). They're intended to document every aspect of the interaction between an actor and a system. Because of this, their overly documentation-centric focus (writing documents for the sake of documents), and their bloated format, use cases have fallen out of favor and been replaced with user stories in agile development.

User stories mark the beginning of the development cycle. Let's continue by looking at a few of the other tools used over the rest of the cycle.

Capturing Design with Test-Driven Development

Test-driven development (TDD) is another agile practice. When using TDD, a developer first writes a test that fails and then implements the code to make the test pass. Designed to require that developers think about what they're trying to code before they code it, TDD (also called test-first development) has been proven to make developers more productive, use their debuggers less, and end up with cleaner code.

Another advantage of TDD is that tests serve as executable documentation. Unlike user stories or other forms of documentation that become stale due to lack of maintenance, automated tests are always updated as part of the ongoing maintenance of the code. If you want to understand how a piece of code is intended to work, you can look at the unit tests for a complete picture of the scenarios in which the developers intended their code to be used.

Although TDD has a number of positives, you won't use it much in this book. It's a great tool for development, but it isn't the best for explaining how things work. However, Chapter 12 looks at testing of all types, from unit testing to functional testing, using open source tools including JUnit, Mockito, and the testing additions in Spring.

Using a Source-Control System

In Chapter 2, you took a quick peek at source control when you used Git to retrieve the source code for Spring Batch. Although it isn't a requirement by any means, you're strongly encouraged to use a source-control system for all your development. Whether you choose to set up a central Subversion repository or use Git locally, the features that source control provides are essential for productive programming.

You're probably thinking, "Why would I use source control for code that I'm going to throw away while I'm learning?" That is the strongest reason I can think of to use it. By using a version-control system, you give yourself a safety net to try things. Commit your working code; try something that may not work. If it does, commit the new revision. If not, roll back to the previous revision with no harm done. Think about the last time you learned a new technology and did so without version control. I'm sure there were times when you coded your way down a path that didn't pan out and were then stuck to debug your way out of it because you didn't have a previously working copy. Save yourself the headache and allow yourself to make mistakes in a controlled environment by using version control.

Working with a True Development Environment

There are many other pieces to development in an agile environment. Get yourself a good IDE. Because this book is purposely written to be IDE agnostic, it won't go into pros and cons of each. However, be sure you have a good one, and learn it well, including the keyboard shortcuts.

Although spending a lot of time setting up a continuous integration environment may not make sense for you while you learn a given technology, it may be worth setting one up to use in general for your personal development. You never know when that widget you're developing on the side will be the next big thing, and you'd hate to have to go back and set up source control and continuous integration, etc when things are starting to get exciting. A few good continuous integration systems are available for free, but I strongly recommend Hudson (or its brother Jenkins). Both of them are easy to use and highly extendable, so you can configure all kinds of additional functionality including things like integrating with Sonar and other code-analysis tools and executing automated functional tests.

Understanding the Requirements of the Statement Job

Now that you've seen the pieces of the development process you're encouraged to use as you learn Spring Batch, let's look at what you'll develop in this book. Figure 3-1 shows what you expect to get in the mail from your stockbroker each quarter as your brokerage account statement.

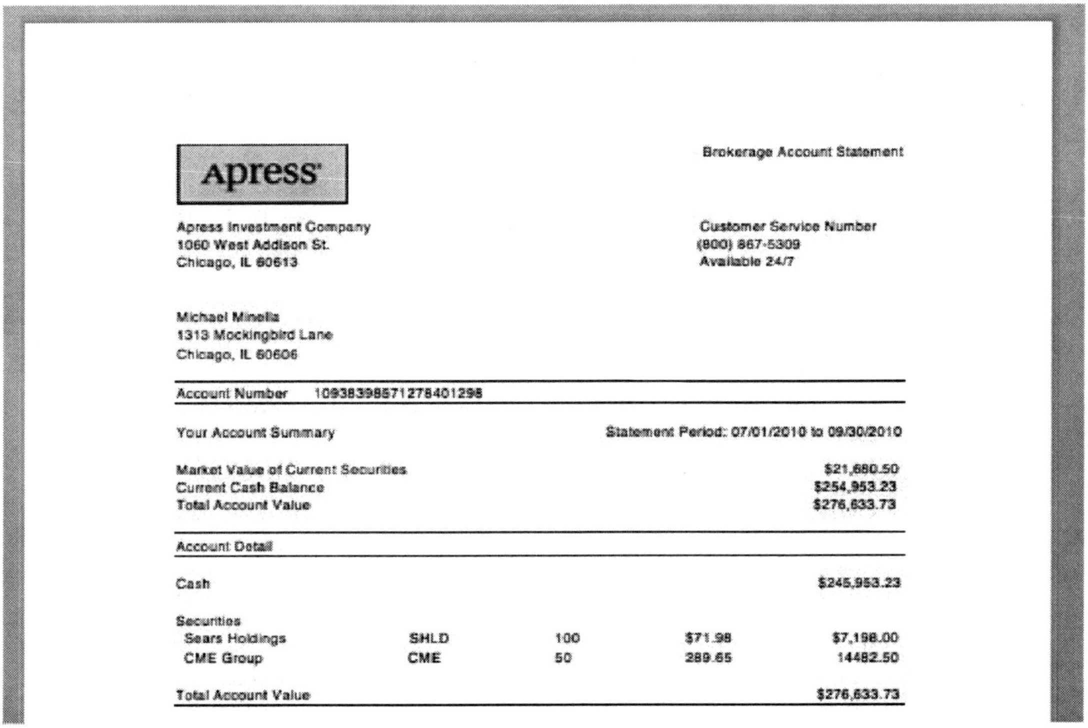

Figure 3-1. *Brokerage statement, formatted and printed on letterhead*

If you break down how the statement is created, there are really two pieces to it. The first is nothing more than a pretty piece of paper on which the second piece is printed. It's the second piece, shown in Figure 3-2, that you create in this book.

Brokerage Account Statement

Apress Investment Company
1060 West Addison St.
Chicago, IL 60613

Customer Service Number
(800) 867-5309
Available 24/7

Michael Minella
1313 Mockingbird Lane
Chicago, IL 60606

Account Number   10938398571278401298

Your Account Summary   Statement Period: 07/01/2010 to 09/30/2010

Market Value of Current Securities $21,680.50
Current Cash Balance $254,953.23
Total Account Value $276,633.73

Account Detail

Cash $245,953.23

Securities
  Sears Holdings   SHLD   100 $71.98 $7,198.00
  CME Group   CME   50   289.65   14482.50

Total Account Value $276,633.73

Figure 3-2. Plain-text brokerage statement

Typically, statements are created as follow. A batch process creates a print file consisting of little more than text. That print file is then sent to a printer that prints the text onto the decorated paper, producing the final statement. The print file is the piece you create using Spring Batch. Your batch process will perform the following functions:

1. Import a file of customer information and related transactions.

2. Retrieve from a web service the closing stock prices for all the stocks included in the database.

3. Import the previously downloaded stock prices into the database.

4. Calculate the pricing level for each of the accounts.

5. Calculate the transaction fees for each transaction based on the level calculated in the previous step.

6. Print the file for the brokerage account for the past month.

Let's look at what each of these features entails. Your job is provided with a customer-transaction flat file that consists of information about a customer and their transactions for the month. Your job updates existing customer information and adds their transactions to the database. When the transactions have been imported, the job obtains the latest prices for each of the stocks in the database from a web service, in order to calculate each account's current value. The job imports the downloaded prices into the database.

After the initial imports are complete, your job can begin calculating transaction fees. The brokerage makes its money by charging a fee for each transaction it does. These fees are based on how many transactions a customer has in a month. The more transactions a customer has, the less they're charged per transaction. The first step in calculating the transaction fees is to determine what level or tier the user falls into; then you can calculate the price for the customer's transactions. When all the calculations have been completed, you can generate the user's monthly statement.

This list of features is intended to provide a complete view into how Spring Batch is used in a real-world problem. Throughout the book, you learn about the features Spring Batch provides to help you develop batch processes like the one required for this scenario. In Chapter 10, you implement the batch job to meet the requirements outlined in the following user stories:

> *Import Transactions:* As the batch process, I will import the customer information and their related transactions into the database for future processing. Acceptance criteria:

- The batch job will import a predefined customer/transaction file into a database table.

- After the file has been imported, it will be deleted.

- The customer/transaction file will have two record formats. The first will be to identify the customer the subsequent transactions belong to. The second will be the individual transaction records.

- The format for the customer record is a comma-delimited record of the following fields:

Name	Required	Format
Customer Tax ID	True	\d{9}
Customer First Name	False	\w+
Customer Last Name	False	\w+
Customer Address 1	False	\w+
Customer City	False	\w+
Customer State	False	[A-Z]{2}
Customer Zip	False	\d{4}
Customer Account Number	False	\d{16}

- A customer record will look like the following:

205866465,Joshua,Thompson,3708 Park,Fairview,LA,58517,3276793917668488

- The format for the transaction records is a comma-delimited record of the following fields:

Name	Required	Format
Customer Account Number	True	\d{16}
Stock Symbol	True	\w+
Quantity True		\d+
Price True		\d+\.\d{2}
Transaction Timestamp	True MM\DD\YYYY	hh:mm:ss.ss

- An transaction record looks like the following:

3276793917668488,KSS,5767,7074247,2011-04-02 07:00:08

- All transactions will be imported as new transactions.

- An error file will be created with any customer records that aren't valid.

- Any transaction records that aren't valid will be written to the error file with the customer record

*Get Stocks Closing Price: A*s the batch process, at the prescheduled execution time, I will query the Yahoo stock web service to obtain the closing prices of all stocks held over the course of the previous month by our customers. I will build a file with this data for future import. Acceptance criteria

- The process will output a file each time it's run.

- The file will consist of one record per stock symbol.

- Each record in the file will have the following fields comma delimited:

Name	Required	Format
Stock Symbol	True	\w+
Closing Price	True	\d+\.\d{,2}

- The file of stock quotes will be obtained from the URL http://download.finance.yahoo.com/d/quotes.csv?s=<QUOTES>&f=sl1, where <QUOTES> is a list of ticker symbols delimited by pluses (+) and sl1 indicates that I want the stock ticker and the last price traded.[1]

---

[1] You can find more information about this web service at www.gummy-stuff.org/Yahoo-data.htm.

- An example record of what is returned using the URL
  `http://download.finance.yahoo.com/d/quotes.csv?s=HD&f=sl1` is:
  `"HD",31.46`.

Import Stock Prices: As the batch process, when I receive the stock price file, I
will import the file into the database for future processing. Acceptance criteria:

- The process will read the file that was downloaded by a previous step in the
  job.

- The stock prices for each of the stocks will be stored in the database for
  reference by each transaction.

- After the file has been successfully imported, it will be deleted.

- The record format of the file can be found in the story Get Stocks Closing Price.

- Any records that are ill formed will be logged in a separate error file for future
  analysis.

Calculate Pricing Tiers: As the batch process, after all input has been imported, I
will calculate the pricing tier each customer falls into and store it for future use.
Acceptance criteria:

- The process will calculate the price per trade based on the number of trades
  the customer has made over the course of the month.

- Each tier will be determined by the following thresholds:

Tier	Trades
I <=	10
II <=	100
III <=1,	000
IV >	10,000

- The tier value will be stored in relation to the customer for future fee
  calculations.

Calculate Fee Per Transaction: As the batch process, after I have completed
calculating pricing tiers, I will calculate a brokerage fee per trade that the
customer will be charged. Acceptance criteria:

- The process will calculate a fee for each transaction based on the tier the
  customer is in (as calculated in the Calculate Pricing Tiers story).

- The formula for calculating the price per trade is as follows:

Tier	Formula
I	$9 + .1% of purchase
II $3	
III $2	
IV $1	

Print Account Summary: As the batch process, after all calculations have been completed, I will print out a summary for each customer. This summary will provide an overview of the customer's account and a breakdown of what makes up the total value of their portfolio. Acceptance criteria:

- The process will generate a single file for each customer.

- The summary will begin with a line that states the following, fully justified

```
Your Account Summary                              Statement Period:<BEGIN_DATE> to <END_DATE>
```

- where BEGIN_DATE is the first calendar date of the previous month and END_DATE is the last of the previous month.

- After the summary title, there will be a single line item for each security type (securities and cash) and the current value of it for the account.

- After each of the detail items, a total account value will be printed. Following is an example of this section:

```
Your Account Summary                              Statement Period: 07/01/2010 to 09/30/2010
Market Value of Current Securities
$21,680.50
Current Cash Balance                                                          $254,953.23
Total Account Value                                                          $276,633.73
```

Print Account Detail: As the batch process, after each account summary I will print the detail makeup of each account. The account detail will provide the customer with a detailed look into the makeup of their account and how their investments are doing. Acceptance criteria:

- The account detail will be appended onto each customer's account summary.

- The detail will begin with a header stating "Account Detail," left justified.

- On a new line, the cash balance of the account will be specified.

- Below the cash balance, a header stating "Securities" will be displayed, left justified.

- For each stock held by the customer, the following fields will be displayed:

Name	Required	Format
Stock Symbol	True	\w+
Quantity True		\d+
Price True		\d+\.\d{2}
Total Value	True	Quantity * price in dollar format

- Below is an example of this section.

```
Account Detail
Cash          $245,953.23

Securities
  SHLD        100     $71.98  $7,198.00
  CME          50     289.65  14482.50

Total Account Value    $276,633.73
```

Print Statement Header: As the batch process, at the top of each page I will print a header. This will provide generic information about the account, the customer, and the brokerage. Acceptance criteria:

- The header is all static text except for the customer's address and account number.

- Following is an example of the header, where the Michael Minella name and address are the customer's name and address, and the account number is the customer's account number:

```
Brokerage Account Statement

Apress Investment Company        Customer              Service Number
1060 West Addison St.            (800)                 867-5309
Chicago, IL 60613               Available                24/7

Michael Minella
1313 Mockingbird Lane
Chicago, IL 60606

Account Number    10938398571278401298
```

That does it for the requirements. If your head is spinning about now, that's ok. In the next section, you begin to outline how to tackle this statement process with Spring Batch. Then, over the rest of this book, you learn how to implement the various pieces required to make it work.

Designing a Batch Job

As stated before, the goal of this project is to take a real-world example and work through it using the features that Spring Batch provides to create a robust, maintainable solution. In order to accomplish this goal, the example includes elements that may seem a bit complex right now, such as headers, multiple file format imports, and complex output including subheadings. The reason is that Spring Batch provides facilities exactly for these features. Let's dig into how you structure this batch process by outlining the job and describing its steps.

Job Description

In order to implement the statement-generation process, you build a single job with six steps. Figure 3-3 shows the flow of the batch job for this process, and the following sections describe the steps.

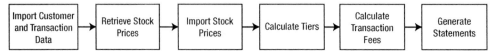

Figure 3-3. *Stock statement jobflow*

Importing Customer Transaction Data

To start the job, you begin by importing the customer and transaction data. Contained in a flat file, this data has a complex format consisting of two record types. The first record type is that of the customer, consisting of the customer's name, address, and account information. The second record type consists of detailed information about each transaction, including the stock ticker, the price paid, the quantity purchased or sold, and the timestamp when the transaction occurred. Using Spring Batch's ability to read multiline records allows you to process this file with minimal coding. You write a data access object (DAO) for the JDBC persistence of the imported data, as shown in Listing 3-1.

Listing 3-1. *Customer/Transaction Input File*

```
392041928,William,Robinson,9764 Jeopardy Lane,Chicago,IL,60606
HD,31.09,200,08:38:05
WMT,53.38,500,09:25:55
ADI,35.96,-300,10:56:10
REGN,29.53,-500,10:56:22
938472047,Robert,Johnson,1060 Addison St,Chicago,IL,60657
CABN,0.890,10000,14:52:15
NUAN,17.11,15000,15:02:45
```

Retrieving Stock Closing Prices

After you've imported the customer's information and transactions, you move on to obtaining the stock price information. This is a simple step that retrieves all the closing values for the stocks that have been traded over the previous month. To do this, you create a tasklet (as you did last chapter for the Hello, World batch process) to call the Yahoo web service specified in the requirements, and you download a CSV with the required stock data. This step writes the output to a file similar to that in Listing 3-2, for the next step to process.

Listing 3-2. *Stock Closing Price Input File*

```
SHLD,71.98
```

```
CME,289.65
GOOG,590.83
F,16.28
```

Importing Stock Prices into Database

This step reads the file and imports the data into the database. This step showcases the strengths of the declarative I/O provided by Spring Batch. Both the input and output of this job require no code on your part. Spring Batch provides the ability to read the CSV file you downloaded in the previous step via stock components of the framework as well as to update the database.

You may wonder why you don't import the data directly. The reason is error handling. You're importing data that was provided to you by a third-party source. Because you can't be sure of the quality of the data, you need to be able to handle any errors that may occur during the import. By writing the data to a file for a future step to process, you can restart the step without having to re-download the stock prices.

Calculating Transaction Fee Tiers

Up to this point, you haven't had to do any real processing of the data you're reading and writing. All you've done is pipe data from a file to a database (with some validation for good measure). When you're finished importing the required data, you begin doing the required calculations. Your brokerage company charges fees based on how much a customer trades. The more the customer trades, the less they're charged per trade. The amounts customers are charged are assigned via tiers; each tier is defined by the number of trades performed over the previous month and has a dollar amount associated with it.

In this step, you introduce an item processor between the reader and writer to determine the tier to which the customer belongs. You declare the reader via XML to load the customer's trade information and the writer to update the customer's account in the same manner.

Calculating Transaction Fees

When you've determined the tier for each customer, you can calculate the fee for each trade. In the previous step, you processed records at the customer level, with each customer being assigned a tier. In this step, you process records at the individual transaction level. As you can imagine, you process many more records in this step than in any previous step; you examine this step in further detail later, when the book talks about scalability options. However, to start, this step looks almost exactly like the previous one, but with different SQL for the reader, different logic in the item processor, and yet another JdbcItemWriter for the writer.

Generating Customer Monthly Statements

The last step seems to be the most complex—but as you know, looks can be deceiving. This step involves the generation of the statements themselves. It demonstrates some of the beauty of applying decoupled solutions to batch problems. By providing a custom-coded formatter, you can do virtually all the work with a single simple class. This step also uses the callbacks for the headers.

All of this sounds great in theory but leaves a lot of questions to be answered. That's good. You'll spend the rest of the book working through how these features are implemented in the processes as well as examining things like exception handling and restart/retry logic. One final item you should be familiar with before you move on, though, is the data model. That will help clear the air regarding how this system is structured. Let's take a look.

Understanding the Data Model

You've seen all the different pieces of the job you create throughout this book. Let's move on to the last piece of the puzzle before you get into actual development. Batch processes are data driven. Because there are no user interfaces, the various datastores end up being the only external interaction the process has. This section looks at the data model used for the sample application.

Figure 3-4 outlines the application-specific tables for this batch process. To be clear, this diagram doesn't encompass all the tables required for this batch job to run. Chapter 2 took a brief look at the tables Spring Batch uses in the job repository. All of those tables will exist in addition to these in your database. Because it isn't uncommon to deploy the batch schema separately, and you reviewed it in the last chapter, I've chosen to leave it out of Figure 3-4.

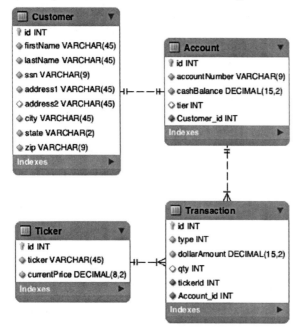

Figure 3-4. Sample application data model

For the batch application, you have four tables: Customer, Account, Transaction, and Ticker. When you look at the data in the tables, notice that you aren't storing all the required fields to generate the statement. There are fields (such as the totals in the account summary) that you calculate during processing. Other than that, the data model should appear relatively straightforward:

- *Customer:* This record contains all the customer-specific information, including name and tax identification number.

- *Account.* For every customer, an account is maintained. For your purposes, each account has a number and a running cash balance from which fees are deducted as needed. The customer's transaction fee tier is also stored at this level.

- *Transaction.* Each trade has a corresponding record in the Transactions table. The data here is used to determine the current state of the account (how many shares are held, and so on).

- *Ticker.* For each stock that has been traded by the brokerage company's customers, a record exists in this table containing the ticker and the most recent closing price for the stock.

Summary

This chapter discussed the agile development process and how you can apply it to batch development. The chapter continued along those lines by defining requirements via user stories for the sample application you build throughout the course of this book. From this point, the book switches from the "what" and "why" of Spring Batch to the "how."

In the next chapter, you take a deep dive into Spring Batch's concepts of jobs and steps and look at a number of other-specific examples.

Understanding Jobs and Steps

In Chapter 2, you created your first job. You walked through the configuration of a job and steps, executed the job, and configured a database to store your job repository. In that "Hello, World!" example, you began to scratch the surface of what jobs and steps are in Spring Batch. This chapter continues to explore jobs and steps at a much deeper level. You begin by learning what a job and a step are in relation to the Spring Batch framework.

From there, you dive into great detail about what happens when jobs or steps are executed, from loading them and validating that they're valid to running all the way through their completion. Then, you dig into some code, see the various parts of jobs and steps that you can configure, and learn best practices along the way. Finally, you see how different pieces of the batch puzzle can pass data to each other via the various scopes involved in a Spring Batch process.

Although you dive deep into steps in this chapter, the largest parts of a step are their readers and writers, which aren't covered here. Chapters 7 and 9 explore the input and output functionality available in Spring Batch. This chapter keeps the I/O aspects of each step as simple as possible so you can focus on the intricacies of steps in a job.

Introducing a Job

With the proliferation of web applications, you may have become used to the idea of an application being broken up into requests and responses. Each request contains the data for a single unique piece of processing that occurs. The result of the request is typically a view of some kind being returned to the user. A web application can be made up of dozens to literally hundreds of unique interactions like this, each structured the same way, as shown in Figure 4-1.

http://www.apress.com/some_page?param=value

<html><body><p>Some Text</p></body></html>

Figure 4-1. Request/Response processing of a web application

Yet when you think about batch jobs, you're really talking about a collection of actions. The term *flow*[1] is a good way to describe a job. Using the web application example again, think about how the checkout process of a shopping cart application works. When you click Check Out with items in your cart, you're walked through a series of steps: register or sign in, confirm shipping address, enter billing information, confirm order, submit order. This flow is similar to what a job is.

For the purpose of this book, a job is defined as a unique, ordered list of steps that can be executed from start to finish independently. Let's break down this definition so you can get a better understanding of what you're working with:

- *Unique:* Jobs in Spring Batch are configured via XML similar to how beans are configured using the core Spring framework and are reusable as a result. You can execute a job as many times as you need to with the same configuration. Because of this there is no reason to define the same job multiple times.

- *Ordered list of steps:*[2] Going back to the checkout flow example, the order of the steps matter. You can't validate your shipping address if you haven't registered one in the first place. You can't execute the checkout process if your shopping cart is empty. The order of steps in your job is important. You can't generate a customer's statement until their transactions have been imported into your system. You can't calculate the balance of an account until you've calculated all of your fees. You structure jobs in a sequence that allows all steps to be executed in a logical order.

- *Can be executed from start to finish:* Chapter 1 defined a batch process as a process that can run without additional interaction to some form of completion. A job is a series of steps that can be executed without external dependencies. You don't structure a job so that the third step is to wait until a file is sent to a directory to be processed. Instead, you have a job begin when the file has arrived.

- *Independently:* Each batch job should be able to execute without external dependencies affecting it. This doesn't mean a job can't have dependencies. On the contrary, there are not many practical jobs (except "Hello, World") that don't have external dependencies. However, the job should be able to manage those dependencies. If a file isn't there, it handles the error gracefully. It doesn't wait for a file to be delivered (that's the responsibility of a scheduler, and so on). A job can handle all elements of the process it's defined to do.

As a comparison, Figure 4-2 shows how a batch process executes versus the web application in Figure 4-1.

---

[1] For those familiar with the Spring Web Flow framework, a job is very similar in structure to a flow within a web application.

[2] Although most jobs consist of an ordered list of steps, Spring Batch does support the ability to execute steps in parallel. This feature is discussed later.

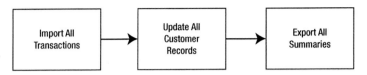

Figure 4-2. Flow of data through a batch process

As you can see in Figure 4-2, a batch process is executed with all of the input available for it as it runs. There are no user interactions. Each step is executed to completion against a dataset before the next step is executed. Before you dig deeply into how to configure the various features of a job in Spring Batch, let's talk about a job's execution lifecycle.

Tracing a Job's Lifecycle

When a job is executed, it goes through a lifecycle. Knowledge of this lifecycle is important as you structure your jobs and understand what is happening as they run. When you define a job in XML, what you're really doing is providing the blueprint for a job. Just like writing the code for a Java class is like defining a blueprint for the JVM from which to create an instance, your XML definition of a job is a blueprint for Spring Batch to create an instance of your job.

The execution of a job begins with a job runner. The job runner is intended to execute the job requested by name with the parameters passed. Spring Batch provides two job runners:

- CommandLineJobRunner: This job runner is intended to be used from a script or directly from the command line. When used, the CommandLineJobRunner bootstraps Spring and executes the job requested with the parameters passed.

- JobRegistryBackgroundJobRunner: When using a scheduler like Quartz or a JMX hook to execute a job, typically Spring is bootstrapped and the Java process is live before the job is to be executed. In this case, a JobRegistry is created when Spring is bootstrapped containing the jobs available to run. The JobRegistryBackgroundJobRunner is used to create the JobRegistry.

CommandLineJobRunner and JobRegistryBackgroundJobRunner (both located in the org.springframework.batch.core.launch.support package) are the two job runners provided by the framework. You used CommandLineJobRunner in Chapter 2 to run the "Hello, World!" job, and you continue to use it through out the book.

Although the job runner is what you use to interface with Spring Batch, it's not a standard piece of the framework. There is no JobRunner interface because each scenario would require a different implementation (although both of the two job runners provided by Spring Batch use main methods to start). Instead, the true entrance into the framework's execute is an implementation of the org.springframework.batch.core.launch.JobLauncher interface.

Spring Batch provides a single JobLauncher, the org.springframework.batch.core.launch.support.SimpleJobLauncher. This class uses the TaskExecutor interface from Core Spring to execute the requested job. You see in a bit at how this is configured, but it's important to note that there are multiple ways to configure the org.springframework.core.task.TaskExecutor in Spring. If an org.springframework.core.task.SyncTaskExecutor is used, the job is executed in the same thread as the JobLauncher. Any other option executes the job in its own thread.

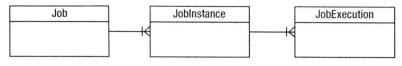

Figure 4-3. *The relationship between a* Job, JobInstance, *and* JobExecution

When a batch job is run, an org.springframework.batch.core.JobInstance is created. A JobInstance represents a logical run of the job and is identified by the job name and the parameters passed to the job for this run. A run of the job is different than an attempt at executing the job. If you have a job that is expected to run daily, you would have it configured once in your XML (defining the blueprint). Each day you would have a new run or JobInstance because you pass a new set of parameters into the job (one of which is the date). Each JobInstance would be considered complete when it has an attempt or JobExecution that has successfully completed.

■**Note** A JobInstance can only be executed once to a successful completion. Because a JobInstance is identified by the job name and parameters passed in, this means you can only run a job once with the same parameters.

You're probably wondering how Spring Batch knows the state of a JobInstance from attempt to attempt. In Chapter 2, you took a look at the job repository, and in it there was a batch_job_instance table. This table is the base from which all other tables are derived. It's the batch_job_instance and batch_job_params that identify a JobInstance (the batch_job_instance.job_key is actually a hash of the name and parameters).

An is an actual attempt to run the job. If a job runs from start to finish the first time, there is only one JobExecution related to a given JobInstance. If a job ends in an error state after the first run, a new JobExecution is created each time an attempt is made to run the JobInstance (by passing in the same parameters to the same job). For each JobExecution that Spring Batch creates for your job, a record in the batch_job_execution table is created. As the JobExecution executes, its state is maintained in the batch_job_execution_context as well. This allows Spring Batch to restart a job at the correct point if an error occurs.

Configuring a Job

Enough about theory. Let's get into some code. This section digs into the various ways to configure a job. As mentioned in Chapter 2, as with all of Spring, Spring Batch configurations are done via XML. With that in mind, one of the very welcome features added to Spring Batch 2 was the addition of a batch XSD to make configuration of batch jobs more concise.

■**Note** A good best practice is to configure each job in its own XML file named after the name of the job.

Basic Job Configuration

Listing 4-1 shows the shell of a basic Spring Batch job. For the record, this isn't a valid job. A job in Spring Batch is required to have at least one step or be declared abstract.[3] In any case, the focus here is on the job and not the steps, so you add steps to the job later in this chapter.

You used this format in Chapter 2's "Hello, World!" job, and it should look familiar to anyone who has used Spring before. Just like most other extensions of the Spring framework, you configure beans like any other use of Spring and have an XSD that defines domain-specific tags. In this case, you include the XSD for Spring Batch in the beans tag.

Listing 4-1. basicJob.xml

```xml
<?xml version="1.0" encoding="UTF-8"?>
<beans xmlns:batch="http://www.springframework.org/schema/batch"
       xmlns="http://www.springframework.org/schema/beans"
       xmlns:xsi="http://www.w3.org/2001/XMLSchema-instance"
       xsi:schemaLocation="http://www.springframework.org/schema/beans
           http://www.springframework.org/schema/beans/spring-beans-3.0.xsd
           http://www.springframework.org/schema/batch
           http://www.springframework.org/schema/batch/spring-batch-2.1.xsd">

    <import resource="../launch-context.xml"/>

    <batch:job id="basicJob">
        ...
    </batch:job>
</beans>
```

The first piece of the basicJob.xml file after the beans tag is an import for the launch-context.xml file, which is located in the src/main/resources directory of your project. You used this file in Chapter 2 without really going into it, so let's look at it now. Listing 4-2 shows launch-context.xml. Notice that this launch-context.xml is a significantly slimmed-down version of what came out of the zip file. This book discusses the rest of the file as you use its parts in future chapters. For now, let's focus on the pieces that you need to make Spring Batch work.

Listing 4-2. launch-context.xml

```xml
<?xml version="1.0" encoding="UTF-8"?>
<beans xmlns="http://www.springframework.org/schema/beans"
       xmlns:p="http://www.springframework.org/schema/p"
       xmlns:xsi="http://www.w3.org/2001/XMLSchema-instance"
       xsi:schemaLocation="http://www.springframework.org/schema/beans
           http://www.springframework.org/schema/beans/spring-beans-3.0.xsd">

    <bean id="dataSource" class="org.apache.commons.dbcp.BasicDataSource">
        <property name="driverClassName" value="${batch.jdbc.driver}" />
        <property name="url" value="${batch.jdbc.url}" />
        <property name="username" value="${batch.jdbc.user}" />
```

---

[3] Later, this chapter looks at abstract jobs.

```xml
            <property name="password" value="${batch.jdbc.password}" />
    </bean>

    <bean id="transactionManager"
    class="org.springframework.jdbc.datasource.DataSourceTransactionManager"
    lazy-init="true">
        <property name="dataSource" ref="dataSource" />
    </bean>

    <bean id="placeholderProperties"
class="org.springframework.beans.factory.config.PropertyPlaceholderConfigure"
>
        <property name="location" value="classpath:batch.properties" />
        <property name="systemPropertiesModeName"
            value="SYSTEM_PROPERTIES_MODE_OVERRIDE" />
        <property name="ignoreUnresolvablePlaceholders" value="true" />
        <property name="order" value="1" />
    </bean>

    <bean id="jobRepository"
class="org.springframework.batch.core.repository.support.JobRepositoryFactoryBean"
p:dataSource-ref="dataSource" p:transactionManager-ref="transactionManager" />

    <bean id="jobLauncher"
    class="org.springframework.batch.core.launch.support.SimpleJobLauncher">
        <property name="jobRepository" ref="jobRepository" />
    </bean>
</beans>
```

launch-context.xml has most of the elements discussed in the previous section and their dependencies. It starts with a datasource. You use standard Spring configuration to configure a datasource that Spring Batch uses to access the job repository and that is also available for any other database access your batch processes may require. It's important to note that the database used by Spring Batch for the JobRepository isn't required to be the same as the schema (or schemas) used for business processing.

transactionManager also is configured in this file. Transaction processing is important in batch jobs given that you process large volumes of data in chunks and each chunk being committed at once. This again is a standard configuration using core Spring components.

Notice that you're using properties to specify values that may change from environment to environment. After transactionManager, you configure Spring's PropertyPlaceholderConfigurer to handle the population of these properties at runtime. You're using the batch.properties file to specify the values, which is included in the source provided in the zip file.

Next you have jobRepository. This is the first Spring Batch component you're going to configure in the launch-context.xml file. jobRepository is used to maintain the state of the job and each step for Spring Batch. In this case, you're configuring the handle that the framework uses to perform CRUD operations on the database. Chapter 5 goes over some advanced configurations of jobRepository including changing schema prefixes, and so on. This example configuration provides its two required dependencies: a datasource and a transaction manager.

The last piece of launch-context.xml you have here is the jobLauncher bean. As the previous section said, the job launcher is the gateway into Spring Batch framework from an execution standpoint. It is configured with the jobRepository as a dependency.

With the common components defined, let's go back to basicJob.xml. With regard to configuration, 90% of the configuration of a job is the ordered definition of the steps, which is covered later in this chapter. Note about the basicJob that you haven't configured any reference to a job repository or a transaction manager. This is because by default, Spring uses the jobRepository with the name jobRepository and the transaction manager named transactionManager. You see how to specifically configure these elements in Chapter 5, which discusses using JobRepository and its metadata.

Job Inheritance

Most of the options related to configuring a job are related to execution, so you see those later when you cover job execution. However, there is one instance when you can alter the job configuration that makes sense to discuss here: the use of inheritance.

Like most other object-oriented aspects of programming, the Spring Batch framework allows you to configure common aspects of your jobs once and then extend the base job with other jobs. Those other jobs inherit the properties of the job they're extending. But there are some caveats to inheritance in Spring Batch. Spring Batch allows the inheritance of all job-level configurations from job to job. This is an important point. You can't define a job that has common steps you can inherit. Things you're allowed to inherit are the ability to restart a job, job listeners, and a validator for any parameters passed in. To do so, you do two things: declare the parent job abstract and specify it as the parent job in any job that wants to inherit functionality from it.

Listing 4-3 configures a parent job to be restartable[4] and then extends it with sampleJob. Because sampleJob extends baseJob, it's also restartable. Listing 4-4 shows how you can configure an abstract job that has a parameter validator configured and extend it to inherit the validator as well.

Listing 4-3. inheritanceJob.xml with Job Inheritance

```
<job id="baseJob" abstract="true" restartable="true">
</job>

<job id="inheritanceJob" parent="baseJob">
    ...
</job>
```

Listing 4-4. Parameter Validator Inheritance

```
<job id="baseJob" abstract="true" restartable="true">
    <validator ref="myParameterValidator"/>
</job>

<job id="sampleJob1" parent="baseJob">
    ...
</job>
```

Although most of a job's configuration can be inherited from a parent job, not all of it is. Following is a list of the things you can define in a parent job that are inherited by its children:

- *Restartable:* Specifies whether a job is restartable or not

---

[4] Restartability is covered in greater detail in Chapter 6.

- *A parameter incrementer:* Increments job parameters with each JobExecution

- *Listeners:* Any job-level listeners

- *Job parameter validator:* Validates that the parameters passed to a job meet any requirements

All of these concepts are new and are discussed later in this chapter. For now, all you need to be aware of is that when these values are set on an abstract job, any job extending the parent job inherits them. Things the child doesn't inherit include step configurations, step flows, and decisions. These must be defined in any job using them.

Inheritance can be helpful not only to consolidate the configuration of common attributes but also to standardize how certain things are done. Because the last example began looking at parameters and their validation, that seems like a logical next topic.

Job Parameters

You've read a few times that a JobInstance is identified by the job name and the parameters passed into the job. You also know that because of that, you can't run the same job more than once with the same parameters. If you do, you receive an org.springframework.batch.core.launch.JobInstanceAlreadyCompleteException telling you that if you'd like to run the job again, you need to change the parameters (as shown in Listing 4-5).

Listing 4-5. What Happens When You Try to Run a Job Twice with the Same Parameters

```
2010-11-28 21:06:03,598 ERROR
org.springframework.batch.core.launch.support.CommandLineJobRunner.main()
[org.springframework.batch.core.launch.support.CommandLineJobRunner] - <Job Terminated in
error: A job instance already exists and is complete for parameters={}.  If you want to run
this job again, change the parameters.>
org.springframework.batch.core.repository.JobInstanceAlreadyCompleteException: A job instance
already exists and is complete for parameters={}.  If you want to run this job again, change
the parameters.
      at
org.springframework.batch.core.repository.support.SimpleJobRepository.createJobExecution(Simpl
eJobRepository.java:122)
      at sun.reflect.NativeMethodAccessorImpl.invoke0(Native Method)
...
```

So how do you pass parameters to your jobs? Spring Batch allows you not only to pass parameters to your jobs but also to automatically increment them[5] or validate them before your job runs. You start by looking at how to pass parameters to your jobs.

Passing parameters to your job depends on how you're calling your job. One of the functions of the job runner is to create an instance of org.springframework.batch.core.JobParameters and pass it to the JobLauncher for execution. This makes sense because the way you pass parameters is different if you

---

[5] It may make sense to have a parameter that is incremented for each JobInstance. For example, if the date the job is run is one of its parameters, this can be addressed automatically via a parameter incrementer.

launch a job from a command line than if you launch your job from a Quartz scheduler. Because you've been using CommandLineJobRunner up to now, let's start there.

Passing parameters to CommandLineJobRunner is as simple as passing key=value pairs on the command line. Listing 4-6 shows how to pass parameters to a job using the way you've been calling jobs up to this point.

Listing 4-6. Passing Parameters to the CommandLineJobRunner

```
java -jar sample-application-0.0.1-SNAPSHOT.jar jobs/sampleJob.xml sampleJob name=Michael
```

In Listing 4-6, you pass one parameter, name. When you pass parameter into your batch job, your job runner creates an instance of JobParameters, which serves as a container for all the parameters the job received.

JobParameters isn't much more than a wrapper for a java.util.Map<String, JobParameter> object. Notice that although you're passing in Strings in this example, the value of the Map is an org.springframework.batch.core.JobParameter instance. The reason for this is type. Spring Batch provides for type conversion of parameters, and with that, type-specific accessors on the JobParameter class. If you specify the type of parameter to be a long, it's available as a java.lang.Long. String, Double, and java.util.Date are all available out of the box for conversion. In order to utilize the conversions, you tell Spring Batch the parameter type in parentheses after the parameter name, as shown in Listing 4-7. Notice that Spring Batch requires that the name of each be all lowercase.

Listing 4-7. Specifying the Type of a Parameter

```
java -jar sample-application-0.0.1-SNAPSHOT.jar jobs/sampleJob.xml sampleJob
param1(string)=Spring param2(long)=33
```

To view what parameters have been passed into your job, you can look in the job repository. Chapter 2 noted that there is a table for job parameters called batch_job_params, but because you didn't pass any parameters to your job, it was empty. If you explore the table after executing the examples in Listings 4-6 and 4-7, you should see what is shown in Table 4-1.

Table 4-1. Contents of `BATCH_JOB_PARAMS`

JOB_ INSTANCE_ ID	TYPE_CD	KEY_NAME	STRING_VAL	DATE_VAL	LONG_VAL	DOUBLE_VAL
1	STRING	name	Michael			
2	STRING	param1	Spring			
2	LONG param2				33	

Now that you know how to get parameters into your batch jobs, how do you access them once you have them? If you take a quick look at the `ItemReader`, `ItemProcessor`, `ItemWriter`, and `Tasklet` interfaces, you quickly notice that all the methods of interest don't receive a `JobParameters` instance as one of their parameters. There are a few different options depending on where you're attempting to access the parameter:

- `ChunkContext`: If you look at the `HelloWorld` tasklet, you see that the execute method receives two parameters. The first parameter is `org.springframework.batch.core.StepContribution`, which contains information about where you are in the step (write count, read count, and so on). The second parameter is an instance of `ChunkContext`. It provides the state of the job at the point of execution. If you're in a tasklet, it contains any information about the chunk you're processing. Information about that chunk includes information about the step and job. As you might guess, `ChunkContext` has a reference to `org.springframework.batch.core.scope.context.StepContext`, which contains your `JobParameters`.

- *Late binding:* For any piece of the framework that isn't a tasklet, the easiest way to get a handle on a parameter is to inject it via the Spring Configuration. Given that `JobParameters` are immutable, binding them during bootstrapping makes perfect sense.

Listing 4-8 shows an updated `HelloWorld` tasklet that utilizes a name parameter in the output as an example of how to access parameters from `ChunkContext`.

Listing 4-8. Accessing JobParameters in a Tasklet

```
package com.apress.springbatch.chapter4;

import org.springframework.batch.core.StepContribution;
import org.springframework.batch.core.scope.context.ChunkContext;
import org.springframework.batch.core.step.tasklet.Tasklet;
import org.springframework.batch.repeat.RepeatStatus;
import org.springframework.batch.item.ExecutionContext;

public class HelloWorld implements Tasklet {
    private static final String HELLO_WORLD = "Hello, %s";
```

```
        public RepeatStatus execute( StepContribution step,
                                     ChunkContext context ) throws Exception {
            String name =
                (String) context.getStepContext().getJobParameters().get("name");
            System.out.println( String.format(HELLO_WORLD, name) );
            return RepeatStatus.FINISHED;
        }
}
```

Although Spring Batch stores the job parameters in an instance of the JobParameter class, when you obtain the parameters this way getJobParameters() returns a Map<String, Object>. Because of this, the previous cast is required.

Listing 4-9 shows how to use Spring's late binding to inject job parameters into components without having to reference any of the JobParameters code. Besides the use of Spring's EL (Expression Language) to pass in the value, any bean that is going to be configured with late binding is required to have the scope set to step.

Listing 4-9. Obtaining Job Parameters via Late Binding

```
<bean id="helloWorld" class="com.apress.springbatch.chapter4.HelloWorld"
    scope="step">
    <property name="name" value="#{jobParameters[name]}"/>
</bean>
```

It's important to note that in order for the configuration in Listing 4-9 to work, the HelloWorld class needs to be updated to accept the new parameter. Listing 4-10 shows the updated code for this method of parameter association.

Listing 4-10. Updated HelloWorld Tasklet

```
package com.apress.springbatch.chapter4;

import org.springframework.batch.core.StepContribution;
import org.springframework.batch.core.scope.context.ChunkContext;
import org.springframework.batch.core.step.tasklet.Tasklet;
import org.springframework.batch.repeat.RepeatStatus;
import org.springframework.batch.item.ExecutionContext;

public class HelloWorld implements Tasklet {

    private static final String HELLO_WORLD = "Hello, %s";

    private String name;

    public RepeatStatus execute( StepContribution step,
                                 ChunkContext context ) throws Exception {
        String name =
            (String) context.getStepContext().getJobParameters().get("name");
        System.out.println( String.format(HELLO_WORLD, name) );
        return RepeatStatus.FINISHED;
    }
```

```
    public void setName(String newName) {
        name = newName;
    }

    public String getName() {
        return name;
    }
}
```

With the ability to pass parameters into your jobs as well as put them to use, two parameter-specific pieces of functionality are built into the Spring Batch framework that the chapter discusses next: parameter validation and the ability to increment a given parameter with each run. Let's start with parameter validation because it's been alluded to in previous examples.

Validating Job Parameters

Whenever a piece of software obtains outside input, it's a good idea to be sure the input is valid for what you're expecting. The web world uses client-side JavaScript as well as various server-side frameworks to validate user input, and validation of batch parameters is no different. Fortunately, Spring has made it very easy to validate job parameters. To do so, you just need to implement the org.springframework.batch.core.JobParametersValidator interface and configure your implementation in your job. Listing 4-11 shows an example of a job parameter validator in Spring Batch.

Listing 4-11. A Parameter Validator that Validates the Parameter Name Is a String

```
package com.apress.springbatch.chapter4;

import java.util.Map;
import org.springframework.batch.core.*;
import org.apache.commons.lang.StringUtils;

public class ParameterValidator implements JobParametersValidator{

    public void validate(JobParameters params) throws
        JobParametersInvalidException {
        String name = params.getString("name");
        if(!StringUtils.isAlpha(name)) {
            throw new
                JobParametersInvalidException("Name is not alphabetic");
        }
    }
}
```

As you can see, the method of consequence is the validate method. Because this method is void, the validation is considered passing as long as a JobParametersInvalidException isn't thrown. In this example, if you pass the name 4566, the exception is thrown and the job completes with a status of COMPLETED. This is important to note. Just because the parameters you passed in weren't valid doesn't mean the job didn't complete correctly. In the case where invalid parameters are passed, the job is marked as COMPLETED because it did all valid processing for the input it received. And when you think about this, it makes sense. A JobInstance is identified by the job name and the parameters passed into the job. If you pass in invalid parameters, you don't want to repeat that, so it's ok to declare the job completed.

In addition to implementing your own custom parameter validator as you did earlier, Spring Batch offers a validator to confirm that all the required parameters have been passed: org.springframework.batch.core.job.DefaultJobParametersValidator. To use it, you configure it the same way you would your custom validator. DefaultJobParametersValidator has two optional dependencies: requiredKeys and optionalKeys. Both are String arrays that take in a list of parameter names that are either required or are the only optional parameters allowed. Listing 4-12 shows two configurations for DefaultJobParametersValidator as well as how to add it to your job.

Listing 4-12. DefaultJobParametersValidator Configuration in parameterValidatorJob.xml

```
<beans:bean id="requiredParamValidator"
    class="org.springframework.batch.core.job.DefaultJobParametersValidator">
    <beans:property name="requiredKeys" value="batch.name,batch.runDate"/>
</beans:bean>

<beans:bean id="optionalParamValidator"
    class="org.springframework.batch.core.job.DefaultJobParametersValidator">
    <beans:property name="requiredKeys" value="batch.name,batch.runDate"/>
    <beans:property name="optionalKeys" value="batch.address"/>
</beans:bean>

<job id="parameterValidatorJob">
    ...
    <validator ref="requiredParamValidator"/>
</job>
```

If you use requiredParamValidator, your job throws an exception if you don't pass the parameters batch.name and batch.runDate. You're allowed to pass more parameters in if required, but those two can't be null. On the other hand, if you use optionalParamValidator, the job once again throws an exception if batch.name and batch.runDate aren't passed to the job, but it also throws an exception if any parameters in addition to batch.address are passed. The difference between the two validators is that the first one can accept any parameters in addition to the required ones. The second one can only accept the three specified. In either case, if the invalid scenario occurs, a JobParametersInvalidException is thrown and the job is marked as completed as previously discussed.

Incrementing Job Parameters

Up to now, you've been running under the limitation that a job can only be run once with a given set of parameters. If you've been following along with the examples, you've probably hit what happens if you attempt to run the same job twice with the same parameters as shown in Listing 4-5. However, there is a small loophole: using JobParametersIncrementer.

org.springframework.batch.core.JobParametersIncrementer is an interface that Spring Batch provides to allow you to uniquely generate parameters for a given job. You can add a timestamp to each run. You may have some other business logic that requires a parameter to be incremented with each run. The framework provides a single implementation of the interface, which increments a single long parameter with the default name run.id.

Listing 4-13 shows how to configure a JobParametersIncrementer for your job by adding the reference to the job.

Listing 4-13. Using a JobParametersIncrementer in a Job

```
<beans:bean id="idIncrementer"
    class="org.springframework.batch.core.launch.support.RunIdIncrementer"/>

<job id="baseJob" incrementer="idIncrementer">
    ...
</job>
```

Once you've configured JobParametersIncrementer (the framework provides org.springframework.batch.core.launch.support.RunIdIncrementer in this case), there are two more things you need to do to make this work. First you need to add the configuration for a JobExplorer implementation. Chapter 5 goes into detail about what JobExplorer is and how to use it. For now, just know that Spring Batch needs it to increment parameters. Listing 4-14 shows the configuration, but it's already configured in the launch-context.xml that is included in the zip file distribution.

Listing 4-14. Configuration for JobExplorer

```
<bean id="jobExplorer"
class="org.springframework.batch.core.explore.support.JobExplorerFactoryBean">
    <property name="dataSource" ref="dataSource"/>
</bean>
```

The last piece of the puzzle to use a JobParametersIncrementer affects how you call your job. When you want to increment a parameter, you need to add the parameter -next to the command when you call your job. This tells Spring Batch to use the incrementer as required.

Now when you run your job with the command in Listing 4-15, you can run it as many times as you want with the same parameters.

Listing 4-15. Command to Run a Job and Increment Parameters

```
 java –jar sample-application-0.0.1-SNAPSHOT.jar jobs/sampleJob.xml
sampleJob name=Michael -next
```

In fact, go ahead and give it a try. When you've run the sampleJob three or four times, look in the batch_job_params table and see how Spring Batch is executing your job with two parameters: one String named name with the value *Michael*, and one long named run.id. run.id's value changes each time, increasing by one with each execution.

You saw earlier that you may want to have a parameter be a timestamp with each run of the job. This is common in jobs that run once a day. To do so, you need to create your own implementation of JobParametersIncrementer. The configuration and execution are the same as before. However, instead of using RunIdIncrementer, you use DailyJobTimestamper, the code for which is in Listing 4-16.

Listing 4-16. DailyJobTimestamper.java

```
package com.apress.springbatch.chapter4;

import org.springframework.batch.core.JobParameters;
import org.springframework.batch.core.JobParametersBuilder;
import org.springframework.batch.core.JobParametersIncrementer;

import java.util.Date;

import org.apache.commons.lang.time.DateUtils;
```

```
public class DailyJobTimestamper implements JobParametersIncrementer {

/**
* Increment the current.date parameter.
*/
public JobParameters getNext( JobParameters parameters ) {
Date today = new Date();

if ( parameters != null && !parameters.isEmpty() ) {
Date oldDate = parameters.getDate( "current.date", new Date() );
today = DateUtils.addDays(oldDate, 1);
}

return new JobParametersBuilder().addDate( "current.date", today )
                                 .toJobParameters();
}
}
```

It's pretty obvious that job parameters are an important part of the framework. They allow you to specify values at runtime for your job. They also are used to uniquely identify a run of your job. You use them more throughout the book for things like configuring the dates for which to run the job and reprocessing error files. For now, let's look at another powerful feature at the job level: job listeners.

Working with Job Listeners

When you use a web application, feedback is essential to the user experience. A user clicks a link, and the page refreshes within a few seconds. However, as you've seen, batch processes don't provide much in the way of feedback. You launch a process, and it runs. That's it. Yes, you can query the job repository to see the current state of your job, and there is the Spring Batch Admin web application, but many times you may want something to happen at a given point in your job. Say you want to send an email if a job fails. Maybe you want to log the beginning and ending of each job to a special file. Any processing you want to occur at the beginning (once the JobExecution is created and persisted but before the first step is executed) or end of a job is done with a job listener.

There are two ways to create a job listener. The first is by implementing the org.springframework.batch.core.JobExecutionListener interface. This interface has two methods of consequence: beforeJob and afterJob. Each takes JobExecution as a parameter, and they're executed— you guessed it, before the job executes and after the job executes, respectively. One important thing to note about the afterJob method is that it's called regardless of the status the job finishes in. Because of this, you may need to evaluate the status in which the job ended to determine what to do. Listing 4-17 has an example of a simple listener that prints out some information about the job being run before and after as well as the status of the job when it completed.

Listing 4-17. JobLoggerListener.java

```
package com.apress.springbatch.chapter4;

import org.springframework.batch.core.JobExecution;
import org.springframework.batch.core.JobExecutionListener;

public class JobLoggerListener implements JobExecutionListener {
```

```
    public void beforeJob(JobExecution jobExecution) {
        System.out.println(jobExecution.getJobInstance().getJobName()
                + " is beginning execution");
    }

    public void afterJob(JobExecution jobExecution) {
        System.out.println(jobExecution.getJobInstance()
                                      .getJobName()
                                      + " has completed with the status " +
                                      jobExecution.getStatus());
    }
}
```

If you remember, the book previously stated that Spring Batch doesn't support annotations yet for its configuration. That was a lie. A small number of annotations are supported, and @BeforeJob and @AfterJob are two of them. When using the annotations, the only difference, as shown in Listing 4-18, is that you don't need to implement the JobExecutionListener interface.

Listing 4-18. JobLoggerListener.java

```java
package com.apress.springbatch.chapter4;

import org.springframework.batch.core.JobExecution;
import org.springframework.batch.core.JobExecutionListener;
import org.springframework.batch.core.annotation.AfterJob;
import org.springframework.batch.core.annotation.BeforeJob;

public class JobLoggerListener {

    @BeforeJob
    public void beforeJob(JobExecution jobExecution) {
        System.out.println(jobExecution.getJobInstance().getJobName()
                + " is beginning execution");
    }

    @AfterJob
    public void afterJob(JobExecution jobExecution) {
        System.out.println(jobExecution.getJobInstance()
                                      .getJobName()
                                      + " has completed with the status " +
                                      jobExecution.getStatus());
    }
}
```

The configuration of these two options is the same in either case. Back in the world of XML, you can configure multiple listeners in your job, as shown in Listing 4-19.

Listing 4-19. Configuring Job Listeners in `listenerJob.xml`

```
<beans:bean id="loggingListener"
    class="com.apress.springbatch.chapter4.JobLoggerListener"/>

<job id="listenerJob" incrementer="idIncrementer">
    ...
    <listeners>
        <listener ref="loggingListener"/>
    </listeners>
</job>
```

Earlier, this chapter discussed job inheritance. This inheritance has an impact on how you configure listeners within your job. When you have a job that has listeners and it has a parent that also has listeners, you have two options. The first option is to let the child's listeners override the parent's. If this is what you want, then you do nothing different. However, if you want both the parent's and the child's listeners to be executed, then when you configure the child's list of listeners, you use the merge attribute as shown in Listing 4-20.

Listing 4-20. Merging Listeners Configured in a Parent and Child Job

```
<beans:bean id="loggingListener"
    class="com.apress.springbatch.chapter4.JobLoggerListener"/>

<beans:bean id="theEndListener"
    class="com.apress.springbatch.chapter4.JobEndingListener"/>

<job id="baseJob">
    ...
    <listeners>
        <listener ref="loggingListener"/>
    </listeners>
</job>

<job id="listenerJob" parent="baseJob">
    ...
    <listeners merge="true">
        <listener ref="theEndListener"/>
    </listeners>
</job>
```

Listeners are a useful tool to be able to execute logic at certain points of your job. Listeners are also available for many other pieces of the batch puzzle, such as steps, readers, writers, and so on. You see each of those as you cover their respective components later in the book. For now, there is just one more piece to cover that pertains to jobs: ExecutionContext.

ExecutionContext

Batch processes are stateful by their nature. They need to know what step they're on. They need to know how many records they have processed within that step. These and other stateful elements are vital to not only the ongoing processing for any batch process but also restarting it if the process failed before.

For example, suppose a batch process that processes a million transactions a night goes down after processing 900,000 of those records. Even with periodic commits along the way, how do you know where to pick back up when you restart? The idea of reestablishing that execution state can be daunting, which is why Spring Batch handles it for you.

You read earlier about how a JobExecution represents an actual attempt at executing the job. It's this level of the domain that requires state to be maintained. As a JobExecution progresses through a job or step, the state changes. This state is maintained in ExecutionContext.

If you think about how web applications store state, typically it's through the HttpSession.[6] ExecutionContext is essentially the session for your batch job. Holding nothing more than simple key-value pairs, ExecutionContext provides a way to store state within your job in a safe way. One difference between a web application's session and ExecutionContext is that you actually have multiple ExecutionContexts over the course of your job. JobExecution has an ExecutionContext, as does each StepExecution (which you'll see later in this chapter). This allows data to be scoped at the appropriate level (either data-specific for the step or global data for the entire job). Figure 4-4 shows how these elements are related.

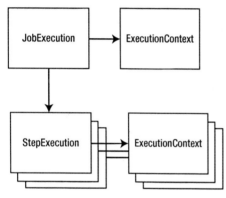

Figure 4-4. The relationship between ExecutionContexts

ExecutionContext provides a "safe" way to store data. The storage is safe because everything that goes into an ExecutionContext is persisted in the job repository. You briefly looked at the batch_job_execution_context and batch_step_execution_context tables in Chapter 2, but they didn't contain any meaningful data at the time. Let's look at how to add data to and retrieve data from the ExecutionContext and what it looks like in the database when you do.

Manipulating the ExecutionContext

The ExecutionContext is part of the JobExecution or StepExecution as mentioned earlier. Because of this, to get a handle on the ExecutionContext, you obtain it from the JobExecution or StepExecution based on which you want to use. Listing 4-21 shows how to get a handle on ExecutionContext in the HelloWorld tasklet and add to the context the name of the person you're saying hello to.

---

[6] This chapter ignores web frameworks that maintain state in some form of client form (cookies, thick client, and so on).

Listing 4-21. Adding a Name to the Job's ExecutionContext

```
package com.apress.springbatch.chapter4;

import org.springframework.batch.core.StepContribution;
import org.springframework.batch.core.scope.context.ChunkContext;
import org.springframework.batch.core.step.tasklet.Tasklet;
import org.springframework.batch.repeat.RepeatStatus;
import org.springframework.batch.item.ExecutionContext;

public class HelloWorld implements Tasklet {
    private static final String HELLO_WORLD = "Hello, %s";

    public RepeatStatus execute( StepContribution step,
                                    ChunkContext context ) throws Exception {
        String name =
            (String) context.getStepContext()
                            .getJobParameters()
                            .get("name");

        ExecutionContext jobContext = context.getStepContext()
                                            .getStepExecution()
                                            .getJobExecution()
                                            .getExecutionContext();
        jobContext.put("user.name", name);

        System.out.println( String.format(HELLO_WORLD, name) );
        return RepeatStatus.FINISHED;
    }
}
```

Notice that you have to do a bit of traversal to get to the job's ExecutionContext. All you're doing in this case is going from the chunk to the step to the job, working your way up the tree of scopes. If you look at the API for StepContext, you see that there is a getJobExecutionContext() method. This method returns a Map<String, Object> that represents the current state of the job's ExecutionContext. Although this is a handy way to get access to the current values, it has one limiting factor in its use: updates made to the Map returned by the StepContext.getJobExecutionContext() method aren't persisted to the actual ExecutionContext. Thus any changes you make to that Map that aren't also made to the real ExecutionContext are lost in the event of an error.

Listing 4-21's example showed using the job's ExecutionContext, but the ability to obtain and manipulate the step's ExecutionContext works the same way. In that case, you get the ExecutionContext directly from the StepExecution instead of the JobExecution. Listing 4-22 shows the code updated to use the step's ExecutionContext instead of the job's.

Listing 4-22. Adding a Name to the Job's ExecutionContext

```
package com.apress.springbatch.chapter4;

import org.springframework.batch.core.StepContribution;
import org.springframework.batch.core.scope.context.ChunkContext;
import org.springframework.batch.core.step.tasklet.Tasklet;
```

```
import org.springframework.batch.repeat.RepeatStatus;
import org.springframework.batch.item.ExecutionContext;

public class HelloWorld implements Tasklet {
    private static final String HELLO_WORLD = "Hello, %s";

    public RepeatStatus execute( StepContribution step,
                                 ChunkContext context ) throws Exception {
        String name =
            (String) context.getStepContext()
                            .getJobParameters()
                            .get("name");

        ExecutionContext jobContext = context.getStepContext()
                                             .getStepExecution()
                                             .getExecutionContext();
        jobContext.put("user.name", name);

        System.out.println( String.format(HELLO_WORLD, name) );
        return RepeatStatus.FINISHED;
    }
}
```

ExecutionContext Persistence

As your jobs process, Spring Batch persists your state as part of committing each chunk. Part of that persistence is the saving of the job and current step's ExecutionContexts. Chapter 2 went over the layout of the tables. Let's go ahead and execute the sampleJob job with the updates from Listing 4-21 to see what the values look like persisted in the database. Table 4-2 shows what the batch_job_execution_context table has in it after a single run with the name parameter set as Michael.

Table 4-2. Contents of BATCH_JOB_EXECUTION_CONTEXT

JOB_EXECUTION_ID	SHORT_CONTEXT	SERIALIZED_CONTEXT
1	{"map":{"entry":{"string":["user.name"," Michael"]}}}	NULL

Table 4-2 consists of three columns. The first is a reference to the JobExecution that this ExecutionContext is related to. The second is a JSON representation of the Job's ExecutionContext. This field is updated as processing occurs. Finally, the SERIALIZED_CONTEXT field contains a serialized Java object. The SERIALIZED_CONTEXT is only populated while a job is running or when it has failed.

This section of the chapter has gone through different pieces of what a job is in Spring Batch. In order for a job to be valid, however, it requires at least one step, which brings you to the next major piece of the Spring Batch framework: steps.

Working with Steps

If a job defines the entire process, a step is the building block of a job. It's an independent, sequential batch processor. I call it a batch processor for a reason. A step contains all of the pieces a job requires. It handles its own input. It has its own processor. It handles its own output. Transactions are self-contained within a step. It's by design that steps are as disjointed as they're. This allows you as the developer to structure your job as freely as needed.

In this section you take the same style deep dive into steps that you did with jobs in the previous section. You cover the way Spring Batch breaks processing down in a step by chunks and how that has changed because previous versions of the framework. You also look at a number of examples on how to configure steps within your job including how to control the flow from step to step and conditional step execution. Finally you configure the steps required for your statement job. With all of this in mind, let's start looking at steps by looking at how steps process data.

Chunk vs. Item Processing

Batch processes in general are about processing data. When you think about what a unit of data to be processed is, there are two options: an individual item or a chunk of items. An individual item consists of a single object that typically represents a single row in a database or file. Item-based processing, therefore, is the reading, processing, and then writing of your data one row, record, or object at a time, as Figure 4-5 shows.

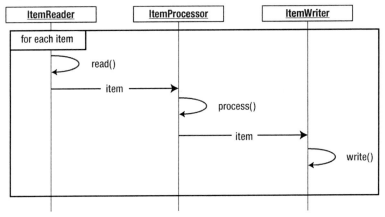

Figure 4-5. Item-based processing

As you can imagine, there can be significant overhead with this approach. The inefficiency of writing individual rows when you know you'll be committing large numbers of rows to a database or writing them to a file can be enormous.

When Spring Batch 1.x came out in 2008, item-based processing was the way records were processed. Since then the guys at SpringSource and Accenture have upgraded the framework, and in Spring Batch 2, they introduced the concept of chunk-based processing. A *chunk* in the world of batch processing is a subset of the records or rows that need to be processed, typically defined by the commit interval. In Spring Batch, when you're working with a chunk of data, it's defined by how many rows are processed between each commit.

Figure 4-6 shows how data flows through a batch process when designed for chunk processing. Here you see that although each row is still read and processed individually, all the writing for a single chunk occurs at once when it's time to be committed. This small tweak in processing allows for large performance gains and opens up the world to many other processing capabilities.

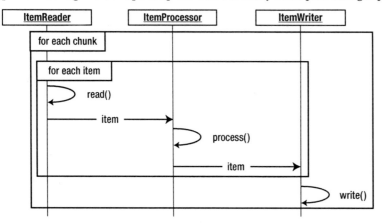

Figure 4-6. Chunk-based processing

One of the things that chunk-based processing allows you to do is to process chunks remotely. When you consider things like networking overhead, it's cost prohibitive to process individual items remotely. However, if you can send over an entire chunk of data at once to a remote processor, then instead of making performance worse, it can improve performance dramatically.

As you learn more about steps, readers, writers, and scalability throughout the book, keep in mind the chunk-based processing that Spring Batch is based on. Let's move on by digging into how to configure the building blocks of your jobs: steps.

Step Configuration

By now, you've identified that a job is really not much more than an ordered list of steps to be executed. Because of this, steps are configured by listing them within a job. Let's examine how to configure a step and the various options that are available to you.

Basic Step

When you think about steps in Spring Batch, there are two different types: a step for chunk-based processing and a tasklet step. Although you used a tasklet step previously in the "Hello, World!" job, you see more detail about it later. For now, you start by looking at how to configure chunk-based steps.

As you saw earlier, chunks are defined by their commit intervals. If the commit interval is set to 50 items, then your job reads in 50 items, processes 50 items, and then writes out 50 items at once. Because of this, the transaction manager plays a key part in the configuration of a chunk-based step. Listing 4-23 shows how to configure a basic step for chunk-oriented processing.

Listing 4-23. stepJob.xml

```xml
<?xml version="1.0" encoding="UTF-8"?>
<beans:beans xmlns="http://www.springframework.org/schema/batch"
    xmlns:beans="http://www.springframework.org/schema/beans"
    xmlns:xsi="http://www.w3.org/2001/XMLSchema-instance"
    xsi:schemaLocation="http://www.springframework.org/schema/beans
        http://www.springframework.org/schema/beans/spring-beans-3.0.xsd
        http://www.springframework.org/schema/batch
        http://www.springframework.org/schema/batch/spring-batch-2.1.xsd">

    <beans:import resource="../launch-context.xml"/>

    <beans:bean id="inputFile"
        class="org.springframework.core.io.FileSystemResource" scope="step">
        <beans:constructor-arg value="#{jobParameters[inputFile]}"/>
    </beans:bean>

    <beans:bean id="outputFile"
        class="org.springframework.core.io.FileSystemResource" scope="step">
        <beans:constructor-arg value="#{jobParameters[outputFile]}"/>
    </beans:bean>

    <beans:bean id="inputReader"
        class="org.springframework.batch.item.file.FlatFileItemReader">
        <beans:property name="resource" ref="inputFile"/>
        <beans:property name="lineMapper">
            <beans:bean
  class="org.springframework.batch.item.file.mapping.PassThroughLineMapper"/>
        </beans:property>
    </beans:bean>

    <beans:bean id="outputWriter"
        class="org.springframework.batch.item.file.FlatFileItemWriter">
        <beans:property name="resource" ref="outputFile"/>
        <beans:property name="lineAggregator">
            <beans:bean
class="org.springframework.batch.item.file.transform.PassThroughLineAggregator"/>
        </beans:property>
    </beans:bean>

    <job id="stepJob">
        <step id="step1">
            <tasklet>
                <chunk reader="inputReader" writer="outputWriter"
                        commit-interval="50"/>
            </tasklet>
        </step>
    </job>
</beans:beans>
```

Listing 4-23 may look intimidating, but let's focus on the job and step configuration at the end. The rest of the file is the configuration of a basic ItemReader and ItemWriter, which are covered in Chapters 7 and 9, respectively. When you look through the job in Listing 4-23, you see that the step begins with the step tag. All that is required is the id or name, like any other Spring Bean. Within the step tag is a tasklet tag. The org.springframework.batch.core.step.tasklet.Tasklet interface is really a strategy interface for the type of step you're going to execute. In this case, you're configuring org.springframework.batch.core.step.item.ChunkOrientedTasklet<I>. You don't have to worry about configuring the class specifically here; just be aware that other types of tasklets can be used. The last piece of the example step is the chunk tag. Here you're defining what a chunk is for your step. You're saying to use the inputReader bean (an implementation of the ItemReader interface) as the reader and the outputWriter bean (an implementation of the ItemWriter interface) as the writer, and that a chunk consists of 50 items.

■**Note** When you're configuring beans with Spring, it's better to use the id attribute than the name attribute. They both have to be unique for Spring to work, but using the id attribute allows XML validators to enforce it.

It's important to note the commit-interval attribute. It's set at 50 in the example. This means no records will be written until 50 records are read and processed. If an error occurs after processing 49 items, Spring Batch will roll back the current chunk (transaction) and mark the job as failed. If you were to set the commit-interval value to 1, your job would read in a single item, process that item, and then write that item. Essentially, you would be going back to item based processing. The issue with this is that there is more than just that single item being persisted at the commit-interval. The state of the job is being updated in the job repository as well. You experiment with the commit-interval later in this book but you needed to know now that it's important to set commit-interval as high as reasonably possible.

Understanding the Other Types of Tasklets

Although the majority of your steps will be chunk-based processing and therefore use ChunkOrientedTasklet, that isn't the only option. Spring Batch provides three other implementations of the Tasklet interface: CallableTaskletAdapter, MethodInvokingTaskletAdapter, and SystemCommandTasklet. Let's look at CallableTaskletAdapter first.

CallableTaskletAdapter

org.springframework.batch.core.step.tasklet.CallableTaskletAdapter is an adapter that allows you to configure an implementation of the java.util.concurrent.Callable<RepeatStatus> interface. If you're unfamiliar with this newer interface, the Callable<V> interface is similar to the java.lang.Runnable interface in that it's intended to be run in a new thread. However, unlike the Runnable interface, which doesn't return a value and can't throw checked exceptions, the Callable interface can return a value (a RepeatStatus, in this case) and can throw checked exceptions.

The adapter is actually extremely simple in its implementation. It calls the call() method on your Callable object and returns the value that the call() method returns. That's it. Obviously you would use this if you wanted to execute the logic of your step in another thread than the thread in which the step is being executed. If you look at Listing 4-24, you can see that to use this adapter, you configure CallableTaskletAdapter as a normal Spring bean and then reference it in the tasklet tag. In the configuration of the CallableTaskletAdapter bean shown in Listing 4-24, CallableTaskletAdapter contains a single dependency: the callable object itself.

Listing 4-24. Using CallableTaskletAdapter

```
<?xml version="1.0" encoding="UTF-8"?>
<beans:beans xmlns="http://www.springframework.org/schema/batch"
xmlns:beans="http://www.springframework.org/schema/beans"
    xmlns:xsi="http://www.w3.org/2001/XMLSchema-instance"
    xsi:schemaLocation="http://www.springframework.org/schema/beans
        http://www.springframework.org/schema/beans/spring-beans-3.0.xsd
        http://www.springframework.org/schema/batch
        http://www.springframework.org/schema/batch/spring-batch-2.1.xsd">

    <beans:import resource="../launch-context.xml"/>

    <beans:bean id="callableObject"
        class="com.apress.springbatch.chapter4.CallableLogger"/>

    <beans:bean id="callableTaskletAdapter"
  class="org.springframework.batch.core.step.tasklet.CallableTaskletAdapter">
        <beans:property name="callable" ref="callableObject"/>
    </beans:bean>

    <job id="callableJob">
        <step id="step1">
            <tasklet ref="callableTaskletAdapter"/>
        </step>
    </job>
</beans:beans>
```

One thing to note with CallableTaskletAdapter is that although the tasklet is executed in a different thread than the step itself, this doesn't parallelize your step execution. The execution of this step won't be considered complete until the Callable object returns a valid RepeatStatus object. Until this step is considered complete, no other steps in the flow in which this step is configured will execute. You see how to parallelize processing in a number of ways, including executing steps in parallel, later in this book.

MethodInvokingTaskletAdapter

The next Tasklet implementation is org.springframework.batch.core.step.tasklet.MethodInvokingTaskletAdapter. This class is similar to a number of utility classes available in the Spring framework. It allows you to execute a preexisting method on another class as the step of your job. Say for example you already have a service that does a piece of logic that you want to run once in your batch job. Instead of writing an implementation of the Tasklet interface that really just wraps that method call, you can use MethodInvokingTaskletAdapter to call the method. Listing 4-25 shows an example of the configuration for MethodInvokingTaskletAdapter.

Listing 4-25. Using MethodInvokingTaskletAdapter

```xml
<?xml version="1.0" encoding="UTF-8"?>
<beans:beans xmlns="http://www.springframework.org/schema/batch"
    xmlns:beans="http://www.springframework.org/schema/beans"
    xmlns:xsi="http://www.w3.org/2001/XMLSchema-instance"
    xsi:schemaLocation="http://www.springframework.org/schema/beans
        http://www.springframework.org/schema/beans/spring-beans-3.0.xsd
        http://www.springframework.org/schema/batch
        http://www.springframework.org/schema/batch/spring-batch-2.1.xsd">

    <beans:import resource="../launch-context.xml"/>

    <beans:bean id="service"
        class="com.apress.springbatch.chapter4.ChapterFourService"/>

    <beans:bean id="methodInvokingTaskletAdapter"
class="org.springframework.batch.core.step.tasklet.MethodInvokingTaskletAdapter">
        <beans:property name="targetObject" ref="service"/>
        <beans:property name="targetMethod" value="serviceMethod"/>
    </beans:bean>

    <job id="methodInvokingJob">
        <step id="step1">
            <tasklet ref="methodInvokingTaskletAdapter"/>
        </step>
    </job>
</beans:beans>
```

The example shown in Listing 4-25 specifies an object and a method. With this configuration, the adapter calls the method with no parameters and returns an ExitStatus.COMPLETED result unless the method specified also returns the type org.springframework.batch.core.ExitStatus. If it does return an ExitStatus, the value returned by the method is returned from the tasklet. If you want to configure a static set of parameters, you can use the late-binding method of passing job parameters that you read about earlier in this chapter, as shown in Listing 4-26.

Listing 4-26. Using MethodInvokingTaskletAdapter with Parameters

```xml
    <beans:bean id="methodInvokingTaskletAdapter"
class="org.springframework.batch.core.step.tasklet.MethodInvokingTaskletAdapter"
        scope="step">
        <beans:property name="targetObject" ref="service"/>
        <beans:property name="targetMethod" value="serviceMethod"/>
        <beans:property name="arguments" value="#{jobParameters[message]}"/>
    </beans:bean>

    <job id="methodInvokingJob">
        <step id="step1">
            <tasklet ref="methodInvokingTaskletAdapter"/>
        </step>
    </job>
```

```
</beans:beans>
```

SystemCommandTasklet

The last type of Tasklet implementation that Spring Batch provides is
org.springframework.batch.core.step.tasklet.SystemCommandTasklet. This tasklet is used to—you
guessed it—execute a system command! The system command specified is executed asynchronously.
Because of this, the timeout value (in milliseconds) as shown in Listing 4-27 is important. The
interruptOnCancel attribute in the listing is optional but indicates to Spring Batch whether to kill the
thread the system process is associated with if the job exits abnormally.

Listing 4-27. Using SystemCommandTasklet

```xml
<?xml version="1.0" encoding="UTF-8"?>
<beans:beans xmlns="http://www.springframework.org/schema/batch"
            xmlns:beans="http://www.springframework.org/schema/beans"
            xmlns:xsi=http://www.w3.org/2001/XMLSchema-instance
            xsi:schemaLocation="http://www.springframework.org/schema/beans
        http://www.springframework.org/schema/beans/spring-beans-3.0.xsd
        http://www.springframework.org/schema/batch
        http://www.springframework.org/schema/batch/spring-batch-2.1.xsd">

    <beans:import resource="../launch-context.xml" />

    <beans:bean id="tempFileDeletionCommand"
    class="org.springframework.batch.core.step.tasklet.SystemCommandTasklet">
        <beans:property name="command" value="rm - rf /temp.txt " />
        <beans:property name="timeout" value="5000" />
        <beans:property name="interruptOnCancel" value="true" />
    </beans:bean>

    <job id="systemCommandJob">
        <step id="step1">
            <tasklet ref="tempFileDeletionCommand" />
        </step>
    </job>
</beans:beans>
```

SystemCommandTasklet allows you to configure a number of parameters that can have an effect on
how a system command executes. Listing 4-28 shows a more robust example.

Listing 4-28. Using SystemCommandTasklet with Full Environment Configuration

```xml
    <beans:bean id="touchCodeMapper"
class="org.springframework.batch.core.step.tasklet.SimpleSystemProcessExitCodeMapper"/>

    <beans:bean id="taskExecutor"
        class="org.springframework.core.task.SimpleAsyncTaskExecutor"/>

    <beans:bean id="robustFileDeletionCommand"
    class="org.springframework.batch.core.step.tasklet.SystemCommandTasklet">
```

```
            <beans:property name="command" value="touch temp.txt" />
            <beans:property name="timeout" value="5000" />
            <beans:property name="interruptOnCancel" value="true" />
            <beans:property name="workingDirectory"
                value="/Users/mminella/spring-batch" />
            <beans:property name="systemProcessExitCodeMapper"
                ref="touchCodeMapper"/>
            <beans:property name="terminationCheckInterval" value="5000" />
            <beans:property name="taskExecutor" ref="taskExecutor" />
            <beans:property name="environmentParams"
                value="JAVA_HOME=/java,BATCH_HOME=/Users/batch" />
        </beans:bean>

        <job id="systemCommandJob">
            <step id="step1">
                <tasklet ref="robustFileDeletionCommand" />
            </step>
        </job>
    </beans:beans>
```

Listing 4-28 includes five more optional parameters in the configuration:

workingDirectory: This is the directory from which to execute the command. In this example, it's the equivalent of executing cd ~/spring-batch before executing the actual command.

systemProcessExitCodeMapper: System codes may mean different things depending on the command you're executing. This property allows you to use an implementation of the org.springframework.batch.core.step.tasklet.SystemProcessExitCodeMapper interface to map what system-return codes go with what Spring Batch status values. Spring provides two implementations of this interface by default: org.springframework.batch.core.step.tasklet.ConfigurableSystemProcessExitCodeMapper, which allows you to configure the mapping in your XML configuration, and org.springframework.batch.core.step.tasklet.SimpleSystemProcessExitCodeMapper, which returns ExitStatus.FINISHED if the return code was 0 and ExitStatus.FAILED if it was anything else.

terminationCheckInterval: Because the system command is executed in an asynchronous way by default, the tasklet checks periodically to see if it has completed. By default, this value is set to one second, but you can configure it to any value you wish in milliseconds.

taskExecutor: This allows you to configure your own TaskExecutor to execute the system command. You're highly discouraged from configuring a synchronous task executor due to the potential of locking up your job if the system command causes problems.

environmentParams: This is a list of environment parameters you can set prior to the execution of your command.

You've seen over the previous section that many different tasklet types are available in Spring Batch. Before moving off the topic, however, there is one other tasklet type to discuss: the tasklet step.

Tasklet Step

The tasklet step is different than the others you've seen. But it should be the most familiar to you, because it's what you used in the "Hello, World!" job. The way it's different is that in this case, you're writing your own code to be executed as the tasklet. Using MethodInvokingTaskletAdapter is one way to define a tasklet step. In that case, you allow Spring to forward the processing to your code. This lets you develop regular POJOs and use them as steps.

The other way to create a tasklet step is to implement the Tasklet interface as you did when you created the HelloWorld tasklet in Chapter 2. There, you implement the execute method required in the interface and return a RepeatStatus object to tell Spring Batch what to do after you completed processing. Listing 4-29 has the HelloWorld tasklet code as you constructed it in Chapter 2.

Listing 4-29. HelloWorld Tasklet

```
package com.apress.springbatch.chapter2;

import org.springframework.batch.core.StepContribution;
import org.springframework.batch.core.scope.context.ChunkContext;
import org.springframework.batch.core.step.tasklet.Tasklet;
import org.springframework.batch.repeat.RepeatStatus;

public class HelloWorld implements Tasklet {

    private static final String HELLO_WORLD = "Hello, world!";

    public RepeatStatus execute( StepContribution arg0,
                                 ChunkContext arg1 ) throws Exception {
        System.out.println( HELLO_WORLD );
        return RepeatStatus.FINISHED;
    }
}
```

When processing is complete in your Tasklet implementation, you return an org.springframework.batch.repeat.RepeatStatus object. There are two options with this: RepeatStatus.CONTINUABLE and RepeatStatus.FINISHED. These two values can be confusing at first glance. If you return RepeatStatus.CONTINUABLE, you aren't saying that the job can continue. You're telling Spring Batch to run the tasklet again. Say, for example, that you wanted to execute a particular tasklet in a loop until a given condition was met, yet you still wanted to use Spring Batch to keep track of how many times the tasklet was executed, transactions, and so on. Your tasklet could return RepeatStatus.CONTINUABLE until the condition was met. If you return RepeatStatus.FINISHED, that means the processing for this tasklet is complete (regardless of success) and to continue with the next piece of processing.

You configure a tasklet step as you configure any of the other tasklet types. Listing 4-30 shows HelloWorldJob configured using the HelloWorld tasklet.

Listing 4-30. HelloWorldJob

```
<beans:bean id="helloWorld" class="com.apress.springbatch.chapter2.HelloWorld/>

    <job id="helloWorldJob">
        <step id="helloWorldStep">
            <tasklet ref="helloWorld"/>
        </step>
    </job>
...
```

You may be quick to point out that this listing isn't the same as it was in Chapter 2, and you would be correct. The reason is that you haven't seen one other feature used in Chapter 2: step inheritance.

Step Inheritance

Like jobs, steps can be inherited from each other. Unlike jobs, steps don't have to be abstract to be inherited. Spring Batch allows you to configure fully defined steps in your configuration and then have other steps inherit them. Let's start discussing step inheritance by looking at the example used in Chapter 2, the HelloWorldJob in Listing 4-31.

Listing 4-31. HelloWorldJob

```
<beans:bean id="helloWorld"
    class="com.apress.springbatch.chapter2.HelloWorld"/>

<step id="helloWorldStep">
    <tasklet ref="helloWorld"/>
</step>

<job id="helloWorldJob">
    <step id="step1" parent="helloWorldStep"/>
</job>
```

In Listing 4-31, you configure the tasklet implementation (the helloWorld bean), and then you configure the step that references the tasklet (helloWorldStep). Spring Batch doesn't require that the step element be nested in a job tag. Once you're defined your step, helloWorldStep, you can then inherit it when you declare the steps in sequence in your actual job, helloWorldJob. Why would you do this?

In this simple example, there is little benefit to this approach. However, as steps become more complex, experience shows that it's best to configure your steps outside the scope of your job and then inherit them with the steps in the job. This allows the actual job declaration to be much more readable and maintainable.

Obviously, readability isn't the only reason to use inheritance, and that isn't all that is going on even in this example. Let's dive deeper. In this example, what you're really doing in step1 is inheriting the step helloWorldStep and all its attributes. However, step1 chooses not to override any of them.

Step inheritance provides a more complete inheritance model than that of job inheritance. In step inheritance you can fully define a step, inherit the step, and then add or override any of the values you wish. You can also declare a step abstract and place only common attributes there.

Listing 4-32 shows an example of how steps can add and override attributes configured in their parent. You start with the parent step, vehicleStep, which declares a reader, writer, and commit-interval. You then create two steps that inherit from vehicleStep: carStep and truckStep. Each uses the same reader and writer that has been configured in vehicleStep. In each case, they add an item processor that does different things. carStep has chosen to use the inherited commit-interval of 50 items, whereas truckStep has overridden the commit-interval and set it to 5 items.

Listing 4-32. Adding Attributes in Step Inheritance

```
<step id="vehicleStep">
<tasklet>
<chunk reader="vehicleReader" writer="vehicleWriter" commit-interval="50"/>
</tasklet>
</step>

<step id="carStep" parent="vehicleStep">
<tasklet>
<chunk processor="carProcessor"/>
</tasklet>
</step>

<step id="truckStep" parent="vehicleStep">
<tasklet>
<chunk processor="truckProcessor" commit-interval="5"/>
</tasklet>
</step>

<job id="exampleJob">
<step id="step1" parent="carStep" next="step2"/>
<step id="step2" parent="truckStep"/>
</job>
```

By declaring a step abstract, as in Java, you're allowed to leave things out that would otherwise be required. In an abstract step, as in Listing 4-33, you're allowed to leave off the reader, writer, processor, and tasklet attributes. This would normally cause an initialization error when Spring tried to build the step; but because it's declared abstract, Spring knows that those will be populated by the steps that inherit it.

Listing 4-33. An Abstract Step and Its Implementations

```
<beans:bean id="inputFile"
    class="org.springframework.core.io.FileSystemResource" scope="step">
    <beans:constructor-arg value="#{jobParameters[inputFile]}"/>
</beans:bean>

<beans:bean id="outputFile"
    class="org.springframework.core.io.FileSystemResource" scope="step">
    <beans:constructor-arg value="#{jobParameters[outputFile]}"/>
</beans:bean>

<beans:bean id="inputReader"
    class="org.springframework.batch.item.file.FlatFileItemReader">
    <beans:property name="resource" ref="inputFile"/>
    <beans:property name="lineMapper">
```

```
                <beans:bean
    class="org.springframework.batch.item.file.mapping.PassThroughLineMapper"/>
            </beans:property>
        </beans:bean>

        <beans:bean id="outputWriter"
            class="org.springframework.batch.item.file.FlatFileItemWriter">
            <beans:property name="resource" ref="outputFile"/>
            <beans:property name="lineAggregator">
                <beans:bean
    class="org.springframework.batch.item.file.transform.PassThroughLineAggregator"/>
            </beans:property>
        </beans:bean>

        <step id="commitIntervalStep" abstract="true">
            <tasklet>
                <chunk commit-interval="15"/>
            </tasklet>
        </step>

        <step id="copyStep" parent="commitIntervalStep">
            <tasklet>
                <chunk reader="inputReader" writer="outputWriter" />
            </tasklet>
        </step>

        <job id="stepInheritanceJob">
            <step id="step1" parent="copyStep" />
        </job>
</beans:beans>
```

In Listing 4-33, commitIntervalStep is an abstract step that is used to configure the commit interval for any step that extends this step. You configure the required elements of a step in the step that extends the abstract step, copyStep. Here you specify a reader and writer. copyStep has the same commit-interval of 15 that commitIntervalStep has, without the need to repeat the configuration.

Step inheritance allows you to configure common attributes that can be reused from step to step as well as structure your XML configuration in a maintainable way. The last example of this section used a couple of attributes that were chunk specific. To better understand them, let's go over how you can use the different features that Spring Batch provides in its chunk-based processing.

Chunk-Size Configuration

Because chunk-based processing is the foundation of Spring Batch 2, it's important to understand how to configure its various options to take full advantage of this important feature. This section covers the two options for configuring the size of a chunk: a static commit count and a CompletionPolicy implementation. All other chunk configuration options relate to error handling and are discussed in that section.

To start looking at chunk configuration, Listing 4-34 has a basic example of nothing more than a reader, writer, and commit-interval configured. The reader is an implementation of the ItemReader interface, and the writer an implementation of ItemWriter. Each of these interfaces has its own dedicated chapter later in the book, so this section doesn't go into detail about them. All you need to know is that they supply input and output, respectively, for the step. The commit-interval defines how many items make up a chunk (50 items, in this case).

Listing 4-34. *A Basic Chunk Configuration*

```xml
<?xml version="1.0" encoding="UTF-8"?>
<beans:beans xmlns="http://www.springframework.org/schema/batch"
             xmlns:beans="http://www.springframework.org/schema/beans"
             xmlns:xsi="http://www.w3.org/2001/XMLSchema-instance"
             xsi:schemaLocation="http://www.springframework.org/schema/beans
        http://www.springframework.org/schema/beans/spring-beans-3.0.xsd
        http://www.springframework.org/schema/batch
     http://www.springframework.org/schema/batch/spring-batch-2.1.xsd">

    <beans:import resource="../launch-context.xml" />

    <beans:bean id="inputFile"
        class="org.springframework.core.io.FileSystemResource" scope="step">
        <beans:constructor-arg value="#{jobParameters[inputFile]}"/>
    </beans:bean>

    <beans:bean id="outputFile"
        class="org.springframework.core.io.FileSystemResource" scope="step">
        <beans:constructor-arg value="#{jobParameters[outputFile]}"/>
    </beans:bean>

    <beans:bean id="inputReader"
        class="org.springframework.batch.item.file.FlatFileItemReader">
        <beans:property name="resource" ref="inputFile"/>
        <beans:property name="lineMapper">
            <beans:bean
class="org.springframework.batch.item.file.mapping.PassThroughLineMapper"/>
        </beans:property>
    </beans:bean>

    <beans:bean id="outputWriter"
        class="org.springframework.batch.item.file.FlatFileItemWriter">
        <beans:property name="resource" ref="outputFile"/>
        <beans:property name="lineAggregator">
            <beans:bean
class="org.springframework.batch.item.file.transform.PassThroughLineAggregator"/>
        </beans:property>
    </beans:bean>

    <step id="copyStep">
        <tasklet>
            <chunk reader="inputReader" writer="outputWriter"
                commit-interval="50"/>
        </tasklet>
    </step>

    <job id="chunkConfigurationJob">
```

```
            <step id="step1" parent="copyStep" />
        </job>
</beans:beans>
```

Although typically you define the size of a chunk based on a hard number configured with the `commit-interval` attribute as configured in Listing 4-34, that isn't always a robust enough option. Say that you have a job that needs to process chunks that aren't all the same size (processing all transactions for an account in a single transaction, for example). Spring Batch provides the ability to programmatically define when a chunk is complete via an implementation of the `org.springframework.batch.repeat.CompletionPolicy` interface.

The `CompletionPolicy` interface allows the implementation of decision logic to decide if a given chunk is complete. Spring Batch comes with a number of implementations of this interface. By default it uses `org.springframework.batch.repeat.policy.SimpleCompletionPolicy`, which counts the number of items processed and flags a chunk complete when the configured threshold is reached. Another out-of-the-box implementation is `org.springframework.batch.repeat.policy.TimeoutTerminationPolicy`. This allows you to configure a timeout on a chunk so that it may exit gracefully after a given amount of time. What does "exit gracefully" mean in this context? It means that the chunk is considered complete and all transaction processing continues normally.

As you can undoubtedly deduce, there are few times when a timeout by itself is enough to determine when a chunk of processing will be complete. `TimeoutTerminationPolicy` is more likely to be used as part of `org.springframework.batch.repeat.policy.CompositeCompletionPolicy`. This policy lets you configure multiple polices that determine whether a chunk has completed. When you use `CompositeCompletionPolicy`, if any of the policies consider a chunk complete, then the chunk is flagged as complete. Listing 4-35 shows an example of using a timeout of 3 milliseconds along with the normal commit count of 200 items to determine if a chunk is complete.

Listing 4-35. Using a Timeout Along With a Regular Commit Count

```xml
<?xml version="1.0" encoding="UTF-8"?>
<beans:beans xmlns="http://www.springframework.org/schema/batch"

    xmlns:beans="http://www.springframework.org/schema/beans"
    xmlns:util="http://www.springframework.org/schema/util"
    xmlns:xsi="http://www.w3.org/2001/XMLSchema-instance"
    xsi:schemaLocation="http://www.springframework.org/schema/beans
        http://www.springframework.org/schema/beans/spring-beans-3.0.xsd
        http://www.springframework.org/schema/util
        http://www.springframework.org/schema/util/spring-util.xsd
        http://www.springframework.org/schema/batch
        http://www.springframework.org/schema/batch/spring-batch-2.1.xsd">

    <beans:import resource="../launch-context.xml" />

    <beans:bean id="inputFile"
        class="org.springframework.core.io.FileSystemResource" scope="step">
        <beans:constructor-arg value="#{jobParameters[inputFile]}" />
    </beans:bean>

    <beans:bean id="outputFile"
        class="org.springframework.core.io.FileSystemResource" scope="step">
        <beans:constructor-arg value="#{jobParameters[outputFile]}" />
    </beans:bean>
```

```xml
    <beans:bean id="inputReader"
        class="org.springframework.batch.item.file.FlatFileItemReader">
        <beans:property name="resource" ref="inputFile" />
        <beans:property name="lineMapper">
            <beans:bean
class="org.springframework.batch.item.file.mapping.PassThroughLineMapper" />
        </beans:property>
    </beans:bean>

    <beans:bean id="outputWriter"
        class="org.springframework.batch.item.file.FlatFileItemWriter">
        <beans:property name="resource" ref="outputFile" />
        <beans:property name="lineAggregator">
            <beans:bean
class="org.springframework.batch.item.file.transform.PassThroughLineAggregator" />
        </beans:property>
    </beans:bean>

    <beans:bean id="chunkTimeout"
    class="org.springframework.batch.repeat.policy.TimeoutTerminationPolicy">
        <beans:constructor-arg value="3" />
    </beans:bean>

    <beans:bean id="commitCount"
      class="org.springframework.batch.repeat.policy.SimpleCompletionPolicy">
        <beans:property name="chunkSize" value="200" />
    </beans:bean>

    <beans:bean id="chunkCompletionPolicy"
    class="org.springframework.batch.repeat.policy.CompositeCompletionPolicy">
        <beans:property name="policies">
            <util:list>
                <beans:ref bean="chunkTimeout" />
                <beans:ref bean="commitCount" />
            </util:list>
        </beans:property>
    </beans:bean>

    <step id="copyStep">
        <tasklet>
            <chunk reader="inputReader" writer="outputWriter"
                    chunk-completion-policy="chunkCompletionPolicy"/>
        </tasklet>
    </step>

    <job id="chunkConfigurationJob">
        <step id="step1" parent="copyStep" />
    </job>
</beans:beans>
```

Using the implementations of the CompletionPolicy interface isn't your only option to determine how large a chunk is. You can also implement it yourself. Before you look at an implementation, let's go over the interface.

The CompletionPolicy interface requires four methods: two versions of isComplete, start, and update. If you look at this through the lifecycle of the class, first the start method is called first. This method initializes the policy so that it knows the chunk is starting. It's important to note that an implementation of the CompletionPolicy interface is intended to be stateful and should be able to determine if a chunk has been completed by its own internal state. The start method resets this internal state to whatever is required by the implementation at the beginning of the chunk. Using SimpleCompletionPolicy as an example, the start method resets an internal counter to 0 at the beginning of a chunk. The update method is called once for each item that has been processed to update the internal state. Going back to the SimpleCompletionPolicy example, update increments the internal counter by one after each item. Finally, there are two isComplete methods. The first isComplete method signature accepts a RepeatContext as its parameter. This implementation is intended to use its internal state to determine if the chunk has completed. The second signature takes the RepeatContext and also the RepeatStatus as parameters. This implementation is expected to determine based on the status whether a chunk has completed. Listing 4-36 shows an example of a CompletionPolicy implementation that considers a chunk complete once a random number of items fewer than 20 have been processed; Listing 4-37 showing the configuration.

Listing 4-36. *Random Chunk Size CompletionPolicy Implementation*

```
package com.apress.springbatch.chapter4;

import java.util.Random;

import org.springframework.batch.repeat.CompletionPolicy;
import org.springframework.batch.repeat.RepeatContext;
import org.springframework.batch.repeat.RepeatStatus;

public class RandomChunkSizePolicy implements CompletionPolicy {

    private int chunkSize;
    private int totalProcessed;

    public boolean isComplete(RepeatContext context) {
        return totalProcessed >= chunkSize;
    }

    public boolean isComplete(RepeatContext context, RepeatStatus status) {
        if (RepeatStatus.FINISHED == status) {
            return true;
        } else {
            return isComplete(context);
        }
    }

    public RepeatContext start(RepeatContext context) {
        Random random = new Random();

        chunkSize = random.nextInt(20);
```

```
        totalProcessed = 0;

        System.out.println("The chunk size has been set to " + chunkSize);

        return context;
    }

    public void update(RepeatContext context) {
        totalProcessed++;
    }
}
```

Listing 4-37. Configuring RandomChunkSizePolicy

```
<beans:bean id="randomChunkSizer"
    class="com.apress.springbatch.chapter4.RandomChunkSizePolicy" />

<step id="copyStep">
    <tasklet>
        <chunk reader="inputReader" writer="outputWriter"
            chunk-completion-policy="randomChunkSizer" />
    </tasklet>
</step>

<job id="chunkConfigurationJob">
    <step id="step1" parent="copyStep" />
</job>
```

You explore the rest of chunk configuration when you get to error handling. That section covers retry and skip logic, which the majority of the remaining options center around. The next step elements that this chapter looks at also carry over from a job: listeners.

Step Listeners

When you looked at job listeners, earlier this chapter, you saw the two events they can fire on: the start and end of a job. Step listeners cover the same types of events (start and end), but for individual steps instead of an entire job. This section covers the org.springframework.batch.core.StepExecutionListener and org.springframework.batch.core.ChunkListener interfaces, both of which allow the processing of logic at the beginning and end of a step and chunk respectively. Notice that the Step's listener is named the StepExecutionListener and not just StepListener. There actually is a StepListener interface, however it's just a marker interface that all step related listeners extend.

Both the StepExecutionListener and ChunkListener provide methods that are similar to the ones in the JobExecutionListener interface. StepExecutionListener has a beforeStep and an afterStep, and ChunkListener has a beforeChunk and an afterChunk, as you would expect. All of these methods are void except afterStep. afterStep returns an ExitStatus because the listener is allowed to modify the ExitStatus that was returned by the step itself prior to it being returned to the job. This feature can be useful when a job requires more than just knowing whether an operation was successful to determine if the processing was successful. An example would be doing some basic integrity checks after importing a file (whether the correct number of records were written to the database, and so on). The ability to configure listeners via annotations also continues to be consistent, with Spring Batch providing

@BeforeStep, @AfterStep, @BeforeChunk, and @AfterChunk annotations to simplify the implementation. Listing 4-38 shows a StepListener that uses annotations to identify the methods.

Listing 4-38. Logging Step Start and Stop Listeners

```
package com.apress.springbatch.chapter4;

import org.springframework.batch.core.ExitStatus;
import org.springframework.batch.core.StepExecution;
import org.springframework.batch.core.annotation.AfterStep;
import org.springframework.batch.core.annotation.BeforeStep;

public class LoggingStepStartStopListener {

    @BeforeStep
    public void beforeStep(StepExecution execution) {
        System.out.println(execution.getStepName() + " has begun!");
    }

    @AfterStep
    public ExitStatus afterStep(StepExecution execution) {
        System.out.println(execution.getStepName() + " has ended!");

        return execution.getExitStatus();
    }
}
```

The configuration for all the step listeners is combined into a single list in the step configuration. Similar to the job listeners, inheritance works the same way, allowing you to either override the list or merge them together. Listing 4-39 configures the LoggingStepStartStopListener that you coded earlier.

Listing 4-39. Configuring LoggingStepStartStopListener

```
...
<beans:bean id="loggingStepListener"
    class="com.apress.springbatch.chapter4.LoggingStepStartStopListener"/>

<job id="stepListenerJob">
    <step id="step1">
        <tasklet>
            <chunk reader="inputReader" writer="outputWriter"
                commit-interval="50"/>
            <listeners>
                <listener ref="loggingStepListener"/>
            </listeners>
        </tasklet>
    </step>
</job>
...
```

As you can see, listeners are available at just about every level of the Spring Batch framework to allow you to hang processing off your batch jobs. They're commonly used not only to perform some form of preprocessing before a component or evaluate the result of a component but also in error handling, as you see in a bit.

The next section covers the flow of steps. Although all your steps up to this point have been processed sequentially, that isn't a requirement in Spring Batch. You learn how to perform simple logic to determine what step to execute next and how to externalize flows for reuse.

Step Flow

A single file line: that is what your jobs have looked like up to this point. You've lined up the steps and allowed them to execute one after another using the next attribute. However, if that were the only way you could execute steps, Spring Batch would be very limited. Instead, the authors of the framework provided a robust collection of options for customizing the flow of your jobs.

To start, let's look at how you can decide what step to execute next or even if you execute a given step at all. This occurs using Spring Batch's conditional logic.

Conditional Logic

Within a job in Spring Batch, steps are executed in the order you specify using the next attribute of the step tag. The only requirement is that the first step be configured as the first step in the job. If you want to execute steps in a different order, it's quite easy: all you need to do is use the next tag. As Listing 4-40 shows, you can use the next tag to direct a job to go from step1 to step2a if things go ok or to step2b if step1 returns an ExitStatus of FAILED.

Listing 4-40. If/Else Logic in Step Execution

```xml
<?xml version="1.0" encoding="UTF-8"?>
<beans:beans xmlns="http://www.springframework.org/schema/batch"
    xmlns:beans="http://www.springframework.org/schema/beans"
    xmlns:xsi="http://www.w3.org/2001/XMLSchema-instance"
    xsi:schemaLocation="http://www.springframework.org/schema/beans
        http://www.springframework.org/schema/beans/spring-beans-3.0.xsd
        http://www.springframework.org/schema/batch
        http://www.springframework.org/schema/batch/spring-batch-2.1.xsd">

    <beans:import resource="../launch-context.xml"/>

    <beans:bean id="passTasklet"
        class="com.apress.springbatch.chapter4.LogicTasklet">
        <beans:property name="success" value="true"/>
    </beans:bean>

    <beans:bean id="successTasklet"
        class="com.apress.springbatch.chapter4.MessageTasklet">
        <beans:property name="message" value="The step succeeded!"/>
    </beans:bean>

    <beans:bean id="failTasklet"
        class="com.apress.springbatch.chapter4.MessageTasklet">
        <beans:property name="message" value="The step failed!"/>
    </beans:bean>
```

```xml
<job id="conditionalStepLogicJob">
    <step id="step1">
        <tasklet ref="passTasklet"/>
        <next on="*" to="step2a"/>
        <next on="FAILED" to="step2b"/>
    </step>
    <step id="step2a">
        <tasklet ref="successTasklet"/>
    </step>
    <step id="step2b">
        <tasklet ref="failTasklet"/>
    </step>
</job>
</beans:beans>
```

The next tag uses the on attribute to evaluate the ExitStatus of the step and determine what to do. It's important to note that you've seen both org.springframework.batch.core.ExitStatus and org.springframework.batch.core.BatchStatus over the course of this chapter. BatchStatus is an attribute of the JobExecution or StepExecution that identifies the current state of the job or step. ExitStatus is the value returned to Spring Batch at the end of a job or step. The on attribute evaluates the ExitStatus for its decisions. So, the example in Listing 4-40 is the XML equivalent of saying, "If the exit code of step1 doesn't equal FAILED, go to step2a, else go to step2b."

Because the values of the ExitStatus are really just Strings, the ability to use wildcards can make things interesting. Spring Batch allows for two wildcards in on criteria:

- * matches zero or more characters. For example, C* matches *C*, *COMPLETE*, and *CORRECT*.

- ? matches a single character. In this case, ?AT matches *CAT* or *KAT* but not *THAT*.

Although evaluating the ExitStatus gets you started in determining what to do next, it may not take you all the way. For example, what if you didn't want to execute a step if you skipped any records in the current step? You wouldn't know that from the ExitStatus alone.

■**Note** Spring Batch helps you when it comes to configuring transitions. It automatically orders the transitions from most to least restrictive and applies them in that order.

Spring Batch has provided a programmatic way to determine what to do next. You do this by creating an implementation of the org.springframework.batch.core.job.flow.JobExecutionDecider interface. This interface has a single method, decide, that takes both the JobExecution and the StepExecution and returns a FlowExecutionStatus (a wrapper for a BatchStatus/ExitStatus pair). With both the JobExecution and StepExecution available for evaluation, all information should be available to you to make the appropriate decision about what your job should do next. Listing 4-41 shows an implementation of the JobExecutionDecider that randomly decides what the next step should be.

Listing 4-41. RandomDecider

```
package com.apress.springbatch.chapter4;

import java.util.Random;

import org.springframework.batch.core.JobExecution;
import org.springframework.batch.core.StepExecution;
import org.springframework.batch.core.job.flow.FlowExecutionStatus;
import org.springframework.batch.core.job.flow.JobExecutionDecider;

public class RandomDecider implements JobExecutionDecider {

    private Random random = new Random();

    public FlowExecutionStatus decide(JobExecution jobExecution,
            StepExecution stepExecution) {

        if (random.nextBoolean()) {
            return new
                FlowExecutionStatus(FlowExecutionStatus.COMPLETED.getName());
        } else {
            return new
                FlowExecutionStatus(FlowExecutionStatus.FAILED.getName());
        }
    }
}
```

To use RandomDecider, you configure an extra attribute on your step called decider. This attribute refers to the Spring bean that implements JobExecutionDecider. Listing 4-42 shows RandomDecider configured. You can see that the configuration maps the values you return in the decider to steps available to execute.

Listing 4-42. If/Else Logic in Step Execution

```
...
<beans:bean id="decider"
    class="com.apress.springbatch.chapter4.RandomDecider"/>

<beans:bean id="successTasklet"
    class="com.apress.springbatch.chapter4.MessageTasklet">
    <beans:property name="message" value="The step succeeded!"/>
</beans:bean>

<beans:bean id="failTasklet"
    class="com.apress.springbatch.chapter4.MessageTasklet">
    <beans:property name="message" value="The step failed!"/>
</beans:bean>

<job id="conditionalLogicJob">
    <step id="step1" next="decision">
        <tasklet>
            <chunk reader="inputReader" writer="outputWriter"
                commit-interval="20"/>
```

```
            </tasklet>
        </step>
        <decision decider="decider" id="decision">
            <next on="*" to="step2a"/>
            <next on="FAILED" to="step2b"/>
        </decision>
        <step id="step2a">
            <tasklet ref="successTasklet"/>
        </step>
        <step id="step2b">
            <tasklet ref="failTasklet"/>
        </step>
    </job>
    ...
```

Because you now know how to direct your processing from step to step either sequentially or via logic, you won't always want to just go to another step. You may want to end or pause the job. The next section covers how to handle those scenarios.

Ending a Job

You learned earlier that a JobInstance can't be executed more than once to a successful completion and that a JobInstance is identified by the job name and the parameters passed into it. Because of this, you need to be aware of the state in which you end your job if you do it programmatically. In reality, there are three states in which you can programmatically end a job in Spring Batch:

> *Completed:* This end state tells Spring Batch that processing has ended in a successful way. When a JobInstance is completed, it isn't allowed to be rerun with the same parameters.

> *Failed:* In this case, the job hasn't run successfully to completion. Spring Batch allows a job in the failed state to be rerun with the same parameters.

> *Stopped:* In the stopped state, the job can be restarted. The interesting part about a job that is stopped is that the job can be restarted from where it left off, although no error has occurred. This state is very useful in scenarios when human intervention or some other check or handling is required between steps.

It's important to note that these states are identified by Spring Batch evaluating the ExitStatus of the step to determine what BatchStatus to persist in the JobRepository. ExitStatus can be returned from a step, chunk, or job. BatchStatus is maintained in StepExecution or JobExecution and persisted in the JobRepository. Let's begin looking at how to end the job in each state with the completed state.

To configure a job to end in the completed state based on the exit status of a step, you use the end tag. In this state, you can't execute the same job again with the same parameters. Listing 4-43 shows that the end tag has a single attribute that declares the ExitStatus value that triggers the job to end.

Listing 4-43. Ending a Job in the Completed State

```xml
<?xml version="1.0" encoding="UTF-8"?>
<beans:beans xmlns="http://www.springframework.org/schema/batch"
    xmlns:beans="http://www.springframework.org/schema/beans"
    xmlns:xsi="http://www.w3.org/2001/XMLSchema-instance"
```

```
xsi:schemaLocation="http://www.springframework.org/schema/beans
    http://www.springframework.org/schema/beans/spring-beans-3.0.xsd
    http://www.springframework.org/schema/batch
    http://www.springframework.org/schema/batch/spring-batch-2.1.xsd">

<beans:import resource="../launch-context.xml"/>

<beans:bean id="passTasklet"
    class="com.apress.springbatch.chapter4.LogicTasklet">
    <beans:property name="success" value="false"/>
</beans:bean>

<beans:bean id="successTasklet"
    class="com.apress.springbatch.chapter4.MessageTasklet">
    <beans:property name="message" value="The step succeeded!"/>
</beans:bean>

<beans:bean id="failTasklet"
    class="com.apress.springbatch.chapter4.MessageTasklet">
    <beans:property name="message" value="The step failed!"/>
</beans:bean>

<job id="conditionalStepLogicJob">
    <step id="step1">
        <tasklet ref="passTasklet"/>
        <end on="*"/>
        <next on="FAILED" to="step2b"/>
    </step>
    <step id="step2b">
        <tasklet ref="failTasklet"/>
    </step>
</job>
</beans:beans>
```

Once you run conditionalStepLogicJob, as you would expect, the batch_step_execution table contains the ExitStatus returned by the step, and batch_job_execution contains COMPLETED regardless of the path taken.

For the failed state, which allows you to rerun the job with the same parameters, the configuration looks similar. Instead of using the end tag, you use the fail tag. Listing 4-44 shows that the fail tag has an additional attribute: exit-code. It lets you add extra detail when causing a job to fail.

Listing 4-44. *Ending a Job in the Failed State*

```
<?xml version="1.0" encoding="UTF-8"?>
<beans:beans xmlns="http://www.springframework.org/schema/batch"
    xmlns:beans="http://www.springframework.org/schema/beans"
    xmlns:xsi="http://www.w3.org/2001/XMLSchema-instance"
    xsi:schemaLocation="http://www.springframework.org/schema/beans
        http://www.springframework.org/schema/beans/spring-beans-3.0.xsd
        http://www.springframework.org/schema/batch
        http://www.springframework.org/schema/batch/spring-batch-2.1.xsd">
```

```
    <beans:import resource="../launch-context.xml"/>

    <beans:bean id="passTasklet"
        class="com.apress.springbatch.chapter4.LogicTasklet">
        <beans:property name="success" value="true"/>
    </beans:bean>

    <beans:bean id="successTasklet"
        class="com.apress.springbatch.chapter4.MessageTasklet">
        <beans:property name="message" value="The step succeeded!"/>
    </beans:bean>

    <beans:bean id="failTasklet"
        class="com.apress.springbatch.chapter4.MessageTasklet">
        <beans:property name="message" value="The step failed!"/>
    </beans:bean>

    <job id="conditionalStepLogicJob">
        <step id="step1">
            <tasklet ref="passTasklet"/>
            <next on="*" to="step2a"/>
            <fail on="FAILED" exit-code="STEP-1-FAILED"/>
        </step>
        <step id="step2a">
            <tasklet ref="successTasklet"/>
        </step>
    </job>
</beans:beans>
```

When you rerun conditionalStepLogicJob with the configuration in Listing 4-44, the results are a bit different. This time, if step1 ends with the ExitStatus FAILURE, the job is identified in the jobRepository as failed, which allows it to be reexecuted with the same parameters.

The last state you can leave a job in when you end it programmatically is the stopped state. In this case, you can restart the job; and when you do, it restarts at the step you configure. Listing 4-45 shows an example.

Listing 4-45. *Ending a Job in the Stopped State*

```
<?xml version="1.0" encoding="UTF-8"?>
<beans:beans xmlns="http://www.springframework.org/schema/batch"
    xmlns:beans="http://www.springframework.org/schema/beans"
    xmlns:xsi="http://www.w3.org/2001/XMLSchema-instance"
    xsi:schemaLocation="http://www.springframework.org/schema/beans
        http://www.springframework.org/schema/beans/spring-beans-3.0.xsd
        http://www.springframework.org/schema/batch
        http://www.springframework.org/schema/batch/spring-batch-2.1.xsd">

    <beans:import resource="../launch-context.xml"/>

    <beans:bean id="passTasklet"
        class="com.apress.springbatch.chapter4.LogicTasklet">
        <beans:property name="success" value="true"/>
```

```
    </beans:bean>

    <beans:bean id="successTasklet"
        class="com.apress.springbatch.chapter4.MessageTasklet">
        <beans:property name="message" value="The step succeeded!"/>
    </beans:bean>

    <beans:bean id="failTasklet"
        class="com.apress.springbatch.chapter4.MessageTasklet">
        <beans:property name="message" value="The step failed!"/>
    </beans:bean>

    <job id="conditionalStepLogicJob">
        <step id="step1">
            <tasklet ref="passTasklet"/>
            <next on="*" to="step2a"/>
            <stop on="FAILED" restart="step2a"/>
        </step>
        <step id="step2a">
            <tasklet ref="successTasklet"/>
        </step>
    </job>
</beans:beans>
```

Executing conditionalStepLogicJob with this final configuration, as in Listing 4-45, allows you to rerun the job with the same parameters. However, this time, if the FAILURE path is chosen, when the job is restarted execution begins at step2a.

The flow from one step to the next isn't just another layer of configuration you're adding to potentially complex job configurations; it's also configurable in a reusable component. The next section discusses how to encapsulate flows of steps into reusable components.

Externalizing Flows

You've already identified that a step doesn't need to be configured within a job tag in your XML. This lets you extract the definition of your steps from a given job into reusable components. The same goes for the order of steps. In Spring Batch, there are three options for how to externalize the order of steps. The first is to create a flow, which is an independent sequence of steps. The second is to use the flow step; although the configuration is very similar, the state persistence in the JobRepository is slightly different. The last way is to actually call another job from within your job. This section covers how all three of these options work.

A flow looks a lot like a job. It's configured the same way, but with a flow tag instead of a job tag. Listing 4-46 shows how to define a flow using the flow tag, giving it an id and then referencing it in your job using the flow tag.

Listing 4-46. Defining a Flow

```
<?xml version="1.0" encoding="UTF-8"?>
<beans:beans xmlns="http://www.springframework.org/schema/batch"
    xmlns:beans="http://www.springframework.org/schema/beans"
    xmlns:xsi="http://www.w3.org/2001/XMLSchema-instance"
    xsi:schemaLocation="http://www.springframework.org/schema/beans
```

```
            http://www.springframework.org/schema/beans/spring-beans-3.0.xsd
            http://www.springframework.org/schema/batch
            http://www.springframework.org/schema/batch/spring-batch-2.1.xsd">

    <beans:import resource="../launch-context.xml"/>

    <beans:bean id="loadStockFile"
        class="com.apress.springbatch.chapter4.MessageTasklet">
        <beans:property name="message"
            value="The stock file has been loaded"/>
    </beans:bean>

    <beans:bean id="loadCustomerFile"
        class="com.apress.springbatch.chapter4.MessageTasklet">
        <beans:property name="message"
            value="The customer file has been loaded" />
    </beans:bean>

    <beans:bean id="updateStart"
        class="com.apress.springbatch.chapter4.MessageTasklet">
        <beans:property name="message"
            value="The stock file has been loaded" />
    </beans:bean>

    <beans:bean id="runBatchTasklet"
        class="com.apress.springbatch.chapter4.MessageTasklet">
        <beans:property name="message" value="The batch has been run" />
    </beans:bean>

    <flow id="preProcessingFlow">
        <step id="loadFileStep" next="loadCustomerStep">
            <tasklet ref="loadStockFile"/>
        </step>
        <step id="loadCustomerStep" next="updateStartStep">
            <tasklet ref="loadCustomerFile"/>
        </step>
        <step id="updateStartStep">
            <tasklet ref="updateStart"/>
        </step>
    </flow>

    <job id="flowJob">
        <flow parent="preProcessingFlow" id="step1" next="runBatch"/>
        <step id="runBatch">
            <tasklet ref="runBatchTasklet"/>
        </step>
    </job>
</beans:beans>
```

When you execute a flow as part of a job and look at the jobRepository, you see the steps from the flow recorded as part of the job as if they were configured there in the first place. In the end, there is no difference between using a flow and configuring the steps within the job itself from a JobRepository perspective.

The next option for externalizing steps is to use the flow step. With this technique, the configuration of a flow is the same. But instead of using the flow tag to include the flow in your job, you use a step tag and its flow attribute. Listing 4-47 demonstrates how to use a flow step to configure the same example Listing 4-46 used.

Listing 4-47. Using a Flow Step

```
...
<flow id="preProcessingFlow">
    <step id="loadFileStep" next="loadCustomerStep">
        <tasklet ref="loadStockFile"/>
    </step>
    <step id="loadCustomerStep" next="updateStartStep">
        <tasklet ref="loadCustomerFile"/>
    </step>
    <step id="updateStartStep">
        <tasklet ref="updateStart"/>
    </step>
</flow>

<job id="flowJob">
    <step id="initializeBatch" next="runBatch">
        <flow parent="preProcessingFlow"/>
    </step>
    <step id="runBatch">
        <tasklet ref="runBatchTasklet"/>
    </step>
</job>
...
```

What is the difference between using the flow tag and the flow step? It comes down to what happens in the JobRepository. Using the flow tag ends up with the same results as if you configured the steps in your job. Using a flow step adds an additional entry. When you use a flow step, Spring Batch records the step that includes the flow as a separate step. Why is this a good thing? The main benefit is for monitoring and reporting purposes. Using a flow step allows you to see the impact of the flow as a whole instead of having to aggregate the individual steps.

The last way to externalize the order in which steps occur is to not externalize them at all. In this case, instead of creating a flow, you call a job from within another job. Similar to the flow step, which creates a StepExecutionContext for the execution of the flow and each step within it, the job step creates a JobExecutionContext for the step that calls the external job. Listing 4-48 shows the configuration of a job step.

Listing 4-48. Using a Job Step

```
<job id="preProcessingJob">
    <step id="step1" parent="loadStockFile" next="step2"/>
    <step id="step2" parent="loadCustomerFile" next="step3"/>
    <step id="step3" parent="updateStartOfBatchCycle"/>
</job>

<beans:bean id="jobParametersExtractor"
class="org.springframework.batch.core.step.job.DefaultJobParametersExtractor">
```

```
        <beans:property name="keys" value="job.stockFile,job.customerFile"/>
    </beans:bean>

    <job id="subJobJob">
        <step id="step0" next="step4 ">
            <job ref="preProcessingJob"
                job-parameters-extractor="jobParametersExtractor "/>
        </step>
        <step id="step4" parent="runBatch"/>
    </job>
```

You might be wondering about the jobParametersExtractor bean in Listing 4-48. When you launch a job, it's identified by the job name and the job parameters. In this case, you aren't passing the parameters to your sub job, preProcessingJob, by hand. Instead, you define a class to extract the parameters from either the JobParameters of the parent job or the ExecutionContext (the DefaultJobParameterExtractor checks both places) and pass those parameters to the child job. Your extractor pulls the values from the job.stockFile and job.customerFile job parameters and passes those as parameters to preProcessingJob.

When preProcessingJob executes, it's identified in the JobRepository just like any other job. It has its own job instance, execution context, and related database records.

A word of caution about using the job-step approach: this may seem like a good way to handle job dependencies. Creating individual jobs and being able to then string them together with a master job is a powerful feature. However, this can severely limit the control of the process as it executes. It isn't uncommon in the real world to need to pause a batch cycle or skip jobs based on external factors (another department can't get you a file in time to have the process finished in the required window, and so on). However, the ability to manage jobs exists at a single job level. Managing entire trees of jobs that could be created using this functionality is problematic and should be avoided. Linking jobs together in this manner and executing them as one master job severely limits the capability to handle these types of situations and should also be avoided.

The last piece of the flow puzzle is the ability Spring Batch provides to execute multiple flows in parallel, which is covered next.

Parallelization of Flows

Although you learn about parallelization later in this book, this section covers the Spring Batch functionality to execute step flows in parallel. One of the strengths of using Java for batch processing and the tools that Spring Batch provides is the ability to bring multithreaded processing to the batch world in a standardized way. One of the easiest ways to execute steps in parallel is to split them in your job.

The split flow is a step that allows you to list flows that you want to execute in parallel. Each flow is started at the same time, and the step isn't considered complete until all the flows within it have completed. If any one of the flows fails, the split flow is considered to have failed. To see how the split step works, look at Listing 4-49.

Listing 4-49. Parallel Flows Using a Split Step

```
<job id="flowJob">
    <split id="preprocessingStep" next="batchStep">
        <flow>
            <step id="step1" parent="loadStockFile" next="step2"/>
            <step id="step2" parent="loadCustomerFile"/>
```

```
        </flow>
        <flow>
            <step id="step3" parent="loadTransactionFile"/>
        </flow>
    </split>
    <step id="batchStep" parent="runBatch"/>
</job>
```

In Listing 4-49, you identify two separate flows: one that loads two files and one that loads one file. Each of these flows is executed in parallel. After all three steps (step1, step2, and step3) have completed, Spring Batch executes batchStep.

That's it. It's amazing how simple it is to do basic parallelization using Spring Batch, as this example shows. And given the potential performance boosts,[7] you can begin to see why Spring Batch can be a very effective tool in high-performance batch processing.

Later chapters cover a variety of error-handling scenarios including error handling at the entire job level down to errors at the transaction level. But because steps are all about processing chunks of items, the next topic is some of the error-handling strategies available when processing a single item.

Item Error Handling

Spring Batch 2 is based on the concept of chunk-based processing. Because chunks are based on transaction-commit boundaries, the book discusses how to handle errors for chunks when it covers transactions in the ItemReader and ItemWriter chapters. However, individual items are usually the cause of an error, and Spring Batch provides a couple of error-handling strategies at the item level for your use. Specifically, Spring Batch lets you either skip the processing of an item or try to process an item again after a failure.

Let's start by looking at retrying to process an item before you give up on it via skipping.

Item Retry

When you're processing large amounts of data, it isn't uncommon to have errors due to things that don't need human intervention. If a database that is shared across systems has a deadlock, or a web service call fails due to a network hiccup, stopping the processing of millions of items is a pretty drastic way to handle the situation. A better approach is to allow your job to try to process a given item again.

There are three ways to implement retry logic in Spring Batch: configuring retry attempts, using RetryTemplate, and using Spring's AOP features. The first approach lets Spring Batch define a number of allowed retry attempts and exceptions that trigger the new attempt. Listing 4-50 show the basic retry configuration for an item when a RemoteAccessException is thrown in the course of executing the remoteStep.

---

[7] Not all parallelization results in an increase in performance. Under the incorrect situations, executing steps in parallel can negatively affect the performance of your job.

Listing 4-50. Basic Retry Configuration

```
<job id="flowJob">
    <step id="retryStep">
        <tasklet>
            <chunk reader="itemReader" writer="itemWriter"
                processor="itemProcessor" commit-interval="20"
                retry-limit="3">
                <retryable-exception-classes>
                    <include
                class="org.springframework.remoting.RemoteAccessException"/>
                </retryable-exception-classes>
            </chunk>
        </tasklet>
    </step>
</job>
```

In the flowJob's retryStep, when a RemoteAccessException is thrown by any of the components in the step (itemReader, itemWriter, or itemProcessor) the item is retried up to three times before the step fails.

Another way to add retry logic to your batch job is to do it yourself via org.springframework.batch.retry.RetryTemplate. Like most other templates provided in Spring, this one simplifies the development of retry logic by providing a simple API to encapsulate the retryable logic in a method that is then managed by Spring. In the case of RetryTemplate, you need to develop two pieces: the org.springframework.batch.retry.RetryPolicy interface and the org.springframework.batch.retry.RetryCallback interface. RetryPolicy allows you to define under what conditions an item's processing is to be retried. Spring provides a number of implementations, including ones for retrying based on an exception being thrown (which you used by default in Listing 4-50), timeout, and others. The other piece of coding retry logic is the use of the RetryCallback interface. This interface provides a single method, doWithRetry(RetryContext context), that encapsulates the logic to be retried. When you use RetryTemplate, if an item is to be retried, the doWithRetry method is called as long as RetryPolicy specifies it to be. Let's look at an example.

Listing 4-51 shows the code to retry a call to a database with a timeout policy of 30 seconds. This means it will continue to try executing the database call until it works or until 30 seconds has passed.

Listing 4-51. Using RetryTemplate and RetryCallback

```
package com.apress.springbatch.chapter4;

import java.util.List;
import org.springframework.batch.item.ItemWriter;
import org.springframework.batch.retry.support.RetryTemplate;
import org.springframework.batch.retry.RetryCallback;
import org.springframework.batch.retry.RetryContext;

public class RetryItemWriter implements ItemWriter<Customer> {

    private CustomerDAO customerDao;
    private RetryTemplate retryTemplate;

    public void write(List<? extends Customer> customers) throws Exception {
```

```
        for (Customer customer : customers) {
            final Customer curCustomer = customer;

            retryTemplate.execute(new RetryCallback<Customer>() {
                public Customer doWithRetry(RetryContext retryContext) {
                    return customerDao.save(curCustomer);
                }
            });
        }
    }
    ...
}
```

The code in Listing 4-51 depends significantly on elements that need to be injected (getters and setters were left out of the example). To get a better view of what is happening here, Listing 4-52 shows the configuration for this example.

Listing 4-52. Configuration for CustomerDao Retry

```xml
<beans:bean id="timeoutPolicy"
    class="org.springframework.batch.retry.policy.TimeoutRetryPolicy">
    <beans:property name="timeout" value="30000"/>
</beans:bean>

<beans:bean id="timeoutRetryTemplate"
    class="org.springframework.batch.retry.support.RetryTemplate">
    <beans:property name="retryPolicy" ref="timeoutPolicy"/>
</beans:bean>

<beans:bean id="retryItemWriter"
    class="com.apress.springbatch.chapter4.RetryItemWriter">
    <beans:property name="customerDao" ref="customerDao"/>
    <beans:property name="retryTemplate" ref="timeoutRetryTemplate"/>
</beans:bean>

<job id="flowJob">
    <step id="retryStep">
        <tasklet>
            <chunk reader="itemReader" writer="retryItemWriter"
                    processor="itemProcessor" commit-interval="20"/>
        </tasklet>
    </step>
</job>
```

Most of the configuration in Listing 4-52 should be straightforward. You configure the org.springframework.batch.retry.policy.TimeoutRetryPolicy bean with a timeout value set to 30 seconds; you inject that into RetryTemplate as the retryPolicy and inject the template into the ItemWriter you wrote for Listing 4-51. One thing that is interesting about the configuration of this retry, however, is that there is no retry configuration in the job. Because you write your own retry logic, you don't use the retry-limit and so on in the chunk configuration.

The final way to configure item-retry logic is to use Spring's AOP facilities and Spring Batch's org.springframework.batch.retry.interceptor.RetryOperationsInterceptor to declaratively apply retry logic to elements of your batch job. Listing 4-53 shows how to declare the aspect's configuration to apply retry logic to any save methods.

Listing 4-53. *Applying Retry Logic Using AOP*

```
<aop:config>
    <aop:pointcut id="saveRetry"
    expression="execution(* com.apress.springbatch.chapter4.*.save(..))"/>
    <aop:advisor pointcut-ref="saveRetry" advice-ref="retryAdvice"
        order="-1"/>
</aop:config>

<beans:bean id="retryAdvice"
    class="org.springframework.batch.retry.interceptor.RetryOperationsInterceptor"/>
```

This configuration leaves out the definition of how many retries to attempt, and so on. To add those, all you need to do is configure the appropriate `RetryPolicy` into `RetryOperationsInterceptor` (which has an optional dependency for a `RetryPolicy` implementation).

`RetryPolicy` is similar to `CompletionPolicy` earlier in that it allows you to programmatically decide something—in this case, when to retry. The `org.springbatch.retry.RetryPolicy` used in either the AOP interceptor or in the regular retry approaches is important, but one thing to note is that you may not want to just retry over and over if it isn't working. For example, when Google's Gmail can't connect back to the server, it first tries to reconnect immediately, then it waits 15 seconds, then 30 seconds, and so on. This approach can prevent multiple retries from stepping on each other's toes. Fortunately, Spring Batch provides a `BackoffPolicy` interface to implement this type of decay. You can implement an algorithm yourself by implementing the `BackoffPolicy` interface or use the `ExponentialBackOffPolicy` provided by the framework. Listing 4-54 shows the configuration required for `BackOffPolicy`.

Listing 4-54. *Applying Retry Logic Using AOP*

```
<beans:bean id="timeoutPolicy"
    class="org.springframework.batch.retry.policy.TimeoutRetryPolicy">
    <beans:property name="timeout" value="30000"/>
</beans:bean>

<beans:bean id="backoutPolicy"

class="org.springframework.batch.retry.backoff.ExponentialBackOffPolicy"/>

<beans:bean id="timeoutRetryTemplate"
    class="org.springframework.batch.retry.support.RetryTemplate">
    <beans:property name="retryPolicy" ref="timeoutPolicy"/>
    <beans:property name="backOffPolicy" ref="backOffPolicy"/>
</beans:bean>

<beans:bean id="retryItemWriter"
    class="com.apress.springbatch.chapter4.RetryItemWriter">
    <beans:property name="customerDao" ref="customerDao"/>
    <beans:property name="retryTemplate" ref="timeoutRetryTemplate"/>
</beans:bean>

<job id="flowJob">
```

```
        <step id="retryStep">
            <tasklet>
                <chunk reader="itemReader" writer="retryItemWriter"
                        processor="itemProcessor"
                         commit-interval="20"/>
            </tasklet>
        </step>
</job>
```

The last aspect of retry logic is that, like most available events in Spring Batch, retry has the ability to register listeners to when an item is being retried. There are two differences, however, between all the other listeners and org.springframework.batch.retry.RetryListener. First, RetryListener has no annotation equivalent of the interface, so if you want to register a listener on retry logic, you have to implement the RetryListener interface. The other difference is that instead of two methods in the interface for the start and end, there are three in this interface. In RetryListener, the open method is called when the retry block is about to be called, onError is called once for each retry, and close is called when the full retry block is complete.

That covers it for retry logic. The other way to handle item-specific error handling is to skip the item altogether.

Item Skip

One of the greatest things in Spring Batch is the ability to skip an item that is causing problems. This feature can easily prevent a phone call in the middle of the night to deal with a production problem if the item can be addressed the next day. Configuring the ability to skip an item is similar to configuring retry logic. All you need to do is use the skip-limit attribute on the chunk tag and specify the exceptions that should cause an item to be skipped. Listing 4-55 demonstrates how to configure a step to allow a maximum of 10 items to be skipped via skip-limit. It then states that any item that causes any subclass of java.lang.Exception except for java.lang.NullPointerException is allowed to be skipped. Any item that throws a NullPointerException causes the step to end in error.

Listing 4-55. Skip Logic Configuration

```
<job id="flowJob">
    <step id="retryStep">
        <tasklet>
            <chunk reader="itemReader" writer="itemWriter"
                processor="itemProcessor" commit-interval="20"
                skip-limit="10">
                <skippable-exception-classes>
                    <include class="java.lang.Exception"/>
                    <exclude class="java.lang.NullPointerException"/>
                </skippable-exception-classes>
            </chunk>
        </tasklet>
    </step>
</job>
```

When using item-based error handling, whether it's retrying to process an item or skipping it, there can be transactional implications. You learn what those are and how to address them when the book gets into reading and writing items in Chapters 7 & 9.

Summary

This chapter covered a large amount of material. You learned what a job is and saw its lifecycle. You looked at how to configure a job and how to interact with it via job parameters. You wrote and configured listeners to execute logic at the beginning and end of a job, and you worked with the ExecutionContext for a job and step.

You began looking at the building blocks of a job: its steps. As you looked at steps, you explored one of the most important concepts in Spring Batch: chunk-based processing. You learned how to configure chunks and some of the more advanced ways to control them (through things like policies). You learned about listeners and how to use them to execute logic at the start and end of a step. You walked through how to order steps either using basic ordering or logic to determine what step to execute next. The chapter briefly touched on parallelization using the split tag and finished discussing steps by covering item-based error handling including skip and retry logic.

The job and step are structural components of the Spring Batch framework. They're used to lay out a process. The majority of the book from here on covers all the different things that go into the structure laid out by these pieces.

CHAPTER 5

Job Repository and Metadata

When you look into writing a batch process, the ability to execute processes without a UI in a stand-alone manner isn't that hard. When you dig into Spring Batch, the execution of a job amounts to nothing more than using an implementation of Spring's TaskExecutor to run a separate task. You don't need Spring Batch to do that.

Where things get interesting, however, is when things go wrong. If your batch job is running and an error occurs, how do you recover? How does your job know where it was in processing when the error occurred, and what should happen when the job is restarted? State management is an important part of processing large volumes of data. This is one of the key features that Spring Batch brings to the table. Spring Batch, as discussed previously in this book, maintains the state of a job as it executes in a job repository. It then uses this information when a job is restarted or an item is retried to determine how to continue. The power of this feature can't be overstated.

Another aspect of batch processing in which the job repository is helpful is monitoring. The ability to see how far a job is in its processing as well as trend elements such as how long operations take or how many items were retried due to errors is vital in the enterprise environment. The fact that Spring Batch does the number gathering for you makes this type of trending much easier.

This chapter covers job repositories in detail. It goes over ways to configure a job repository for most environments by using either a database or an in-memory repository. You also look briefly at performance impacts on the configuration of the job repository. After you have the job repository configured, you learn how to put the job information stored by the job repository to use using the JobExplorer and the JobOperator.

Configuring the Job Repository

In order for Spring Batch to be able to maintain state, the job repository needs to be available. Spring offers two options by default: an in-memory repository and a persisted repository in a database. This section looks at how to configure each of those options as well as the performance impacts of both options. Let's start with more simpler option, the in-memory job repository.

Using an In-Memory Job Repository

The opening paragraphs of this chapter laid out a list of benefits for the job repository, such as the ability to maintain state from execution to execution and trend run statistics from run to run. However, you'll almost never use an in-memory repository for those reasons. That's because when the process ends, all of that data is lost. So, why would you use an in-memory repository at all?

The answer is that sometimes you don't need to persist the data. For example, in development, it's common to run jobs with an in-memory repository so that you don't have to worry about maintaining the job schema in a database. This also allows you to execute the same job multiple times with the same parameters, which is a must-have in development. You might also run a job using the in-memory repository for performance reasons. There is a cost to maintaining job state in a database that may not be needed. Say, for instance, that you're using Spring Batch to do a data migration, moving data from one database table to another; the destination table is empty to start, and you have a small amount of data to migrate. In a case like this, the overhead of setting up a Spring Batch schema and using it may not make sense. Situations that don't need Spring Batch to manage restarts and so on can use the in-memory option.

The JobRepository you've been using so far is configured in the launch-context.xml file. In the previous examples, you've configured the job repository using MySQL. To configure your job to use an in-memory repository, you use the org.springframework.batch.core.repository.support.MapJobRepositoryFactoryBean, as shown in Listing 5-1. Notice that a transaction manager is still required. This is because the data the JobRepository stores is still dependent on transaction semantics (rollback, and so on), and business logic may depend on transactional stores as well. The transaction manager configured in the listing, org.springframework.batch.support.transaction.ResourcelessTransactionManager, actually doesn't do anything with transactions; it's a dummy transaction manager that provides a dummy transaction.

Listing 5-1. *Configuring an In-Memory Job Repository*

```xml
<?xml version="1.0" encoding="UTF-8"?>
<beans:beans xmlns="http://www.springframework.org/schema/batch"
    xmlns:beans="http://www.springframework.org/schema/beans"
    xmlns:xsi="http://www.w3.org/2001/XMLSchema-instance"
    xsi:schemaLocation="http://www.springframework.org/schema/beans
        http://www.springframework.org/schema/beans/spring-beans-3.0.xsd
        http://www.springframework.org/schema/batch
        http://www.springframework.org/schema/batch/spring-batch-2.1.xsd">
    <beans:bean id="transactionManager"
class="org.springframework.batch.support.transaction.
ResourcelessTransactionManager"/>

    <beans:bean id="jobRepository"
class="org.springframework.batch.core.repository.support.
MapJobRepositoryFactoryBean" p:transactionManager-ref="transactionManager" />
...
```

If you take the HelloWorld example from Chapter 2 and configure it to use the in-memory elements of Listing 5-1, you see that you can run the job over and over without Spring Batch throwing an exception for running the same job with the same parameters multiple times.

You should keep in mind a couple of limitations when using an in-memory job repository. First, as already stated, because the storage of data is in memory, once a JVM is restarted the data is lost. Second, because synchronization occurs in the memory space of a particular JVM, there is no guarantee that a given job won't be executed with the same given parameters by executing the same job in two JVMs. Finally, if your job is using any of the multithreading options (multithreaded step, parallel flows, and so on) provided by Spring Batch, this option won't work.

That's it for the in-memory option. By making a small configuration tweak, you can prevent yourself from having to deal with setting up a database to run your batch jobs. However, given the limitations of this approach and the features that a persistent job repository provides, most of the time you'll use a database to back your job repository. With that in mind, let's look at configuring the job repository in a database.

Database

Using a Database Repository is the predominant way to configure a job repository. It allows you to utilize all the benefits of a persistent store with little impact on your job's overall performance. Later, this chapter looks at some hard numbers to illustrate the cost of using a database.

For now, however, let's start by looking at the MySQL configuration you've been using in the examples. You can see the configuration in Listing 5-2. In this case, you begin with the datasource. This example uses the org.apache.commons.dbcp.BasicDataSource provided by Apache Commons, but any datasource you want to use is ok. Listing 5-2 sets the values of the various properties (driver class, database URL, username, and password) via properties in the batch.properties file. This allows you to configure those properties specific to the environment you're working in (your production environment has different values than your test environment, which has different values than your local development).

Listing 5-2. Job Repository Configuration in launch-context.xml Using a Database

```
<beans:bean id="dataSource" class="org.apache.commons.dbcp.BasicDataSource">
    <beans:property name="driverClassName" value="${batch.jdbc.driver}" />
    <beans:property name="url" value="${batch.jdbc.url}" />
    <beans:property name="username" value="${batch.jdbc.user}" />
    <beans:property name="password" value="${batch.jdbc.password}" />
</beans:bean>

<beans:bean id="transactionManager"
    class="org.springframework.jdbc.datasource.DataSourceTransactionManager"
    lazy-init="true">
    <beans:property name="dataSource" ref="dataSource" />
</beans:bean>

<job-repository id="jobRepository" data-source="dataSource"
    transaction-manager="transactionManager"/>
```

The next thing you configure is the transaction manager. Again, you keep it simple here by using the basic DataSourceTransactionManager provided by Spring, but any transaction manager will do. DataSourceTransactionManager has a single dependency: an actual datasource that you've configured. The last aspect of the transaction manager is that it's configured to be lazily initialized[1] which is optional per the Spring documentation but because Spring Batch's shell project has it configured this way, there is no reason to change it.

Finally you come to the job repository factory. The first thing to call out about this configuration is that you don't use the regular bean tag. Instead, Spring Batch provides a tag specific for configuring the job repository. In order to configure the job repository this way, you need to add references to the Spring Batch XSD to launch-context.xml as you did in Listing 5-1, because it isn't included by default. With the job-repository tag, the only attribute that is required is id. By default, Spring autowires the data-source and transaction-manager attributes of JobRepositoryFactoryBean with beans named dataSource and transactionManager, respectively.

---

[1] By default, Spring instantiates all singleton beans on startup. Because you don't know what will happen, there is no reason to go through the work of creating a transaction manager if it won't be used.

In either configuration, using the bean tag or the `job-repository` tag, you reference the second of two job repository factories provided with Spring Batch. The first is `org.springframework.batch.core.repository.support.MapJobRepositoryFactoryBean`, which you use for an in-memory job repository. The second is `org.springframework.batch.core.repository.support.JobRepositoryFactoryBean`. The `JobRepositoryFactoryBean` that this configuration demonstrates uses a database as the method for maintaining state in the job repository. To access the underlying database, you need to satisfy its two dependencies: a datasource and a transaction manager, both of which are configured in Listing 5-2.

Database Schema Configuration

Spring does a good job of allowing you to be flexible with your configurations. One of the things Spring Batch allows you to change up is the table prefix. By default, every table is prefixed with *BATCH_*, but this may not be what you or your enterprise want. With that in mind, the developers of Spring Batch let you configure the table prefix for the tables in the job repository. To do that, you use the `table-prefix` attribute of the `job-repository` tag as shown in Listing 5-3. With the configuration updated as it is in the example, Spring Batch expects the tables to be named SAMPLE_JOB_EXECUTION, and so on.

Listing 5-3. Changing the Table Prefix

```
<job-repository id="jobRepository" data-source="dataSource"
    transaction-manager="transactionManager" table-prefix="SAMPLE_"/>
```

■**Note** Spring Batch only lets you configure the table prefix. You can't change the complete name of the tables or column names.

The other aspect of the database schema that Spring Batch allows you to configure is the maximum length of the varchar data type. By default, the schema scripts in Spring Batch set the length of the larger varchar columns to 2500 (EXIT_MESSAGE columns in the execution tables and the SHORT_CONTEXT columns in the execution context tables). If you're using a character set that uses more than a byte for a character, or modify the schema, you can use this to allow Spring Batch to store larger values. Listing 5-4 shows the job repository being configured for 3000 as the maximum.

Listing 5-4. Configuring the Maximum varchar Length

```
<job-repository id="jobRepository" data-source="dataSource"
    transaction-manager="transactionManager" max-varchar-length="3000"/>
```

It's important to note that the `max-varchar-length` configuration in Listing 5-4 doesn't actually change the database. Instead, it truncates any messages that are too long to fit in the EXIT_MESSAGE column. The last and probably most important piece of configuring the job repository is how transactions are configured, which you look at next.

Transaction Configuration

The use of the job repository is based on transactions. The repository is updated when each chunk of processing completes, which triggers the end of a transaction. You've seen that there are two ways to configure the job repository, one with the regular Spring bean tag and one using the Spring Batch namespace's job-repository tag. How transactions are configured depends on which of these options you choose.

When you use the job-repository tag from the Spring Batch namespace, Spring Batch uses Spring's AOP features to wrap the repository with a transaction. The only thing to configure when using this approach is the transaction isolation level for the createJobExecution method of the job repository interface. The intent of this configuration is to prevent multiple executions of a JobInstance at the same time. To address this issue, Spring Batch sets the transaction's isolation level at its most aggressive value, SERIALIZABLE, by default. However, your environment may not require a level this aggressive, so Spring Batch lets you configure the transaction level for the createJobExecution method with the isolation-level-for-create attribute of the job-repository tag. Listing 5-5 shows how to lower the isolation level when using the job-repository tag.

Listing 5-5. Setting the Create Transaction Level

```
<job-repository id="jobRepository" transaction-manager="transactionManager"
    data-source="dataSource" isolation-level-for-create="READ_COMMITTED"/>
```

If you configure your job repository using the Spring bean tag as you did with the in-memory option, the framework doesn't handle any of the transactions for you. In this case, you need to configure transactional advice by hand, as shown in Listing 5-6. Here you use Spring's AOP namespace to configure the transaction advice and apply it to all the methods in the job repository interface.

Listing 5-6. Configuring Job Repository Transactions by Hand

```
<beans:bean id="dataSource" class="org.apache.commons.dbcp.BasicDataSource">
    <beans:property name="driverClassName" value="${batch.jdbc.driver}" />
    <beans:property name="url" value="${batch.jdbc.url}" />
    <beans:property name="username" value="${batch.jdbc.user}" />
    <beans:property name="password" value="${batch.jdbc.password}" />
</beans:bean>

<beans:bean id="transactionManager"
    class="org.springframework.jdbc.datasource.DataSourceTransactionManager"/>

<aop:config>
    <aop:advisor
pointcut="execution(*org.springframework.batch.core.repository..*Repository+.*(..))"/>
    <advice-ref="txAdvice" />
</aop:config>

<tx:advice id="txAdvice" transaction-manager="transactionManager">
    <tx:attributes>
        <tx:method name="*" />
    </tx:attributes>
</tx:advice>
```

```
<beans:bean id="jobRepository"
class="org.springframework.batch.core.repository.support.JobRepositoryFactoryBean"
p:transactionManager-ref="transactionManager" p:dataSource-ref="dataSource" />
```

The job repository is the central piece of the safety net that Spring Batch provides for your processing. However, it's much more than just a tool for the Spring Batch framework's own use. You have as much access to the data as the framework does, along with the ability to manipulate that data. This next section shows you how how.

Using Job Metadata

Although Spring Batch accesses the job repository tables through a collection of DAOs, they expose a much more practical API for the use of the framework and for you to use. This section you look at the two ways Spring Batch exposes the data in the job repository. First you look at the JobExplorer, an item you configured last chapter, how to configure it and read data from the repository using it. From there you move onto the JobOperator. You look at how to configure the operator as well as use it to manipulate the data contained in the job repository. Let's start with the JobExplorer.

The JobExplorer

The `org.springframework.batch.core.explore.JobExplorer` interface is the starting point for all access to historical and active data in the job repository. Figure 5-1 shows that although most of the framework accesses the information stored about job execution through the JobRepository, the JobExplorer accesses it directly from the database itself.

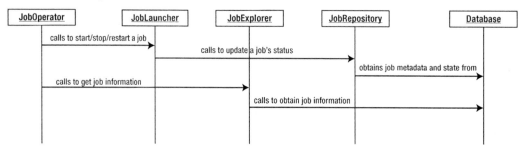

Figure 5-1. *The relationship between the job administration components*

The underlying purpose of the JobExplorer is to provide read-only access to the data in the job repository. The interface provides seven methods you can use to obtain information about job instances and executions. Table 5-1 lists the available methods and their use.

Table 5-1. Methods of the JobExplorer

Method	Description
`java.util.Set<JobExecution>findRunningjobExecutions(java.lang.String jobName)`	Returns all JobExecutions without an end time.
`JobExecution getJobExecution(java.lang.Long executionId)`	Returns the JobExecution identified by the supplied id and null if not found.
`java.util.List<JobExecution> getJobExecutions( JobInstance instance)`	Returns a list of all JobExecutions related to the JobInstance supplied.
`JobInstance getJobInstance(java.lang.Long instanceId)`	Returns the JobInstance identified by the supplied id or null if none is found.
`java.util.List<JobInstance> getJobInstances( java.lang.String jobName, int start, int count)`	Returns a range of JobInstances starting with the index specified (the start parameter). The final parameter specifies the maximum number of JobInstances to return.
`java.util.List<java.lang.String> getJobNames()`	Returns all unique job names from the job repository in alphabetical order.
`StepExecution getStepExecution(java.lang.Long jobExecutionId, java.lang.Long stepExecutionId)`	Returns the specified StepExecution based on the id of the StepExecution and the id of its parent JobExecution.

As you can see, the entire job repository is available from the methods exposed by the JobExplorer interface. However, before you can put the JobExplorer to use, you need to configure it. Listing 5-7 shows how to configure the JobExplorer in the launch-context.xml file.

Listing 5-7. JobExplorer Configuration

```
<beans:bean id="jobExplorer"
class="org.springframework.batch.core.explore.support.JobExplorerFactoryBean"
p:dataSource-ref="dataSource" />
```

The JobExplorer is configured just like any other Spring bean with a single dependency—a datasource—so it can be injected into any of your other elements. Note that unlike most of the other Spring Batch components you've configured that have a dependency of the JobRepository, this one depends on a datasource. The reason is that, as mentioned earlier, the JobExplorer doesn't obtain its information from the JobRepository. Instead, it goes directly to the database for its information.

To see how the JobExplorer works, you can inject it into the HelloWorld tasklet from the previous examples. From there, you can see what you can use the JobExplorer for. In Listing 5-8, you configure the HelloWorld tasklet with the JobExplorer injected.

Listing 5-8. Configuration of the HelloWorld tasklet and JobExplorer

```
<?xml version="1.0" encoding="UTF-8"?>
<beans xmlns:batch="http://www.springframework.org/schema/batch"
    xmlns="http://www.springframework.org/schema/beans"
    xmlns:xsi="http://www.w3.org/2001/XMLSchema-instance"
    xsi:schemaLocation="http://www.springframework.org/schema/beans
        http://www.springframework.org/schema/beans/spring-beans-3.0.xsd
        http://www.springframework.org/schema/batch
        http://www.springframework.org/schema/batch/spring-batch-2.1.xsd">

    <import resource="../launch-context.xml"/>

    <bean id="helloWorld"
        class="com.apress.springbatch.chapter5.HelloWorld">
        <property name="explorer" ref="jobExplorer"/>
    </bean>

    <batch:step id="helloWorldStep">
        <batch:tasklet ref="helloWorld"/>
    </batch:step>

    <batch:job id="helloWorldJob">
        <batch:step id="step1" parent="helloWorldStep"/>
    </batch:job>
</beans>
```

With the JobExplorer configured, there are a number of things you can do with it. Within the Spring Batch framework, you can use the JobExplorer in the RunIdIncrementer you looked at in Chapter 4 to look up the previous run.id parameter value. Another place it's used is in the Spring Batch Admin web application to determine whether a job is currently running before launching a new instance. In the example, you use it to determine whether this is the first time you've run this JobInstance. If it is, you print the message "Hello, Michael!" where Michael is a value passed in. If it isn't the first time you've run the job, you update the message to "Welcome back Michael!" Listing 5-9 has the updated code for this tasklet.

Listing 5-9. Updated HelloWorld Tasklet

```java
package com.apress.springbatch.chapter5;

import java.util.List;

import org.springframework.batch.core.JobInstance;
import org.springframework.batch.core.StepContribution;
import org.springframework.batch.core.explore.JobExplorer;
import org.springframework.batch.core.scope.context.ChunkContext;
import org.springframework.batch.core.step.tasklet.Tasklet;
import org.springframework.batch.repeat.RepeatStatus;

public class HelloWorld implements Tasklet {

private static final String HELLO = "Hello, %s!";
    private static final String WELCOME = "And then we have %s!";
    private static final String JOB_NAME = "helloWorldJob";

    private JobExplorer explorer;

    public RepeatStatus execute(StepContribution stepContribution,
                                ChunkContext chunkContext) throws Exception {
        List<JobInstance>instances =
            explorer.getJobInstances(JOB_NAME, 0, Integer.MAX_VALUE);

        String name = (String) chunkContext.getStepContext()
                                    .getJobParameters()
                                    .get("name");

        if (instances != null && instances.size() > 1) {
            System.out.println(String.format(WELCOME, name));
        } else {
            System.out.println(String.format(HELLO, name));
        }

        return RepeatStatus.FINISHED;
    }

    public void setExplorer(JobExplorer explorer) {
        this.explorer = explorer;
    }
}
```

The code in Listing 5-9 begins by obtaining all the JobInstances for helloWorldJob. Once it has the list, it determines whether the job has been run before. If it has, you use the "Welcome back" message. If this is the first time the job is being run, you use the "Hello" message.

With the code and configuration in place, run the job twice so you can see both halves of the if statement execute. Listing 5-10 shows the important output for each job.

Listing 5-10. HelloWorld Job Output from Both Runs

```
Run 1 executed with the command java -jar metadata-0.0.1-SNAPSHOT.jar name=Michael
2010-12-17 22:42:50,613 DEBUG
org.springframework.batch.core.launch.support.CommandLineJobRunner.main()
[org.springframework.batch.core.scope.context.StepContextRepeatCallback] - <Chunk execution
starting: queue size=0>

Hello, Michael!

2010-12-17 22:42:50,619 DEBUG
org.springframework.batch.core.launch.support.CommandLineJobRunner.main()
[org.springframework.batch.core.step.tasklet.TaskletStep] - <Applying contribution:
[StepContribution: read=0, written=0, filtered=0, readSkips=0, writeSkips=0, processSkips=0,
exitStatus=EXECUTING]>

Run 2 executed with the command java -jar metadata-0.0.1-SNAPSHOT.jar name=John
2010-12-17 22:44:49,960 DEBUG
org.springframework.batch.core.launch.support.CommandLineJobRunner.main()
[org.springframework.batch.core.scope.context.StepContextRepeatCallback] - <Chunk execution
starting: queue size=0>

And then we have John!

2010-12-17 22:44:49,965 DEBUG
org.springframework.batch.core.launch.support.CommandLineJobRunner.main()
[org.springframework.batch.core.step.tasklet.TaskletStep] - <Applying contribution:
[StepContribution: read=0, written=0, filtered=0, readSkips=0, writeSkips=0, processSkips=0,
exitStatus=EXECUTING]>
```

This section looked at how to access data in the job repository via the JobExplorer. You use APIs like the JobExplorer to access the data to use it in a safe way. Although it isn't considered good practice to manipulate the job repository directly, that doesn't mean the data it maintains is hands-off. In fact, you can control what happens in your jobs programmatically by manipulating the job repository. You do this using the JobOperator.

The JobOperator

The JobOperator is very similar to the JobExplorer when you look at the method names. However, whereas the JobExplorer provides a read-only look into the data in the job repository, the JobOperator exposes only as much as required to take action on it. The org.springframework.batch.core.launch.JobOperator interface lets you execute basic administrative tasks programmatically in a job.

The JobOperator's interface consists of 11 methods, which are outlined in Table 5-2.

Table 5-2. Methods Available on the JobOperator

Method	Description
`java.util.List<java.lang.Long> getExecutions( long instanceId )`	Returns an ordered list of JobExecution ids associated with the JobInstance identified. The list in order of creation/execution from newest to oldest.
`java.util.List<java.lang.Long> getJobInstances( java.lang.String jobName, int start, int count)`	Returns the ids for each JobInstance for the job name requested starting with the index provided via the `start` parameter, in reverse chronological order (newest to oldest). The count is the maximum number of ids to be returned.
`java.util.Set<java.lang.String> getJobNames()`	Returns all job names available to be executed via the `JobOperator.start` method.
`java.lang.String getParameters(long executionId)`	Returns the job parameters used for the requested JobExecution in a human-readable string.
`java.util.Set<java.lang.Long> getRunningExecutions( java.lang.String jobName )`	Returns the ids of all currently running (no end time) JobExecutions for the job with the name passed.
`java.util.Map<java.lang.Long, java.lang.String> getStepExecutionSummaries( long executionId )`	Provides a summary (status, start and end times, and so on) of the each StepExecution related to the JobExecution specified.
`java.lang.String getSummary( long executionId )`	Returns a summary of the JobExecution specified (status, start and end times, and so on).
`java.lang.Long restart( long executionId )`	Restarts a JobExecution in the `FAILED` or `STOPPED` state.
`java.lang.Long start(java.lang.String jobName, java.lang.String parameters)`	Starts a new JobInstance of the job specified with the parameters passed.
`java.lang.Long startNextInstance (java.lang.String jobName )`	Performs the programmatic equivalent of running a job with the –next parameter and a `JobParametersIncrementer` configured.

`boolean stop( long executionId )`	Sends a stop signal to the JobExecution identified. It's important to note that this doesn't mean the job has stopped, only that the request to stop has been made.

Up to now this book has been using a basic java command line command to launch Spring Batch's CommandLineJobRunner to run jobs. To see the JobOperator in action, you create a JMX JobRunner that allows you to execute a job via a JMX console. To get started, you have to write a main method that keeps the Spring application running without actually doing anything. Listing 5-11 shows how you do that.

Listing 5-11. Bootstrapping a Spring Application

```
package com.apress.springbatch.chapter5;

import org.springframework.context.ApplicationContext;
import org.springframework.context.support.ClassPathXmlApplicationContext;

public class Batch {

    @SuppressWarnings("unused")
    public static void main(String[] args) {
        try {
            ApplicationContext context =
                new ClassPathXmlApplicationContext("launch-context.xml");

            Object lock = new Object();

            synchronized (lock) {
                lock.wait();
            }
        } catch (Exception e) {
            e.printStackTrace();
        }
    }
}
```

When you have the code written to launch your Spring application and keep it running, you can write JMXJobRunner. To do this, all you do is write a POJO that starts a job based on the job name passed in. As you can see in Listing 5-12, the code to accomplish this isn't much more than a wrapper around a JobOperator instance.

Listing 5-12. JMXJobRunner

```
package com.apress.springbatch.chapter5;

import org.springframework.batch.core.JobParametersInvalidException;
import org.springframework.batch.core.launch.JobInstanceAlreadyExistsException;
import org.springframework.batch.core.launch.JobOperator;
import org.springframework.batch.core.launch.NoSuchJobException;
```

```
public class JMXJobRunner {

    private JobOperator operator;

    public void runJob(String name) throws NoSuchJobException,
                                     JobInstanceAlreadyExistsException,
                                     JobParametersInvalidException {
        operator.start(name, null);
    }
    public void setOperator(JobOperator operator) {
        this.operator = operator;
    }
}
```

In Listing 5-12, you use the JobOperator.start method to launch a job with the name provided and no parameters; the job is configured within the previously loaded ApplicationContext. With the JMXJobRunner and Batch classes written, the only thing left is to wire them up with Spring. All of the configuration for these elements is in launch-context.xml, as shown in Listing 5-13.

Listing 5-13. launch-context.xml

```
<?xml version="1.0" encoding="UTF-8"?>
<beans:beans xmlns:beans="http://www.springframework.org/schema/beans"
    xmlns="http://www.springframework.org/schema/batch"
    xmlns:p="http://www.springframework.org/schema/p"
    xmlns:xsi="http://www.w3.org/2001/XMLSchema-instance"
    xsi:schemaLocation="http://www.springframework.org/schema/beans
        http://www.springframework.org/schema/beans/spring-beans-3.0.xsd
        http://www.springframework.org/schema/batch
        http://www.springframework.org/schema/batch/spring-batch-2.1.xsd">

    <beans:bean id="jobOperator"
      class="org.springframework.batch.core.launch.support.SimpleJobOperator"
      p:jobLauncher-ref="jobLauncher" p:jobExplorer-ref="jobExplorer"
      p:jobRepository-ref="jobRepository" p:jobRegistry-ref="jobRegistry" />

    <beans:bean id="jobExplorer"
class="org.springframework.batch.core.explore.support.JobExplorerFactoryBean"
        p:dataSource-ref="dataSource" />

    <beans:bean id="taskExecutor"
        class="org.springframework.core.task.SimpleAsyncTaskExecutor" />

    <beans:bean id="jobLauncher"
      class="org.springframework.batch.core.launch.support.SimpleJobLauncher">
        <beans:property name="jobRepository" ref="jobRepository" />
        <beans:property name="taskExecutor" ref="taskExecutor" />
    </beans:bean>

    <job-repository id="jobRepository"
        data-source="dataSource" transaction-manager="transactionManager" />
```

```
    <beans:bean id="jobRegistry"
class="org.springframework.batch.core.configuration.support.MapJobRegistry" />

    <beans:bean
class="org.springframework.batch.core.configuration.support.AutomaticJobRegistrar">
        <beans:property name="applicationContextFactories">
            <beans:bean
class="org.springframework.batch.core.configuration.support.
ClasspathXmlApplicationContextsFactoryBean">
                <beans:property name="resources"
                    value="classpath*:/jobs/helloWorld.xml" />
            </beans:bean>
        </beans:property>
        <beans:property name="jobLoader">
            <beans:bean
                class="org.springframework.batch.core.configuration.support.DefaultJobLoader">
                <beans:property name="jobRegistry" ref="jobRegistry" />
            </beans:bean>
        </beans:property>
    </beans:bean>

    <beans:bean id="jobRunner"
        class="com.apress.springbatch.chapter5.JMXJobRunnerImpl"
        p:operator-ref="jobOperator" />

    <beans:bean id="exporter"
        class="org.springframework.jmx.export.MBeanExporter"
        lazy-init="false">
        <beans:property name="beans">
            <map>
                <entry key="bean:name=myJobRunner" value-ref="jobRunner" />
            </map>
        </beans:property>
        <beans:property name="assembler" ref="assembler" />
    </beans:bean>

    <beans:bean id="assembler"
        class="org.springframework.jmx.export.assembler.
        InterfaceBasedMBeanInfoAssembler">
        <beans:property name="managedInterfaces">
            <list>
                <value>com.apress.springbatch.chapter5.JMXJobRunner
                </value>
            </list>
        </beans:property>
    </beans:bean>

    <beans:bean id="registry"
        class="org.springframework.remoting.rmi.RmiRegistryFactoryBean">
        <beans:property name="port" value="1099" />
    </beans:bean>
```

```
    <beans:bean id="dataSource"
        class="org.apache.commons.dbcp.BasicDataSource">
        <beans:property name="driverClassName"
            value="${batch.jdbc.driver}" />
        <beans:property name="url" value="${batch.jdbc.url}" />
        <beans:property name="username" value="${batch.jdbc.user}" />
        <beans:property name="password" value="${batch.jdbc.password}" />
    </beans:bean>

<beans:bean id="transactionManager"
    class="org.springframework.jdbc.datasource.DataSourceTransactionManager"
    lazy-init="true">
        <beans:property name="dataSource" ref="dataSource" />
    </beans:bean>

    <beans:bean id="placeholderProperties"
        class="org.springframework.beans.factory.config.
        PropertyPlaceholderConfigurer">
        <beans:property name="location" value="classpath:batch.properties" />
        <beans:property name="systemPropertiesModeName"
            value="SYSTEM_PROPERTIES_MODE_OVERRIDE" />
        <beans:property name="ignoreUnresolvablePlaceholders"
            value="true" />
        <beans:property name="order" value="1" />
    </beans:bean>
</beans:beans>
```

This launch-context.xml file has a lot going on, so let's take it from the top. In order for the JMXJobLauncher to be able to start a job, you need a reference to a JobOperator. The first bean in this file is that configuration. SimpleJobOperator is the only implementation of the JobOperator interface provided by the Spring Batch framework. You configure it to have access to the JobExplorer, JobLauncher, JobRepository, and JobRegistry. Given what the JobOperator can do, these dependencies are all needed.

The JobExplorer is next, to provide read-only access to the JobRepository for many of the objects in this configuration. After the JobExplorer is a TaskExecutor configuration along with the JobLauncher used by the JobOperator. The JobLauncher does the work of starting the job and is managed by the JobOperator for your environment. You configure the JobRepository next; as discussed, this is used by Spring Batch to maintain the state of your jobs.

The JobRegistry is the next bean configured. Spring Batch provides the ability to register a collection of jobs in a JobRegistry to be executed on demand. The JobRegistry contains all the jobs that are eligible to be run in this JVM. In the case of this configuration, you're using Spring Batch's MapJobRegistry, which is a Map of jobs available to be run. In order to populate the JobRegistry on startup, you configure an instance of AutomaticJobRegistrar. This class, as configured in Listing 5-13, reads all the jobs configured in the /jobs/helloWorldJob.xml file and loads them into the JobRegistry for future use.

The final piece from a Spring Batch perspective in this launch-context.xml file is the configuration of JMXJobLauncher itself. The rest of the configuration found in this file consists of the datasource, transaction manager, properties loader, and required elements to expose JMXJobLauncher as an MBean.

With all of the configuration and coding complete, you can now run the main class, Batch, and look at the beans exposed via JMX with the JConsole application provided by the JDK. To launch the Batch program, you need to make one last tweak, however. When you create a shell project by using Spring Batch's simple-cli-archetype, the *cli* stands for command line interface. The Project Object Model

(POM) in this project is preconfigured to create a jar file, with CommandLineJobRunner defined as the main class by default. For this example, you update the POM to use the Batch class from Listing 5-11 as the main method for your jar. Listing 5-14 shows the snippet that needs to be updated.

Listing 5-14. Maven Jar Plug-in Configured to Run Batch

```
<plugin>
    <groupId>org.apache.maven.plugins</groupId>
    <artifactId>maven-jar-plugin</artifactId>
    <configuration>
        <archive>
            <index>false</index>
            <manifest>
                <mainClass>com.apress.springbatch.chapter5.Batch</mainClass>
                <addClasspath>true</addClasspath>
                <classpathPrefix>lib/</classpathPrefix>
            </manifest>
            <manifestFile>
                ${project.build.outputDirectory}/META-INF/MANIFEST.MF
            </manifestFile>
        </archive>
    </configuration>
</plugin>
```

With the POM updated, you can use the same command you have in the past to launch the program: java -jar metadata-0.0.1-SNAPSHOT.jar.

Notice that when you run the program, the output is quite different. This time, no job runs. Instead, you see Spring bootstrap and register the job helloWorldJob from the helloWorld.xml file, as shown in Listing 5-16.

Listing 5-16. The registration of the helloWorld job.

```
2010-12-16 21:17:41,390 DEBUG com.apress.springbatch.chapter5.Batch.main()
[org.springframework.batch.core.configuration.support.DefaultJobLoader] - <Registering job:
helloWorldJob1 from context: file:/Users/mminella/Documents/SpringBatch/Chapter5/batch-
test/target/classes/jobs/helloWorld.xml>
```

With the Batch process running, you view the beans exposed via JMX using Java's JConsole. JConsole is a free Java monitoring and management tool provided with the JDK. It allows you to monitor the JVM in a number of ways, including CPU utilization and memory allocation, and it lets you perform management tasks including interacting with JMX beans. When you launch JConsole, you're presented with a screen that asks you which Java process you would like to connect to, as shown in Figure 5-2.

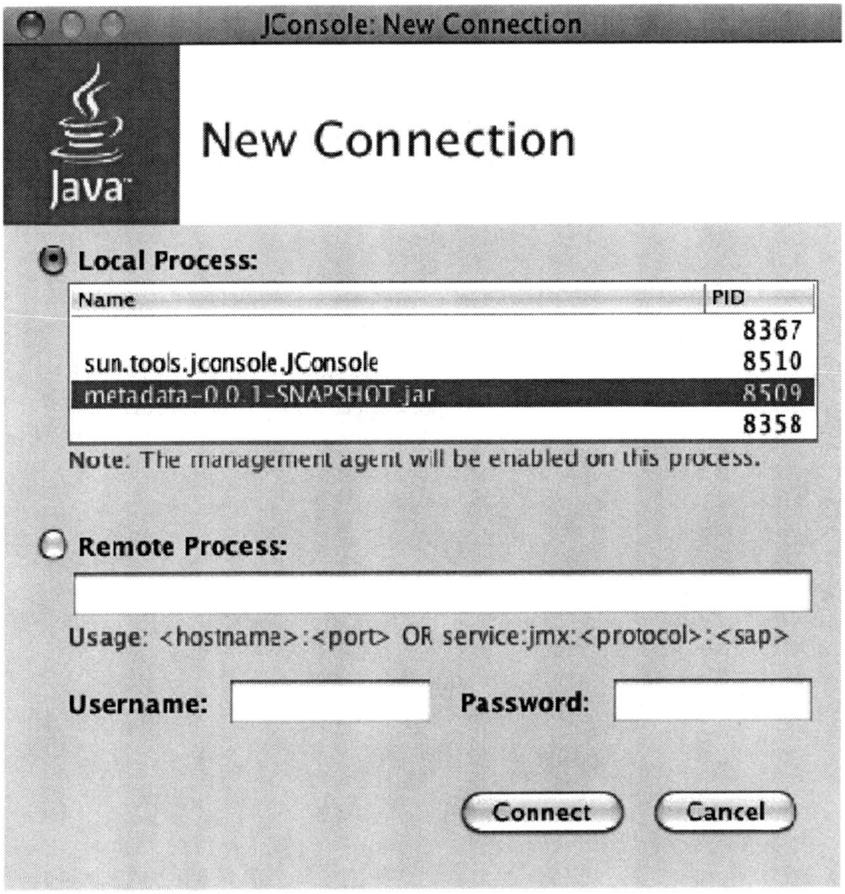

Figure 5-2. The JConsole main screen

In this case, select the local process (you can use JConsole to administer remote Java processes as well) with the name org.codehaus.classworlds.Launcher "exec:java". This is the Java process you launched with the maven command in Listing 5-15. Clicking connect allows JConsole to connect to the JVM.

After you connect, JConsole shows you a screen like the one in Figure 5-3. At the top are six tabs: Overview, Memory, Threads, Classes, VM Summary, and MBeans. Below the tabs, JConsole lets you select the time range for which to display the overview data. Finally, there are four quadrants of data: the amount of JVM heap memory usage, the number of threads being used, the number of classes currently loaded by the JVM, and the CPU usage during the time selected. The tab you're interested in is MBeans.

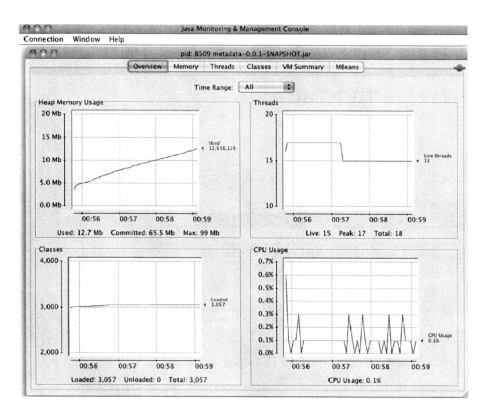

Figure 5-3. *Overview of the JVM*

When you select the MBeans tab, you're presented with a tree navigation on the left and a main panel in the rest of the window. In Listing 5-13 you configured the bean to be in the namespace bean and have the name myJobRunner. Sure enough, Figure 5-4 shows the bean namespace in the tree navigation with a bean myJobRunner available.

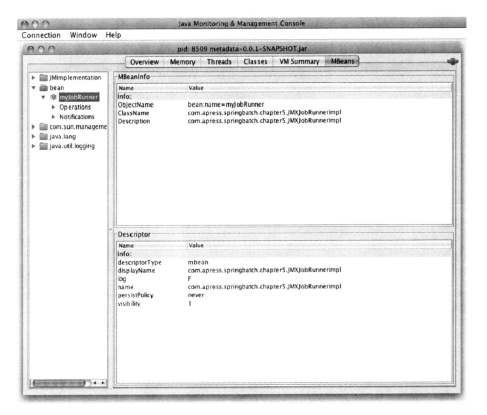

Figure 5-4. JMXJobRunner exposed in JConsole

For any bean exposed, there are up to three sections: attributes that allow you to modify public attributes (which you don't have in this case); Operations, which lets you execute public methods; and Notifications, to show you any JMX notifications (messages sent from the bean to anyone listening via JMX). To run your batch job, go to Operations, as shown in Figure 5-5. There you see the only public method on JMXJobRunner: runJob. It's void and takes a single parameter. To invoke the job, all you need to do is enter the job name in the box and click RunJob.

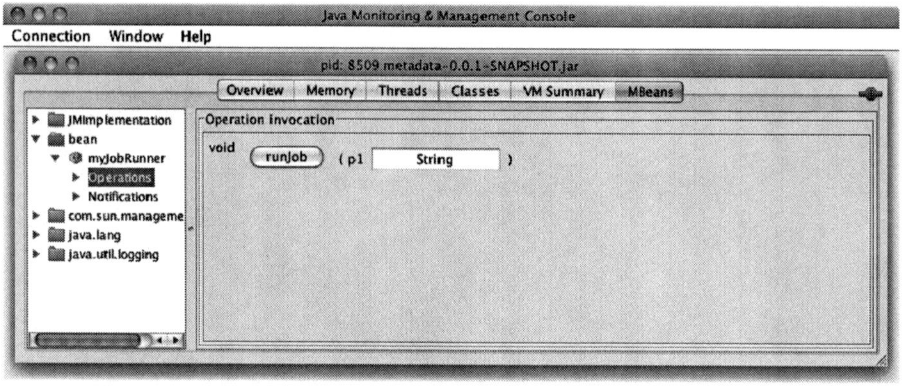

Figure 5-5. The `JMXJobRunner.runJob` *method exposed in JConsole*

When you click the Runjob button, you see in the console in which you're currently running your Java process that the job runs, giving you the output you expect with `helloWorldJob`.

```
2010-12-17 17:06:09,444 DEBUG RMI TCP Connection(1)-192.168.1.119
[org.springframework.batch.core.scope.context.StepContextRepeatCallback] - <Chunk execution
starting: queue size=0>

Hello, World!

2010-12-17 17:06:09,450 DEBUG RMI TCP Connection(1)-192.168.1.119
[org.springframework.batch.core.step.tasklet.TaskletStep] - <Applying contribution:
[StepContribution: read=0, written=0, filtered=0, readSkips=0, writeSkips=0, processSkips=0,
exitStatus=EXECUTING]>
```

In this example, you wrote a job runner that you were able to expose via JMX. Other uses would be to develop a step listener that stops the job based on a given condition. In Chapter 6, you expand this example to accept parameters and use the JobOperator to stop and restart jobs programmatically.

Summary

Spring Batch's ability to manage metadata about a job as well as maintain the state of the job as it runs for error handling is one of the primary reasons, if not the primary reason, to use Spring Batch for enterprise batch processing. Not only does it provide the ability for robust error handling, but it also allows processes to make decisions about what to do based on what has happened elsewhere in the job. In the next chapter, you put this metadata to further use as well as the JobOperator as you take a deep look at how to start, stop, and restart jobs in a variety of environments.

## CHAPTER 6

Running a Job

Normally, you don't have to think about how to run an application in Java. If you have a web application, you run it in some form of container. To run the application, you start the container, which starts the application. If you want to run a stand-alone Java program, you either create an executable jar file or call the class directly. In either case you might write a shell script to launch the process.

However, running a batch job is different. This is partially because a batch job can be run either as a thread within an existing process (as it has been up to now) or within the main execution thread. It can be run within a container or as a stand-alone process. You can start a JVM with each execution, or you can have a JVM loaded and call into it via something like JMX to launch the job (as you did in Chapter 5).

You also have the consideration of what should happen when things go wrong and your job stops. Does the entire job need to be rerun, or can you start at the step where it left off? If the step is processing a million rows, do they all need to be reprocessed, or can you restart at the chunk where the error occurred?

With all this to think about when running a batch job, this chapter covers how to start a job in a variety of environments. It discusses the different job runners provided with the Spring Batch framework, as well as integrating the starting and running of jobs with a container like Tomcat and a scheduler like Quartz.

Running a job isn't all you learn about here. You also see how to programmatically stop a job once it has begun in a way that allows it to be restarted. Finally, you finish this chapter by seeing what it takes to be able to restart a job.

Starting a Job

In the chapters up to now, you've almost exclusively run a job each time you start a JVM. However, when you execute a job as you have been with SimpleJobLauncher, things are a little more complex than meets the eye. This section looks at what happens when you launch a job via the SimpleJobLauncher. You then take a detailed look at all the job runners and launchers Spring Batch provides. You see how to execute jobs in a variety of environments, including from within a servlet container, using the Spring Batch Admin administration application and via the open source scheduler Quartz.

Job Execution

When you think about launching a batch job in Spring Batch, you may think that what is happening is Spring Batch executing the job as part of the main execution thread. When it finishes, the process ends. However, it isn't that simple. The org.springframework.batch.core.launch.JobLauncher interface, which is responsible for the work of starting a job, can be implemented in a number of ways, exposing any number of execution options (web, JMX, command line, and so on).

Because the JobLauncher interface doesn't guarantee whether a job is run synchronously or asynchronously, SimpleJobLauncher (the only JobLauncher implementation provided by Spring Batch) leaves it up to the developer by running the job in Spring's TaskExecutor. By default, SimpleJobLauncher uses Spring's SyncTaskExecutor, which executes the job in the current thread. Although this is ok in many instances, this option is a limiting factor for the number of jobs you run within a single JVM.

Let's look at how SimpleJobLauncher is configured. Listing 6-1 shows its configuration with the optional taskExecutor property set. This property allows you, as said previously, to specify the algorithm used for launching jobs. In this case, you're using Spring's SimpleAsyncTaskExecutor to launch the job in a new thread. However, you can easily configure this to use ThreadPoolTaskExecutor to control the number of threads available

Listing 6-1. SimpleJobLauncher Configured with a Task Executor

```
<bean id="taskExecutor"
    class="org.springframework.core.task.SimpleAsyncTaskExecutor"/>

<bean id="jobLauncher"
    class="org.springframework.batch.core.launch.support.SimpleJobLauncher">
    <property name="jobRepository" ref="jobRepository" />
    <property name="taskExecutor" ref="taskExecutor"/>
</bean>
```

Although the JobLauncher kicks off the job and defines how it's run (synchronously, asynchronously, in a thread pool, and so on), it's the job runner that you interact with when you want to launch a job (as you did in the last chapter's JMX job runner). Next you look at the two job runners that Spring Batch provides out of the box: CommandLineJobRunner and JobRegistryBackgroundJobRunner.

Spring Batch Job Runners

When you look at the Spring Batch API, although theoretically there are many ways to run a job (launch it via a servlet, the command line, JMX, and so on), the framework provides only the two runners org.springframework.batch.core.launch.support.CommandLineJobRunner and org.springframework.batch.core.launch.support.JobRegistryBackgroundJobRunner. All other options— servlet, JMX, and so forth—must be custom developed. Let's look at how CommandLineJobRunner and JobRegistryBackgroundJobRunner are used and why, starting with CommandLineJobRunner.

CommandLineJobRunner

CommandLineJobRunner is the runner you've been using up to now. It serves as an interface for your batch processes via the command line. It's useful for calling jobs from either a terminal or, more commonly, shell scripts. It provides four features:

- Loads the appropriate ApplicationContext based on the passed parameter

- Parses command-line arguments into a JobParameters object

- Locates the job requested based on the parameters passed

- Uses the configured JobLauncher to execute the requested job

When you call `CommandLineJobRunner` from a command line or script, there are three required parameters and four optional ones, as detailed in Table 6-1.

Table 6-1. CommandLineJobRunner Parameters

Parameter	Use
jobPath	Provides the path to the `ApplicationContext` configuration containing a job configuration.
-restart	Tells Spring Batch to execute the last failed execution for the job identified
-stop	Stops an already running `JobExecution`
-abandon	Tells Spring Batch to abandon a previously stopped execution
-next	Increments the required parameter in the sequence configured by the `JobParametersIncrementer` of the job specified
jobIdentifier	Gives the name or id of the job as it's specified in the `ApplicationContext`. (used in conjunction with the –stop, -abandon, and -restart parameters)
jobParameters	Specifies a list of key=value pairs to be passed into the job as `JobParameters`

Although you've used `CommandLineJobRunner` almost exclusively to execute jobs up to now, as you can see, there is more that this small tool can do for you. The path to your job's XML file, and the -next and job parameter options, should all be familiar because they have been covered previously.

The build process you've been using with the Project Object Model (POM) included in `simple-cli` builds a jar file with `CommandLineJobRunner` configured as the main class. To use it, you need the jar file in a directory with a lib folder containing all dependencies. If you look at the `<project_home>/target/` directory, you see the jar file that has been built along with the `lib` directory with the required dependencies; however, the name may not be the most intuitive (for example, `spring-batch-simple-cli-2.1.3.RELEASE.jar`). To update the build process to build a more appropriate jar name, you can change the POM file to generate your artifact with the appropriate name. Listing 6-2 shows the POM update that changes the name of the jar to `helloWorld.jar`.

Listing 6-2. Renaming the Maven Artifact to helloWorld.jar

```
...
<build>
    <finalName>helloWorld</finalName>
    ...
</build>
...
```

With your jar file named something that makes sense for your application (helloWorld in this case), you can run the job using the jar file itself from the <project_home>/target directory. Listing 6-3 shows an example of how to run the HelloWorld job you've been running up to now using the Java command.

Listing 6-3. Basic Call to CommandLineJobRunner Contained in helloWorld.jar

```
java –jar helloWorld.jar jobs/helloWorld.xml helloWorldJob
```
You pass two parameters in: the path to the job's configuration and the name of the job to run. Using the –next parameter (from Chapter 4), as shown in Listing 6-4, invokes any configured JobParametersIncrementers.

Listing 6-4. Using the –next Parameter

```
java –jar helloWorld.jar jobs/helloWorld.xml helloWorldJob -next
```
Although Table 6-1 shows seven parameters are available for CommandLineJobRunner, this chapter only covers the four you have for now. Later in this chapter, you revisit CommandLineJobRunner and see how to stop, abandon, and restart jobs with it. For now, you move on to the other job runner that Spring Batch provides: JobRegistryBackgroundJobRunner.

JobRegistryBackgroundJobRunner

JobRegistryBackgroundJobRunner actually isn't a job runner at all. You don't execute jobs through this runner as you do CommandLineJobRunner. Instead, this class is intended to be used to bootstrap Spring and build a JobRegistry for others to consume. In Chapter 5, you wrote your own version of a class that has a similar function to bootstrap Spring and your jobs for the JMXJobRunner.

But you didn't have to write your own. org.springframework.batch.core.launch.support.JobRegistryBackgroundJobRunner is a command-line interface, like CommandLineJobRunner. However, instead of running a job that is specified, this job runner takes a list of configuration files. Once the configuration files have been bootstrapped, JobRegistryBackgroundJobRunner pauses until a key is pressed.

Let's look at an example of how this works. To start, back to the JMXJobRunner example from Chapter 5. Up to now, you've linked the job XML file (<project_home>/src/main/resources/jobs/helloWorld.xml) with the main or parent application context (<project_home>/src/main/resources/launch-context.xml). When using a JobRegistry, however, this isn't typically the case. The reason is that when a JobRegistry is loaded, the jobs aren't executed immediately. Instead, you load all possible jobs that can be executed into a Map that so they can be launched at any time. To configure your job correctly, you need to remove a single line: the import of the launch-context.xml file in the helloWorld.xml file. You do this to prevent a circular reference. If you leave the reference to the launch-context.xml file in your helloWorld.xml file, the JobRegistryBackgroundJobRunner will load launch-context.xml and then load the jobs in helloWorld.xml. Because launch-context.xml is already loaded at that point, you don't want or need to load it again.

The other modification you need to do is to remove the AutomaticJobRegistrar bean from launch-context.xml. JobRegistryBackgroundJobRunner takes two parameters from the command line: a base configuration (called the *parent*) that contains all general components including things like the JobRepository, JobLauncher, and so on; and a list of configuration files containing the jobs you want to run. JobRegistryBackgroundJobRunner registers the jobs it finds in the configuration you pass, so there is no need for AutomaticJobRegistrar.

▪Note Passing in a configuration that has a job that has already been referenced leads to a `DuplicateJobException` being thrown.

Instead of using the `Batch` class you wrote in the previous chapter, you use `JobRegistryBackgroundJobRunner` to bootstrap your job. Because `JobRegistryBackgroundJobRunner` is included in the `spring-batch-core` jar file (the main Spring Batch dependency), the only change you need to make to execute the jar file with `JobRegistryBackgroundJobRunner` is to change the POM file to reference `JobRegistryBackgroundJobRunner` as the main class. Listing 6-5 highlights the change.

Listing 6-5. Changing the Main Class in `pom.xml`

```
<plugin>
    <groupId>org.apache.maven.plugins</groupId>
    <artifactId>maven-jar-plugin</artifactId>
    <configuration>
        <archive>
            <index>false</index>
            <manifest>
                <mainClass>
org.springframework.batch.core.launch.support.JobRegistryBackgroundJobRunner
                </mainClass>
                <addClasspath>true</addClasspath>
                <classpathPrefix>lib/</classpathPrefix>
            </manifest>
            <manifestFile>
                ${project.build.outputDirectory}/META-INF/MANIFEST.MF
            </manifestFile>
        </archive>
    </configuration>
</plugin>
```

That small change in `pom.xml` is all that you need to make to be able to execute the jar file using `JobRegistryBackgroundJobRunner`. When the jar file is rebuilt, you can execute it with the command in Listing 6-6.

Listing 6-6. Executing `JobRegistryBackgroundJobRunner`

```
java -jar helloWorld.jar launch-context.xml jobs/helloWorld.xml
```
Notice that you don't specify the name of the job you want to be run on the command line as you have in the past. The reason is that you're only bootstrapping Spring and Spring Batch with this command and not initiating the execution of a job. When you execute the jar, you see your normal Spring bootstrap output, finishing with what is shown in Listing 6-7 Then the application waits. And waits. It continues to run until either it's killed or the `JobRegistryBackgroundJobRunner.stop()` method is called programmatically. With the process now running, you can use JConsole as you did in Chapter 5 to execute the job.

Listing 6-7. Output from JobRegistryBackgroundJobRunner

```
2011-04-30 01:36:24,105 DEBUG main
[org.springframework.batch.core.configuration.support.ClassPathXmlApplication
ContextFactory$ResourceXmlApplicationContext] - <Unable to locate
LifecycleProcessor with name 'lifecycleProcessor': using default
[org.springframework.context.support.DefaultLifecycleProcessor@d3ade7]>

2011-04-30 01:36:24,106 DEBUG main
[org.springframework.batch.core.configuration.support.DefaultJobLoader] -
<Registering job: helloWorldJob from context:
org.springframework.batch.core.configuration.support.ClassPathXmlApplicationC
ontextFactory$ResourceXmlApplicationContext@1c6a99d>

Started application. Interrupt (CTRL-C) or call
JobRegistryBackgroundJobRunner.stop() to exit.
```

JobRegistryBackgroundJobRunner is a useful tool for bootstrapping Spring and your jobs from a command line without executing them immediately. This is a much more typical scenario found in production-like environments. However, most production environments don't fire up a Java process and let it run and kick off jobs by hand. Instead, jobs are scheduled. They may be run in a servlet container for consistency of deployment, and they may need to be managed by the Spring Admin project. The next section covers how to do all that.

Third-Party Integration

Spring Batch is an excellent tool to develop batch processes, but it's rarely administered on its own. Enterprises need the ability for batch jobs to be administered by operations teams. They need to be able to deploy jobs in a consistent way for the enterprise. They need to be able to start, stop, and schedule jobs in a way that doesn't require programming (typically through an enterprise scheduler of some kind). This section looks at how to schedule batch jobs with the open source scheduler Quartz, how to deploy Spring Batch jobs in the Tomcat servlet container, and finally how to start jobs with the administration tool Spring Batch Admin.

Scheduling with Quartz

Many enterprise schedulers are available. They range from the crude but very effective crontab to enterprise automation platforms that can run into the millions of dollars. The scheduler you use here is an open source scheduler called Quartz (www.quartz-scheduler.org/). This scheduler is commonly used in Java environments of all sizes. In addition to its power and solid community support, it has an established history of Spring integration that is helpful in executing jobs.

Given the scope of Quartz, this book won't cover all of it here. However, a brief introduction to how it works and how it integrates with Spring is warranted. Figure 6-1 shows the components of Quartz and their relationships.

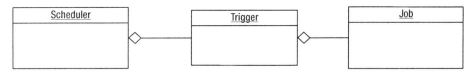

Figure 6-1. *The Quartz scheduler*

As you can see, Quartz has three main components: a scheduler, a job, and a trigger. A scheduler, which is obtained from a `SchedulerFactory`, serves as a registry of `JobDetails` (a reference to a Quartz job) and triggers and is responsible for executing a job when its associated trigger fires. A *job* is a unit of work that can be executed. A *trigger* defines when a job is to be run. When a trigger fires, telling Quartz to execute a job, a `JobDetails` object is created to define the individual execution of the job.

Does this sound familiar? It should. The model of defining a job and a `JobDetails` object is very similar to the way Spring Batch defines a job and a `JobInstance`. In order to integrate Quartz with your Spring Batch process, you need to do the following:

- Add the required dependencies to your `pom.xml` file.

- Write your own Quartz job to launch your job using Spring's `QuartzJobBean`.

- Configure a `JobDetailBean` provided by Spring to create a Quartz `JobDetail`.

- Configure a trigger to define when your job should run.

To show how Quartz can be used to periodically execute a job, let's create a new job, `deleteFilesJob`, that empties a directory each time it runs. This is a common practice with batch jobs or any instance where data is stored and needs to be periodically removed (database purges, and so on). In this case, you're deleting all files in a temporary directory.

You begin by adding the required dependencies to your POM file. In this case, there are three new dependencies. The first is the Quartz framework itself. The second dependency you add is for the `spring-context-support` artifact. This package from Spring provides the classes required to integrate Quartz easily with Spring. Finally, to help with some of the configuration hoops you're jumping through for this example, you include the Apache Commons Collections library. The configuration for the dependency is found in Listing 6-8.

Listing 6-8. *Adding the Quartz-Related Dependencies to the POM*

```xml
<dependency>
    <groupId>org.springframework</groupId>
    <artifactId>spring-context-support</artifactId>
    <version>${spring.framework.version}</version>
</dependency>
<dependency>
    <groupId>org.quartz-scheduler</groupId>
    <artifactId>quartz</artifactId>
    <version>1.8.3 /version>
</dependency>
<dependency>
    <groupId>commons-collections</groupId>
    <artifactId>commons-collections</artifactId>
    <version>3.2.1</version>
</dependency>
```

125

The configuration in Listing 6-8 assumes you're using the POM file that is included in the Spring Batch project. If you aren't, you need to include the version number in place of the property provided.

With the appropriate code now available on your classpath, you can write SpringBatchQuartzJobLauncher. Before you write the code, however, let's talk about what it's going to do. In this case, SpringBatchQuartzJobLauncher takes the place of JMXJobLauncher from Chapter 5 and then some. JMXJobLauncher didn't accept any job parameters as part of the job execution. For this example, your job requires two parameters: the path to the directory you wish to empty and the age of a file that you want to delete. For the sake of simplicity, you delete all files that haven't been modified for the given period of time.

Not only can your Quartz job runner accept incoming parameters, but to prevent the job from not being able to be run more than once, you use Spring Batch's parameter-incrementer functionality (discussed in Chapter 4) to have a unique set of parameters with each run. Listing 6-9 shows SpringBatchQuartzJobLauncher in its entirety.

Listing 6-9. SpringBatchQuartzJobLauncher

```
package com.apress.springbatch.chapter6;

import java.util.List;
import java.util.Map;

import org.quartz.JobExecutionContext;
import org.quartz.JobExecutionException;
import org.slf4j.Logger;
import org.slf4j.LoggerFactory;
import org.springframework.batch.core.Job;
import org.springframework.batch.core.JobInstance;
import org.springframework.batch.core.JobParameter;
import org.springframework.batch.core.JobParameters;
import org.springframework.batch.core.JobParametersBuilder;
import org.springframework.batch.core.JobParametersIncrementer;
import org.springframework.batch.core.configuration.JobLocator;
import org.springframework.batch.core.explore.JobExplorer;
import org.springframework.batch.core.launch.JobLauncher;
import org.springframework.batch.core.launch.JobParametersNotFoundException;
import org.springframework.scheduling.quartz.QuartzJobBean;

public class SpringBatchQuartzJobLauncher extends QuartzJobBean {

    private JobLauncher jobLauncher;
    private JobLocator jobLocator;
    private JobExplorer jobExplorer;
    private Map<String, String> jobParameters;
    public static final String JOB_NAME = "jobName";

    private static final Logger log = LoggerFactory
            .getLogger(SpringBatchQuartzJobLauncher.class);

    @Override
    @SuppressWarnings("unchecked")
    protected void executeInternal(JobExecutionContext context)
```

```
        throws JobExecutionException {
    Map<String, Object> jobDataMap = context.getMergedJobDataMap();
    String jobName = (String) jobDataMap.get(JOB_NAME);

    try {
        Job job = jobLocator.getJob(jobName);
        JobParameters allParams = translateParams(job, jobParameters);

        jobLauncher.run(job, allParams);
    } catch (Exception e) {
        log.error("Could not execute job.", e);
    }
}

private JobParameters translateParams(Job job,
                                      Map<String, String> params)
                                      throws Exception {
    JobParametersBuilder builder = new JobParametersBuilder();

    JobParameters incrementedParams = getNextJobParameters(job);

    for (Map.Entry<String, JobParameter> param :
            incrementedParams.getParameters().entrySet()) {
        builder.addParameter(param.getKey(), param.getValue());
    }

    for (Map.Entry<String, String> param : params.entrySet()) {
        builder.addString(param.getKey(), param.getValue());
    }

    return builder.toJobParameters();
}

private JobParameters getNextJobParameters(Job job)
        throws JobParametersNotFoundException {
    String jobIdentifier = job.getName();
    JobParameters jobParameters;
    List<JobInstance> lastInstances =
        jobExplorer.getJobInstances(jobIdentifier, 0, 1);

    JobParametersIncrementer incrementer =
        job.getJobParametersIncrementer();
    if (incrementer == null) {
        throw new JobParametersNotFoundException(
                "No job parameters incrementer found for job="
                        + jobIdentifier);
    }

    if (lastInstances.isEmpty()) {
        jobParameters = incrementer.getNext(new JobParameters());
        if (jobParameters == null) {
            throw new JobParametersNotFoundException(
```

```
                        "No bootstrap parameters found from incrementer for job="
                                + jobIdentifier);
            }
        } else {
            jobParameters = incrementer.getNext(lastInstances.get(0)
                                    .getJobParameters());
        }
        return jobParameters;
    }

    public void setJobLauncher(JobLauncher jobLauncher) {
        this.jobLauncher = jobLauncher;
    }

    public void setJobLocator(JobLocator jobLocator) {
        this.jobLocator = jobLocator;
    }

    public void setJobParameters(Map<String, String> jobParameters) {
        this.jobParameters = jobParameters;
    }

    public void setJobExplorer(JobExplorer jobExplorer) {
        this.jobExplorer = jobExplorer;
    }
}
```

As you look over this code, notice that there are many clashes in class names between Quartz and Spring Batch. To understand what is going on, let's start by looking at the execution environment's structure. You have a single class that extends Spring's QuartzJobBean. This implementation of Quartz's org.quartz.Job interface is a helpful class that allows you to implement only the pieces of logic that pertain to your work, leaving the manipulation of the scheduler and so on to Spring. In this case, you override the executeInternal method from which to execute the job.

Within the executeInternal method, you begin by obtaining the JobDataMap, which is a Map of parameters you pass in to the Quartz job via your Spring configuration (you look at the configuration after this class is covered). This Map contains all the dependencies that are injected into the SpringBatchQuartzJobLauncher class as well as any additional parameters you may want to reference. In this case, you want to reference one other parameter: the name of the job.

With the name of the job obtained, you use the JobLocator to retrieve the Spring Batch job from the JobRegistry. Before you can execute the job you need to convert the parameters passed via Spring as a Map of <String, String> into a Spring Batch JobParameters collection. Once that is complete, you can execute the job using the JobLauncher.

Notice that the actual execution of the job in this class doesn't take much in the way of code. The vast majority of this class is dedicated to the conversion and incrementing of the job's parameters. The other two methods, translateParams and getNextJobParameters are used to translate the parameters you receive from Spring into JobParameters and call the configured parameter incrementer.

translateParams begins by creating an instance of Spring Batch's org.springframework.batch.core.JobParametersBuilder. This class is used to take key value pairs and convert them into JobParameter instances. To begin the conversion, you call the getNextJobParameters[1] method to increment any parameters that are required to be incremented. Because that process returns a JobParameters instance, you then add those parameters to the JobParametersBuilder you're currently working with. With the incremented parameters added, you add the Spring-passed parameters. In this case, you know they're all Strings, and you can simplify the code accordingly.

With SpringBatchQuartzJobLauncher written, you can move on to writing the tasklet that is the base of this job. In this case, you have a simple tasklet (similar to the HelloWorld tasklet you wrote in Chapter 2) that deletes all files in a specified directory that haven't been modified in longer than a given period of time. Listing 6-10 shows the code to accomplish this.

Listing 6-10. DeleteFilesTasklet

```
package com.apress.springbatch.chapter6;

import java.io.File;
import java.util.Date;
import java.util.Map;

import org.springframework.batch.core.StepContribution;
import org.springframework.batch.core.scope.context.ChunkContext;
import org.springframework.batch.core.step.tasklet.Tasklet;
import org.springframework.batch.repeat.RepeatStatus;

public class DeleteFilesTasklet implements Tasklet {

    public RepeatStatus execute(StepContribution step, ChunkContext chunk)
            throws Exception {
        Map<String, Object> params =
            chunk.getStepContext().getJobParameters();
        String path = (String) params.get("path");
        Long age = Long.valueOf((String) params.get("age"));

        File tempDirectory = new File(path);

        File[] files = tempDirectory.listFiles();

        Date now = new Date();
        long oldesttime = now.getTime() - age;

        for (File file : files) {
            if (file.lastModified() < oldesttime) {
                file.delete();
            }
        }
```

---

[1] The source code of the getNextJobParameters method comes from Spring Batch's CommandLineJobRunner. Unfortunately, there is no standard way of starting a job that requires parameters and incremented parameters (JobOperator calls an incrementer but doesn't accept parameters, and JobLauncher takes parameters but doesn't call an incrementer).

```
        return RepeatStatus.FINISHED;
    }
}
```

The code for DeleteFilesTasklet in Listing 6-10 shouldn't come as any surprise. In implementing the Tasklet interface, you implement the execute method to do all your work. For DeleteFilesTasklet's work, you need to know where to delete the files from and how long they have been idle. When you have that information, you can proceed with deleting the files.

The first three lines of the execute method retrieve the job parameters so you can get the path to the directory from which you're to delete the files (path) and the time in milliseconds that a file hasn't been modified (age). When you have the job parameters, you can open a directory and delete all files or directories that meet your requirements. With processing complete, you return RepeatStatus.FINISHED to tell Spring Batch that the step has completed.

All you have left to do to make this happen is the configuration. Again, you're using the JobRegistryBackgroundJobRunner, so the configuration files are separate: launch-context.xml is located in the <project_home>/src/main/resources directory, and deleteFilesJob.xml is in <project_home>/src/main/resources/jobs. Looking at the deleteFilesJob.xml file first, in Listing 6-11, shows you the configuration for the job itself.

Listing 6-11. deleteFilesJob.xml

```xml
<?xml version="1.0" encoding="UTF-8"?>
<beans:beans xmlns="http://www.springframework.org/schema/batch"
    xmlns:beans="http://www.springframework.org/schema/beans"
    xmlns:xsi="http://www.w3.org/2001/XMLSchema-instance"
    xsi:schemaLocation="http://www.springframework.org/schema/beans
        http://www.springframework.org/schema/beans/spring-beans-3.0.xsd
        http://www.springframework.org/schema/batch
        http://www.springframework.org/schema/batch/spring-batch-2.1.xsd">

    <beans:bean id="deleteFilesTasklet"
        class="com.apress.springbatch.chapter6.DeleteFilesTasklet" />

    <step id="deleteFilesStep">
        <tasklet ref="deleteFilesTasklet" />
    </step>

    <beans:bean id="idIncrementer"
     class="org.springframework.batch.core.launch.support.RunIdIncrementer"/>

    <job id="deleteFilesJob" incrementer="idIncrementer">
        <step id="step1" parent="deleteFilesStep" />
    </job>
</beans:beans>
```

As with your other jobs, you define the tasklet itself, then have a step that uses the tasklet, and then finish with the definition of the job, a single step that deletes the files when the job runs. The only additional piece of configuration this job receives is the addition of RunIdIncrementer, as discussed in Chapter 4, so you can run this job via Quartz multiple times without having to change the job parameters.

launch-context.xml consists mostly of the usual Spring Batch suspects, as shown in Listing 6-12. You need to add just three beans to make the Quartz interaction work: jobDetail, cronTrigger, and schedule.

Listing 6-12. Updates to launch-context.xml

```
...
<bean id="jobDetail"
    class="org.springframework.scheduling.quartz.JobDetailBean">
    <property name="jobClass"
        value="com.apress.springbatch.chapter6.SpringBatchQuartzJobLauncher"/>
    <property name="jobDataAsMap">
        <map>
            <entry key="jobName" value="deleteFilesJob" />
            <entry key="jobLocator" value-ref="jobRegistry" />
            <entry key="jobLauncher" value-ref="jobLauncher" />
            <entry key="jobExplorer" value-ref="jobExplorer"/>
            <entry key="jobParameters">
                <map>
                    <entry key="path" value="${batch.temp.dir}" />
                    <entry key="age" value="${batch.temp.age}" />
                </map>
            </entry>
        </map>
    </property>
</bean>

<bean id="cronTrigger"
    class="org.springframework.scheduling.quartz.CronTriggerBean">
    <property name="jobDetail" ref="jobDetail" />
    <property name="cronExpression" value="0/10 * * * * ?" />
</bean>

<bean id="schedule"
    class="org.springframework.scheduling.quartz.SchedulerFactoryBean">
    <property name="triggers" ref="cronTrigger"/>
</bean>
...
```

The first bean of consequence in launch-context.xml for the Quartz example is the jobDetail bean. Here is where you configure SpringBatchQuartzJobLauncher. It's important to note how the relationship between Spring's JobDetailBean and the SpringBatchQuartzJobLauncher bean is used. You configure a JobDetailBean as a Spring bean in launch-context.xml. Each time your Quartz job is executed, the JobDetailBean creates a new instance of SpringBatchQuartzJobLauncher. When configuring the JobDetailBean, jobDetail, you set two properties:

- jobClass: This is the class that is instantiated and executed each time the Quartz job runs.

- jobDataAsMap: This Map is a collection of all the objects that are injected into SpringBatchQuartzJobLauncher and any other parameters the Quartz job needs to run (the location of the files to be deleted and how old they need to be to be).

When the Quartz job is triggered and Spring creates a new instance of SpringBatchQuartzJobLauncher, Spring uses jobDataAsMap to inject any required dependencies as required. In this case, you inject the location of the files to be deleted and how old they need to be.

The second bean to look at in launch-context.xml is the cronTrigger bean. You saw earlier how Quartz uses a trigger to determine when to execute the job. The trigger you're using here determines when to run based on a cron string. To configure the trigger, you create a org.springframework.scheduling.quartz.CronTriggerBean with two dependencies: jobDetail references the jobDetail bean, and cronExpression is the cron string used to determine when the job runs. In this case, you execute deleteFilesJob once every 10 seconds.

The final bean to configure is the one that does all the work: the scheduler. Using Spring's org.springframework.scheduling.quartz.SchedulerFactoryBean, you register your trigger with the scheduler. From there, Spring and Quartz take care of the rest.

To get things started, use JobRegistryBackgroundJobRunner to bootstrap the process. Launching this process using the command in Listing 6-13, you bootstrap Spring, register deleteFilesJob in the JobRegistry, and start Quartz. With Quartz running, the job executes every 10 seconds as configured.

Listing 6-13. *Executing the Job via Quartz*

```
java -jar deleteFiles.jar launch-context.xml jobs/deleteFilesJob.xml
```

Running jobs via Quartz or another scheduler is a common way to administer batch processes in an enterprise. Another common aspect of running jobs in an enterprise is the way they're deployed. Given that many enterprises deploy all or most Java applications to containers of some kind, you should look at how Spring Batch processes can be run in a container.

Running in a Container

Unlike web applications, batch processes don't require a container to execute. You can build robust and completely independent batch jobs using readily available frameworks for things like database-connection pooling, transaction management, and JMS without the need of an application server or servlet container. That being said, however, there are just as many reasons to run a job in a container as not.

In an enterprise, there is typically a more robust base of expertise around the configuration and deployment of container-based applications, where plain Java applications deployed as a collection of jar files may cause some operations teams pause. Also, resources like database connections (and their security), JMS queues, and so on may be easier to manage with a standardized configuration within a container. Let's look at how to deploy and execute jobs from within Tomcat.

Although the ability to configure a large number of resources through the application server is possible with Spring, their configuration is outside of the scope of this book. Instead, you focus on bootstrapping a Spring Batch JobRegistry with the required jobs and triggering their execution.

Bootstrapping the job registry from within a container is easier than what you've been doing up to now. Instead of relying on CommandLineJobRunner or JobRegistryBackgroundJobRunner for a main method and to bootstrap your process, Tomcat serves as the means of starting the Java process, and you can use standard web techniques to bootstrap Spring Batch in your container.

Let's look at how to deploy deleteFilesJob to Tomcat. There are four steps:

1. Update the POM file to a package application as a war file instead of a jar.

2. Add the required Spring web-related dependencies to your POM file.

3. Create web.xml in a new directory <project_home>/src/main/webapp/WEB-INF with ContextLoaderListener to bootstrap Spring.

4. Configure AutomaticJobRegistrar to register the jobs with the JobRegistry.

You start by updating the POM file. In order for Spring to be bootstrapped in a servlet container like Tomcat, you need to add the Spring framework's web dependencies. Listing 6-14 shows how to configure the additional dependencies required for this job including Spring's web module, SLF4J, and log4j.

Listing 6-14. Additional Dependencies for pom.xml

```
<dependency>
    <groupId>org.springframework</groupId>
    <artifactId>spring-web</artifactId>
    <version>${spring.framework.version}</version>
</dependency>
<dependency>
    <groupId>org.slf4j</groupId>
    <artifactId>slf4j-log4j12</artifactId>
    <version>1.5.8</version>
</dependency>
<dependency>
    <groupId>log4j</groupId>
    <artifactId>log4j</artifactId>
    <version>1.2.14</version>
</dependency>
```

Instead of creating a jar file for you to execute independently, you want to create a war file that you can deploy to Tomcat. To do this, you need to update the packaging in your POM file from jar to war. You also replace the reference to maven-jar-plugin with maven-war-plugin. Listing 6-15 shows how to configure the POM file so your application is packaged correctly.

Listing 6-15. Revised pom.xml

```
<plugin>
    <artifactId>maven-war-plugin</artifactId>
    <version>2.1-beta-1</version>
    <configuration>
        <attachClasses>true</attachClasses>
        <warName>deleteFiles</warName>
    </configuration>
</plugin>
```

As Listing 6-15 shows, configuring Maven to generate your war file is very easy. Unfortunately, the changes to the pom.xml file won't work until you create a web.xml file and put it in the correct place. For web.xml, you configure a single listener, Spring's org.springframework.web.context.ContextLoaderListener. It bootstraps Spring as well as the JobRegistry for you. Listing 6-16 shows the web.xml file.

Listing 6-16. web.xml

```xml
<?xml version="1.0" encoding="UTF-8"?>
<!DOCTYPE web-app PUBLIC
    "-//Sun Microsystems, Inc.//DTD Web Application 2.3//EN"
    "http://java.sun.com/dtd/web-app_2_3.dtd">
<web-app>
    <display-name>Spring Batch Webapp</display-name>
    <description>A web application that wraps Spring Batch jobs</description>

    <context-param>
        <param-name>contextConfigLocation</param-name>
        <param-value>classpath:launch-context.xml</param-value>
    </context-param>

    <listener>
        <listener-class>
            org.springframework.web.context.ContextLoaderListener
        </listener-class>
    </listener>
</web-app>
```

The web.xml file exists in the <project_home>/src/main/webapp/WEB-INF/ directory. With the POM file updated and the web.xml file defined in the correct place, you can generate a war file using the standard mvn clean install.

Now that you have a working war file, let's configure AutomaticJobRegistrar to register the jobs on startup in your JobRegistry. Just as in previous examples, AutomaticJobRegistrar is configured to register all jobs that are listed in the /jobs/ directory of your classpath. From there, you can use Quartz as you did earlier in this chapter to launch the job. Listing 6-17 shows launch-context.xml configured with both the previous Quartz configuration and AutomaticJobRegistrar.

Listing 6-17. Updates to launch-context.xml

```xml
...
<bean
    class="org.springframework.batch.core.configuration.support.
AutomaticJobRegistrar">
    <property name="applicationContextFactories">
        <bean
            class="org.springframework.batch.core.configuration.support.
ClasspathXmlApplicationContextsFactoryBean">
            <property name="resources"
                value="classpath*:/jobs/deleteFilesJob.xml" />
        </bean>
    </property>
    <property name="jobLoader">
        <bean class="org.springframework.batch.core.configuration.support.
DefaultJobLoader">
            <property name="jobRegistry" ref="jobRegistry" />
        </bean>
    </property>
```

```
</bean>
...
```

With the job configured and built, all you need to do is deploy it on a Tomcat server. When you copy the war file to `<TOMCAT_HOME>/webapps` and start up the server by executing the `./startup.sh` command in `<TOMCAT_HOME>/bin`, the application starts and the job is executed every 10 seconds via Quartz. How do you know it's running? You can confirm that files are being deleted as expected and validate the output in the `<TOMCAT_HOME>/logs/catalina.out` file as shown in Listing 6-18.

Listing 6-18. Job Output in `catalina.out`

```
2011-01-04 21:07:50,103 DEBUG SimpleAsyncTaskExecutor-2
[org.springframework.batch.core.job.AbstractJob] - <Job execution complete:
JobExecution: id=151, startTime=Tue Jan 04 21:07:50 CST 2011, endTime=null,
lastUpdated=Tue Jan 04 21:07:50 CST 2011, status=COMPLETED,
exitStatus=exitCode=COMPLETED;exitDescription=, job=[JobInstance: id=144,
JobParameters=[{age=9000, run.id=49, path=/Users/mminella/temp}],
Job=[deleteFilesJob]]>

2011-01-04 21:07:50,105 INFO SimpleAsyncTaskExecutor-2
[org.springframework.batch.core.launch.support.SimpleJobLauncher] - <Job:
[FlowJob: [name=deleteFilesJob]] completed with the following parameters:
[{age=9000, run.id=49, path=/Users/mminella/temp}] and the following status:

[COMPLETED]>
```

Running Spring Batch jobs in a container provides a number of advantages in an enterprise environment including standardized packaging and deployment and more robust management options. Another aspect of running a job in an enterprise environment is the ability to monitor and administer a job by operations. Let's look at how you can use the Spring Batch Admin project to launch jobs.

Launching with Spring Batch Admin

Spring Batch Admin is a recent addition to how Spring Batch works. It's less an administration tool and more an administration framework. Having gone 1.0 in early 2010, it's still evolving in its capabilities and its role in the Spring family. However, it's a useful tool that can not only put a web interface onto the JobRepository but also allow the execution of jobs via a web interface.

To look at Spring Batch Admin, add it to the existing `deleteFiles` application. Because you already have the structure to deploy jobs via Tomcat, adding Spring Batch Admin provides a web interface for you to view the JobRepository as well as administer jobs (start, stop, and so on). It's important to note that you don't need to package jobs with Spring Batch Admin to be able to browse Spring Batch's JobRepository—you only need to manage their execution.

To add Spring Batch Admin to your application, do the following:

1. Update your POM file to include the required jar files in your war file.

2. Update `web.xml` to include the elements required to bootstrap Spring Batch Admin.

3. Move the `launch-context.xml` file so it's used by Spring Batch Admin to override its components.

With Spring Batch, if you haven't noticed, the POM file that comes with the sample project you've been working with builds with Spring version 2.5.6. Obviously, this is an older version of Spring. Spring Batch runs fine with the newer Spring 3.0.x; and because Spring Batch Admin requires a newer version of Spring, your first update to the POM file is to update the version of Spring you're using to 3.0.5.RELEASE, as shown in Listing 6-19.

Listing 6-19. *Updated Properties in pom.xml*

```
...
<properties>
<maven.test.failure.ignore>true</maven.test.failure.ignore><spring.framework.version>3.0.
5.RELEASE</spring.framework.version>
    <spring.batch.version>2.1.2.RELEASE</spring.batch.version>
    <dependency.locations.enabled>false</dependency.locations.enabled>
</properties>
...
```

You need to make one other version change, to the AspectJ dependencies. Instead of the 1.5.4 dependencies that your shell came with, you need to use the newer 1.6.6 version. Finally, add the dependencies to the Spring Batch Admin jar files. Listing 6-20 shows the new and updated dependencies in pom.xml.

Listing 6-20. *New and Updated Dependencies*

```
...
<dependency>
    <groupId>org.aspectj</groupId>
    <artifactId>aspectjrt</artifactId>
    <version>1.6.6</version>
</dependency>
<dependency>
    <groupId>org.aspectj</groupId>
    <artifactId>aspectjweaver</artifactId>
    <version>1.6.6</version>
</dependency>
<dependency>
    <groupId>org.springframework.batch</groupId>
    <artifactId>spring-batch-admin-manager</artifactId>
    <version>1.2.0.RELEASE</version>
</dependency>
<dependency>
    <groupId>org.springframework.batch</groupId>
    <artifactId>spring-batch-admin-resources</artifactId>
    <version>1.2.0.RELEASE</version>
</dependency>
<dependency>
    <groupId>org.springframework.batch</groupId>
    <artifactId>spring-batch-integration</artifactId>
    <version>1.2.0.RELEASE</version>
</dependency>
```

```
</dependency>
...
```

Now that the project has the correct dependencies and versions, you can update web.xml. For the deleteFilesJob you used earlier, you had a single listener, Spring's ContextLoaderListener, that you used to bootstrap the Spring configuration. For Spring Batch Admin, you need a few more things, as shown in Listing 6-21.

Listing 6-21. Updated web.xml

```xml
<?xml version="1.0" encoding="UTF-8"?>
<!DOCTYPE web-app PUBLIC
    "-//Sun Microsystems, Inc.//DTD Web Application 2.3//EN"
    "http://java.sun.com/dtd/web-app_2_3.dtd">
<web-app>
    <display-name>Spring Batch Webapp</display-name>
    <description>A web application that wraps Spring Batch jobs</description>

    <context-param>
        <param-name>contextConfigLocation</param-name>
        <param-value>
  classpath*:/org/springframework/batch/admin/web/resources/webapp-config.xml
        </param-value>
    </context-param>

    <filter>
        <filter-name>hiddenHttpMethodFilter</filter-name>
        <filter-class>
            org.springframework.web.filter.HiddenHttpMethodFilter
        </filter-class>
    </filter>

    <filter-mapping>
        <filter-name>hiddenHttpMethodFilter</filter-name>
        <url-pattern>/*</url-pattern>
    </filter-mapping>

    <listener>
        <listener-class>
            org.springframework.web.context.ContextLoaderListener
        </listener-class>
    </listener>

    <servlet>
        <servlet-name>Batch Servlet</servlet-name>
        <servlet-class>
            org.springframework.web.servlet.DispatcherServlet
        </servlet-class>
        <init-param>
            <param-name>contextConfigLocation</param-name>
            <param-value>
  classpath*:/org/springframework/batch/admin/web/resources/servlet-config.xml
```

```
                </param-value>
            </init-param>
            <load-on-startup>1</load-on-startup>
        </servlet>

        <servlet-mapping>
            <servlet-name>Batch Servlet</servlet-name>
            <url-pattern>/*</url-pattern>
        </servlet-mapping>
    </web-app>
```

From the beginning of the web.xml file shown in Listing 6-21, you have the display name and description for your application. After that, you configure the location of the base Spring context configuration. In this case, you're using one that is included in the spring-batch-admin-resources-1.2.0.RELEASE jar file, webapp-config.xml. This file contains the beans required for Spring Batch Admin to run and also provides a facility for you to override and extend any of the components you wish.

The next two elements, which configure hiddenHttpMethodFilter, are used as a workaround for browsers that don't support all of the standard HTTP methods.[2] Because Spring Batch Admin exposes a number of features via a RESTful API, it uses this filter to support a common technique for indicating the HTTP method being invoked via a request header.

You configure ContextLoaderListener next to bootstrap Spring as in any normal Spring-based web application. Finally, you have the servlet that does the heavy lifting for the Spring Batch Admin application. As with most Spring-based web applications, you use org.springframework.web.servlet.DispatcherServlet to direct requests to beans as configured. In this case, Spring Batch Admin comes with a configuration (again found in the spring-batch-admin-resources-1.2.0.RELEASE.jar) servlet-config.xml that contains the required mappings.

The last piece of the Spring Batch Admin puzzle is to move launch-context.xml. You may be wondering why you need to move it. The reason is that the Spring Batch Admin application has an embedded configuration for a number of beans that you've already configured by default (JobExplorer, JobRepository, a datasource, and so on). However, it also provides you the ability to override those configurations by placing the overriding configurations in the <WAR_ROOT>/META-INF/spring/batch/override directory of your war file. In this case, the easy way to handle the overrides you want is to move launch-context.xml from the <PROJECT_ROOT>/src/main/resources directory to the <PROJECT_ROOT>/src/main/resources/META-INF/spring/batch/override directory. When Spring Batch Admin launches, it uses your configurations over the defaults provided.

All that is left is to build your war file and deploy it to Tomcat just as you did previously. Using the mvn clean install command, you end up with a war file that you can drop into Tomcat's webapps directory and start Tomcat. With Tomcat running, fire up a browser and navigate to http://localhost:8080/deleteFiles to see the administration application as shown in Figure 6-2.

---

[2] Most modern browsers only support HTTP POST and GET, but true RESTful implementations require the support of PUT and DELETE as well.

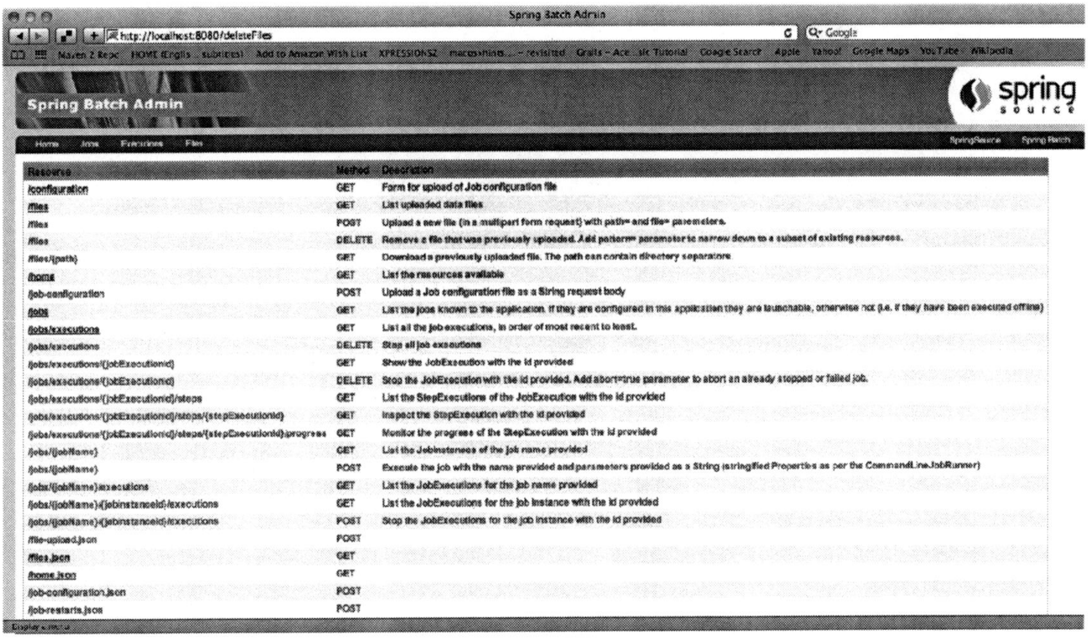

Figure 6-2. Home page of the Spring Batch Admin application

The home page of the Spring Batch Admin application shows a listing of the REST APIs available. The tabs across the top let you access the jobs that have been executed in the JobRepository, see what JobExecutions have occurred or are currently running, and upload new configuration files.

To look at the jobs you've run in the past as well as any you can administer from Spring Batch Admin, click the Jobs tab. Doing so takes you to a page like that shown in Figure 6-3.

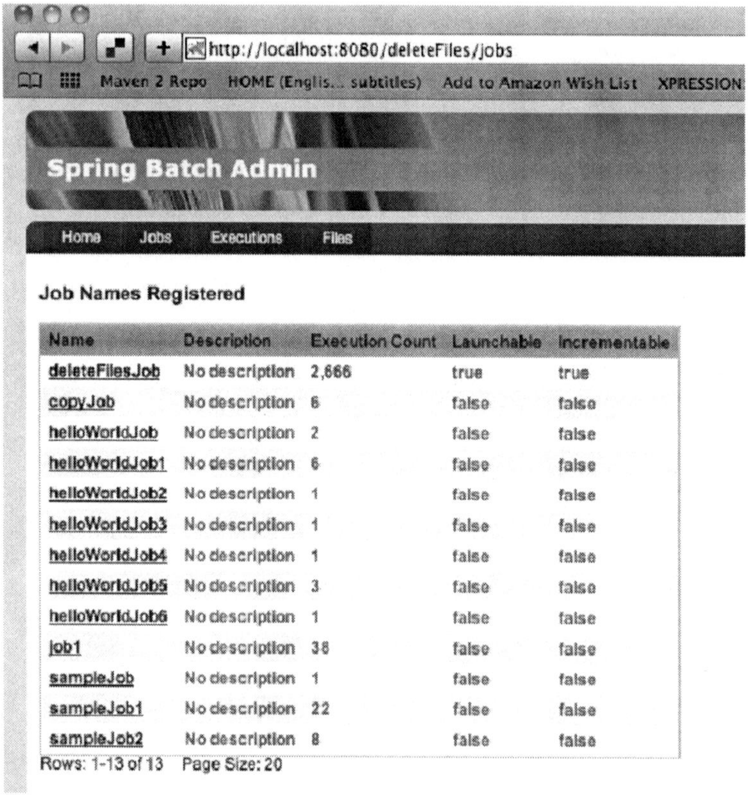

Figure 6-3. *The list of jobs in the JobRepository*

The Jobs page lists all the jobs that appear in the JobRepository. The number of times each job has been executed, whether the job can be executed through the current configuration,and whether it has a JobParametersIncrementer configured or not are all displayed on this page. Notice in this example that deleteFilesJob has been executed 2,666 times (every 10 seconds adds up quickly). deleteFilesJob is also the only job that is launchable, so click that link to see how to execute it.

The page for deleteFilesJob, shown in Figure 6-4, starts with the controls required to execute the job, including a button to launch the job and a text box populated with the job parameters from the last run. In the case of deleteFilesJob, because it has a JobParametersIncrementer configured, you can pass the same parameters to the job; Spring Batch handles incrementing the run.id parameter so you have a unique JobInstance.

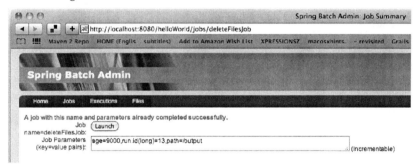

Figure 6-4. *The Job page for* `deleteFilesJob`

To execute `deleteFilesJob` from this page, all you need to do is click the Launch button. Spring Batch executes the `JobParametersIncrementer` so that everything works. If you launch a job with a duplicate set of parameters, an error is displayed, and no JobInstance or JobExecution is created, as shown in Figure 6-5.

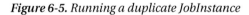

Figure 6-5. *Running a duplicate JobInstance*

As you've seen, there are a number of ways to launch a Spring Batch job: via `CommandLineJobRunner` at the command line, using another protocol like JMX and a custom job runner as you saw in Chapter 5, using a scheduler like Quartz, or even using the Spring Batch Admin web application. However, and pardon the pun, starting a job is only the beginning. How a job ends can have a big impact on a number of things. The next section looks at the different ways a Spring Batch job can end and how those scenarios affect how you configure or execute jobs.

Stopping a Job

A job can stop for a number of reasons, each of which has its own affect on what happens next. It can run to completion naturally (as all the examples have up to this point). You can programmatically stop the execution of a job during processing for some reason. You can stop a job externally (say, someone realizes something is wrong, and they need to stop the job to fix it). And of course, although you may never admit it, errors can occur that cause a job to stop execution. This section looks at how each of these scenarios plays out using Spring Batch and your options for what to do when each occurs. Let's begin with the most basic: a job running to its natural completion.

The Natural End

Up to this point, all of your jobs have run to their natural completion. That is, each job has run all of its steps until they returned a COMPLETED status and the job itself returned an exit code of COMPLETED. What does this mean for a job?

As you've seen, a job can't be executed with the same parameter values more than once successfully. This is the *successfully* part of that statement. When a job has been run to the COMPLETED exit code, a new JobInstance can't be created using the same JobParameters again. This is important to note because it dictates how you execute jobs. You've used the JobParametersIncrementer to increment parameters based on their run, which is a good idea, especially in jobs that are run based on a schedule of some kind. For example, if you have a job that is run daily, developing a JobParametersIncrementer implementation that increments a timestamp as a parameter makes sense. That way, each time the job is executed via the schedule, you use the -next flag to increment the job accordingly. If anything occurred that caused the job to not run to its natural completion, you could execute the job without the -next flag, providing the same parameters (you see how to restart jobs later in this chapter).

Not all jobs execute to their natural ending every time. There are situations when you want to stop a job based on something that happens during processing (an integrity check at the end of a step fails, for example). In cases like this, you want to stop the job programmatically. The next section goes over this technique.

Programmatic Ending

Batch processing requires a series of checks and balances to be effective. When you're dealing with large amounts of data, you need to be able to validate what is happening as things are processing. It's one thing for a user to update their profile with the wrong address on a web application. That affects one user. However, what if your job is to import a file containing 1 million records, and the import step completes after importing only 10,000? Something is wrong, and you need to fix it before the job goes any further. This section looks at how to stop a job programmatically. First you look at a more real-world example of using the <stop> tag introduced in Chapter 4; you join its use with some new attributes in order to restart the job. You also look at how to set a flag to end a job.

Using the <stop> Tag

To begin, let's look at constructing a job that is configured to stop using the <stop> tag and how where to restart is addressed. Let's create a three-step job to process a file:

1. Import a simple transaction file (transaction.csv). Each transaction consists of an account number, a timestamp, and an amount (positive is a credit,

negative is a debit). The file ends with a single summary record containing the number of records in the file.

2. After importing the transactions into a transaction table, apply them to a separate account summary table that consists of the account number and the current account balance.

3. Generate a summary file (summary.csv) that lists the account number and balance for each account.

Looking at these steps from a design perspective, you want to validate that the number of records you import matches the summary file before applying the transactions to each user's account. This integrity check can save you many hours of recovery and reprocessing when dealing with large amounts of data.

To start this job, let's look at the file formats and data model. The file format for this job is simple comma-separated value (CSV) files. This lets you easily configure the appropriate readers and writers with no code. Listing 6-22 shows example record formats for each of the two files you're using (transaction.csv and summary.csv, respectively).

Listing 6-22. Sample Records for Each of the Two Files

```
Transaction file:
3985729387,2010-01-08 12:15:26,523.65
3985729387,2010-01-08 1:28:58,-25.93
2

Summary File:
3985729387,497.72
```

For this example, you also keep the data model simple, consisting of only two tables: Transaction and Account_Summary. Figure 6-6 shows the data model.

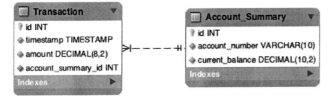

Figure 6-6. Transaction data model

To create the job, begin with a fresh copy of the Spring Batch shell from the zip distribution as covered in previous chapters. With your project set up, configure batch.properties to use your MySQL instance as you have up to now.

When the boilerplate shell is ready to go, you can configure the job. Create a new file, transactionJob.xml, in the <PROJECT_HOME>/src/main/resources/jobs directory, and configure the job as shown in Listing 6-23.

Listing 6-23. transactionJob.xml

```
<?xml version="1.0" encoding="UTF-8"?>
<beans:beans xmlns="http://www.springframework.org/schema/batch"
```

```xml
    xmlns:beans="http://www.springframework.org/schema/beans"
    xmlns:util="http://www.springframework.org/schema/beans"
    xmlns:xsi="http://www.w3.org/2001/XMLSchema-instance"
    xsi:schemaLocation="http://www.springframework.org/schema/beans
        http://www.springframework.org/schema/beans/spring-beans-3.0.xsd
        http://www.springframework.org/schema/util
        http://www.springframework.org/schema/util/spring-util.xsd
        http://www.springframework.org/schema/batch
        http://www.springframework.org/schema/batch/spring-batch-2.1.xsd">

    <beans:import resource="../launch-context.xml"/>

    <beans:bean id="transactionFile"
        class="org.springframework.core.io.FileSystemResource" scope="step">
        <beans:constructor-arg value="#{jobParameters[transactionFile]}"/>
    </beans:bean>

    <beans:bean id="transactionFileReader"
        class="com.apress.springbatch.chapter6.TransactionReader">
        <beans:property name="fieldSetReader" ref="fileItemReader"/>
    </beans:bean>

    <beans:bean id="fileItemReader"
        class="org.springframework.batch.item.file.FlatFileItemReader">
        <beans:property name="resource" ref="transactionFile" />
        <beans:property name="lineMapper">
            <beans:bean
                class="org.springframework.batch.item.file.mapping.
DefaultLineMapper">
                <beans:property name="lineTokenizer">
                    <beans:bean
                        class="org.springframework.batch.item.file.transform.
DelimitedLineTokenizer">
                        <beans:property name="delimiter" value=","/>
                    </beans:bean>
                </beans:property>
                <beans:property name="fieldSetMapper">
                    <beans:bean
                        class="org.springframework.batch.item.file.mapping.
PassThroughFieldSetMapper" />
                </beans:property>
            </beans:bean>
        </beans:property>
    </beans:bean>

    <beans:bean id="transactionWriter"
        class="org.springframework.batch.item.database.JdbcBatchItemWriter">
        <beans:property name="assertUpdates" value="true" />
        <beans:property name="itemSqlParameterSourceProvider">
            <beans:bean class="org.springframework.batch.item.database.
BeanPropertyItemSqlParameterSourceProvider" />
        </beans:property>
```

```
            <beans:property name="sql" value="INSERT INTO TRANSACTION
(ACCOUNT_SUMMARY_ID, TIMESTAMP, AMOUNT) VALUES ((SELECT ID FROM
ACCOUNT_SUMMARY WHERE ACCOUNT_NUMBER = :accountNumber), :timestamp, :amount)"
/>
            <beans:property name="dataSource" ref="dataSource" />
    </beans:bean>

    <step id="importTransactionFileStep">
        <tasklet allow-start-if-complete="true">
            <chunk reader="transactionFileReader" writer="transactionWriter"
                commit-interval="100">
                <streams>
                    <stream ref="fileItemReader"/>
                </streams>
            </chunk>
            <listeners>
                <listener ref="transactionFileReader"/>
            </listeners>
        </tasklet>
    </step>
...
```

The first step of this job consists of the input file, two ItemReaders (one to do the actual file work and another to apply some interpretation) and an ItemWriter. The configuration begins with the definition of the input file, a wrapper for the FlatFileItemReader used to read the file itself and the related FlatFileItemReader. (Chapters 7 and 9 cover ItemReaders and ItemWriters, respectively.) All you need to worry about for this example is that this is the configuration for the input file and the way you read it. The reason for the wrapper is twofold. First, it's used to determine whether the record is a regular transaction record or the summary record at the end of the file. Second, it's used as a StepListener to determine whether the correct number of records were processed. If they were, no changes to ExitStatus are made. If the number of records doesn't match the summary record of your file, ExitStatus is changed to return STOPPED. The code for this is covered later in this section. It's important to note that the tasklet for this step is configured with the allow-start-if-complete attribute set to true. By configuring the step in this way, when the job is stopped for any reason, the job can reexecute this step even if it has been successfully completed. By default, this value is false; and if the step was successfully completed, it would be skipped on a retry.

The configuration of the transactionJob continues in Listing 6-24, where you configure the second step (applyTransactionStep) and its components.

Listing 6-24. Configuration of applyTransactionStep and Its Components

```
...
<beans:bean id="accountSummaryReader"
    class="org.springframework.batch.item.database.JdbcCursorItemReader">
    <beans:property name="dataSource" ref="dataSource"/>
    <beans:property name="sql" value="select account_number, current_balance
from account_summary a where a.id in (select distinct t.account_summary_id
from transaction t) order by a.account_number"/>
    <beans:property name="rowMapper">
        <beans:bean
            class="com.apress.springbatch.chapter6.AccountSummaryRowMapper"/>
    </beans:property>
```

```
</beans:bean>

<beans:bean id="transactionDao"
    class="com.apress.springbatch.chapter6.TransactionDaoImpl">
    <beans:property name="dataSource" ref="dataSource"/>
</beans:bean>

<beans:bean id="transactionApplierProcessor"
    class="com.apress.springbatch.chapter6.TransactionApplierProcessor">
    <beans:property name="transactionDao" ref="transactionDao"/>
</beans:bean>

<beans:bean id="accountSummaryUpdater"
    class="org.springframework.batch.item.database.JdbcBatchItemWriter">
    <beans:property name="assertUpdates" value="true" />
    <beans:property name="itemSqlParameterSourceProvider">
        <beans:bean class="org.springframework.batch.item.database.
BeanPropertyItemSqlParameterSourceProvider" />
    </beans:property>
    <beans:property name="sql" value="UPDATE ACCOUNT_SUMMARY SET
CURRENT_BALANCE = :currentBalance WHERE ACCOUNT_NUMBER = :accountNumber" />

<step id="applyTransactionsStep">
    <tasklet>
        <chunk reader="accountSummaryReader"
            processor="transactionApplierProcessor"
            writer="accountSummaryUpdater" commit-interval="100"/>
    </tasklet>
</step>
...
```

The second step of this job applies the transactions to the user's account. The configuration for this step begins with the ItemReader you use to read the account summary records from the database. As each item is read, you update the currentBalance field with each of the transactions you imported in the previous step in the transactionApplierProcessor. This ItemProcessor uses a data access object (DAO) to look up the transactions for the account as they're processed. Finally, the account is updated with the new currentBalance value using the accountSummaryUpdater ItemWriter. The configuration for the step itself links the ItemReader, ItemProcessor, and ItemWriter together at the end of Listing 6-24.

The last step in the job, generateAccountSummaryStep, consists of the same accountSummaryReader configured in Listing 6-24, but it adds a new ItemWriter that writes the summary file. Listing 6-25 shows the configuration of the new ItemWriter and the related step.

Listing 6-25. generateAccountSummaryStep Configuration

```
...
<beans:bean id="summaryFile"
    class="org.springframework.core.io.FileSystemResource" scope="step">
    <beans:constructor-arg value="#{jobParameters[summaryFile]}"/>
</beans:bean>

<beans:bean id="accountSummaryWriter"
    class="org.springframework.batch.item.file.FlatFileItemWriter"
```

```
        scope="step">
        <beans:property name="lineAggregator">
            <beans:bean
                class="org.springframework.batch.item.file.transform.
DelimitedLineAggregator">
                <beans:property name="delimiter" value=","/>
                <beans:property name="fieldExtractor">
                    <beans:bean
                        class="org.springframework.batch.item.file.transform.
BeanWrapperFieldExtractor">
                        <beans:property name="names"
                            value="accountNumber,currentBalance"/>
                    </beans:bean>
                </beans:property>
            </beans:bean>
        </beans:property>
        <beans:property name="resource" ref="summaryFile" />
</beans:bean>

<step id="generateAccountSummaryStep">
    <tasklet>
        <chunk reader="accountSummaryReader" writer="accountSummaryWriter"
            commit-interval="100"/>
    </tasklet>
</step>
...
```

With all the steps configured, you can finally configure the job itself. In the job, you configure the three steps as discussed. However, for step1, if the step returns STOPPED, you stop the job. If the job is restarted, it reexecutes step1. If step1 returns any other successful value, the job continues with step2 and finally step3. Listing 6-26 shows the configuration for this logic using the <stop> tag.

Listing 6-26. Configuring a Job Using the <stop> Tag

```
...
    <job id="transactionJob">
        <step id="step1" parent="importTransactionFileStep">
            <stop on="STOPPED" restart="step1"/>
            <next on="*" to="step2"/>
        </step>
        <step id="step2" parent="applyTransactionsStep" next="step3"/>
        <step id="step3" parent="generateAccountSummaryStep"/>
    </job>
</beans:beans>
```

How do you perform the check to be sure you read in the correct number of records? In this case, you develop a custom reader that also serves as a step listener. The code in Listing 6-27 shows how the reader reads in all the records and keeps a count of how many are read in. When the step is complete, the listener validates that the number of records read in matches the number of records expected. If they match, the ExitStatus that was determined by the regular processing is returned. If they don't match, you override the ExitStatus by returning your own ExitStatus.STOPPED value.

Listing 6-27. TransactionReader.java

```
package com.apress.springbatch.chapter6;

import org.springframework.batch.core.ExitStatus;
import org.springframework.batch.core.StepExecution;
import org.springframework.batch.core.annotation.AfterStep;
import org.springframework.batch.item.ItemReader;
import org.springframework.batch.item.NonTransientResourceException;
import org.springframework.batch.item.ParseException;
import org.springframework.batch.item.UnexpectedInputException;
import org.springframework.batch.item.file.transform.FieldSet;

public class TransactionReader implements ItemReader<Object> {

    private ItemReader<FieldSet> fieldSetReader;
    private int recordCount = 0;
    private int expectedRecordCount = 0;

    public Object read() throws Exception,
                                UnexpectedInputException,
                                ParseException,
                                NonTransientResourceException {
        Transaction record = process(fieldSetReader.read());

        return record;
    }

    private Transaction process(FieldSet fieldSet) {
        Transaction result = null;

        if(fieldSet.getFieldCount() > 1) {
            result = new Transaction();
            result.setAccountNumber(fieldSet.readString(0));
            result.setTimestamp(fieldSet.readDate(1, "yyyy-MM-DD HH:mm:ss"));
            result.setAmount(fieldSet.readDouble(2));

            recordCount++;
        } else {
            expectedRecordCount = fieldSet.readInt(0);
        }

        return result;
    }

    public void setFieldSetReader(ItemReader<FieldSet> fieldSetReader) {
        this.fieldSetReader = fieldSetReader;
    }

    @AfterStep
    public ExitStatus afterStep(StepExecution execution) {
```

```
            if(recordCount == expectedRecordCount) {
                return execution.getExitStatus();
            } else {
                return ExitStatus.STOPPED;
            }
        }
    }
}
```

For the job to execute, four other classes are required: Transaction, AccountSummary, TransactionApplierProcessor, and TransactionDaoImpl. The first two, Transaction and AccountSummary, are nothing more than the POJOs used to represent the two record formats. Transaction has four fields to represent both the transaction input file record format and its related Transaction database table format. The fields represented in the Transaction class are as follows:

- id: An int representing the primary key for the database

- accountNumber: A String representing the account number for the transaction as found in the transaction input file

- timestamp: A java.util.Date representing the timestamp as found in the transaction input file

- amount: A double representing the amount of the transaction as found in the transaction input file

The AccountSummary class represents the format of the Account_Summary database table and the subsequent accountSummary output file. The fields found in the AccountSummary class (with the appropriate getters and setters) are as follows:

- id: An int representing the primary key of the Account_Summary database table

- accountNumber: A String representing the account number

- currentBalance: A double representing the current balance of the account

The other two classes are related to step2 of the job. This step applies each of the transactions to its appropriate account's balance. To do this, the step reads in each of account that has any transactions associated with it, loads all the related transactions, updates the record, and writes the updated record to the database. The reader and writer for this step are declared in the XML from Listing 6-19, but the processor is something you have to write yourself. Listing 6-28 shows the ItemProcessor, TransactionApplierProcessor.

Listing 6-28. TransactionApplierProcessor

```
package com.apress.springbatch.chapter6;

import java.util.List;

import org.springframework.batch.item.ItemProcessor;

public class TransactionApplierProcessor implements
        ItemProcessor<AccountSummary, AccountSummary> {

    private TransactionDao transactionDao;
```

```
    public AccountSummary process(AccountSummary summary) throws Exception {
        List<Transaction> transactions = transactionDao
                .getTransactionsByAccountNumber(summary.getAccountNumber());

        for (Transaction transaction : transactions) {
            summary.setCurrentBalance(summary.getCurrentBalance()
                    + transaction.getAmount());
        }
        return summary;
    }

    public void setTransactionDao(TransactionDao transactionDao) {
        this.transactionDao = transactionDao;
    }
}
```

As Listing 6-28 shows, to apply the transactions to each of the account summary records, you load all of the Transactions related to AccountSummary's account number. From there, you loop through the Transactions, adjusting the current balance by each transaction's amount before returning the AccountSummary to be updated in the database.

The final piece of the puzzle for this job is TransactionDaoImpl, as shown in Listing 6-29. Using Spring's org.springframework.jdbc.core.JdbcTemplate, you query the Transaction table for Transaction records that are associated with the requested account number.

Listing 6-29. TransactionDaoImpl

```
package com.apress.springbatch.chapter6;

import java.sql.ResultSet;
import java.sql.SQLException;
import java.util.List;

import org.springframework.jdbc.core.JdbcTemplate;
import org.springframework.jdbc.core.RowMapper;

public class TransactionDaoImpl extends JdbcTemplate implements TransactionDao {

    @SuppressWarnings("unchecked")
    @Override
    public List<Transaction> getTransactionsByAccountNumber(
                                                    String accountNumber) {
        return query(
                "select t.id, t.timestamp, t.amount from transaction t " +
                "inner join account_summary a on a.id = t.account_summary_" +
                "id where a.account_number = ?",
                new Object[] { accountNumber },
                new RowMapper() {
                    public Object mapRow(ResultSet rs, int rowNum)
                                                    throws SQLException{
                        Transaction trans = new Transaction();
                        trans.setAmount(rs.getDouble("amount"));
```

```
                            trans.setTimestamp(rs.getDate("timestamp"));
                            return trans;
                        }
                    }
            );
        }
}
```

Now, execute the job twice. The first time, execute the job with a `transaction.csv` that has an invalid integrity record. In other words, you run the job with an input file of 100 records plus an integrity record at the end. The integrity record is any number other than 100; here you use the number 20. When the job executes, the StepListener validates that the number of records you read in (100) doesn't match the number expected (20) and returns the value `ExitStatus.STOPPED`, stopping the job. You can see the results of the first run via Spring Batch Admin in Figure 6-7.

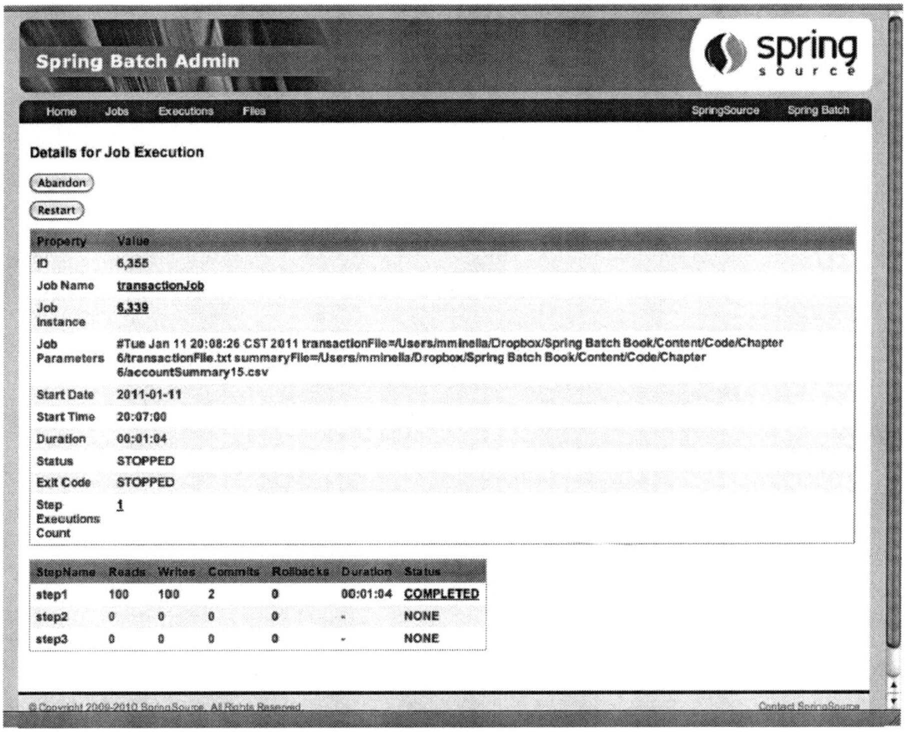

Figure 6-7. *Results of the first run of* transactionJob

When the job stops, delete the contents of the Transaction table and update your transaction file to have 100 records and an integrity record say 100 as well. This time, when you execute the job, as Figure 6-8 shows, it runs to completion successfully.

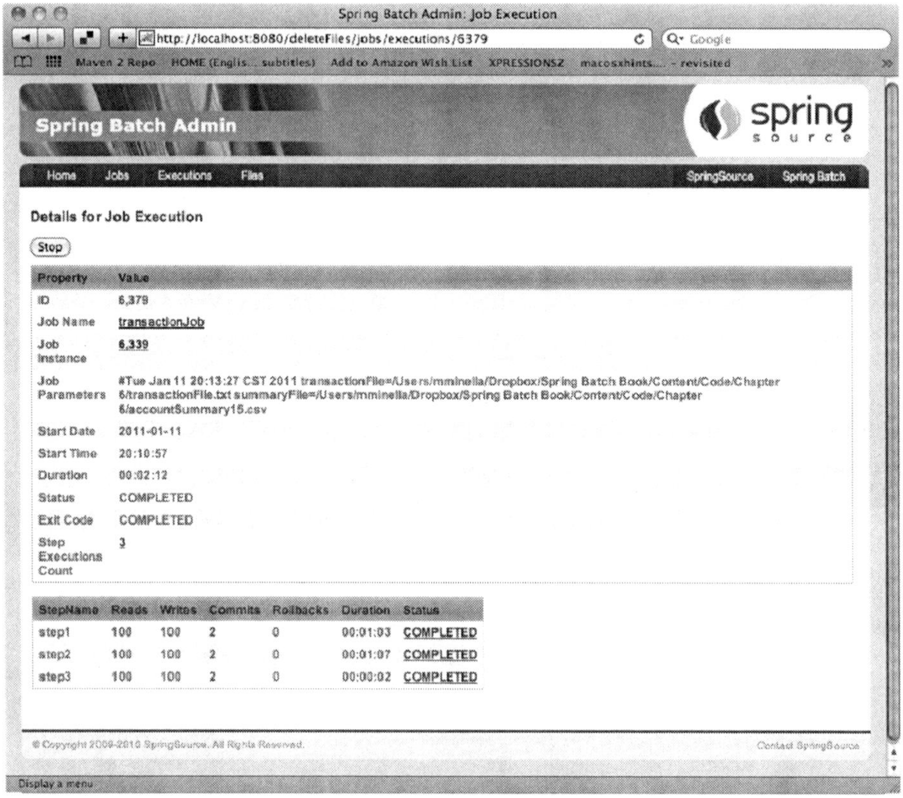

Figure 6-8. Results of the second run of transactionJob

Using the <stop> tag along with configuring the ability to reexecute steps in the job is a useful way to allow for issues to be fixed based on checks in the execution of a job. In the next section, you refactor the listener to use the StepExecution.setTerminateOnly() method to communicate to Spring Batch to end the job.

Stopping with StepExecution

In the transactionJob example, you manually handled stopping the job by using the ExitStatus of a StepListener and the configured transitions in the job. Although this approach works, it requires you to specially configure the job's transitions and override the step's ExitStatus.

There is a slightly cleaner approach. In the StepListener, you have access to the StepExecution. With this, as you see in Listing 6-30, you can call the StepExecution.setTerminateOnly() method. This method sets a flag that tells Spring Batch to end after the step is complete.

Listing 6-30. TransactionReader with setTerminateOnly() Call

```
package com.apress.springbatch.chapter6;
```

```java
import org.springframework.batch.core.ExitStatus;
import org.springframework.batch.core.StepExecution;
import org.springframework.batch.core.annotation.AfterStep;
import org.springframework.batch.item.ItemReader;
import org.springframework.batch.item.NonTransientResourceException;
import org.springframework.batch.item.ParseException;
import org.springframework.batch.item.UnexpectedInputException;
import org.springframework.batch.item.file.transform.FieldSet;

public class TransactionReader implements ItemReader<Object> {

    private ItemReader<FieldSet> fieldSetReader;
    private int recordCount = 0;
    private int expectedRecordCount = 0;

    public Object read() throws Exception, UnexpectedInputException,
                            ParseException, NonTransientResourceException {
        Transaction record = process(fieldSetReader.read());

        return record;
    }

    private Transaction process(FieldSet fieldSet) {
        Transaction result = null;

        if(fieldSet.getFieldCount() > 1) {
            result = new Transaction();
            result.setAccountNumber(fieldSet.readString(0));
            result.setTimestamp(fieldSet.readDate(1, "yyyy-MM-DD HH:mm:ss"));
            result.setAmount(fieldSet.readDouble(2));

            recordCount++;
        } else {
            expectedRecordCount = fieldSet.readInt(0);
        }

        return result;
    }

    public void setFieldSetReader(ItemReader<FieldSet> fieldSetReader) {
        this.fieldSetReader = fieldSetReader;
    }

    @AfterStep
    public ExitStatus afterStep(StepExecution execution) {
        if(recordCount != expectedRecordCount) {
            execution.setTerminateOnly();
        }

        return execution.getExitStatus();
    }
```

```
}
```

Although the code is only marginally cleaner (you eliminate the else statement—that's it), the configuration becomes cleaner as well by allowing you to remove the configuration required for the transitions. Listing 6-31 shows the updated job configuration.

Listing 6-31. Reconfigured transactionJob

```
...
<job id="transactionJob">
    <step id="step1" parent="importTransactionFileStep" next="step2"/>
    <step id="step2" parent="applyTransactionsStep" next="step3"/>
    <step id="step3" parent="generateAccountSummaryStep"/>
</job>
...
```

You can now execute the job again with the same test (running it the first time with an incorrect number of records in the transaction file and then a second time with the correct number) and see the same results. The only difference is in the output of the job on the console. Instead of the job returning a STOPPED status, Spring Batch throws a JobInterruptedException, as shown in Listing 6-32.

Listing 6-32. Results of the First Execution of your updated job

```
2011-01-11 20:08:04,724 ERROR
[org.springframework.batch.core.job.AbstractJob] - <Encountered interruption
executing job>

org.springframework.batch.core.JobInterruptedException: Step requested
termination: StepExecution: id=6379, version=4, name=step1, status=COMPLETED,
exitStatus=COMPLETED, readCount=100, filterCount=0, writeCount=100
readSkipCount=0, writeSkipCount=0, processSkipCount=0, commitCount=2,
rollbackCount=0, exitDescription=
        at
org.springframework.batch.core.job.flow.JobFlowExecutor.executeStep(JobFlowExccutor.java:67)
        at
org.springframework.batch.core.job.flow.support.state.StepState.handle(StepState.java:60)
        at
org.springframework.batch.core.job.flow.support.SimpleFlow.resume(SimpleFlow.java:144)
        at
org.springframework.batch.core.job.flow.support.SimpleFlow.start(SimpleFlow.java:124)
        at org.springframework.batch.core.job.flow.FlowJob.doExecute(FlowJob.java:135)
        at org.springframework.batch.core.job.AbstractJob.execute(AbstractJob.java:281)
        at
org.springframework.batch.core.launch.support.SimpleJobLauncher$1.run(SimpleJ
obLauncher.java:120)
        at org.springframework.core.task.SyncTaskExecutor.execute(SyncTaskExecutor.java:49)
        at
org.springframework.batch.core.launch.support.SimpleJobLauncher.run(SimpleJob
Launcher.java:114)
        at
org.springframework.batch.core.launch.support.CommandLineJobRunner.start(Comm
```

```
andLineJobRunner.java:348)
     at
org.springframework.batch.core.launch.support.CommandLineJobRunner.main(Comma
ndLineJobRunner.java:565)

2011-01-11 20:08:04,727 INFO
[org.springframework.batch.core.launch.support.SimpleJobLauncher] - <Job:
[FlowJob: [name=transactionJob]] completed with the following parameters:
[{transactionFile=/Users/mminella/Dropbox/Spring Batch
Book/Content/Code/Chapter 6/transactionFile.txt,
summaryFile=/Users/mminella/Dropbox/Spring Batch Book/Content/Code/Chapter
6/accountSummary15.csv}] and the following status: [STOPPED]>
```

Stopping a job programmatically is an important tool when you're designing batch jobs. Unfortunately, not all batch jobs are perfect, and you sometimes need to shut down a job when it's running. The next section discusses the ways you can stop a Spring Batch job without doing a kill -9 on the process.

External Stoppage

There aren't many worse feelings. You've done your homework. You've run your tests, and all looks good. You start the job, which you know will take hours to complete. Only a couple of minutes later, you realize that you made a mistake and you need to stop the job—but you can't just kill it. You need it to end gracefully so your database and processing are left in a state that can be restarted. Luckily for you, the authors of Spring Batch have gone through your pain and have developed a couple of ways to stop an already running job. The two you look at here are using Spring Batch Admin and CommandLineJobRunner. Let's start with Spring Batch Admin.

Stopping via Spring Batch Admin

Having an instance of Spring Batch Admin pointed at your JobRepository is by far the easiest way to stop jobs. To see this in action, start the transactionJob job with a large transaction file (100 records in this case). With the job running, if you go to the page for the job's execution, as shown in Figure 6-9, you see a Stop button in the upper-left corner.

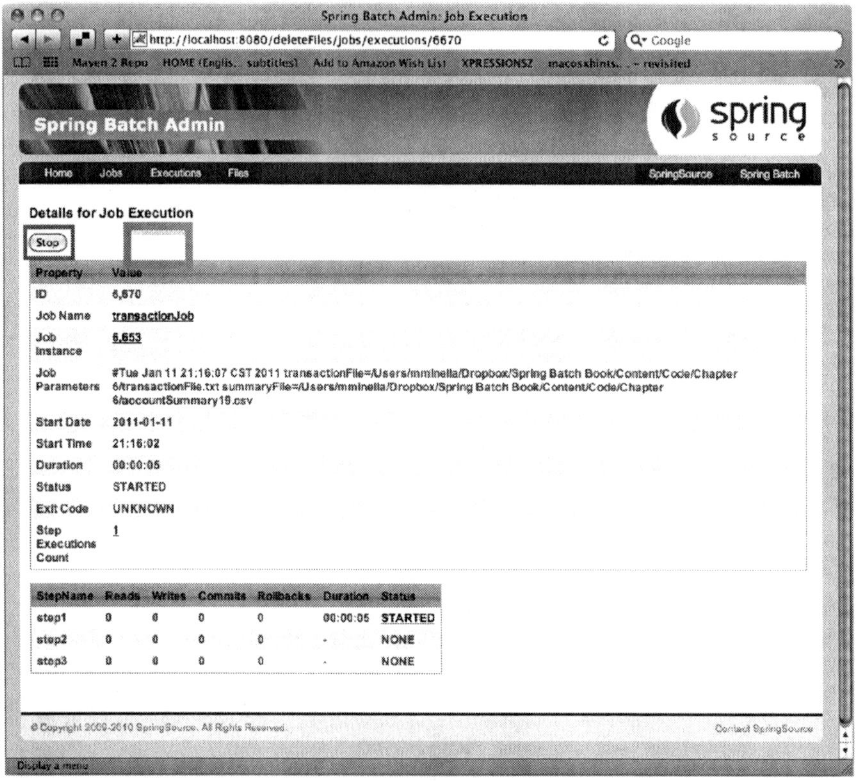

Figure 6-9. *Stopping a job via Spring Batch Admin*

When you click the Stop button, Spring Batch throws a JobInterruptedException, stopping the job. It's important to note what happens here. With the way you have the job configured, the chunk that is currently being processed when the Stop button is clicked is rolled back. When the job is restarted, Spring Batch uses the previous job's various ExecutionContexts (job and step) to determine where it was in the processing of step1 and restart where it left off. Figure 6-10 shows how the first time the job was executed, 50 records were processed in step1; the second time the job was executed, the second 50 records were processed.

StepName	Reads	Writes	Commits	Rollbacks	Duration	Status
step1	50	50	1	0	00:00:33	STOPPED
step2	0	0	0	0	-	NONE
step3	0	0	0	0	-	NONE

StepName	Reads	Writes	Commits	Rollbacks	Duration	Status
step1	50	50	1	0	00:00:31	COMPLETED
step2	100	100	2	0	00:01:07	COMPLETED
step3	100	100	2	0	00:00:02	COMPLETED

Figure 6-10. *Results for two executions of transactionJob*

Clicking a button. It's hard to think of a simpler way to stop a job. The next technique, although not as easy, doesn't require you to deploy anything else for it to work.

Stopping Using CommandLineJobRunner

Earlier in this chapter, you saw that a number of command-line options are available for CommandLineJobRunner that you haven't explored yet. Two of them are related to stopping and restarting jobs. This section looks at how to stop and restart jobs with CommandLineJobRunner.

When you execute jobs via CommandLineJobRunner, you build a jar file and execute it via the standard Java -jar command, as covered earlier. When a job is running, you can stop it gracefully by executing the command shown in Listing 6-33.

Listing 6-33. *Calling* CommandLineJobRunner *to Stop a Job*

```
java -jar transactionJob.jar jobs/transactionJob.xml 7007 -stop
```

The command should look similar to all the others you've used. You call the executable jar file (transactionJob.jar in this case) that has CommandLineJobRunner configured as its main class in META-INF. CommandLineJobRunner requires two parameters: the path to an XML file that defines a job and either a job name (as it's been called up to now) or a job execution id. In this case, you're passing it the job execution id (7007 is the id for this execution, as found in the BATCH_JOB_EXECUTION table or via Spring Batch Admin) to specify which job execution to stop. If you choose to pass in the job name in this situation, all running instances of the job are stopped.

After a job is stopped this way, how do you restart it? One of the other options for CommandLineJobRunner should give you a hint. There is a -restart option that you haven't seen yet. As you can guess, you can restart execution with the same command you used to stop it, changing only -stop to -restart, as shown in Listing 6-34.

Listing 6-34. *Calling* CommandLineJobRunner *to Restart a Stopped Job*

```
java -jar transactionJob.jar jobs/transactionJob.xml 7007 -restart
```

Starting, stopping, and restarting a job from the command line are common occurrences. Up to this point, this chapter has talked about stopping jobs in a way that occurs by your choice: you choose to stop the job programmatically, or you choose to stop the job via Spring Batch Admin. However, some situations are outside of your control. Errors occur. The next section discusses how stopping a job works when an Exception is thrown.

Error Handling

No job is perfect—not even yours. Errors happen. You may receive bad data. You may forget one null check that causes a NullPointerException at the worst of times. How you handle errors using Spring Batch is important. This section discusses the options for what to do when an exception is thrown during your batch job and how to implement them.

Stopping the Job

It should come as little surprise that the default behavior of Spring Batch is probably the safest: stopping the job and rolling back the current chunk. This is one of the driving concepts of chunk-based processing. It allows you to commit the work you've successfully completed and pick up where you left off when you restart.

By default, Spring Batch considers a step and job failed when any exception is thrown. You can see this in action by tweaking TransactionReader as shown in Listing 6-35. In this case, you throw a org.springframework.batch.item.ParseException after reading 510 records, stopping the job in a Failed status.

Listing 6-35. TransactionReader Set Up to Throw an Exception

```
package com.apress.springbatch.chapter6;

import org.springframework.batch.core.ExitStatus;
import org.springframework.batch.core.StepExecution;
import org.springframework.batch.core.annotation.AfterStep;
import org.springframework.batch.item.ItemReader;
import org.springframework.batch.item.NonTransientResourceException;
import org.springframework.batch.item.ParseException;
import org.springframework.batch.item.UnexpectedInputException;
import org.springframework.batch.item.file.transform.FieldSet;

public class TransactionReader implements ItemReader<Object> {

    private ItemReader<FieldSet> fieldSetReader;
    private int recordCount = 0;

    public Object read() throws Exception, UnexpectedInputException,
                            ParseException, NonTransientResourceException {

        if(recordCount == 510) {
            throw new ParseException("This isn't what I hoped to happen");
        }

        Transaction record = process(fieldSetReader.read());

        return record;
    }

    private Transaction process(FieldSet fieldSet) {
        Transaction result = null;

        result = new Transaction();
        result.setAccountNumber(fieldSet.readString(0));
        result.setTimestamp(fieldSet.readDate(1, "yyyy-MM-DD HH:mm:ss"));
        result.setAmount(fieldSet.readDouble(2));

        recordCount++;

        return result;
    }

    public void setFieldSetReader(ItemReader<FieldSet> fieldSetReader) {
        this.fieldSetReader = fieldSetReader;
```

```
    }

    @AfterStep
    public ExitStatus afterStep(StepExecution execution) {
        return execution.getExitStatus();
    }
}
```

With no other configuration changes from the previous runs, when you execute transactionJob, it throws a ParseException after it reads the record 510 of the transaction file. After this exception is thrown, Spring Batch considers the step and job failed. If you look at the job execution in Spring Batch Admin and click the FAILED status of step1, you're shown statistics about the job as it ran as well as the exception that caused the failure. Figure 6-11 shows the result of this execution.

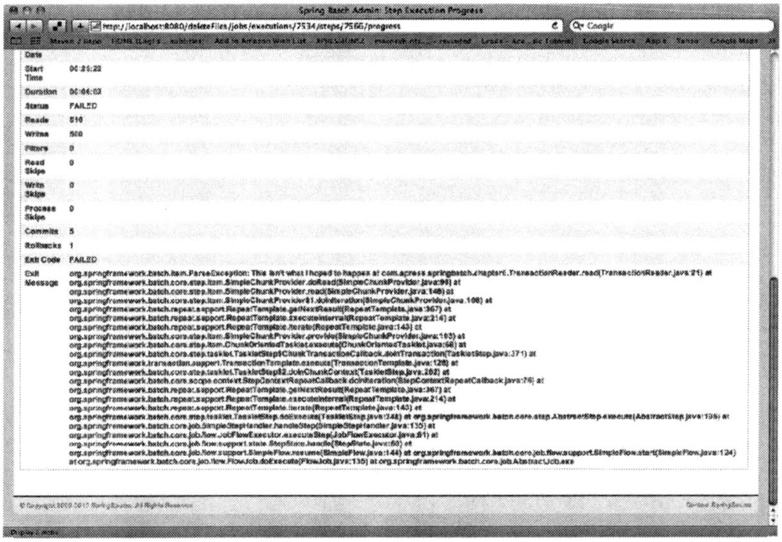

Figure 6-11. A failed job

There is a big difference between the examples of stopping via StepExecution and stopping the job with an exception. That difference is the state in which the job is left. In the StepExecution example, the job was stopped after a step is complete in the STOPPED ExitStatus. In the exception case, the step didn't finish. In fact, it was part way through the step when the exception was thrown. Because of this, the step and job are labeled with the ExitStatus FAILED.

When a step is identified as FAILED, Spring Batch doesn't start the step over from the beginning. Instead, Spring Batch is smart enough to remember what chunk you were on when the exception was thrown. When you restart the job, Spring Batch picks up at the chunk it left off on. As an example, let's say the job is processing chunk 5 of 10, with each chunk consisting of 5 items. An exception is thrown on the fourth item of the second chunk. Items 1–4 of the current chunk are rolled back, and when you restart, Spring Batch skips chunks one and two.

Although Spring Batch's default method of handling an exception is to stop the job in the failed status, there are other options at your disposal. Because most of those depend on input/output-specific scenarios, the next few chapters cover them together with I/O.

Controlling Restart

Spring Batch provides many facilities to address stopping and restarting a job, as you've seen. However, it's up to you to determine what can and can't be restarted. If you have a batch process that imports a file in the first step ,and that job fails in the second step, you probably don't want to reimport the file. There are scenarios where you may only want to retry a step a given number of times. This section looks at how to configure a job to be restartable and how to control how it's restarted.

Preventing a Job from Being Rerun

All the jobs up to now could be executed again if they failed or were stopped. This is the default behavior for Spring Batch. But what if you have a job that can't be rerun? You give it one try, and if it works, great. If not, you don't run it again. Spring Batch provides the ability to configure jobs to not be restartable using the restartable attribute of the job tag.

If you look at the transactionJob configuration, by default the restartable attribute is true. However, if you choose to configure it to be false, as shown in Listing 6-36, then when the job fails or is stopped for any reason, you won't be able to reexecute it.

Listing 6-36. transactionJob Configured to Not Be Restartable

```
...
<job id="transactionJob" restartable="false">
    <step id="step1" parent="importTransactionFileStep" next="step2"/>
    <step id="step2" parent="applyTransactionsStep" next="step3"/>
    <step id="step3" parent="generateAccountSummaryStep"/>
</job>
...
```

Now if you attempt to run the job after a failure, you're told by Spring Batch that the JobInstance already exists and isn't restartable, as shown in Listing 6-37.

Listing 6-37. Results from Reexecuting a Non-Restartable Job

```
2011-01-13 19:50:30,559 ERROR
[org.springframework.batch.core.launch.support.CommandLineJobRunner] - <Job
Terminated in error: JobInstance already exists and is not restartable>

org.springframework.batch.core.repository.JobRestartException: JobInstance
already exists and is not restartable
        at org.springframework.batch.core.launch.support.SimpleJobLauncher.run(SimpleJob
Launcher.java:97)
        at org.springframework.batch.core.launch.support.CommandLineJobRunner.start(Comm
andLineJobRunner.java:348)
        at org.springframework.batch.core.launch.support.CommandLineJobRunner.main(Comma
ndLineJobRunner.java:565)
```

Being able to execute a job once or else may be a bit extreme for some scenarios. Spring Batch also lets you configure the number of times a job can be run, as you see next.

Configuring the Number of Restarts

There can be situations where a job doesn't run successfully for some reason outside of your control. Say for example that the job downloads a file from a web site as one of its steps, and the web site is down. If the download fails the first time, it may work if you try again in 10 minutes. However, you probably don't want to try that download indefinitely. Because of this, you may want to configure the job so it can be executed only five times. After the fifth time, it can't be rerun any more.

Spring Batch provides this facility at the step level instead of the job level. Again, looking at the transactionJob example, if you only want to attempt to import an input file twice, you modify the step configuration as in Listing 6-38.

Listing 6-38. *Allowing the File Import to Be Attempted Only Once*

```
...
<step id="importTransactionFileStep">
    <tasklet start-limit="2">
        <chunk reader="transactionFileReader" writer="transactionWriter"
            commit-interval="10">
            <streams>
                <stream ref="fileItemReader"/>
            </streams>
        </chunk>
        <listeners>
            <listener ref="transactionFileReader"/>
        </listeners>
    </tasklet>
</step>...
```

In this case, if you attempt to restart this job more than once, because the start-limit attribute has been configured to 2, you can't reexecute this job. The initial run takes up one attempt you're allowed allowing you one other try. You receive an org.springframework.batch.core.StartLimitExceededException, as shown in Listing 6-39, if you attempt to execute the job again.

Listing 6-39. *Results from Reexecuting* transactionJob *More Than Once*

```
2011-01-13 20:10:05,127 ERROR
[org.springframework.batch.core.job.AbstractJob] - <Encountered fatal error
executing job>

org.springframework.batch.core.JobExecutionException: Flow execution ended
unexpectedly
        at org.springframework.batch.core.job.flow.FlowJob.doExecute(FlowJob.java:141)
        at org.springframework.batch.core.job.AbstractJob.execute(AbstractJob.java:281)
        at
org.springframework.batch.core.launch.support.SimpleJobLauncher$1.run(SimpleJ
obLauncher.java:120)
        at org.springframework.core.task.SyncTaskExecutor.execute(SyncTaskExecutor.java:49)
        at
org.springframework.batch.core.launch.support.SimpleJobLauncher.run(SimpleJob
```

```
Launcher.java:114)
        at
org.springframework.batch.core.launch.support.CommandLineJobRunner.start(Comm
andLineJobRunner.java:348)
        at
org.springframework.batch.core.launch.support.CommandLineJobRunner.main(Comma
ndLineJobRunner.java:565)
Caused by: org.springframework.batch.core.job.flow.FlowExecutionException:
Ended flow=transactionJob at state=transactionJob.step1 with exception
        at
org.springframework.batch.core.job.flow.support.SimpleFlow.resume(SimpleFlow.
java:152)
        at
org.springframework.batch.core.job.flow.support.SimpleFlow.start(SimpleFlow.j
ava:124)
        at
org.springframework.batch.core.job.flow.FlowJob.doExecute(FlowJob.java:135)
        ... 6 more
Caused by: org.springframework.batch.core.StartLimitExceededException:
Maximum start limit exceeded for step: step1StartMax: 1
        at
org.springframework.batch.core.job.SimpleStepHandler.shouldStart(SimpleStepHa
ndler.java:216)
        at
org.springframework.batch.core.job.SimpleStepHandler.handleStep(SimpleStepHan
dler.java:117)
        at
org.springframework.batch.core.job.flow.JobFlowExecutor.executeStep(JobFlowEx
ecutor.java:61)
        at
org.springframework.batch.core.job.flow.support.state.StepState.handle(StepSt
ate.java:60)
        at
org.springframework.batch.core.job.flow.support.SimpleFlow.resume(SimpleFlow.
java:144)
        ... 8 more
```

The last configuration aspect that you can use when determining what should happen when your batch job is reexecuted, you've seen before: the allow-start-if-complete attribute.

Rerunning a Complete Step

One of Spring Batch's features (or detriments, depending on how you choose to look at it) is that the framework allows you to execute a job only once successfully with the same parameters. There is no way around this. However, that rule doesn't necessarily apply to steps.

You can override the framework's default configuration and execute a step that has been completed more than once. You did it previously using transactionJob. To tell the framework that you want to be able to reexecute a step even if it has been completed, you use the allow-start-if-complete attribute of the tasklet. Listing 6-40 shows an example.

Listing 6-40. Configuring a Step to Be Reexecuted if Complete

```
...
<step id="importTransactionFileStep">
    <tasklet allow-start-if-complete="true">
        <chunk reader="transactionFileReader" writer="transactionWriter"
            commit-interval="10">
            <streams>
                <stream ref="fileItemReader"/>
            </streams>
        </chunk>
        <listeners>
            <listener ref="transactionFileReader"/>
        </listeners>
    </tasklet>
</step>
```

In this case, when the step is executed for the second time within a job that failed or was stopped on the previous execution, the step starts over. Because it completed the previous time, there is no middle ground at which to restart, which is why it begins again at the beginning.

■**Note** If the job has the ExitStatus of COMPLETE, the JobInstance can't be rerun regardless of whether you configure all the steps to allow-start-if-complete="true".

When you're configuring batch processes, Spring Batch offers many different options for stopping and restarting jobs. Some scenarios can have the full job reexecuted. Others can be tried again, but only a given number of times. And some can't be restarted at all. However, it's you, the developer, who must design your batch jobs in a way that is safe for your scenario.

Summary

Starting or stopping a program isn't a topic that typically gets much press. But as you've seen, controlling the execution of a Spring Batch process provides many options. And when you think about the variety of scenarios that must be supported by batch processes, those options make sense.
The next section of this book covers the meat of the framework: ItemReaders, ItemProcessors, and ItemWriters.

CHAPTER 7

Readers

The three R's, Reading, wRiting and aRithmetic, are considered the basis of the skills children learn in schools. When you think about it, these same concepts apply to software as well. The foundations of any programs—whether web applications, batch jobs, or anything else—are the input of data, the processing of it in some way, and the output of data.

This concept is no more obvious than when you use Spring Batch. Each step consists of an ItemReader, an ItemProcessor, and an ItemWriter. Reading in any system isn't always straight forward, however. There are a number of different formats in which input can be provided; flat files, XML, and databases are just some of the potential input sources.

Spring Batch provides standard ways to handle most forms of input without the need to write code as well as the ability to develop your own readers for formats that are not supported, like reading a web service. This chapter will walk through the different features ItemReaders provide within the Spring Batch framework.

The ItemReader Interface

Up to this chapter we have vaguely discussed the concept of an ItemReader but we have not looked at the interface that Spring Batch uses to define input operations. The `org.springframework.batch.item.ItemReader<T>` interface defines a single method, read that is used to provide input for a step. Listing 7-1 shows the ItemReader interface.

Listing 7-1. org.springframework.batch.item.ItemReader<T>

```
package org.springframework.batch.item;

public interface ItemReader<T> {

    T read() throws Exception, UnexpectedInputException, ParseException,
                    NonTransientResourceException;
}
```

The ItemReader interface shown in Listing 7-1 is a strategy interface. Spring Batch provides a numer of implementations based on the type of input to be processed. Flat files, databases, JMS resources and other sources of input all have implementations provided by Spring Batch. You can also implement your own ItemReader by implementing the ItemReader or any one of its subinterfaces.

The read method of the ItemReader interface returns a single item to be processed by your step as it is called by Spring Batch. This item is what your step will count as it maintains how many items within a chunk has been processed. The item will be passed to any configured ItemProcessor before being sent as part of a chunk to the ItemWriter.

The best way to understand how to use the ItemReader interface is to put it to use. In the next section you will begin to look at the many ItemReader implementations provided by Spring Batch by working with the FlatFileItemReader.

File Input

When I think of file IO in Java, I can't help but cringe. The API for IO is marginally better than the API for handling dates in this language, and you all know how good that is. Luckily, the guys at Spring Batch have addressed most of this by providing a number of declarative readers that allow you to declare the format of what you're going to read and they handle the rest. In this section, you'll be looking at the declarative readers that Spring Batch provides and how to configure them for file-based IO.

Flat Files

When I talk about flat files in the case of batch processes, I'm talking about any file that has one or more records. Each record can take up one or more lines. The difference between a flat file and an XML file is that the data within the file is non-descriptive. In other words, there is no meta information within the file itself to define the format or meaning of the data. In contrast, in XML, you use tags to give the data meaning.

Before you get into actually configuring an ItemReader for a flat file, let's take a look at the pieces of reading a file in Spring Batch. The authors of the framework did a good job in creating an API that makes sense and can be easily related to concepts that most of us already know.

Figure 7-2 shows the components of the FlatFileItemReader. The org.springframework.batch.item.file.FlatFileItemReader consists of two main components: a Spring Resource that represents the file to be read and an implementation of the org.springfamework.batch.item.file.LineMapper interface. The LineMapper serves a similar function as the RowMapper does in Spring JDBC. When using a RowMapper in Spring JDBC, a ResultSet representing a collection of fields is provided for you map to objects.

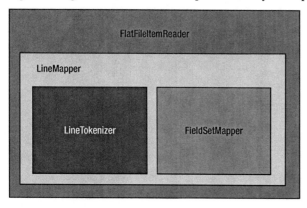

Figure 7-2. FlatFileItemReader pieces

The FlatFileItemReader allows you to configure a number of attributes about the file you're reading. Table 7-1 shows the options that you are likely to use and explains their meanings.

Table 7-1. FlatFileItemReader Configuration Options

Option	Type	Default	Description
Comments	String []	null	This array of strings indicates what prefixes will be considered line comments and skipped during file parsing.
Encoding	String	ISO-8859-1	The character encoding for the file.
lineMapper	LineMapper	null (required)	This class will take each line of a file as a String and convert it into a domain object (item) to be processed.
linesToSkip	**int**	**0**	When running a job, the FlatFileItemReader can be configured to skip lines at the beginning of the file before parsing. This number indicates how many.
recordSeparatorPolicy	RecordSeparatorPolicy	DefaultRecordSeparator Policy	Used to determine the end of each record. By default, an end of line character indicates the end of a record; however, this can be used to determine how to handle things like quoted strings across lines.
Resource	Resource	null (required)	The resource to be read.
skippedLinesCallback	LineCallbackHandler	null	Callback interface called with the line skipped. Every line skipped will be passed to this callback.
Strict	boolean	false	An Exception will be thrown if the resource is

	not found in strict mode.

With Spring Batch's LineMapper interface, a String is provided, representing a single record from a file. With the raw String from the file, there is a two-step process for getting it to the domain object you will later work with. These two steps are handled by the LineTokenizer and FieldSetMapper.

- A LineTokenizer implementation parses the line into a `org.springframework.batch.item.file.FieldSet`. The provided String represents the entire line from the file. In order to be able to map the individual fields of each record to your domain object, you need to parse the line into a collection of fields. The FieldSet in Spring Batch represents that collection of fields for a single row.

- The FieldSetMapper implementation maps the FieldSet to a domain object. With the line divided into individual fields, you can now map each input field to the field of your domain object just like a RowMapper would map a ResultSet row to the domain object.

Sounds simple doesn't it? It really is. The intricacies come from how to parse the line and when you look at objects that are built out of multiple records from your file. Let's take a look at reading files with fixed-width records first.

Fixed-Width Files

When dealing with legacy mainframe systems, it is common to have to work with fixed-width files due to the way COBOL and other technologies declare their storage. Because of this, you need to be able to handle fixed with files as well.

You can use a customer file as your fixed-width file. Consisting of a customer's name and address, Table 7-2 outlines the format of your customer file.

Table 7-2. Customer File Format

Field	Length	Description
First Name	10	Your customer's first name.
Middle Initial	1	The customer's middle initial.
Last Name	10	The last name of the customer.
Address Number	6	The street number piece of the customer's address.
Street	20	The name of the street where the customer lives.
City	10	The city the customer is from.

State	2	The two letter state abbreviation.
Zip Code	5	The customer's postal code.

Defining the format for a fixed with file is important. A delimited file describes its fields with its delimiters. XML or other structured files are self-describing given the metadata the tags provide. Database data has the metadata from the database describing it. However, fixed-width files are different. They provide zero metadata to describe their format. If you look at Listing 7-1, you can see an example of what the previous description looks like as your input file.

Listing 7-1. customer.txt, the Fixed-Width File

```
Michael   TMinella   123   4th Street      Chicago  IL60606
Warren    QGates     11    Wall Street      New York NY10005
Ann       BDarrow    350   Fifth Avenue     New York NY10118
Terrence  HDonnelly  4059  Mt. Lee Drive    HollywoodCA90068
```

To demonstrate how each of these readers work, you will create a single-step job that reads in a file and writes it right back out. For this job, copyJob, you will create a copyJob.xml file with the following beans:

- *customerFile*: The input file.

- *outputFile*: The file you will copy the input file to.

- *customerReader*: The FlatFileItemReader.

- *outputWriter*: The FlatFileItemWriter.

- *copyStep*: The step definition for your job.

- *copyJob*: The job definition.

Your customerFile and outputFile beans will be nothing more than Spring's org.springframework.core.io.FileSystemResource beans. Each of the file-related beans has the scope step because they can't be bound until the step begins (unlike normal Spring beans, which are instantiated and wired upon the application's startup)[1]. The customerReader is an instance of the FlatFileItemReader. As covered previously, the FlatFileItemReader consists of two pieces, a resource to read in (in this case, the customerFile) and a way to map each line of the file (a LineMapper implementation).

▨**Note** The "step" scope is a new bean scope provided by Spring Batch. This scope allows bean properties to be set when the step is excuted instead of on application startup (as is the default in Spring).

---

[1] Late binding of JobParameters was discussed in Chapter 4.

For the LineMapper implementation, you are going to use Spring Batch's `org.springframework.batch.item.file.DefaultLineMapper`. This LineMapper implementation is intended for the two-step process of mapping lines to domain objects you talked about previously: parsing the line into a FieldSet and then mapping the fields of the FieldSet to a domain object, the Customer object in your case.

To support the two step mapping process, the DefaultLineMapper takes two dependencies: a LineTokenizer implementation which will parse the String that is read in from your file into a FieldSet and a FieldSetMapper implementation to map the fields in your FieldSet to the fields in your domain object. Listing 7-2 shows the customerFile and customerReader bean definitions.

Listing 7-2. customerFile and customerReader in copyJob.xml

```
<?xml version="1.0" encoding="UTF-8"?>
<beans:beans xmlns="http://www.springframework.org/schema/batch"
    xmlns:beans="http://www.springframework.org/schema/beans"
    xmlns:util="http://www.springframework.org/schema/beans"
    xmlns:xsi="http://www.w3.org/2001/XMLSchema-instance"
    xsi:schemaLocation="http://www.springframework.org/schema/beans
        http://www.springframework.org/schema/beans/spring-beans-3.0.xsd
        http://www.springframework.org/schema/util
        http://www.springframework.org/schema/util/spring-util.xsd
        http://www.springframework.org/schema/batch
        http://www.springframework.org/schema/batch/spring-batch-2.1.xsd">

  <beans:import resyource="../launch-context.xml"/>


  <beans:bean id="customerFile"
    class="org.springframework.core.io.FileSystemResyource" scope="step">
    <beans:constructor-arg value="#{jobParameters[customerFile]}"/>
  </beans:bean>

  <beans:bean id="customerReader"
    class="org.springframework.batch.item.file.FlatFileItemReader">
    <beans:property name="resyource" ref="customerFile" />
    <beans:property name="lineMapper">
      <beans:bean
        class="org.springframework.batch.item.file.mapping.
DefaultLineMapper">
        <beans:property name="lineTokenizer">
          <beans:bean
            class="org.springframework.batch.item.file.transform.
FixedLengthTokenizer">
            <beans:property name="names"
              value="firstName,middleInitial,lastName,addressNumber,street,
city,state,zip"/>
            <beans:property name="columns"
              value="1-10,11,12-21,22-27,28-47,48-56,57-58,59-63"/>
          </beans:bean>
        </beans:property>
        <beans:property name="fieldSetMapper">
          <beans:bean
```

```
                class="org.springframework.batch.item.file.mapping.
BeanWrapperFieldSetMapper">
                <beans:property name="prototypeBeanName" value="customer"/>
              </beans:bean>
          </beans:property>
        </beans:bean>
    </beans:property>
  </beans:bean>

  <beans:bean id="customer" class="com.apress.springbatch.chapter7.Customer"
    scope="prototype"/>
...
```

Listing 7-2 begins with the customerFile, which is a reference to the file that will be read in by the customerReader. Note that the actual name of the customer file will be passed in as a job parameter at runtime.

From there you have your customerReader. The reader, as noted previously, consists of two pieces: the file to be read in and a LineMapper instance. When you look at the LineMapper interface, as shown in Listing 7-3, you can see that it's nearly identical to Spring's RowMapper.

Listing 7-3. *The LineMapper Interface*

```
package org.springframework.batch.item.file;

import org.springframework.batch.item.file.mapping.FieldSetMapper;
import org.springframework.batch.item.file.transform.LineTokenizer;

public interface LineMapper<T> {

        T mapLine(String line, int lineNumber) throws Exception;
}
```

For each line in your file, Spring Batch will call the mapLine method of the LineMapper implementation configured. In your case, that method will do two things; first, it will use the org.springframework.batch.item.file.transform.FixedLengthTokenizer to divide the string up into a FieldSet based upon the columns you configured. Then it will pass the FieldSet to the org.springframework.batch.item.file.mapping.BeanWrapperFieldSetMapper, which will use the names of each field to map the fields to the bean you requested (Customer in this case).

When working with fixed-width files, you use the FixedLengthTokenizer to parse your records into FieldSets. This implementation of the LineTokenizer interface takes three parameters:

- *columns* *(required)*: The column number ranges that define each field.

- *names (optional)*: A name to associate with each of the ranges specified in the list of columns.

- *strict (optional)*: A Boolean telling the reader if an exception should be thrown if a line of an invalid length is passed in (fixed-width files are expected to have all records be the same length).

With the LineTokenizer configured, you have a way to parse your line into a FieldSet. Now you need to map the FieldSet into the fields of your domain object. In this case, you are going to use the BeanWrapperFieldSetMapper. This implementation of the FieldSetMapper interface uses the bean spec to map fields in the FieldSet to fields in the domain object by name (the Customer object will have a getFirstName() and a setFirstName(String name), etc). The only thing you need to supply for the BeanWrapperFieldSetMapper is a reference to the bean it will be using, in your case it is the reference to the customer bean.

■**Note** The FixedLengthTokenizer doesn't trim any leading or trailing characters (spaces, zeros, etc) within each field. To do this, you'll have to implement your own LineTokenizer or you can trim in your own FieldSetMapper.

To put your reader to use, you need to configure your step and job. You will also need to configure a writer so that you can see that everything works. You will be covering writers in depth in the next chapter so you can keep the writer for this example simple. Listing 7-4 shows how to configure a simple writer to output the domain objects to a file.

Listing 7-4. A Simple Writer

```
...
<beans:bean id="outputFile"
  class="org.springframework.core.io.FileSystemResyource" scope="step">
  <beans:constructor-arg value="#{jobParameters[outputFile]}"/>
</beans:bean>

<beans:bean id="outputWriter"
  class="org.springframework.batch.item.file.FlatFileItemWriter">
  <beans:property name="resource" ref="outputFile" />
  <beans:property name="lineAggregator">
    <beans:bean class="org.springframework.batch.item.file.transform.
FormatterLineAggregator">
      <beans:property name="fieldExtractor">
        <beans:bean class="org.springframework.batch.item.file.transform.
BeanWrapperFieldExtractor">
          <beans:property name="names" value="firstName,middleInitial,
lastName,addressNumber,street,city,state,zip" />
        </beans:bean>
      </beans:property>
      <beans:property name="format" value=" %s %s. %s, %s %s, %s %s %s" />
    </beans:bean>
  </beans:property>
</beans:bean>
...
```

Looking at the output file resource and the writer in Listing 7-4, you can see a pattern between the readers and writers. The writer has two dependencies: the file resource to write to and a lineAggregator. The lineAggregator is used to take an object and convert it to the string that will be written to the file.

Your job configuration is very simple. As shown in Listing 7-5, a simple step that consists of the reader and writer with a commit count of 10 records is all you need. Your job uses that single step.

Listing 7-5. *The copyFileStep and copyFileJob*

```
...
  <step id="copyFileStep">
    <tasklet>
      <chunk reader="customerFileReader" writer="outputWriter"
        commit-interval="10"/>
    </tasklet>
  </step>

  <job id="copyJob">
    <step id="step1" parent="copyFileStep"/>
  </job>
</beans:beans>
```

The interesting piece of all of this is the small amount of code required to read and write this file. In this example, the only code you need to write is the domain object itself (Customer). Once you build your application, you can execute it with the command shown in Listing 7-6.

Listing 7-6. *Executing the copyJob*

```
java -jar copyJob.jar jobs/copyJob.xml copyJob customerFile=/input/customer.txt
outputFile=/output/output.txt
```

The output of the job is the same contents of the input file formatted according to the format string of the writer, as shown in Listing 7-7.

Listing 7-7. *Results of the copyJob*

```
Michael T. Minella, 123 4th Street, Chicago IL 60606
Warren Q. Gates, 11 Wall Street, New York NY 10005
Ann B. Darrow, 350 Fifth Avenue, New York NY 10118
Terrence H. Donnelly, 4059 Mt. Lee Drive, Hollywood CA 90068
```

Fixed-width files are a form of input provided for batch processes in many enterprises. As you can see, parsing the file into objects via FlatFileItemReader and FixedLengthTokenizer makes this process easy. In the next section you will look at a file format that provides a small amount of metadata to tell us how the file is to be parsed.

Delimited Files

Delimited files are files that provide a small amount of metadata within the file to tell us what the format of the file is. In this case, a character acts as a divider between each field in your record. This metadata provides us with the ability to not have to know what defines each individual field. Instead, the file dictates to use what each field consists of by dividing each record with a delimiter.

As with fixed-width records, the process is the same to read a delimited record. The record will first be tokenized by the LineTokenizer into a FieldSet. From there, the FieldSet will be mapped into your domain object by the FieldSetMapper. With the process being the same, all you need to do is update the LineTokenizer implementation you use to parse your file based upon a delimiter instead of premapped columns. Let's start by looking at an updated customerFile that is delimited instead of fixed-width. Listing 7-8 shows your new input file.

Listing 7-8. *A Delimited customerFile*

```
Michael,T,Minella,123,4th Street,Chicago,IL,60606
Warren,Q,Gates,11,Wall Street,New York,NY,10005
Ann,B,Darrow,350,Fifth Avenue,New York,NY,10118
Terrence,H,Donnelly,4059,Mt. Lee Drive,Hollywood,CA,90068
```

You'll notice right away that there are two changes between the new file and the old one. First, you are using commas to delimit the fields. Second, you have trimmed all of the fields. Typically when using delimited files, each field is not padded to a fixed-width like they are in fixed-width files. Because of that, the record length can vary, unlike the fixed-width record length.

As mentioned, the only configuration update you need to make to use the new file format is how each record is parsed. For fixed-width records, you used the FixedLengthTokenizer to parse each line. For the new delimited records, you will use the org.springframework.batch.item.file.transform.DelimitedLineTokenizer to parse the records into a FieldSet. Listing 7-9 shows the configuration of the reader updated with the DelimitedLineTokenizer.

Listing 7-9. *customerFileReader with the DelimitedLineTokenizer*

```
...
<beans:bean id="customerFile"
  class="org.springframework.core.io.FileSystemResyource" scope="step">
  <beans:constructor-arg value="#{jobParameters[customerFile]}"/>
</beans:bean>

<beans:bean id="customerFileReader"
  class="org.springframework.batch.item.file.FlatFileItemReader">
  <beans:property name="resyource" ref="customerFile" />
  <beans:property name="lineMapper">
    <beans:bean
      class="org.springframework.batch.item.file.mapping.DefaultLineMapper">
      <beans:property name="lineTokenizer">
            <beans:bean
class="org.springframework.batch.item.file.transform.DelimitedLineTokenizer">
              <beans:property name="names"
value="firstName,middleInitial,lastName,addressNumber,street,city,state,zip"/>
              <beans:property name="delimiter" value=","/>
            </beans:bean>
      </beans:property>
      <beans:property name="fieldSetMapper">
        <beans:bean class="org.springframework.batch.item.file.mapping.
BeanWrapperFieldSetMapper">
          <beans:property name="prototypeBeanName" value="customer"/>
        </beans:bean>
      </beans:property>
    </beans:bean>
  </beans:property>
</beans:bean>
```

```
<beans:bean id="customer" class="com.apress.springbatch.chapter7.Customer"
  scope="prototype"/>
…
```

The DelimitedLineTokenizer allows for two options that you'll find very useful. The first is the ability to configure the delimiter. A comma is the default value; however, any single character can be used. The second option is the ability to configure what value will be used as a quote character. When this option is used, that value will be used instead of " as the character to indicate quotes. This character will also be able to escape itself. Listing 7-10 shows an example of how a string is parsed when you use # character as quote character.

Listing 7-10. Parsing a Delimited File with the Quote Character Configured

```
Michael,T,Minella,#123,4th Street#,Chicago,IL,60606
Is parsed as
Michael
T
Minella
123,4th Street
Chicago
IL
60606
```

Although that's all that is required to process delimited files, it's not the only option you have. The current example maps address numbers and streets to two different fields. However, what if you wanted to map them together into a single field as represented in the domain object in Listing 7-11?

Listing 7-11. Customer with a Single Street Address Field

```
package com.apress.springbatch.chapter7;

public class Customer {
    private String firstName;
    private String middleInitial;
    private String lastName;
    private String addressNumber;
    private String street;
    private String city;
    private String state;
    private String zip;

    // Getters & setters go here
…
}
```

With the new object format, you will need to update how the FieldSet is mapped to the domain object. To do this, you will create your own implementation of the `org.springframework.batch.item.file.mapping.FieldSetMapper` interface. The FieldSetMapper interface, as shown in Listing 7-12, consists of a single method, `mapFieldSet`, that allows you to map the FieldSet as it is returned from the LineTokenizer to the domain object fields.

Listing 7-12. *The FieldSetMapper Interface*

```
package org.springframework.batch.item.file.mapping;

import org.springframework.batch.item.file.transform.FieldSet;
import org.springframework.validation.BindException;

public interface FieldSetMapper<T> {

    T mapFieldSet(FieldSet fieldSet) throws BindException;
}
```

To create your own mapper, you will implement the FieldSetMapper interface with the type defined as Customer. From there, as shown in Listing 7-13, you can map each field from the FieldSet to the domain object, concatenating the addressNumber and street fields into a single address field per your requirements.

Listing 7-13. *Mapping Fields from the FieldSet to the Customer Object*

```
package com.apress.springbatch.chapter7;

import org.springframework.batch.item.file.mapping.FieldSetMapper;
import org.springframework.batch.item.file.transform.FieldSet;
import org.springframework.validation.BindException;

public class CustomerFieldSetMapper implements FieldSetMapper<Customer> {

    public Customer mapFieldSet(FieldSet fieldSet) throws BindException {
        Customer customer = new Customer();

        customer.setAddress(fieldSet.readString("addressNumber") +
                            " " + fieldSet.readString("street"));
        customer.setCity(fieldSet.readString("city"));
        customer.setFirstName(ficldSet.readString("firstName"));
        customer.setLastName(fieldSet.readString("lastName"));
        customer.setMiddleInitial(fieldSet.readString("middleInitial"));
        customer.setState(fieldSet.readString("state"));
        customer.setZip(fieldSet.readString("zip"));

        return customer;
    }
}
```

The FieldSet methods are very similar to the ResultSet methods of the JDBC realm. Spring provides a method for each of the primitive data types, String (trimmed or untrimmed), BigDecimal, and java.util.Date. Each of these different methods has two different varieties. The first takes an integer as the parameter where the integer represents the index of the field to be retrieved in the record. The other version, shown in Listing 7-14, takes the name of the field. Although this approach requires you to name the fields in the job configuration, it's a more maintainable model in the long run. Listing 7-14 shows the FieldSet interface.

Listing 7-14. FieldSet Interface

```java
package org.springframework.batch.item.file.transform;

import java.math.BigDecimal;
import java.sql.ResultSet;
import java.util.Date;
import java.util.Properties;

public interface FieldSet {

 String[]        getNames();
 boolean         hasNames();
 String[]         getValues();
        String readString(int index);
        String readString(String name);
        String readRawString(int index);
        String readRawString(String name);
        boolean readBoolean(int index);
        boolean readBoolean(String name);
        boolean readBoolean(int index, String trueValue);
        boolean readBoolean(String name, String trueValue);
        char readChar(int index);
        char readChar(String name);
        byte readByte(int index);
        byte readByte(String name);
        short readShort(int index);
        short readShort(String name);
        int readInt(int index);
        int readInt(String name);
        int readInt(int index, int defaultValue);
        int readInt(String name, int defaultValue);
        long readLong(int index);
        long readLong(String name);
        long readLong(int index, long defaultValue);
        long readLong(String name, long defaultValue);
        float readFloat(int index);
        float readFloat(String name);
        double readDouble(int index);
        double readDouble(String name);
        BigDecimal readBigDecimal(int index);
        BigDecimal readBigDecimal(String name);
        BigDecimal readBigDecimal(int index, BigDecimal defaultValue);
        BigDecimal readBigDecimal(String name, BigDecimal defaultValue);
        Date readDate(int index);
        Date readDate(String name);
        Date readDate(int index, Date defaultValue);
        Date readDate(String name, Date defaultValue);
        Date readDate(int index, String pattern);
        Date readDate(String name, String pattern);
        Date readDate(int index, String pattern, Date defaultValue);
```

```
        Date readDate(String name, String pattern, Date defaultValue);
  int        getFieldCount();
  Properties        getProperties();
}
```

■**Note** Unlike the JDBC ResultSet, which begins indexing columns at 1, the index used by Spring Batch's FieldSet is zero-based.

To put the CustomerFieldSetMapper to use, you need to update the configuration to use it. Replace the BeanWrapperFieldSetMapper reference with your own bean reference, as shown in Listing 7-15.

Listing 7-15. customerFileReader Configured with the CustomerFieldSetMapper

```
...
<beans:bean id="customerFile"
  class="org.springframework.core.io.FileSystemResource" scope="step">
  <beans:constructor-arg value="#{jobParameters[customerFile]}"/>
</beans:bean>

<beans:bean id="customerFileReader"
  class="org.springframework.batch.item.file.FlatFileItemReader">
  <beans:property name="resource" ref="customerFile" />
  <beans:property name="lineMapper">
    <beans:bean
      class="org.springframework.batch.item.file.mapping.DefaultLineMapper">
      <beans:property name="lineTokenizer">
        <beans:bean class="org.springframework.batch.item.file.transform.
DelimitedLineTokenizer">
          <beans:property name="names"
            value="firstName,middleInitial,lastName,addressNumber,street,
city,state,zip"/>
          <beans:property name="delimiter" value=","/>
        </beans:bean>
      </beans:property>
      <beans:property name="fieldSetMapper">
        <beans:bean
          class="com.apress.springbatch.chapter7.CustomerFieldSetMapper"/>
      </beans:property>
    </beans:bean>
  </beans:property>
</beans:bean>
...
```

Note that with your new CustomerFieldSetMapper, you don't need to configure the reference to the Customer bean. Since you handle the instantiation yourselves, this is no longer needed.

Parsing files with the standard Spring Batch parsers, as you have shown, requires nothing more than a few lines of XML. However, not all files consist of Unicode characters laid out in a format that is easy for Java to understand. When dealing with legacy systems, it's common to come across data storage techniques that require custom parsing. In the next section, you will look at how to implement your own LineTokenizer to be able to handle custom file formats.

Custom Record Parsing

In the previous section you looked at how to address the ability to tweak the mapping of fields in your file to the fields of your domain object by creating a custom FieldSetMapper implementation. However, that is not the only option. Instead, you can create your own LineTokenizer implementation. This will allow you to parse each record however you need.

Like the FieldSetMapper interface, the org.springframework.batch.item.file.transform.LineTokenizer interface has a single method: tokenize. Listing 7-16 shows the LineTokenizer interface.

Listing 7-16. LineTokenizer interface

```
package org.springframework.batch.item.file.transform;

public interface LineTokenizer {

    FieldSet tokenize(String line);
}
```

For this approach you will use the same delimited input file you used previously; however, since the domain object has the address number and the street combined into a single field, you will combine those two tokens into a single field in the FieldSet. Listing 7-17 shows the CustomerFileLineTokenizer.

Listing 7-17. CustomerFileLineTokenizer

```
package com.apress.springbatch.chapter7;

import java.util.ArrayList;
import java.util.List;

import org.springframework.batch.item.file.transform.DefaultFieldSetFactory;
import org.springframework.batch.item.file.transform.FieldSet;
import org.springframework.batch.item.file.transform.FieldSetFactory;
import org.springframework.batch.item.file.transform.LineTokenizer;

public class CustomerFileLineTokenizer implements LineTokenizer {

    private String delimiter;
    private String names;
    private FieldSetFactory fieldSetFactory = new DefaultFieldSetFactory();

    public FieldSet tokenize(String record) {

        String[] fields = record.split(delimiter);

        List<String> parsedFields = new ArrayList<String>();
```

```
            for (int i = 0; i < fields.length; i++) {
                if (i == 4) {
                    parsedFields.set(i - 1,
                                     parsedFields.get(i - 1) + " " + fields[i]);
                } else {
                    parsedFields.add(fields[i]);
                }
            }

            FieldSet fieldSet =
                fieldSetFactory.create(parsedFields.toArray(new String [0]),
                                       names.split(","));

            return fieldSet;
        }

        public void setDelimiter(String delimiter) {
            this.delimiter = delimiter;
        }

        public void setNames(String names) {
            this.names = names;
        }
    }
```

The tokenize method of the CustomerFileLineTokenizer takes each record and splits it based upon the delimiter that was configured with Spring. You loop through the fields, combining the third and fourth fields together so that they are a single field. You then create a FieldSet using the DefaultFieldSetFactory, passing it the one required parameter (an array of values to be your fields) and one optional parameter (an array of names for the fields). This LineTokenizer names your fields so that you can use the BeanWrapperFieldSetMapper to do your FieldSet to domain object mapping without any additional code.

Configuring the CustomerFileLineTokenizer is identical to the configuration for the DelimitedLineTokenizer with only the class name to change. Listing 7-18 shows the updated configuration.

Listing 7-18. Configuring the CustomerFileLineTokenizer

```
...
<beans:bean id="customerFile"
  class="org.springframework.core.io.FileSystemResyource" scope="step">
  <beans:constructor-arg value="#{jobParameters[customerFile]}"/>
</beans:bean>

<beans:bean id="customerFileReader"
  class="org.springframework.batch.item.file.FlatFileItemReader">
  <beans:property name="resource" ref="customerFile" />
  <beans:property name="lineMapper">
    <beans:bean
      class="org.springframework.batch.item.file.mapping.DefaultLineMapper">
      <beans:property name="lineTokenizer">
            <beans:bean class="com.apress.springbatch.chapter7.CustomerFileLineTokenizer">
              <beans:property name="names"
                value="firstName,middleInitial,lastName,address,city,state,zip"/>
              <beans:property name="delimiter" value=","/>
            </beans:bean>
      </beans:property>
      <beans:property name="fieldSetMapper">
        <beans:bean class="org.springframework.batch.item.file.mapping.
BeanWrapperFieldSetMapper">
          <beans:property name="prototypeBeanName" value="customer"/>
        </beans:bean>
      </beans:property>
    </beans:bean>
  </beans:property>
</beans:bean>

<beans:bean id="customer" class="com.apress.springbatch.chapter7.Customer"
  scope="prototype"/>
...
```

The sky's the limit with what you can do with your own LineTokenizer and FieldSetMapper. Other uses for custom LineTokenizers could include:

- Parsing legacy file encodings like EBCDIC.

- Parsing third party file formats like Microsoft's Excel Worksheets.

- Handling special type conversion requirements.

However, not all files are as simple as the customer one you have been working with. What if your file contains multiple record formats? The next section will discuss how Spring Batch can choose the appropriate LineTokenizer to parse each record it comes across.

Multiple Record Formats

Up to this point you have been looking at a customer file that contains a collection of customer records. Each record in the file has the exact same format. However, what if you received a file that had customer information as well as transaction information? Yes, you could implement a single custom LineTokenizer. However there are two issues with this approach.

1. *Complexity.* If you have a file that has three, four, five, or more line formats—each with a large number of fields—this single class can get out of hand quickly.

2. *Separation of concerns.* The LineTokenizer is intended to parse a record. That's it. It should not need to determine what the record type is prior to the parsing.

With this in mind, Spring Batch provides another LineMapper implementation: the org.springframework.batch.item.file.mapping.PatternMatchingCompositeLineMapper. The previous examples used the DefaultLineMapper, which provided the ability to use a single LineTokenizer and a single FileSetMapper. With the PatternMatchingCompositeLineMapper, you will be able to define a Map of LineTokenizers and a corresponding Map of FieldSetMappers. The key for each map will be a pattern that the LineMapper will use to identify which LineTokenizer to use to parse each record.

Let's start this example by looking at the updated input file. In this case, you still have the same customer records. However, interspersed between each customer record is a random number of transaction records. To help identify each record, you have added a prefix to each record. Listing 7-19 shows the updated input file.

Listing 7-19. The Updated customerInputFile

```
CUST,Warren,Q,Darrow,8272 4th Street,New York,IL,76091
TRANS,1165965,2011-01-22 00:13:29,51.43
CUST,Ann,V,Gates,9247 Infinite Loop Drive,Hollywood,NE,37612
CUST,Erica,I,Jobs,8875 Farnam Street,Aurora,IL,36314
TRANS,8116369,2011-01-21 20:40:52,-14.83
TRANS,8116369,2011-01-21 15:50:17,-45.45
TRANS,8116369,2011-01-21 16:52:46,-74.6
TRANS,8116369,2011-01-22 13:51:05,48.55
TRANS,8116369,2011-01-21 16:51:59,98.53
```

In the file shown in Listing 7-19, you have two comma-delimited formats. The first consists of the standard customer format you have been working to up to now with the concatenated address number and street. These records are indicated with the prefix CUST. The other records are transaction records; each of these records, prefixed with the TRANS, prefix, are also comma-delimited, with the following three fields:

1. *Account number.* The customer's account number.

2. *Date:* The date the transaction occurred. The transactions may or may not be in date order.

3. *Amount.* The amount in dollars for the transaction. Negative values symbolize debits and positive amounts symbolize credits.

Listing 7-20 shows the code for the Transaction domain object.

Listing 7-20. Transaction Domain Object Code

```java
package com.apress.springbatch.chapter7;

import java.text.DateFormat;
import java.text.SimpleDateFormat;
import java.util.Date;

public class Transaction {

    private String accountNumber;
    private Date transactionDate;
    private Double amount;

    private DateFormat formatter = new SimpleDateFormat("MM/dd/yyyy");

    public String getAccountNumber() {
        return accountNumber;
    }
    public void setAccountNumber(String accountNumber) {
        this.accountNumber = accountNumber;
    }
    public Date getTransactionDate() {
        return transactionDate;
    }
    public void setTransactionDate(Date transactionDate) {
        this.transactionDate = transactionDate;
    }
    public Double getAmount() {
        return amount;
    }
    public void setAmount(Double amount) {
        this.amount = amount;
    }
    public String getDateString() {
        return formatter.format(transactionDate);
    }

}
```

With the record formats identified, you can look at the reader. Listing 7-21 shows the configuration for the updated customerFileReader. As mentioned, using the PatternMatchingCompositeLineMapper, you map two instances of the DelimitedLineTokenizer, each with the correct record format configured. You'll notice that you have an additional field named prefix for each of the LineTokenizers. This is to address the string at the beginning of each record (CUST and TRANS). Spring Batch will parse the prefix and name it prefix in your FieldSet; however, since you don't have a prefix field in either of your domain objects, it will be ignored in the mapping.

Listing 7-21. *Configuring the customerFileReader with Multiple Record Formats*

```
...
<beans:bean id="customerFile"
  class="org.springframework.core.io.FileSystemResyource" scope="step">
  <beans:constructor-arg value="#{jobParameters[customerFile]}"/>
</beans:bean>

<beans:bean id="customerFileReader"
  class="org.springframework.batch.item.file.FlatFileItemReader">
  <beans:property name="resyource" ref="customerFile" />
  <beans:property name="lineMapper">
    <beans:bean class="org.springframework.batch.item.file.mapping.
PatternMatchingCompositeLineMapper">
      <beans:property name="tokenizers">
        <beans:map>
          <beans:entry key="CUST*" value-ref="customerLineTokenizer"/>
          <beans:entry key="TRANS*" value-ref="transactionLineTokenizer"/>
        </beans:map>
      </beans:property>
      <beans:property name="fieldSetMappers">
        <beans:map>
          <beans:entry key="CUST*" value-ref="customerFieldSetMapper"/>
          <beans:entry key="TRANS*" value-ref="transactionFieldSetMapper"/>
        </beans:map>
      </beans:property>
    </beans:bean>
  </beans:property>
</beans:bean>

<beans:bean id="customerLineTokenizer"
  class="org.springframework.batch.item.file.transform.
DelimitedLineTokenizer">
  <beans:property name="names"
    value="prefix,firstName,middleInitial,lastName,address,city,state,zip"/>
  <beans:property name="delimiter" value=","/>
</beans:bean>

<beans:bean id="transactionLineTokenizer"
  class="org.springframework.batch.item.file.transform.
DelimitedLineTokenizer">
  <beans:property name="names"
    value="prefix,accountNumber,transactionDate,amount"/>
  <beans:property name="delimiter" value=","/>
</beans:bean>

<beans:bean id="customerFieldSetMapper"
  class="org.springframework.batch.item.file.mapping.
BeanWrapperFieldSetMapper">
  <beans:property name="prototypeBeanName" value="customer"/>
  <beans:property name="strict" value="false"/>
```

```
</beans:bean>

<beans:bean id="transactionFieldSetMapper"
  class="com.apress.springbatch.chapter7.TransactionFieldSetMapper"/>

<beans:bean id="customer" class="com.apress.springbatch.chapter7.Customer"
  scope="prototype"/>
...
```

The configuration of the customerFileReader is beginning to get a bit verbose. Let's walk through what will actually happen when this reader is executed. If you look at Figure 7-2, you can follow the flow of how the customerFileReader will process each line.

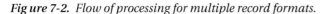

Fig ure 7-2. Flow of processing for multiple record formats.

As Figure 7-2 shows, the PatternMatchingCompositeLineMapper will look at each record of the file and apply your pattern to it. If the record begins with CUST,* (where * is zero or more characters), it will pass the record to the customerLineTokenizer for parsing. Once the record is parsed into a FieldSet, it will be passed to the customerFieldSetMapper to be mapped to the domain object. However, if the record begins with TRANS,*, it will be passed to the transactionLineTokenizer for parsing with the resulting FieldSet being passed to the custom transactionFieldSetMapper.

But why do you need a custom FieldSetMapper? It's necessary for custom type conversion. By default, the BeanWrapperFieldSetMapper doesn't do any special type conversion. The Transaction domain object consists of an accountNumber field, which is a String; however, the other two fields, transactionDate and amount, are a java.util.Date and a Double, respectively. Because of this, you will need to create a custom FieldSetMapper to do the required type conversions. Listing 7-22 shows the TransactionFieldSetMapper.

Listing 7-22. TransactionFieldSetMapper

```java
package com.apress.springbatch.chapter7;

import org.springframework.batch.item.file.mapping.FieldSetMapper;
import org.springframework.batch.item.file.transform.FieldSet;
import org.springframework.validation.BindException;

public class TransactionFieldSetMapper implements FieldSetMapper<Transaction> {

    public Transaction mapFieldSet(FieldSet fieldSet) throws BindException {
        Transaction trans = new Transaction();
```

```
        trans.setAccountNumber(fieldSet.readString("accountNumber"));
        trans.setAmount(fieldSet.readDouble("amount"));
        trans.setTransactionDate(fieldSet.readDate("transactionDate",
                                    "yyyy-MM-dd HH:mm:ss"));

        return trans;
    }
}
```

As you can see, the FieldSet interface, like the ResultSet interface of the JDBC world, provides custom methods for each data type. In the case of the Transaction domain object, you use the readDouble method to have the String in your file converted into a Java.lang.Double and you use the readDate method to parse the string contained in your file into a Java.util.Date. For the date conversion, you specify not only the field's name but also the format of the date to be parsed.

Unfortunately, with two different item types now being processed by the step at the same time, you won't be able to use the same ItemWriter you have been up to now. I would love to be able to tell you that Spring Batch has the equivalent delegator for the writer side as it does with the reader side and the PatternMatchingCompositeLineMapper. Unfortunately, it doesn't. Instead, you will need to create a custom ItemWriter that will delegate to the appropriate writer based upon the type of item to be printed. Chapter 9 covers the details of this writer implementation. However, to be able to see the results of the job, Listing 7-23 shows the implementation of the LineAggregator interface that will delegate the items accordingly.

Listing 7-23. *CustomerLineAggregator*

```
package com.apress.springbatch.chapter7;

import org.springframework.batch.item.file.transform.LineAggregator;

public class CustomerLineAggregator implements LineAggregator<Object> {

    private LineAggregator<Customer> customerLineAggregator;
    private LineAggregator<Transaction> transactionLineAggregator;

    public String aggregate(Object record) {
        if(record instanceof Customer) {
            return customerLineAggregator.aggregate((Customer) record);
        } else {
            return transactionLineAggregator.aggregate((Transaction) record);
        }
    }

    public void setCustomerLineAggregator(
            LineAggregator<Customer> customerLineAggregator) {
        this.customerLineAggregator = customerLineAggregator;
    }

    public void setTransactionLineAggregator(
            LineAggregator<Transaction> transactionLineAggregator) {
        this.transactionLineAggregator = transactionLineAggregator;
```

```
        }

}
```

The LineAggregator implementation in Listing 7-23 is quite simple. It takes an item, determines its type, and passes the item to the appropriate LineAggregator implementation based upon the type. The configuration for the previous LineAggregator is shown in Listing 7-24.

Listing 7-24. outputWriter Configuration

```
…
<beans:bean id="outputFile"
  class="org.springframework.core.io.FileSystemResource" scope="step">
  <beans:constructor-arg value="#{jobParameters[outputFile]}"/>
</beans:bean>

<beans:bean id="outputWriter"
  class="org.springframework.batch.item.file.FlatFileItemWriter">
  <beans:property name="resource" ref="outputFile" />
  <beans:property name="lineAggregator">
    <beans:bean
      class="com.apress.springbatch.chapter7.CustomerLineAggregator">
      <beans:property name="customerLineAggregator"
        ref="customerLineAggregator" />
      <beans:property name="transactionLineAggregator"
        ref="transactionLineAggregator" />
    </beans:bean>
  </beans:property>
</beans:bean>

<beans:bean id="customerLineAggregator"
  class="org.springframework.batch.item.file.transform.
FormatterLineAggregator">
  <beans:property name="fieldExtractor">
    <beans:bean class="org.springframework.batch.item.file.transform.
BeanWrapperFieldExtractor">
      <beans:property name="names" value="firstName,middleInitial,lastName,
address,city,state,zip" />
    </beans:bean>
  </beans:property>
  <beans:property name="format" value="%s %s. %s, %s, %s %s %s" />
</beans:bean>

<beans:bean id="transactionLineAggregator" class="org.springframework.batch.
item.file.transform.FormatterLineAggregator">
  <beans:property name="fieldExtractor">
    <beans:bean class="org.springframework.batch.item.file.transform.
BeanWrapperFieldExtractor">
      <beans:property name="names" value="accountNumber,amount,dateString" />
    </beans:bean>
  </beans:property>
  <beans:property name="format" value="%s had a transaction of %.2f on %s" />
```

```
</beans:bean>
…
```

As you can see from Listing 7-24, configuring each of the two LineAggregators to which the CustomerLineAggregator delegates are based upon the same configuration that you used previously. The only difference is you have a delegation step in front of them.

When you execute the job, you're able to read in the two different record formats, parse them into their respective domain objects, and print them out into two, different record formats. A sample of the results of this job is shown in Listing 7-25.

Listing 7-25. *Results of Running the copyJob Job with Multiple Record Formats*

```
Warren Q. Darrow, 8272 4th Street, New York IL 76091
1165965 had a transaction of 51.43 on 01/22/2011
Ann V. Gates, 9247 Infinite Loop Drive, Hollywood NE 37612
Erica I. Jobs, 8875 Farnam Street, Aurora IL 36314
8116369 had a transaction of -14.83 on 01/21/2011
8116369 had a transaction of -45.45 on 01/21/2011
8116369 had a transaction of -74.60 on 01/21/2011
8116369 had a transaction of 48.55 on 01/22/2011
8116369 had a transaction of 98.53 on 01/21/2011
```

The ability to process multiple records from a single file is a common requirement in batch processing. However, this example assumes that there was no real relationship between the different records. What if there is? The next section will look at how to read multiline records into a single item.

Multiline Records

In the last example, you looked at the processing of two different record formats into two different, unrelated items. However, if you take a closer look at the file format you were using, you can see that the records you were reading were actually related (as shown in the output of the job). While not related by a field in the file, the transaction records are the transaction records for the customer record above it. Instead of processing each record independently, doesn't it make more sense to have a Customer object that has a collection of Transaction objects on it?

To make this work, you will need to perform a small bit of trickery. The examples provided with Spring Batch use a footer record to identify the true end of a record. Although convenient, many files seen in batch do not have that trailer record. With your file format, you run into the issue of not knowing when a record is complete without reading the next row. To get around this, you can implement your own ItemReader that adds a bit of logic around the customerFileReader you configured in the previous section. Figure 7-3 shows the flow of logic you will use within your custom ItemReader.

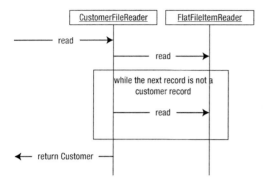

Figure 7-3. CustomerFileReader flow

As Figure 7-3 shows, your read method will begin by determining if a Customer object has already been read. If it hasn't, it will attempt to read one from the FlatFileItemReader. Assuming you read a record (you won't have read one once you reach the end of the file), you will initialize the transaction List on the Customer object. While the next record you read is a Transaction, you will add it to the Customer object. Listing 7-26 shows the implementation of the CustomerFileReader.

Listing 7-26. CustomerFileReader

```java
package com.apress.springbatch.chapter7;

import Java.util.ArrayList;

import org.springframework.batch.item.ExecutionContext;
import org.springframework.batch.item.ItemStreamException;
import org.springframework.batch.item.ItemStreamReader;
import org.springframework.batch.item.ParseException;
import org.springframework.batch.item.UnexpectedInputException;

public class CustomerFileReader implements ItemStreamReader<Object> {

    private Object curItem = null;

    private ItemStreamReader<Object> delegate;

    public Object read() throws Exception {
        if(curItem == null) {
            curItem = (Customer) delegate.read();
        }

        Customer item = (Customer) curItem;
        curItem = null;

        if(item != null) {
            item.setTransactions(new ArrayList<Transaction>());

            while(peek() instanceof Transaction) {
```

```
                    item.getTransactions().add((Transaction) curItem);
                    curItem = null;
                }
            }

        return item;
    }

    public Object peek() throws Exception, UnexpectedInputException,
            ParseException {
        if (curItem == null) {
            curItem = delegate.read();
        }
        return curItem;
    }

    public void setDelegate(ItemStreamReader<Object> delegate) {
        this.delegate = delegate;
    }

    public void close() throws ItemStreamException {
        delegate.close();
    }

    public void open(ExecutionContext arg0) throws ItemStreamException {
        delegate.open(arg0);
    }

    public void update(ExecutionContext arg0) throws ItemStreamException {
        delegate.update(arg0);
    }
}
```

The CustomerFileReader has two key methods that you should look at. The first is the read() method. This method is responsible for implementing the logic involved in reading and assembling a single Customer item including its child transaction records. It does so by reading in a customer record from the file you are reading. It then reads the related transaction records until the next record is the next customer record. Once the next customer record is found, the current customer is considered complete and returned by your ItemReader. This type of logic is called control break logic.

The other method of consequence is the peak method. This method is used to read ahead while still working on the current Customer. It caches the current record. If the record has been read but not processed, it will return the same record again. If the record has been processed (indicated to this method by setting curItem to null), it will read in the next record[2].

You should notice that your custom ItemReader does not implement the ItemReader interface. Instead, it implements on of its subinterfaces, the ItemStreamReader interface. The reason for this is that when using one of the Spring Batch ItemReader implementations, they handle the opening and

---

[2] It is important to note that there is an ItemReader subiterface called the org.springframework.batch.item.PeekableItemReader<T>. Since the CustomerFileReader not firmly meet the contract defined by that interface here we do not implement it.

closing of the resource being read as well as maintaining the ExecutionContext as records are being read. However, if you implement your own, you need to manage that yourself. Since you are just wrapping a Spring Batch ItemReader (the FlatFileItemReader), you can use it to maintain those resources.

To configure the CustomerFileReader, the only dependency you have is the delegate. The delegate in this case is the reader that will do the actual reading and parsing work for you. Listing 7-27 shows the configuration for the CustomerFileReader.

Listing 7-27. *CustomerFileReader Configuration*

```
...
<beans:bean id="customerFile"
  class="org.springframework.core.io.FileSystemResyource" scope="step">
  <beans:constructor-arg value="#{jobParameters[customerFile]}"/>
</beans:bean>

<beans:bean id="customerFileReader"
class="com.apress.springbatch.chapter7.CustomerFileReader">
  <beans:property name="delegate" ref="trueCustomerFileReader"/>
</beans:bean>

<beans:bean id="trueCustomerFileReader"
  class="org.springframework.batch.item.file.FlatFileItemReader">
  <beans:property name="resource" ref="customerFile" />
  <beans:property name="lineMapper">
    <beans:bean class="org.springframework.batch.item.file.mapping.
PatternMatchingCompositeLineMapper">
      <beans:property name="tokenizers">
        <beans:map>
          <beans:entry key="CUST*" value-ref="customerLineTokenizer"/>
          <beans:entry key="TRANS*" value-ref="transactionLineTokenizer"/>
        </beans:map>
      </beans:property>
      <beans:property name="fieldSetMappers">
        <beans:map>
          <beans:entry key="CUST*" value-ref="customerFieldSetMapper"/>
          <beans:entry key="TRANS*" value-ref="transactionFieldSetMapper"/>
        </beans:map>
      </beans:property>
    </beans:bean>
  </beans:property>
</beans:bean>

<beans:bean id="customerLineTokenizer"
  class="org.springframework.batch.item.file.transform.
DelimitedLineTokenizer">
  <beans:property name="names" value="prefix,firstName,middleInitial,
lastName,address,city,state,zip"/>
  <beans:property name="delimiter" value=","/>
</beans:bean>

<beans:bean id="transactionLineTokenizer"
  class="org.springframework.batch.item.file.transform.
```

```
DelimitedLineTokenizer">
  <beans:property name="names"
    value="prefix,accountNumber,transactionDate,amount"/>
  <beans:property name="delimiter" value=","/>
</beans:bean>

<beans:bean id="customerFieldSetMapper"
  class="org.springframework.batch.item.file.mapping.
BeanWrapperFieldSetMapper">
  <beans:property name="prototypeBeanName" value="customer"/>
</beans:bean>

<beans:bean id="transactionFieldSetMapper"
  class="com.apress.springbatch.chapter7.TransactionFieldSetMapper"/>

<beans:bean id="customer" class="com.apress.springbatch.chapter7.Customer"
  scope="prototype"/>
...
```

The configuration in Listing 7-27 should look familiar. It's essentially the exact same as the configuration you used for multiple record formats (see Listing 7-19). The only addition, as highlighted in bold, is the configuration of your new CustomerFileReader with its reference to the old ItemReader and renaming the old ItemReader.

With the updated object model, the previous method for writing to your output file won't work for this example. Because of this, I chose to use Spring Batch's PassThroughLineAggregator to write the output for this example. It calls the item's toString() method and writes the output to the output file. Listing 7-28 shows the updated ItemWriter configuration.

Listing 7-28. *Updated outputWriter Configuration*

```
...
<beans:bean id="outputFile"
  class="org.springframework.core.io.FileSystemResyource" scope="step">
  <beans:constructor-arg value="#{jobParameters[outputFile]}"/>
</beans:bean>

<beans:bean id="outputWriter"
  class="org.springframework.batch.item.file.FlatFileItemWriter">
  <beans:property name="resource" ref="outputFile" />
  <beans:property name="lineAggregator">
    <beans:bean class="org.springframework.batch.item.file.transform.
PassThroughLineAggregator"/>
  </beans:property>
</beans:bean>
...
```

For each Customer object, it will print how many transactions the user has. This will provide enough detail for you to verify that your reading worked correctly. With the PassThroughLineAggregator configured as it is, you only need to override the Customer's toString() method to format the output. Listing 7-29 shows the updated method.

Listing 7-29. *Customer's toString() Method*

```
...
    @Override
    public String toString() {
        StringBuilder output = new StringBuilder();

        output.append(firstName);
        output.append(" ");
        output.append(middleInitial);
        output.append(". ");
        output.append(lastName);

        if(transactions != null&& transactions.size() > 0) {
            output.append(" has ");
            output.append(transactions.size());
            output.append(" transactions.");
        } else {
            output.append(" has no transactions.");
        }

        return output.toString();
    }
...
```

With a run of the job, you can see each of your customers and the number of transaction records you read in. It's important to note that when reading records in this way, the customer record and all the subsequent transaction records are considered a single item. The reason for this is that Spring Batch considers an item to be any object that is returned by the ItemReader. In this case, the Customer object is the object returned by the ItemReader so it is the item used for things like commit counts, etc. Each Customer object will be processed once by any configured ItemProcessor you add and once by any configured ItemWriter. The output from the job configured with the new ItemReaders can be seen in Listing 7-30.

Listing 7-30. *Output from Multiline Job*

```
Warren Q. Darrow has 1 transactions.
Ann V. Gates has no transactions.
Erica I. Jobs has 5 transactions.
```

Multiline records are a common element in batch processing. Although they are a bit more complex than basic record processing, as you can see from this example, there is still only a minimal amount of actual code that needs to be written to handle these robust situations.

The last piece of the flat file puzzle is to look at input situations where you read in from multiple files. This is a common requirement in the batch world and it's covered in the next section.

Multiple Sources

The examples up to this point have been based around a customer file with transactions for each customer. Many companies have multiple departments or locations that sell things. Take, for example, a restaurant chain with restaurants nationwide. Each location may contribute a file with the same format to be processed. If you were to process each one with a separate writer like you have been up to now, there would be a number of issues from performance to maintainability. So how does Spring Batch provide for the ability to read in multiple files with the same format?

Using a similar pattern to the one you just used in the multiline record example, Spring Batch provides an ItemReader called the MultiResourceItemReader. This reader wraps another ItemReader like the CustomerFileItemReader did; however, instead of defining the resource to be read as part of the child ItemReader, a pattern that defines all of the files to be read is defined as a dependency of the MultiResourceItemReader. Let's take a look.

You can use the same file format as you did in your multi-record example (as shown in Listing 7-19), which will allow you to use the same ItemReader configuration you created in the multiline example as well. However, if you have five of these files with the filenames customerFile1.txt, customerFile2.txt, customerFile3.txt, customerFile4.txt, and customerFile5.txt, you need to make two small updates. The first is to the configuration. You need to tweak your configuration to use the MultiResyourceItemReader with the correct resource pattern. You will also remove the reference to the input resource (<beans:property name="resource" ref="customerFile" />) from the FlatFileItemReader that you have used up to this point. Listing 7-31 shows the updated configuration.

Listing 7-31. Configuration to Process Multiple Customer Files

```
...
<beans:bean id="customerFileReader"
  class="org.springframework.batch.item.file.MultiResourceItemReader">
  <beans:property name="resources" value="file:/Users/mminella/temp/customerFile*.csv"/>
  <beans:property name="delegate" ref="fullCustomerFileReader"/>
</beans:bean>

<beans:bean id="fullCustomerFileReader"
  class="com.apress.springbatch.chapter7.CustomerFileReader">
  <beans:property name="delegate" ref="trueCustomerFileReader"/>
</beans:bean>

<beans:bean id="trueCustomerFileReader"
  class="org.springframework.batch.item.file.FlatFileItemReader">
  <beans:property name="lineMapper">
    <beans:bean
      class="org.springframework.batch.item.file.mapping.
PatternMatchingCompositeLineMapper">
      <beans:property name="tokenizers">
        <beans:map>
          <beans:entry key="CUST*" value-ref="customerLineTokenizer"/>
          <beans:entry key="TRANS*" value-ref="transactionLineTokenizer"/>
        </beans:map>
      </beans:property>
      <beans:property name="fieldSetMappers">
        <beans:map>
          <beans:entry key="CUST*" value-ref="customerFieldSetMapper"/>
          <beans:entry key="TRANS*" value-ref="transactionFieldSetMapper"/>
        </beans:map>
      </beans:property>
    </beans:bean>
  </beans:property>
```

```
</beans:bean>

<beans:bean id="customerLineTokenizer"
  class="org.springframework.batch.item.file.transform.
DelimitedLineTokenizer">
  <beans:property name="names" value="prefix,firstName,middleInitial,
lastName,address,city,state,zip"/>
  <beans:property name="delimiter" value=","/>
</beans:bean>

<beans:bean id="transactionLineTokenizer"
  class="org.springframework.batch.item.file.transform.
DelimitedLineTokenizer">
  <beans:property name="names"
    value="prefix,accountNumber,transactionDate,amount"/>
  <beans:property name="delimiter" value=","/>
</beans:bean>

<beans:bean id="customerFieldSetMapper"
  class="org.springframework.batch.item.file.mapping.
BeanWrapperFieldSetMapper">
  <beans:property name="prototypeBeanName" value="customer"/>
  <beans:property name="strict" value="false"/>
</beans:bean>

<beans:bean id="transactionFieldSetMapper"
  class="com.apress.springbatch.chapter7.TransactionFieldSetMapper"/>

<beans:bean id="customer" class="com.apress.springbatch.chapter7.Customer"
  scope="prototype"/>
...
```

The other change you need to make is to the CustomerFileReader code. Previously, you were able to use the ItemStreamReader interface as what you implemented and the delegate's type. However, that won't be specific enough this time around. Instead, you are going to need to use one of the ItemStreamResource's sub interfaces. The ResourceAwareItemReaderItemStream interface is for any ItemReader that reads its input from resources. The reason you will want to make the two changes is that you will need to be able to inject multiple Resources into the ItemReader.

By implementing org.springframework.batch.item.file.ResourceAwareItemStreamItemReader, you will be required to add one additional method: setResource. Like the open, close and update methods of the ItemStreamReader interface, you will just be calling the setResource method on the delegate in your implementation. The other change you need to make is to have your delegate be of the type ResourceAwareItemStreamItemReader. Since you are using the FlatFileItemReader as your delegate, you won't need to use a different ItemReader as the delegate. The updated code is listed in Listing 7-32.

Listing 7-32. CustomerFileReader

```
package com.apress.springbatch.chapter7;

import java.util.ArrayList;

import org.springframework.batch.item.ExecutionContext;
import org.springframework.batch.item.ItemStreamException;
import org.springframework.batch.item.ParseException;
import org.springframework.batch.item.UnexpectedInputException;
import org.springframework.batch.item.file.ResourceAwareItemReaderItemStream;
import org.springframework.core.io.Resource;

public class CustomerFileReader implements
        ResourceAwareItemReaderItemStream<Object> {

    private Object curItem = null;

    private ResourceAwareItemReaderItemStream<Object> delegate;

    public Object read() throws Exception {
        if (curItem == null) {
            curItem = (Customer) delegate.read();
        }

        Customer item = (Customer) curItem;
        curItem = null;

        if (item != null) {
            item.setTransactions(new ArrayList<Transaction>());

            while (peek() instanceof Transaction) {
                item.getTransactions().add((Transaction) curItem);
                curItem = null;
            }
        }

        return item;
    }

    public Object peek() throws Exception, UnexpectedInputException,
            ParseException {
        if (curItem == null) {
            curItem = delegate.read();
        }
        return curItem;
    }

    public void setDelegate(
        ResourceAwareItemReaderItemStream<Object> delegate) {
        this.delegate = delegate;
```

```
    }

    public void close() throws ItemStreamException {
        delegate.close();
    }

    public void open(ExecutionContext arg0) throws ItemStreamException {
        delegate.open(arg0);
    }

    public void update(ExecutionContext arg0) throws ItemStreamException {
        delegate.update(arg0);
    }

    public void setResource(Resyource arg0) {
        delegate.setResource(arg0);
    }
}
```

The sole difference from a processing standpoint between what is shown in Listing 7-33 and what you originally wrote in Listing 7-26 is the ability to inject a Resource. This allows Spring Batch to create each of the files as needed and inject them into the ItemReader instead of the ItemReader itself being responsible for file management.

When you run this example, Spring Batch will iterate through all of the resources that match your provided pattern and execute your reader for each file. The output for this job is nothing more than a larger version of the output from the multiline record example.

Listing 7-33. Output from Multiline Job

```
Warren Q. Darrow has 1 transactions.
Ann V. Gates has no transactions.
Erica I. Jobs has 5 transactions.
Joseph Z. Williams has 2 transactions.
Estelle Y. Laflamme has 3 transactions.
Robert X. Wilson has 1 transactions.
Clement A. Blair has 1 transactions.
Chana B. Meyer has 1 transactions.
Kay C. Quinonez has 1 transactions.
Kristen D. Seibert has 1 transactions.
Lee E. Troupe has 1 transactions.
Edgar F. Christian has 1 transactions.
```

It is important to note that when dealing with multiple files like this, Spring Batch provides no added safety around things like restart. So in this example, if your job started with files customerFile1.csv, customerFile2.csv, and customerFile3.csv and it were to fail after processing customerFile2.csv, and you added a customerFile4.csv before it was restated, customerFile4.csv would be processed as part of this run even though it didn't exist when the job was first executed. To safeguard against this, it's a common practice to have a directory for each batch run. All files that are to be processed for the run go into the appropriate directory and are processed. Any new files go into a new directory so that they have no impact on the currently running execution.

I have covered many scenarios involving flat files—from fixed-width records, delimited records, multiline records, and even input from multiple files. However, flat files are not the only type of files that you are likely to see. You have spent a large amount of this book (and will still spend a large amount more) looking at XML, yet you haven't even looked at how Spring Batch processes it. Let's see what Spring Batch can do for you when you're faced with XML files.

XML

When I began talking about file-based processing at the beginning of this chapter, I talked about how different file formats have differing amounts of metadata that describe the format of the file. I said that fixed-width records have the least amount of metadata, requiring the most information about the record format to be known in advance. XML is at the other end of the spectrum. XML uses tags to describe the data in the file, providing a full description of the data it contains.

Two XML parsers are commonly used: DOM and SAX. The DOM parser loads the entire file into memory in a tree structure for navigation of the nodes. This approach is not useful for batch processing due to the performance implications. This leaves you with the SAX parser. SAX is an event-based parser that fires events when certain elements are found.

In Spring Batch, you use a StAX parser. Although this is an event-based parser similar to SAX, it has the advantage of allowing for the ability to parse sections of your document independently. This relates directly with the item oriented reading you do. A SAX parser would parse the entire file in a single run; the StAX parser allows you to read each section of a file that represents an item to be processed at a time.

Before you look at how to parse XML with Spring Batch, let's look at a sample input file. To see how the XML parsing works with Spring Batch, you will be working with the same input: your customer file. However, instead of the data in the format of a flat file, you will structure it via XML. Listing 7-34 shows a sample of the input.

Listing 7-34. *Customer XML File Sample*

```
<customers>
  <customer>
    <firstName>Laura</firstName>
    <middleInitial>O</middleInitial>
    <lastName>Minella</lastName>
    <address>2039 Wall Street</address>
    <city>Omaha</city>
    <state>IL</state>
    <zip>35446</zip>
    <transaction>
      <account>829433</account>
      <transactionDate>2010-10-14 05:49:58</transactionDate>
      <amount>26.08</amount>
    </transaction>
  </customer>
  <customer>
    <firstName>Michael</firstName>
    <middleInitial>T</middleInitial>
    <lastName>Buffett</lastName>
    <address>8192 Wall Street</address>
    <city>Omaha</city>
    <state>NE</state>
    <zip>25372</zip>
```

```
<transaction>
  <account>8179238</account>
  <transactionDate>2010-10-27 05:56:59</transactionDate>
  <amount>-91.76</amount>
</transaction>
<transaction>
  <account>8179238</account>
  <transactionDate>2010-10-06 21:51:05</transactionDate>
  <amount>-25.99</amount>
</transaction>
    </customer>
</customers>
```

The customer file is structured as a collection of customer sections. Each of these contains a collection of transaction sections. Spring Batch parses lines in flat files into FieldSets. When working with XML, Spring Batch parses XML fragments that you define into your domain objects. What is a fragment? As Figure 7-4 shows, an XML fragment is a block of XML from open to close tag. Each time the specified fragment exists in your file, it will be considered a single record and converted into an item to be processed.

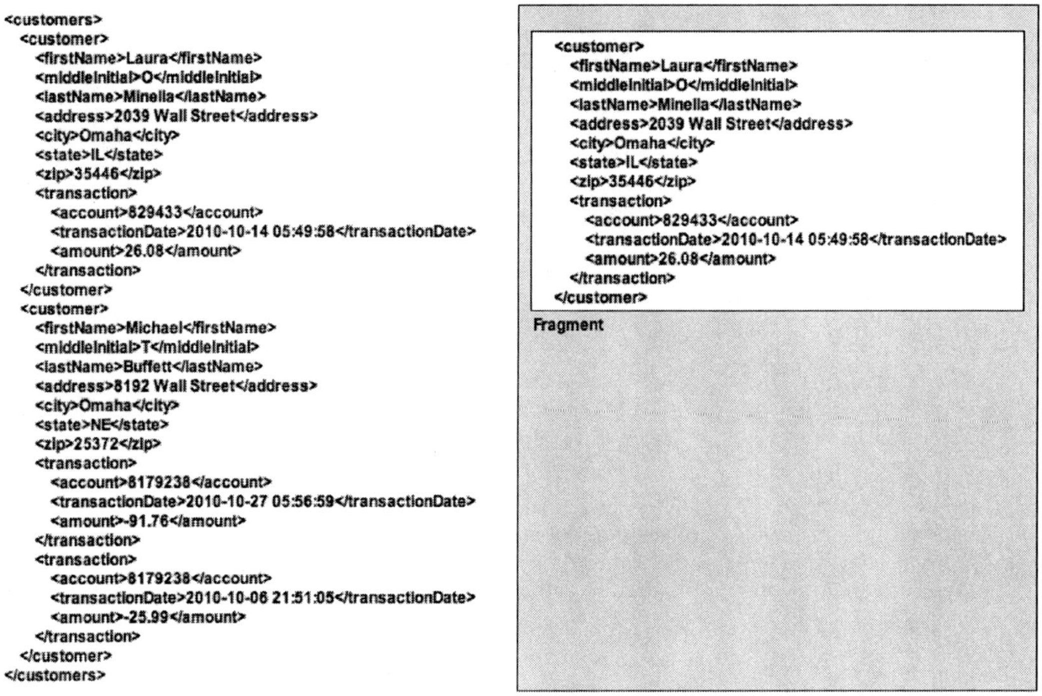

Figure 7-4. XML fragments as Spring Batch sees them

In the customer input file, you have the same data at the customer level. You also have a collection of transaction elements within each customer, representing the list of transactions you put together in the multiline example previously.

To parse your XML input file, you will use the
org.springframework.batch.item.xml.StaxEventItemReader that Spring Batch provides. To use it, you
define a fragment root element name, which identifies the root element of each fragment considered an
item in your XML. In your case, this will be the customer tag. It also takes a resource, which will be the
same your customerFile bean as it has been previously. Finally, it takes an
org.springframework.oxm.Unmarshaller implementation. This will be used to convert the XML to your
domain object. Listing 7-35 shows the configuration of your customerFileReader using the
StaxEventItemReader implementation.

Listing 7-35. *customerFileReader Configured with the StaxEventItemReader*

```
...
<beans:bean id="customerFile"
  class="org.springframework.core.io.FileSystemResource" scope="step">
  <beans:constructor-arg value="#{jobParameters[customerFile]}"/>
</beans:bean>

<beans:bean id="customerFileReader"
  class="org.springframework.batch.item.xml.StaxEventItemReader">
  <beans:property name="fragmentRootElementName" value="customer" />
  <beans:property name="resource" ref="customerFile" />
  <beans:property name="unmarshaller" ref="customerMarshaller" />
</beans:bean>
...
```

Spring Batch is not picky about the XML binding technology you choose to use. Spring provides
Unmarshaller implementations that use Castor, JAXB, JiBX, XMLBeans, and XStream in their oxm
package. For this example, you will use the XStream binding framework.

For your customerMarshaller configuration, you will use the
org.springframework.oxm.xstream.XStreamMarshaller implementation provided by Spring. To parse
your customer file, there are three things you will need to configure on the XStreamMarshaller instance.

1. *Aliases*: This is a map of tag names to fully qualified class names that tells the
   unmarshaller what each tag maps to.

2. *implicitCollection*: This is a map of fields to fully qualified classes that indicate
   what fields on the class specified are collections consisting of another type.

3. *Converters*: Although XStream is pretty smart and can figure out how to
   convert most of your XML file from the Strings it sees in the file to the required
   data type in your objects, you need to help it out on the transaction date. For
   XStream to be able to parse the transaction date, you will need to provide a
   DateConverter instance configured with the correct date format.

Listing 7-36 shows how to configure your XStreamMarshaller with these dependencies.

Listing 7-36. *customerMarshaller Configuration*

```
...
<beans:bean id="customerMarshaller"
  class="org.springframework.oxm.xstream.XStreamMarshaller">
  <beans:property name="aliases">
    <beans:map>
```

```
      <beans:entry key="customer"
        value="com.apress.springbatch.chapter7.Customer" />
      <beans:entry key="transaction"
        value="com.apress.springbatch.chapter7.Transaction" />
      <beans:entry key="account" value="java.lang.String"/>
      <beans:entry key="zip" value="java.lang.String"/>
    </beans:map>
  </beans:property>
  <beans:property name="implicitCollection">
    <beans:map>
      <beans:entry key="transactions"
        value="com.apress.springbatch.chapter7.Customer"/>
    </beans:map>
  </beans:property>
  <beans:property name="converters">
    <beans:list>
      <beans:ref local="dateConverter"/>
    </beans:list>
  </beans:property>
</beans:bean>

<beans:bean id="dateConverter"
  class="com.thoughtworks.xstream.converters.basic.DateConverter">
  <beans:constructor-arg value="yyyy-MM-dd HH:mm:ss"/>
  <beans:constructor-arg value="yyyy-MM-dd HH:mm:ss"/>
</beans:bean>
...
```

As you can see in Listing 7-36, you configure the aliases to tell your parser what each tag maps to. Note that you don't need to map every tag since the parser can figure out most of the Strings. However, in the case of the zip code and account number, you need to let XStream know that those are not any type of number field. You also let your parser know what each of the two root tags map to: transaction maps to the Transaction class and customer maps to the Customer class. The implicitCollection dependency identifies that the field transactions on the Customer object is a collection. Finally, you provide a list of converters for XStream to use when it finds types that it can't parse by default. In your case, you provide the com.thoughtworks.xstream.converters.basic.DateConverter with the correct format for the dates found in your file.

That's all you need to parse XML into items in Spring Batch! By running this job, you will get the same output as you did from the multiline record job.

Over the course of this section, you have covered a wide array of input formats. Fixed length files, delimited files, and various record configurations as well as XML are all available to be handled via Spring Batch with no or very limited coding, as you have seen. However, not all input will come from a file. Relational databases will provide a large amount of the input for your batch processes. The next section will cover the facilities that Spring Batch provides for database input.

Database Input

Databases serve as a great source of input for batch processes for a number of reasons. They provide transactionality built in, they are typically more performant, and they scale better than flat files. They also provide better recovery features out of the box than most other input formats. When you consider all of the above and the fact that most enterprise data is stored in relational databases to begin with, your batch processes will need to be able to handle input from databases. In this section, you will look at some of the facilities that Spring Batch provide out of the box to handle reading input data from a database including JDBC, Hibernate, and JPA.

JDBC

In the Java world, database connectivity begins with JDBC. We all go through the pain of writing the JDBC connection code when we learn it, then quickly forget those lines when we realize that most frameworks handle things like connections for us. One of the Spring framework's strengths is encapsulating the pain points of things like JDBC in ways that allow developers to concentrate only on the business-specific details.

In this tradition, the developers of the Spring Batch framework have extended the Spring framework's JDBC functionality with the features that are needed in the batch world. But what are those features and how has Spring Batch addressed them?

When working with batch processes, the need to process large amounts of data is common. If you have a query that returns millions of records, you probably don't want all of that data loaded into memory at once. However, if you use Spring's JdbcTemplate, that is exactly what you would get. The JdbcTemplate loops through the entire ResultSet, mapping every row to the required domain object in memory.

Instead, Spring Batch provides two different methods for loading records one at a time as they are processed: a cursor and paging. A cursor is actually the default functionality of the JDBC ResultSet. When a ResultSet is opened, every time the next() method is called a record from the database is returned. This allows records to be streamed from the database on demand, which is the behavior that you need for a cursor.

Paging, on the other hand, takes a bit more work. The concept of paging is that you retrieve records from the database in chunks called pages. As you read through each page, a new page is read from the database. Figure 7-5 shows the difference between the two approaches.

Figure 7-5. Cursor vs. paging

As you can see in Figure 7-5, the first read in the cursor returns a single record and advances the record you point at to the next record, streaming a single record at a time, whereas in the pagination approach, you receive 10 records from the database at a time. You will look at both approaches (cursor implementations as well as paging) for each of the database technologies you will look at. Let's start with straight JDBC.

JDBC Cursor Processing

For this example, you'll be using a Customer table. Using the same fields you have been working with up to now, you will create a database table to hold the data. Figure 7-6 shows the database model for the new Customer table.

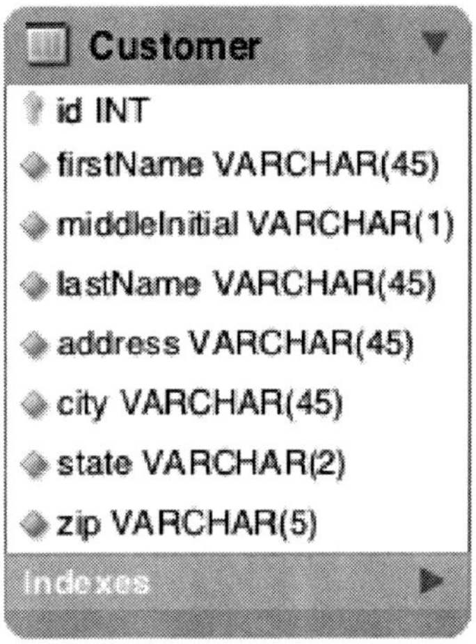

Figure 7-6. Customer data model

To implement a JDBC reader (either cursor-based or page-based), you will need to do two things: configure the reader to execute the query that is required and create a RowMapper implementation just like the Spring JdbcTemplate requires to map your ResultSet to your domain object. Since the RowMapper implementation will be the same for each approach, you can start there.

A RowMapper is exactly what it sounds like. It takes a row from a ResultSet and maps the fields to a domain object. In your case, you will be mapping the fields of the Customer table to the Customer domain object. Listing 7-37 shows the CustomerRowMapper you'll use for your JDBC implementations.

Listing 7-37. CustomerRowMapper

```
package com.apress.springbatch.chapter7;

import java.sql.ResultSet;
import java.sql.SQLException;

import org.springframework.jdbc.core.RowMapper;

public class CustomerRowMapper implements RowMapper {

    public Customer mapRow(ResultSet resultSet, int rowNumber) throws
        SQLException {
        Customer customer = new Customer();

        customer.setId(resultSet.getLong("id"));
        customer.setAddress(resultSet.getString("address"));
        customer.setCity(resultSet.getString("city"));
        customer.setFirstName(resultSet.getString("firstName"));
        customer.setLastName(resultSet.getString("lastName"));
        customer.setMiddleInitial(resultSet.getString("middleInitial"));
        customer.setState(resultSet.getString("state"));
        customer.setZip(resultSet.getString("zip"));

        return customer;
    }
}
```

With the ability to map your query results to a domain object, you need to be able to execute a query by opening a cursor to return results on demand. To do that, you will use Spring Batch's `org.springframework.batch.item.database.JdbcCursorItemReader`. This ItemReader opens a cursor (by creating a ResultSet) and have a row mapped to a domain object each time the read method is called by Spring Batch. To configure the JdbcCursorItemReader, you provide a minimum of three dependencies: a datasource, the query you want to run, and your RowMapper implementation. Listing 7-38 shows the configuration for your customerItemReader.

Listing 7-38. JDBC Cursor-Based customerItemReader

```
...
<beans:bean id="customerItemReader"
  class="org.springframework.batch.item.database.JdbcCursorItemReader">
  <beans:property name="dataSource" ref="dataSource"/>
  <beans:property name="sql" value="select * from customer"/>
  <beans:property name="rowMapper" ref="customerRowMapper"/>
</beans:bean>

<beans:bean id="customerRowMapper"
  class="com.apress.springbatch.chapter7.CustomerRowMapper"/>
...
```

I should point out that while the rest of the configurations for the job do not need to be changed (the same ItemWriter will work fine), you will need to update the reference to the customerFileReader in the copyFileStep to reference your new customerItemReader instead.

For this example, you will ignore the Transaction data that you have been working with in previous examples. Because of that, you will need to update your Customer's toString to print out valid output. Instead of printing the number of transactions each customer had, you will print out a formatted address for each customer. Listing 7-39 shows the updated toString method you can use.

Listing 7-39. Customer.toString

```
...
    @Override
    public String toString() {
        StringBuilder output = new StringBuilder();

        output.append(firstName + " " +
                    middleInitial + ". " +
                    lastName + "\n");
        output.append(address + "\n");
        output.append(city + ", " + state + "\n");
        output.append(zip);

        return output.toString();
    }
...
```

With the configuration you have now, each time Spring Batch calls the read() method on the JdbcCursorItemReader, the database will return a single row to be mapped to your domain object and processed.

To run your job, you use the same command you have been using: Java -jar copyJob.jar jobs/copyJob.xml copyJob outputFile=/output/jdbcOutput.txt. This command will execute your job generating the same type of output you have in your previous examples.

Although this example is nice, it lacks one key ingredient. The SQL is hardcoded. I can think of very few instances where SQL requires no parameters. Using the JdbcCursorItemReader, you use the same functionality to set parameters in your SQL as you would using the JdbcTemplate and a PreparedStatement. To do this, you need to write an org.springframework.jdbc.core.PreparedStatementSetter implementation. A PreparedStatementSetter is similar to a RowMapper; however, instead of mapping a ResultSet row to a domain object, you are mapping parameters to your SQL statement. If you wanted to get all of the customers in a given city, your configuration would look like Listing 7-40.

Listing 7-40. Processing Only Customers by a Given City

```
<beans:bean id="customerItemReader"
  class="org.springframework.batch.item.database.JdbcCursorItemReader">
  <beans:property name="dataSource" ref="dataSource"/>
  <beans:property name="sql" value="select * from customer where city = ?"/>
  <beans:property name="rowMapper" ref="customerRowMapper"/>
  <beans:property name="preparedStatementSetter" ref="citySetter"/>
</beans:bean>
```

```
<beans:bean id="citySetter"
  class="com.apress.springbatch.chapter7.CitySetter" scope="step">
  <beans:property name="city" value="#{jobParameters[city]}"/>
</beans:bean>

<beans:bean id="customerRowMapper"
  class="com.apress.springbatch.chapter7.CustomerRowMapper"/>
```

Notice that in the SQL, there is a ? where your parameter will go. This is nothing more than a standard PreparedStatement. Spring Batch will use your CitySetter to set the value of the city to be processed. This is the same processing paradigm as the JdbcTemplate in Spring Core uses. Listing 7-41 shows your CitySetter implementation.

Listing 7-41. CitySetter

```
package com.apress.springbatch.chapter7;

import java.sql.PreparedStatement;
import java.sql.SQLException;

import org.springframework.jdbc.core.PreparedStatementSetter;

public class CitySetter implements PreparedStatementSetter {

    private String city;

    public void setValues(PreparedStatement ps) throws SQLException {
        ps.setString(1, city);
    }

    public void setCity(String city) {
        this.city = city;
    }
}
```

This job is executed using virtually the same command as the previous example. he only difference is the addition of the city parameter: java -jar copyJob.jar jobs/copyJob.xml copyJob outputFile=/output/jdbcOutput.txt city="Carol Stream".

With the ability to not only stream items from the database but also inject parameters into your queries, this approach is useful in the real world. There are good and bad things about this approach. It can be a good thing to stream records in certain cases; however, when processing a million rows, the individual network overhead for each request can add up, which leads you to the other option, paging.

JDBC Paged Processing

When working with a paginated approach, Spring Batch returns the result set in chunks called pages. Each page is a predefined number of records to be returned by the database. It is important to note that when working with pages, the items your job will process will still be processed individually. There is no difference in the processing of the records. What differs is the way they are retrieved from the database. Instead of retrieving records one at a time, paging will essentially cache a page until they are needed to be processed. In this section, you'll update your configuration to return a page of 10 records in a page.

In order for paging to work, you need to be able to query based on a page size and page number (the number of records to return and which page you are currently processing). For example, if your total number of records is 10,000 and your page size is 100 records, you need to be able to specify that you are requesting the 20^(th) page of 100 records (or records 2,000 through 2100). To do this, you provide an implementation of the `org.springframework.batch.item.database.PagingQueryProvider` interface to the JdbcPagingItemReader. The PagingQueryProvider interface provides all of the functionality required to navigate a paged ResultSet.

Unfortunately, each database offers its own paging implementation. Because of this, you have the following two options:

1. Configure a database-specific implementation of the PagingQueryProvider. As of this writing, Spring Batch provides implementations for DB2, Derby, H2, HSql, MySql, Oracle, Postgres, SqlServer, and Sybase.

2. Configure your reader to use the `org.springframework.batch.item.database.support.SqlPagingQueryProviderF actoryBean`. This factory detects what database implementation to use.

Although the easier route is definitely the SqlPagingQueryProviderFactoryBean, it is important to note that each of the different databases implement paging in a different way. Because of this, you may want to use database specific options when tuning your jobs. Given that the analysis of each database type is out of the scope for this book, you will use the SqlPagingQueryProviderFactoryBean for your example.

To configure the JdbcPagingItemReader, you have four dependencies: a datasource, the PagingQueryProvider implementation, your RowMapper implementation, and the size of your page. You also have the opportunity to configure your SQL statement's parameters to be injected by Spring. Listing 7-42 shows the configuration for the JdbcPagingItemReader.

Listing 7-42. JdbcPagingItemReader Configuration

```
...
<beans:bean id="customerItemReader"
  class="org.springframework.batch.item.database.JdbcPagingItemReader"
  scope="step">
  <beans:property name="dataSource" ref="dataSource"/>
  <beans:property name="queryProvider">
    <beans:bean class="org.springframework.batch.item.database.support.
SqlPagingQueryProviderFactoryBean">
      <beans:property name="selectClause" value="select *"/>
      <beans:property name="fromClause" value="from Customer"/>
      <beans:property name="whereClause" value="where city = :city"/>
      <beans:property name="sortKey" value="lastName"/>
      <beans:property name="dataSource" ref="dataSource"/>
    </beans:bean>
  </beans:property>
  <beans:property name="parameterValues">
    <beans:map>
      <beans:entry key="city" value="#{jobParameters[city]}"/>
    </beans:map>
  </beans:property>
  <beans:property name="pageSize" value="10"/>
  <beans:property name="rowMapper" ref="customerRowMapper"/>
```

```
</beans:bean>

<beans:bean id="customerRowMapper"
  class="com.apress.springbatch.chapter7.CustomerRowMapper"/>
```

As you can see, to configure your JdbcPagingItemReader, you provide it a datasource, PagingQueryProvider, the parameters to be injected into your SQL, the size of each page, and the RowMapper implementation that will be used to map your results.

Within the PagingQueryProvider's configuration, you provide five pieces of information. The first three are the different pieces of your SQL statement: the select clause, the from clause, and the where clause of your statement. The next property you set is the sort key. It is important to sort your results when paging since instead of a single query being executed and the results being streamed, a paged approach will typically execute a query for each page. In order for the record order to be guaranteed across query executions, an order by is recommended and is applied to the generated SQL statement for any fields that are listed in the sortKey. Finally, you have a dataSource reference. You may wonder why you need to configure it in both the SqlPagingQueryProviderFactoryBean and the JdbcPagingItemReader. The SqlPagingQueryProviderFactoryBean uses the dataSource to determine what type of database it's working with. From there, it provides the appropriate implementation of the PagingQueryProvider to be used for your reader.

The use of parameters in a paging context is different than it is in the previous cursor example. Instead of creating a single SQL statement with question marks as parameter placeholders, you build your SQL statement in pieces. Within the whereClause string, you have the option of using either the standard question mark placeholders or you can use the named parameters as I did in the customerItemReader in Listing 7-42. From there, you can inject the values to be set as a map in your configuration. In this case, the city entry in the parameterValues map maps to the named parameter city in your whereClause string. If you wanted to use question marks instead of names, you would use the number of the question mark as the key for each parameter. With all of the pieces in place, Spring Batch will construct the appropriate query for each page each time it is required.

As you can see, straight JDBC interaction with a database for reading the items to be processed is actually quite simple. With not much more than a few lines of XML, you can have a performant ItemReader in place that allows you to input data to your job. However, JDBC isn't the only way to access database records. Object Relational Mapping (ORM) technologies like Hibernate and MyBatis have become popular choices for data access given their well-executed solution for mapping relational database tables to objects. You will take a look at how to use Hibernate for data access next.

Hibernate

Hibernate is the leading ORM technology in Java today. Written by Gaven King back in 2001, Hibernate provides the ability to map the object oriented model you use in your applications to a relational database. Hibernate uses XML files or annotations to configure mappings of objects to database tables; it also provides a framework for querying the database by object. This provides the ability to write queries based on the object structure with little or no knowledge of the underlying database structure. In this section, you will look at how to use Hibernate as your method of reading items from a database.

Using Hibernate in batch processing is not as straightforward as it is for web applications. For web applications, the typical scenario is to use the session in view pattern. In this pattern, the session is opened as a request comes into the server, all processing is done using the same session, and then the session is closed as the view is returned to the client. Although this works well for web applications that typically have small independent interactions, batch processing is different.

For batch processing, if you use Hibernate naively, you would use the normal stateful session implementation, read from it as you process your items, and write to it as you complete your processing closing the session once the step is complete. However, as mentioned, the standard session within

Hibernate is stateful. If you are reading a million items, processing them, then writing those same million items, the Hibernate session will cache the items as they are read and an OutOfMemoryException will occur.

Another issue with using Hibernate as a persistence framework for batch processing is that Hibernate incurs larger overhead than straight JDBC does. When processing millions of records, every millisecond can make a big difference[3].

I'm not trying to persuade you from against using Hibernate for your batch processing. In environments where you have the Hibernate objects mapped previously for another system, it can be a great way to get things up and running. Also, Hibernate does solve the fundamental issue of mapping objects to database tables in a very robust way. It's up to you and your requirements to determine if Hibernate or any ORM tool is right for your job.

Cursor processing with Hibernate

To use Hibernate with a cursor, you will need to configure the sessionFactory, your Customer mapping, the HibernateCursorItemReader, and add the Hibernate dependencies to your pom.xml file. Let's start with updating your pom.xml file.

Using Hibernate in your job will require three additional dependencies to be added to your POM. Listing 7-43 shows the addition of the hibernate-core, hibernate-entity manager, and the hibernate-annotations to pom.xml.

Listing 7-43. *Hibernate Dependencies in POM*

```
...
<dependency>
  <groupId>org.hibernate</groupId>
  <artifactId>hibernate-core</artifactId>
  <version>3.3.0.SP1</version>
</dependency>
<dependency>
  <groupId>org.hibernate</groupId>
  <artifactId>hibernate-entitymanager</artifactId>
  <optional>true</optional>
  <version>3.3.2.GA</version>
</dependency>
<dependency>
  <groupId>org.hibernate</groupId>
  <artifactId>hibernate-annotations</artifactId>
  <optional>true</optional>
  <version>3.4.0.GA</version>
</dependency>
<dependency>
  <groupId>org.springframework</groupId>
  <artifactId>spring-orm</artifactId>
  <version>${spring.framework.version}</version>
```

---

[3] A one millisecond increase per item over the course of a million items can add over 15 minutes of processing time to a single step.

```
</dependency>
...
```

With the Hibernate framework added to your project, you can map your Customer object to the Customer table in the database. To keep things simple, you will use Hibernate's annotations to configure the mapping. Listing 7-44 shows the updated Customer object mapped to the Customer table.

Listing 7-44. Customer Object Mapped to the Customer Table via Hibernate Annotations

```java
package com.apress.springbatch.chapter7;

import java.util.List;

import javax.persistence.Entity;
import javax.persistence.Id;
import javax.persistence.Table;

@Entity
@Table(name="customer")
public class Customer {
    @Id private long id;
    private String firstName;
    private String middleInitial;
    private String lastName;
    private String address;
    private String city;
    private String state;
    private String zip;
    @Transient
    List<Transaction> transactions;

    // Accessors go here
    ...

    @Override
    public String toString() {
        StringBuilder output = new StringBuilder();

        output.append(firstName + " " +
                    middleInitial + ". " +
                    lastName + "\n");
        output.append(address + "\n");
        output.append(city + ", " + state + "\n");
        output.append(zip);

        return output.toString();
    }
}
```

The Customer class's mapping consists of identifying the object as an Entity using the JPA annotation @Entity, specifying the table the entity maps to using the @Table annotation, and finally identifying the ID for the table with the @Id tag. All other attributes on the Customer will be mapped automatically by

Hibernate since you have named the columns in the database the same as the attributes in your object. For simplicity, you will mark the Transaction attribute as @Transient so that Hibernate ignores it.

Once you have Hibernate as part of your project and map your classes, you can configure Hibernate. To configure Hibernate, you will need to configure a SessionFactory, update your transaction manager, and create a hibernate.cfg.xml to tell Hibernate where to find the domain objects. Let's look at the updates to the launch-context.xml file first. Here you will add the session factory as well as change the transaction manager to use Spring's HibernateTransactionManager. Listing 7-45 shows the updates to the launch-context.xml.

Listing 7-45. Launch-config.xml Updates

```
...
<bean id="sessionFactory"
  class="org.springframework.orm.hibernate3.LocalSessionFactoryBean">
  <property name="dataSyource" ref="dataSyource" />
  <property name="configLocation">
    <value>classpath:hibernate.cfg.xml</value>
  </property>
  <property name="configurationClass">
    <value>org.hibernate.cfg.AnnotationConfiguration</value>
  </property>
  <property name="hibernateProperties">
    <props>
      <prop key="hibernate.show_sql">true</prop>
      <prop key="hibernate.format_sql">true</prop>
    </props>
  </property>
</bean>

<bean id="transactionManager"
  class="org.springframework.orm.hibernate3.HibernateTransactionManager"
  lazy-init="true">
  <property name="sessionFactory" ref="sessionFactory" />
</bean>
...
```

The SessionFactory you are using requires three things: a dataSource to provide a database connection to the Hibernate Session it creates, the location of the Hibernate configuration file (which is in the root of your class path in this case), and, since you are using Hibernate's annotations to map your domain objects, the org.hibernate.cfg.AnnotationConfiguration class for Hibernate to be able to read the mappings. The only other dependency you provide for the SessionFactory is configuring Hibernate to log and format the SQL it generates via the hibernateProperties.

The other change you made to the launch-context.xml file is to change the transactionManager implementation you are using. You will be using Spring's org.springframework.orm.hibernate.HibernateTransactionManager instead of the org.springframework.jdbc.datasource.DataSourceTransactionManager you have been using up to this point.

To configure Hibernate itself, you need to provide a hibernate.cfg.xml file in the root of your classpath. To do this, you create a new file in <myprojectname>/src/main/resources called hibernate.cfg.xml. Listing 7-46 shows that its sole use in your example is to list your domain classes for Hibernate.

Listing 7-46. hibernate.cfg.xml

```
<!DOCTYPE hibernate-configuration PUBLIC
"-//Hibernate/Hibernate Configuration DTD 3.0//EN"
 "http://hibernate.sourceforge.net/hibernate-configuration-3.0.dtd">

<hibernate-configuration>
  <session-factory>
    <mapping class="com.apress.springbatch.chapter7.Customer"/>
  </session-factory>
</hibernate-configuration>
```

Last but not least, you need to actually configure the
org.springframework.batch.item.database.HibernateCusorItemReader. Probably the simplest piece of
the puzzle, this ItemReader implementation requires only two dependencies: a Hibernate
SessionFactory and the HQL string to be executed. Listing 7-47 shows the configuration of the
HibernateCusorItemReader with those two dependencies included as well as injecting query parameters
the same way you did in the JdbcPagingItemReader earlier in this chapter.

Listing 7-47. Configuring the HibernateCursorItemReader

```
...
<beans:bean id="customerItemReader"
  class="org.springframework.batch.item.database.HibernateCursorItemReader"
  scope="step">
  <beans:property name="sessionFactory" ref="sessionFactory"/>
  <beans:property name="queryString"
    value="from Customer where city = :city"/>
  <beans:property name="parameterValues">
    <beans:map>
      <beans:entry key="city" value="#{jobParameters[city]}"/>
    </beans:map>
  </beans:property>
</beans:bean>
...
```

In this example, you used an HQL query as your method of querying the database. There are two
other ways to specify the query to execute. Table 7-3 covers all three options.

Table 7-3. *Hibernate Query Options*

Option	Type	Description
queryName	String	This references a named Hibernate query as configured in your Hibernate configurations.
queryString	String	This is an HQL query specified in your Spring configuration.
queryProvider	HibernateQueryProvider	This provides the ability to programmatically build your Hibernate Query.

That's all that is required to implement the Hibernate equivalent to JdbcCursorItemReader. Executing this job will output the same output as your previous job.

Paged Database Access with Hibernate

Hibernate, like JDBC, supports both cursor database access as well as paged database access. The only change required is to specify the HibernatePagingItemReader instead of the HibernateCursorItemReader in your copyJob.xml file and specify a page size for your ItemReader. Listing 7-48 shows the updated ItemReader using paged database access with Hibernate.

Listing 7-48. *Paging Database Access with Hibernate*

```
...
<beans:bean id="customerItemReader"
  class="org.springframework.batch.item.database.HibernatePagingItemReader"
  scope="step">
  <beans:property name="sessionFactory" ref="sessionFactory"/>
  <beans:property name="queryString"
    value="from Customer where city = :city"/>
  <beans:property name="parameterValues">
    <beans:map>
      <beans:entry key="city" value="#{jobParameters[city]}"/>
    </beans:map>
  </beans:property>
  <beans:property name="pageSize" value="10"/>
</beans:bean>
...
```

Using Hibernate can speed up development of batch processing in situations where the mapping already exists as well as simplify the mapping of relational data to domain objects. However, Hibernate is not the only kid on the ORM block. The Java Persistence API (or JPA for short) is the native Java implementation of ORM persistence. You'll look at that next.

JPA

Over the past few years, the majority of innovation in the Java world has been in the open source space. Spring, Hibernate, the various JVM languages like Clojure, Scala, and JRuby that have come onto the scene. All of these have been products of the open source movement. As those products have shown their usefulness, Sun (now Oracle) has integrated similar approaches into the native Java API. JPA is one such example. In this case, Gavin King (the original author of Hibernate) was one of the driving forces in the development of JSR 220. In this section, you will look at how to use the JPA as your method of database access for your batch processes.

Although, as you will see, JPA has a number of similarities to Hibernate, it is not a drop-in replacement. One of the notable features missing from the JPA capabilities that Hibernate supports is the ability to use a cursor for database access. JPA supports paging but not cursor driven access. In this example, you will use JPA to provide paged database access similar to the Hibernate paged example you used previously.

To configure JPA, you will need to create the JPA version of the `hibernate.cfg.xml`, the `persistence.xml` as well as update `launch-context.xml` and `copyJob.xml`. It is important to note that since you used the JPA annotations in your Hibernate example, there will be no need to change your Customer object itself. Let's get started by creating the `persistence.xml` file.

The `persistence.xml` file must reside in the `META-INF` folder of your built jar file per the Java spec. To get it there, you will create your file in the `<project_root>/src/main/resources/META-INF` directory. Maven will take care of getting this directory in the correct spot of your jar file when you build it later. The contents of your `persistence.xml` file are about as simple as you can get. The only thing you need it for is to define your persistence unit (a customer object) and associate it with the correct class (your Customer class). Listing 7-49 shows the `persistence.xml` file you will use.

Listing 7-49. `persistence.xml`

```
<persistence xmlns="http://java.sun.com/xml/ns/persistence"
  xmlns:xsi="http://www.w3.org/2001/XMLSchema-instance"
  xsi:schemaLocation="http://java.sun.com/xml/ns/persistence
    http://java.sun.com/xml/ns/persistence/persistence_1_0.xsd"
  version="1.0">

  <persistence-unit name="customer" transaction-type="RESOURCE_LOCAL">
    <class>com.apress.springbatch.chapter7.Customer</class>
  </persistence-unit>
</persistence>
```

With the `persistence.xml` file configured, you can update your `launch-context.xml` to use Spring's `org.springframework.orm.jpa.JpaTransactionManager` and its EntityManager, and to update the jobRepository. The configuration for your JpaTransactionManager and EntityManager should look very familiar. They are almost identical to the Hibernate configurations for the HibernateTransactionManager and SessionFactory, respectively. The small tweak you need to make to your jobRepository implementation is that you need to define the transaction isolation level to create ISOLATION_DEFAULT. Listing 7-50 shows launch-context.xml configured to use JPA for persistence.

Listing 7-50. `launch-context.xml`

```
<?xml version="1.0" encoding="UTF-8"?>
<beans xmlns="http://www.springframework.org/schema/beans"
  xmlns:p="http://www.springframework.org/schema/p"
```

```xml
  xmlns:xsi="http://www.w3.org/2001/XMLSchema-instance"
  xsi:schemaLocation="http://www.springframework.org/schema/beans
    http://www.springframework.org/schema/beans/spring-beans-3.0.xsd">

  <bean id="jobOperator"
    class="org.springframework.batch.core.launch.support.SimpleJobOperator"
    p:jobLauncher-ref="jobLauncher" p:jobExplorer-ref="jobExplorer"
    p:jobRepository-ref="jobRepository" p:jobRegistry-ref="jobRegistry" />

  <bean
    id="jobExplorer"class="org.springframework.batch.core.explore.support.
JobExplorerFactoryBean" p:dataSource-ref="dataSource" />

  <bean
    id="jobRegistry"class="org.springframework.batch.core.configuration.
support.MapJobRegistry" />

  <bean class="org.springframework.batch.core.configuration.support.
JobRegistryBeanPostProcessor">
    <property name="jobRegistry" ref="jobRegistry"/>
  </bean>

  <bean id="jobLauncher"
    class="org.springframework.batch.core.launch.support.SimpleJobLauncher">
    <property name="jobRepository" ref="jobRepository" />
  </bean>

  <bean id="dataSource" class="org.apache.commons.dbcp.BasicDataSource">
    <property name="driverClassName" value="${batch.jdbc.driver}" />
    <property name="url" value="${batch.jdbc.url}" />
    <property name="username" value="${batch.jdbc.user}" />
    <property name="password" value="${batch.jdbc.password}" />
  </bean>

  <bean id="transactionManager"
class="org.springframework.orm.jpa.JpaTransactionManager">
    <property name="entityManagerFactory" ref="entityManagerFactory" />
  </bean>

  <bean id="entityManagerFactory"
    class="org.springframework.orm.jpa.LocalContainerEntityManagerFactoryBean">
    <property name="dataSource" ref="dataSource" />
    <property name="persistenceUnitName" value="customer" />
    <property name="jpaVendorAdapter">
      <bean class="org.springframework.orm.jpa.vendor.HibernateJpaVendorAdapter">
        <property name="showSql" value="false" />
      </bean>
    </property>
    <property name="jpaDialect">
      <bean class="org.springframework.orm.jpa.vendor.HibernateJpaDialect" />
    </property>
  </bean>
```

215

```
  <bean id="jobRepository"
    class="org.springframework.batch.core.repository.support.
JobRepositoryFactoryBean">
    <property name="isolationLevelForCreate" value="ISOLATION_DEFAULT" />
    <property name="dataSource" ref="dataSource" />
    <property name="transactionManager" ref="transactionManager" />
  </bean>

  <bean id="placeholderProperties"
    class="org.springframework.beans.factory.config.
PropertyPlaceholderConfigurer">
    <property name="location" value="classpath:batch.properties" />
    <property name="systemPropertiesModeName"
      value="SYSTEM_PROPERTIES_MODE_OVERRIDE" />
    <property name="ignoreUnresolvablePlaceholders" value="true" />
    <property name="order" value="1" />
  </bean>
</beans>
```

The transactionManager relationship to the entityManagerFactoryBean is the same as Hibernate's relationship between the HibernateTransactionManager and the SessionFactory. For the EntityManager configuration, you specify a datasource like you did in Hibernate; however, since the JPA spec defines where to look for the persistence.xml file (in the META-INF directory), you don't need to configure that. You do need to tell your EntityManager the persistence unit name and configure the vendor implementation. Since Hibernate implements the JPA spec, you will use it for this example.

The last piece of the JPA puzzle is to configure your ItemReader. As mentioned, JPA does not support cursor database access but it does support paging database access. The ItemReader will be the org.springframework.batch.item.database.JpaPagingItemReader which uses three dependencies: the entityManager you configured in the launch-context.xml, a query to execute, and in your case, your query has a parameter, so you will inject the value of the parameter as well. Listing 7-51 shows the customerItemReader configured for JPA database access.

Listing 7-51. customerItemReader with JPA

```
...
<beans:bean id="customerItemReader"
  class="org.springframework.batch.item.database.JpaPagingItemReader"
  scope="step">
  <beans:property name="entityManagerFactory" ref="entityManagerFactory" />
  <beans:property name="queryString"
    value="select c from Customer c where c.city = :city" />
  <beans:property name="parameterValues">
    <beans:map>
      <beans:entry key="city" value="#{jobParameters[city]}"/>
    </beans:map>
  </beans:property>
</beans:bean>
...
```

Executing the job as it currently is configured will output a file containing all of the customers' names and addresses within the city specified at the command line. There's another way to specify

queries in JPA: the Query object. To use JPA's Query API, you need to implement the
org.springframework.batch.item.database.orm.JpaQueryProvider interface. The interface, which
consists of a createQuery() method and a setEntityManager(EntityManager em) method is used by the
JpaPagingItemReader to obtain the required Query to be executed. To make things easier, Spring batch
provides an abstract base class for you to extend, the
org.springframework.batch.item.database.orm.AbstractJpaQueryProvider. Listing 7-52 shows what the
implementation to return the same query (as configured in Listing 7-51) looks like.

Listing 7-52. CustomerByCityQueryProvider

```
package com.apress.springbatch.chapter7;

import javax.persistence.EntityManager;
import javax.persistence.Query;

import org.springframework.batch.item.database.orm.AbstractJpaQueryProvider;
import org.springframework.util.Assert;

public class CustomerByCityQueryProvider extends AbstractJpaQueryProvider {

    private String cityName;

    public Query createQuery() {
        EntityManager manager = getEntityManager();

        Query query =
            manager.createQuery("select c from Customer " +
                                "c where c.city = :city");
        query.setParameter("city", cityName);

        return query;
    }

    public void afterPropertiesSet() throws Exception {
        Assert.notNull(cityName);
    }

    public void setCityName(String cityName) {
        this.cityName = cityName;
    }
}
```

For the CustomerByCityQueryProvider, you use the AbstractJpaQueryProvider base class to handle
obtaining an EntityManager for you. From there, you create the JPA query, populate any parameters in
the query and return it to Spring Batch for execution. To configure your ItemReader to use the
CustomerByCityQueryProvider instead of the query string you provided previously, you simply swap the
queryString parameter with the queryProvider parameter, as shown in Listing 7-53.

Listing 7-53. Using the JpaQueryProvider

```
...
<beans:bean id="customerItemReader"
```

```
      class="org.springframework.batch.item.database.JpaPagingItemReader"
      scope="step">
      <beans:property name="entityManagerFactory" ref="entityManagerFactory" />
      <beans:property name="queryProvider">
        <beans:bean
          class="com.apress.springbatch.chapter7.CustomerByCityQueryProvider">
          <beans:property name="cityName" value="#{jobParameters[city]}"/>
        </beans:bean>
      </beans:property>
    </beans:bean>
    ...
```

Using JPA can limit an application's dependencies on third party libraries while still providing many of the benefits of ORM libraries like Hibernate.

Up to this point you have covered file and database input sources and the variety of ways you can obtain your input data from them. However, a common scenario concerns existing Java services that provide the data you need. In the next section, you will cover how to obtain data from your existing Java services.

Existing Services

Many companies have Java applications (web or otherwise) currently in production. These applications have gone through strenuous amounts of analysis, development, testing, and bug fixing. The code that comprises these applications is battle tested and proven to work.

So why can't you use that code in your batch processes? Let's use the example that your batch process requires you to read in customer objects. However, instead of a Customer object mapping to a single table or file like it has been up to now, your customer data is spread across multiple tables in multiple databases. Also, you never physically delete customers; instead you flag them as being deleted. A service to retrieve the customer objects already exists in your web-based application. How do you use that in your batch process? In this section you will look at how to call existing Spring services to provide data for your ItemReader.

Back in Chapter 4, you learned about a few adapters that Spring Batch provides for tasklets to be able to do different things, specifically the org.springframework.batch.core.step.tasklet.CallableTaskletAdapter, org.springframework.batch.core.step.tasklet.MethodInvokingTaskletAdapter and the org.springframework.batch.core.step.tasklet.SystemCommandTasklet. All three of these were used to wrap some other element in a way that Spring Batch could interact with it. To use an existing service within Spring Batch, the same pattern is used.

In this case, you will be using the org.springframework.batch.item.adapter.ItemReaderAdapter. This class takes two dependencies when it is configured: a reference to the service to call and the name of the method to call. You need to keep the following two things in mind when using the ItemReaderAdapter:

1. The object returned from each call is the object that will be returned by the ItemReader. If your service returns a single Customer, then that single Customer object will be the object passed onto the ItemProcessor and finally the ItemWriter. If a collection of Customer objects is returned by the service, it will be passed as a single item to the ItemProcessor and ItemWriter and it will be your responsibility to iterate over the collection.

2. Once the input is exhausted, the service method must return a null. This indicates to Spring Batch that the input is exhausted for this step.

For this example, you will use a service hardcoded to return a Customer object for each call until the list is exhausted. Once the List is exhausted, null will be returned for every call after. The CustomerService in Listing 7-54 generates a random list of Customer objects for your use.

Listing 7-54. CustomerService

```
package com.apress.springbatch.chapter7;

import Java.util.ArrayList;
import Java.util.List;
import Java.util.Random;

public class CustomerService {

    private List<Customer> customers;
    private int curIndex;

    private String [] firstNames = {"Michael", "Warren", "Ann", "Terrence",
                                    "Erica", "Laura", "Steve", "Larry"};
    private String middleInitial = "ABCDEFGHIJKLMNOPQRSTUVWXYZ";
    private String [] lastNames = {"Gates", "Darrow", "Donnelly", "Jobs",
                                   "Buffett", "Ellison", "Obama"};
    private String [] streets = {"4th Street", "Wall Street", "Fifth Avenue",
                                 "Mt. Lee Drive", "Jeopardy Lane",
                                 "Infinite Loop Drive", "Farnam Street",
                                 "Isabella Ave", "S. Greenwood Ave"};
    private String [] cities = {"Chicago", "New York", "Hollywood", "Aurora",
                                "Omaha", "Atherton"};
    private String [] states = {"IL", "NY", "CA", "NE"};

    private Random generator = new Random();

    public CustomerService() {
        curIndex = 0;

        customers = new ArrayList<Customer>();

        for(int i = 0; i < 100; i++) {
            customers.add(buildCustomer());
        }
    }

    private Customer buildCustomer() {
        Customer customer = new Customer();

        customer.setFirstName(
            firstNames[generator.nextInt(firstNames.length - 1)]);
        customer.setMiddleInitial(
            String.valueOf(middleInitial.charAt(
```

```
                    generator.nextInt(middleInitial.length() - 1))));
        customer.setLastName(
            lastNames[generator.nextInt(lastNames.length - 1)]);
        customer.setAddress(generator.nextInt(9999) + " " +
                            streets[generator.nextInt(streets.length - 1)]);
        customer.setCity(cities[generator.nextInt(cities.length - 1)]);
        customer.setState(states[generator.nextInt(states.length - 1)]);
        customer.setZip(String.valueOf(generator.nextInt(99999)));

        return customer;
    }

    public Customer getCustomer() {
        Customer cust = null;

        if(curIndex < customers.size()) {
            cust = customers.get(curIndex);
            curIndex++;
        }

        return cust;
    }
}
```

Finally, to use the service you have developed in Listing 7-54, using the ItemReaderAdapter, you configure your customerItemReader to call the getCustomer method for each item. Listing 7-55 shows the configuration for this.

Listing 7-55. *Configuring the ItemReaderAdapter to Call the CustomerService*

```
...
<beans:bean id="customerItemReader"
  class="org.springframework.batch.item.adapter.ItemReaderAdapter">
  <beans:property name="targetObject" ref="customerService"/>
  <beans:property name="targetMethod" value="getCustomer"/>
</beans:bean>

<beans:bean id="customerService"
  class="com.apress.springbatch.chapter7.CustomerService"/>
...
```

That's all that is required to use one of your existing services as the source of data for your batch job. Using existing services can allow you to reuse code that is tested and proven instead of running the risk of introducing new bugs by rewriting existing processes.

Spring Batch provides a wide array of ItemReader implementations, many of which you have covered up to now. However, there is now way the developers of the framework can plan for every possible scenario. Because of this, they provide the facilities for you to create your own ItemReader implementations. The next section will look at how to implement your own custom ItemReader.

Custom Input

Spring Batch provides readers for just about every type of input Java applications normally face, however if you are using a form of input that Spring Batch provides an ItemReader, you will need to create one yourself. Implementing the ItemReader interface's read() method is the easy part. However, what happens when you need to be able to restart your reader? How do you maintain state across executions? This section will look at how to implement an ItemReader that can handle state across executions.

As mentioned, implementing Spring Batch's ItemReader interface is actually quite simple. In fact, with a small tweak, you can convert the CustomerService you used in the previous section to an ItemReader. All you need to do is implement the interface and rename the method getCustomer() to read(). Listing 7-56 shows the updated code.

Listing 7-56. CustomerItemReader

```java
package com.apress.springbatch.chapter7;

import java.util.ArrayList;
import java.util.List;
import java.util.Random;

import org.springframework.batch.item.ItemReader;

public class CustomerItemReader implements ItemReader<Customer> {

    private List<Customer> customers;
    private int curIndex;

    private String [] firstNames = {"Michael", "Warren", "Ann", "Terrence",
                                    "Erica", "Laura", "Steve", "Larry"};
    private String middleInitial = "ABCDEFGHIJKLMNOPQRSTUVWXYZ";
    private String [] lastNames = {"Gates", "Darrow", "Donnelly", "Jobs",
                                   "Buffett", "Ellison", "Obama"};
    private String [] streets = {"4th Street", "Wall Street", "Fifth Avenue",
                                 "Mt. Lee Drive", "Jeopardy Lane",
                                 "Infinite Loop Drive", "Farnam Street",
                                 "Isabella Ave", "S. Greenwood Ave"};
    private String [] cities = {"Chicago", "New York", "Hollywood", "Aurora",
                                "Omaha", "Atherton"};
    private String [] states = {"IL", "NY", "CA", "NE"};

    private Random generator = new Random();

    public CustomerItemReader () {
        curIndex = 0;

        customers = new ArrayList<Customer>();

        for(int i = 0; i < 100; i++) {
            customers.add(buildCustomer());
        }
    }
```

```
        private Customer buildCustomer() {
            Customer customer = new Customer();

            customer.setFirstName(
                firstNames[generator.nextInt(firstNames.length - 1)]);
            customer.setMiddleInitial(
                String.valueOf(middleInitial.charAt(
                    generator.nextInt(middleInitial.length() - 1))));
            customer.setLastName(
                lastNames[generator.nextInt(lastNames.length - 1)]);
            customer.setAddress(generator.nextInt(9999) + " " +
                            streets[generator.nextInt(streets.length - 1)]);
            customer.setCity(cities[generator.nextInt(cities.length - 1)]);
            customer.setState(states[generator.nextInt(states.length - 1)]);
            customer.setZip(String.valueOf(generator.nextInt(99999)));

            return customer;
        }

    public Customer read() {
        Customer cust = null;

        if(curIndex < customers.size()) {
            cust = customers.get(curIndex);
            curIndex++;
        }

        return cust;
    }
}
```

Even if you ignore the fact that your CustomerItemReader builds a new list with each run, the CustomerItemReader as it is written in Listing 7-56 will restart at the beginning of your list each time the job is executed. Although this will be the behavior you want in many cases, it will not always be the case. Instead, if there is an error after processing half a million records out of a million, you will want to start over again in that same chunk.

To provide the ability for Spring Batch to maintain the state of your reader in the jobRepository and restart your reader where you left off, you need to implement an additional interface, the ItemStream interface. Shown in Listing 7-57, the ItemStream interface consists of three methods: open, update, and close.

Listing 7-57. *The ItemStream Interface*

```
package org.springframework.batch.item;

public interface ItemStream {

  void open(ExecutionContext executionContext) throws ItemStreamException;
  void update(ExecutionContext executionContext) throws ItemStreamException;
  void close() throws ItemStreamException;
}
```

Each of the three methods of the ItemStream interface are called by Spring Batch during the execution of a step. open is called to initialize any required state within your ItemReader. This includes the opening of any files or database connections as well as when restarting a job. The open method could be used to reload the number of records that had been processed so they could be skipped during the second execution. update is used by Spring Batch as processing occurs to update that state. Keeping track of how many records or chunks have been processed is a use for the update method. Finally, the close method is used to close any required resources (close files, etc).

You will notice that the open and update provide access to the ExecutionContext that you did not have a handle on in your ItemReader implementation. This is because Spring Batch will use the open method to reset the state of the reader when a job is restarted. It will also use the update method to learn the current state of the reader (which record you are currently on) as each item is processed. Finally, the close method is used to clean up any resources used in the ItemStream.

Now you may be wondering how you can use the ItemStream interface for your ItemReader if it doesn't have the read method. Short answer: you don't. Instead you'll use a utility interface, org.springframework.batch.item.ItemStreamReader, that extends both the ItemStream and the ItemReader interfaces. This will allow you to implement the ItemReader functionality as well as maintain the state of your reader via Spring Batch. Listing 7-58 shows your CustomerItemReader updated to implement the ItemStreamReader interface.

Listing 7-58. CustomerItemReader Implementing the ItemStreamReader Interface

```
package com.apress.springbatch.chapter7;

import java.util.ArrayList;
import java.util.List;
import java.util.Random;

import org.springframework.batch.item.ExecutionContext;
import org.springframework.batch.item.ItemStreamException;
import org.springframework.batch.item.ItemStreamReader;

public class CustomerItemReader implements ItemStreamReader<Customer> {

    private List<Customer> customers;
    private int curIndex;
    private String INDEX_KEY = "current.index.customers";

    private String [] firstNames = {"Michael", "Warren", "Ann", "Terrence",
                                    "Erica", "Laura", "Steve", "Larry"};
    private String middleInitial = "ABCDEFGHIJKLMNOPQRSTUVWXYZ";
    private String [] lastNames = {"Gates", "Darrow", "Donnelly", "Jobs",
                                   "Buffett", "Ellison", "Obama"};
    private String [] streets = {"4th Street", "Wall Street", "Fifth Avenue",
                                 "Mt. Lee Drive", "Jeopardy Lane",
                                 "Infinite Loop Drive", "Farnam Street",
                                 "Isabella Ave", "S. Greenwood Ave"};
    private String [] cities = {"Chicago", "New York", "Hollywood", "Aurora",
                                "Omaha", "Atherton"};
    private String [] states = {"IL", "NY", "CA", "NE"};
```

```
    private Random generator = new Random();

    public CustomerItemReader() {
        customers = new ArrayList<Customer>();

        for(int i = 0; i < 100; i++) {
            customers.add(buildCustomer());
        }
    }

    private Customer buildCustomer() {
        Customer customer = new Customer();

        customer.setFirstName(
            firstNames[generator.nextInt(firstNames.length - 1)]);
        customer.setMiddleInitial(
            String.valueOf(middleInitial.charAt(
                generator.nextInt(middleInitial.length() - 1))));
        customer.setLastName(
            lastNames[generator.nextInt(lastNames.length - 1)]);
        customer.setAddress(generator.nextInt(9999) + " " +
                            streets[generator.nextInt(streets.length - 1)]);
        customer.setCity(cities[generator.nextInt(cities.length - 1)]);
        customer.setState(states[generator.nextInt(states.length - 1)]);
        customer.setZip(String.valueOf(generator.nextInt(99999)));

        return customer;
    }

    public Customer read() {
        Customer cust = null;

        if(curIndex == 50) {
            throw new RuntimeException("This will end your execution");
        }

        if(curIndex < customers.size()) {
            cust = customers.get(curIndex);
            curIndex++;
        }

        return cust;
    }

    public void close() throws ItemStreamException {
    }

    public void open(ExecutionContext executionContext) throws ItemStreamException {
        if(executionContext.containsKey(INDEX_KEY)) {
            int index = executionContext.getInt(INDEX_KEY);

            if(index == 50) {
```

```
                curIndex = 51;
            } else {
                curIndex = index;
            }
        } else {
            curIndex = 0;
        }
    }

    public void update(ExecutionContext executionContext) throws ItemStreamException {
        executionContext.putInt(INDEX_KEY, curIndex);
    }
}
```

The bold sections of Listing 7-58 show the updates to the CustomerItemReader. First, the class was changed to implement the ItemStreamReader interface. Then the close, open and update methods were added. In the update method, you add a key value pair to the executionContext that indicates the current record being processed. The open method will check to see if that value has been set. If it has been set, that means that this is the restart of your job. In the run method, to force the job to end, you added code to throw a RuntimeException after the 50th customer. In the open method, if the index being restored is 50, you'll know it was due to your previous code so you will just skip that record. Otherwise, you'll try again.

The other piece you need to do is configure your new ItemReader implementation. In this case, your ItemReader has no dependencies so all you will need to do is define the bean with the correct name (so it is referred to in your existing copyJob). Listing 7-59 shows the configuration of the CustomerItemReader.

Listing 7-59. CustomerItemReader Configuration

```
…
<beans:bean id="customerItemReader"
  class="com.apress.springbatch.chapter7.CustomerItemReader"/>
…
```

That really is it. Now if you execute your job, after you process 50 records, your CustomerItemReader will throw an Exception causing your job to fail. However, if you look in the BATCH_STEP_EXECUTION_CONTEXT table of your jobRepository, you will be happy to see what is listed in Listing 7-60.

Listing 7-60. The Step Execution Context

```
mysql> select * from BATCH_STEP_EXECUTION_CONTEXT where STEP_EXECUTION_ID = 8495;
+------------------+-----------------------------------------------------------------------
-----+-----------------------+
| STEP_EXECUTION_ID | SHORT_CONTEXT
| SERIALIZED_CONTEXT |
+------------------+-----------------------------------------------------------------------
-----+-----------------------+
|              8495 |
{"map":{"entry":[{"string":"FlatFileItemWriter.current.count","long":2655},{"string":"FlatFi
leItemWriter.written","long":50},{"string":"current.index.customers","int":50}]}} | NULL
|
```

Although a bit hard to read, you'll notice that Spring Batch has saved your commit count in the jobRepository. Because of this and your logic to skip the 50th customer the second time around, you can re-execute your job knowing that Spring Batch will start back where it left off and your writer will skip the item that caused the error.

Files, databases, services and even your own custom ItemReaders—Spring Batch provides you with a wide array of input options of which you have truly only scratched the surface here. Unfortunately, not all of the data you work with in the real world is as pristine as the data you have been working with here. However, not all errors are ones that need to stop processing. In the next section you will look at some of the ways that Spring Batch allows you to deal with input errors.

Error Handling

Things can go wrong in any part of a Spring Batch application—on startup, when reading input, processing input, or writing output. In this section, you will look at ways to handle different errors that can occur during batch processing.

Skipping Records

When there is an error reading a record from your input, you have a couple different options. First, an Exception can be thrown that causes processing to stop. Depending on how many records need to be processed and the impact of not processing this single record, this may be a drastic resolution. Instead, Spring Batch provides the ability to skip a record when a specified Exception is thrown. This section will look at how to use this technique to skip records based upon specific Exceptions.

There are two pieces involved in choosing when a record is skipped. The first is under what conditions to skip the record, specifically what exceptions you will ignore. When any error occurs during the reading process, Spring Batch throws an exception. In order to determine what to skip, you need to identify what exceptions to skip.

The second part of skipping input records is how many records you will allow the step to skip before considering the step execution failed. If you skip one or two records out of a million, not a big deal; however, skipping half a million out of a million is probably wrong. It's your responsibility to determine the threshold.

To actually skip records, all you need to do is tweak your configuration to specify the exceptions you want to skip and how many times it's okay to do so. Say you want to skip the first 10 records that throw any `org.springframework.batch.item.ParseException`. Listing 7-61 shows the configuration for this scenario.

Listing 7-61. *Configuring to Skip 10 ParseExceptions*

```
<step id="copyFileStep">
  <tasklet>
    <chunk reader="customerItemReader" writer="outputWriter"
      commit-interval="10" skip-limit="10">
      <skippable-exception-classes>
        <include class="org.springframework.batch.item.ParseException"/>
      </skippable-exception-classes>
    </chunk>
  </tasklet>
</step>
```

In this scenario, you have a single exception that you want to be able to skip. However, sometimes this can be a rather exhaustive list. The configuration in Listing 7-61 allows the skipping of a specific exception, but it might be easier to configure the ones you don't want to skip instead of the ones you do. To do this, you use a combination of the include tag like Listing 7-61 did and the exclude tag. Listing 7-62 shows how to configure the opposite of your previous example (skipping all exceptions except for the ParseException).

Listing 7-62. Configuring to Skip All Exceptions Except the ParseException

```
<step id="copyFileStep">
  <tasklet>
    <chunk reader="customerItemReader" writer="outputWriter"
      commit-interval="10" skip-limit="10">
      <skippable-exception-classes>
        <include class="java.lang.Exception"/>
        <exclude class="org.springframework.batch.item.ParseException"/>
      </skippable-exception-classes>
    </chunk>
  </tasklet>
</step>
```

The configuration in Listing 7-62 specifies that any Exception that extends java.lang.Exception except for org.springframework.batch.item.ParseException will be skipped up to 10 times.

There is a third way to specify what Exceptions to skip and how many times to skip them. Spring Batch provides an interface called org.springframework.batch.core.step.skip.SkipPolicy. This interface, with its single method shouldSkip, takes the Exception that was thrown and the number of times records have been skipped. From there, any implementation can determine what Exceptions they should skip and how many times. Listing 7-63 shows a SkipPolicy implementation that will not allow a java.io.FileNotFoundException to be skipped but 10 ParseExceptions to be skipped.

Listing 7-63. FileVerificationSkipper

```
package com.apress.springbatch.chapter7;

import java.io.FileNotFoundException;

import org.springframework.batch.core.step.skip.SkipLimitExceededException;
import org.springframework.batch.core.step.skip.SkipPolicy;
import org.springframework.batch.item.ParseException;

public class FileVerificationSkipper implements SkipPolicy {

    public boolean shouldSkip(Throwable exception, int skipCount)
        throws SkipLimitExceededException {

        if(exception instanceof FileNotFoundException) {
            return false;
        } else if(exception instanceof ParseException && skipCount <= 10) {
            return true;
        } else {
            return false;
        }
```

```
        }
}
```

Skipping records is a common practice in batch processing. It allows what is typically a much larger process than a single record to continue with minimal impact. Once you can skip a record that has an error, you may want to do something additional like log it for future evaluation. The next section discusses an approach for just that.

Logging Invalid Records

While skipping problematic records is a useful tool, by itself it can raise an issue. In some scenarios, the ability to skip a record is okay. Say you are mining data and come across something you can't resolve; it's probably okay to skip it. However, when you get into situations where money is involved, say when processing transactions, just skipping a record probably will not be a robust enough solution. In cases like these, it is helpful to be able to log the record that was the cause of the error. In this section, you will look at using an ItemListener to record records that were invalid.

The ItemReadListener interface consists of three methods: beforeRead, afterRead, and onReadError. For the case of logging invalid records as they are read in, you can use the ItemListenerSupport class and override the onReadError to log what happened. It's important to point out that Spring Batch does a good job building its Exceptions for file parsing to inform you of what happened and why. On the database side, things are a little less in the framework's hands as most of the actual database work is done by other frameworks (Spring itself, Hibernate, etc). It is important that as you develop your own processing (custom ItemReaders, RowMappers, etc) that you include enough detail for you to diagnose the issue from the Exception itself.

In this example, you will read data in from the Customer file from the beginning of the chapter. When an Exception is thrown during input, you will log the record that caused the exception and the exception itself. To do this, the CustomerItemListener will take the exception thrown and if it is a FlatFileParseException, you will have access to the record that caused the issue and information on what went wrong. Listing 7-64 shows the CustomerItemListener.

Listing 7-64. *CustomerItemListener*

```java
package com.apress.springbatch.chapter7;

import org.apache.log4j.Logger;
import org.springframework.batch.core.listener.ItemListenerSupport;
import org.springframework.batch.item.file.FlatFileParseException;

public class CustomerItemListener extends
    ItemListenerSupport<Customer, Customer> {

    private Logger logger = Logger.getLogger(CustomerItemListener.class);

    @Override
    public void onReadError(Exception e) {
        if(e instanceof FlatFileParseException) {
            FlatFileParseException ffpe = (FlatFileParseException) e;

            StringBuilder errorMessage = new StringBuilder();
            errorMessage.append("An error occured while processing the " +
                            ffpe.getLineNumber() +
```

```
                         " line of the file.  Below was the faulty " +
                         "input.\n");
              errorMessage.append(ffpe.getInput() + "\n");

              logger.error(errorMessage.toString(), ffpe);
          } else {
              logger.error("An error has occured", e);
          }
      }
  }
}
```

Configuring your listener requires you to update the step reading the file. In your case, you have only one step in your copyJob. Listing 7-65 shows the configuration for this listener.

Listing 7-65. *Configuring the CustomerItemListener*

```
...
<beans:bean id="customerItemLogger"
    class="com.apress.springbatch.chapter7.CustomerItemListener"/>

<job id="copyJob">
    <step id="copyFileStep">
        <tasklet>
            <chunk reader="customerFileReader" writer="outputWriter"
                commit-interval="10" skip-limit="100">
                <skippable-exception-classes>
                    <include class="java.lang.Exception"/>
                </skippable-exception-classes>
            </chunk>
            <listeners>
                <listener ref="customerItemLogger"/>
            </listeners>
        </tasklet>
    </step>
</job>
...
```

If you use the fixed length record job as an example and execute it with a file that contains an input record longer than 63 characters, an exception will be thrown. However, since you have configured your job to skip all exceptions that extend Exception, the exception will not affect your job's results, yet your customerItemLogger will be called and log the item as required. When you execute this job, you see two things. The first is a FlatFileParseException for each record that is invalid. The second are your log messages. Listing 7-66 shows an example of the log messages your job generates on error.

Listing 7-66. *Output of the CustomerItemLogger*

```
2011-05-03 23:49:22,148 ERROR main [com.apress.springbatch.chapter7.CustomerItemListener] -
<An error occured while processing the 1 line of the file.  Below was the faulty input.
Michael   TMinella   123   4th Street           Chicago  IL60606ABCDE
>
```

Using nothing more that log4j, you can get the input that failed to parse from the FlatFileParseException and log it to your log file. However, this by itself does not accomplish your goal of logging the error record to a file and continuing on. In this scenario, your job will log the record that caused the issue and fail. In the last section, you will look at how to handle having no input when your jobs run.

Dealing with No Input

A SQL query that returns no rows is not an uncommon occurrence. Empty files exist in many situations. But do they make sense for your batch process? In this section, you will look at how Spring Batch handles reading input sources that have no data.

When a reader attempts to read from an input source and a null is returned the first time, by default this is treated like any other time a reader receives a null; it considers the step complete. While this approach may work in the majority of the scenarios, you may need to know when a given query returns zero rows or a file is empty.

If you want to cause your step to fail or take any other action (send an e-mail, etc) when no input has been read, you use a StepListener. In Chapter 4, you used a StepListener to log the beginning and end of your step. In this case, you can use the StepListener's @AfterStep method to see how many records were read and react accordingly. Listing 7-67 shows how you would mark a step failed if no records were read.

Listing 7-67. *EmptyInputStepFailer*

```
package com.apress.springbatch.chapter7;

import org.springframework.batch.core.ExitStatus;
import org.springframework.batch.core.StepExecution;
import org.springframework.batch.core.annotation.AfterStep;

public class EmptyInputStepFailer {

    @AfterStep
    public ExitStatus afterStep(StepExecution execution) {
        if(execution.getReadCount() > 0) {
            return execution.getExitStatus();
        } else {
            return ExitStatus.FAILED;
        }
    }
}
```

To configure your listener, you configure it like you would any other StepListener. Listing 7-68 covers the configuration in this instance.

Listing 7-68. *Configuring the EmptyInputStepFailer*

```
...
<beans:bean id="emptyFileFailer"
  class="com.apress.springbatch.chapter7.EmptyInputStepFailer"/>

<step id="copyFileStep">
```

```
<tasklet>
  <chunk reader="customerItemReader" writer="outputWriter"
    commit-interval="10"/>
  <listeners>
    <listener ref="emptyFileFailer"/>
  </listeners>
</tasklet>
</step>
...
```

By running a job with this step configured, instead of your job ending with the status COMPLETED if no input was found, the job will fail, allowing you to obtain the expected input and rerun the job.

Summary

Reading and writing take up the vast majority of a batch process and as such, is one of the most important pieces of the Spring Batch framework. In this chapter, you took a thorough (but not exhaustive) look at the ItemReader options within the framework. Now that you can read in an item, you need to be able to do something with it. ItemProcessors, which make things happen, are covered in the next chapter.

## CHAPTER 8

Item Processors

In the previous chapter, you learned how to read various types of input using the components of Spring Batch. Obviously, obtaining the input for any piece of software is an important aspect of the project; however, it doesn't mean much if you don't do something with it. Item processors are the component within Spring Batch where you do something with your input. In this chapter, you will look at the ItemProcessor interface and see how you can use it to develop your own processing of batch items.

- In the "Introduction to ItemProcessors" section,,you'll start with a quick overview of what an ItemProcessor is and how it fits into the flow of a step.

- Spring Batch provides utility ItemProcessors like the ItemProcessorAdapter, which uses existing services as your ItemProcessor implementation. In the "Using Spring Batch's ItemProcessors" section, you'll take and in-depth look at each of the processors the framework provides.

- In many cases, you will want to develop your own ItemProcessor implementation. In the "Writing Your Own ItemProcessors" section, you will look at different considerations as you implement an example ItemProcessor.

- A common use of an ItemProcessor is to filter out items that were read in by an ItemReader from being written by the step's ItemWriter. In the "Filtering Items" section, you'll look at an example of how this is accomplished.

Introduction to ItemProcessors

In Chapter 7, you looked at ItemReaders, the input facility you use within Spring Batch. Once you have received your input, you have two options. The first is to just write it back out as you did in the examples in the last chapter. There are many times when that will make sense. Migrating data from one system to another or loading data into a database initially are two examples of where reading input and writing it directly without any additional processing makes sense.

However, in most scenarios, you are going to need to do something with the data you read in. Spring Batch has broken up the pieces of a step to allow a good separation of concerns between reading, processing, and writing. Doing this allows you the opportunity to do a couple unique things, such as the following:

- *Validate input:* In the original version of Spring Batch, validation occurred at the ItemReader by subclassing the ValidatingItemReader class. The issue with this approach is that none of the provided readers subclassed the ValidatingItemReader class so if you wanted validation, you couldn't use any of the included readers. Moving the validation step to the ItemProcessor allows validation to occur on an object before processing, regardless of the input method. This makes much more sense from a division-of-concerns perspective.

- *Reuse existing services:* Just like the ItemReaderAdapter you looked at in Chapter 7 to reuse services for your input, Spring Batch provides an ItemProcessorAdapter for the same reason.

- *Chain ItemProcessors:* There are situations where you will want to perform multiple actions on a single item within the same transaction. Although you could write your own custom ItemProcessor to do all of the logic in a single class, that couples your logic to the framework, which is something you want to avoid. Instead, Spring Batch allows you to create a list of ItemProcessors that will be executed in order against each item.

To accomplish this, the org.springframework.batch.item.ItemProcessor interface consists of a single method process shown in Listing 8-1. It takes an item as read from your ItemReader and returns another item.

Listing 8-1. ItemProcessor Interface

```
package org.springframework.batch.item;

public interface ItemProcessor<I, O> {

    O process(I item) throws Exception;
}
```

It's important to note that the type the ItemProcessor receives as input does not need to be the same type it returns. The framework allows for you to read in one type of object and pass it to an ItemProcessor and have the ItemProcessor return a different type for writing. With this feature, you should note that the type the final ItemProcessor returns is required to be the type the ItemWriter takes as input. You should also be aware that if an ItemProcessor returns null, all processing of the item will stop. In other words, any further ItemProcessors for that item will not be called nor shall the ItemWriter for the step. However, unlike returning null from an ItemReader, which indicates to Spring Batch that all input has been exhausted, processing of other items will continue when an ItemProcessor returns null.

■**Note** The type an ItemProcessor returns doesn't need to be the same as it takes in as input.

Let's take a look at how to use ItemProcessors for your jobs. To start, you'll dig into the ones provided by the framework.

Using Spring Batch's ItemProcessors

When you looked at the ItemReaders previously, there was a lot of ground to cover regarding what was provided from Spring Batch because input and output are two relatively standard things. Reading from a file is the same in most cases. Writing to a database works the same with most databases. However, what you do to each item is different based upon your business requirements. This is really what makes each job different. Because of this, the framework can only provide you with the facility to either implement your own or wrap existing logic. This section will cover the ItemProcessors that are included in the Spring Batch framework.

ValidatingItemProcessor

You'll start your look at Spring Batch's ItemProcessor implementations with where you left off in Chapter 7. Previously, you handled obtaining input for your jobs; however, just because you can read it doesn't mean it's valid. Data validation with regards to types and format can occur within an ItemReader; however, validation via business rules is best left once the item has been constructed. That's why Spring Batch provides an ItemProcessor implementation for validating input called the ValidatingItemProcessor. In this section, you will look at how to use it to validate your input.

Input Validation

The `org.springframework.batch.item.validator.ValidatingItemProcessor` is an implementation of the ItemProcessor interface that allows you to set an implementation of Spring Batch's Validator interface[1] to be used to validate the incoming item prior to processing. If the item passes validation, it will be processed. If not, an `org.springframework.batch.item.validator.ValidationException` is thrown, causing normal Spring Batch error handling to kick in.

JSR 303 is the Java specification for bean validation. Because it only came out in late 2009, it hasn't been as widely integrated as I would like; however, I consider it a better alternative to the Spring Modules[2] examples show in most Spring Batch documentation. The validation performed via the `javax.validation.*` code is configured via annotations. There is a collection of annotations that predefine validation functions out of the box; you also have the ability to create your own validation functions. Let's start by looking at how you would validate a `Customer` class like the one in Listing 8-2.

Listing 8-2. Customer Class

```
package com.apress.springbatch.chapter8;

public class Customer {
    private String firstName;
    private String middleInitial;
    private String lastName;
    private String address;
    private String city;
```

---

[1] Although Spring does have a Validator interface of its own, the ValidatingItemProcessor uses one from Spring Batch instead.
[2] The Spring Modules project was retired as of late 2010 in favor of the Spring Extensions project.

```
    private String state;
    private String zip;

    // Getters & setters go here
...
}
```

If you look at the Customer class in Listing 8-2, you can quickly determine some basic validation rules.

- Not null: firstName, lastName, address, city, state, zip.

- Alphabetic: firstName, middleInitial, lastName, city, state.

- Numeric: zip.

- Size: middleInitial should be no longer than one character; state should be no longer than two characters; and zip should be no longer than five characters.

There are further validations you can perform on the data provided zip is a valid ZIP code for the city and state. However, this provides you with a good start. Now that you have identified the things you want to validate, you can describe them to your validator via annotations on the Customer object. Specifically, you will be using the @NotNull, @Size, and @Pattern annotations for these rules. To use these, you will need to update your pom to reference a new library. You will use the Hibernate implementation of the JSR 303 annotations, so you will need to add it to your project. Listing 8-3 shows the dependency you need to add.

Listing 8-3. *Hibernate Implementation of JSR 303 Dependency*

```
<dependency>
    <groupId>org.hibernate</groupId>
    <artifactId>hibernate-validator</artifactId>
    <version>4.0.2.GA</version>
</dependency>
```

With the dependency in place, you can actually update your code to use the annotations. Listing 8-4 shows their use on the Customer object.

Listing 8-4. *Customer Object with Validation Annotations*

```
package com.apress.springbatch.chapter8;

import javax.validation.constraints.NotNull;
import javax.validation.constraints.Pattern;
import javax.validation.constraints.Size;

public class Customer {

    @NotNull
    @Pattern(regexp="[a-zA-Z]+")
    private String firstName;

    @Size(min=1, max=1)
```

```
    private String middleInitial;

    @NotNull
    @Pattern(regexp="[a-zA-Z]+")
    private String lastName;

    @NotNull
    @Pattern(regexp="[0-9a-zA-Z\\. ]+")
    private String address;

    @NotNull
    @Pattern(regexp="[a-zA-Z\\. ]+")
    private String city;

    @NotNull
    @Size(min=2,max=2)
    @Pattern(regexp="[A-Z]{2}")
    private String state;

    @NotNull
    @Size(min=5,max=5)
    @Pattern(regexp="\\d{5}")
    private String zip;

    // Accessors go here
    ...
}
```

A quick look at the rules defined in Listing 8-4 may make you ask why use both the @Size annotation and the @Pattern one when the regular expression defined in the @Pattern would satisfy both. You are correct. However, each annotation allows you to specify a unique error message (if you want); moreover, being able to identify if the field was the wrong size vs. the wrong format may be helpful in the future.

At this point, you have defined the validation rules you will use for your Customer item. However, there is no Validator implementation within Spring yet that handles the execution of these rules. Because of this, you will have to create your own. Fortunately, it only requires a couple lines of code to create a universal validator for the basic JSR 303 validations. To do this, you will implement Spring Batch's org.springframework.batch.item.validator.Validator interface and use Hibernate's implementation of the javax.validation.Validator to validate your item. Listing 8-5 shows the code for the validator.

Listing 8-5. *BeanValidator*

```
package com.apress.springbatch.chapter8;

import java.util.Set;

import javax.validation.ConstraintViolation;
import javax.validation.Validation;
import javax.validation.ValidatorFactory;
```

```
import org.springframework.batch.item.validator.ValidationException;
import org.springframework.batch.item.validator.Validator;
import org.springframework.beans.factory.InitializingBean;

@SuppressWarnings("rawtypes")
public class BeanValidator implements Validator, InitializingBean {

    private javax.validation.Validator validator;

    public void afterPropertiesSet() throws Exception {
        ValidatorFactory validatorFactory = Validation.buildDefaultValidatorFactory();
        validator = validatorFactory.usingContext().getValidator();
    }

    public void validate(Object target) throws ValidationException {

        Set<ConstraintViolation<Object>> constraintViolations = validator.validate(target);

        if(constraintViolations.size() > 0) {
            buildValidationException(constraintViolations);
        }
    }

    private void buildValidationException(
            Set<ConstraintViolation<Object>> constraintViolations) {
        StringBuilder message = new StringBuilder();

        for (ConstraintViolation<Object> constraintViolation : constraintViolations) {
            message.append(constraintViolation.getMessage() + "\n");
        }

        throw new ValidationException(message.toString());
    }
}
```

Implementing Spring Batch's Validator interface as well as Spring's
org.springframework.beans.factory.InitializingBean interface allows you to obtain an instance of the
Java validator in the afterPropertiesSet method and execute the validation within the validate
method. Once you have validated the object, you can construct a ValidationException out of the
messages you received if any attributes failed validation.

■**Note** The Validator interface included in the Spring Batch framework is not the same as the Validator interface
that is part of the core Spring framework. Spring Batch provides an adapter class, SpringValidator, to handle
the differences.

Let's see how all of this works together by creating a job to put them to use. Your job will read a
comma-delimited file into your Customer object, which will then be valided as part of the

ValidatingItemProcessor and written out to a csv, as you did in Chapter 7. To start, Listing 8-6 shows an example of the input you will process.

Listing 8-6. customer.csv

```
Richard,N,Darrow,5570 Isabella Ave,St. Louis,IL,58540
Warren,L,Darrow,4686 Mt. Lee Drive,St. Louis,NY,94935
Barack,G,Donnelly,7844 S. Greenwood Ave,Houston,CA,38635
Ann,Z,Benes,2447 S. Greenwood Ave,Las Vegas,NY,55366
Laura,9S,Minella,8177 4th Street,Dallas,FL,04119
Erica,Z,Gates,3141 Farnam Street,Omaha,CA,57640
Warren,M,Williams,6670 S. Greenwood Ave,Hollywood,FL,37288
Harry,T,Darrow,3273 Isabella Ave,Houston,FL,97261
Steve,O,Darrow,8407 Infinite Loop Drive,Las Vegas,WA,90520
Erica,Z,Minella,513 S. Greenwood Ave,Miami,IL,12778
```

Note on line 5 of your input the middle initial field is 9S, which is invalid. This should cause your validation to fail at this point. With your input file defined, you can configure the job. The job you will be running will consist of a single step that reads in the input, passes it to an instance of the ValidatingItemProcessor, and then writes it to an output file. Listing 8-7 shows the configuration for the job.

Listing 8-7. copyJob.xml

```xml
<?xml version="1.0" encoding="UTF-8"?>
<beans:beans xmlns="http://www.springframework.org/schema/batch"
    xmlns:beans="http://www.springframework.org/schema/beans"
    xmlns:util="http://www.springframework.org/schema/beans"
    xmlns:xsi="http://www.w3.org/2001/XMLSchema-instance"
    xsi:schemaLocation="http://www.springframework.org/schema/beans
        http://www.springframework.org/schema/beans/spring-beans-3.0.xsd
        http://www.springframework.org/schema/util
        http://www.springframework.org/schema/util/spring-util.xsd
        http://www.springframework.org/schema/batch
        http://www.springframework.org/schema/batch/spring-batch-2.1.xsd">

    <beans:import resource="../launch-context.xml"/>

    <beans:bean id="customerFile" class="org.springframework.core.io.FileSystemResource"
scope="step">
        <beans:constructor-arg value="#{jobParameters[customerFile]}"/>
    </beans:bean>

    <beans:bean id="customerFileReader"
class="org.springframework.batch.item.file.FlatFileItemReader">
        <beans:property name="resource" ref="customerFile" />
        <beans:property name="lineMapper">
            <beans:bean class="org.springframework.batch.item.file.mapping.DefaultLineMapper">
                <beans:property name="lineTokenizer">
                    <beans:bean
class="org.springframework.batch.item.file.transform.DelimitedLineTokenizer">
                        <beans:property name="names"
```

```
                            value="firstName,middleInitial,lastName,address,city,state,zip"/>
                    <beans:property name="delimiter" value=","/>
                </beans:bean>
            </beans:property>
            <beans:property name="fieldSetMapper">
                <beans:bean
class="org.springframework.batch.item.file.mapping.BeanWrapperFieldSetMapper">
                    <beans:property name="prototypeBeanName" value="customer"/>
                </beans:bean>
            </beans:property>
        </beans:bean>
    </beans:property>
</beans:bean>

<beans:bean id="customer" class="com.apress.springbatch.chapter8.Customer"
scope="prototype"/>

<beans:bean id="outputFile" class="org.springframework.core.io.FileSystemResource"
scope="step">
    <beans:constructor-arg value="#{jobParameters[outputFile]}"/>
</beans:bean>

<beans:bean id="outputWriter"
class="org.springframework.batch.item.file.FlatFileItemWriter">
    <beans:property name="resource" ref="outputFile" />
    <beans:property name="lineAggregator">
        <beans:bean
class="org.springframework.batch.item.file.transform.PassThroughLineAggregator"/>
    </beans:property>
</beans:bean>

<beans:bean id="customerValidatingProcessor"
    class="org.springframework.batch.item.validator.ValidatingItemProcessor">
    <beans:property name="validator">
        <beans:bean class="com.apress.springbatch.chapter8.BeanValidator"/>
    </beans:property>
</beans:bean>

<step id="copyFileStep">
    <tasklet>
        <chunk reader="customerFileReader" processor="customerValidatingProcessor"
            writer="outputWriter" commit-interval="10"/>
    </tasklet>
</step>

<job id="copyJob">
    <step id="step1" parent="copyFileStep"/>
</job>
</beans:beans>
```

To walk through the copyJob.xml file listed in Listing 8-7, let's start with definitions of the input file and the reader. This reader is a simple delimited file reader that maps the fields of the file to your

Customer object. Next is the output configuration, which consists of defining the file and its writer. With the input and output defined, the bean customerValidatingProcessor will serve as your ItemProcessor. By default, the ValidatingItemProcessor just passes the item through from the ItemReader to the ItemWriter, which will work for this example. The only dependency you inject for your ItemProcessor is the reference to the BeanValidator you write in Listing 8-5. With all of the beans defined, you can build your step, which is the next piece of the file. All you need for your step is to define the reader, processor, and writer. With your step defined, you finish the file by configuring the job itself.

To run the job, use the command in Listing 8-8 from the target directory of your project.

Listing 8-8. Running the copyJob

```
java -jar itemProcessors-0.0.1-SNAPSHOT.jar jobs/copyJob.xml copyJob
customerFile=/tmp/customer.csv outputFile=/tmp/output.csv
```

As mentioned, you have some bad input that will not pass validation. When you run the job, it fails due to the ValidationException that is thrown. To get the job to complete successfully, you have to fix your input to pass validation. Listing 8-9 shows the results of your job when the input fails validation.

Listing 8-9. copyJob Output

```
2011-02-13 16:31:11,030 DEBUG main [org.springframework.batch.core.step.tasklet.TaskletStep]
- <Applying contribution: [StepContribution: read=10, written=0, filtered=0, readSkips=0,
writeSkips=0, processSkips=0, exitStatus=EXECUTING]>
2011-02-13 16:31:11,031 DEBUG main [org.springframework.batch.core.step.tasklet.TaskletStep]
- <Rollback for RuntimeException:
org.springframework.batch.item.validator.ValidationException: size must be between 1 and 1
>
2011-02-13 16:31:11,031 DEBUG main [org.springframework.batch.repeat.support.RepeatTemplate]
- <Handling exception: org.springframework.batch.item.validator.ValidationException, caused
by: org.springframework.batch.item.validator.ValidationException: size must be between 1 and
1
>
2011-02-13 16:31:11,031 DEBUG main [org.springframework.batch.repeat.support.RepeatTemplate]
- <Handling fatal exception explicitly (rethrowing first of 1):
org.springframework.batch.item.validator.ValidationException: size must be between 1 and 1
>
2011-02-13 16:31:11,032 ERROR main [org.springframework.batch.core.step.AbstractStep] -
<Encountered an error executing the step>
org.springframework.batch.item.validator.ValidationException: size must be between 1 and 1

  at
com.apress.springbatch.chapter8.BeanValidator.buildValidationException(BeanValidator.java:40
)
  at       com.apress.springbatch.chapter8.BeanValidator.validate(BeanValidator.java:28)
  at
org.springframework.batch.item.validator.ValidatingItemProcessor.process(ValidatingItemProce
ssor.java:77)
```

That is all that is required to add item validation to your jobs in Spring Batch. JSR 303 provides the ability to add custom checks as well as a number of additional annotations out of the box to be able to

create even more robust validation. To read more about JSR 303 and validation using it within a Spring application, visit the Spring documentation on validation at
http://static.springsource.org/spring/docs/current/spring-framework-reference/html/validation.html.

Before you move on, however, the previous example only applied the validation itself to the input. It did not apply any processing to the item once it did pass validation. This next section will look at how to apply business logic once an item has passed validation.

Subclassing the ValidatingItemProcessor

Although in the previous section you were able to perform item validation, you didn't actually process the item once it did pass validation. In this section, you will look at how to subclass the ValidatingItemProcessor to apply logic to each item as it passes validation.

By subclassing the ValidatingItemProcessor class, you can override the process method to apply your logic to each item. If you use the same example as you did for the validation, you can add the ability to output the customer's name and the number record he was in your implementation. Listing 8-10 shows the code for the CustomerValidatingItemProcessor.

Listing 8-10. CustomerValidatingItemProcessor

```
package com.apress.springbatch.chapter8;

import org.springframework.batch.item.validator.ValidatingItemProcessor;

public class CustomerValidatingItemProcessor extends ValidatingItemProcessor<Customer> {

    private int recordCount = 0;

    @Override
    public Customer process(Customer customer) {
        recordCount++;

        System.out.println(customer.getFirstName() + " " +
                                   customer.getLastName() + " was record number " +
                                   recordCount + " in your file.");

        return customer;
    }
}
```

With the validation logic already addressed with your BeanValidator class and the annotations on the Customer class, the CustomerValidatingItemProcessor only needs to concern itself with the actual logic required for this step. In this case, you keep a running count of the number of items you receive and print them out to standard out with each item. To use your implementation of the ValidatingItemProcessor, the only configuration change you need to do is update the class identified in the customerValidatingProcessor bean. Listing 8-11 shows the updated configuration.

Listing 8-11. Updated Configuration for the customerValidatingProcessor Bean

```
...
<beans:bean id="customerValidatingProcessor"
    class="com.apress.springbatch.chapter8.CustomerValidatingItemProcessor">
    <beans:property name="validator">
        <beans:bean class="com.apress.springbatch.chapter8.BeanValidator"/>
    </beans:property>
</beans:bean>
...
```

When you run the job with your new configuration and your input is updated to pass validation by removing the 9 from the middleInitial field of the fifth record, Listing 8-12 shows the results you get.

Listing 8-12. Results of New Logic Applied to the Customer Item

```
2011-02-13 17:35:00,234 DEBUG main [org.springframework.batch.repeat.support.RepeatTemplate]
- <Repeat operation about to start at count=9>
2011-02-13 17:35:00,234 DEBUG main [org.springframework.batch.repeat.support.RepeatTemplate]
- <Repeat operation about to start at count=10>
2011-02-13 17:35:00,234 DEBUG main [org.springframework.batch.repeat.support.RepeatTemplate]
- <Repeat is complete according to policy and result value.>
Richard Darrow was record number 1 in your file.
Warren Darrow was record number 2 in your file.
Barack Donnelly was record number 3 in your file.
Ann Benes was record number 4 in your file.
Laura Minella was record number 5 in your file.
Erica Gates was record number 6 in your file.
Warren Williams was record number 7 in your file.
Harry Darrow was record number 8 in your file.
Steve Darrow was record number 9 in your file.
Erica Minella was record number 10 in your file.
2011-02-13 17:35:00,235 DEBUG main [org.springframework.batch.item.file.FlatFileItemWriter]
- <Writing to flat file with 10 items.>
2011-02-13 17:35:00,236 DEBUG main
[org.springframework.batch.core.step.item.ChunkOrientedTasklet] - <Inputs not busy, ended:
false>
```

The ValidatingItemProcessor is useful for being able to apply validation to your items as they are processed. However, it is only one of the three implementations of the ItemProcessor interface provided by Spring Batch. In the next section you will look at the ItemProcessorAdapter and how it allows you to use existing services as ItemProcessors.

ItemProcessorAdapter

In Chapter 7, you looked at the ItemReaderAdapter as a way to use existing services to provide input to your jobs. Spring Batch also allows you to put to use the various services you already have developed as ItemProcessors as well by using the org.springframework.batch.item.adapter.ItemProcessorAdapter.

In this section, you will look at the ItemProcessorAdapter and see how it lets you use existing services as processors for your batch job items.

Let's use an example where you read in customers, use the ItemProcessor to lookup their account executive, and pass the AccountExecutive object to the ItemWriter. Before you get into the code itself, let's take a look at the updated data model showing the relationship between the AccountExecutive and the Customer. Figure 8-1 shows the updated data model.

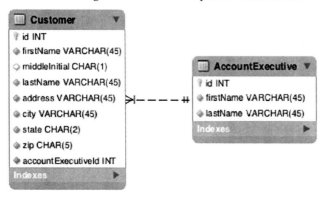

Figure 8-1. *Data model for the Customer-AccountExecutive relationship*

These tables will require a domain object each. While the Customer object you previously used will work fine with the additions of the ID field and the accountExecutive reference, you will need to create a new AccountExecutive domain object. Listing 8-13 show the code for both domain objects.

Listing 8-13. *Customer and AccountExecutive Domain Objects*

Customer

```
package com.apress.springbatch.chapter8;

import javax.validation.constraints.NotNull;
import javax.validation.constraints.Pattern;
import javax.validation.constraints.Size;

public class Customer {

    private long id;

    @NotNull
    @Pattern(regexp="[a-zA-Z]+")
    private String firstName;

    @Size(min=1, max=1)
    private String middleInitial;

    @NotNull
    @Pattern(regexp="[a-zA-Z]+")
    private String lastName;
```

```java
    @NotNull
    @Pattern(regexp="[0-9a-zA-Z\\. ]+")
    private String address;

    @NotNull
    @Pattern(regexp="[a-zA-Z\\. ]+")
    private String city;

    @NotNull
    @Size(min=2,max=2)
    @Pattern(regexp="[A-Z]{2}")
    private String state;

    @NotNull
    @Size(min=5,max=5)
    @Pattern(regexp="\\d{5}")
    private String zip;

    private AccountExecutive accountExecutive;

    // Accessors go here
    ...

    @Override
    public String toString() {
        StringBuilder output = new StringBuilder();
        output.append(firstName);
        output.append(" ");
        output.append(middleInitial);
        output.append(" ");
        output.append(lastName);
        output.append(" lives at ");
        output.append(address);
        output.append(" ");
        output.append(city);
        output.append(", ");
        output.append(state);
        output.append(" ");
        output.append(zip);
        output.append(" and has ");

        if(accountExecutive != null) {
            output.append(accountExecutive.getFirstName());
            output.append(" ");
            output.append(accountExecutive.getLastName());
            output.append(" as their account exec");
        } else {
            output.append("no account exec");
        }

        return output.toString();
    }
```

```
}
```

AccountExecutive

```
package com.apress.springbatch.chapter8;

public class AccountExecutive {

    private long id;
    private String firstName;
    private String lastName;

    // Accessors go here
    ...
}
```

To support the need to be able to read from this table, you will implement a new DAO that extends Spring's JdbcTemplate. This DAO will have a single method used to get an AccountExecutive object from the database based upon the Customer provided. Listing 8-14 shows the implementation of the AccountExecutiveDaoImpl.

Listing 8-14. AccountExecutiveDaoImpl

```
package com.apress.springbatch.chapter8;

import java.sql.ResultSet;
import java.sql.SQLException;

import org.springframework.jdbc.core.JdbcTemplate;
import org.springframework.jdbc.core.RowMapper;

public class AccountExecutiveDaoImpl extends JdbcTemplate implements
        AccountExecutiveDao {

    private String BY_CUSTOMER = "select a.* from accountExccutive a inner join " +
        "customer c on a.id = c.accountExecutiveId where c.id = ?";

    public AccountExecutive getAccountExecutiveByCustomer(Customer customer) {
        return (AccountExecutive) queryForObject(BY_CUSTOMER,
                                        new Object [] {customer.getId()},
                                        new RowMapper()
            {
              public Object mapRow(ResultSet rs, int arg1) throws SQLException {
                AccountExecutive result = new AccountExecutive();

                result.setFirstName(rs.getString("firstName"));
                result.setLastName(rs.getString("lastName"));
                result.setId(rs.getLong("id"));

                return result;
              }
            });
    }
```

```
}
```

As Listing 8-14 shows, the AccountExecutiveDaoImpl consists of a single method to look up the AccountExecutive by the Customer's information. The ResultSet you receive back is mapped by the RowMapper implementation you coded inline.

To put this Dao to use, you could do two things. The first would be to implement the ItemProcessor interface and perform the logic of looking up the AccountExecutive there. However, this doesn't provide any portability when it comes to reusing this code outside of your batch jobs. Instead, you'll implement a service that you can wrap with the ItemProcessorAdapter as well as use in non-Spring Batch applications. Listing 8-15 shows the code for the service you will use.

Listing 8-15. `CustomerServiceImpl`

```
package com.apress.springbatch.chapter8;

public class CustomerServiceImpl {

    private AccountExecutiveDao acctExecDao;

    public AccountExecutive getAccountExecutiveForCustomer(Customer customer) {
        return acctExecDao.getAccountExecutiveByCustomer(customer);
    }

    public void setAcctExecDao(AccountExecutiveDao execDao) {
        acctExecDao = execDao;
    }
}
```

In order to use this service, you can configure the ItemProcessorAdapter to call the getAccountExecutiveForCustomer method. By default, Spring Batch will use the item the ItemProcessor receives when its process method is called as the parameter to the method on the service you call. In this case, the ItemProcessor you configure will receive a Customer object as the parameter to the process method. Spring Batch will take that Customer object and call your service with that object as the parameter. To make this happen, you configure your ItemProcessor to use the ItemProcessorAdapter as the class and satisfy two required dependencies:

- *targetObject*: The object that contains the method to be called.

- *targetMethod*: The name of the method to be called (as a String).

The configuration for this is shown in Listing 8-16.

Listing 8-16. *ItemProcessor Configuration*

```
...
<beans:bean id="accountExecutiveDao"
class="com.apress.springbatch.chapter8.AccountExecutiveDaoImpl">
    <beans:property name="dataSource" ref="dataSource"/>
</beans:bean>

<beans:bean id="customerService" class="com.apress.springbatch.chapter8.CustomerServiceImpl">
    <beans:property name="acctExecDao" ref="accountExecutiveDao"/>
```

```
    </beans:bean>

    <beans:bean id="customerProcessor"
        class="org.springframework.batch.item.adapter.ItemProcessorAdapter">
        <beans:property name="targetObject" ref="customerService"/>
        <beans:property name="targetMethod" value="getAccountExecutiveForCustomer"/>
    </beans:bean>

    <step id="copyFileStep">
        <tasklet>
            <chunk reader="customerFileReader" processor="accountExecutiveItemProcessor"
writer="outputWriter"
                commit-interval="10"/>
        </tasklet>
    </step>

    <job id="copyJob">
        <step id="step1" parent="copyFileStep"/>
    </job>
    …
```

With the job configured to use your new ItemProcessor, the ItemProcessorAdapter, and your job will call the CustomerServiceImpl with each Customer item you input and pass the returned AccountExecutive object to the ItemWriter. As mentioned, the framework allows for an ItemProcessor to accept one type as input and another as output.

The idea of applying a single action to an item within a transaction can be limiting in certain situations. For example, if you have a set of calculations that need to be done on some of the items, you may want to filter out the ones that don't need to be processed. In the next section, you will look at how to configure Spring Batch to execute a list of ItemProcessors on each item within a step.

CompositeItemProcessor

You break up a step into three phases (reading, processing, and writing) to divide responsibilities between components. However, the business logic that needs to be applied to a given item may not make sense to couple into a single ItemProcessor. Spring Batch allows you to maintain that same division of responsibilities within your business logic by chaining ItemProcessors within a step. In this section, you will look at how to chain ItemProcessors within a single step using Spring Batch's CompositeItemProcessor.

The org.springframework.batch.item.support.CompositeItemProcessor is an implementation of the ItemProcessor interface that delegates processing to each of a list of ItemProcessor implementations in order. As each processor returns its result, that result is passed onto the next processor until they all have been called. This pattern occurs regardless of the types returned so if the first ItemProcessor takes a String as input it can return a Product object as output as long as the next ItemProcessor takes a Product as input. At the end, the result is passed to the ItemWriter configured for the step. It is important to note that just like any other ItemProcessor, if any of the processors this one delegates to returns null, the item will not be process further. Figure 8-2 shows how the processing within the CompositeItemProcessor occurs.

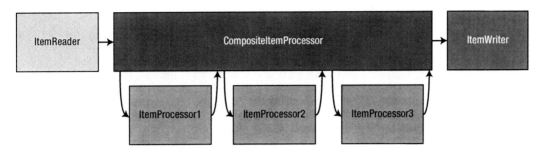

Figure 8-2. CompositeItemProcessor processing

As Figure 8-2 shows, the CompositeItemProcessor serves as a wrapper for multiple ItemProcessors, calling them in order. As one completes, the next one is called with the item returned from the previous one. Let's take a look at how this looks in practice.

In this example, you are going to take a Customer item that was read in from an input file, look it up in the database to get its database ID in the first ItemProcessor, and then pass it onto a second ItemProcessor to lookup its AccountExecutive. You will update the Customer object with its AccountExecutive reference and pass that to the writer to be written to a file.

The data model for this example will be the same as the one you used in the ItemProcessorAdapter example, consisting of two tables: a customer table containing all of the basic customer information (name and address) as well as a reference to an account executive. For this example, the account executive will consist only of its name.

As mentioned, this step will first look up the customer and set the ID on the customer, then look up the customer's account executive and update the item with that as well. In both cases, the ItemProcessor really does nothing more than do a database lookup and update the item appropriately. Let's look at the first ItemProcessor, the CustomerItemProcessor. Listing 8-17 shows the code involved.

Listing 8-17. CustomerItemProcessor

```java
package com.apress.springbatch.chapter8;

import org.springframework.batch.item.ItemProcessor;

public class CustomerItemProcessor implements ItemProcessor<Customer, Customer> {

    private CustomerDao customerDao;

    public Customer process(Customer customer) {
        Customer currentCustomer =
          customerDao.getCustomerByNameAndZip(customer.getFirstName(),
                                              customer.getLastName(),
                                              customer.getZip());

        customer.setId(currentCustomer.getId());

        return customer;
    }

    public void setCustomerDao(CustomerDao customerDao) {
```

```
        this.customerDao = customerDao;
    }
}
```

As you can see in Listing 8-17, the CustomItemProcessor implements the ItemProcessor interface, both accepting and returning a `Customer` object as the item. When the processor receives the item, it looks up the customer by name and ZIP code and updates the item you received with the ID in the database. The `Customer` is then returned to be processed by the next ItemProcessor, which in this case is the AccountExecutiveItemProcessor shown in Listing 8-18.

Listing 8-18. AccountExecutiveItemProcessor

```
package com.apress.springbatch.chapter8;

import org.springframework.batch.item.ItemProcessor;

public class AccountExecutiveItemProcessor implements ItemProcessor<Customer, Customer> {

    private AccountExecutiveDao accountExecutiveDao;

    public Customer process(Customer customer) {
      customer.setAccountExecutive(
         accountExecutiveDao.getAccountExecutiveByCustomer(customer));

      return customer;
    }

    public void setAccountExecutiveDao(AccountExecutiveDao accountExecutiveDao) {
        this.accountExecutiveDao = accountExecutiveDao;
    }
}
```

Same process, different domain. In the AccountExecutiveItemProcessor, you again take a Customer object as input. However, this time you look up which AccountExecutive it's associated with and update the item with the correct association. You then return the same Customer object to be written to your output file.

The last piece of this puzzle from a code perspective is the two DAOs you used in the ItemProcessors: the CustomerDao and the AccountExecutiveDao. In each case, you extend Spring's JdbcTemplate to make accessing the database easier. All you need to do is define your query, inject the parameters, and build a RowMapper implementation. Listing 8-19 has the CustomerDao's implementation.

Listing 8-19. `CustomerDao`

```
package com.apress.springbatch.chapter8;

import java.sql.ResultSet;
import java.sql.SQLException;

import org.springframework.jdbc.core.JdbcTemplate;
import org.springframework.jdbc.core.RowMapper;
```

```
public class CustomerDaoImpl extends JdbcTemplate implements CustomerDao {

    private static final String BY_ATTRIBUTES =
        "select * from customer where firstName = ? " +
        "and lastName = ? and zip = ?";

    @SuppressWarnings("unchecked")
    public Customer getCustomerByNameAndZip(String firstName, String lastName, String zip) {
        List<Customer> customers = query(BY_ATTRIBUTES,
                                         new Object []{
                                             firstName,
                                             lastName,
                                             zip},
                                         new RowMapper() {

            public Object mapRow(ResultSet rs, int arg1) throws SQLException {
                Customer result = new Customer();

                result.setFirstName(rs.getString("firstName"));
                result.setLastName(rs.getString("lastName"));
                result.setAddress(rs.getString("address"));
                result.setCity(rs.getString("city"));
                result.setState(rs.getString("state"));
                result.setZip(rs.getString("zip"));
                result.setId(rs.getLong("id"));

                return result;
            }});

        if(customers != null && customers.size() > 0) {
            return customers.get(0);
        } else {
            return null;
        }
    }
}
```

The CustomerDao queries the Customer table via first name, last name, and ZIP code to find the customer you received. From there, it uses Spring's RowMapper to create a new Customer object containing the results of the query. Although you probably don't need the full object returned in this scenario, since the Customer object is not a very large object, passing the entire object back allows this method to be a little more reusable.

The AccountExecutiveDao is the other DAO you are using and is listed in Listing 8-20.

Listing 8-20. *AccountExecutiveDao*

```
package com.apress.springbatch.chapter8;

import java.sql.ResultSet;
import java.sql.SQLException;
```

```
import org.springframework.jdbc.core.JdbcTemplate;
import org.springframework.jdbc.core.RowMapper;

public class AccountExecutiveDaoImpl extends JdbcTemplate implements
        AccountExecutiveDao {

    private String BY_CUSTOMER = "select a.* from accountExecutive a inner join customer c " +
                                "on a.id = c.accountExecutiveId where c.id = ?";

    public AccountExecutive getAccountExecutiveByCustomer(Customer customer) {
        return (AccountExecutive) queryForObject(BY_CUSTOMER,
                                            new Object [] {
                                                customer.getId()},
                                            new RowMapper() {
            public Object mapRow(ResultSet rs, int arg1) throws SQLException {
                AccountExecutive result = new AccountExecutive();

                result.setFirstName(rs.getString("firstName"));
                result.setLastName(rs.getString("lastName"));
                result.setId(rs.getLong("id"));

                return result;
            }
        });
    }
}
```

As you did in the `CustomerDaoImpl` in Listing 8-19, the `AccountExecutiveDaoImpl` queries the database using Spring's JdbcTemplate. Using Spring's RowMapper facilities, you are able to map the results of the query to the new AccountExecutive object and return it to your ItemProcessor.

With your code written, you can wire up this job and see how it runs. The configuration for this job—including the two DAOs, the two ItemProcessors, one reader, one writer, the step, and the job—can all be found in Listing 8-21.

Listing 8-21. *Configuring a Step with a CompositeItemProcessor*

```xml
<?xml version="1.0" encoding="UTF-8"?>
<beans:beans xmlns="http://www.springframework.org/schema/batch"
    xmlns:beans="http://www.springframework.org/schema/beans"
    xmlns:util="http://www.springframework.org/schema/beans"
    xmlns:xsi="http://www.w3.org/2001/XMLSchema-instance"
    xsi:schemaLocation="http://www.springframework.org/schema/beans
        http://www.springframework.org/schema/beans/spring-beans-3.0.xsd
        http://www.springframework.org/schema/util
        http://www.springframework.org/schema/util/spring-util.xsd
        http://www.springframework.org/schema/batch
        http://www.springframework.org/schema/batch/spring-batch-2.1.xsd">

    <beans:import resource="../launch-context.xml"/>

    <beans:bean id="customerFile" class="org.springframework.core.io.FileSystemResource"
scope="step">
```

```
            <beans:constructor-arg value="#{jobParameters[customerFile]}"/>
        </beans:bean>

    <beans:bean id="customerFileReader"
class="org.springframework.batch.item.file.FlatFileItemReader">
        <beans:property name="resource" ref="customerFile" />
        <beans:property name="lineMapper">
            <beans:bean class="org.springframework.batch.item.file.mapping.DefaultLineMapper">
                <beans:property name="lineTokenizer">
                    <beans:bean
class="org.springframework.batch.item.file.transform.DelimitedLineTokenizer">
                        <beans:property name="names"
                            value="firstName,middleInitial,lastName,address,city,state,zip"/>
                        <beans:property name="delimiter" value=","/>
                    </beans:bean>
                </beans:property>
                <beans:property name="fieldSetMapper">
                    <beans:bean
class="org.springframework.batch.item.file.mapping.BeanWrapperFieldSetMapper">
                        <beans:property name="prototypeBeanName" value="customer"/>
                    </beans:bean>
                </beans:property>
            </beans:bean>
        </beans:property>
    </beans:bean>

    <beans:bean id="customer" class="com.apress.springbatch.chapter8.Customer"
scope="prototype"/>

    <beans:bean id="outputFile" class="org.springframework.core.io.FileSystemResource"
scope="step">
        <beans:constructor-arg value="#{jobParameters[outputFile]}"/>
    </beans:bean>

    <beans:bean id="outputWriter"
class="org.springframework.batch.item.file.FlatFileItemWriter">
        <beans:property name="resource" ref="outputFile" />
        <beans:property name="lineAggregator">
            <beans:bean
class="org.springframework.batch.item.file.transform.PassThroughLineAggregator"/>
        </beans:property>
    </beans:bean>

    <beans:bean id="accountExecutiveDao"
        class="com.apress.springbatch.chapter8.AccountExecutiveDaoImpl">
        <beans:property name="dataSource" ref="dataSource"/>
    </beans:bean>

    <beans:bean id="customerDao" class="com.apress.springbatch.chapter8.CustomerDaoImpl">
        <beans:property name="dataSource" ref="dataSource"/>
    </beans:bean>
```

```xml
    <beans:bean id="customerIdItemProcessor"
        class="com.apress.springbatch.chapter8.CustomerItemProcessor">
        <beans:property name="customerDao" ref="customerDao"/>
    </beans:bean>

    <beans:bean id="accountExecutiveItemProcessor"
        class="com.apress.springbatch.chapter8.AccountExecutiveItemProcessor">
        <beans:property name="accountExecutiveDao" ref="accountExecutiveDao"/>
    </beans:bean>

    <beans:bean id="completeItemProcessor"
        class="org.springframework.batch.item.support.CompositeItemProcessor">
        <beans:property name="delegates">
            <util:list>
                <beans:ref bean="customerIdItemProcessor"/>
                <beans:ref bean="accountExecutiveItemProcessor"/>
            </util:list>
        </beans:property>
    </beans:bean>

    <step id="copyFileStep">
        <tasklet>
            <chunk reader="customerFileReader" processor="completeItemProcessor"
writer="outputWriter"
                commit-interval="10"/>
        </tasklet>
    </step>

    <job id="copyJob">
        <step id="step1" parent="copyFileStep"/>
    </job>
</beans:beans>
```

There is a lot of XML here, so let's start at the top. Beginning with the normal Spring configuration file imports and the inclusion of your normal launch-context.xml file, this file contains 10 uniquely configured beans (not including nested beans of the actual step or job). Table 8-1 walks through each of the beans configured in this file.

Table 8-1. Beans Configured for the CompositeItemProcessor Example

Bean	Description	Dependencies
customerFile	The input file to be read (the actual file name will be passed in as a parameter of the job).	None
customerFileReader	The FlatFileItemReader used for the step in this job.	• customerFile (the file to be read by this reader)

		• A LineMapper implementation
Customer	The bean that the ItemReader will return for each record read.	None
outputFile	The output file to be written to (the actual file name will be passed in as a parameter of the job).	None
outputWriter	The FlatFileItemWriter used for the step in this job	• outputFile (the file to be written to by this writer). • A LineAggregator implementation.
accountExecutiveDao	The DAO implementation used to look up AccountExecutive's from the database.	A dataSource to be used by the JdbcTemplate.
customerDao	The DAO implementation used to look up Customers from the database.	A dataSource to be used by the JdbcTemplate
customerIdItemProcessor	The implementation of the ItemProcessor interface that you will use to populate the Customer's database ID field.	customerDao
accountExecutiveItemProcessor	The implementation of the ItemProcessor interface that you will use to associate a Customer with their AccountExecutive.	accountExecutiveDao
completeItemProcessor	This will execute each of the ItemProcessor implementations provided to it in order on the item it receives.	A list of ItemProcessor implementations to be executed in order.
copyFileStep	The Spring Batch step	customerFileReader,

used to configure the ItemReader, ItemProcessor, and ItemWriter to be executed within a single transaction.	completeItemProcessor, and outputWriter.

The configuration for even a simple CompositeItemProcessor job is not short. However, the amount of code you need to develop—and even more importantly the amount of code you need to write that depends on Spring Batch—is minimal to none[3].

By executing this job, Spring Batch will read in each of your customer records into Customer objects, apply the logic of both ItemProcessors, and write out the Customer object to your output file for each record. An example of the output generated by this batch job can be found in Listing 8-22.

Listing 8-22. *Sample Output of the CompositeItemProcessor Example*

```
Richard N Darrow lives at 5570 Isabella Ave St. Louis, IL 58540 and has Manuel Castro as
their account exec
Warren L Darrow lives at 4686 Mt. Lee Drive St. Louis, NY 94935 and has Manuel Castro as
their account exec
Ann Z Benes lives at 2447 S. Greenwood Ave Las Vegas, NY 55366 and has Manuel Castro as
their account exec
Laura S Johnson lives at 8177 4th Street Dallas, FL 04119 and has Manuel Castro as their
account exec
Erica Z Gates lives at 3141 Farnam Street Omaha, CA 57640 and has Manuel Castro as their
account exec
Harry T Darrow lives at 3273 Isabella Ave Houston, FL 97261 and has Anita Jordan as their
account exec
```

The CompositeItemProcessor allows you to apply multiple flows of logic to each item within a transaction. This approach gives you the opportunity to keep your logical concerns separate for maintainability and reuse.

In the next section, you will look at writing your own ItemProcessor to filter items from the ItemWriter. Although you have written your own ItemProcessors in this section, you have passed all of the records you received to the writer up to this point. In the next section, you will look at how to change that.

Writing Your Own ItemProcessor

The ItemProcessor is really the easiest piece of the Spring Batch framework to implement yourself. This is by design. Input and output is standard across environments and business cases. Reading a file is the same regardless of if it contains financial data or scientific data. Writing to a database works the same

---

[3] You could have implemented the CustomerItemProcessor and the AccountExecutiveItemProcessors as services and used the ItemProcessorAdapter to reference them. This approach would isolate your code completely from the Spring Batch framework.

regardless of what the object looks like. However, the ItemProcessor is where the business logic of your process exists. Because of this, you will virtually always need to create custom implementations of them. In this section, you will look at how to create a custom ItemProcessor implementation that filters certain items that were read from begin written.

Filtering Items

In the previous section, you created two of your own ItemProcessors: a CustomerItemProcessor that updated the item it received with the corresponding database ID and the AccountExecutiveItemProcessor that associates the customer's AccountExecutive with the Customer item so that information about the customer and the account executive can be written in the output file.

However, you didn't do a good job with error handling in the previous example. What happens if the Customer is not found and the ID is not updated in the CustomerItemProcessor? In this scenario, you probably want to filter the item out so the job does not try the account executive lookup. So how do you tell Spring Batch not to process the item anymore?

Spring Batch has you covered. It is actually very easy to tell Spring Batch not to continue processing an item. To do so, instead of the ItemProcessor returning an item, it returns null. So in this case, if you can't find a customer in your database, you will want the CustomerItemProcessor to return null so that the AccountExecutiveItemProcessor doesn't throw an exception by not having a Customer to look up by. The updated code for this is shown in Listing 8-23.

Listing 8-23. CustomerItemProcessor that Handles Nonexistent Customers

```
package com.apress.springbatch.chapter8;

import org.springframework.batch.item.ItemProcessor;

public class CustomerItemProcessor implements ItemProcessor<Customer, Customer> {

    private CustomerDao customerDao;

    public Customer process(Customer customer) {
        Customer currentCustomer =
          customerDao.getCustomerByNameAndZip(customer.getFirstName(),
                                              customer.getLastName(),
                                              customer.getZip());
        if(currentCustomer != null) {
            customer.setId(currentCustomer.getId());
            return customer;
        } else {
            return null;
        }
    }

    public void setCustomerDao(CustomerDao customerDao) {
        this.customerDao = customerDao;
    }
}
```

With just this small change to your job, you can now run it without fear that the AccountExecutiveItemProcessor will fail because it doesn't have a customer number to look up. If you run this job with an input file that has customers that are not in the database, Spring Batch will keep track (as always) of the items read and written as well as the items filtered by your ItemProcessor. Looking at the results of your job via Spring Batch Admin in Figure 8-3, you can see just that.

Details for Step Execution

Property	Value
ID	8,543
Job Execution	8,506
Job Name	copyJob
Step Name	step1
Start Date	2011-02-19
Start Time	23:21:10
Duration	00:00:00
Status	COMPLETED
Reads	13
Writes	10
Filters	3
Read Skips	0
Write Skips	0
Process Skips	0
Commits	2
Rollbacks	0
Exit Code	COMPLETED
Exit Message	

Figure 8-3. *Results from a job that filtered three items*

In Chapter 4, you learned about skipping items, which used exceptions to identify records that were not to be processed. The difference between these two approaches is that this approach is intended for records that are technically valid records. Your customer had no records that the customerFileReader could not parse into an object. Instead, your business rules prevented you from being able to process this record so you decided to filter it out of the steps results.

Although a simple concept, ItemProcessors are a piece of the Spring Batch framework that any batch developer will spend large amounts of time in. This is where the business logic lives and is applied to the items being processed.

Summary

ItemProcessors are where business logic can be applied to the items being processed in your jobs. Spring Batch, instead of trying to help you, does what it should do for this piece of the framework: it gets out of your way and lets you determine how to apply the logic of your business as needed. In the next chapter, you will finish your look at the core components of Spring Batch by taking a deep dive into ItemWriters.

CHAPTER 9

Item Writers

It's amazing what computers can do. The numbers they can crunch. The images they can process. Yet it doesn't mean a thing unless the computer can communicate what it has done via its output. ItemWriters are the output facility for Spring Batch. And when you need a format to output the results of the Spring Batch process, Spring Batch delivers. In this chapter, you look at the different types of ItemWriters provided by Spring Batch as well as how to develop ItemWriters for situations that are more specific to your needs. Topics discussed include the following:

- *Introduction to ItemWriters:* Similar to the ItemReaders at the other end of step execution, ItemWriters have their own special nuances. This chapter talks about how ItemWriters work from a high level.

- *File-based ItemWriters:* File-based output is the easiest method to set up and is one of the most common forms used in batch processing. Because of this, you begin your exploration of ItemWriters by looking at writing to flat files as well as XML files.

- *Database ItemWriters:* The relational database is king in the enterprise when it comes to data storage. However, databases create their own unique challenges when you're working with high volumes of data. You look at how Spring Batch handles these challenges with its unique architecture.

- *Alternative output destination ItemWriters:* Files and databases aren't the only media to which enterprise software outputs. Systems send e-mails, write to JMS endpoints, and save data via other systems. This section looks at some of the less common but still very useful output methods that Spring Batch supports.

- Multipart ItemWriters: Unlike reading, where data typically comes from a single source, it's common to send output to multiple sources. Spring Batch provides ways to write to multiple systems as well as structure a single ItemWriter as a collaborative effort of multiple ItemWriters. This section looks at ItemWriters tasked with working with either multiple resources or multiple output formats.

- *Statement writers:* This chapter finishes the development of the statement job by implementing the required writers for each step.

To start with ItemWriters, let's look at how they work and how they fit into a step.

Introduction to ItemWriters

The ItemWriter is the output mechanism used in Spring Batch. When Spring Batch first came out, ItemWriters were essentially the same as ItemReaders. They wrote each item out as it was processed. However, with Spring Batch 2 and the introduction of chunk-based processing, the role of the ItemWriter changed. Writing out each item as it's processed no longer makes sense.

With chunked-based processing, an ItemWriter doesn't write a single item: it writes a chunk of items. Because of this, the `org.springframework.batch.item.ItemWriter` interface is slightly different than the ItemReader interface. Listing 9-1 shows that the ItemWriter's `write` method takes a list of items, whereas the ItemReader interface you looked at in Chapter 7 returns only a single item from the `read` method.

***Listing 9-1.** ItemWriter*

```
package org.springframework.batch.item;

import java.util.List;

public interface ItemWriter<T> {
    void write(List<? extends T> items) throws Exception;
}
```

To illustrate the flow of how an ItemWriter fits into the step, Figure 9-1 shows a sequence diagram that walks through the processing within a step. The step reads each item individually via the ItemReader and passes it to the ItemProcessor for processing. This interaction continues until the number of items in a chunk has been processed. With the processing of a chunk complete, the items are passed into the ItemWriter to be written accordingly.

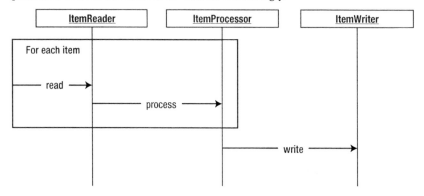

***Figure 9-1.** Step interaction with an ItemWriter*

Since chunk-based processing was introduced, the number of calls to an ItemWriter is much less than it was. However, you need to handle things a bit differently. Take for example working with nontransactional resources like files. If a write to a file fails, there is no way to roll back what was already written. Because of that, if you write a custom writer, you should buffer the output and flush all at once to the file to prevent an item from being half written, leaving the file in an inconsistent state.

Spring Batch provides a number of writers to handle the vast majority of output scenarios. Let's start with writers at the same place you started with readers: `FlatFileItemWriter`.

File-Based ItemWriters

Large amounts of data are moved via files in enterprise batch processing. There is a reason for this: files are simple and reliable. Backups are easy. So is recovery if you need to start over. This section looks at how to generate flat files in a variety of formats including formatted records (fixed width or other) and delimited files as well as how Spring Batch handles the issue of file creation.

FlatFileItemWriter

org.springframework.batch.item.file.FlatFileItemWriter is the ItemWriter implementation provided to generate text file output. Similar to FlatFileItemReader in many respects, this class addresses the issues with file-based output in Java with a clean, consistent interface for you to use. Figure 9-2 shows how the FlatFileItemWriter is constructed.

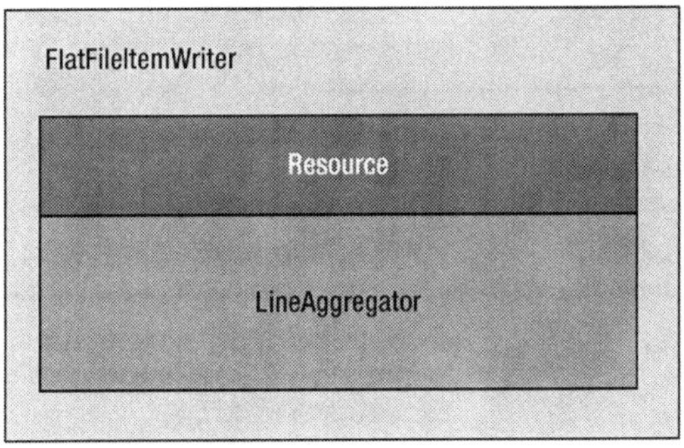

Figure 9-2. FlatFileItemWriter pieces

FlatFileItemWriter, as shown in Figure 9-2 consists of a resource to write to and a LineAggregator implementation. The org.springframework.batch.item.file.transform.LineAggregator interface replaces the LineMapper of the FlatFileItemReader discussed in Chapter 7. Here, instead of parsing a String into an object as the LineMapper is responsible for doing, the LineAggregator is responsible for the generating of an output String based on an object.

In many of the previous examples, you used PassThroughLineAggregator to generate the output files. This particular implementation of the LineAggregator interface just calls the item's toString() method to generate the output. But there are other implementations that you look at in the coming sections.

FlatFileItemWriter has a number of interesting configuration options, which are reviewed in Table 9-1.

Table 9-1. FlatFileItemWriterCconfiguration Options

Option	Type	Default	Description
encoding String		UTF-8	Character encoding for the file.
footerCallback FlatFileFooterCall back		null	Executed after the last item of a file has been written.
headerCallback FlatFileHeaderCall back		null	Executed before the first item of a file has been written.
lineAggregator LineAggregator		null (required)	Used to convert an individual item to a String for output.
lineSeparator String		System's line.separator	Generated file's newline character.
resource Resource		null (required)	File or stream to be written to.
saveState boolean		true	Determines if the state of the writer should be stored in the ExecutionContext as processing occurs.
shouldDeleteIfEmpty boolean		false	If true and no records are written (not including header/footer records), the file is deleted on the close of the reader.
appendAllowed boolean		false	If true and the file to be written to already exists, the output is appended to it instead of replacing the file. If true, shouldDeleteIfExists is automatically set to false.
shouldDeleteIfExists boolean		true	If true and the file to be written to exists prior to the run of the job, the file is deleted and a new file is created.
transactional boolean		true	If true and a transaction is currently active, the writing of the data to the file is delayed

	until the transaction is committed.

Unlike the `LineMapper` of `FlatFileItemReader`, the `LineAggregator` doesn't have any hard dependencies. However, a related interface to be aware of is `org.springframework.batch.item.file.transform.FieldExtractor`. This interface is used in most of the provided `LineAggregator` implementations as a way to access the required fields from a given item. Spring Batch provides two implementations of the `FieldExtractor` interface: `org.springframework.batch.item.file.transform.BeanWrapperFieldExtractor`, which uses the getters on the class to access the properties per the JavaBean spec, and `org.springframework.batch.item.file.transform.PassThroughFieldExtractor`, which returns the item (useful for items that are just a `String`, for example).

You look at a few of the `LineAggregator` implementations over the rest of this section. Let's begin with using `FlatFileItemWriter` with `FormatterLineAggregator` to create formatted files.

Formatted Text Files

When you looked at text files from the input side, you had three different types: fixed width, delimited, and XML. From the output side of things, you still have delimited and XML, but fixed width isn't just fixed width. In this case, it's really a formatted record. This section looks at how to construct batch output as a formatted text file.

Why the difference between a fixed-width input file and a formatted output file? Well, technically there is no difference. They're both files that contain a fixed format record of some kind. However, typically input files have records that contain nothing but data and are defined via columns, whereas output files can be either fixed width or more robust (as you see later in this chapter with the statement job).

This example generates a list of customers and where they live. To begin, let's look at the input you're working with. Listing 9-2 shows an example of the `customer.csv` file.

Listing 9-2. `customer.csv`

```
Richard,N,Darrow,5570 Isabella Ave,St. Louis,IL,58540
Warren,L,Darrow,4686 Mt. Lee Drive,St. Louis,NY,94935
Barack,G,Donnelly,7844 S. Greenwood Ave,Houston,CA,38635
Ann,Z,Benes,2447 S. Greenwood Ave,Las Vegas,NY,55366
Erica,Z,Gates,3141 Farnam Street,Omaha,CA,57640
Warren,M,Williams,6670 S. Greenwood Ave,Hollywood,FL,37288
Harry,T,Darrow,3273 Isabella Ave,Houston,FL,97261
Steve,O,Darrow,8407 Infinite Loop Drive,Las Vegas,WA,90520
```

As Listing 9-2 shows, you're working with a file similar to the customer files you've been using up to this point in the book. However, the output for this job will be slightly different. In this case, you want to output a full sentence for each customer: "Richard Darrow lives at 5570 Isabella Ave in St. Louis, IL." Listing 9-3 shows an example of what the output file looks like.

Listing 9-3. Formatted Customer Output

```
Richard N Darrow lives at 5570 Isabella Ave in St. Louis, IL.
Warren L Darrow lives at 4686 Mt. Lee Drive in St. Louis, NY.
Barack G Donnelly lives at 7844 S. Greenwood Ave in Houston, CA.
Ann Z Benes lives at 2447 S. Greenwood Ave in Las Vegas, NY.
Laura 9S Minella lives at 8177 4th Street in Dallas, FL.
Erica Z Gates lives at 3141 Farnam Street in Omaha, CA.
Warren M Williams lives at 6670 S. Greenwood Ave in Hollywood, FL.
Harry T Darrow lives at 3273 Isabella Ave in Houston, FL.
Steve O Darrow lives at 8407 Infinite Loop Drive in Las Vegas, WA.
Erica Z Minella lives at 513 S. Greenwood Ave in Miami, IL.
```

How do you do this? For this example, you'll use a single step job that reads in the input file and writes it to the output file; you don't need an ItemProcessor. Because the only code you need to write is that for the Customer class, you can start there; see Listing 9-4.

Listing 9-4. Customer.java

```java
package com.apress.springbatch.chapter9;

import java.io.Serializable;

public class Customer implements Serializable {
    private static final long serialVersionUID = 1L;

    private long id;
    private String firstName;
    private String middleInitial;
    private String lastName;
    private String address;
    private String city;
    private String state;
    private String zip;

    // Accessors go here
    ...
}
```

As you can see in Listing 9-4, the fields of the Customer object map to the fields in the customer.csv file.[1] With the item coded, you can begin configuring the job.[2] The input side should be familiar from Chapter 7. Listing 9-5 shows the configuration of the input file as a resource (the value is passed in via a job parameter), the FlatFileItemReader configuration, and the required reference to the Customer object.

---

[1] The Customer object has an id attribute that you use later; it has no data in the file.

[2] As with all the previous examples in this book, batch.properties for the project is the same as it was using MySQL in Chapter 2. Also, unless otherwise specified, launch-context.xml is the same as well.

Listing 9-5. Configuring the Format Job's Input

```
...
<beans:bean id="customerFile"
  class="org.springframework.core.io.FileSystemResource" scope="step">
  <beans:constructor-arg value="#{jobParameters[customerFile]}"/>
</beans:bean>

<beans:bean id="customerFileReader"
  class="org.springframework.batch.item.file.FlatFileItemReader">
  <beans:property name="resource" ref="customerFile"/>
  <beans:property name="lineMapper">
    <beans:bean
      class="org.springframework.batch.item.file.mapping.DefaultLineMapper">
      <beans:property name="lineTokenizer">
        <beans:bean
          class="org.springframework.batch.item.file.transform.
DelimitedLineTokenizer">
          <beans:property name="names"
            value="firstName,middleInitial,lastName,address,city,state,zip"/>
          <beans:property name="delimiter" value=","/>
        </beans:bean>
      </beans:property>
      <beans:property name="fieldSetMapper">
        <beans:bean class="org.springframework.batch.item.file.mapping.
BeanWrapperFieldSetMapper">
          <beans:property name="prototypeBeanName" value="customer"/>
        </beans:bean>
      </beans:property>
    </beans:bean>
  </beans:property>
</beans:bean>

<beans:bean id="customer" class="com.apress.springbatch.chapter9.Customer"
  scope="prototype"/>
...
```

There shouldn't be a lot of surprises in the configuration in Listing 9-4. You begin by configuring customerFile as a resource for the ItemReader to read from. Next is customerFileReader, which consists of a FlatFileItemReader. customerFileReader references customerFile as well as a LineMapper implementation to convert each record of the file into a Customer object. Because you're processing a basic CSV file, you're able to use DelimitedLineTokenizer to parse each record and BeanWrapperFieldSetMapper to take the resulting FieldSet and populate a customer instance. The final piece of the input configuration is a reference to the Customer object that the ItemReader uses to create new Customer objects.

For the output side of things, you need to configure the output file, FlatFileItemWriter, and a LineAggregator. This example uses the org.springframework.batch.itemfile.transform.FormatterLineAggregator provided by Spring Batch. Listing 9-6 shows the configuration for the job's output.

Listing 9-6. Output Configuration for Format Job

```
...
<beans:bean id="outputFile"
  class="org.springframework.core.io.FileSystemResource" scope="step">
  <beans:constructor-arg value="#{jobParameters[outputFile]}"/>
</beans:bean>

<beans:bean id="flatFileOutputWriter"
  class="org.springframework.batch.item.file.FlatFileItemWriter">
  <beans:property name="resource" ref="outputFile"/>
  <beans:property name="lineAggregator" ref="formattedLineAggregator"/>
</beans:bean>

<beans:bean id="formattedLineAggregator"
  class="org.springframework.batch.item.file.transform.
FormatterLineAggregator">
  <beans:property name="fieldExtractor">
    <beans:bean class="org.springframework.batch.item.file.transform.
BeanWrapperFieldExtractor">
      <beans:property name="names"
        value="firstName,lastName,address,city,state,zip"/>
    </beans:bean>
  </beans:property>
  <beans:property name="format" value="%s %s lives at %s %s in %s, %s."/>
</beans:bean>
...
```

As Listing 9-6 shows, the configuration for the output side of this step is actually smaller than the input. You begin by configuring of the output file; again, the name of the file is passed in as a job parameter. Next you have the configuration of the FlatFileItemWriter. flatFileOutputWriter takes two dependencies: a resource (the file to write to) and the LineAggregator implementation. The last piece of the output puzzle is the LineAggregator implementation: FormatterLineAggregator in this case. It takes two dependencies: a FieldExtractor implementation and a format.

The org.springframework.batch.item.file.transform.FieldExtractor interface is intended to abstract the process of taking the fields of an object tree and convert them into an Object array. With the objects to be written into an array, the FormatterLineAggregator uses Java's String.format() method in conjunction with the string provided in the format dependency to generate the formatted String to be written to the file. In this case, BeanWrapperFieldExtractor uses the getters for each of the properties defined and returns the results, in order, in an Object array to be formatted according to the format string. In the case of Listing 9-6, you're extracting the firstName, lastName, address, city, state, and zip from each item. It's important to note that there is no key/value pairing during the formatting process. If you want a bean property to appear twice in the formatted String, you need to include it twice, in order, in the names list.

With all of the input and output configured, all you need to do to complete the job is configure the step and job. Listing 9-7 shows the complete configuration of formatJob including the previous input and output.

Listing 9-7. formatJob.xml

```xml
<?xml version="1.0" encoding="UTF-8"?>
<beans:beans xmlns="http://www.springframework.org/schema/batch"
  xmlns:beans="http://www.springframework.org/schema/beans"
  xmlns:xsi="http://www.w3.org/2001/XMLSchema-instance"
  xsi:schemaLocation="http://www.springframework.org/schema/beans
    http://www.springframework.org/schema/beans/spring-beans-3.0.xsd
    http://www.springframework.org/schema/batch
    http://www.springframework.org/schema/batch/spring-batch-2.1.xsd">

  <beans:import resource="../launch-context.xml"/>

  <beans:bean id="customerFile"
    class="org.springframework.core.io.FileSystemResource" scope="step">
    <beans:constructor-arg value="#{jobParameters[customerFile]}"/>
  </beans:bean>

  <beans:bean id="customerFileReader"
    class="org.springframework.batch.item.file.FlatFileItemReader">
    <beans:property name="resource" ref="customerFile"/>
    <beans:property name="lineMapper">
      <beans:bean
       class="org.springframework.batch.item.file.mapping.DefaultLineMapper">
        <beans:property name="lineTokenizer">
          <beans:bean class="org.springframework.batch.item.file.transform.
DelimitedLineTokenizer">
            <beans:property name="names"
              value="firstName,middleInitial,lastName,address,city,state,zip"/>
            <beans:property name="delimiter" value=","/>
          </beans:bean>
        </beans:property>
        <beans:property name="fieldSetMapper">
          <beans:bean class="org.springframework.batch.item.file.mapping.
BeanWrapperFieldSetMapper">
            <beans:property name="prototypeBeanName" value="customer"/>
          </beans:bean>
        </beans:property>
      </beans:bean>
    </beans:property>
  </beans:bean>

  <beans:bean id="customer" class="com.apress.springbatch.chapter9.Customer"
    scope="prototype"/>

  <beans:bean id="outputFile"
    class="org.springframework.core.io.FileSystemResource" scope="step">
    <beans:constructor-arg value="#{jobParameters[outputFile]}"/>
  </beans:bean>

  <beans:bean id="flatFileOutputWriter"
```

```
      class="org.springframework.batch.item.file.FlatFileItemWriter">
      <beans:property name="resource" ref="outputFile"/>
      <beans:property name="lineAggregator" ref="formattedLineAggregator"/>
    </beans:bean>

  <beans:bean id="formattedLineAggregator"
    class="org.springframework.batch.item.file.transform.
FormatterLineAggregator">
    <beans:property name="fieldExtractor">
      <beans:bean class="org.springframework.batch.item.file.transform.
BeanWrapperFieldExtractor">
        <beans:property name="names"
          value="firstName,lastName,address,city,state,zip"/>
      </beans:bean>
    </beans:property>
    <beans:property name="format" value="%s %s lives at %s %s in %s, %s."/>
  </beans:bean>

  <step id="formatStep">
    <tasklet>
      <chunk reader="customerFileReader" writer="flatFileOutputWriter"
        commit-interval="10"/>
    </tasklet>
  </step>

  <job id="formatJob">
    <step id="step1" parent="formatStep"/>
  </job>
</beans:beans>
```

After you build the project using Maven's mvn clean install command, you can execute the example using CommandLineJobRunner with the command shown in Listing 9-8.

Listing 9-8. *How to Execute formatJob from the Command Line*

```
java -jar itemWriters-0.0.1-SNAPSHOT.jar jobs/formatJob.xml formatJob
customerFile=/input/customer.csv outputFile=/output/formattedCustomers.txt
```

When you run the job with the input specified in Listing 9-2, the result is a new file, formattedCustomers.txt, with the contents listed in Listing 9-9.

Listing 9-9. *formattedCustomers.txt*

```
Richard Darrow lives at 5570 Isabella Ave St. Louis in IL, 58540.
Warren Darrow lives at 4686 Mt. Lee Drive St. Louis in NY, 94935.
Barack Donnelly lives at 7844 S. Greenwood Ave Houston in CA, 38635.
Ann Benes lives at 2447 S. Greenwood Ave Las Vegas in NY, 55366.
Erica Gates lives at 3141 Farnam Street Omaha in CA, 57640.
Warren Williams lives at 6670 S. Greenwood Ave Hollywood in FL, 37288.
Harry Darrow lives at 3273 Isabella Ave Houston in FL, 97261.
Steve Darrow lives at 8407 Infinite Loop Drive Las Vegas in WA, 90520.
```

This method of formatting output can be used for a number of different requirements. Whether it's formatting items into human-readable output as you did here, or formatting them into a fixed-width file as you used for input in Chapter 7, all that needs to change is the format String you configure for the LineAggregator.

The other main type of flat file you see on a regular basis is the delimited file. customer.csv is a comma-delimited file, for example. The next section looks at how to output files that contain delimited output.

Delimited Files

Unlike the formatted files you looked at in the previous section, delimited files don't have a single predefined format. Instead, a delimited file consists of a list of values separated by a predefined separator character. This section looks at how to use Spring Batch to generate a delimited file.

To see how generating a delimited file works, you use the same input for this job. For the output, you refactor the ItemWriter to generate the new, delimited output. In this case, you change the order of the fields and change the delimiter from a comma (,) to a semicolon (;). Listing 9-10 shows some sample output with the updated formatJob.

Listing 9-10. Output for Delimited formatJob

```
58540;IL;St. Louis;5570 Isabella Ave;Darrow;Richard
94935;NY;St. Louis;4686 Mt. Lee Drive;Darrow;Warren
38635;CA;Houston;7844 S. Greenwood Ave;Donnelly;Barack
55366;NY;Las Vegas;2447 S. Greenwood Ave;Benes;Ann
57640;CA;Omaha;3141 Farnam Street;Gates;Erica
37288;FL;Hollywood;6670 S. Greenwood Ave;Williams;Warren
97261;FL;Houston;3273 Isabella Ave;Darrow;Harry
90520;WA;Las Vegas;8407 Infinite Loop Drive;Darrow;Steve
```

To generate the output in Listing 9-10, all you need to do is update the configuration of the LineAggregator. Instead of using FormatterLineAggregator, you use Spring Batch's org.springframework.batch.item.file.transform.DelimitedLineAggregator implementation. Using the same BeanWrapperFieldExtractor to extract an Object array, the DelimitedLineAggregator concatenates the elements of the array with the configured delimiter between each element. Listing 9-11 shows the updated configuration for the ItemWriter.

Listing 9-11. flatFileOutputWriter Configuration

```
...
<beans:bean id="flatFileOutputWriter"
  class="org.springframework.batch.item.file.FlatFileItemWriter">
  <beans:property name="resource" ref="outputFile"/>
  <beans:property name="lineAggregator" ref="delimitedLineAggregator"/>
</beans:bean>

<beans:bean id="delimitedLineAggregator"
  class="org.springframework.batch.item.file.transform.
DelimitedLineAggregator">
  <beans:property name="fieldExtractor">
    <beans:bean class="org.springframework.batch.item.file.transform.
BeanWrapperFieldExtractor">
```

```
    <beans:property name="names"
      value="zip,state,city,address,lastName,firstName"/>
  </beans:bean>
</beans:property>
<beans:property name="delimiter" value=";"/>
</beans:bean>
...
```

By changing the configuration of the FormatterLineAggregator to use Spring Batch's DelimitedLineAggregator, the only other change you have to make is removing the format dependency and including the definition of a delimiter character. After building the project with the same mvn clean install you used previously, you can run the job with the command in Listing 9-12.

Listing 9-12. Running formatJob to Generate Delimited Output

```
java -jar itemWriters-0.0.1-SNAPSHOT.jar jobs/formatJob.xml formatJob
customerFile=/input/customer.csv outputFile=/output/delimitedCustomers.txt
```

The results of the formatJob with the updated configuration are shown in Listing 9-13.

Listing 9-13. formatJob results for delimited file writing

```
58540;IL;St. Louis;5570 Isabella Ave;Darrow;Richard

94935;NY;St. Louis;4686 Mt. Lee Drive;Darrow;Warren

38635;CA;Houston;7844 S. Greenwood Ave;Donnelly;Barack

55366;NY;Las Vegas;2447 S. Greenwood Ave;Benes;Ann

57640;CA;Omaha;3141 Farnam Street;Gates;Erica

37288;FL;Hollywood;6670 S. Greenwood Ave;Williams;Warren

97261;FL;Houston;3273 Isabella Ave;Darrow;Harry

90520;WA;Las Vegas;8407 Infinite Loop Drive;Darrow;Steve
```

It's easy to create flat files with Spring Batch. With zero lines of code outside of the domain object, you can read in a file and convert its format to either a formatted file or a delimited file. Both of the examples for flat-file processing have assumed that the file is a new file to be created each time. The next section looks at some of the more advanced options Spring Batch provides for handling what file to write to.

File Creation Options

Unlike reading from an input file where the file must exist or it's considered an error condition, an output file may or may not exist, and that may or may not be ok. Spring Batch provides the ability to configure how to handle each of these scenarios based on your needs. This section looks at how to configure FlatFileItemWriter to handle multiple file creation scenarios.

In Table 9-1, there were two options for FlatFileItemWriter that pertain to file creation: shouldDeleteIfEmpty and shouldDeleteIfExists. shouldDeleteIfEmpty actually deals with what to do when a step is complete. It's set to false by default. If a step executes, no items were written (a header and footer may have been, but no item records were written), and shouldDeleteIfEmpty is set to true, the file is deleted on the completion of the step. By default, the file is created and left empty. You can look at this behavior with the formatJob you ran in the previous section. By updating the configuration of flatFileOutputWriter to set shouldDeleteIfEmpty to true as shown in Listing 9-14, you can process an empty file and see that no output file is left behind.

Listing 9-14. Configuring formatJob to Delete the Output File if No Items Are Written

```
...
<beans:bean id="flatFileOutputWriter"
  class="org.springframework.batch.item.file.FlatFileItemWriter">
  <beans:property name="resource" ref="outputFile"/>
  <beans:property name="lineAggregator" ref="delimitedLineAggregator"/>
  <beans:property name="shouldDeleteIfEmpty" value="true"/>
</beans:bean>
...
```

If you execute formatJob with the updated file and pass it an empty customer.csv file as input, no output is left behind. It's important to note that the file is still created, opened, and closed. In fact, if the step is configured to write a header and/or footer in the file, that is written as well. However, if the number of items written to the file is zero, the file is deleted at the end of the step.

The next configuration parameter related to file creation/deletion is the shouldDeleteIfExists flag. This flag, set to true by default, deletes a file that has the same name as the output file the step intends to write to. For example, if you're going to run a job that writes to a file /output/jobRun.txt, and that file already exists when the job starts, Spring Batch deletes the file and creates a new one. If this file exists and the flag is set to false, an org.springframework.batch.item.ItemStreamException is thrown when the step attempts to create the new file. Listing 9-15 shows formatJob's flatFileOutputWriter configured to not delete the output file if it exists.

Listing 9-15. Configuring formatJob to Not Delete the Output File if It Already Exists

```
...
<beans:bean id="flatFileOutputWriter"
  class="org.springframework.batch.item.file.FlatFileItemWriter">
  <beans:property name="resource" ref="outputFile"/>
  <beans:property name="lineAggregator" ref="delimitedLineAggregator"/>
  <beans:property name="shouldDeleteIfExists" value="false"/>
</beans:bean>
...
```

By running the job as it's configured in Listing 9-15, you receive the previously mentioned ItemStreamException as shown in Listing 9-16.

Listing 9-16. Results of a Job that Writes to an Existing File that Shouldn't Be There

```
2011-03-06 12:32:51,006 DEBUG main
[org.springframework.batch.core.scope.StepScope] - <Creating object in
scope=step, name=scopedTarget.outputFile>
2011-03-06 12:32:51,065 ERROR main
[org.springframework.batch.core.step.AbstractStep] - <Encountered an error
executing the step>
```

```
org.springframework.batch.item.ItemStreamException: File already exists:
[/output/overwriteThisFile.txt]
      at org.springframework.batch.item.util.FileUtils.setUpOutputFile(FileUtils.java:62)
 at
org.springframework.batch.item.file.FlatFileItemWriter$OutputState.initialize
BufferedWriter(FlatFileItemWriter.java:497)
 at
org.springframework.batch.item.file.FlatFileItemWriter$OutputState.access$000
(FlatFileItemWriter.java:354)
 at
org.springframework.batch.item.file.FlatFileItemWriter.doOpen(FlatFileItemWri
ter.java:291)
 at
org.springframework.batch.item.file.FlatFileItemWriter.open(FlatFileItemWrite
r.java:281)
 at
org.springframework.batch.item.support.CompositeItemStream.open(CompositeItem
Stream.java:98)
 at
org.springframework.batch.core.step.tasklet.TaskletStep.open(TaskletStep.java
:288)
      at org.springframework.batch.core.step.AbstractStep.execute(AbstractStep.java:193)
 at
org.springframework.batch.core.job.SimpleStepHandler.handleStep(SimpleStepHan
dler.java:135)
 at
org.springframework.batch.core.job.flow.JobFlowExecutor.executeStep(JobFlowEx
ecutor.java:61)
```

The use of this parameter is a good idea in an environment where you want to preserve the output of each run. This prevents an accidental overwrite of your old file.

The final option related to file creation is the appendAllowed parameter. When this flag (which defaults to false) is set to true, Spring Batch automatically sets the shouldDeleteIfExists flag to false, creates a new file if one doesn't exist, and appends the data if it does. This option can be useful if you have an output file that you need to write to from multiple steps. Listing 9-17 shows formatJob configured to append data if the file exists.

Listing 9-17. Appending Data if the Output File Exists

```
...
<beans:bean id="flatFileOutputWriter"
  class="org.springframework.batch.item.file.FlatFileItemWriter">
  <beans:property name="resource" ref="outputFile"/>
  <beans:property name="lineAggregator" ref="delimitedLineAggregator"/>
  <beans:property name="appendAllowed" value="true"/>
</beans:bean>
...
```

With this configuration, you can run the job multiple times using the same output file (with different input files), and Spring Batch appends the output of the current job to the end of the existing output file.

As you can see, there are a number of options available to handle flat file-based output, from being able to format your records any way you want to generating delimited files and even providing options for how Spring Batch handles files that already exist. However, flat files aren't the only type of file output. XML is the other type of file output that Spring Batch provides for, and you look at it next.

StaxEventItemWriter

When you looked at reading XML back in Chapter 7, you explored how Spring Batch views XML documents in fragments. Each of these fragments is the XML representation of a single item to be processed. On the ItemWriter side, the same concept exists. Spring Batch generates an XML fragment for each of the items the ItemWriter receives and writes the fragment to the file. This section looks at how Spring Batch handles XML as an output medium.

To handle writing XML using Spring Batch, you use `org.springframework.batch.item.xml.StaxEventItemWriter`. Just like the ItemReader, the Streaming API for XML (StAX) implementation allows Spring Batch to write fragments of XML as each chunk is processed. Just like `FlatFileItemWriter`, `StaxEventItemWriter` generates the XML a chunk at a time and writes it to the file after the local transaction has been committed; this prevents rollback issues if there is an error writing to the file.

The configuration of the `StaxEventItemReader` consists of a resource (file to read from), a root element name (the root tag for each fragment), and an unmarshaller to be able to convert the XML input into an object. The configuration for `StaxEventItemWriter` is almost identical, with a resource to write to, a root element name (the root tag for each fragment you generate), and a marshaller to convert each item into an XML fragment.

`StaxEventItemWriter` has a collection of configurable attributes that are covered in Table 9-2.

Table 9-2. Attributes Available in `StaxEventItemWriter`

Option	Type	Default	Description
`encoding String`		UTF-8	Character encoding for the file.
`footerCallback StaxWriterCallback`		null	Executed after the last item of a file has been written.
`headerCallback StaxWriterCallback`		null	Executed before the first item of a file has been written.
`marshaller Marshaller`		null (required)	Used to convert an individual item to an XML fragment for output.
`overwriteOutput boolean`		true	By default, the file is replaced if the output file already exists. If this is set to true and the file exists, an `ItemStreamException` is thrown.
`resource Resource`		null (required)	File or stream to be written to.

rootElementAttributes Map<String,	String>	null	This key/value pairing is appended to the root tag of each fragment with the keys as the attribute names and value as their values.
rootTagName String		null (required)	Defines the root XML tag the XML document.
saveState boolean		true	Determines if Spring Batch keeps track of the state of the ItemWriter (number of items written, and so on).
transactional boolean		true	If true, the writing of the output is delayed until the transaction is committed, to prevent rollback issues.
version String		"1.0"	Version of XML the file is written in.

To look at how `StaxEventItemWriter` works, let's update `formatJob` to output the customer output in XML. Using the same input from the previous examples, Listing 9-18 shows the new output you create when you update the job.

Listing 9-18. `customer.xml`

```
<?xml version="1.0" encoding="UTF-8"?>
<customers>
  <customer>
    <id>0</id>
    <firstName>Richard</firstName>
    <middleInitial>N</middleInitial>
    <lastName>Darrow</lastName>
    <address>5570 Isabella Ave</address>
    <city>St. Louis</city>
    <state>IL</state>
    <zip>58540</zip>
  </customer>
  ...
</customers>
```

In order to generate the output shown in Listing 9-18, you reuse the `formatJob` configuration but replace `flatFileOutputWriter` with a new `xmlOutputWriter` that uses the `StaxEventItemWriter` ItemWriter implementation. To configure the new ItemWriter, you provide three dependencies as shown in Listing 9-19: a resource to write to, a reference to an `org.springframework.oxm.Marshaller` implementation, and a root tag name (`customer` in this case).

Listing 9-19. Configuration for formatJob with StaxEventItemWriter

```xml
<?xml version="1.0" encoding="UTF-8"?>
<beans:beans xmlns="http://www.springframework.org/schema/batch"
  xmlns:beans="http://www.springframework.org/schema/beans"
  xmlns:util="http://www.springframework.org/schema/beans"
  xmlns:xsi="http://www.w3.org/2001/XMLSchema-instance"
  xsi:schemaLocation="http://www.springframework.org/schema/beans
    http://www.springframework.org/schema/beans/spring-beans-3.0.xsd
    http://www.springframework.org/schema/util
    http://www.springframework.org/schema/util/spring-util.xsd
    http://www.springframework.org/schema/batch
    http://www.springframework.org/schema/batch/spring-batch-2.1.xsd">

  <beans:import resource="../launch-context.xml"/>

  <beans:bean id="customerFile"
    class="org.springframework.core.io.FileSystemResource" scope="step">
    <beans:constructor-arg value="#{jobParameters[customerFile]}"/>
  </beans:bean>

  <beans:bean id="customerFileReader"
    class="org.springframework.batch.item.file.FlatFileItemReader">
    <beans:property name="resource" ref="customerFile"/>
    <beans:property name="lineMapper">
      <beans:bean
        class="org.springframework.batch.item.file.mapping.DefaultLineMapper">
        <beans:property name="lineTokenizer">
          <beans:bean class="org.springframework.batch.item.file.transform.
DelimitedLineTokenizer">
            <beans:property name="names"
              value="firstName,middleInitial,lastName,address,city,state,zip"/>
            <beans:property name="delimiter" value=","/>
          </beans:bean>
        </beans:property>
        <beans:property name="fieldSetMapper">
          <beans:bean class="org.springframework.batch.item.file.mapping.
BeanWrapperFieldSetMapper">
            <beans:property name="prototypeBeanName" value="customer"/>
          </beans:bean>
        </beans:property>
      </beans:bean>
    </beans:property>
  </beans:bean>

  <beans:bean id="customer" class="com.apress.springbatch.chapter9.Customer"
    scope="prototype"/>

  <beans:bean id="outputFile"
    class="org.springframework.core.io.FileSystemResource" scope="step">
    <beans:constructor-arg value="#{jobParameters[outputFile]}"/>
```

```
    </beans:bean>

    <beans:bean id="xmlOutputWriter"
      class="org.springframework.batch.item.xml.StaxEventItemWriter">
      <beans:property name="resource" ref="outputFile" />
      <beans:property name="marshaller" ref="customerMarshaller" />
      <beans:property name="rootTagName" value="customers" />
    </beans:bean>

    <beans:bean id="customerMarshaller"
      class="org.springframework.oxm.xstream.XStreamMarshaller">
      <beans:property name="aliases">
        <util:map>
          <beans:entry key="customer"
            value="com.apress.springbatch.chapter9.Customer" />
        </util:map>
      </beans:property>
    </beans:bean>

    <step id="formatStep">
      <tasklet>
        <chunk reader="customerFileReader" writer="xmlOutputWriter"
          commit-interval="10"/>
      </tasklet>
    </step>

    <job id="formatJob">
      <step id="step1" parent="formatStep"/>
    </job>
</beans:beans>
```

Of the 69 lines of XML that it took to configure the original formatJob as shown in Listing 9-7, the formatJob in Listing 9-19 has changed only 14 lines (shortening the file overall by one line). The changes begin with the definition of a new ItemWriter, xmlOutputWriter. This bean is a reference to the StaxEventItemWriter the section has been talking about and defines three dependencies: the resource to write to, the Marshaller implementation, and the root tag name for each XML fragment the Marshaller will generate.

Just below xmlOutputWriter is customerMarshaller. This bean is used to generate an XML fragment for each item the job processes. Using Spring's org.springframework.oxm.xtream.XStreamMarshaller class, the only further configuration you're required to provide is a Map of aliases to use for each type the Marshaller comes across. By default, the Marshaller uses the attribute's name as the tag name, but you provide an alias for the Customer class because the XStreamMarshaller uses the fully qualified name for the class by default as the root tag of each fragment (com.apress.springbatch.chatper8.Customer instead of just customer).

In order for the job to be able to compile and run, you need to make one more update. The POM file needs a new dependency to handle the XML processing, a reference to Spring's Object/XML Mapping (OXM) library. Listing 9-20 shows the update to the POM that is required.

Listing 9-20. Spring's OXM Library Maven Dependency

```
...
<dependency>
  <groupId>org.springframework.ws</groupId>
  <artifactId>spring-oxm</artifactId>
  <version>1.5.9</version>
</dependency>
...
```

▧**Note** Although Spring Batch considers itself compatible with Spring 3, and you're using Spring 3 for all examples in this book, this is one area where it isn't compatible and depends on an older version of OXM.

With the POM updated and the job configured, you're ready to build and run formatJob to generate XML as the output. After running a mvn clean install from the command line, you can use the command listed in Listing 9-21 to execute the job.

Listing 9-21. Executing formatJob to Generate XML

```
java -jar itemWriters-0.0.1-SNAPSHOT.jar jobs/formatJob.xml formatJob
customerFile=/input/customer.csv outputFile=/output/xmlCustomer.xml
```

When you look at the results of the XML, notice that it was obviously generated by a library in that there is no formatting applied. But by running it through XML Tidy, you can see clearly that the output is what you expected. Listing 9-22 shows a sample of the generated output XML.

Listing 9-22. formatJob XML Results

```
<?xml version="1.0" encoding="UTF-8"?>
<customers>
<customer>
<id>0</id>
<firstName>Richard</firstName>
<middleInitial>N</middleInitial>
<lastName>Darrow</lastName>
<address>5570 Isabella Ave</address>
<city>St. Louis</city>
<state>IL</state>
<zip>58540</zip>
</customer>
    ...
</customers>
```

With not much more than a couple lines of XML, you can easily generate XML output with the full power of any Spring-supported XML marshaller.

The ability to process XML as both input and output is important in today's enterprise environment, as isthe ability to process flat files. However, although files play a large part in batch processing, they en't as prevalent in other processing in today's enterprise. Instead, the relational database has taken over. As such, the batch process must be able to not only read from a database (as you saw in Chapter 7) but write to it as well. The next section looks at the more common ways to handle writing to a database using Spring Batch.

Database-Based ItemWriters

Writing to a database offers a different set of constraints than file-based output. First, databases are transactional resources, unlike files. Because of this, you can include the physical write as part of the transaction instead of segmenting it as file-based processing does. Also, there are many different options for how to access a database. JDBC, Java Persistence API (JPA), and Hibernate all offer unique yet compelling models for handling writing to a database. This section looks at how to use JDBC, Hibernate, and JPA to write the output of a batch process to a database.

JdbcBatchItemWriter

The first way you can write to the database is the way most people learn how to access a database with Spring in general, via JDBC. Spring Batch's JdbcBatchItemWriter uses the JdbcTemplate and its batch SQL execution capabilities to execute all of the SQL for a single chunk at once. This section looks at how to use JdbcBatchItemWriter to write a step's output to a database.

org.springframework.batch.item.database.JdbcBatchItemWriter isn't much more than a thin wrapper around Spring's org.springframework.jdbc.support.JdbcTemplate, using the JdbcTemplate.batchUpdate or JdbcTemplate.execute method depending on if named parameters are used in the SQL to execute mass database insert/updates. The important thing to note about this is that Spring uses PreparedStatement's batch-update capabilities to execute all the SQL statements for a single chunk at once instead of using multiple calls. This greatly improves performance while still allowing all the executions to execute within the current transaction.

To see how the JdbcBatchItemWriter works, again you work with the same input you used with the file-based writers, but you use it to populate a customer database table instead of writing a file. Figure 9-3 shows the design of the table into which you're inserting the customer information.

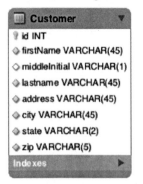

Figure 9-3. Customer table design

As you can see in Figure 9-3, the columns of the Customer table match up virtually one-to-one with the elements in the customer.csv file. The only difference is the id field, which you let the database populate for you. In order to insert the values into the table, you need to build the SQL in either of two ways: using question marks (?) as placeholders for the values or using named parameters (:name, for example) as placeholders. Each of these two options requires a slightly different approach in populating the values. You start with the question mark as shown in the sample SQL statement in Listing 9-23.

Listing 9-23. Prepared Statement for Inserting into the Customer Table

```
insert into customer (firstName, middleInitial, lastName, address, city,
state, zip) values (?, ?, ?, ?, ?, ?, ?)
```

As you can see, there is nothing unusual about the prepared statement. However, providing the SQL statement is only one of the configuration options for JdbcBatchItemWriter. Table 9-3 lists all the configuration options.

Table 9-3. JdbcBatchItemWriter Configuration Options

Option	Type	Default	Description
assertUpdates	boolean	true	If true, causes JdbcBatchItemWriter to validate that every item resulted in an insert or update. If any item didn't trigger an insert or an update of a record, an EmptyResultDataAccessException is thrown.

dataSource DataSource		null (required)	Provides access to the required database.
itemPreparedStatementSetter	ItemPreparedStatement Setter	null	If a standard PreparedStatement is provided (using ? for parameters), JdbcBatchItemWriter uses this class to populate the parameter values.
itemSqlParameterSourceProvi der	ItemSqlParameter SourceProvider	null	If named parameters are used in the SQL provided, the JdbcBatchItemWriter uses this class to populate the parameter values.
simpleJdbcTemplate SimpleJdbcTemplate		null	Allows you to inject an implementation of the SimpleJdbcOperations interface.
sql String		null (required)	SQL to be executed for each item.

To use JdbcBatchItemWriter in formatJob, you replace xmlOutputWriter with a new jdbcBatchWriter bean. Because you begin with a standard PreparedStatement syntax for the query (using question marks), you need to provide it with a dataSource, the SQL to be executed, and an implementation of the org.springframework.batch.item.database.ItemPreparedStatementSetter interface. Yes, you're correct if you realized that you're going to have to write some code to make this one work.

ItemPreparedStatementSetter is a simple interface used to abstract the extraction of values from each item and set them on the PreparedStatement. It contains a single method, as shown in Listing 9-24.

Listing 9-24. ItemPreparedStatementSetter Interface

```
package org.springframework.batch.item.database;

import java.sql.PreparedStatement;
import java.sql.SQLException;

import org.springframework.jdbc.core.RowMapper;

public interface ItemPreparedStatementSetter<T> {
    void setValues(T item, PreparedStatement ps) throws SQLException;
}
```

To implement the ItemPreparedStatementSetter interface, you create your own CustomerItemPreparedStatementSetter. This class implements the single setValues method that is required by the ItemPreparedStatementSetter interface by using the normal PreparedStatement API to populate each value of the PreparedStatement with the appropriate value from the item. Listing 9-25 shows the code for CustomerItemPreparedStatementSetter.

Listing 9-25. CustomerItemPreparedStatementSetter.java

```java
package com.apress.springbatch.chapter9;

import java.sql.PreparedStatement;
import java.sql.SQLException;

import org.springframework.batch.item.database.ItemPreparedStatementSetter;

public class CustomerItemPreparedStatementSetter implements
        ItemPreparedStatementSetter<Customer> {

    public void setValues(Customer customer, PreparedStatement ps)
            throws SQLException {

        ps.setString(1, customer.getFirstName());
        ps.setString(2, customer.getMiddleInitial());
        ps.setString(3, customer.getLastName());
        ps.setString(4, customer.getAddress());
        ps.setString(5, customer.getCity());
        ps.setString(6, customer.getState());
        ps.setString(7, customer.getZip());
    }
}
```

As Listing 9-25 shows, there is no magic involved in setting the values for each PreparedStatement. With this code, you can update formatJob's configuration to write its output to the database. Listing 9-26 shows the configuration for the new ItemWriter.

Listing 9-26. jdbcBatchWriter's Configuration

```xml
...
<beans:bean id="jdbcBatchWriter"
  class="org.springframework.batch.item.database.JdbcBatchItemWriter">
  <beans:property name="dataSource" ref="dataSource"/>
  <beans:property name="sql" value="insert into customer (firstName,
middleInitial, lastName, address, city, state, zip) values (?, ?, ?, ?, ?, ?,
?)"/>
  <beans:property name="itemPreparedStatementSetter"
    ref="preparedStatementSetter"/>
</beans:bean>

<beans:bean id="preparedStatementSetter"
class="com.apress.springbatch.chapter9.CustomerItemPreparedStatementSetter"/>
...
```

As you can see in Listing 9-26, the new jdbcBatchItemWriter references the dataSource bean from the launch-context.xml file (the customer table is in the same schema as the Spring Batch tables you use for the JobRepository). The SQL value is the same as the SQL statement you previously defined in Listing 9-23. The last dependency you provide is the reference to the CustomerItemPreparedStatementSetter.

The final piece of the puzzle to configure the new ItemWriter is to update the configuration for the step to reference the new ItemWriter. To do this, all you need to do is update formatStep's configuration reference the jdbcBatchWriter bean in place of its current reference to the xmlOutputWriter from the previous section. Listing 9-27 shows the full listing of formatJob.xml configured to write to the database.

Listing 9-27. formatJob.xml Configured for JDBC Database Writing

```xml
<?xml version="1.0" encoding="UTF-8"?>
<beans:beans xmlns="http://www.springframework.org/schema/batch"
  xmlns:beans="http://www.springframework.org/schema/beans"
  xmlns:util="http://www.springframework.org/schema/beans"
  xmlns:xsi="http://www.w3.org/2001/XMLSchema-instance"
  xsi:schemaLocation="http://www.springframework.org/schema/beans
    http://www.springframework.org/schema/beans/spring-beans-3.0.xsd
    http://www.springframework.org/schema/util
    http://www.springframework.org/schema/util/spring-util.xsd
    http://www.springframework.org/schema/batch
    http://www.springframework.org/schema/batch/spring-batch-2.1.xsd">

  <beans:import resource="../launch-context.xml"/>

  <beans:bean id="customerFile"
    class="org.springframework.core.io.FileSystemResource" scope="step">
    <beans:constructor-arg value="#{jobParameters[customerFile]}"/>
  </beans:bean>

  <beans:bean id="customerFileReader"
    class="org.springframework.batch.item.file.FlatFileItemReader">
    <beans:property name="resource" ref="customerFile"/>
    <beans:property name="lineMapper">
      <beans:bean
       class="org.springframework.batch.item.file.mapping.DefaultLineMapper">
        <beans:property name="lineTokenizer">
          <beans:bean class="org.springframework.batch.item.file.transform.
DelimitedLineTokenizer">
            <beans:property name="names"
             value="firstName,middleInitial,lastName,address,city,state,zip"/>
            <beans:property name="delimiter" value=","/>
          </beans:bean>
        </beans:property>
        <beans:property name="fieldSetMapper">
          <beans:bean class="org.springframework.batch.item.file.mapping.
BeanWrapperFieldSetMapper">
            <beans:property name="prototypeBeanName" value="customer"/>
          </beans:bean>
        </beans:property>
      </beans:bean>
    </beans:property>
  </beans:bean>

  <beans:bean id="customer" class="com.apress.springbatch.chapter9.Customer"
    scope="prototype"/>

  <beans:bean id="jdbcBatchWriter"
```

```
    class="org.springframework.batch.item.database.JdbcBatchItemWriter">
    <beans:property name="dataSource" ref="dataSource"/>
    <beans:property name="sql" value="insert into customer (firstName,
middleInitial, lastName, address, city, state, zip) values (?, ?, ?, ?, ?, ?,
?)"/>
    <beans:property name="itemPreparedStatementSetter"
      ref="preparedStatementSetter"/>
  </beans:bean>

  <beans:bean id="preparedStatementSetter"
    class="com.apress.springbatch.chapter9.
CustomerItemPreparedStatementSetter"/>

  <step id="formatStep">
    <tasklet>
      <chunk reader="customerFileReader" writer="jdbcBatchWriter"
        commit-interval="10"/>
    </tasklet>
  </step>

  <job id="formatJob">
    <step id="step1" parent="formatStep"/>
  </job>
</beans:beans>
```

Because you already have the JDBC drivers configured in the POM and the dataSource configured for the JobRepository, all you need to do is execute an mvn clean install and execute the command in Listing 9-28 to see the results of the updated formatJob.

Listing 9-28. Command to Execute formatJob

```
java -jar itemWriters-0.0.1-SNAPSHOT.jar jobs/formatJob.xml formatJob
customerFile=/input/customer.csv
```

The output of this job isn't in a file this time but in the database. You can confirm the execution in two ways. The first is by going to the database to validate the input. Listing 9-29 shows the results of the job in the database.

Listing 9-29. Job Results with jdbcBatchWriter

```
mysql> select * from customer;
+------+-----------+---------------+----------+-------------------------+---
--------+-------+-------+
| id   | firstName | middleInitial | lastName | address                 |
city       | state | zip   |
+------+-----------+---------------+----------+-------------------------+---
--------+-------+-------+
| 1607 | Richard   | N             | Darrow   | 5570 Isabella Ave       |
St. Louis | IL    | 58540 |
| 1608 | Warren    | L             | Darrow   | 4686 Mt. Lee Drive      |
St. Louis | NY    | 94935 |
| 1609 | Barack    | G             | Donnelly | 7844 S. Greenwood Ave   |
```

```
Houston   | CA  | 38635 |
| 1610 | Ann     | Z         | Benes    | 2447 S. Greenwood Ave   |
Las Vegas | NY  | 55366 |
| 1612 | Erica   | Z         | Gates    | 3141 Farnam Street      |
Omaha     | CA  | 57640 |
| 1613 | Warren  | M         | Williams | 6670 S. Greenwood Ave   |
Hollywood | FL  | 37288 |
| 1614 | Harry   | T         | Darrow   | 3273 Isabella Ave       |
Houston   | FL  | 97261 |
| 1615 | Steve   | O         | Darrow   | 8407 Infinite Loop Drive |
Las Vegas | WA  | 90520 |
```

The other way to check the output of the job is to look at the results via the Spring Batch Admin application. Figure 9-4 shows Spring Batch Admin's display of the results.

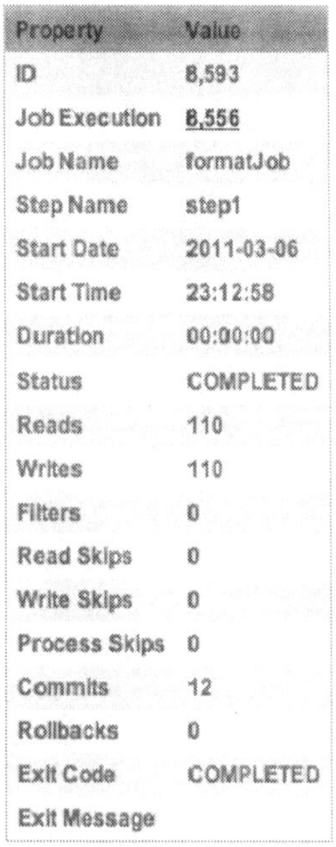

Details for Step Execution

Property	Value
ID	8,593
Job Execution	8,556
Job Name	formatJob
Step Name	step1
Start Date	2011-03-06
Start Time	23:12:58
Duration	00:00:00
Status	COMPLETED
Reads	110
Writes	110
Filters	0
Read Skips	0
Write Skips	0
Process Skips	0
Commits	12
Rollbacks	0
Exit Code	COMPLETED
Exit Message	

Figure 9-4. Spring Batch Admin's display of the results for the step

The PreparedStatement notation is useful given most Java developers' familiarity with it. However, the named parameter approach provided by Spring's JdbcTemplate is a much safer way to go and is the preferred way to populate parameters in most Spring environments. With that in mind, you can put this feature to use by making two small updates to the configuration:

1. Update the configuration to remove the ItemPreparedStatementSetter implementation you wrote and replace it with an implementation of the ItemSqlParameterSourceProvider interface.

    2.   Update the SQL to use named parameters instead of question marks for parameters.

The `org.springframework.batch.item.database.ItemSqlParameterSourceProvider` interface is slightly different from the `ItemPreparedStatementSetter` interface in that it doesn't set the parameters on the statement to be executed. Instead, an implementation of the `ItemSqlParameterSourceProvider`'s responsibility is to extract the parameter values from an item and return them as an `org.springframework.jdbc.core.namedparam.SqlParameterSource` object.

The nice thing about this approach is that not only is it the safer approach (no concerns about needing to keep the SQL in the XML file in synch with the code of the `ItemPreparedStatementSetter` implementation) but Spring Batch provides implementations of this interface that allow you to use convention over code to extract the values from the items. In this example, you use Spring Batch's `BeanPropertyItemSqlParameterSourceProvider` (try saying that three times fast) to extract the values from the items to be populated in the SQL. Listing 9-30 shows the updated `jdbcBatchWriter` configuration for this change.

Listing 9-30. jdbcBatchWriter using BeanPropertyItemSqlParameterSourceProvider

```
...
<beans:bean id="jdbcBatchWriter"
  class="org.springframework.batch.item.database.JdbcBatchItemWriter">
  <beans:property name="dataSource" ref="dataSource"/>
  <beans:property name="sql" value="insert into customer (firstName, middleInitial, lastName,
address, city, state, zip) values (:firstName, :middleInitial, :lastName, :address, :city,
:state, :zip)"/>
  <beans:property name="itemSqlParameterSourceProvider">
    <beans:bean
      class="org.springframework.batch.item.database.
BeanPropertyItemSqlParameterSourceProvider"/>
  </beans:property>
</beans:bean>
...
```

You can quickly note in Listing 9-30 that there is no reference to the `ItemPreparedStatementSetter` implementation. By using this configuration, you don't need any custom code. Yet the results are the same.

Although JDBC is known for its speed compared to other persistence framework that lie on top of it, other frameworks are popular in the enterprise. Next you look at how to use the most popular of those to do database writing: Hibernate.

HibernateItemWriter

When you have most of your database tables and applications already mapped with Hibernate, reusing all that is a logical choice to start. You saw how Hibernate works as a competent reader in Chapter 7. This section looks at how you can use `HibernateItemWriter` to write the changes to a database.

Like `JdbcBatchItemWriter`, `org.springframework.batch.item.database.HibernateItemWriter` serves as a thin wrapper to Spring's `org.springframework.orm.hibernate3.HibernateTemplate`. When a chunk completes, the list of items is passed to `HibernateItemWriter` where `HibernateTemplate`'s `saveOrUpdate` method is called for each item. When all the items have been saved or updated, `HibernateItemWriter` makes a single call to `HibernateTemplate`'s `flush` method, executing all the changes at once. This provides a batching functionality similar to JdbcBatchItemWriter's implementation without dealing directly with the SQL.

Configuring HibernateItemWriter is simple. All but the configuration of the actual ItemWriter should be familiar, because it's the same as the configuration and coding you did for the Hibernate-supported ItemReaders. To modify formatJob to use Hibernate, you need to update the following:

- *The pompom:* The POM needs to incorporate the Hibernate dependencies.

- Customer.java: You use annotations to configure the mapping for the Customer object, so you need to add those to the Customer class.

- SessionFactory: You need to configure both the SessionFactory and a new TransactionManager to support Hibernate.

- HibernateItemWriter: You can configure the new ItemWriter using HibernateItemWriter.

Let's start with the POM updates. For Hibernate to work with Spring Batch, you need to include the Hibernate dependencies as well as Spring's ORM-supporting dependencies. Listing 9-31 shows the additions you need to make to the POM.

Listing 9-31. Pom Additions for Supporting Hibernate

```
...
<dependency>
  <groupId>org.hibernate</groupId>
  <artifactId>hibernate-core</artifactId>
  <version>3.3.0.SP1</version>
</dependency>
<dependency>
  <groupId>org.hibernate</groupId>
  <artifactId>hibernate-entitymanager</artifactId>
  <optional>true</optional>
  <version>3.3.2.GA</version>
</dependency>
<dependency>
  <groupId>org.hibernate</groupId>
  <artifactId>hibernate-annotations</artifactId>
  <optional>true</optional>
  <version>3.4.0.GA</version>
</dependency>
<dependency>
  <groupId>org.springframework</groupId>
  <artifactId>spring-orm</artifactId>
  <version>${spring.framework.version}</version>
</dependency>
<dependency>
  <groupId>org.springframework</groupId>
  <artifactId>spring-context-support</artifactId>
  <version>${spring.framework.version}</version>
</dependency>
...
```

Now you can begin updating formatJob. Let's begin with the only code you need to write: the annotations you add to the Customer class to map it to the database. Listing 9-32 shows the Customer class updated.

Listing 9-32. Customer.java Mapped to the Customer Table

```java
package com.apress.springbatch.chapter9;

import java.io.Serializable;

import javax.persistence.Entity;
import javax.persistence.GeneratedValue;
import javax.persistence.GenerationType;
import javax.persistence.Id;
import javax.persistence.Table;

@Entity
@Table(name="customer")
public class Customer implements Serializable {
    private static final long serialVersionUID = 1L;

    @Id
    @GeneratedValue(strategy = GenerationType.IDENTITY)
    private long id;
    private String firstName;
    private String middleInitial;
    private String lastName;
    private String address;
    private String city;
    private String state;
    private String zip;

    // Accessors go here
    ....
}
```

The annotations you use here are the same as the ones you used in the ItemReader example in Chapter 7. The mapping for the Customer class is pretty straightforward because the column names of the Customer table match those of the Customer class. The other thing to notice is that you aren't using any Hibernate-specific annotations. All the annotations used here are JPA-supported annotations, which allows you to switch from Hibernate to any JPA-supported implementation if you choose with no code changes required.

Next, you can move on to configuring the SessionFactory. Again, the configuration here is the same that you used in Chapter 7 for Hibernate's ItemReader implementations. You configure the SessionFactory and the Hibernate-supported transaction manager both in the launch-context.xml file. In addition, you add a hibernate.cfg.xml file to the root of the resources directory. Listing 9-33 shows the configuration updates you need to make to the launch-context.xml file.

Listing 9-33. Launch-context.xml Configured for Hibernate Support

```
...
<bean id="sessionFactory"
  class="org.springframework.orm.hibernate3.LocalSessionFactoryBean">
  <property name="dataSource" ref="dataSource" />
  <property name="configLocation">
    <value>classpath:hibernate.cfg.xml</value>
  </property>
  <property  name="configurationClass">
    <value>org.hibernate.cfg.AnnotationConfiguration</value>
  </property>
  <property name="hibernateProperties">
    <props>
      <prop key="hibernate.show_sql">true</prop>
      <prop key="hibernate.format_sql">true</prop>
    </props>
  </property>
</bean>

<bean id="transactionManager"
  class="org.springframework.orm.hibernate3.HibernateTransactionManager"
  lazy-init="true">
  <property name="sessionFactory" ref="sessionFactory" />
</bean>
...
```

Again, this configuration should be familiar because it matches what you used in Chapter 7. You begin the configuration with the SessionFactory. It relies on a dataSource (you recycle the same one you've been using up to now); the location of the configuration, which in the case is a hibernate.cfg.xml file in the root of the classpath; and a configurationClass to identify that you're using Hibernate's annotation support to handle the mapping. Finally, you want to see the SQL that is being executed, so you add the properties to tell Hibernate to log and format all SQL it generates.

The second part of the configuration in Listing 9-33 is the configuration of Hibernate's transaction manager. It's important to note that you want to remove the one you've used up to now (and that's included in launch-context.xml) when you use Hibernate's transaction manager. This allows Spring Batch and the Hibernate code to use the same transaction manager.

The second part of the SessionFactory configuration is the addition of a hibernate.cfg.xml file into the <PROJECT_HOME>/src/main/resources directory. Listing 9-34 shows the contents of this file.

Listing 9-34. hibernate.cfg.xml

```
<!DOCTYPE hibernate-configuration PUBLIC
  "-//Hibernate/Hibernate Configuration DTD 3.0//EN"
  "http://hibernate.sourceforge.net/hibernate-configuration-3.0.dtd">

<hibernate-configuration>
  <session-factory>
    <mapping class="com.apress.springbatch.chapter9.Customer"/>
  </session-factory>
</hibernate-configuration>
```

The very simple hibernate.cfg.xml file shown in Listing 9-34 serves only to tell Hibernate where to look for classes that are annotated as entities.

Finally you can configure HibernateItemWriter. It's probably the easiest ItemWriter to configure given that other components and the Hibernate framework do all the work. HibernateItemWriter requires a single dependency and has one optional dependency. The required dependency is a reference to the SessionFactory you configured previously in Listing 9-31. The optional dependency (which you aren't using in this case) is a reference to a HibernateOperations implementation via the property hibernateTemplate.[3]Listing 9-35 show the configuration of the job complete with the new HibernateItemWriter configuration.

Listing 9-35. formatJob.xml Using Hibernate

```
<?xml version="1.0" encoding="UTF-8"?>
<beans:beans xmlns="http://www.springframework.org/schema/batch"
  xmlns:beans="http://www.springframework.org/schema/beans"
  xmlns:util="http://www.springframework.org/schema/beans"
  xmlns:xsi="http://www.w3.org/2001/XMLSchema-instance"
  xsi:schemaLocation="http://www.springframework.org/schema/beans
    http://www.springframework.org/schema/beans/spring-beans-3.0.xsd
    http://www.springframework.org/schema/util
    http://www.springframework.org/schema/util/spring-util.xsd
    http://www.springframework.org/schema/batch
    http://www.springframework.org/schema/batch/spring-batch-2.1.xsd">

  <beans:import resource="../launch-context.xml"/>

  <beans:bean id="customerFile"
    class="org.springframework.core.io.FileSystemResource" scope="step">
    <beans:constructor-arg value="#{jobParameters[customerFile]}"/>
  </beans:bean>

  <beans:bean id="customerFileReader"
    class="org.springframework.batch.item.file.FlatFileItemReader">
    <beans:property name="resource" ref="customerFile"/>
    <beans:property name="lineMapper">
      <beans:bean
        class="org.springframework.batch.item.file.mapping.DefaultLineMapper">
        <beans:property name="lineTokenizer">
          <beans:bean class="org.springframework.batch.item.file.transform.
DelimitedLineTokenizer">
            <beans:property name="names"
            value="firstName,middleInitial,lastName,address,city,state,zip"/>
            <beans:property name="delimiter" value=","/>
          </beans:bean>
        </beans:property>
        <beans:property name="fieldSetMapper">
          <beans:bean class="org.springframework.batch.item.file.mapping.
BeanWrapperFieldSetMapper">
```

---

[3] This option is rarely used. Typically it's used for testing purposes only.

```
                <beans:property name="prototypeBeanName" value="customer"/>
              </beans:bean>
            </beans:property>
          </beans:bean>
        </beans:property>
      </beans:bean>

      <beans:bean id="customer" class="com.apress.springbatch.chapter9.Customer"
        scope="prototype"/>

      <beans:bean id="hibernateBatchWriter"
        class="org.springframework.batch.item.database.HibernateItemWriter">
        <beans:property name="sessionFactory" ref="sessionFactory"/>
      </beans:bean>

      <step id="formatStep">
        <tasklet>
          <chunk reader="customerFileReader" writer="hibernateBatchWriter"
            commit-interval="10"/>
        </tasklet>
      </step>

      <job id="formatJob">
        <step id="step1" parent="formatStep"/>
      </job>
    </beans:beans>
```

The configuration for this job changes only with the configuration of hibernateBatchWriter and its reference in the formatStep. As you saw previously, HibernateItemWriter requires only a reference to a SessionFactory, which is provided via the configuration in launch-context.xml. Executing this job returns the same results as the JdbcBatchItemWriter example previously.

When other frameworks do all of the heavy lifting, the Spring Batch configuration is quite simple, as this Hibernate example shows. Hibernate's official spec cousin, JPA, is the other database access framework you can use to do database writing.

JpaItemWriter

The Java Persistence API (JPA) provides very similar functionality and requires almost the exact same configuration as its Hibernate cousin. It, like Hibernate, does the heavy lifting in the case of writing to the database, so the Spring Batch piece of the puzzle is very small. This section looks at how to configure JPA to perform database writing.

When you look at the org.springframework.batch.item.writer.JpaItemWriter, it serves as a thin wrapper around JPA's javax.persistence.EntityManager. When a chunk completes, the list of items within the chunk is passed to JpaItemWriter. The writer loops over the items in the list, calling the EntityManager's merge method on each item before calling flush after all the items have been saved.

To see JpaItemWriter in action, you use the same customer input as earlier and insert it into the same Customer table. To hook JPA into the job, you need to do the following four things:

1. Add a persistence.xml file. The persistence.xml file in JPA is used to configure the EntityManager. For you to be able to use JPA, you need to add one to the project.

2. Configure `EntityManagerFactory` and the JPA Transaction Manager.
    `EntityManagerFactory` is the source of an `EntityManager` for the job. It along
    with a JPA-supported transaction manager is required.

3. Map the `Customer` class. You use annotations to configure the mapping of the
    `Customer` class to the Customer table.

4. Configure the `JpaItemWriter`. The last step is to configure the new ItemWriter
    to save the items read in the job.

Let's start with the `persistence.xml` file, which is shown in Listing 9-36. This file needs to live in the
`<PROJECT_HOME>/src/main/resources/META-INF/` directory with the name `persistence.xml` per the JPA
specification.

Listing 9-36. persistence.xml

```xml
<persistence xmlns="http://java.sun.com/xml/ns/persistence"
  xmlns:xsi="http://www.w3.org/2001/XMLSchema-instance"
  xsi:schemaLocation="http://java.sun.com/xml/ns/persistence
    http://java.sun.com/xml/ns/persistence/persistence_1_0.xsd"
    version="1.0">

  <persistence-unit name="customer" transaction-type="RESOURCE_LOCAL">
    <class>com.apress.springbatch.chapter9.Customer</class>
  </persistence-unit>
</persistence>
```

The `persistence.xml` file required for this example is about as simple as you can create. The
persistence unit is named customer with the application controlling the transactions. You have a single
class mapped with annotations, the `Customer` class. To get started with JPA, that is really all you need for
a `persistence.xml` file.

Next you can update the `launch-context.xml` file with an `EntityManagerFactory` and Spring's
`JpaTransactionManager`. Listing 9-37 shows the additions you need to make to a base `launch-context.xml`
file to incorporate the JPA components.

Listing 9-37. Launch-context.xml Updates for JPA

```xml
...
<bean id="entityManagerFactory"
  class="org.springframework.orm.jpa.LocalContainerEntityManagerFactoryBean">
  <property name="dataSource" ref="dataSource" />
  <property name="persistenceUnitName" value="customer" />
  <property name="jpaVendorAdapter">
    <bean
      class="org.springframework.orm.jpa.vendor.HibernateJpaVendorAdapter">
      <property name="showSql" value="true" />
    </bean>
  </property>
  <property name="jpaDialect">
    <bean class="org.springframework.orm.jpa.vendor.HibernateJpaDialect" />
  </property>
</bean>
```

```
<bean id="transactionManager"
  class="org.springframework.orm.jpa.JpaTransactionManager">
  <property name="entityManagerFactory" ref="entityManagerFactory" />
</bean>
...
```

You begin looking at the configuration for launch-context.xml with the EntityManagerFactory. Configuring Spring's org.springframework.orm.jpa.LocalContainerEntityManagerFactoryBean requires four dependencies:

- *A datasource:* The EntityManager uses this to connect to the database.

- *A persistence unit name*: This defines the group of persistable classes for the EntityManager.

- jpaVendorAdapter: JPA is just a specification like JDBC or JavaServer Faces (JSF). Someone needs to implement the specification in order for you to use it. In this example, you're using Hibernate's implementation of JPA.

- jpaDialect: This gives you a vendor-dependent way of handling things that JPA doesn't provide for (accessing the underlying database connection, for example).

Next, you configure Spring's org.springframework.orm.jpa.JpaTransactionManager with its single dependency, the EntityManagerFactory you just configured.

The next piece of the JPA puzzle is mapping the Customer object to the Customer table. You use annotations for this as you have in the past. The nice thing about the way you mapped the Customer class previously is that you used all JPA annotations for the Hibernate example. This allows you to reuse the Customer object unchanged for JPA. Listing 9-38 shows the Customer class mapped using the JPA annotations.

Listing 9-38. Customer.java Mapped with JPA Annotations

```
package com.apress.springbatch.chapter9;

import java.io.Serializable;

import javax.persistence.Entity;
import javax.persistence.GeneratedValue;
import javax.persistence.GenerationType;
import javax.persistence.Id;
import javax.persistence.Table;

@Entity
@Table(name="customer")
public class Customer implements Serializable {
    private static final long serialVersionUID = 1L;

    @Id
    @GeneratedValue(strategy = GenerationType.IDENTITY)
    private long id;
    private String firstName;
    private String middleInitial;
    private String lastName;
```

```
    private String address;
    private String city;
    private String state;
    private String zip;

    // Accessors go here
    ...
}
```

The code in Listing 9-38 is the same that is in Listing 9-32. By avoiding the Hibernate annotations in the previous example, you're able to see how switching persistence frameworks requires no code changes.

The final aspect of configuring the job to use JPA is to configure JpaItemWriter. It requires only a single dependency—a reference to EntityManagerFactory—so that it can obtain an EntityManager to work with. Listing 9-39 shows the configuration for the new ItemWriter and the job updated to use it.

Listing 9-39. *formatJob Configured to Use JpaItemWriter*

```
...
<beans:bean id="jpaBatchWriter"
  class="org.springframework.batch.item.database.JpaItemWriter">
  <beans:property name="entityManagerFactory" ref="entityManagerFactory"/>
</beans:bean>

<step id="formatFileStep">
  <tasklet>
    <chunk reader="customerFileReader" writer="jpaBatchWriter"
      commit-interval="10"/>
  </tasklet>
</step>

<job id="formatJob">
  <step id="step1" parent="formatFileStep"/>
</job>
...
```

You can now build the job with a quick mvn clean install. To execute the job, use the command in Listing 9-40, which returns the results you've seen in the other database examples.

Listing 9-40. *Command to Execute formatJob with JPA Configured*

```
java -jar itemWriters-0.0.1-SNAPSHOT.jar jobs/formatJob.xml formatJob
customerFile=/input/customer.csv
```

The relational database rules in the modern enterprise, for better or worse. As you can see, writing job results to a database is easy with Spring Batch. But files and databases aren't the only forms of output that are available both from Spring Batch or needed in an enterprise. The next section looks at other examples of the wide range of output options Spring Batch provides.

Alternative Output Destination ItemWriters

Files and databases aren't the only ways you can communicate the end result of an item being processed. Enterprises use a number of other means to store an item after it has been processed. In Chapter 7, you looked at Spring Batch's ability to call an existing Spring service to obtain data. It should come as no surprise then that the framework offers similar functionality on the writing end. Spring Batch also exposes Spring's powerful JMS interactions with a `JmsItemWriter`. Finally, if you have a requirement to send e-mails from a batch process, Spring Batch can handle that too. This section looks at how to call existing Spring services, write to a JMS destination, and send e-mail using provided Spring Batch ItemWriters.

ItemWriterAdapter

In most enterprises that use Spring, there are a number of existing services already written and battle-tested in production. There is no reason they can't be reused in your batch processes. In Chapter 7, you looked at how to use them as sources of input for the jobs. This section looks at how the `ItemWriterAdapter` allows you to use existing Spring services as ItemWriters as well.

`org.springframework.batch.item.adapter.ItemWriterAdapter` is nothing more than a thin wrapper around the service you configure. As with any other ItemWriter, the `write` method receives a list of items to be written. `ItemWriterAdapter` loops through the list calling the service method configured for each item in the list. It's important to note that the method being called by `ItemWriterAdapter` can only accept the item type being processed. For example, if the step is processing `Car` objects, the method being called must take a single argument of type `Car`.

To configure an `ItemWriterAdapter`, two dependencies are required:

- `targetObject`: The Spring bean that contains the method to be called

- `targetMethod`: The method to be called with each item

■**Note** The method being called by `ItemWriterAdapter` must take a single argument of the type that is being processed by the current step.

Let's look at an example of `ItemWriterAdapter` in action. Listing 9-41 shows the code for a service that logs `Customer` items to `System.out`.

Listing 9-41. CustomerServiceImpl.java

```
package com.apress.springbatch.chapter9;

public class CustomerServiceImpl {

public void logCustomer(Customer cust) {
        System.out.println("I just saved " + cust);
    }
}
```

As you can see in Listing 9-41, CustomerServiceImpl is short, sweet, and to the point. But it serves the purpose for the example. To put this service to work in formatJob, you can configure it to be the target of a new ItemWriterAdapter. Using the same input configuration you've used in the other jobs this chapter, Listing 9-42 shows the configuration for the ItemWriter using the CustomerServiceImpl's logCustomer method and job referencing it.

Listing 9-42. ItemWriterAdapter Configuration

```
    ...
<beans:bean id="customerService"
  class="com.apress.springbatch.chapter9.CustomerServiceImpl"/>

<beans:bean id="itemWriterAdapter"
  class="org.springframework.batch.item.adapter.ItemWriterAdapter">
  <beans:property name="targetObject" ref="customerService"/>
  <beans:property name="targetMethod" value="logCustomer"/>
</beans:bean>

<step id="formatFileStep">
  <tasklet>
    <chunk reader="customerFileReader" writer="itemWriterAdapter"
      commit-interval="10"/>
  </tasklet>
</step>

<job id="formatJob">
  <step id="step1" parent="formatFileStep"/>
</job>
...
```

Listing 9-42 starts with the configuration of customerService. The ItemWriter is next as the itemWriterAdapter. The two dependencies it uses are a reference to customerService and the name of the logCustomer method. Finally, you reference the itemWriterAdapter in the step to be used by the job.

To execute this job, you build it, like all jobs, with a mvn clean install from the command line. With the job built, you can execute it by executing the jar file as you've done in the past. A sample of the output of this job is shown in Listing 9-43.

Listing 9-43. ItemWriterAdapter Output

```
2011-03-09 22:43:56,526 DEBUG main
[org.springframework.batch.repeat.support.RepeatTemplate] - <Repeat operation
about to start at count=10>
2011-03-09 22:43:56,526 DEBUG main
[org.springframework.batch.repeat.support.RepeatTemplate] - <Repeat is
complete according to policy and result value.>
I just saved Richard N. Darrow
5570 Isabella Ave
St. Louis, IL
58540
I just saved Warren L. Darrow
4686 Mt. Lee Drive
```

St. Louis, NY
94935

As you would expect, calling an existing service with the item you've processed in your step is made easy with Spring Batch. However, what if your service doesn't take the same object you're processing? If you want to be able to extract values out of your item and pass them to your service, Spring Batch has you covered. `PropertyExtractingDelegatingItemWriter` (yes, that really is its name) is next.

PropertyExtractingDelegatingItemWriter

The use case for `ItemWriterAdapter` is pretty simple. Take the item being processed, and pass it to an existing Spring service. However, software is rarely that straightforward. Because of that, Spring Batch has provided a mechanism to extract values from an item and pass them to a service as parameters. This section looks at `PropertyExtractingDelegatingItemWriter` and how to use it with an existing service.

Although it has a long name, `org.springframework.batch.item.adapter.PropertyExtractingDelegatingItemWriter` is a lot like the `ItemWriterAdapter`. Just like `ItemWriterAdapter`, it calls a specified method on a referenced Spring service. The difference is that instead of blindly passing the item being processed by the step, `PropertyExtractingDelegatingItemWriter` passes only the attributes of the item that are requested. For example, if you have an item of type `Product` that contains fields for a database id, name, price, and SKU number, you're required to pass the entire `Product` object to the service method as with `ItemWriterAdapter`. But with `PropertyExtractingDelegatingItemWriter`, you can specify that you only want the database id and price to be passed as parameters to the service.

To look at this as an example, you can use the same customer input that you're familiar with by this point. You add a method to the `CustomerServiceImpl` that allows you to log the address of the `Customer` item being processed and use `PropertyExtractingDelegatingItemWriter` to call the new method. Let's start by looking at the updated `CustomerServiceImpl` (see Listing 9-44).

Listing 9-44. CustomerServiceImpl with logAddress()

```
package com.apress.springbatch.chapter9;

public class CustomerServiceImpl {

    public void logCustomer(Customer cust) {
        System.out.println("I just saved " + cust);
    }

    public void logAddress(String address,
                           String city,
                           String state,
                           String zip) {
        System.out.println("I just saved the address:\n" + address + "\n" +
                           city + ", " + state + "\n" + zip);
    }
}
```

As you can see in Listing 9-44, the `logAddress` method doesn't take the `Customer` item. Instead it takes values that you have within it. To use this method, you use `PropertyExtractingDelegatingItemWriter` to extract the address fields (address, city, state, and zip) from each `Customer` item and call the service with the values it receives. To configure this ItemWriter, you pass in an ordered list of properties to extract from the item along with the target object and method to be called. The list you pass in in the same order as the parameters required for the property; Spring does support dot notation (`address.city`, for example) as well as index properties (`e-mail[5]`). Just like the `ItemWriterAdapter`, this `ItemWriter` implementation also exposes an `arguments` property that isn't used because the arguments are extracted by the writer dynamically. Listing 9-45 shows the job updated to call the `logAddress` method instead of handling the entire `Customer` item.

Listing 9-45. formatJob Configured to Call the logAddress Method on CustomerServiceImpl

```
    ...
<beans:bean id="parameterizedItemWriterAdapter"
  class="org.springframework.batch.item.adapter.
PropertyExtractingDelegatingItemWriter">
  <beans:property name="targetObject" ref="customerService"/>
  <beans:property name="targetMethod" value="logAddress"/>
  <beans:property name="fieldsUsedAsTargetMethodArguments"
    value="address,city,state,zip"/>
</beans:bean>

<step id="formatFileStep">
  <tasklet>
    <chunk reader="customerFileReader"
      writer="parameterizedItemWriterAdapter" commit-interval="10"/>
  </tasklet>
</step>

<job id="formatJob">
  <step id="step1" parent="formatFileStep"/>
</job>
...
```

When you run the job, the output of it consists of a sentence written to `System.out` with a formatted address. Listing 9-46 shows a sample of the output you can expect.

Listing 9-46. Output of formatJob Using PropertyExtractingDelegatingItemWriter

```
2011-03-10 22:14:46,744 DEBUG main
[org.springframework.batch.repeat.support.RepeatTemplate] - <Repeat operation
about to start at count=9>
2011-03-10 22:14:46,744 DEBUG main
[org.springframework.batch.repeat.support.RepeatTemplate] - <Repeat operation
about to start at count=10>
2011-03-10 22:14:46,745 DEBUG main
[org.springframework.batch.repeat.support.RepeatTemplate] - <Repeat is
complete according to policy and result value.>
I just saved the address:
5570 Isabella Ave
St. Louis, IL
58540
I just saved the address:
4686 Mt. Lee Drive
```

St. Louis, NY
94935

Spring Batch provides the ability to reuse just about any existing Spring service you've created as an ItemWriter, with good reason. The code your enterprise has is battle tested in production, and reusing it is less likely to introduce new bugs and also speeds up development time. The next section looks at using JMS resources as the destination of items processed within a step.

JmsItemWriter

Java Messaging Service (JMS) is a message-oriented method of communicating between two or more endpoints. By using either point-to-point communication (a JMS queue) or a publish-subscribe model (JMS topic), Java applications can communicate with any other technology that can interface with the messaging implementation. This section looks at how you can put messages on a JMS queue using Spring Batch's JmsItemWriter.

Spring has made great progress in simplifying a number of common Java concepts. JDBC and integration with the various ORM frameworks come to mind as examples. But Spring's work in simplifying interfacing with JMS resources is just as impressive. In order to work with JMS, you need to use a JMS broker. This example uses Apache's ActiveMQ.

Apache ActiveMQ is one of the most popular and powerful open source JMS implementations available. It has the ability to interface with a number of different languages (Java, C, C++, C#, Ruby, and so on), provides a full JMS 1.1 implementation, and yet still is one of the easier message brokers to work with.

Before you can work with ActiveMQ, you need to add its dependencies and Spring's JMS dependencies to the POM so that it's available. This example works with ActiveMQ version 5.4.2, which is the most current version as of this writing. Listing 9-47 shows the dependencies you need to add to the POM.

Listing 9-47. Dependencies for ActiveMQ and Spring JMS

```
...
<dependency>
  <groupId>org.apache.activemq</groupId>
  <artifactId>activemq-core</artifactId>
  <version>5.4.2</version>
  <exclusions>
    <exclusion>
      <groupId>org.apache.activemq</groupId>
      <artifactId>activeio-core</artifactId>
    </exclusion>
  </exclusions>
</dependency>
<dependency>
  <groupId>org.springframework</groupId>
  <artifactId>spring-jms</artifactId>
  <version>${spring.framework.version}</version>
</dependency>
...
```

Now you can begin to put ActiveMQ to work. Before you get into the code, however, let's look at the processing for this job because it's slightly different than before.

In previous examples in this chapter, you have had a single step that read in the customer.csv file and wrote it out using the appropriate ItemWriter for the example. For this example, however, that won't be enough. If you read in the items and write them to the JMS queue, you won't know that everything got onto the queue correctly because you can't see what is in the queue. Instead, as Figure 9-5 shows, you use two steps for this job. The first one reads the customer.csv file and writes it to the ActiveMQ queue. The second step reads from the queue and writes the records out to an XML file.

Figure 9-5. Processing for jmsFormatJob

It's important to note that you don't want to do this in an actual production environment because a message isn't pulled off the queue until all of them have been put on it. This could lead to running out of room in your queue depending on how it's configured and the resources available. However, for this example and given the small number of customers you're processing, this approach demonstrates the point.

To begin using org.springframework.batch.item.jms.JmsItemWriter, you need to configure a couple of JMS-related beans in launch-context.xml. Luckily, Spring makes this very easy.[4] You need to configure three beans:

- *A queue:* This is the destination for JmsItemWriter. It's a queue provided by ActiveMQ.

- *A connection factory:* The job needs to be able to obtain a connection to the queue (similar to a connection to a database).

- *A JmsTemplate:* This is the Spring component that is does all the heavy lifting for you.

Let's start by looking at the queue. Although ActiveMQ offers a number of options for configuring a queue, it makes things simple to get up and running by allowing you to configure a JMS queue via Spring. You will configure the queue to be dynamically created on startup and serve as the destination.

With the queue itself configured, you can configure the connection factory to access it. Just like the queue itself, ActiveMQ exposes a class that allows you to configure the connection factory via Spring. To do that, all you need to do is define a URL in which the connection factory can find the broker. In this case, you're telling it to look at the local JVM.

Finally you can create JmsTemplate. This is Spring's way of exposing JMS functionality in a way that's easy to use and understand. To put it to use here, you need to provide three dependencies: a reference to the connection factory, a reference to the queue, and a timeout value for how long the reader will wait when listening for messages. Listing 9-48 shows the configuration of the JMS resources in launch-context.xml.

Listing 9-48. JMS Resource Configuration in launch-context.xml

---

[4] Entire books have been devoted to the subject of JMS, not to mention volumes on the topic of Spring integrating with JMS. This book keeps things simple to emphasize the integration of Spring Batch and JMS. For more information on Spring and JMS, check out *Pro Spring Integration* (Apress, 2011).

```
...
<bean id="destination" class="org.apache.activemq.command.ActiveMQQueue">
  <constructor-arg value="customerQueue"/>
</bean>

<bean id="jmsConnectionFactory"
  class="org.apache.activemq.ActiveMQConnectionFactory">
  <property name="brokerURL" value="vm://localhost"/>
</bean>

<bean id="jmsTemplate" class="org.springframework.jms.core.JmsTemplate">
  <property name="connectionFactory" ref="jmsConnectionFactory"/>
  <property name="defaultDestination" ref="destination"/>
  <property name="receiveTimeout" value="5000"/>
</bean>
...
```

Now you can configure the job. You use the same reader you've used up to this point in the chapter for the first step and the same writer you used in the XML example earlier in the chapter for the writer in the second step. Their configuration can be found in Listing 9-49.

Listing 9-49. Input and Output of jmsFormatJob

```
<beans:bean id="customerFile"
  class="org.springframework.core.io.FileSystemResource" scope="step">
  <beans:constructor-arg value="#{jobParameters[customerFile]}"/>
</beans:bean>

<beans:bean id="customerFileReader"
  class="org.springframework.batch.item.file.FlatFileItemReader">
  <beans:property name="resource" ref="customerFile"/>
  <beans:property name="lineMapper">
    <beans:bean
      class="org.springframework.batch.item.file.mapping.DefaultLineMapper">
      <beans:property name="lineTokenizer">
        <beans:bean class="org.springframework.batch.item.file.transform.
DelimitedLineTokenizer">
          <beans:property name="names"
            value="firstName,middleInitial,lastName,address,city,state,zip"/>
          <beans:property name="delimiter" value=","/>
        </beans:bean>
      </beans:property>
      <beans:property name="fieldSetMapper">
        <beans:bean class="org.springframework.batch.item.file.mapping.
BeanWrapperFieldSetMapper">
          <beans:property name="prototypeBeanName" value="customer"/>
        </beans:bean>
      </beans:property>
    </beans:bean>
  </beans:property>
</beans:bean>
```

```
<beans:bean id="customer" class="com.apress.springbatch.chapter9.Customer"
  scope="prototype"/>

<beans:bean id="outputFile"
  class="org.springframework.core.io.FileSystemResource" scope="step">
  <beans:constructor-arg value="#{jobParameters[outputFile]}"/>
</beans:bean>

<beans:bean id="xmlOutputWriter"
  class="org.springframework.batch.item.xml.StaxEventItemWriter">
  <beans:property name="resource" ref="outputFile" />
  <beans:property name="marshaller" ref="customerMarshaller" />
  <beans:property name="rootTagName" value="customers" />
</beans:bean>

<beans:bean id="customerMarshaller"
  class="org.springframework.oxm.xstream.XStreamMarshaller">
  <beans:property name="aliases">
    <util:map>
      <beans:entry key="customer"
        value="com.apress.springbatch.chapter9.Customer" />
    </util:map>
  </beans:property>
</beans:bean>
...
```

JmsReader and JmsWriter are configured the same way. Both of them are basic Spring beans with a reference to the JmsTemplate configured in Listing 9-48. In Listing 9-50, you see the configuration of JmsItemReader, JmsItemWriter, and the job to put all the readers/writers to work.

Listing 9-50. JmsItemReader and JmsItemWriter and the Job that Uses Them

```
    ...
<beans:bean id="jmsReader"
  class="org.springframework.batch.item.jms.JmsItemReader">
  <beans:property name="jmsTemplate" ref="jmsTemplate"/>
</beans:bean>

<beans:bean id="jmsWriter"
  class="org.springframework.batch.item.jms.JmsItemWriter">
  <beans:property name="jmsTemplate" ref="jmsTemplate"/>
</beans:bean>

<step id="formatFileInputStep">
  <tasklet>
    <chunk reader="customerFileReader" writer="jmsWriter"
      commit-interval="10"/>
  </tasklet>
</step>

<step id="formatFileOutputStep">
  <tasklet>
```

```
      <chunk reader="jmsReader" writer="xmlOutputWriter" commit-interval="10"/>
    </tasklet>
</step>

<job id="formatJob">
  <step id="step1" parent="formatFileInputStep" next="step2"/>
  <step id="step2" parent="formatFileOutputStep"/>
</job>
...
```

That's all it takes! With all the resources configured, building and running this job is no different than any of the others you've executed. However, when you run this job, notice that nothing obvious is outputted from step 1 to tell you that anything happened besides looking into the JobRepository or browsing the queue before the second step executes. When you look at the XML generated in step 2, you can see that the messages have successfully been passed through the queue as expected. Listing 9-51 shows a sample of the XML generated by this job.

Listing 9-51. Sample Output from the JMS Version of formatJob

```xml
<?xml version="1.0" encoding="UTF-8"?>
<customers>
<customer>
<id>0</id>
<firstName>Richard</firstName>
<middleInitial>N</middleInitial>
<lastName>Darrow</lastName>
<address>5570 Isabella Ave</address>
<city>St. Louis</city>
<state>IL</state>
<zip>58540</zip>
</customer>
<customer>
<id>0</id>
<firstName>Warren</firstName>
<middleInitial>L</middleInitial>
<lastName>Darrow</lastName>
<address>4686 Mt. Lee Drive</address>
<city>St. Louis</city>
<state>NY</state>
<zip>94935</zip>
</customer>
    ...
</customers>
```

By using Spring's JmsTemplate, Spring Batch exposes the full power of Spring's JMS processing capabilities to the batch processes with minimal effort. The next section looks at a writer you may not have thought about: it lets you send e-mail from batch processes.

SimpleMailMessageItemWriter

The ability to send an e-mail may sound very useful. Heck, when a job completes, it might be handy to receive an e-mail that things ended nicely. However, that isn't what this ItemWriter is for. It's an

ItemWriter, which means it's called once for each item processed in the step where it's used. If you want to run your own spam operation, this is the ItemWriter for you! This section looks at how to use Spring Batch's SimpleMailMessageItemWriter to send e-mails from jobs.

Although you probably won't be using this ItemWriter to write a spam-processing program, you can use it for other things as well. Let's say the customer file you've been processing up to this point is really a customer import file; after you import all the new customers, you want to send a welcome e-mail to each one. Using the org.springframework.batch.item.mail.SimpleMailMessageItemWriter is a perfect way to do that.

For this example, you have a two-step process as you did in the JMS example. The first step imports the customer.csv file into the customer database table. The second step reads all the customers that have been imported and sends them the welcome e-mail. Figure 9-6 shows the flow for this job.

Figure 9-6. Flow for the customerImport job

Before you begin coding, let's look at SimpleMailMessageItemWriter. Like all other ItemWriters, it implements the ItemWriter interface by executing a single write method that takes a list of objects. However, unlike the ItemWriters you've looked at up to this point, SimpleMailMessageItemWriter doesn't take just any item. Sending an e-mail requires more information than the text of the e-mail. It needs a subject, a to address, and a from address. Because of this, SimpleMailMessageItemWriter requires that the list of objects it takes contain objects that extend Spring's SimpleMailMessage. By doing this, SimpleMailMessageItemWriter has all the information it needs to build the e-mail message.

But does that mean any item you read in must extend SimpleMailMessage? That seems like a poor job of decoupling e-mail functionality from business logic—which is why you don't have to do that. If you remember, Chapter 8 talked about how ItemProcessors don't need to return an object of the same type they receive. For example, you can receive a Car object but return an object of type House. In this case, you create an ItemProcessor that takes in the Customer object and returns the required SimpleMailMessage.

To make this work, you reuse the same input file format with a single field appended to the end: the customer's e-mail address. Listing 9-52 shows an example of the input file you're processing.

Listing 9-52. customerWithEmail.csv

```
Ann,A,Smith,2501 Mt. Lee Drive,Miami,NE,62935,ASmith@yahoo.com
Laura,B,Jobs,9542 Isabella Ave,Aurora,FL,62344,LJobs@yahoo.com
Harry,J,Williams,1909 4th Street,Seattle,TX,48548,HWilliams@hotmail.com
Larry,Y,Minella,7839 S. Greenwood Ave,Miami,IL,65371,LMinella@hotmail.com
Richard,Q,Jobs,9732 4th Street,Chicago,NV,31320,RJobs@gmail.com
Ann,P,Darrow,4195 Jeopardy Lane,Aurora,CA,24482,ADarrow@hotmail.com
Larry,V,Williams,3075 Wall Street,St. Louis,NY,34205,LWilliams@hotmail.com
Michael,H,Gates,3219 S. Greenwood Ave,Boston,FL,24692,MGates@gmail.com
Harry,H,Johnson,7520 Infinite Loop Drive,Hollywood,MA,83983,HJohnson@hotmail.com
Harry,N,Ellison,6959 4th Street,Hollywood,MO,70398,HEllison@gmail.com
```

To handle the need for an e-mail address per customer, you need to add an e-mail field to the Customer object as well. Listing 9-53 shows the updated Customer class.

303

Listing 9-53. Customer.java Updated with an E-mail Field

```java
package com.apress.springbatch.chapter9;

import java.io.Serializable;

import javax.persistence.Entity;
import javax.persistence.GeneratedValue;
import javax.persistence.GenerationType;
import javax.persistence.Id;
import javax.persistence.Table;

@Entity
@Table(name="customer")
public class Customer implements Serializable {
    private static final long serialVersionUID = 1L;

    @Id
    @GeneratedValue(strategy = GenerationType.IDENTITY)
    private long id;
    private String firstName;
    private String middleInitial;
    private String lastName;
    private String address;
    private String city;
    private String state;
    private String zip;
    private String email;

    // Accessors go here
    ...
}
```

Because the job is storing the customer information in the database, let's take a quick look at how that interaction works. To start, Figure 9-7 has the data model for the Customer table you use in this example.

Figure 9-7. Customer table

To write to the database, you use JdbcBatchItemWriter as you did earlier in this chapter. If you remember, JdbcBatchItemWriter depends on three things: a datasource, a prepared statement, and an implementation of the ItemPreparedStatementSetter interface to populate the prepared statement with values from the Customer item. Listing 9-54 has the code for CustomerItemPreparedStatementSetter.

Listing 9-54. CustomerItemPreparedStatementSetter.java

```
package com.apress.springbatch.chapter9;

import java.sql.PreparedStatement;
import java.sql.SQLException;

import org.springframework.batch.item.database.ItemPreparedStatementSetter;

public class CustomerItemPreparedStatementSetter implements
        ItemPreparedStatementSetter<Customer> {

    public void setValues(Customer customer, PreparedStatement ps)
            throws SQLException {

        ps.setString(1, customer.getFirstName());
        ps.setString(2, customer.getMiddleInitial());
        ps.setString(3, customer.getLastName());
        ps.setString(4, customer.getAddress());
        ps.setString(5, customer.getCity());
        ps.setString(6, customer.getState());
        ps.setString(7, customer.getZip());
        ps.setString(8, customer.getEmail());

    }
}
```

On the flip side, after you've imported the Customer items into the database, you need to read them out again in the second step. For this step, you use the JdbcCursorItemReader discussed back in Chapter 7. Like JdbcBatchItemWriter, JdbcCursorItemReader also depends on a datasource. However, this ItemReader only needs an SQL statement instead of a prepared statement, and it needs a RowMapper implementation to map the returned ResultSet into items you can process. The CustomerRowMapper implementation is shown in Listing 9-55.

Listing 9-55. CustomerRowMapper.java

```
package com.apress.springbatch.chapter9;

import java.sql.ResultSet;
import java.sql.SQLException;

import org.springframework.jdbc.core.RowMapper;

public class CustomerRowMapper implements RowMapper<Customer> {
```

```
    @Override
    public Customer mapRow(ResultSet rs, int arg1) throws SQLException {
        Customer customer = new Customer();

        customer.setAddress(rs.getString("address"));
        customer.setCity(rs.getString("city"));
        customer.setEmail(rs.getString("email"));
        customer.setFirstName(rs.getString("firstName"));
        customer.setId(rs.getLong("id"));
        customer.setLastName(rs.getString("lastName"));
        customer.setMiddleInitial(rs.getString("middleInitial"));
        customer.setState(rs.getString("state"));
        customer.setZip(rs.getString("zip"));

        return customer;
    }
}
```

Now that the Customer class can handle e-mails, you need to do one other piece of coding for the job before you wire it up. As mentioned previously, this job needs an ItemProcessor to convert the Customer objects into the required SimpleMailMessages. Listing 9-56 shows the simple converter you use for this.

Listing 9-56. CustomerEmailConverter.java

```
package com.apress.springbatch.chapter9;

import org.springframework.batch.item.ItemProcessor;
import org.springframework.mail.SimpleMailMessage;

public class CustomerEmailConverter implements
    ItemProcessor<Customer, SimpleMailMessage> {

    private static final String EMAIL_TEMPLATE =
        "Welcome %s,\nYou were imported into the system using Spring Batch!";

    @Override
    public SimpleMailMessage process(Customer customer) throws Exception {
        SimpleMailMessage mail = new SimpleMailMessage();

        mail.setFrom("prospringbatch@gmail.com");
        mail.setTo(customer.getEmail());
        mail.setSubject("Welcome!");
        mail.setText(String.format(EMAIL_TEMPLATE,
            new Object[] {customer.getFirstName(), customer.getLastName()}));

        return mail;
    }
}
```

That's all the code you need to write! However, to get it to compile, you need to update the POM file to include the Java mail dependencies. Listing 9-57 shows the additions required to build the updated project.

Listing 9-57. Java Mail Dependency

```
...
<dependency>
    <groupId>javax.mail</groupId>
    <artifactId>mail</artifactId>
    <version>1.4</version>
</dependency>
...
```

To wire all this up, start by configuring Spring to be able to send e-mails in the first place. Using Spring's `org.springframework.mail.javamail.JavaMailSenderImpl` lets you configure where the SMTP server is and the appropriate values for it. Listing 9-58 shows the configuration that goes in `launch-context.xml` for this bean.

Listing 9-58. Configuring JavaMailSenderImpl

```
...
<bean id="javaMailSender"
  class="org.springframework.mail.javamail.JavaMailSenderImpl">
  <property name="host" value="smtp.gmail.com"/>
  <property name="port" value="587"/>
  <property name="username" value="someusername"/>
  <property name="password" value="somepassword"/>
  <property name="javaMailProperties">
    <props>
      <prop key="mail.smtp.auth">true</prop>
      <prop key="mail.smtp.starttls.enable">true</prop>
    </props>
  </property>
</bean>
...
```

To be able to test the e-mail sending capabilities, you use Google's Gmail SMTP functionality as the mail server. Listing 9-58 shows the configuration required. All you need to do is replace the username and password with your Gmail username and password.[5]

Next, you can move on to configuring the job to process the new customers. To configure the input for the first step, you configure a resource to read from that is passed from the command line, and a `FlatFileItemReader` that reads in the `customerWithEmail.csv` file. The writer for step 1 consists of the previously mentioned `JdbcBatchItemWriter` using the `dataSource`, a provided `preparedStatement`, and the `CustomerItemPreparedStatementSetter` coded in Listing 9-54. Listing 9-59 shows how you wire that up for the first step in the job.

---

[5] Unlike most SMTP servers used by enterprises, the Gmail server you're using for this example ignores the `from` attribute of the e-mail when it's sent and replaces it with the name of the account from which you logged in.

Listing 9-59. ItemReader and ItemWriter for Step 1

```
...
<beans:bean id="customerFile"
  class="org.springframework.core.io.FileSystemResource" scope="step">
  <beans:constructor-arg value="#{jobParameters[customerFile]}"/>
</beans:bean>

<beans:bean id="customerFileReader"
  class="org.springframework.batch.item.file.FlatFileItemReader">
  <beans:property name="resource" ref="customerFile"/>
  <beans:property name="lineMapper">
  <beans:bean
    class="org.springframework.batch.item.file.mapping.DefaultLineMapper">
    <beans:property name="lineTokenizer">
      <beans:bean class="org.springframework.batch.item.file.transform.
DelimitedLineTokenizer">
        <beans:property name="names"
          value="firstName,middleInitial,lastName,address,city,state,zip,
email"/>
        <beans:property name="delimiter" value=","/>
      </beans:bean>
    </beans:property>
    <beans:property name="fieldSetMapper">
      <beans:bean class="org.springframework.batch.item.file.mapping.
BeanWrapperFieldSetMapper">
        <beans:property name="prototypeBeanName" value="customer"/>
      </beans:bean>
    </beans:property>
  </beans:bean>
  </beans:property>
</beans:bean>

<beans:bean id="customer" class="com.apress.springbatch.chapter9.Customer"
  scope="prototype"/>

<beans:bean id="jdbcBatchWriter"
  class="org.springframework.batch.item.database.JdbcBatchItemWriter">
  <beans:property name="dataSource" ref="dataSource"/>
  <beans:property name="sql" value="insert into customer (firstName, middleInitial, lastName,
address, city, state, zip, email) values (?, ?, ?, ?, ?, ?, ?, ?)"/>
  <beans:property name="itemPreparedStatementSetter"
    ref="preparedStatementSetter"/>
</beans:bean>

<beans:bean id="preparedStatementSetter"
  class="com.apress.springbatch.chapter9.
CustomerItemPreparedStatementSetter"/>
...
```

None of the configuration in Listing 9-59 should be new, because you've seen it previously. The new parts come when you configure step 2. For step 2, you're using a JdbcCursorItemReader with the

CustomerRowMapper you coded in Listing 9-55, along with the CustomerEmailConverter from Listing 9-56 as the ItemProcessor, and finally SimpleMailMessageItemWriter as the ItemWriter. Listing 9-60 shows the configuration of the beans required for step 2 along with the job configuration.

Listing 9-60. Step2 and the Job Configuration

```
...
<beans:bean id="customerItemReader"
  class="org.springframework.batch.item.database.JdbcCursorItemReader">
  <beans:property name="dataSource" ref="dataSource"/>
  <beans:property name="sql" value="select * from customer"/>
  <beans:property name="rowMapper" ref="customerRowMapper"/>
</beans:bean>

<beans:bean id="customerRowMapper"
  class="com.apress.springbatch.chapter9.CustomerRowMapper"/>

<beans:bean id="simpleEmailWriter"
  class="org.springframework.batch.item.mail.SimpleMailMessageItemWriter">
  <beans:property name="mailSender" ref="javaMailSender"/>
</beans:bean>

<beans:bean id="emailConverter"
  class="com.apress.springbatch.chapter9.CustomerEmailConverter"/>

<step id="importFileStep">
  <tasklet>
    <chunk reader="customerFileReader" writer="jdbcBatchWriter"
      commit-interval="10"/>
  </tasklet>
</step>

<step id="emailCustomersStep">
  <tasklet>
    <chunk reader="customerItemReader" processor="emailConverter"
      writer="simpleEmailWriter" commit-interval="10"/>
  </tasklet>
</step>

<job id="formatJob">
  <step id="step1" parent="importFileStep" next="step2"/>
  <step id="step2" parent="emailCustomersStep"/>
</job>
...
```

That's all there is to it! You can build this job with mvn clean install from the command line and run it with the command listed in Listing 9-61 to process the input file and send out the e-mails.

Listing 9-61. Executing the E-mail Job

```
java -jar itemWriters-0.0.1-SNAPSHOT.jar jobs/emailFormatJob.xml formatJob
customerFile=/input/customerWithEmail.csv
```

When the job is complete, you can check your e-mail inbox as shown in Figure 9-8 to see that the customers have successfully received their e-mails.

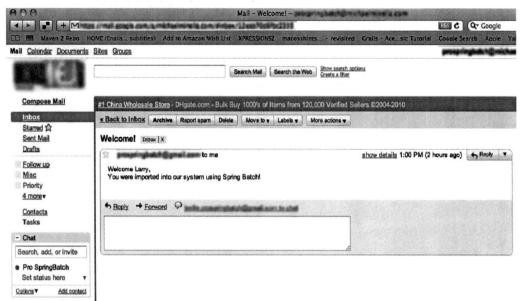

Figure 9-8. *The result of the e-mail job*

Spring Batch provides a full collection of ItemWriters to handle the vast majority of output handling that you need to be able to do. The next section looks at how you can use the individual features of each of these ItemWriters together to address more complex output scenarios, such as writing to multiple places based on a number of scenarios.

Multipart ItemWriters

As part of your new system, you have the requirement to extract customer data into two different formats. You need an XML file for the Sale's department's customer relationship management (CRM) application. You also need a CSV for the billing department's database import system. The issue is, you expect to extract one million customers.

Using the tools discussed up to this point, you would be stuck looping through the one million items twice (once for a step that outputs the XML file and once for the step that outputs the CSV file) or creating a custom ItemWriter implementation to write to each file as an item is processed. Neither option is what you're looking for. The first will take too long, tying up resources; and the other requires you to code and test something that the framework should already provide. Fortunately for you, it does. This section looks at how you can use the various composite ItemWriters available in Spring Batch to address more complex output scenarios.

MultiResourceItemWriter

Chapter 7 looked at Spring Batch's ability to read from multiple files with the same format in a single step. Spring Batch provides a similar feature on the ItemWriter side as well. This section looks at how to generate multiple resources based on the number of items written to a file.

Spring Batch offers the ability to create a new resource after a given number of records has been processed. Say you want to extract all the customer records and write them to XML files with only 10 customers per file. To do that, you use `MultiResourceItemWriter`.

`MultiResourceItemWriter` dynamically creates output resources based on the number of records it has processed. It passes each item it processes to a delegate writer so that the actual writing piece is handled there. All `MultiResourceItemWriter` is responsible for is maintaining the current count and creating new resources as items are processed. Figure 9-9 shows the flow of a step using `org.springframework.batch.item.file.MultiResourceItemWriter`.

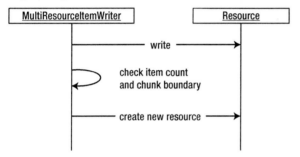

Figure 9-9. Processing using a `MultiResourceItemWriter`

When the `write` method on `MultiResourceItemWriter` is called, it verifies that the current resource has been created and is open (if not, it creates and opens a new file) and passes the items to the delegate ItemWriter. Once the items have been written, it checks to see if the number of items written to the file has reached the configured threshold for a new resource. If it has, the current file is closed.

It's important to note that when `MultiResourceItemWriter` is processing, it doesn't create a new resource mid-chunk. It waits for the end of the chunk before creating a new resource. For example, if the writer is configured to roll the file after 15 items have been processed but the chunk size is configured to 20, `MultiResourceItemWriter` writes the 20 items in the chunk before creating a new resource.

`MultiResourceItemWriter` has five available dependencies you can configure. Table 9-4 shows each one and how they're used.

Table 9-4. `MultiResourceItemWriter` Configuration Options

Option	Type	Default	Description
delegate ResourceAware	ItemWriterIte mStream	null (required)	The delegate ItemWriter that the `MultiResourceItemWriter` uses to write each item.
itemCountLimitPerResource int		Integer.MAX_VA LUE	The number of items to write to each resource.

resource Resource	null (required)	A prototype of the resources to be created by MultiResourceItemWriter.
resourceSuffixCreator ResourceSuffixCreator	null	Optionally, MultiResourceItemWriter can use this class to append a suffix to the end of the file names it creates.
saveState Boolean	true	If false, the state of the ItemWriter isn't maintained in the JobRepository.

To see how this works, you extract customers from the database and create XML files containing 10 customers each. To make this work, you don't need to develop any new code (you created the XML). All you need to do is wire everything up. Let's start working with this example by looking at the configuration for the job.

Listing 9-62 shows the configuration for the ItemReader in this example. In this case, it's a simple JdbcCursorItemReader configured to select all customers. From there, you pass the customers you receive from the database to the ItemWriter you configure next.

Listing 9-62. The multiResource formatJob's ItemReader

```
...
<beans:bean id="customerItemReader"
  class="org.springframework.batch.item.database.JdbcCursorItemReader">
  <beans:property name="dataSource" ref="dataSource"/>
  <beans:property name="sql" value="select * from customer"/>
  <beans:property name="rowMapper" ref="customerRowMapper"/>
</beans:bean>

<beans:bean id="customerRowMapper"
  class="com.apress.springbatch.chapter9.CustomerRowMapper"/>
...
```

The configuration for this ItemWriter is in layers. First you configure the StaxEventItemWriter that you use for the XML generation. With that configured you layer MultiResourceItemWriter on top to generate multiple resources the StaxEventItemWriter writes to. Listing 9-63 shows the configuration of the output half of the job as well as the step and job configuration.

Listing 9-63. ItemWriters and Step and Job Configuration

```
...
<beans:bean id="outputFile"
  class="org.springframework.core.io.FileSystemResource" scope="step">
  <beans:constructor-arg value="#{jobParameters[outputFile]}"/>
</beans:bean>

<beans:bean id="xmlOutputWriter"
```

```
  class="org.springframework.batch.item.xml.StaxEventItemWriter">
  <beans:property name="marshaller" ref="customerMarshaller" />
  <beans:property name="rootTagName" value="customers" />
</beans:bean>

<beans:bean id="customerMarshaller"
  class="org.springframework.oxm.xstream.XStreamMarshaller">
  <beans:property name="aliases">
    <util:map>
      <beans:entry key="customer"
        value="com.apress.springbatch.chapter9.Customer" />
    </util:map>
  </beans:property>
</beans:bean>

<beans:bean id="multiResourceItemWriter"
  class="org.springframework.batch.item.file.MultiResourceItemWriter">
  <beans:property name="resource" ref="outputFile"/>
  <beans:property name="delegate" ref="xmlOutputWriter"/>
  <beans:property name="itemCountLimitPerResource" value="10"/>
</beans:bean>

<step id="formatFileStep">
  <tasklet>
    <chunk reader="customerItemReader" writer="multiResourceItemWriter"
      commit-interval="10"/>
  </tasklet>
</step>

<job id="formatJob">
  <step id="step1" parent="formatFileStep"/>
</job>
...
```

As you saw earlier, the configuration of the output for this job begins with the outputFile configuration. Although the file is generated by MultiResourceItemWriter, MultiResourceItemWriter uses this as a template for each new file (file location and file name specifically). In the case, the outputFile bean in Listing 9-63 serves as the template for the output file definition. With the file name configured, you can configure xmlOutputWriter and customerMarshaller to generate the XML as required. Although similar, it's important to note that xmlOutputWriter doesn't have a direct reference to the output file. Instead, multiResourceItemWriter provides it when needed.

For this example, multiResourceItemWriter uses three dependencies: the resource you configured previously, the xmlOutputWriter that does the actual work of writing to the files it creates, and the number of customers that the ItemWriter writes per file (itemCountLimitPerResource)—10 in this case. The last piece for this job is configuring the step and job to put them to use. The configuration for the job itself is straightforward, as Listing 9-63 shows. To use this job, you use the command listed in Listing 9-64.

Listing 9-64. *Command Used to Execute the* multiResource *Job*

```
java -jar itemWriters-0.0.1-SNAPSHOT.jar jobs/multiResourceFormatJob.xml
formatJob outputFile=/output/custOutputs
```

When you look at the output of this job, you find in the /output directory one file for every 10 customers currently loaded in the database. However, Spring Batch did something interesting. First, note that you didn't pass in a file extension on the outputFile parameter you passed into the job. This was for a reason. If you look at the directory listing shown in Listing 9-65, you see that MultiResourceItemWriter added a .X to each file, where X is the number of the file that was created.

Listing 9-65. File Names Created by the Job

```
michael-minellas-macbook-pro:temp mminella$ ls /output/
custOutputs.1custOutputs.2custOutputs.4custOutputs.6custOutputs.8
custOutputs.10   custOutputs.3custOutputs.5custOutputs.7custOutputs.9
```

Although it makes sense that you need to distinguish each file name from another, this may or may not be a workable solution for how to name the files (they don't exactly open nicely with your favorite editor by default). Because of that, Spring Batch lets you to configure the suffix for each file created. You do that by implementing the org.springframework.batch.item.file.ResourceSuffixCreator interface and adding that as a dependency to the multiResourceItemWriter bean. When the MultiResourceItemWriter is creating a new file, it uses ResourceSuffixCreator to generate a suffix that it tacks onto the end of the new file's name. Listing 9-66 shows the suffix creator for the example.

Listing 9-66. CustomerOutputFileSuffixCreator

```
package com.apress.springbatch.chapter9;

import org.springframework.batch.item.file.ResourceSuffixCreator;

public class CustomerOutputFileSuffixCreator implements ResourceSuffixCreator {

    @Override
    public String getSuffix(int arg0) {
        return arg0 + ".xml";
    }
}
```

In Listing 9-66, you implement the ResourceSuffixCreator's only method, getSuffix, and return a suffix of the number provided and an .xml extension. The number provided is the number file that is being created. If you were to re-create the same extension as the default, you would return a dot plus the number provided.

To use CustomerOutputFileSuffixCreator, you configure it as a bean and add it as a dependency to the multiResourceItemWriter bean using the property resourceSuffixCreator. Listing 9-67 shows the added configuration.

Listing 9-67. Configuring CustomerOutputFileSuffixCreator

```
...
<beans:bean id="customerSuffixCreator"
  class="com.apress.springbatch.chapter9.CustomerOutputFileSuffixCreator"/>

<beans:bean id="multiResourceItemWriter"
  class="org.springframework.batch.item.file.MultiResourceItemWriter">
  <beans:property name="resource" ref="outputFile"/>
```

```
    <beans:property name="delegate" ref="xmlOutputWriter"/>
    <beans:property name="itemCountLimitPerResource" value="10"/>
    <beans:property name="resourceSuffixCreator" ref="customerSuffixCreator"/>
</beans:bean>
...
```

By running the job again with the additional configuration provided in Listing 9-67, you get a slightly different result, as shown in Listing 9-68.

Listing 9-68. *Results Using ResourceSuffixCreator*

```
michael-minellas-macbook-pro:output mminella$ ls /output/
custOutputs1.xml      custOutputs2.xml      custOutputs4.xml      custOutputs6.xml
custOutputs8.xml
custOutputs10.xml     custOutputs3.xml      custOutputs5.xml      custOutputs7.xml
custOutputs9.xml
```

You surely agree that the file names in Listing 9-68 are more like what you would expect when generating XML files.

Header and Footer XML Fragments

When creating files, whether a single file for a step/job or multiple files as you saw in the previous example, it's common to need to be able to generate a header or footer on the file. You can use a header to define the format of a flat file (what fields exist in a file or in what order) or include a separate, non-item-related section in an XML file. A footer may include the number of records processed in the file or totals to use as integrity checks after a file has been processed. This section looks at how to generate header and footer records using Spring Batch's callbacks available for them.

When opening or closing a file, Spring Batch provides the ability to add either a header or footer (whichever is appropriate) to your file. Adding a header or footer to a file means different things based on whether it's a flat file or an XML file. For a flat file, adding a header means adding one or more records to the top or bottom of the file. For an XML file, you may want to add an XML segment at either the top or bottom of the file. Because the generation of plain text for a flat file is different from generating an XML segment for an XML file, Spring Batch offers two different interfaces to implement and make this happen. Let's begin by looking at the XML callback interface, org.springframework.batch.item.xml.StaxWriterCallback.

The StaxWriterCallback interface consists of a single write method that is used to add XML to the current XML document. Spring Batch executes a configured callback once at either the header or footer of the file (based on the configuration). To see how this works, in this example you write a StaxWriterCallback implementation that adds an XML fragment containing the name of the person who wrote the job (me). Listing 9-69 shows the code for the implementation.

Listing 9-69. *CustomerXmlHeaderCallback*

```
package com.apress.springbatch.chapter9;

import java.io.IOException;

import javax.xml.stream.XMLEventFactory;
import javax.xml.stream.XMLEventWriter;
```

```
import javax.xml.stream.XMLStreamException;

import org.springframework.batch.item.xml.StaxWriterCallback;

public class CustomerXmlHeaderCallback implements StaxWriterCallback {

    @Override
    public void write(XMLEventWriter writer) throws IOException {
        XMLEventFactory factory = XMLEventFactory.newInstance();

        try {
            writer.add(factory.createStartElement("", "", "identification"));
            writer.add(factory.createStartElement("", "", "author"));
            writer.add(factory.createAttribute("name", "Michael Minella"));
            writer.add(factory.createEndElement("", "", "author"));
            writer.add(factory.createEndElement("", "", "identification"));
        } catch (XMLStreamException xmlse) {
            System.err.println("An error occured: " + xmlse.getMessage());
            xmlse.printStackTrace(System.err);
        }
    }
}
```

Listing 9-69 shows CustomerXmlHeaderCallback. In the callback, you add two tags to the XML file: an identification section and a single author section. The author section contains a single attribute called name with the value Michael Minella. To create a tag, you use the javax.xml.stream.XMLEventFactory's createStartElement and createEndElement methods. Each of these methods takes three parameters: a prefix, a namespace, and the name of the tag. Because you aren't using a prefix or namespace, you pass in empty strings for those. To put this implementation to use, you need to configure StaxEventItemWriter to call the callback as the headerCallback. Listing 9-70 shows the configuration for this example.

Listing 9-70. XML Configuration for `CustomerXmlHeaderCallback`

```
...
<beans:bean id="xmlOutputWriter"
  class="org.springframework.batch.item.xml.StaxEventItemWriter">
  <beans:property name="marshaller" ref="customerMarshaller" />
  <beans:property name="rootTagName" value="customers" />
  <beans:property name="headerCallback" ref="customerHeaderCallback"/>
</beans:bean>

<beans:bean id="customerHeaderCallback"
  class="com.apress.springbatch.chapter9.CustomerXmlHeaderCallback"/>
...
```

When you execute the multiresource job from the previous example using the header configuration in Listing 9-70, each of the output files begins with the XML fragment as shown in Listing 9-71.

Listing 9-71. XML Header

```
<?xml version="1.0" encoding="UTF-8"?>
<customers>
<identification>
<author name="Michael Minella"/>
</identification>
<customer>
    ...
```

As you can see, adding an XML fragment at either the start or end of an XML file is quite easy. Implement the StaxWriterCallback interface and configure the ItemWriter to call it as either the header or the footer, and you're done!

Header and Footer Records in a Flat File

Next you can look at adding headers and footers to a flat file. Unlike the XML header and footer generation that use the same interface for either, writing a header in a flat file requires the implementation of a different interface than that of a footer. For the header, you implement the org.springframework.batch.item.file.FlatFileHeaderCallback interface; and for the footer, you implement the org.springframework.batch.item.file.FlatFileFooterCallback interface. Both consist of a single method: writeHeader and writeFooter, respectively. Let's look at how to write a footer that writes the number of records you've processed in the current file.

For this example, you use the MultiResourceItemWriter to write files with 10 formatted records in each record plus a single footer record that states how many records were written in each file. To be able to keep count of the number of items you've written into a file, you need to decorate the writers with the appropriate functionality. Figure 9-10 shows the layering of the ItemWriters required for the example.

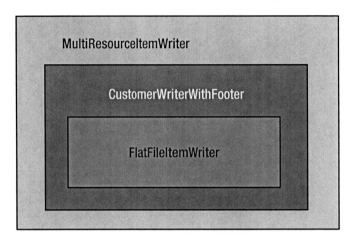

Figure 9-10. *Using multiple layers of ItemWriters to accomplish writing the footers*

As Figure 9-10 shows, the writer that does the heavy lifting in this example is a regular
FlatFileItemWriter. But you decorate that ItemWriter with your own implementation that keeps track
of the number of items that have been written and implement the FlatFileFooterCallback interface.
Finally you use MultiResourceItemWriter to create the resources as needed.

Because the only code you need to write for this example is the CustomerWriterWithFooter class, you
can start there. This class implements two interfaces: FlatFileFooterCallback as well as
org.springframework.batch.item.file.ResourceAwareItemWriterItemStream. You implement
FlatFileFooterCallback so you can use the data compiled while you write the items to write the footer.
The ResourceAwareItemWriterItemStream interface is implemented so MultiResourceItemWriter can
inject the resource into the ItemWriter as they're created. If you didn't use this interface, you would be
required to inject a single resource at startup, which is not what you require. For all practical purposes,
the methods required by the ResourceAwareItemWriterItemStream interface are just passthroughs to the
FlatFileItemWriter it wraps. Listing 9-72 shows the implementation of the CustomerWriterWithFooter
class.

Listing 9-72. CustomerWriterWithFooter

```java
package com.apress.springbatch.chapter9;

import java.io.IOException;
import java.io.Writer;
import java.util.List;

import org.springframework.batch.item.ExecutionContext;
import org.springframework.batch.item.ItemStreamException;
import org.springframework.batch.item.file.FlatFileFooterCallback;
import org.springframework.batch.item.file.ResourceAwareItemWriterItemStream;
import org.springframework.core.io.Resource;

public class CustomerWriterWithFooter implements
    ResourceAwareItemWriterItemStream<Customer>, FlatFileFooterCallback {

    private ResourceAwareItemWriterItemStream<Customer> delegate;
    private int itemsProcessedSoFar = 0;

    @Override
    public void writeFooter(Writer writer) throws IOException {
        writer.write("At the end of this file, you have written " +
                        itemsProcessedSoFar + " items");
    }

    @Override
    public void write(List<? extends Customer> items) throws Exception {
        itemsProcessedSoFar += items.size();

        delegate.write(items);
    }

    public void setDelegate(
        ResourceAwareItemWriterItemStream<Customer> delegate) {
        this.delegate = delegate;
    }

    @Override
    public void close() throws ItemStreamException {
        delegate.close();
    }

    @Override
    public void open(ExecutionContext executionContext)
        throws ItemStreamException {
        if(executionContext.containsKey("records.processed")) {
            itemsProcessedSoFar = Integer.parseInt(executionContext
                                    .get("records.processed").toString());
        }
```

```
        delegate.open(executionContext);
    }

    @Override
    public void update(ExecutionContext executionContext)
        throws ItemStreamException {
        executionContext.put("records.processed", itemsProcessedSoFar);
        delegate.update(executionContext);
    }

    @Override
    public void setResource(Resource arg0) {
        itemsProcessedSoFar = 0;
        delegate.setResource(arg0);
    }
}
```

As you can see in Listing 9-72 when a resource is set on the ItemWriter, the counter (itemsProcessedSoFar) is set to 0. As items are written via the write method, the counter is incremented accordingly. When the writeFooter method is called, the counter is used in the footer output to list the number of records that are in the file that is being closed.

There are three other methods to take note of in this implementation: open, update, and close. The open and update methods end up being more than just passthroughs to make this ItemWriter restartable. Because the ItemWriter has its own state (the number of records that have been processed in the current file), you want to save that in the ExecutionContext in case the job fails. The update method is used to save that value during processing. The open method is used to reset where you left off in the event the job is restarted. The close method serves as only a passthrough to the delegate so that it can close the file as required.

To configure the various ItemWriters required for this example, Listing 9-73 shows the required XML. You begin with the input, reading the customer records out of the Customer table. From there, you configure the three ItemWriter implementations. The first is FlatFileItemWriter and its required LineAggregator. From there, you configure customerWriter, which is the implementation of the ItemWriter (ResourceAwareItemReaderItemStream is a sub-interface of the ItemReader interface) in Listing 9-72. Finally, you have the multiResourceItemWriter you've used previously. Listing 9-73 finishes with the configuration of the step and job.

Listing 9-73. customerFooterFormatJob.xml

```xml
<?xml version="1.0" encoding="UTF-8"?>
<beans:beans xmlns="http://www.springframework.org/schema/batch"
  xmlns:beans="http://www.springframework.org/schema/beans"
  xmlns:util="http://www.springframework.org/schema/beans"
  xmlns:xsi="http://www.w3.org/2001/XMLSchema-instance"
  xsi:schemaLocation="http://www.springframework.org/schema/beans
    http://www.springframework.org/schema/beans/spring-beans-3.0.xsd
    http://www.springframework.org/schema/util
    http://www.springframework.org/schema/util/spring-util.xsd
    http://www.springframework.org/schema/batch
    http://www.springframework.org/schema/batch/spring-batch-2.1.xsd">

    <beans:import resource="../launch-context.xml"/>
```

```xml
<beans:bean id="customerItemReader"
  class="org.springframework.batch.item.database.JdbcCursorItemReader">
  <beans:property name="dataSource" ref="dataSource"/>
  <beans:property name="sql" value="select * from customer"/>
  <beans:property name="rowMapper" ref="customerRowMapper"/>
</beans:bean>

<beans:bean id="customerRowMapper"
  class="com.apress.springbatch.chapter9.CustomerRowMapper"/>

<beans:bean id="outputFile"
  class="org.springframework.core.io.FileSystemResource" scope="step">
  <beans:constructor-arg value="#{jobParameters[outputFile]}"/>
</beans:bean>

<beans:bean id="flatFileOutputWriter"
  class="org.springframework.batch.item.file.FlatFileItemWriter">
  <beans:property name="lineAggregator" ref="formattedLineAggregator"/>
  <beans:property name="appendAllowed" value="true"/>
  <beans:property name="footerCallback" ref="customerWriter"/>
</beans:bean>

<beans:bean id="formattedLineAggregator"
  class="org.springframework.batch.item.file.transform.
FormatterLineAggregator">
  <beans:property name="fieldExtractor">
    <beans:bean class="org.springframework.batch.item.file.transform.
BeanWrapperFieldExtractor">
      <beans:property name="names"
        value="firstName,lastName,address,city,state,zip"/>
    </beans:bean>
  </beans:property>
  <beans:property name="format" value="%s %s lives at %s %s in %s, %s."/>
</beans:bean>

<beans:bean id="customerWriter"
  class="com.apress.springbatch.chapter9.CustomerWriterWithFooter">
  <beans:property name="delegate" ref="flatFileOutputWriter"/>
</beans:bean>

<beans:bean id="multiResourceItemWriter"
  class="org.springframework.batch.item.file.MultiResourceItemWriter">
  <beans:property name="resource" ref="outputFile"/>
  <beans:property name="delegate" ref="customerWriter"/>
  <beans:property name="itemCountLimitPerResource" value="10"/>
</beans:bean>

<step id="formatFileStep">
  <tasklet>
    <chunk reader="customerItemReader" writer="multiResourceItemWriter"
      commit-interval="10"/>
  </tasklet>
```

```
      </step>

    <job id="formatJob">
      <step id="step1" parent="formatFileStep"/>
    </job>
</beans:beans>
```

Writing to multiple files based on the number of records per file is made easy using MultiResourceItemWriter. Spring's ability to add a header and/or footer record is also managed in a simple and practical way using the appropriate interfaces and configuration. The next section looks at how to write the same item to multiple writers with the addition of no code.

CompositeItemWriter

Although it may not seem like it, the examples you've reviewed in this chapter up to this point have been simple. A step writes to a single output location. That location may be a database, a file, an e-mail, and so on, but they each have written to one endpoint. However, it's not always that simple. An enterprise may need to write to a database that a web application uses as well as a data warehouse. While items are being processed, various business metrics may need to be recorded. Spring Batch allows you to write to multiple places as you process each item of a step. This section looks at how the CompositeItemWriter lets a step write items to multiple ItemWriters.

Like most things in Spring Batch, the ability to call multiple ItemWriters for each item you process is quite easy. Before you get into the code, however, let's look at the flow of writing to multiple ItemWriters with the same item. Figure 9-11 shows a sequence diagram of the process.

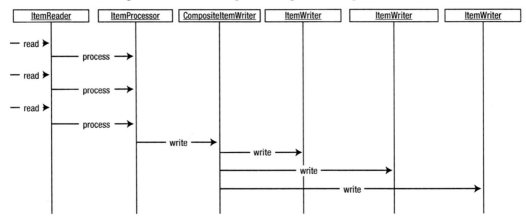

Figure 9-11. Sequence diagram of writing to multiple ItemWriters

As Figure 9-11 shows, reading in occurs one at a time, as does processing. However, the diagram also shows that writing occurs in chunks as you would expect, calling each ItemWriter with the items in the current chunk in the order they're configured.

To look at how this feature works, you create a job that reads in the customerWithEmail.csv file from earlier in the chapter. let's start with the input. Listing 9-74 shows the configuration to read in the customerWithEmail.csv file.

Listing 9-74. Reading in the `customerWithEmail.csv` File

```
...
<beans:bean id="customerFile"
  class="org.springframework.core.io.FileSystemResource" scope="step">
  <beans:constructor-arg value="#{jobParameters[customerFile]}"/>
</beans:bean>

<beans:bean id="customerFileReader"
  class="org.springframework.batch.item.file.FlatFileItemReader">
  <beans:property name="resource" ref="customerFile"/>
  <beans:property name="lineMapper">
    <beans:bean
      class="org.springframework.batch.item.file.mapping.DefaultLineMapper">
      <beans:property name="lineTokenizer">
        <beans:bean class="org.springframework.batch.item.file.transform.
DelimitedLineTokenizer">
          <beans:property name="names"
            value="firstName,middleInitial,lastName,address,city,state,zip,
email"/>
          <beans:property name="delimiter" value=","/>
        </beans:bean>
      </beans:property>
      <beans:property name="fieldSetMapper">
        <beans:bean class="org.springframework.batch.item.file.mapping.
BeanWrapperFieldSetMapper">
          <beans:property name="prototypeBeanName" value="customer"/>
        </beans:bean>
      </beans:property>
    </beans:bean>
  </beans:property>
</beans:bean>

<beans:bean id="customer" class="com.apress.springbatch.chapter9.Customer"
  scope="prototype"/>
...
```

Nothing in Listing 9-74 should be unfamiliar. You're using the same input file you used in the previous examples in this chapter. The configuration consists of the file reference (`Resource`), the configuration of the `FlatFileItemReader` using `DelimitedLineTokenizer` and `BeanWrapperFieldSetMapper` to read the file, and a reference to the `Customer` bean to create them as required.

On the output side, you need to create three ItemWriters: the XML writer and its dependencies, the JDBC writer and its dependencies, and the `CompositeItemWriter` that wraps both of the other writers. Listing 9-75 shows the configuration for the output of this step as well as the configuration for the step and job.

Listing 9-75. Output, Step, and Job Configuration

```
...
<beans:bean id="outputFile"
  class="org.springframework.core.io.FileSystemResource" scope="step">
```

```
    <beans:constructor-arg value="#{jobParameters[outputFile]}"/>
  </beans:bean>

  <beans:bean id="xmlOutputWriter"
    class="org.springframework.batch.item.xml.StaxEventItemWriter">
    <beans:property name="resource" ref="outputFile" />
    <beans:property name="marshaller" ref="customerMarshaller" />
    <beans:property name="rootTagName" value="customers" />
  </beans:bean>

  <beans:bean id="customerMarshaller"
    class="org.springframework.oxm.xstream.XStreamMarshaller">
    <beans:property name="aliases">
      <util:map>
        <beans:entry key="customer"
          value="com.apress.springbatch.chapter9.Customer" />
      </util:map>
    </beans:property>
  </beans:bean>

  <beans:bean id="jdbcBatchWriter"
    class="org.springframework.batch.item.database.JdbcBatchItemWriter">
    <beans:property name="dataSource" ref="dataSource"/>
    <beans:property name="sql" value="insert into customer (firstName, middleInitial, lastName,
address, city, state, zip, email) values (?, ?, ?, ?, ?, ?, ?, ?)"/>
    <beans:property name="itemPreparedStatementSetter"
      ref="preparedStatementSetter"/>
  </beans:bean>

  <beans:bean id="preparedStatementSetter"
    class="com.apress.springbatch.chapter9.
CustomerItemPreparedStatementSetter"/>

  <beans:bean id="customerCompositeWriter"
    class="org.springframework.batch.item.support.CompositeItemWriter">
    <beans:property name="delegates">
      <util:list>
        <util:ref bean="xmlOutputWriter"/>
        <util:ref bean="jdbcBatchWriter"/>
      </util:list>
    </beans:property>
  </beans:bean>

  <step id="formatFileStep">
    <tasklet>
      <chunk reader="customerFileReader" writer="customerCompositeWriter"
        commit-interval="10"/>
    </tasklet>
  </step>

  <job id="formatJob">
    <step id="step1" parent="formatFileStep"/>
```

```
</job>
...
```

The configuration for the ItemWriters is about what you would expect. You begin the configuration with the configuration of the output file (outputFile). From there, the XML writer you're using (xmlOutputWriter) is configured as in the example earlier on in the chapter. The JDBC ItemWriter is next, with the prepared statement configured and an ItemPreparedStatementSetter configured to set the values onto the PreparedStatement. Finally you get to the CompositeItemWriter definition (customerCompositeWriter). For customerCompositeWriter, you configure a list of ItemWriters for the wrapper to call. It's important to note that the ItemWriters is called in the order they're configured with all of the items in a chunk. So if there are 10 items in a chunk, the first ItemWriter is called with all 10 items followed by the next ItemWriter and so on. It's important to note that although the execution of the writing is serial (one writer at a time), all of the writes across all of the ItemWriters occur in the same transaction. Because of that, if an item fails to be written at any point in the chunk, the entire chunk is rolled back.

When you run this job as configured via the command java -jar itemWriters-0.0.1-SNAPSHOT.jar jobs/formatJob.xml formatJob customerFile=/input/customerWithEmail.csv outputFile=/output/xmlCustomer.xml, you can see that the output consists of all the records being written to both the database and an XML file. You would think that if the file had 100 customers in it, Spring Batch would consider this to be 200 writes. But if you look at what Spring Batch recorded in the JobRepository, it says that 100 writes were executed, as shown in Figure 9-12.

Details for Step Execution

Property	Value
ID	8,624
Job Execution	8,584
Job Name	formatJob
Step Name	step1
Start Date	2011-03-16
Start Time	02:46:45
Duration	00:00:01
Status	COMPLETED
Reads	100
Writes	100
Filters	0
Read Skips	0
Write Skips	0
Process Skips	0
Commits	11
Rollbacks	0
Exit Code	COMPLETED
Exit Message	

Figure 9-12. Spring Batch Admin recording of writing 100 customers

The reasoning is that Spring Batch is counting the number of items that were written. It doesn't care how many places you write the item to. If the job fails, the restart point depends on how many items you read and processed, not how many you wrote to each location (because those are rolled back anyway).

The CompositeItemWriter makes writing all the items to multiple locations easy. But sometimes you want to write some things to one place and some things to another place. The last ItemWriter you look at in this chapter is ClassifierCompositeItemWriter, which handles just that.

ClassifierCompositeItemWriter

In Chapter 7, you looked at the scenario where you had a single file that contained multiple record types. Handling the ability to map different types of lines to different parsers and mappers so that each would end up in the correct object was no trivial task. But on the writing side, Spring Batch has made life a bit easier. This section looks at how ClassifierCompositeItemWriter allows you to choose where to write items based on a predetermined criteria.

org.springframework.batch.item.support.ClassifierCompositeItemWriter is used to look at items of different types, determine what ItemWriter they should be written to, and forward them accordingly. This functionality is based on two things: ClassifierCompositeItemWriter and an implementation of the org.springframework.batch.classify.Classifier interface. Let's start by looking at the Classifier interface.

The Classifier interface, shown in Listing 9-76, consists of a single method, classify. In the case of what ClassifierCompositeItemWriter uses a Classifier implementation for, the classify method accepts an item as input and returns the ItemWriter to write the item to. In essence, the Classifier implementation serves as a context, with the ItemWriters as strategy implementations.

Listing 9-76. The Classifier Interface

```
package org.springframework.batch.classify;


public interface Classifier<C, T> {

    T classify(C classifiable);
}
```

ClassifierCompositeItemWriter takes a single dependency, an implementation of the Classifier interface. From there it gets the ItemWriter required for each item as it's processed.

Unlike the regular CompositeItemWriter, which writes all items to all ItemWriters, ClassifierCompositeItemWriter ends up with a different number of items written to each ItemWriter. Let's look at an example where you write all customers who live in a state that starts with the letters *A* through *M* to a flat file and items with a state name starting with the letters *N* through *Z* to the database.

As you've probably gathered, the Classifier implementation is the key to making CompositeItemWriter work, so that is where you start. To implement this Classifier as Listing 9-77 shows, you take a Customer object as the sole parameter to the classify method. From there, you use a regular expression to determine whether it should be written to a flat file or the database and return the ItemWriter as required.

Listing 9-77. CustomerClassifier

```
package com.apress.springbatch.chapter9;

import org.springframework.batch.classify.Classifier;
```

```java
import org.springframework.batch.item.ItemWriter;

public class CustomerClassifier implements
    Classifier<Customer, ItemWriter<Customer>> {

    private ItemWriter<Customer> fileItemWriter;
    private ItemWriter<Customer> jdbcItemWriter;

    @Override
    public ItemWriter<Customer> classify(Customer customer) {
        if(customer.getState().matches("^[A-M].*")) {
            return fileItemWriter;
        } else {
            return jdbcItemWriter;
        }
    }

    public void setFileItemWriter(ItemWriter<Customer> fileItemWriter) {
        this.fileItemWriter = fileItemWriter;
    }

    public void setJdbcItemWriter(ItemWriter<Customer> jdbcItemWriter) {
        this.jdbcItemWriter = jdbcItemWriter;
    }
}
```

With the CustomerClassifier coded, you can configure the job and ItemWriters. You reuse the same input and individual ItemWriters you used in the CompositeItemWriter example in the previous section, leaving only ClassifierCompositeItemWriter to configure. The configuration for ClassifierCompositeItemWriter and CustomerClassifier is shown in Listing 9-78.

Listing 9-78. Configuration of the ClassifierCompositeItemWriter and Dependencies

```xml
    ...
<beans:bean id="customerClassifier"
  class="com.apress.springbatch.chapter9.CustomerClassifier">
  <beans:property name="fileItemWriter" ref="xmlOutputWriter"/>
  <beans:property name="jdbcItemWriter" ref="jdbcBatchWriter"/>
</beans:bean>

<beans:bean id="classifierWriter" class="org.springframework.batch.item.
support.ClassifierCompositeItemWriter">
  <beans:property name="classifier" ref="customerClassifier"/>
</beans:bean>

<step id="formatFileStep">
  <tasklet>
    <chunk reader="customerFileReader" writer="classifierWriter"
      commit-interval="10"/>
  </tasklet>
</step>
```

```
<job id="classifierFormatJob">
  <step id="step1" parent="formatFileStep"/>
</job>
...
```

When you build and run classifierFormatJob via the statement java -jar itemWriters-0.0.1-SNAPSHOT.jar jobs/formatJob.xml formatJob customerFile=/input/customerWithEmail.csv outputFile=/output/xmlCustomer.xml, you're met with a bit of a surprise. It doesn't work. Instead of the normal output of Spring telling you the job completed as expected, you're met with an exception, as shown in Listing 9-79.

Listing 9-79. Results of classifierFormatJob

```
2011-03-15 22:46:53,647 DEBUG main [org.springframework.batch.core.step.tasklet.TaskletStep]
- <Applying contribution: [StepContribution: read=10, written=0, filtered=0, readSkips=0,
writeSkips=0, processSkips=0, exitStatus=EXECUTING]>

2011-03-15 22:46:53,647 DEBUG main
[org.springframework.batch.core.step.tasklet.TaskletStep] - <Rollback for
RuntimeException: java.lang.IllegalArgumentException: StaxResult contains
neither XMLStreamWriter nor XMLEventConsumer>
2011-03-15 22:46:53,648 DEBUG main
[org.springframework.batch.repeat.support.RepeatTemplate] - <Handling
exception: java.lang.IllegalArgumentException, caused by:
java.lang.IllegalArgumentException: StaxResult contains neither
XMLStreamWriter nor XMLEventConsumer>
2011-03-15 22:46:53,648 DEBUG main
[org.springframework.batch.repeat.support.RepeatTemplate] - <Handling fatal
exception explicitly (rethrowing first of 1):
java.lang.IllegalArgumentException: StaxResult contains neither
XMLStreamWriter nor XMLEventConsumer>
2011-03-15 22:46:53,649 ERROR main
[org.springframework.batch.core.step.AbstractStep] - <Encountered an error
executing the step>
java.lang.IllegalArgumentException: StaxResult contains neither
XMLStreamWriter nor XMLEventConsumer
 at
org.springframework.oxm.AbstractMarshaller.marshalStaxResult(AbstractMarshall
er.java:217)
    at org.springframework.oxm.AbstractMarshaller.marshal(AbstractMarshaller.java:91)
    at org.springframework.batch.item.xml.StaxEventItemWriter.write(StaxEventItemWri
ter.java:573)
 at
org.springframework.batch.item.support.ClassifierCompositeItemWriter.write(Cl
assifierCompositeItemWriter.java:65)
 at
org.springframework.batch.core.step.item.SimpleChunkProcessor.writeItems(Simp
leChunkProcessor.java:171)
    at org.springframework.batch.core.step.item
```

What went wrong? All you really did was swap out the CompositeItemWriter you used in the previous section with the new ClassifierCompositeItemWriter. The issue centers around the ItemStream interface.

The ItemStream Interface

The ItemStream interface serves as the contract to be able to periodically store and restore state. Consisting of three methods, open, update, and close, the ItemStream interface is implemented by any stateful ItemReader or ItemWriter. In cases, for example, where a file is involved in the input or output, the open method opens the required file, and the close method closes the required file. The update method records the current state (number of records written, and so on) as each chunk is completed.

The reason for the difference between CompositeItemWriter and ClassifierCompositeItemWriter is that CompositeItemWriter implements the org.springframework.batch.item.ItemStream interface. In CompositeItemWriter, the open method loops through the delegate ItemWriters and calls the open method on each of them as required. The close and update methods work the same way. However, ClassifierCompositeItemWriter doesn't implement the ItemStream method. Because of this, the XML file is never opened or XMLEventFactory (or the underlying XML writing) created, throwing the exception shown in Listing 9-79.

How do you fix this error? Spring Batch provides the ability to register ItemStreams to be handled in a step manually. If an ItemReader or ItemWriter implements ItemStream, the methods are handled for you. If they don't (as in the case of ClassifierCompositeItemWriter), you're required to register the ItemReader or ItemWriter as a stream to be able to work with it if it maintains state. Listing 9-80 shows the updated configuration for the job, registering the xmlOutputWriter as an ItemStream.[6]

Listing 9-80. Updated Configuration Registering the Appropriate ItemStream for Processing

```
    ...
<step id="formatFileStep">
  <tasklet>
    <chunk reader="customerFileReader" writer="classifierWriter"
      commit-interval="10">
      <streams>
        <stream ref="xmlOutputWriter"/>
      </streams>
    </chunk>
  </tasklet>
</step>

<job id="formatJob">
  <step id="step1" parent="formatFileStep"/>
</job>
...
```

If you rebuild and rerun the job with the updated configuration, you see that all the records are processed as expected.

---

[6] You only need to register the xmlOutputWriter as a stream. JdbcBatchItemWriter doesn't implement the ItemStream interface because it doesn't maintain any state.

Summary

Spring Batch's ItemWriters provide a wide range of output options. From writing to a simple flat file to choosing which items get written to which ItemWriters on the fly, there aren't many scenarios that aren't covered by the components Spring Batch provides out of the box.

This chapter has covered the majority of the ItemWriters available in Spring Batch. You also looked at how to use the ItemWriters provided by the framework to complete the sample application. In the next chapter, you look at how to use the scalability features of the framework to allow the jobs to scale and perform as required.

CHAPTER 10

Sample Application

Tutorials you find on the Internet in technology can be funny. Most of then rarely extend past a "Hello, World!" level of complexity for any new concept. And although that may be great for a basic understanding of a technology, you know that life is never as simple as a tutorial makes it out to be. Because of this, in this chapter you look at a more real-world example of a Spring Batch job.

This chapter covers the following:

- *Reviewing the statement job*: Before developing any new functionality, you review the goals of the job to be developed, as outlined in Chapter 3.

- *Project setup*: You create a brand-new Spring Batch project from Spring's distribution.

- *Job development:* You walk through the entire development process for the statement job outlined in Chapter 3.

- *Job testing:* You develop a full set of tests for this job, including unit, integration, and functional tests.

Let's get started by reviewing what the statement job you develop is required to do.

Reviewing the Statement Job

The job you develop in this chapter is for a mythical investment firm called Apress Investment Company. Apress Investments has a large number of clients that trade stocks through the company via individual trading accounts. At the end of each month, the clients are assessed a fee based on how many trades they made over the course of a month (the more trades they make, the lower the fee is). The related transaction fees are deducted from their account's current cash balance, and a statement is sent out containing the current values of all their investments as well as the current cash balance of their account.

To accomplish these requirements, you create a job that consists of six steps as outlined in Figure 10-1.

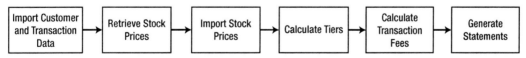

Figure 10-1. The flow for the statement job

The job starts in step 1 with importing customer and transaction data. You do this all in one step because the data is contained within the same file. After the transaction data has been imported, you can use that in step 2 to get a list of stocks that your clients currently have, and download the latest stock prices from the Internet for them. Then, you can update the customer's accounts with the latest values in step 3 so that you can calculate how much money their account is worth. You finish the job by calculating the customer's fees in steps 4 and 5 of the job and print the statement itself in step 6. The rest of the chapter goes into detail about how each of these steps is implemented and why.

To start any project, you need to begin by creating a new project shell. The next section looks at how to take the shell provided by Spring Batch and clean it up to include just what you need.

Setting Up a New Project

To start the statement job, you need to begin with a new project shell. This project shell consists of the Maven project structure, a POM file that addresses your build needs, and the infrastructure configured as required. To create a new project, as you have done in the past, download the zip distribution for Spring Batch and copy the <ZIP_ROOT>/samples/spring-batch-simple-cli directory to your workspace renaming it statement. Figure 10-2 shows the directory structure this provides you with to start.

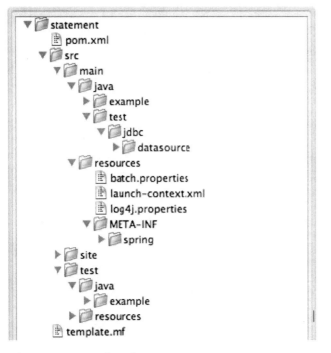

Figure 10-2. Template directory structure

The directory structure that the zip file provides is what you need to use, and the POM file it includes is a good start, but you should clean up a few things that you don't use. The files to delete are as follows:

- `<project_home>/src/main/java/example`: This directory contains sample readers and writers that you don't need in this project.

- `<project_home>/src/main/java/test`: You don't use the `DataSourceInitializer` to initialize the database schema for this project, and it isn't recommended for use in production.

- `<project_home>/src/main/resources/META-INF/spring`: As you have throughout the book, you configure the job XML files in the directory `<project_home>/src/main/resources/jobs`, so this directory and its contents aren't needed.

- `<project_home>/src/test/java/example`: Because you deleted the example ItemReader and ItemWriter included in the shell, you don't need their unit tests.

- `<project_home>/src/test/resources/test-context.xml`: You do the required configuration for the unit tests slightly differently than using this file, so it isn't needed.

With the project now much leaner, you still need to do a bit more pruning. Specifically, the launch-context.xml file has a reference to the `DataSourceInitializer` that you need to remove now that your project no longer includes that class.

After you've removed the pieces that won't be used in the project, you should update some of the remaining files. Specifically, you should update the POM file to use Spring 3 and add the MySQL driver dependency. You also need to remove the reference to the `DataSourceInitializer` from the launch-context.xml file because you deleted it earlier.

Let's start with the POM file updates. Spring does a good job of abstracting the versions of the frameworks you're using, so changing the version of Spring you use requires that you update the `spring.framework.version` property located near the top of the POM file. Listing 10-1 shows the update you need to make.

Listing 10-1. Updating the Spring Version to Spring 3

```
...
<properties>
  <maven.test.failure.ignore>true</maven.test.failure.ignore>
  <spring.framework.version>3.0.5.RELEASE</spring.framework.version>
  <spring.batch.version>2.1.7.RELEASE</spring.batch.version>
  <dependency.locations.enabled>false</dependency.locations.enabled>
</properties>
...
```

You also need to add the MySQL driver to the POM file because, as mentioned earlier, you use MySQL for the project. Listing 10-2 shows the Maven dependency you need to add to the POM file.

Listing 10-2. MySQL Maven Dependency

```
...
<dependency>
  <groupId>mysql</groupId>
  <artifactId>mysql-connector-java</artifactId>
  <version>5.1.3</version>
```

```
</dependency>
...
```

Because you added the MySQL driver to the POM file, let's configure the connection to the database next. As covered in Chapter 2, you configure the database connection both for the JobRepository and the application's database in the `statement/src/main/resources/batch.properties` file. Listing 10-3 shows the contents of this file configured for the statement job.

Listing 10-3. batch.properties

```
# Values to connect to my local
batch.jdbc.driver=com.mysql.jdbc.Driver
batch.jdbc.url=jdbc:mysql://localhost:3306/statement
# use this one for a separate server process so you can inspect the results
# (or add it to system properties with -D to override at run time).
# batch.jdbc.url=jdbc:hsqldb:hsql://localhost:9005/samples
batch.jdbc.user=root
batch.jdbc.password=password
batch.schema=statement
```

The values in the `batch.properties` file are those required in `launch-context.xml`:

- `batch.jdbc.driver`: The fully qualified class name of the JDBC driver for the database you're using. Here, you use MySQL's driver: com.mysql.jdbc.Driver.

- `batch.jdbc.url`: The URL to the database you're connecting to for your JobRepository. For the example application, you use one database schema for all tables.

- `batch.jdbc.user`: The username for the database you're connecting to.

- `batch.jdbc.password`: The password for the database.

- `batch.schema`: In MySQL's case, the database you're using.

The last piece of the project setup is to update the `launch-context.xml` file to prune the beans that you don't need for this job and update the XSDs to use Spring 3 instead of Spring 2.5 (which they come configured to use). Listing 10-4 shows the updated `statement/src/main/resources/launch-context.xml` file.

Listing 10-4. launch-context.xml

```
<?xml version="1.0" encoding="UTF-8"?>
<beans xmlns="http://www.springframework.org/schema/beans"
  xmlns:p="http://www.springframework.org/schema/p"
  xmlns:xsi="http://www.w3.org/2001/XMLSchema-instance"
  xsi:schemaLocation="http://www.springframework.org/schema/beans
    http://www.springframework.org/schema/beans/spring-beans-3.0.xsd">

  <bean id="jobExplorer"
    class="org.springframework.batch.core.explore.support.JobExplorerFactoryBean"
    p:dataSource-ref="dataSource" />
```

```xml
<bean id="jobLauncher"
   class="org.springframework.batch.core.launch.support.SimpleJobLauncher">
   <property name="jobRepository" ref="jobRepository" />
</bean>

<bean id="jobRepository"
   class="org.springframework.batch.core.repository.support.JobRepositoryFactoryBean"
   p:dataSource-/ref="dataSource" p:transactionManager-ref="transactionManager" />

<bean id="dataSource" class="org.apache.commons.dbcp.BasicDataSource">
   <property name="driverClassName" value="${batch.jdbc.driver}" />
   <property name="url" value="${batch.jdbc.url}" />
   <property name="username" value="${batch.jdbc.user}" />
   <property name="password" value="${batch.jdbc.password}" />
</bean>

<bean id="transactionManager"
   class="org.springframework.jdbc.datasource.DataSourceTransactionManager"
   lazy-init="true">
   <property name="dataSource" ref="dataSource" />
</bean>

<bean id="placeholderProperties"
   class="org.springframework.beans.factory.config.PropertyPlaceholderConfigurer">
   <property name="location" value="classpath:batch.properties" />
   <property name="systemPropertiesModeName"
     value="SYSTEM_PROPERTIES_MODE_OVERRIDE" />
   <property name="ignoreUnresolvablePlaceholders" value="true" />
   <property name="order" value="1" />
</bean>
</beans>
```

A quick walkthrough of this file shows that it looks like a normal `applicationContext.xml` file for Spring because … it's a normal `applicationContext.xml` file from Spring. You begin with the standard XML namespace declarations for the file. From there, you define six beans:

- *jobExplorer.* This bean is used by Spring Batch to access the JobRepository in a read-only mode. The JobExplorer's only dependency is a datasource.

- *JobLauncher.* In order to run a job with Spring Batch, a JobLauncher is required. Here you keep things simple and use the `SimpleJobLauncher` that is provided by the framework. Although you could administer this job in a number of ways, in most enterprises jobs are administered by an external scheduler, so there is no reason to get fancy here. The JobLauncher has the JobRepository as its only dependency.

- *JobRepository.* The JobRepository provides CRUD operations for Spring Batch to persist state and other metadata about each job run. Because you use a persistent JobRepository, it requires a datasource and a transaction manager for its processing.

- *Datasource*: There are many ways to obtain a datasource in Spring. In this case, defining one using Spring's `BasicDataSource` suffices. The values for the JDBC connection are stored in the `batch.properties` file, which you update next.

- *TransactionManager*: When you begin reading data from and writing data to the database, this becomes a more important piece of the Spring Batch puzzle. Because you run this locally and with a single datasource, Spring JDBC's `DataSourceTransactionManager` does nicely.

- *PlaceholderProperties*: This bean handles the loading and population of any properties you choose to extract into your `batch.properties` file. For now, the only things you configure are the JDBC connection values.

With that, the setup of the statement job's project is complete. You now have an empty Spring Batch project: the database is configured to point to your database, and all the example code that is included has been removed.

Because Spring Batch jobs are designed to consist of steps that are independent of each other, you can develop them in their entirety independently. Over the course of the remainder of this chapter, you will develop the statement job using the project structure you just configured, the requirements discussed earlier this chapter and in Chapter 3, and the knowledge you've gained over the course of this book. The first step in the job is importing the customer and transaction data which is covered next.

Importing Customer and Transaction Data

As the job begins, it receives a file from another department that contains information about your customers and their transactions. Both types of data are included in the same CSV file. This section looks at how to configure the step to import the customer and transaction data into your database.

Before you get into the code, however, let's review the data model used for this job. The data model for this job consists of four tables. The Customer table contains all customer-related data including name, address, and Social Security number. Each customer is associated with an account in the Account table. The Account table contains information about how much cash a customer has in their account as well as the pricing tier they have been calculated to be part of for the month. As you would expect, the account has a one-to-many relationship to the Transaction table. Each of the customer's trades has a record in the Transaction table. The Transaction table contains information about the trade itself: the stock that was traded, how many shares were traded, how much the fee was, and so on. The final table is the Ticker table. This table is used to abstract the current values of each stock. Figure 10-3 shows the data model for the statement job.

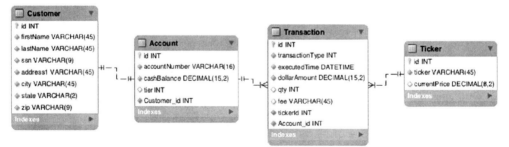

Figure 10-3. Data model for the statement job

In order to import the data you receive, you need to understand the format of the file you configure. The file consists of two record formats: one for the customer and one for the transactions. Listing 10-5 shows a sample of the file format.

Listing 10-5. Sample of the `customerTransaction.csv` File

```
205866465,Joshua,Thompson,3708 Park,Fairview,LA,58517,3276793917668488
3276793917668488,SKT,5534,416811,2011-03-30 00:15:18
3276793917668488,KSS,5767,7074247,2011-04-02 07:00:08
3276793917668488,CSR,3887,6315693,2011-03-14 20:29:20
3276793917668488,EMD,8209,6445091,2011-03-19 18:52:56
3276793917668488,SYY,7980,9524343,2011-03-24 17:26:00
3276793917668488,BYM,4011,6870023,2011-03-05 09:35:18
```

This sample consists of the records for a single customer. The file you process for the example contains records for many customers. The initial customer record consists of eight fields:

- *Social Security number:* This tax id number is unique for each customer. Although it isn't the primary key for the Customer table, it can be used to look up unique customers.

- *First name:* The customer's first name.

- *Last name:* The customer's last name.

- *Address:* The customer's street address.

- *City:* The city the customer lives in.

- *State:* The state the customer lives in.

- *Zip code:* The postal code for the customer.

- *Account number:* The identifying number for the customer's account.

It's important to note that for processing purposes, the customers you process already exist in your database. This file is only used to update existing customers and accounts. Any record for a customer who doesn't exist (identified by their Social Security number) is invalid.

The records after a customer record and before the next customer record are the transaction records for the customer preceding them. Each transaction record consists of five fields:

- *Account number:* The account number the transaction belongs to. This should match the account number of the previous customer record.

- *Stock ticker:* The stock symbol for this transaction. This is used later to obtain the current price for the stock.

- *Price:* The price of the stock when it was traded.

- *Quantity:* The number of shares traded. Positive numbers mean the shares were purchased; negative numbers indicate they were sold.

- *Timestamp:* The date and time when the transaction was executed.

To process this file, you begin by defining the job and its first step. The job configuration, like all the job configurations you've done in this book, is located in the `statement/src/main/resources/jobs` directory in a file called statementJob. This file for now contains the configuration for a single job (statementJob) with the first step configured. Listing 10-6 shows the configuration to start with.

Listing 10-6. statementJob.xml

```xml
<?xml version="1.0" encoding="UTF-8"?>
<beans:beans xmlns="http://www.springframework.org/schema/batch"
  xmlns:beans="http://www.springframework.org/schema/beans"
  xmlns:xsi="http://www.w3.org/2001/XMLSchema-instance"
  xmlns:util="http://www.springframework.org/schema/beans"
  xsi:schemaLocation="http://www.springframework.org/schema/beans
    http://www.springframework.org/schema/beans/spring-beans-3.0.xsd
    http://www.springframework.org/schema/util
    http://www.springframework.org/schema/util/spring-util.xsd
    http://www.springframework.org/schema/batch
    http://www.springframework.org/schema/batch/spring-batch-2.1.xsd">

  <beans:import resource="../launch-context.xml"/>

  <step id="importCustomerAndTransactionData">
    <tasklet>
      <chunk reader="customerTransactionReader" processor="customerLookupItemProcessor"
        writer="customerTransactionItemWriter" commit-interval="100"/>
    </tasklet>
  </step>

  <job id="statementJob">
    <step id="step1" parent="importCustomerAndTransactionData"/>
  </job>
</beans:beans>
```

There are a couple of things to notice right away. The first is that the file in Listing 10-6 won't work by itself. As you can see, you configure the step importCustomerAndTransactionData to use an ItemReader (customerTransactionReader), ItemProcessor (customerLookupItemProcessor), and ItemWriter (customerTransactionWriter). Without these beans configured, the job won't run. The other thing to notice is that you define a few more XSDs than are currently in use. Rest assured that by the end of the chapter, they will all be used.

The configuration for the job as of right now consists of the inclusion of the launch-context.xml file, which you looked at in Listing 10-4, and the definition of the first step (importCustomerAndTransactionData) with its reader, processor and writer. Finally, it has the definition of the job itself, the statementJob. To get development started, let's begin by creating the ItemReader, customerTransactionReader.

Creating the Customer Transaction Reader

When you consider the input file for this step as shown in Listing 10-5 and the data model you need to translate that data into, it quickly becomes apparent that customerTransactionReader isn't a simple FlatFileItemReader. Instead, this ItemReader is built by assembling a number of different components. This section looks at how to read in the input for the importCustomerAndTransactionData step.

The best way to think about customerTransactionReader is to visualize layers similar to your object model. The customer object has an account object, and the account object has many transactions under it. To be able to map your input file to an object model that represents this data model effectively, you need to use a layered approach to building your reader. Figure 10-4 shows how these layers stack up.

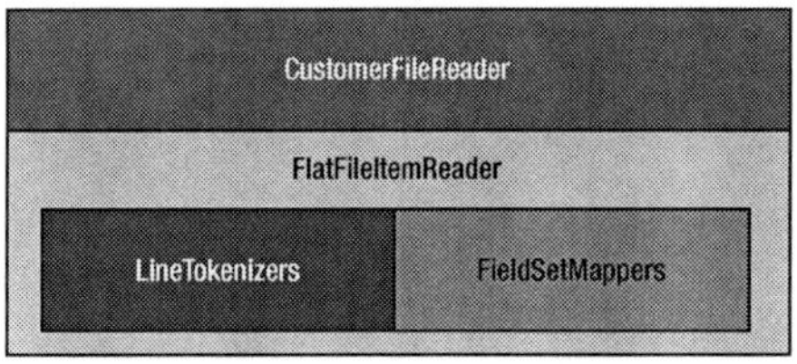

Figure 10-4. How the `CustomerFileReader` *is structured*

There are two essential layers for this reader. The first major layer, the FlatFileItemReader, works with the strings that make up the file you read in. This layer is responsible for parsing each record into objects that you can use in your batch process. The other layer, represented by the CustomerFileReader, is responsible for associating the objects in the correct way. You've looked at these different types of readers previously when you examined delimited files and files with multiple record formats in Chapter 7. Let's start by parsing the basics (`Customer` and `Transaction`). From there, you can add the abstraction of the `Account` and `Address` objects and associate them together.

The first layer of this reader, which handles parsing records, is very similar to the example for multiple record formats in Chapter 7. Before you begin parsing the records, Listing 10-7 shows the `Customer` and `Transaction` domain objects into which you parse the records.

Listing 10-7. Customer and Transaction

```
package com.apress.springbatch.statement.domain;

public class Customer {

    private long id = -1l;
    private String firstName;
    private String lastName;
    private Address address;
    private Account account;
    private String taxId;

    // Accessors removed
    ...

    @Override
    public String toString() {
        String output = "Customer number " + id + ", " + firstName + " " + lastName;

        if(address != null) {
            output = output + " who lives in "
                + address.getCity() + "," + address.getState();
        }

        if(account != null && account.getTransactions() != null) {
            output = output + " has "
```

```
                    + account.getTransactions().size() + " transactions.";
        }

        return output;
    }
}

package com.apress.springbatch.statement.domain;

import java.math.BigDecimal;
import java.util.Date;

public class Transaction {

    private long id;
    private long accountId;
    private String accountNumber;
    private String ticker;
    private long tickerId;
    private long quantity;
    private Date tradeTimestamp;
    private BigDecimal dollarAmount;
    private TransactionType type;

    // Accessors removed
    ...
    @Override
    public String toString() {
        return "Sold " + quantity + " of " + ticker;
    }
}
```

You should immediately notice in the Customer and Transaction classes that they both contain a variety of data types including an Address object and an Account object for the Customer object. Listing 10-8 shows the code for those additional domain objects.

Listing 10-8. Account and Address

```
package com.apress.springbatch.statement.domain;

import java.math.BigDecimal;
import java.util.List;

public class Account {

    private long id = -1;
    private String accountNumber;
    private Customer cust;
    private BigDecimal cashBalance;
    private PricingTier tier;
    private List<Transaction> transactions;
```

```
    // Accessors removed
    ...
}

package com.apress.springbatch.statement.domain;

public class Address {
    private String address1;
    private String city;
    private String state;
    private String zip;

    // Accessors removed
    ...
}
```

The fact that the `Customer` and `Transaction` domain objects have a number of different data types brings up an interesting issue. Although this is good in the world of objects, it should immediately signal to you that you need to write custom FieldSetMappers for each object to handle the appropriate data-type conversions required. Because the `Transaction` FieldSetMapper is simpler, you look at that one first in Listing 10-9.

Listing 10-9. TransactionFieldSetMapper

```
package com.apress.springbatch.statement.reader;

import org.springframework.batch.item.file.mapping.FieldSetMapper;
import org.springframework.batch.item.file.transform.FieldSet;
import org.springframework.validation.BindException;

import com.apress.springbatch.statement.domain.Transaction;

public class TransactionFieldSetMapper implements FieldSetMapper<Transaction> {

    public Transaction mapFieldSet(FieldSet fieldSet) throws BindException {
        Transaction trans = new Transaction();

        trans.setAccountNumber(fieldSet.readString("accountNumber"));
        trans.setQuantity(fieldSet.readLong("quantity"));
        trans.setTicker(fieldSet.readString("stockTicker"));
        trans.setTradeTimestamp(fieldSet.readDate("timestamp", "yyyy-MM-dd HH:mm:ss"));
        trans.setDollarAmount(fieldSet.readBigDecimal("price"));

        return trans;
    }
}
```

As you can see in Listing 10-9, you use the data-type conversion features of the FieldSet implementation to convert the strings read in from your file to the data types required. In this case, you convert the strings to a **long** and a **date** (by specifying the correct pattern for the date). The other FieldSetMapper you need is for the `Customer` object (see Listing 10-10).

Listing 10-10. CustomerFieldSetMapper

```java
package com.apress.springbatch.statement.reader;

import org.springframework.batch.item.file.mapping.FieldSetMapper;
import org.springframework.batch.item.file.transform.FieldSet;
import org.springframework.validation.BindException;

import com.apress.springbatch.statement.domain.Account;
import com.apress.springbatch.statement.domain.Address;
import com.apress.springbatch.statement.domain.Customer;

public class CustomerFieldSetMapper implements FieldSetMapper<Customer> {

    public Customer mapFieldSet(FieldSet fieldSet) throws BindException {
        Customer customer = new Customer();

        customer.setFirstName(fieldSet.readString("firstName"));
        customer.setLastName(fieldSet.readString("lastName"));
        customer.setTaxId(fieldSet.readString("taxId"));
        customer.setAddress(buildAddress(fieldSet));
        customer.setAccount(buildAccount(fieldSet, customer));

        return customer;
    }

    private Account buildAccount(FieldSet fieldSet, Customer cust) {
        Account account = new Account();

        account.setAccountNumber(fieldSet.readString("accountNumber"));
        account.setCust(cust);

        return account;
    }

    private Address buildAddress(FieldSet fieldSet) {
        Address address = new Address();

        address.setAddress1(fieldSet.readString("address"));
        address.setCity(fieldSet.readString("city"));
        address.setState(fieldSet.readString("state"));
        address.setZip(fieldSet.readString("zip"));

        return address;
    }
}
```

CustomerFieldSetMapper has the responsibility of breaking the customer record into three objects: Customer, Address, and Account. As you can see in Listing 10-10, there isn't much to it besides moving the appropriate fields into the appropriate objects and manually building the relationships. Now that you have the ability to map FieldSets to their respective objects, you need to be able to tokenize the lines in the file into the FieldSets. Unfortunately, in this case, it's not quite that simple.

In the example in Chapter 7, you used a file that contained a prefix on each row. This allowed you to use Spring Batch's PatternMatchingCompositeLineMapper to specify a pattern that identifies each that LineTokenizer uses to parse the record. However, PatternMatchingCompositeLineMapper's pattern-matching ability is limited. It allows for only the verification of string literals and two types of wildcards (? for a single character and * for one or more characters). The records contained in your input file are too complex to be mapped using this form of pattern matching. Because of this, you need to create your own version of PatternMatchingCompositeLineMapper that applies a true regular expression to each line to determine what LineTokenizer (and subsequently, which FieldSetMapper) to use. Listing 10-11 shows RegularExpressionLineMapper.

Listing 10-11. RegularExpressionLineMapper

```
package com.apress.springbatch.statement.reader;

import java.util.HashMap;
import java.util.Map;
import java.util.Map.Entry;
import java.util.regex.Matcher;
import java.util.regex.Pattern;

import org.springframework.batch.item.ParseException;
import org.springframework.batch.item.file.LineMapper;
import org.springframework.batch.item.file.mapping.FieldSetMapper;
import org.springframework.batch.item.file.transform.FieldSet;
import org.springframework.batch.item.file.transform.LineTokenizer;
import org.springframework.beans.factory.InitializingBean;

public class RegularExpressionLineMapper implements LineMapper<Object>, InitializingBean {

    private Map<String, LineTokenizer> tokenizers;
    private Map<String, FieldSetMapper<Object>> mappers;
    private Map<Pattern, LineTokenizer> patternTokenizers;
    private Map<LineTokenizer, FieldSetMapper<Object>> patternMappers;

    public Object mapLine(String input, int rowCount) throws Exception {

        LineTokenizer tokenizer = findTokenizer(input);
        FieldSet fields = tokenizer.tokenize(input);
        FieldSetMapper<Object> mapper = patternMappers.get(tokenizer);

        if(mapper != null) {
            return mapper.mapFieldSet(fields);
        }

        throw new ParseException("Unable to parse the input " + input);
    }

    private LineTokenizer findTokenizer(String input) {
        LineTokenizer tokenizer = null;
```

```
            for (Entry<Pattern, LineTokenizer> entry : patternTokenizers.entrySet()) {

                Matcher matcher = entry.getKey().matcher(input);
                if(matcher.find()) {
                    tokenizer = entry.getValue();
                    break;
                }
            }

            if(tokenizer != null) {
                return tokenizer;
            } else {
                throw new ParseException("Unable to locate a tokenizer for " + input);
            }
        }

    public void afterPropertiesSet() throws Exception {
        patternTokenizers = new HashMap<Pattern, LineTokenizer>();
        patternMappers = new HashMap<LineTokenizer, FieldSetMapper<Object>>();

        for (Map.Entry<String, LineTokenizer> entry : tokenizers.entrySet()) {
            Pattern pattern = Pattern.compile(entry.getKey());
            patternTokenizers.put(pattern, entry.getValue());
            patternMappers.put(entry.getValue(), mappers.get(entry.getKey()));
        }
    }

    public void setLineTokenizers(Map<String, LineTokenizer> lineTokenizers) {
        this.tokenizers = lineTokenizers;
    }

    public void setFieldSetMappers(Map<String, FieldSetMapper<Object>> fieldSetMappers) {
        this.mappers = fieldSetMappers;
    }
}
```

RegularExpressionLineMapper is a basic implementation of the LineMapper interface. It implements the one required method, mapLine, to convert a String read in from a flat file to an object. The mapLine method begins by obtaining a LineTokenizer implementation based on the String the method received as input (more on that in a bit). It then uses that LineTokenizer implementation to parse the String into a FieldSet. With the String divided into its individual fields, the appropriate FieldSetMapper is retrieved, and the fields are mapped into a new instance of the object required. The new object is then returned.

To determine which LineTokenizer to use, you do two things. First, the afterPropertiesSet method (from the InitializerBean interface) creates two Maps. The first consists of regular expression keys to LineTokenizer values. The second consists of LineTokenizer keys to FieldSetMapper values. These two Maps are used in delegating to the appropriate implementations. You use these maps by looping through the keys of the patternTokenizers Map, applying each regular expression to the String you're trying to parse. When you find a regular expression that matches, you use the associated LineTokenizer to parse the String. The LineTokenizer from the previous step allows you to get the correct FieldSetMapper from the patternMappers Map and map the FieldSet to the correct object. If for some reason a LineTokenizer or a FieldSetMapper can't be found, a `ParseException` is thrown indicating that the record couldn't be parsed.

The last part of the parsing puzzle is to configure all the pieces. You need to configure the two FieldSetMappers, two LineTokenizers, a `LineMapper` and `ItemReader all` so your step can use them. Listing 10-12 contains the configuration of the pieces you've defined up to now.

Listing 10-12. Configuring the Parsing of the customerTransaction *File*

```
...
<beans:bean id="customerTransactionFile"
class="org.springframework.core.io.FileSystemResource">
  <beans:constructor-arg value="/input/customerTransaction.csv"/>
</beans:bean>

<beans:bean id="customerLineTokenizer"
  class="org.springframework.batch.item.file.transform.DelimitedLineTokenizer">
  <beans:property name="names"
    value="taxId,firstName,lastName,address,city,state,zip,accountNumber"/>
  <beans:property name="delimiter" value=","/>
</beans:bean>

<beans:bean id="transactionLineTokenizer"
  class="org.springframework.batch.item.file.transform.DelimitedLineTokenizer">
  <beans:property name="names" value="accountNumber,stockTicker,price,quantity,timestamp"/>
  <beans:property name="delimiter" value=","/>
</beans:bean>

<beans:bean id="customerFieldSetMapper"
  class="com.apress.springbatch.statement.reader.CustomerFieldSetMapper"/>

<beans:bean id="transactionFieldSetMapper"
  class="com.apress.springbatch.statement.reader.TransactionFieldSetMapper"/>

<beans:bean id="customerTransactionLineMapper"
  class="com.apress.springbatch.statement.reader.RegularExpressionLineMapper">
  <beans:property name="lineTokenizers">
    <beans:map>
      <beans:entry key="^\d+,[A-Z][a-zA-Z]+,[A-Z][a-zA-Z]+,.*"
        value-ref="customerLineTokenizer"/>
      <beans:entry key="^\d+,[A-Z\.\ ]+,\d+.*"
        value-ref="transactionLineTokenizer"/>
    </beans:map>
  </beans:property>
  <beans:property name="fieldSetMappers">
    <beans:map>
      <beans:entry key="^\d+,[A-Z][a-zA-Z]+,[A-Z][a-zA-Z]+,.*"
        value-ref="customerFieldSetMapper"/>
      <beans:entry key="^\d+,[A-Z\.\ ]+,\d+.*"
        value-ref="transactionFieldSetMapper"/>
    </beans:map>
  </beans:property>
```

```
</beans:bean>

<beans:bean id="customerTransactionReader"
  class="org.springframework.batch.item.file.FlatFileItemReader">
  <beans:property name="resource" ref="customerTransactionFile"/>
  <beans:property name="lineMapper" ref="customerTransactionLineMapper"/>
</beans:bean>
...
```

In Listing 10-12, you begin the configuration with the input file configuration. It's a FileSystemResource like all your flat files have been; you specify the path to the file you process. From there, you configure the customer and transaction LineTokenizers. These are simple DelimitedLineTokenizers provided by the framework and configured to parse the comma-separated record format you defined earlier. Next are the customer and transaction FieldSetMappers. These are the two you wrote. Because they have no dependencies, they consist only of the bean definitions. The next (and largest) piece of the configuration is RegularExpressionLineMapper. It has two dependencies: a map of regular expressions to LineTokenizers and a map of the same regular expressions to FieldSetMappers. Each map contains a single entry for each record type. The ItemReader follows in the XML. In this case, you use a regular FlatFileItemReader for the implementation, passing it a reference to your input file and a reference to your LineMapper (RegularExpressionLineMapper).

That's all you need to read the input required for the customerTransaction.csv file. But reading is only half the process. The goal of this step is to get the data into your database. To do that, you need to update each item with some ids for referential integrity to work. You look at the ItemProcessor responsible for these updates in the next section.

Looking Ip Ids

Although the goal of this first step is to read the data from the customerTransaction.csv file and write it to the database, the customer and transaction data needs some processing before you can do the write. Per the requirements in Chapter 3, you need to insert customers if they don't exist currently in the database and update them if they do. In this section, you write an ItemProcessor to update the customer item if it exists in the database.

The items you get from customerTransactionReader can be either Customer objects or Transaction objects. Because of this, the ItemProcessor needs to determine which type it is, update the ticker id and the account id if it's a transaction, or look up the customer by social security number to get the database id to update the Customer object before passing it along. Listing 10-13 has the code for CustomerLookupItemProcessor.

Listing 10-13. CustomerLookupItemProcessor

```
package com.apress.springbatch.statement.processor;

import org.springframework.batch.item.ItemProcessor;

import com.apress.springbatch.statement.dao.AccountDao;
import com.apress.springbatch.statement.dao.CustomerDao;
import com.apress.springbatch.statement.dao.TickerDao;
import com.apress.springbatch.statement.domain.Account;
import com.apress.springbatch.statement.domain.Customer;
import com.apress.springbatch.statement.domain.Ticker;
import com.apress.springbatch.statement.domain.Transaction;
```

```java
import com.apress.springbatch.statement.domain.TransactionType;
import com.apress.springbatch.statement.exception.InvalidItemException;

public class CustomerLookupItemProcessor implements ItemProcessor<Object, Object> {

    private CustomerDao customerDao;
    private TickerDao tickerDao;
    private AccountDao accountDao;

    public Object process(Object curItem) throws Exception {
        if(curItem instanceof Customer) {
            doCustomerUpdate((Customer) curItem);
        } else if(curItem instanceof Transaction){
            doTransactionUpdate((Transaction) curItem);
        } else {
            throw new InvalidItemException("An invalid item was received: " + curItem);
        }

        return curItem;
    }

    private void doTransactionUpdate(Transaction curItem) {
        updateTicker(curItem);
        updateAccount(curItem);

        curItem.setType(TransactionType.STOCK);
    }

    private void updateAccount(Transaction curItem) {
        Account account = accountDao.findAccountByNumber(curItem.getAccountNumber());

        curItem.setAccountId(account.getId());
    }

    private void updateTicker(Transaction curItem) {
        Ticker ticker = tickerDao.findTickerBySymbol(curItem.getTicker());

        if(ticker == null) {
            Ticker newTicker = new Ticker();
            newTicker.setTicker(curItem.getTicker());

            tickerDao.saveTicker(newTicker);
            ticker = tickerDao.findTickerBySymbol(curItem.getTicker());
        }

        curItem.setTickerId(ticker.getId());
    }

    private void doCustomerUpdate(Customer curCustomer) {
        Customer storedCustomer = customerDao.findCustomerByTaxId(curCustomer.getTaxId());
        Account account =
accountDao.findAccountByNumber(curCustomer.getAccount().getAccountNumber());
```

```
            curCustomer.setId(storedCustomer.getId());

            curCustomer.setAccount(account);
        }

        public void setCustomerDao(CustomerDao customerDao) {
            this.customerDao = customerDao;
        }

        public void setTickerDao(TickerDao tickerDao) {
            this.tickerDao = tickerDao;
        }

        public void setAccountDao(AccountDao accountDao) {
            this.accountDao = accountDao;
        }
    }
```

Listing 10-13 looks like it has quite a bit going on, but it's really not that bad. Like any ItemProcessor, the logic begins in the process method. Here you determine what type of item you're processing and pass it to the appropriate method to update that type.

For a Customer object, you look up the customer's database id and update the Customer object with it. You do the same for the customer's Account object before you return it to be written. For a Transaction object, you update the ticker object's id if the ticker is already in the database. If it isn't, you save it to the database for future objects to reference. You also update the account id on the Transaction object as well as identify the type of transaction before you return it to be written.

CustomerLookupItemProcessor requires a few data access objects (DAOs) to look up the ids you populate. First is CustomerDaoJdbc, which looks up the customer's id (see Listing 10-14).

Listing 10-14. CustomerDaoJdbc

```
package com.apress.springbatch.statement.dao.impl;

import java.sql.ResultSet;
import java.sql.SQLException;
import java.util.List;

import org.springframework.jdbc.core.JdbcTemplate;
import org.springframework.jdbc.core.RowMapper;

import com.apress.springbatch.statement.dao.CustomerDao;
import com.apress.springbatch.statement.domain.Address;
import com.apress.springbatch.statement.domain.Customer;

public class CustomerDaoJdbc extends JdbcTemplate implements CustomerDao {

    private static final String FIND_BY_TAX_ID = "select * from customer c where ssn = ?";

    @SuppressWarnings("unchecked")
    public Customer findCustomerByTaxId(String taxId) {
        List<Customer> customers = query(FIND_BY_TAX_ID,
                new Object[] { taxId }, new RowMapper() {
```

```
        public Object mapRow(ResultSet rs, int arg1)

                throws SQLException {
            Customer customer = new Customer();

            customer.setId(rs.getLong("id"));
            customer.setFirstName(rs.getString("firstName"));
            customer.setLastName(rs.getString("lastName"));
            customer.setTaxId(rs.getString("ssn"));
            customer.setAddress(buildAddress(rs));

            return customer;
        }

        private Address buildAddress(ResultSet rs)
                throws SQLException {
            Address address = new Address();

            address.setAddress1(rs.getString("address1"));
            address.setCity(rs.getString("city"));
            address.setState(rs.getString("state"));
            address.setZip(rs.getString("zip"));

            return address;
        }
    });

    if (customers != null && customers.size() > 0) {
        return customers.get(0);
    } else {
        return null;
    }
}
}
```

CustomerDaoJdbc in Listing 10-14 is definitely more robust than it needs to be. As you can see, the findCustomerByTaxId method maps a full Customer object when you really only need its id. However, this approach makes the DAO much more reusable in the long run.

Next on the list of DAOs is AccountDaoJdbc. This is the same situation as the Customer DAO you just looked at. This DAO provides the ability to look up an Account by account number and returns a full Account object including transactions. Listing 10-15 shows the code.

Listing 10-15. AccountDaoJdbc

```
package com.apress.springbatch.statement.dao.impl;

import java.sql.ResultSet;
import java.sql.SQLException;
import java.util.ArrayList;
import java.util.List;

import org.springframework.jdbc.core.JdbcTemplate;
```

```
import org.springframework.jdbc.core.RowMapper;

import com.apress.springbatch.statement.dao.AccountDao;
import com.apress.springbatch.statement.domain.Account;
import com.apress.springbatch.statement.domain.Address;
import com.apress.springbatch.statement.domain.Customer;
import com.apress.springbatch.statement.domain.PricingTier;
import com.apress.springbatch.statement.domain.Transaction;
import com.apress.springbatch.statement.domain.TransactionType;

public class AccountDaoJdbc extends JdbcTemplate implements AccountDao {

    private static final String FIND_BY_ACCOUNT_NUMBER = "select a.id, " +
        "a.accountNumber, a.cashBalance, a.tier, a.customer_id, c.firstName, " +
        "c.lastName, c.ssn, c.address1, c.city, c.state, c.zip, t.id as transaction_id, " +
        "t.transactionType, t.executedTime, t.dollarAmount, t.qty, t.tickerId, t.fee  " +
        "from account a inner join customer c on a.customer_id = c.id left outer join " +
        "transaction t on a.id = t.account_id where accountNumber = ?";

    private final class AccountRowMapper implements RowMapper {
        public Object mapRow(ResultSet rs, int arg1)
                throws SQLException {
            Account account = new Account();

            account.setAccountNumber(rs.getString("accountNumber"));
            account.setCashBalance(rs.getBigDecimal("cashBalance"));
            account.setTier(PricingTier.convert(rs.getInt("tier")));
            account.setId(rs.getLong("id"));
            account.setCust(buildCustomer(rs));
            account.setTransactions(buildTransactions(rs));

            return account;
        }

        private List<Transaction> buildTransactions(ResultSet rs) throws SQLException {
            List<Transaction> transactions = new ArrayList<Transaction>();

            do {
                if(rs.getLong("transaction_id") >= 0) {
                    Transaction curTransaction = new Transaction();
                    curTransaction.setAccountId(rs.getLong("id"));
                    curTransaction.setAccountNumber(rs.getString("accountNumber"));
                    curTransaction.setDollarAmount(rs.getBigDecimal("dollarAmount"));
                    curTransaction.setId(rs.getLong("transaction_id"));
                    curTransaction.setQuantity(rs.getLong("qty"));
                    curTransaction.setTickerId(rs.getLong("tickerId"));
                    curTransaction.setTradeTimestamp(rs.getDate("executedTime"));

curTransaction.setType(TransactionType.fromIntValue(rs.getInt("transactionType")));

                    transactions.add(curTransaction);
                }
```

```
            } while(rs.next());

            if(transactions.size() > 0) {
                rs.previous();
            }

            return transactions;
        }

        private Customer buildCustomer(ResultSet rs) throws SQLException {
            Customer customer = new Customer();

            customer.setId(rs.getLong("customer_id"));
            customer.setFirstName(rs.getString("firstName"));
            customer.setLastName(rs.getString("lastName"));
            customer.setTaxId(rs.getString("ssn"));
            customer.setAddress(buildAddress(rs));

            return customer;
        }

        private Address buildAddress(ResultSet rs)
                throws SQLException {
            Address address = new Address();

            address.setAddress1(rs.getString("address1"));
            address.setCity(rs.getString("city"));
            address.setState(rs.getString("state"));
            address.setZip(rs.getString("zip"));

            return address;
        }
    }

    @SuppressWarnings("unchecked")
    public Account findAccountByNumber(String accountNumber) {
        List<Account> accounts = query(FIND_BY_ACCOUNT_NUMBER,
                new Object[] { accountNumber }, new AccountRowMapper());

        if (accounts != null && accounts.size() > 0) {
            return accounts.get(0);
        } else {
            return null;
        }
    }
}
```

The last DAO you need to implement is the ticker DAO. This one needs to provide a bit more functionality. As you process each of the transactions in the ItemProcessor, you try to update the Transaction object with the id of the ticker involved in the sale. However, if the ticker isn't found, you save a new copy of it and associate the Transaction object with that new Ticker object. Because of this, you need to implement not only the lookup functionality but the save as well. Listing 10-16 shows the code for TickerDaoJdbc.

Listing 10-16. TickerDaoJdbc

```
package com.apress.springbatch.statement.dao.impl;

import java.math.BigDecimal;
import java.sql.ResultSet;
import java.sql.SQLException;
import java.util.List;

import org.springframework.jdbc.core.JdbcTemplate;
import org.springframework.jdbc.core.RowMapper;

import com.apress.springbatch.statement.dao.TickerDao;
import com.apress.springbatch.statement.domain.Ticker;
import com.apress.springbatch.statement.domain.Transaction;

public class TickerDaoJdbc extends JdbcTemplate implements TickerDao {

    private static final String FIND_BY_SYMBOL = "select * from ticker t where ticker = ?";
    private static final String SAVE_TICKER = "insert into ticker (ticker, currentPrice)
values (?,?)";

    @SuppressWarnings("unchecked")
    public Ticker findTickerBySymbol(String symbol) {
        List<Ticker> tickers = query(FIND_BY_SYMBOL, new Object [] {symbol}, new RowMapper() {

            public Object mapRow(ResultSet rs, int arg1) throws SQLException {
                Ticker ticker = new Ticker();

                ticker.setId(rs.getLong("id"));
                ticker.setPrice(rs.getBigDecimal("currentPrice"));
                ticker.setTicker(rs.getString("ticker"));

                return ticker;
            }
        });

        if(tickers != null && tickers.size() > 0) {
            return tickers.get(0);
        } else {
            return null;
        }
    }

    public void saveTicker(Ticker ticker) {
        update(SAVE_TICKER, new Object [] {ticker.getTicker(), ticker.getPrice()});
    }
}
```

By looking up the customer in the ItemProcessor and updating the item with the database id before passing it onto the writer, you allow the writer to be dumb and do nothing more than a typical save-or-update style operation. Without this, your ItemWriter would need to do both a lookup and an insert, which isn't the behavior you're looking for in an ItemWriter.

The configuration for the job needs to be updated to include the new ItemProcessor. To configure the ItemProcessor, you add it to the `statementJob.xml` file as well as the DAOs the ItemProcessor is dependent on. Listing 10-17 shows the configuration to add to the `statementJob.xml` file.

Listing 10-17. Configuration for `customerLookupItemProcessor`

```
...
<beans:bean id="customerLookupItemProcessor"
  class="com.apress.springbatch.statement.processor.CustomerLookupItemProcessor">
  <beans:property name="customerDao" ref="customerDao"/>
  <beans:property name="tickerDao" ref="tickerDao"/>
  <beans:property name="accountDao" ref="accountDao"/>
</beans:bean>

<beans:bean id="customerDao"
  class="com.apress.springbatch.statement.dao.impl.CustomerDaoJdbc">
  <beans:property name="dataSource" ref="dataSource"/>
</beans:bean>

<beans:bean id="tickerDao"
  class="com.apress.springbatch.statement.dao.impl.TickerDaoJdbc">
  <beans:property name="dataSource" ref="dataSource"/>
</beans:bean>

<beans:bean id="accountDao"
  class="com.apress.springbatch.statement.dao.impl.AccountDaoJdbc">
  <beans:property name="dataSource" ref="dataSource"/>
</beans:bean>
...
```

The added configuration shown in Listing 10-17 begins with the configuration of `CustomerLookupItemProcessor` itself. The ItemProcessor is dependent only on the DAOs you coded in this section, which are also configured as the next three beans; each requires only a reference to a datasource.

The last piece of the process to import the customer and transaction data is to write the data to the database. The required ItemWriters are covered in the next section.

Writing the Customer and Transaction Data

The last piece of importing the customer and transaction data is updating the database with your newly read items. This section looks at how to write both the `Customer` items and `Transaction` items processed in this step.

Spring Batch provides a great tool to handle the writing for this step: ClassifierCompositeItemWriter. With its ability to determine which writer to use based on a classifier paired with Spring Batch's SubclassClassifier, which allows you to define class-to-ItemWriter associations, it's a perfect fit for this type of problem. Figure 10-5 shows the structure of the `importCustomerAndTransaction` step as a whole.

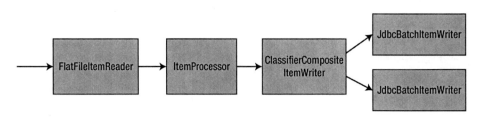

Figure 10-5. *Structure of the* `importCustomerAndTransaction` *step*

Figure 10-5 shows that you have the FlatFileItemReader and your implementation of the ItemProcessor (`CustomerLookupItemProcessor`). It also shows that you define three ItemWriters for this step: `customerImportWriter` as a JdbcBatchItemWriter; followed by the `transactionImportWriter`, which is also a JdbcBatchItemWriter; and the ClassifierCompositeItemWriter defined by the bean `customerTransactionItemWriter`, which wraps those two ItemWriters. This maps `Customer` items to one writer and `Transaction` items to the other.

The nice part about this step's writers is that they require zero code. The JdbcBatchItemWriters both look the same except for the SQL being used. For `customerImportWriter`, you use an `update` statement because this step only updates existing customers' information and doesn't add new customers. However, for `transactionImportWriter`, you insert each one new, so it uses an `insert` statement as expected. Listing 10-18 shows the configuration for all three of this step's ItemWriters.

Listing 10-18. *ItemWriters for the Customer and Transaction Import as Configured in* `statementJob.xml`

```
...
<beans:bean id="customerImportWriter"
  class="org.springframework.batch.item.database.JdbcBatchItemWriter">
  <beans:property name="dataSource" ref="dataSource"/>
  <beans:property name="sql"
    value="update customer set firstName = :firstName, lastName = :lastName, address1 =
:address.address1, city = :address.city, state = :address.state, zip = :address.zip where ssn
= :taxId"/>
  <beans:property name="itemSqlParameterSourceProvider">
    <beans:bean

class="org.springframework.batch.item.database.BeanPropertyItemSqlParameterSourceProvider"/>
  </beans:property>
</beans:bean>

<beans:bean id="transactionImportWriter"
  class="org.springframework.batch.item.database.JdbcBatchItemWriter">
  <beans:property name="dataSource" ref="dataSource"/>
  <beans:property name="sql"
    value="insert into transaction (transactionType, executedTime, dollarAmount, qty,
tickerId, account_id) values (:type.intValue, :tradeTimestamp, :dollarAmount, :quantity,
:tickerId, :accountId)"/>
  <beans:property name="itemSqlParameterSourceProvider">
    <beans:bean

class="org.springframework.batch.item.database.BeanPropertyItemSqlParameterSourceProvider"/>
  </beans:property>
```

```
</beans:bean>

<beans:bean id="customerTransactionItemWriter"
  class="org.springframework.batch.item.support.ClassifierCompositeItemWriter">
  <beans:property name="classifier">
    <beans:bean class="org.springframework.batch.classify.SubclassClassifier">
      <beans:property name="typeMap">
        <beans:map>
          <beans:entry key="com.apress.springbatch.statement.domain.Customer"
            value-ref="customerImportWriter"/>
          <beans:entry key="com.apress.springbatch.statement.domain.Transaction"
            value-ref="transactionImportWriter"/>
        </beans:map>
      </beans:property>
    </beans:bean>
  </beans:property>
</beans:bean>
...
```

Each of the JdbcBatchItemWriters as shown in Listing 10-18 provides the same three dependencies. First, they provide a datasource to be able to connect to the database. Second, they provide the SQL to be executed for each item. In both cases, you provide a statement using named parameters. This allows you to use BeanPropertyItemSqlParameterSourceProvider as your third dependency to set the values for PreparedStatement.

▨ **Note** The BeanPropertyItemSqlParameterSourceProvider supports dot notation when referring to the properties to be set in your SQL, such as address.city and address.state.

The last element of this step's configuration is the driver for the ItemWriters, customerTransactionItemWriter. This ItemWriter sends all items of type Customer to customerImportWriter and all items of type Transaction to the writer transactionImportWriter. Although it isn't used in this example, SubclassClassifier does what it says in that it identifies not only by type but by subtype as well. If you had items that extended Customer (VIPCustomer, for example), those would be routed to customerImportWriter as well.

Believe it or not, that is all you need to be able to import the customer transaction file. If you build the project right now using the mvn clean install command from the root of the project, and then execute it, you see that your customer records are updated, the transactions are imported, and all the stocks that have been traded have a single record in the Ticker table.

The next section looks at the next step, which consists of downloading the current prices for each of the stocks you just imported.

Downloading Current Stock Prices

After you've imported the transactions, you can get the current prices of all the stocks your customers currently hold. This allows you to generate a statement that accurately displays what your customers' current investments are worth. This section looks at how to download the current prices for the stocks your customers hold.

Reading the Tickers

There are a couple different ways you can approach downloading the current stock prices you need:

- You can use an ItemReader that returns an item representing the stock symbol for which you need to get the price. From there, you can get the price for each of the stock tickers and write it to a file to be imported later.

- You can use an ItemReader to read a single stream from the web service, getting all the stock prices at once.

Although the first option fits better with the components of Spring Batch, let's consider what you're attempting to do. The New York Stock Exchange (NYSE) has over 2,000 listed stocks, not to mention bonds, mutual funds, and other securities. To loop through each of these financial products one by one and make a web service call to get a single number (the closing price of the stock) isn't a practical way to process this data. Because of this, this example uses option 2.

This opens up a different can of worms. Although Spring Batch provides a nice array of ItemReader implementations, it doesn't offer one that reads from a URL. To implement this functionality, you have to create your own custom URL reader. This reader loads all the stocks that your customers currently hold, calls a web service to obtain the closing price for each ticker, and returns the response as a single string to be written out as a file by the writer.

To start, let's create a DAO to obtain a list of all the stock tickers your customers currently have. To do this, you add a method to the ticker DAO to return a list of tickers for which you need to get prices. Listing 10-19 shows the updated `TickerDaoJdbc` with the new method.

Listing 10-19. *TickerDaoJdbc*

```
package com.apress.springbatch.statement.dao.impl;

import java.math.BigDecimal;
import java.sql.ResultSet;
import java.sql.SQLException;
import java.util.List;

import org.springframework.jdbc.core.JdbcTemplate;
import org.springframework.jdbc.core.RowMapper;

import com.apress.springbatch.statement.dao.TickerDao;
import com.apress.springbatch.statement.domain.Ticker;
import com.apress.springbatch.statement.domain.Transaction;

public class TickerDaoJdbc extends JdbcTemplate implements TickerDao {

    private static final String FIND_BY_SYMBOL = "select * from ticker t where ticker = ?";
    private static final String SAVE_TICKER =
      "insert into ticker (ticker, currentPrice) values (?,?)";
    private static final String FIND_ALL =
      select distinct ticker from ticker order by ticker limit ?, ?";

    @SuppressWarnings("unchecked")
    public Ticker findTickerBySymbol(String symbol) {
        List<Ticker> tickers = query(FIND_BY_SYMBOL, new Object [] {symbol}, new RowMapper() {
```

```
            public Object mapRow(ResultSet rs, int arg1) throws SQLException {

                Ticker ticker = new Ticker();

                ticker.setId(rs.getLong("id"));
                ticker.setPrice(rs.getBigDecimal("currentPrice"));
                ticker.setTicker(rs.getString("ticker"));

                return ticker;
            }
        });

        if(tickers != null && tickers.size() > 0) {
            return tickers.get(0);
        } else {
            return null;
        }
    }

    public void saveTicker(Ticker ticker) {
        update(SAVE_TICKER, new Object [] {ticker.getTicker(), ticker.getPrice()});
    }

    @SuppressWarnings("unchecked")
    public List<String> getTickersPaged(int page, int pageSize) {
        return queryForList(FIND_ALL,
                            new Object [] {(page * pageSize), pageSize},
                            String.class);
    }
}
```

The new method getTickersPaged returns a list of stock tickers. Notice that you're paginating the results. The reason is that the web service you use can't take large numbers of stock tickers at once, so you break up the list.

After you can get the stock tickers from the Transactions table, you can create your web service call. In this case, you don't need to use a web service client. All you need to do is make a simple HTTP GET request and get the String response. For this, you use Apache Commons' HttpClient. To use it, you have to add the library to your POM file. Listing 10-20 lists the dependency required.

Listing 10-20. HttpClient Dependency

```
...
<dependency>
  <groupId>org.apache.httpcomponents</groupId>
  <artifactId>httpclient</artifactId>
  <version>4.1</version>
</dependency>
...
```

With the dependency addressed, you can write your reader. This reader consists of formatting the URL, making the request to obtain the stock prices, and returning the String response. The only logic you need to be concerned with is storing the results before you return them the first time, because you only want to make the request once in the case of an import failure. If you've already retrieved the results, then the next time you come through, you can return null to indicate that the input has been exhausted. Listing 10-21 shows UrlReader.

Listing 10-21. UrlReader

```
package com.apress.springbatch.statement.reader;

import java.net.URI;
import java.util.List;

import org.apache.commons.io.IOUtils;
import org.apache.commons.lang.StringUtils;
import org.apache.http.HttpEntity;
import org.apache.http.HttpResponse;
import org.apache.http.client.HttpClient;
import org.apache.http.client.methods.HttpGet;
import org.apache.http.impl.client.DefaultHttpClient;
import org.springframework.batch.item.ExecutionContext;
import org.springframework.batch.item.ItemStreamException;
import org.springframework.batch.item.ItemStreamReader;
import org.springframework.batch.item.ParseException;
import org.springframework.batch.item.UnexpectedInputException;

import com.apress.springbatch.statement.dao.TickerDao;

public class UrlReader implements ItemStreamReader<String> {

    private String host;
    private String path;
    private int curPage = -1;
    private int pageSize = 200;
    private TickerDao tickersDao;

    public String read() throws Exception, UnexpectedInputException,
            ParseException {

        HttpClient client = new DefaultHttpClient();

        String buildQueryString = buildQueryString();

        if(buildQueryString == null) {
            return null;
        }

        URI uri = new URI("http", host, path, buildQueryString, null);

        HttpGet get = new HttpGet(uri);

        HttpResponse response = client.execute(get);
```

```java
        HttpEntity entity = response.getEntity();

        String stockPrices = IOUtils.toString(entity.getContent());
        stockPrices = StringUtils.strip(stockPrices);

        if(stockPrices != null && stockPrices.length() > 0) {
            return stockPrices;
        } else {
            return null;
        }
    }

    private String buildQueryString() throws Exception {
        List<String> tickers = tickersDao.getTickersPaged(curPage, pageSize);

        if(tickers == null || tickers.size() == 0) {
            return null;
        }

        StringBuilder tickerList = new StringBuilder("s=");

        for (String ticker : tickers) {
            tickerList.append(ticker + "+");
        }

        tickerList = new StringBuilder(tickerList.substring(0, tickerList.length() - 1));
        return tickerList.append("&f=sl1").toString();
    }

    public void close() throws ItemStreamException {
    }

    public void open(ExecutionContext executionContext) throws ItemStreamException {
        if(executionContext.containsKey("step2.tickers.page")) {
            curPage = (Integer) executionContext.get("step2.tickers.page");
        } else {
            executionContext.put("step2.tickers.page", curPage);
        }
    }

    public void update(ExecutionContext executionContext) throws ItemStreamException {
        executionContext.put("step2.tickers.page", curPage);
        curPage++;
    }

    public void setTickersDao(TickerDao tickersDao) {
        this.tickersDao = tickersDao;
    }

    public void setHost(String host) {
        this.host = host;
    }
```

```
    public void setPath(String path) {

        this.path = path;
    }

    public void setPageSize(int pageSize) {
        this.pageSize = pageSize;
    }
}
```

The UrlReader class, like any ItemReader, begins with the read method. In it, you build a query string and then use HttpClient to send an HTTP GET request to the web service. The results you get back are in a CSV format: *ticker, price.*

To create the query string, you call the ticker DAO to obtain the current page of stock tickers to price. This reader is stateful, so it keeps track of where it is in the list of stocks by page number. You use the ItemStream's open and update methods to reset the page count on a restart and update the current page you're processing, respectively.

The last step of putting this reader to use is to configure it and your DAO. The DAO has a single dependency of a datasource. UrlReader takes three dependencies: a host name, a path, and a reference to the DAO. Finally, you can add the second step, retrieveStockPrices, with references to your reader. The configuration for these pieces is shown in Listing 10-22.

Listing 10-22. Configuring the retrieveStockPrices Step

```
...
<beans:bean id="stockPriceWebServiceReader"
  class="com.apress.springbatch.statement.reader.UrlReader">
  <beans:property name="host" value="download.finance.yahoo.com"/>
  <beans:property name="path" value="/d/quotes.csv"/>
  <beans:property name="tickersDao" ref="tickerDao"/>
</beans:bean>

<step id="retrieveStockPrices">
  <tasklet>
    <chunk reader="stockPriceWebServiceReader" writer="stockFileWriter" commit-interval="1"/>
  </tasklet>
</step>
...
<job id="statementJob">
  <step id="step1" parent="importCustomerAndTransactionData" next="step2"/>
  <step id="step2" parent="retrieveStockPrices"/>
</job>
...
```

With the input side of step 2 complete, let's look at writing the values you get back from the web service to a file. This couldn't be easier using Spring Batch's declarative ItemWriters.

Writing the Stock File

Because the output from the web service is in CSV format when you receive it, all you needed to do is some simple cleanup (removing whitespace at the start and end of each chunk, which was done in your

UrlReader) and you can pass it on. The output you receive from Yahoo! is in CSV format already, so your ItemWriter becomes significantly simplified. In this case, because your item is a **String**, using the FlatFileItemWriter with a PassThroughLineAggregator works perfectly. Listing 10-23 shows the configuration for this ItemWriter.

Listing 10-23. The stockFileWriter *Configuration*

```
...
<beans:bean id="stockFile" class="org.springframework.core.io.FileSystemResource">
  <beans:constructor-arg value="/output/stockFile.csv"/>
</beans:bean>

<beans:bean id="stockFileWriter"
  class="org.springframework.batch.item.file.FlatFileItemWriter">
  <beans:property name="resource" ref="stockFile" />
  <beans:property name="lineAggregator">
    <beans:bean
      class="org.springframework.batch.item.file.transform.PassThroughLineAggregator"/>
  </beans:property>
</beans:bean>
...
```

You can't get much simpler for an ItemWriter. By providing a file to write to and using a **String** as the item, there is nothing for Spring Batch to do other than write the **String** to the file. Short, sweet, and to the point.

When you build and run the job with only the first and second steps fully functional, the end result of step 2 is a CSV file that looks like what is shown in Listing 10-24.

Listing 10-24. Output of Step 2

```
"A",42.94
"AA",16.11
"AAI",7.30
"AAP",64.80
"AAR",24.04
"AAV",8.31
"AB",21.57
"ABA",25.6231
"ABB",23.14
```

As you can see, the file consists of the stock ticker followed by the closing price of the previous day. The next section looks at the process of importing this file into your Ticker table.

Importing Current Stock Prices

In the previous step, you read the results of a web service call and wrote it to disk to import. You might be wondering, why not just read it straight into the database? The main reason is that if something goes wrong with the import step (after you've successfully downloaded the stock prices), you don't have to rerequest the prices. Once you've successfully received the stock prices, you can skip step 2 if the import fails.

Because of this, the third step is dedicated to reading the file generated in the previous step and updating the database with its contents. This section looks at how to write the reader and writer appropriate for the import of the stock price file.

Reading the Stock Price File

Unlike the reader from step 2, which wasn't exactly an ItemReader you need to write every day, this ItemReader is much more off the shelf. For this, you use the FlatFileItemReader and the DelimitedLineTokenizer to read in each stock ticker and parse it into a `Ticker` item. The domain object you use for this step, `Ticker`, consists of nothing more than two fields, ticker and price. Listing 10-25 shows the `Ticker` class.

Listing 10-25. Ticker

```
package com.apress.springbatch.statement.domain;

import java.math.BigDecimal;

public class Ticker {

    private long id;
    private String ticker;
    private BigDecimal price;

    // Accessors go here
    ...

    @Override
    public String toString() {
        return ticker + " closed at " + price;
    }
}
```

For the ItemReader, you define a FlatFileItemReader with a resource (the output file from step 2) and a LineMapper. Because the output you receive from step 2 is comma delimited as shown in Listing 10-24, you use the DefaultLineMapper with a DelimitedLineTokenizer to chop up the line and Spring Batch's BeanWrapperFieldSetMapper to map the FieldSet to your domain object by naming convention. The configuration for your ItemReader and the `importStockPrices` step is in Listing 10-26.

Listing 10-26. Configuration of stockFileReader and the importStockPrices Step

```
...
<beans:bean id="stockFileReader"
class="org.springframework.batch.item.file.FlatFileItemReader">
  <beans:property name="resource" ref="stockFile" />
  <beans:property name="lineMapper">
    <beans:bean class="org.springframework.batch.item.file.mapping.DefaultLineMapper">
      <beans:property name="lineTokenizer">
        <beans:bean
class="org.springframework.batch.item.file.transform.DelimitedLineTokenizer">
          <beans:property name="names"value="ticker,price"/>
```

```
            <beans:property name="delimiter" value=","/>
          </beans:bean>
        </beans:property>
        <beans:property name="fieldSetMapper">
          <beans:bean
            class="org.springframework.batch.item.file.mapping.BeanWrapperFieldSetMapper">
            <beans:property name="prototypeBeanName" value="stock"/>
          </beans:bean>
        </beans:property>
      </beans:bean>
    </beans:property>
  </beans:bean>

  <beans:bean id="stock" class="com.apress.springbatch.statement.domain.Ticker"
    scope="prototype"/>

  <step id="importStockPrices">
    <tasklet>
      <chunk reader="stockFileReader" writer="tickerUpdateWriter" commit-interval="100"/>
    </tasklet>
  </step>

  <job id="statementJob" incrementer="idIncrementer">
    <step id="step1" parent="importCustomerAndTransactionData" next="step2"/>
    <step id="step2" parent="retrieveStockPrices" next="step3"/>
    <step id="step3" parent="importStockPrices"/>
  </job>
  ...
```

With this reader configured, you can now obtain the closing prices for all the stocks your customers currently hold as well as read in the output you receive from the web service so that you can import it into your database. In the next section, you look at how to update the database with the stock prices you received in step 2.

Writing Stock Prices to the Database

With the ability to read stock prices in from your file configured, you can move to updating the database with the values you read. This section looks at the configuration for the ItemWriter required to import the stock prices you download in step 2.

In the previous section, you used a FlatFileItemReader to read in the CSV generated in step 2. To update the tickers stored as part of the process of updating the Transaction in step 1, you again use a simple JdbcBatchItemWriter to update the currentPrice column of the Ticker table. Listing 10-27 shows the configuration of the ItemWriter required for this step.

Listing 10-27. tickerUpdateItemWriter Configuration

```
...
<beans:bean id="tickerUpdateWriter"
  class="org.springframework.batch.item.database.JdbcBatchItemWriter">
  <beans:property name="dataSource" ref="dataSource"/>
  <beans:property name="sql"
```

```
        value="update ticker set currentPrice = :price where ticker = :ticker"/>
    <beans:property name="itemSqlParameterSourceProvider">
        <beans:bean
```

```
class="org.springframework.batch.item.database.BeanPropertyItemSqlParameterSourceProvider"/>
    </beans:property>
</beans:bean>
...
```

With the tickers updated, the data import is complete. From here, you can apply the business rules as required and finally output your customers' statements. The first step of applying business logic for this job is determining the pricing tier to which each of your customers belongs. The next section looks at how to apply that logic to your customers' accounts.

Calculating Pricing Tiers

The Apress Investment Company charges for each transaction a customer chooses to make through it. However, Apress Investments gives discounts based on how many transactions a customer makes in a month. The more transactions the customer makes, the less the company charges. The pricing is divided into four tiers. The number of transactions a customer performed in a month indicates each tier. Pricing for a customer is based on the tier they fall into. In this section you create an ItemProcessor that calculates the tier each customer falls into for the month.

Before you get into the technical aspects of the calculation, Table 10-1 shows how each tier is defined and the related price that each transaction is charged based on the tier.

Table 10-1. Pricing Tiers

Tier	Trades	Fee per Transaction
I	<=1,000	$9 + .1% of the purchase price
II	1,001: 100,000	$3
III	100,001: 1,000,000	$2
IV	> 1,000,000	$1

You may wonder why you need to calculate the tiers prior to calculating the fees and why you can't just do it all in one step. The reasons are twofold. First, processing the tiers requires only the number of transactions a customer performed in a month and not the transactions themselves. Because of this, you don't need to load all the transactions to make this calculation. Second, because knowing the tier is a prerequisite for calculating the fees, it would require a lot of state management to pull off this type of calculation in a single step, and with large numbers of transactions doing so would be impractical. Finally, this approach also provides you with a safer implementation because this step can fail without impacting the pricing of the transactions.

To implement this piece of functionality, you use a JDBC-based ItemReader to read in the data required to determine the pricing tier. Once the data for each account has been read in, it's passed to the ItemProcessor to calculate what tier the customer's account falls into. Finally, a JDBC-based ItemWriter is used to update the account record of the user. This section looks at how to code and configure the required components to implement the pricing tiers' calculation.

Reading How Many Transactions the Customer Had

There are two ways you can get the number of transactions for each account:

1. You can load each account and its list of transactions (similar to how Hibernate would do it) and get the size of the transactions list.

2. You can create a custom object and query just for the account number and the count of transactions the account has had.

The problem with the first option is that it doesn't scale well. As customers accumulate more and more transactions, this approach may work well for counts in the thousands; but when you have customers who literally make millions of trades per month,[1] this approach falls apart in a painful way. Instead, in this example you opt for the second choice.

For this choice, you need to create a special domain object for this step. It contains the account number and the number of transactions the account has had over the given period. Listing 10-28 shows the code for the `AccountTransactionQuantity` domain object.

Listing 10-28. AccountTransactionQuantity

```
package com.apress.springbatch.statement.domain;

public class AccountTransactionQuantity {

    private String accountNumber;
    private long transactionCount;
    private PricingTier tier;

    // Accessors go here
    ..

    @Override
    public String toString() {
        return accountNumber + " has " + transactionCount +
            " transactions this month wich falls into tier " + tier;
    }
}
```

If you remember from the discussion in Chapter 7 about JDBC ItemReaders, there are two possible approaches: cursor based and paged based. For this reader, you a cursor-based implementation. The reasons are that it's the default behavior for Spring Batch and there is no improvement in a case like this from a performance perspective between the two approaches.

To create the ItemReader, you need to create a RowMapper implementation and configure both the RowMapper and the JdbcCursorItemReader. Listing 10-29 has the code for the RowMapper.

---

[1] Customers like this are typically what are known as *algorithmic traders*. These customers use computer models to trigger trades automatically without human intervention.

Listing 10-29. AccountTransactionQuantityRowMapper

```
package com.apress.springbatch.statement.reader;

import java.sql.ResultSet;
import java.sql.SQLException;

import org.springframework.jdbc.core.RowMapper;

import com.apress.springbatch.statement.domain.AccountTransactionQuantity;

public class AccountTransactionQuantityRowMapper implements RowMapper {

    public AccountTransactionQuantity mapRow(ResultSet resultSet, int arg1)
      throws SQLException {
        AccountTransactionQuantity qty = new AccountTransactionQuantity();

        qty.setAccountNumber(resultSet.getString("accountNumber"));
        qty.setTransactionCount(resultSet.getLong("qty"));

        return qty;
    }
}
```

To configure AccountTransactionQuantityRowMapper (wow, that's a mouthful) and the JdbcCursorItemReader is very easy. The JdbcCursorItemReader is the only thing with dependencies, and you configure only the basics here: a datasource, a row mapper, and the SQL statement to be executed. Listing 10-30 contains the configuration for this ItemReader and the calculateTiers step.

Listing 10-30. calculateTiers Step Configuration with ItemReader

```
...
<beans:bean id="accountTransactionQtyItemReader"
  class="org.springframework.batch.item.database.JdbcCursorItemReader">
  <beans:property name="dataSource" ref="dataSource"/>
  <beans:property name="sql"
    value="select a.accountNumber, count(*) as qty from account a inner join transaction t on
t.account_id = a.id group by a.accountNumber"/>
  <beans:property name="rowMapper" ref="accountTransactionQtyRowMapper"/>
</beans:bean>

<beans:bean id="accountTransactionQtyRowMapper"
  class="com.apress.springbatch.statement.reader.AccountTransactionQuantityRowMapper"/>

<step id="calculateTiers">
  <tasklet>
    <chunk reader="accountTransactionQtyItemReader" processor="pricingTiersItemProcessor"
      writer="tiersUpdateWriter" commit-interval="10"/>
  </tasklet>
</step>
```

```
<job id="statementJob" incrementer="idIncrementer">
  <step id="step1" parent="importCustomerAndTransactionData" next="step2"/>
  <step id="step2" parent="retrieveStockPrices" next="step3"/>
  <step id="step3" parent="importStockPrices" next="step4"/>
  <step id="step4" parent="calculateTiers"/>
</job>
...
```

The configuration in Listing 10-30 begins with the definition of the
accountTransactionQtyItemReader—the JdbcCursorItemReader with its three dependencies: a
datasource, the select statement that gets you each account number and the number of transactions
the account has, and a reference to the RowMapper implementation you developed. The configuration
for this RowMapper is next, followed by the step that is configured to use the ItemReader.

Now that you can read in a customer's transaction history, you can calculate the pricing tier they fall
into. In the next section, you look at the ItemProcessor you use to do that calculation.

Calculating the Pricing Tier

In the previous section, you defined an AccountTransactionQuantity object that you use as the item into
which your reader reads the data. It contains two fields: an account number and a transaction count (the
number of transactions the customer performed during the month). To calculate the tiers, you add a
PricingTier reference to the AccountTransactionQuantity object. Listing 10-31 shows the updated
AccountTransactionQuantity object and the related PricingTier enum.

Listing 10-31. AccountTransactionQuantity and PricingTier

```
package com.apress.springbatch.statement.domain;

public class AccountTransactionQuantity {

    private String accountNumber;
    private long transactionCount;
    private PricingTier tier;

    // Accessors go here
    ...

    @Override
    public String toString() {
        return accountNumber + " has " + transactionCount +
            " transactions this month wich falls into tier " + tier;
    }
}

package com.apress.springbatch.statement.domain;

public enum PricingTier {
    UNDEFINED(0), I(1), II(2), III(3), IV(4);

    private int value;
```

```
    PricingTier(int value) {
        this.value = value;
    }

    public int getValue() {
        return value;
    }

    public static PricingTier convert(Integer i) {
        if(i != null && i >= 0) {
            return values()[i];
        } else {
            return UNDEFINED;
        }
    }

    public String toString() {
        return name();
    }
}
```

Now you can create your ItemProcessor. In this case, you assign the PricingTier based on the value of the transactionCount field. With this simple logic, Listing 10-32 has the code for the new PricingTierItemProcessor.

Listing 10-32. PricingTierItemProcessor

```
package com.apress.springbatch.statement.processor;

import java.util.ArrayList;
import java.util.List;

import org.springframework.batch.item.ItemProcessor;

import com.apress.springbatch.statement.domain.AccountTransactionQuantity;
import com.apress.springbatch.statement.domain.PricingTier;

public class PricingTierItemProcessor implements ItemProcessor<AccountTransactionQuantity,
AccountTransactionQuantity> {

    private List<Integer> accountsProcessed = new ArrayList<Integer>();

    public AccountTransactionQuantity process(AccountTransactionQuantity atq)
            throws Exception {

        if(atq.getTransactionCount() <= 1000) {
            atq.setTier(PricingTier.I);
        } else if(atq.getTransactionCount() > 1000 &&
                atq.getTransactionCount() <= 100000) {
            atq.setTier(PricingTier.II);
```

```
        } else if(atq.getTransactionCount() > 100000 && atq.getTransactionCount() <= 1000000)
{
            atq.setTier(PricingTier.III);
        } else {
            atq.setTier(PricingTier.IV);
        }

return atq;
    }
}
```

As with each component of the batch process, you need to configure it. This ItemProcessor obviously doesn't have any dependencies, so the configuration involves nothing more than a bean definition and updating your step to reference the bean. Listing 10-33 shows the updated configuration for the calculateTiers step.

Listing 10-33. calculateTiers Step Configuration

```
...
<beans:bean id="pricingTiersItemProcessor"
  class="com.apress.springbatch.statement.processor.PricingTierItemProcessor"/>
...
```

With the pricing tiers calculated, you need to update the database with the values you've calculated. That database update occurs in the next section.

Updating the Database with the Calculated Tier

Unlike the steps up to this point, which were mostly about moving data around, step 4 is the first step intended to apply business rules to the data you already have. Because of that, the ItemReader and the ItemWriter are simplistic. The logic for this step resides in the ItemProcessor. This section looks at the ItemWriter required for the tier-processing step.

Because most of the work in this step is done in the ItemProcessor, it should come as no surprise that the ItemWriter for this step is, again, quite simple. Its responsibility is only to update the account being processed with the tier you've calculated it to fall into. Using a JdbcBatchItemWriter, you can perform the required updates. Listing 10-34 shows the configuration for the new ItemWriter.

Listing 10-34. Configuration for tiersUpdateWriter

```
...
<beans:bean id="tiersUpdateWriter"
  class="org.springframework.batch.item.database.JdbcBatchItemWriter">
  <beans:property name="dataSource" ref="dataSource"/>
  <beans:property name="sql"
    value="update account set tier = :tier.value where accountNumber = :accountNumber"/>
  <beans:property name="itemSqlParameterSourceProvider">
    <beans:bean

class="org.springframework.batch.item.database.BeanPropertyItemSqlParameterSourceProvider"/>
  </beans:property>
</beans:bean>
...
```

You may wonder about the :tier.value parameter defined in the SQL in this example. Because you define a getValue method on the PricingTier enum, you can use the dot notation and save the value of the tier as its integer value. This is purely a personal preference in this case.

Apress Investments doesn't make its money by moving data around. It makes its money by charging fees per transaction. In the next section, you look at how those fees are calculated.

Calculating Transaction Fees

With the pricing tier determined, you can calculate the cost of each transaction. To do this, you need two pieces of information: the price of the purchase and the pricing tier you calculated in the previous step. This section looks at how to calculate a fee and update the transaction accordingly.

Reading the Transactions

Just as in the previous step, you use a new domain object for this step. In this case, you have a class that extends Transaction but adds a couple of Account fields that you need (pricing tier, specifically) to make the calculations. Listing 10-35 shows the new domain object.

Listing 10-35. AccountTransaction

```
package com.apress.springbatch.statement.domain;

import java.math.BigDecimal;

public class AccountTransaction extends Transaction {

    private String accountNumber;
    private PricingTier tier;
    private BigDecimal fee;
    private long quantity;
    private BigDecimal price;

    // Accessors go here
    ...

    @Override
    public String toString() {
        return getId() + ":" + accountNumber + ":" + getTicker() +
            ":" + getTradeTimestamp().getTime() + ":" + fee;
    }
}
```

Each AccountTransaction represents a transaction that needs a fee to be calculated. When the fee has been calculated, the ItemWriter updates the transaction. The process for creating this ItemReader is no different than creating the one covered in the previous section. You have a JdbcCursorItemReader that executes the SQL query you configure and uses the RowMapper you configure to map the results to the AccountTransaction object. Listing 10-36 shows the code required for the RowMapper.

Listing 10-36. AccountTransactionRowMapper

```
package com.apress.springbatch.statement.reader;

import java.sql.ResultSet;
import java.sql.SQLException;

import org.springframework.jdbc.core.RowMapper;

import com.apress.springbatch.statement.domain.AccountTransaction;
import com.apress.springbatch.statement.domain.PricingTier;

public class AccountTransactionRowMapper implements RowMapper {

    public Object mapRow(ResultSet resultSet, int arg1) throws SQLException {
        AccountTransaction accountTransaction = new AccountTransaction();

        accountTransaction.setAccountId(resultSet.getLong("accountId"));
        accountTransaction.setAccountNumber(resultSet.getString("accountNumber"));
        accountTransaction.setId(resultSet.getLong("transactionId"));
        accountTransaction.setQuantity(resultSet.getLong("qty"));
        accountTransaction.setTicker(resultSet.getString("ticker"));
        accountTransaction.setTier(PricingTier.convert(resultSet.getInt("tier")));
        accountTransaction.setTradeTimestamp(resultSet.getDate("executedTime"));
        accountTransaction.setPrice(resultSet.getBigDecimal("dollarAmount"));

        return accountTransaction;
    }
}
```

With the domain object defined and the RowMapper written, all that is left is to configure the ItemReader and the step of the job used to calculate transaction fees. For the configuration, you use almost the exact same configuration as in the previous step. The only difference is the SQL statement and the ItemReader's reference to the RowMapper implementation. Listing 10-37 shows the configured step with the ItemReader.

Listing 10-37. Configuring the calculateTransactionFees Step and Dependencies

```
...
<beans:bean id="transactionPricingItemReader"
  class="org.springframework.batch.item.database.JdbcCursorItemReader" scope="step">
  <beans:property name="dataSource" ref="dataSource"/>
  <beans:property name="sql"
    value="select a.id as accountId, a.accountNumber, t.id as transactionId, t.qty, tk.ticker,
a.tier, t.executedTime, t.dollarAmount from account a inner join transaction t on a.id =
t.account_id inner join ticker tk on t.tickerId = tk.id and t.processed = false and t.jobId =
#{jobParameters[run.id]} order by t.executedTime"/>
  <beans:property name="rowMapper" ref="transactionPricingRowMapper"/>
</beans:bean>
```

```
<beans:bean id="transactionPricingRowMapper"
  class="com.apress.springbatch.statement.reader.AccountTransactionRowMapper"/>

<step id="calculateTransactionFees">
  <tasklet task-executor="taskExecutor">
    <chunk reader="transactionPricingItemReader" processor="feesItemProcessor"
      writer="applyFeeWriter" commit-interval="100"/>
  </tasklet>
</step>

<job id="statementJob" incrementer="idIncrementer">
  <step id="step1" parent="importCustomerAndTransactionData" next="step2"/>
  <step id="step2" parent="retrieveStockPrices" next="step3"/>
  <step id="step3" parent="importStockPrices" next="step4"/>
  <step id="step4" parent="calculateTiers" next="step5"/>
  <step id="step5" parent="calculateTransactionFees"/>
</job>
...
```

The configuration for the calculateTransactionFees step shown in Listing 10-37 begins with the definition of the ItemReader—a JdbcCursorItemReader in this case. transactionPricingItemReader requires three dependencies: a datasource, the SQL, and a reference to the RowMapper implementation you coded back in Listing 10-36. After the ItemReader configuration, you configure an instance of the RowMapper the ItemReader needs for the dataset it is processing. Finally the configuration for your step is provided. However, just as in the previous steps you've configured, you still have more to do before this is operational. First you need to code and configure the ItemProcessor, which is covered in the next section.

Calculating Transaction Prices

Table 10-1 showed that tiers II through IV all have a flat fee, but tier I's fee consists of a flat fee of $9.00 plus 0.1% of the total cost of the transaction. For example, if the transaction consists of 20 shares of HD stock at $40.00 each, the fee is calculated as

$$(\$40.00 \times 20 \text{ shares})0.001 = \$0.80$$

To calculate what the fee is for each transaction a customer has made, you implement an ItemProcessor to apply that logic. This section looks at how to develop and configure the ItemProcessor required to calculate the customer's transaction fees.

The code for this ItemProcessor is straightforward; Listing 10-37 has the code for FeesItemProcessor.

Listing 10-37. FeesItemProcessor

```
package com.apress.springbatch.statement.processor;

import java.math.BigDecimal;

import org.springframework.batch.item.ItemProcessor;

import com.apress.springbatch.statement.domain.AccountTransaction;
```

```
import com.apress.springbatch.statement.domain.PricingTier;

public class FeesItemProcessor implements
        ItemProcessor<AccountTransaction, AccountTransaction> {

    public AccountTransaction process(AccountTransaction transaction)
            throws Exception {
        if (transaction.getTier() == PricingTier.I) {
            priceTierOneTransaction(transaction);
        } else if (transaction.getTier() == PricingTier.II) {
            priceTierTwoTransaction(transaction);
        } else if (transaction.getTier() == PricingTier.II) {
            priceTierThreeTransaction(transaction);
        } else {
            priceTierFourTransaction(transaction);
        }

        return transaction;
    }

    private void priceTierFourTransaction(AccountTransaction transaction) {
        transaction.setFee(new BigDecimal(1.00));
    }

    private void priceTierThreeTransaction(AccountTransaction transaction) {
        transaction.setFee(new BigDecimal(2.00));
    }

    private void priceTierTwoTransaction(AccountTransaction transaction) {
        transaction.setFee(new BigDecimal(3.00));
    }

    private void priceTierOneTransaction(AccountTransaction transaction) {
        BigDecimal fee = transaction.getPrice()
                .multiply(new BigDecimal(.001));

        fee = fee.add(new BigDecimal(9.00));

        transaction.setFee(fee);
    }
}
```

FeesItemProcessor determines what tier the account for each transaction has been calculated to be. From there, it calls the appropriate method to calculate the price. To configure this ItemProcessor, you use virtually the same configuration you did for pricingTiersItemProcessor. Listing 10-39 has the configuration for feesItemProcessor.

Listing 10-39. Configuration for the calculateTransactionFees Step

```
...
<beans:bean id="feesItemProcessor"
```

```
      class="com.apress.springbatch.statement.processor.FeesItemProcessor"/>
...
```

When you've calculated the fees for each transaction, you need to save them to the database, as you look at next.

Saving Transaction Fees to the Database

After a transaction's fee has been calculated, you need to do two things: update the transaction record and update the account's cash balance, deducting the fee. This section looks at the ItemWriters required to apply transaction fees to a customer's account.

Coming out of the feesItemProcessor in this step, you have an item that has information that needs to be applied to two different locations. The first location where it needs to be applied is the Transaction table. Each transaction stores the fee applied to it. The second place the item's information needs to be applied is in the account's cash balance, where you need to deduct the amount of the fee.

To do this, Spring Batch provides the ability to process a single item with multiple ItemWriters using CompositeItemWriter, as you saw earlier in Chapter 9. CompositeItemWriter is the perfect tool for a scenario like this. Figure 10-6 shows the structure of this step as a whole.

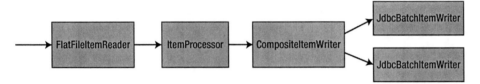

Figure 10-6. calculateTransactionFees step structure

Figure 10-6 shows that you read in each transaction with **transactionPricingItemReader** (the **FlatFileItemReader**) and process it with **feesItemProcessor** (the **ItemProcessor**). However, using CompositeItemWriter, you apply the transaction to the Transaction table with **feesUpdateWriter** and the Account table with **cashBalanceUpdateWriter**. Listing 10-40 shows the configuration for the three required ItemWriters for this step.

Listing 10-40. ItemWriter Configuration for Step 5

```xml
...
<beans:bean id="feesUpdateWriter"
  class="org.springframework.batch.item.database.JdbcBatchItemWriter">
  <beans:property name="dataSource" ref="dataSource"/>
  <beans:property name="sql" value="update transaction set fee = :fee where id = :id"/>
  <beans:property name="itemSqlParameterSourceProvider">
    <beans:bean

class="org.springframework.batch.item.database.BeanPropertyItemSqlParameterSourceProvider"/>
  </beans:property>
</beans:bean>

<beans:bean id="cashBalanceUpdateWriter"
  class="org.springframework.batch.item.database.JdbcBatchItemWriter">
  <beans:property name="dataSource" ref="dataSource"/>
```

```
  <beans:property name="sql"
    value="update account set cashBalance = (cashBalance - :fee) where accountNumber =
:accountNumber"/>
  <beans:property name="itemSqlParameterSourceProvider">
    <beans:bean

class="org.springframework.batch.item.database.BeanPropertyItemSqlParameterSourceProvider"/>
  </beans:property>
</beans:bean>

<beans:bean id="applyFeeWriter"
  class="org.springframework.batch.item.support.CompositeItemWriter">
  <beans:property name="delegates">
    <util:list>
      <util:ref bean="feesUpdateWriter"/>
      <util:ref bean="cashBalanceUpdateWriter"/>
    </util:list>
  </beans:property>
</beans:bean>
...
```

Like the classifying ItemWriter used for step 1, the CompositeItemWriter used in step 5 has two virtually identical ItemWriters it delegates to. Both are JdbcBatchItemWriters, with only the SQL as the difference between the two.

applyFeeWriter handles the delegation of items to each of the registered ItemWriters for this step. In this case, it executes feesUpdateWriter with all the items in the current chunk before moving on to cashBalanceUpdateWriter. As noted in Chapter 9, each ItemWriter in order processes all the items in the chunk at once.

When step 5 has completed, all the business processing is finished. The last step is to generate the customer statements, as covered next.

Generating Monthly Statement

The end goal of this batch job is to generate a statement for each customer with a summary of their account. All the processing up to this point has been about updating and preparing to write the statement. Step 6 is where you do that work. This section looks at the processing involved writing the statements.

Reading the Statement Data

When you look at the expected output of this last step, you quickly realize that a large amount of data needs to be pulled in order to generate the statement. Before you get into how to pull that data, let's look at the domain object you use to represent the data: the Statement object (see Listing 10-41).

Listing 10-41. Statement.java

```
package com.apress.springbatch.statement.domain;

import java.math.BigDecimal;
import java.util.List;
```

```
public class Statement {

    private Customer customer;
    private BigDecimal securityTotal;
    private List<Transaction> stocks;

    // Accessors go here
    ...
}
```

The Statement object consists of the customer's information to display on the statement. It also includes the total value of all the stocks the customer currently holds (the total is easier to get in the database than it is to calculate as you process the statements). Finally, it contains a list the stock holdings the customer currently has. It's important to note that the list of Transaction objects isn't a list of all the customer's actual transactions—you're just reusing an existing domain object because the format is similar.

Because you now know what you need to populate, you can begin to look at how to populate it. When you're designing a complex ItemReader structure like this, begin by thinking about what the item is. In this case, the item or single unit to be processed is the statement. Because of that, your ItemReader returns a Statement object.

By looking at the Statement class in Listing 10-41, you can tell that given the complexity of the data, using a single ItemReader is not going to be practical. Instead, to read the statement data, you layer ItemReaders as you've done in the past. You use a regular JDBC ItemReader to read the customer data. Although you could use a DAO, because each statement is based on a Customer anyway, using an ItemReader makes more sense. From there, you can use DAOs to populate the related data.

However, notice that the Statement has no data. Everything is associated with the Statement, but nothing is Statement specific. Because of that, you use a custom ItemReader to aggregate all the datasources. To start, let's look at the code for the custom ItemReader, CustomerStatementReader (see Listing 10-42).

Listing 10-42. CustomerStatementReader

```
package com.apress.springbatch.statement.reader;

import org.springframework.batch.item.ItemReader;
import org.springframework.batch.item.ParseException;
import org.springframework.batch.item.UnexpectedInputException;

import com.apress.springbatch.statement.dao.TickerDao;
import com.apress.springbatch.statement.domain.Customer;
import com.apress.springbatch.statement.domain.Statement;

public class CustomerStatementReader implements ItemReader<Statement> {

    private ItemReader<Customer> customerReader;
    private TickerDao tickerDao;

    public Statement read() throws Exception, UnexpectedInputException,
            ParseException {

        Customer customer = customerReader.read();
```

```
        if(customer == null) {
            return null;
        } else {
            Statement statement = new Statement();

            statement.setCustomer(customer);
            statement.setSecurityTotal(tickerDao.getTotalValueForCustomer(customer.getId()));
            statement.setStocks(tickerDao.getStocksForCustomer(customer.getId()));

            return statement;
        }
    }

    public void setCustomerReader(ItemReader<Customer> customerReader) {
        this.customerReader = customerReader;
    }

    public void setTickerDao(TickerDao tickerDao) {
        this.tickerDao = tickerDao;
    }
}
```

CustomerStatementReader begins its processing in the **read** method. You read in a customer from the ItemReader you configure. If one isn't found, you consider all the input exhausted and tell Spring Batch that by returning null. If a customer is returned, you create a new **Statement** object for them, including the customer you just received as well as the associated other data, via TickerDaoJdbc.

TickerDao for this step needs two new methods: getTotalValueForCustomer, which returns a BigDecimal value of the total value of the securities the customer currently holds, and getStocksForCustomer, which returns a List of Transaction items representing the customer's current stock holdings. Listing 10-43 shows the updated TickerDao with the new methods.

Listing 10-43. TickerDaoJdbc

```
package com.apress.springbatch.statement.dao.impl;

import java.math.BigDecimal;
import java.sql.ResultSet;
import java.sql.SQLException;
import java.util.List;

import org.springframework.jdbc.core.JdbcTemplate;
import org.springframework.jdbc.core.RowMapper;

import com.apress.springbatch.statement.dao.TickerDao;
import com.apress.springbatch.statement.domain.Ticker;
import com.apress.springbatch.statement.domain.Transaction;

public class TickerDaoJdbc extends JdbcTemplate implements TickerDao {

    private static final String FIND_BY_SYMBOL = "select * from ticker t where ticker = ?";
```

```java
    private static final String SAVE_TICKER =
      "insert into ticker (ticker, currentPrice) values (?,?)";
    private static final String FIND_ALL =
      "select distinct ticker from ticker order by ticker limit ?, ?";
    private static final String TOTAL_VALUE =
      "select SUM(value) as totalValue " +
      "from (select ticker, qty * currentPrice as value " +
      "from (select tk.ticker, SUM(ts.qty) as qty, tk.currentPrice " +
      "from transaction ts inner join " +
      "ticker tk on ts.tickerId = tk.id inner join " +
      "account a on ts.account_id = a.id inner join " +
      "customer c on c.id = a.customer_id " +
      "where c.id = ? " +
      "group by tk.ticker, tk.currentPrice) as stocks) as total";
    private static final String STOCKS_BY_CUSTOMER =
      "select ticker, qty, qty * currentPrice as value " +
      "from (select tk.ticker, SUM(ts.qty) as qty, tk.currentPrice " +
      "from transaction ts inner join  " +
      "ticker tk on ts.tickerId = tk.id inner join  " +
      "account a on ts.account_id = a.id inner join " +
      "customer c on c.id = a.customer_id " +
      "where c.id = ? " +
      "group by tk.ticker, tk.currentPrice) as stocks";

    @SuppressWarnings("unchecked")
    public Ticker findTickerBySymbol(String symbol) {
        List<Ticker> tickers = query(FIND_BY_SYMBOL, new Object [] {symbol}, new RowMapper() {

            public Object mapRow(ResultSet rs, int arg1) throws SQLException {
                Ticker ticker = new Ticker();

                ticker.setId(rs.getLong("id"));
                ticker.setPrice(rs.getBigDecimal("currentPrice"));
                ticker.setTicker(rs.getString("ticker"));

                return ticker;
            }
        });

        if(tickers != null && tickers.size() > 0) {
            return tickers.get(0);
        } else {
            return null;
        }
    }
}
```

```java
    public void saveTicker(Ticker ticker) {
        update(SAVE_TICKER, new Object [] {ticker.getTicker(), ticker.getPrice()});
    }

    @SuppressWarnings("unchecked")
    public List<String> getTickersPaged(int page, int pageSize) {
        return queryForList(FIND_ALL,
                            new Object [] {(page * pageSize), pageSize},
                            String.class);
    }

    public BigDecimal getTotalValueForCustomer(long id) {
        BigDecimal result = (BigDecimal) queryForObject(TOTAL_VALUE,
                            new Object [] {id},
                            BigDecimal.class);

        if(result == null) {
            result = new BigDecimal("0");
        }

        return result;
    }

    @SuppressWarnings("unchecked")
    public List<Transaction> getStocksForCustomer(long id) {
        return query(STOCKS_BY_CUSTOMER, new Object [] {id}, new RowMapper() {

            public Object mapRow(ResultSet rs, int arg1) throws SQLException {
                Transaction transaction = new Transaction();

                transaction.setDollarAmount(rs.getBigDecimal("value"));
                transaction.setQuantity(rs.getLong("qty"));
                transaction.setTicker(rs.getString("ticker"));

                return transaction;
            }
        });
    }
}
```

The hard part in `TickerDaoJdbc` isn't the processing but is in the SQL. The execution of the SQL and the mapping of the results to the objects is nothing more than standard uses of Spring's JdbcTemplate.

To make these three pieces work (the customer reader, `CustomerStatementReader`, and `TickerDaoJdbc`, you need to update your configuration. Listing 10-44 shows the configuration for these three components.

Listing 10-44. Configuring the generateMonthlyStatement Step

```xml
...
<beans:bean id="customerReader"
  class="org.springframework.batch.item.database.JdbcCursorItemReader">
```

```
    <beans:property name="dataSource" ref="dataSource"/>
    <beans:property name="sql"
      value="select a.id as account_id, a.accountNumber, a.cashBalance, a.tier, c.address1 as
address, c.city, c.state, c.zip, c.id as customer_id, c.firstName, c.lastName from customer c
left outer join account a on a.customer_id = c.id order by c.id"/>
    <beans:property name="rowMapper" ref="customerStatementRowMapper"/>
  </beans:bean>

  <beans:bean id="customerStatementRowMapper"
    class="com.apress.springbatch.statement.reader.CustomerStatementRowMapper"/>

  <beans:bean id="customerStatementReader"
    class="com.apress.springbatch.statement.reader.CustomerStatementReader">
    <beans:property name="customerReader" ref="customerReader"/>
    <beans:property name="tickerDao" ref="tickerDao"/>
  </beans:bean>

  <step id="generateMonthlyStatements">
    <tasklet>
      <chunk reader="customerStatementReader" writer="statementsWriter"
        commit-interval="1">
        <streams>
          <stream ref="customerReader"/>
        </streams>
      </chunk>
    </tasklet>
  </step>

  <job id="statementJob" incrementer="idIncrementer">
    <step id="step1" parent="importCustomerAndTransactionData" next="step2"/>
    <step id="step2" parent="retrieveStockPrices" next="step3"/>
    <step id="step3" parent="importStockPrices" next="step4"/>
    <step id="step4" parent="calculateTiers" next="step5"/>
    <step id="step5" parent="calculateTransactionFees" next="step6"/>
    <step id="step6" parent="generateMonthlyStatements"/>
  </job>
  ...
```

The configuration in Listing 10-44 begins with the definition of the JdbcCursorItemReader used to read the customer data. As in any of your JdbcCursorItemReader configurations, you provide a datasource, SQL, and a RowMapper implementation (the customerStatementReader RowMapper). The configuration for the RowMapper on which customerReader depends is next in the list. The CustomerStatementReader configuration is configured next. Its only two dependencies, customerReader and a reference to the TickerDaoJdbc, are both provided.

The last part of Listing 10-44 is the configuration of the final step in the job. Although it looks like a normal step, two aspects of it are unique. First is the registration of customerReader as a stream. As you saw in Chapter 7, if an ItemReader needs to be opened and isn't configured directly as the ItemReader for the step, you need to register it as a stream so Spring Batch calls the open method for you. The second interesting piece for this step is the commit count: it's set to 1. The reason is the ItemWriter you use, as you see next.

Writing the Statements

When you look at the expected output from this step, you may think a very complex system of ItemWriters must be employed. But nothing could be further from the truth. Instead, you use nothing more than a MultiResourceItemWriter (to generate a single file per customer) that delegates to a regular FlatFileItemWriter with a header callback. You obtain the complex formatting by implementing your own LineAggregator to generate the output required. To see the pieces involved, let's start with the code you need to write first: the LineAggregator implementation and the FlatFileHeaderCallback implementation.

Chapter 9 discussed how the LineAggregator interface is similar to the LineMapper interface of the ItemReader side. The LineAggregator's responsibility is to extract the fields required from each item and format them into a record to be written by a FlatFileItemWriter. Listing 10-45 shows the code for StatementFormatter.

Listing 10-45. StatementFormatter

```
package com.apress.springbatch.statement.writer;

import java.text.NumberFormat;

import org.springframework.batch.item.file.transform.LineAggregator;

import com.apress.springbatch.statement.domain.Customer;
import com.apress.springbatch.statement.domain.Statement;
import com.apress.springbatch.statement.domain.Transaction;

public class StatementFormatter implements LineAggregator<Statement> {

    private static final String ADDRESS_FORMAT = "%s %s\n%s\n%s, %s %s\n\n";
    private static final String SUMMARY_HEADER_FORMAT = "Account Number   %s\n"
            + "\nYour Account Summary\n\n";
    private static final String SUMMARY_FORMAT =
            "Market Value of Current Securities" +
            "                      %s\nCurrent Cash Balance                      " +
            "                      %s\nTotal Account Value                       " +
            "                %s\n\n";
    private static final String CASH_DETAIL_FORMAT =
            "Account Detail\n\nCash         " +
            "                                      %s\n\nSecurities\n\n";
    private static final String SECURITY_HOLDING_FORMAT =
            "    %s                    " +
            "    %s                      %s\n";
    private static NumberFormat moneyFormatter = NumberFormat
            .getCurrencyInstance();

    public String aggregate(Statement statement) {
        StringBuilder output = new StringBuilder();

        formatAddress(statement, output);
        formatSummary(statement, output);
        formatDetails(statement, output);
```

```
            return output.toString();

    }

    private void formatDetails(Statement statement, StringBuilder output) {
        output.append(String.format(CASH_DETAIL_FORMAT,
                new Object[] { statement.getCustomer().getAccount()
                        .getCashBalance() }));
        for (Transaction transaction : statement.getStocks()) {
            output.append(String.format(SECURITY_HOLDING_FORMAT, new Object[] {
                    transaction.getTicker(), transaction.getQuantity(),
                    moneyFormatter.format(transaction.getDollarAmount()) }));
        }
    }

    private void formatSummary(Statement statement, StringBuilder output) {
        output.append(String.format(SUMMARY_HEADER_FORMAT,
                new Object[] { statement.getCustomer().getAccount()
                        .getAccountNumber() }));
        output.append(String.format(
                SUMMARY_FORMAT,
                new Object[] {
                        moneyFormatter.format(statement.getSecurityTotal()),
                        moneyFormatter.format(statement.getCustomer()
                                .getAccount().getCashBalance()),
                        moneyFormatter.format(statement.getCustomer()
                                .getAccount().getCashBalance().doubleValue()
                                + statement.getSecurityTotal().doubleValue()) }));
    }

    private void formatAddress(Statement statement, StringBuilder output) {
        Customer customer = statement.getCustomer();

        output.append(String.format(ADDRESS_FORMAT,
                new Object[] { customer.getFirstName(), customer.getLastName(),
                        customer.getAddress().getAddress1(),
                        customer.getAddress().getCity(),
                        customer.getAddress().getState(),
                        customer.getAddress().getZip() }));
    }
}
```

Although there is quite a bit of code here, you can quickly see that all it consists of is multiple calls to String.format for the various types of objects you're working with. When the FlatFileItemWriter calls the aggregate method on the LineAggregator, it gets back the entire statement, formatted and ready to be written to your file.

The main part of the statement is formatted, but you still need to write one other small piece of code. Each statement has a simple header consisting of the name of the statement, the brokerage address, and the customer assistance phone number. To add that information to the top of each statement, you use Spring Batch's FlatFileHeaderCallback (see Listing 10-46).

Listing 10-46. StatementHeaderCallback

```
package com.apress.springbatch.statement.writer;

import java.io.IOException;
import java.io.Writer;

import org.springframework.batch.item.file.FlatFileHeaderCallback;

public class StatementHeaderCallback implements FlatFileHeaderCallback {

    public void writeHeader(Writer writer) throws IOException {
        writer.write("                                            " +
                "                         Brokerage Account Statement\n");
        writer.write("\n\n");
        writer.write("Apress Investment Company                   " +
                "             Customer Service Number\n");
        writer.write("1060 W. Addison St.                        " +
                "               (800) 876-5309\n");
        writer.write("Chicago, IL 60613                          " +
                "             Available 24/7\n");
        writer.write("\n\n");
    }
}
```

StatementHeaderCallback writes some static text to each of your files. Because Spring Batch handles calling it, the job is pretty easy.

The last piece of code that needs to be written for the statement job is a suffix generator. This class will be used by Spring Batch to append a number and the .txt extension on the statement files that are generated. Listing 4-47 shows the code for the StatementSuffixGenerator.

Listing 4-47. StatementSuffixGenerator.

```
package com.apress.springbatch.statement.writer;

import org.springframework.batch.item.file.ResourceSuffixCreator;

public class StatementSuffixGenerator implements ResourceSuffixCreator {

    public String getSuffix(int arg0) {
        return arg0 + ".txt";
    }
}
```

That is all the code you need to write to output the robust statement you require. The configuration is also deceptively simple. It consists of the output resource, a suffix generator so that your files have a nice file name, StatementFormatter, the statement writer, and the MultiResourceItemWriter used to create new files for each customer. The complete configuration is shown in Listing 10-48.

Listing 10-48. Configuration of Writer Components for the Statement

```
...
<beans:bean id="statementFiles"
  class="org.springframework.core.io.FileSystemResource">
  <beans:constructor-arg value="/output/statement"/>
</beans:bean>

<beans:bean id="statementSuffixGenerator"
  class="com.apress.springbatch.statement.writer.StatementSuffixGenerator"/>

<beans:bean id="statementFormatter"
  class="com.apress.springbatch.statement.writer.StatementFormatter"/>

<beans:bean id="statementWriter"
  class="org.springframework.batch.item.file.FlatFileItemWriter">
  <beans:property name="headerCallback">
    <beans:bean class="com.apress.springbatch.statement.writer.StatementHeaderCallback"/>
  </beans:property>
  <beans:property name="lineAggregator" ref="statementFormatter"/>
</beans:bean>

<beans:bean id="statementsWriter"
  class="org.springframework.batch.item.file.MultiResourceItemWriter">
  <beans:property name="resource" ref="statementFiles"/>
  <beans:property name="resourceSuffixCreator" ref="statementSuffixGenerator"/>
  <beans:property name="itemCountLimitPerResource" value="1"/>
  <beans:property name="delegate" ref="statementWriter"/>
</beans:bean>
...
```

As Listing 10-48 shows, there is nothing extravagant for this step's writing. You begin by defining the template resource on which the MultiResourceItemWriter bases each file. From there, you define the configuration for statementSuffixGenerator, which appends a number.txt at the end of each file name. StatementFormatter is configured next with no dependencies as required. Finally, you configure the two ItemWriters involved.

FlatFileItemWriter uses two dependencies: a reference to the header callback and a reference to the LineAggregator. This writer does the majority of the heavy lifting for your output. The final ItemWriter involved in this step is MultiResourceItemWriter. It uses a reference to your resource to create similar files, it uses the suffix generator to make the file names acceptable, and it delegates the writing of the statement to the statementWriter you defined earlier. It's important to note that itemCountLimitPerResource (the number of items per file you write) is set to 1 for this configuration. Because StatementFormatter is designed to write an entire statement, you should write only one per file.

The code is written and configured. When you build and run the job, you're left with one file per customer, with the customer's statement completed. Listing 10-49 shows an example of the statement as it's generated.

Listing 10-49. A Sample Statement

```
Brokerage Account Statement
```

```
Apress Investment Company              Customer Service Number
1060 W. Addison St.                         (800) 876-5309
Chicago, IL 60613                          Available 24/7

Joshua Thompson
3708 Park
Fairview, LA 58517

Account Number    3276793917668488

Your Account Summary

Market Value of Current Securities            $26,193,904,052.27
Current Cash Balance                             ($138,274.56)
Total Account Value                           $26,193,765,777.71

Account Detail

Cash                                   $(138274.56)

Securities

      ABT              9004084               $432,466,154.52
ABX              9392107             $472,610,824.24
      ADI              6493573               $247,535,002.76
```

Summary

Learning how to do something without context makes it hard to take what you've learned and apply it to the real world. This chapter has taken commonly used elements of the Spring Batch framework and put them together into a realistic example of a batch job.

With the basics covered we will dive deeper into the more advanced topics of Spring Batch in the upcoming chapters. In Chapter 11, you will look at how to scale batch jobs beyond a single threaded execution like you have used up to this point.

Scaling and Tuning

The IRS processed over 236 million tax returns in 2010. Atlanta's Hartsfield-Jackson airport handled nearly 90 million passengers in 2010. Facebook has more than 45 million status updates a day. Apple sold more than 1.7 million iPhone 4s in its first three days of availability. The amount of data the world generates every day is staggering. It used to be that as the data increased, so did the processors to process it. If your app wasn't fast enough, you could wait a year and buy a new server, and all was fine.

But that isn't the case anymore. CPUs aren't getting faster at nearly the rate they used to. Instead, by adding cores instead of transistors to a single core, CPUs are getting better at parallel processing instead of becoming faster at a single task. The developers behind Spring Batch understand this and made parallel processing one of the primary focuses of the framework. This chapter looks at the following:

- *Profiling batch jobs:* You see a process for profiling your batch jobs so that the optimization decisions you make positively impact your performance and not the other way around.

- *Evaluating each of the scalability options in Spring Batch:* Spring Batch provides a number of different scalability options, each of which is reviewed in detail.

Profiling Your Batch Process

Michael A. Jackson put forth the best two rules of optimization in his 1975 book *Principals of Program Design*:

> *Rule 1. Don't do it.*
> *Rule 2 (for experts only). Don't do it yet.*

The idea behind this is simple. Software changes over the course of its development. Because of this, it's virtually impossible to make accurate decisions about how to design a system until the system has been developed. After the system has been developed, you can test it for performance bottlenecks and address those as required. By not taking this approach, you risk being described by my second most favorite quote on optimization, this one by W. A. Wulf:

> *More computing sins are committed in the name of efficiency (without necessarily achieving it) than for any other single reason—including blind stupidity.*

To profile any Java application there are many options, ranging from free to very expensive. However, one of the best free options is included in the Java Virtual Machine (JVM): VisualVM. This is the tool you can use to profile batch jobs. Before you begin profiling your jobs, let's take a quick tour of the VisualVM tool.

A Tour of VisualVM

Oracle's VisualVM is a tool that gives you insights into what is going on in your JVM. As JConsole's big brother, VisualVM provides not only JMX administration like JConsole but also information about CPU and memory usage, method execution times, as well as thread management and garbage collection. This section looks at the capabilities of the VisualVM tool.

Before you can try VisualVM, you have to install it. If you're running an Oracle distribution of the JDK version greater than version 6 update 7, then you've already installed it because it comes with the JDK. If you're running a different version of Java, you can obtain VisualVM from Oracle directly at http://visualvm.java.net/download.html.

With VisualVM installed, you can launch it. VisualVM greets you with a menu on the left and a Start Page on the right, as shown in Figure 11-1.

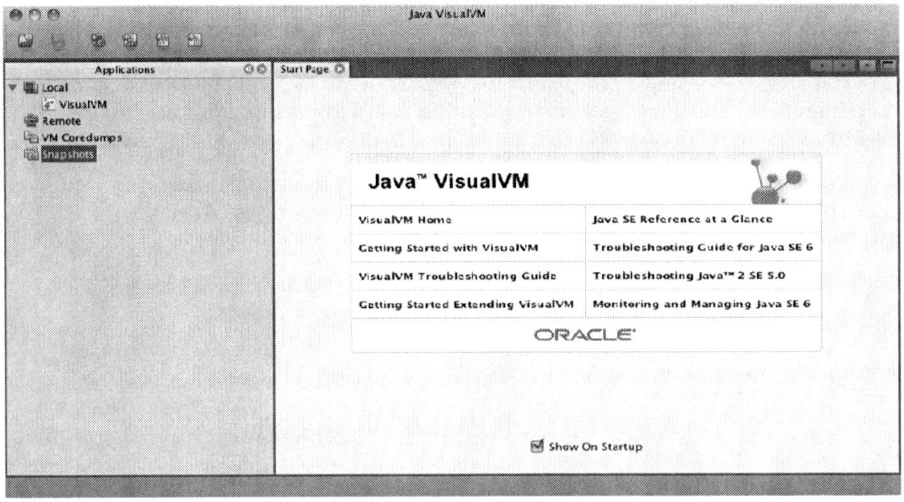

Figure 11-1. The start screen for VisualVM

The menu on the left is broken into four sections: Local and Remote are where you find applications that you can connect to, to profile. When you start VisualVM, because it's itself a Java application, it appears in the Local section. Below the Local and Remote sections are where you can load either Java VM coredumps that you've collected previously that you want to analyze; or snapshots, which are the state of a VM at a certain point in time that you can capture using VisualVM. To see some of the capabilities of the VisualVM tool, let's connect VisualVM to an instance of Eclipse.

When you first connect to a running JVM, VisualVM displays the screen shown in Figure 11-2.

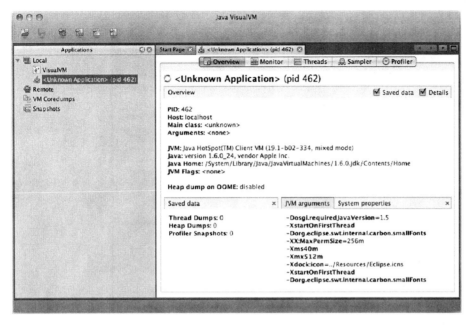

Figure 11-2. Connecting to a Java Process

Along the top of the screen are five tabs:

- *Overview:* Provides an overview of the Java application running, including the main class, application name, process id, and arguments passed into the JVM on startup.

- *Monitor:* Displays charts showing CPU utilization, memory utilization (both heap and PermGen), the number of classes loaded, and the number of live and daemon threads. The Monitor tab also lets you perform garbage collection as well as generate a heap dump for later analysis.

- *Threads:* Displays information about all threads the application has launched and what they're doing (running, sleeping, waiting, or monitoring). This data is shown in either timeline, table, or detail form.

- *Sampler:* Allows you to take a sample of the CPU utilization and memory allocation for your application as well as take snapshots. CPU shows what methods are taking how long to run. Memory utilization shows what classes are taking how much memory.

- *Profiler:* Looks and feels similar to the Sampler tab, but lets you profile the CPU and memory utilization as well as save snapshots of the current state each of these two resources is currently in. You can also compare multiple snapshots.

In addition to the tabs, Overview shows you information about the current Java process that is being analyzed including process id, the host the process is running on, JVM arguments, as well as the full list of system properties the JVM knows.

The second tab is the Monitor tab, as shown in Figure 11-3.

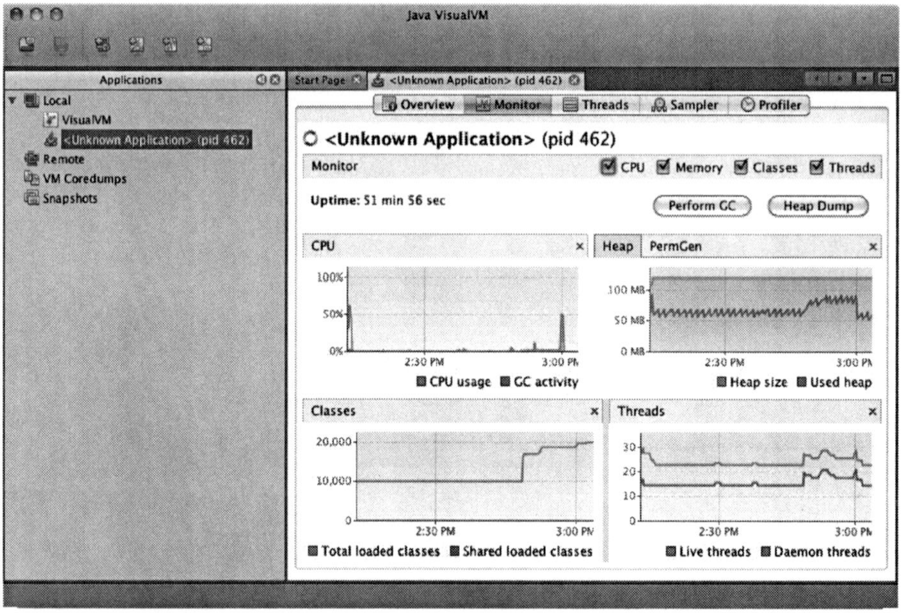

Figure 11-3. *The Monitor tab for an Eclipse instance*

The Monitor tab is where you view the state of the JVM from a memory and CPU perspective as a whole. The other tabs are more useful when you're determining the cause of a problem identified in the Monitor tab (if you keep running out of memory or the CPU is pegged for some reason). All the charts on the Monitor tab are resizable, and they can be hidden as required.

The next tab available in VisualVM is the Threads tab, displayed in Figure 11-4.

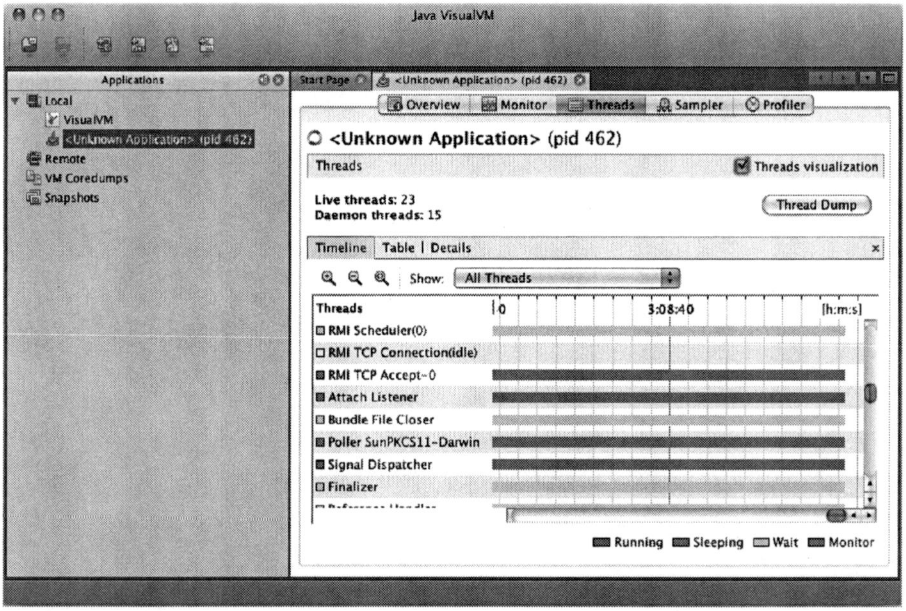

Figure 11-4. The Threads tab in VisualVM

All Java applications are multithreaded. At the least, you have the main execution thread and an additional thread for garbage collection. However, most Java applications spawn many additional threads for various reasons. This tab allows you to see information about the various threads your application has spawned and what they're doing. Figure 11-4 shows the data as a timeline, but the data is also available as a table and as detailed graphs for each thread.

The last two tabs are pretty similar. The first, as shown in Figure 11-5, is the Sampler tab.

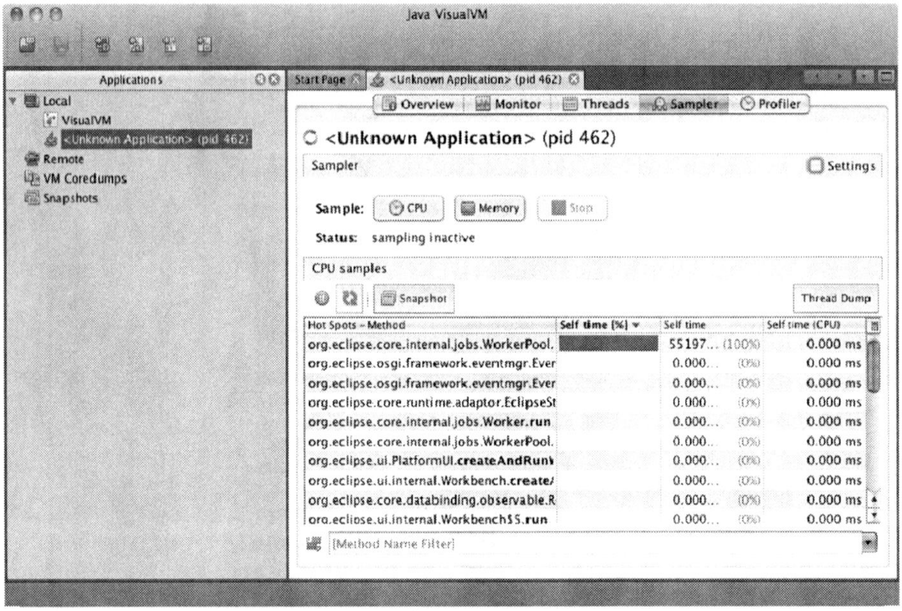

Figure 11-5. VisualVM's Sampler tab

In both tabs, you're presented with the same screen, which includes CPU and Memory buttons as well as a Stop button. To begin sampling either CPU execution by method or memory footprint by class, click the appropriate button. The tables update periodically with the current state of the VM VisualVM is studying. The difference between the two tabs is that the Profiler tab can execute garbage collections and save the data it has collected, but the sampler tab can't.

VisualVM is a powerful and extendable tool. Many plug-ins are available to extend the feature set provided out of the box. You can add things like the ability to view the stack trace of currently executing threads with the Thread Inspector plug-in, visual garbage collection with the Visual GC plug-in, and access to MBeans via the MBean browser, to extend VisualVM's already powerful suite of tools.

Now that you have an idea of what Oracle's VisualVM can do, let's see how you can use it to profile Spring Batch applications.

Profiling Spring Batch Applications

When you profile your applications, you're typically looking at one of two things: how hard the CPU is working and where, and how much memory is being used and on what. The first questions, how hard the CPU is working and where, relate to what your CPU is working on. Is your job computationally difficult? Is your CPU using a lot of its effort in places other than your business logic—for example, is it spending more time working on parsing files than actually doing the calculations you want it to? The second set of questions revolves around memory. Are you using most if not all of the available memory? If so, what is taking up all the memory? Do you have a Hibernate object that isn't lazily loading a collection, which is causing the issues? This section looks at how to see where resources are being used in your Spring Batch applications.

CPU Profiling

It would be nice to have a straightforward checklist of things to check when you're profiling applications. But it just isn't that easy. Profiling an application can, at times, feel more like an art than a science. This section walks through how to obtain data related to the performance of your applications and their utilization of the CPU.

When you look at how a CPU is performing within your application, you typically use the measure of time to determine the hot spots (the areas that aren't performing to your expectations). What areas is the CPU working in the most? For example, if you have an infinite loop somewhere in your code, the CPU will spend a large amount of time there after it's triggered. However, if everything is running fine, you can expect to see either no bottlenecks or at bottlenecks that you would expect (I/O is typically the bottleneck of most modern systems).

To view the CPU profiling functionality at work, let's use the statement job that you completed in the last chapter. This job consists of six steps and interacts with the Internet, files, and a database. Figure 11-6 shows from a high level what the job does as it's currently configured.

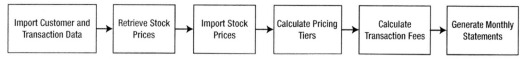

Figure 11-6. Statement job

To execute the job, you use the command java -jar statement-job-1.0.0-SNAPSHOT.jar jobs/statementJob.xml statementJob -next. After you've launched the job, it appears in the VisualVM menu on the left under Local. To connect to it, all you need to do is double-click it.

Now that you've connected to the running statement job, you can begin to look at how things operate within it. Let's first look at the Monitor tab to see how busy the CPU is in the first place. After running the statement job with a customer transaction file containing 100 customers and more than 20,000 transactions, you can see that the CPU utilization for this job is minimal. Figure 11-7 shows the charts from the Monitor tab after a run of the job.

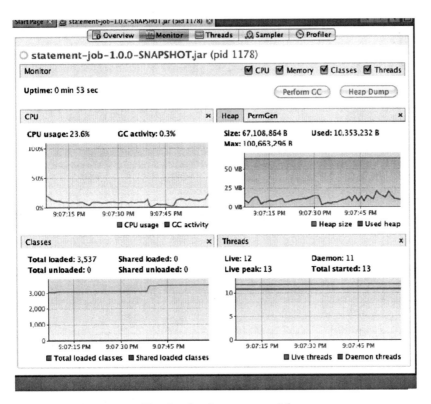

Figure 11-7. Resource utilization for the statement job

As Figure 11-7 shows, the statement job isn't a CPU-intensive process. In fact, if you look at the memory profile, the job isn't very memory intensive either. However, you can easily change that. If you add a small loop into the ItemProcessor used in step 4 (PricingTiersItemProcessor) you can quickly make your CPU busy. Listing 11-1 shows the loop you add.

Listing 11-1. Using PricingTiersItemProcessor to Calculate Prime Numbers

```
package com.apress.springbatch.statement.processor;

import java.math.BigInteger;

import org.springframework.batch.item.ItemProcessor;

import com.apress.springbatch.statement.domain.AccountTransactionQuantity;
import com.apress.springbatch.statement.domain.PricingTier;

public class PricingTierItemProcessor implements
        ItemProcessor<AccountTransactionQuantity, AccountTransactionQuantity> {

    public AccountTransactionQuantity process(AccountTransactionQuantity atq)
            throws Exception {
```

```
    for(int i = 0; i < 1000000; i++){
        new BigInteger(String.valueOf(i)).isProbablePrime(0);
    }

    if(atq.getTransactionCount() <= 1000) {
        atq.setTier(PricingTier.I);
    } else if(atq.getTransactionCount() > 1000 &&
                atq.getTransactionCount() <= 100000) {
        atq.setTier(PricingTier.II);
    } else if(atq.getTransactionCount() > 100000 &&
                atq.getTransactionCount() <= 1000000) {
        atq.setTier(PricingTier.III);
    } else {
        atq.setTier(PricingTier.IV);
    }

    return atq;
    }
}
```

Obviously the loop you added to calculate all the prime numbers between 0 and 1 million as shown in Listing 11-1 is unlikely to end up in your code. But it's exactly the type of accidental looping that could cause a catastrophic impact on the performance of a batch job over the course of processing millions of transactions. Figure 11-8 shows the impact this small loop makes on CPU utilization, according to VirtualVM.

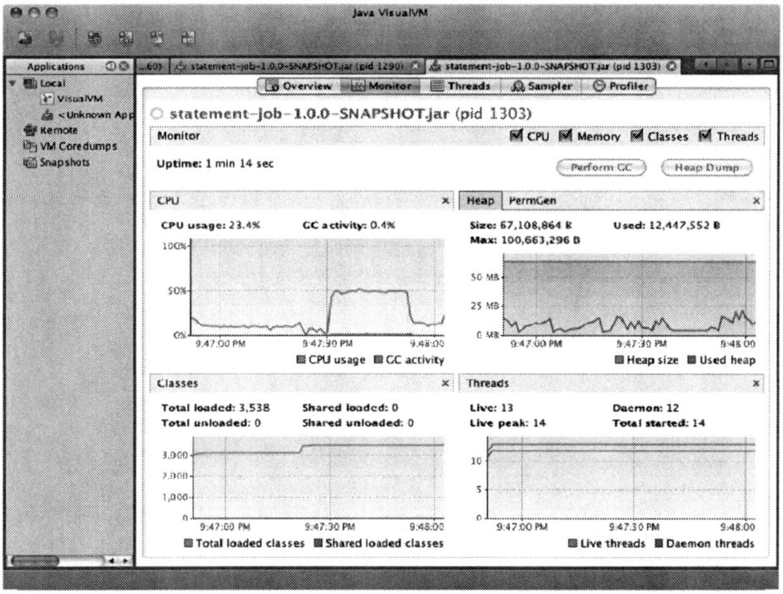

Figure 11-8. CPU utilization for the updated statement job

That is quite a spike for three lines of code. This job went from barely using the CPU at all to pushing it to 50% utilized for that step. But if you didn't know what caused that spike, where would you look next?

With a spike identified like this, the next place to look is in the Sampler tab. By rerunning the job under the same conditions, you can see what individual methods show up as hot spots in the job's execution. In this case, after you begin running the job, the method that stands out immediately is `com.mysql.jdbc.util.ReadAheadInputStream.fill()`. This class is used by the MySQL driver to read from your database. As you saw previously, I/O is typically the main bottleneck for processing in today's business systems, so seeing this class take up the majority of the CPU should come as no surprise. However, at the same time that the spike on the Monitor tab begins, a new class quickly climbs through the ranks of the list of methods using a lot of CPU: `com.apress.springbatch.statement.processor.PricingTierItemProcessor.process()`. By the end of the job, this method has taken up 32.6% of all the CPU time required to execute this job, as shown in Figure 11-9.

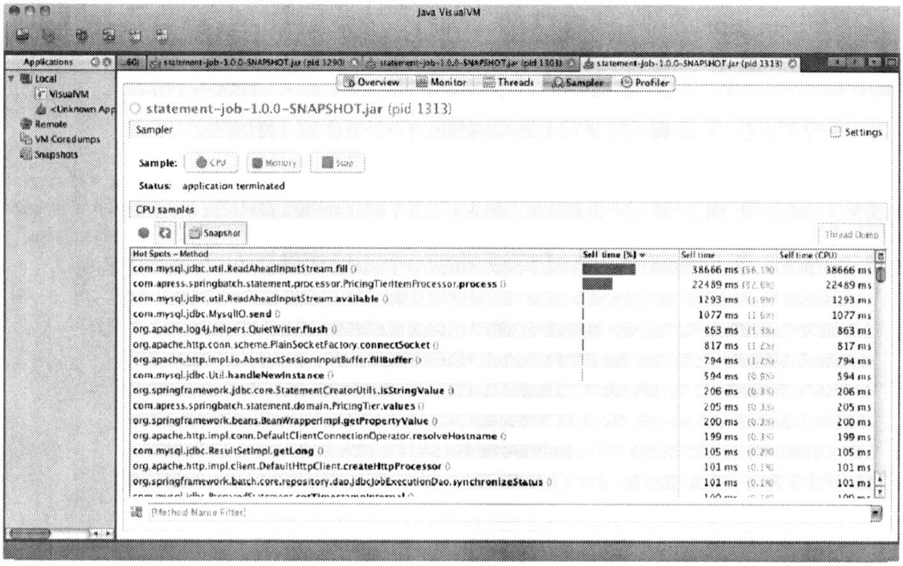

Figure 11-9. *The* `PricingTierItemProcessor` *has taken up quite a bit of CPU.*

When you come across a scenario like this, a better way to view what is eating up CPU execution time is to filter the list by the package name you're using for your code. In this case, you can filter the list on `com.apress.springbatch.statement` to see what classes take up what percentage of the total CPU utilization. Under this filter, the culprit becomes crystal clear in this example: the `PricingTierItemProcessor.process()` method and the `32.6%` of the CPU time it takes up.. The next highest on the list takes up 0.3% (`com.apress.springbatch.statement.domain.PricingTier.values()`). At this point, you have all the information you can get from the tool, and it's time to begin digging through the code to determine what in `PricingTierItemProcessor.process()` is using so much CPU.

Simple, isn't it? Not really. Although the process used here is what you would use to narrow down an issue in any system, the issue is rarely this easy to track down. However, using VisualVM you can progressively narrow down where the issue is in your job. CPU utilization isn't the only piece of performance. The next section looks at how to profile memory using VisualVM.

Memory Profiling

Although CPU utilization may seem like the place you're most likely to see issues, the truth is that it is my experience that memory issues are more likely to pop up in your software. The reason is that you use a number of frameworks that do things behind the scenes. When you use these frameworks incorrectly, large numbers of objects can be created without any indication that it has occurred until you run out of memory completely. This section looks at how to profile memory usage using VisualVM.

To look at how to profile memory, let's tweak the same PricingTierItemProcessor you did previously. However, this time instead of taking up processing time, you update it to simulate creating a collection that is out of control. Although the code example may not be what you see in real-world systems, accidentally creating collections that are larger than you expect is a common reason for memory issues. Listing 11-2 shows the code for the updated PricingTierItemProcessor.

Listing 11-2. PricingTierItemProcessor with a Memory Leak

```java
package com.apress.springbatch.statement.processor;

import java.util.ArrayList;
import java.util.List;

import org.springframework.batch.item.ItemProcessor;

import com.apress.springbatch.statement.domain.AccountTransactionQuantity;
import com.apress.springbatch.statement.domain.PricingTier;

public class PricingTierItemProcessor implements
        ItemProcessor<AccountTransactionQuantity, AccountTransactionQuantity> {

    private List<PricingTier> accountsProcessed = new ArrayList<PricingTier>();

    public AccountTransactionQuantity process(AccountTransactionQuantity atq)
            throws Exception {

        if(atq.getTransactionCount() <= 1000) {
            atq.setTier(PricingTier.I);
        } else if(atq.getTransactionCount() > 1000 && atq.getTransactionCount() <= 100000) {
            atq.setTier(PricingTier.II);
        } else if(atq.getTransactionCount() > 100000 &&
                atq.getTransactionCount() <= 1000000) {
            atq.setTier(PricingTier.III);
        } else {
            atq.setTier(PricingTier.IV);
        }

        for(int i = 0; i <atq.getTransactionCount() * 750; i++) {
            accountsProcessed.add(atq.getTier());
        }

        return atq;
    }
}
```

In the version shown in Listing 11-2, you're creating a `List` of objects that will exist past the currently processing chunk. Under normal processing, most of the objects involved in a given chunk are garbage-collected when the chunk is complete, keeping the memory footprint in check. By doing something like what you have in this example, you would expect the memory footprint to grow out of control.

When you run the statement job with this bug and profile it using VisualVM, you can see that things quickly get out of hand from a memory perspective; an `OutOfMemoryException` is thrown midway through the step. Figure 11-10 shows the VisualVM Monitor tab a run of the statement job with the memory leak.

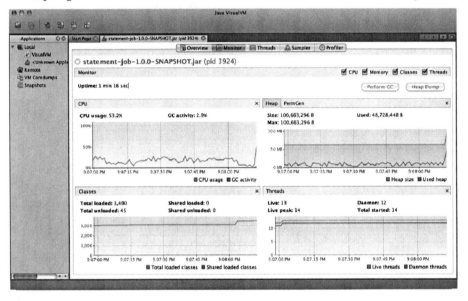

Figure 11-10. Monitoring results of the statement job with a memory leak

Notice at the very end of the memory graph in the upper-right corner of Figure 11-10 that memory usage spikes, causing the `OutOfMemoryException`. But how do you know what caused the spike? If you didn't know, the Sampler tab might be able to shed some light.

You've seen before that the Sampler tab can show what method calls are using up CPU, but it can also tell you what objects are taking up precious memory. To see that, begin by executing your job as you have previously. When it's running, connect to the process using VisualVM and go to the Sampler tab. To determine the cause of a memory leak, you need to determine what changes as the memory usage occurs. For example, in Figure 11-11, each block represents a class instance. The higher the blocks are stacked in each column, the more instances are in memory. Each column represents a snapshot in time within the JVM. When the program begins, the number of instances created is small (one in this case); this number slowly rises over time, occasionally declining when garbage collection occurs. Finally it spikes at the end to nine instances. This is the type of increase in memory usage you look for with VisualVM.

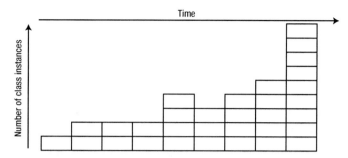

Figure 11-11. Memory utilization over the life of a program

To view this type of change in your batch jobs, you can use VisualVM's snapshot feature. As a job runs, click the Snapshot button in the middle of the screen. VisualVM records the exact state of the JVM when you take that snapshot. You can compare this with other snapshots to determine what changes. Typically, the change indicates the location of the issue. If it isn't the smoking gun, it's definitely where you should start looking.

The ability to scale batch jobs isn't a requirement to be able to address performance bugs as discussed in the previous sections of this chapter. On the contrary, jobs that have bugs like those discussed typically don't scale no matter what you do. Instead, you need to address the issues within your application before applying the scalability features that Spring Batch or any framework provides. When you have a system with none of these issues, the features that Spring Batch offers to scale it beyond a single-threaded, single-JVM approach are some of the strongest of any framework. You spend the rest of this chapter looking at how to use Spring Batch's scalability features.

Scaling a Job

In an enterprise, when things are going well, data gets big. More customers. More transactions. More site hits. More, more, more. Your batch jobs need to be able to keep up. Spring Batch was designed from the ground up to be highly scalable, to fit the needs of both small batch jobs and large enterprise-scale batch infrastructures. This section looks at the four different approaches Spring Batch takes for scaling batch jobs beyond the default flow: multithreaded steps, parallel steps, remote chunking, and partitioning.

Multithreaded Steps

When a step is processed, by default it's processed in a single thread. Although a multithreaded step is the easiest way to parallelize a job's execution, as with all multithreaded environments there are aspects you need to consider when using it. This section looks at Spring Batch's multithreaded step and how to use it safely in your batch jobs.

Spring Batch's multithreaded step concept allows a batch job to use Spring's `org.springframework.core.task.TaskExecutor` abstraction to execute each chunk in its own thread. Figure 11-12 shows an example of how processing works when using the multithreaded step.

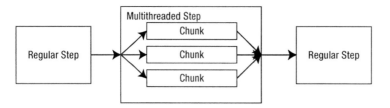

Figure 11-12. Multithreaded step processing

As Figure 11-12 shows, any step in a job can be configured to perform within a threadpool, processing each chunk independently. As chunks are processed, Spring Batch keeps track of what is done accordingly. If an error occurs in any one of the threads, the job's processing is rolled back or terminated per the regular Spring Batch functionality.

To configure a step to execute in a multithreaded manor, all you need to do is configure a reference to a TaskExecutor for the given step. If you use the statement job as an example, Listing 11-3 shows how to configure the calculateTransactionFees step (step 5) to be a multithreaded step.

Listing 11-3. calculateTransactionFees as a Multithreaded Step

```
...
<step id="calculateTransactionFees">
  <tasklet task-executor="taskExecutor">
    <chunk reader="transactionPricingItemReader" processor="feesItemProcessor"
      writer="applyFeeWriter" commit-interval="100"/>
  </tasklet>
</step>

<beans:bean id="taskExecutor"
  class="org.springframework.core.task.SimpleAsyncTaskExecutor">
  <beans:property name="concurrencyLimit" value="10"/>
</beans:bean>
...
```

As Listing 11-3 shows, all that is required to add the power of Spring's multithreading capabilities to a step in your job is to define a TaskExecutor implementation (you use org.springframework.core.task.SimpleAsyncTaskExecutor in this example) and reference it in your step. When you execute the statement job, Spring creates a threadpool of 10 threads, executing each chunk in a different thread or 10 chunks in parallel. As you can imagine, this can be a powerful addition to most jobs.

But there is a catch when working with multithreaded steps. Most ItemReaders provided by Spring Batch are stateful. Spring Batch uses this state when it restarts a job so it knows where processing left off. However, in a multithreaded environment, objects that maintain state in a way that is accessible to multiple threads (not synchronized, and so on) can run into issues of threads overwriting each other's state.

To get around the issue of state, you use the concept of *staging* the records to be processed in your batch run. The concept is quite simple. Before the step begins, you tag all the records in a way that identifies them as the records to be processed in the current batch run (or JobInstance) using a StepListener. The tagging can be by either updating a special column or columns on the database field or copying the records into a staging table. Then, the ItemReader reads the records that were tagged at the beginning of the step normally. As each chunk completes, you use an ItemWriteListener to update the records you just processed as having been processed.

To apply this concept to the statement job's calculateTransactionFees step, you begin by adding two columns to the transaction table: jobId and processed. The jobId stores the run.id of the current run of the statement job. The second column is a boolean with the value true if the record has been processed and false if it hasn't. Figure 11-13 shows the updated table definition.

Figure 11-13. Updated data model for the transaction table with staging columns included

In order to put the columns to use, you need to create a StepListener to update the records you process with the jobId and set the processed flag to false for the records you process. To do this, you create a StepListener called StagingStepListener that updates these columns on whatever table you configure as well as reuse it for other tables. Listing 11-4 shows the code for the StagingStepListener.

Listing 11-4. StagingStepListener

```
package com.apress.springbatch.statement.listener;
import org.springframework.batch.core.StepListener;
import org.springframework.batch.core.annotation.BeforeStep;
import org.springframework.jdbc.core.JdbcTemplate;

public class StagingStepListener extends JdbcTemplate implements StepListener {

    private String SQL = " set jobId = ?, processed = false ";
    private String tableName;
    private String whereClause = "";
    private long jobId;

    @BeforeStep
    public void stageRecords() {
        update("update " + tableName + SQL + whereClause, new Object [] {jobId});
    }

    public void setTableName(String tableName) {
        this.tableName = tableName;
    }
```

```
    public void setJobId(long jobId) {

        this.jobId = jobId;
    }

    public void setWhereClause(String whereClause) {
        if(whereClause != null) {
            this.whereClause = whereClause;
        }
    }
}
```

As you can see, the StepListener in Listing 11-4 updates all the records you identify with the job id you pass in to be processed by your step. On the other end of the step is the ItemWriteListener. This listener interface is called either before or after (here, after) a chunk is written. The method afterWrite takes the same list of items that were previously written by the ItemWriter. Using this lets you update the staged records to be flagged as processed. Listing 11-5 shows the code for this listener.

Listing 11-5. StagingChunkUpdater

```
package com.apress.springbatch.statement.listener;

import java.util.List;

import org.springframework.batch.core.ItemWriteListener;
import org.springframework.jdbc.core.JdbcTemplate;

import com.apress.springbatch.statement.domain.AccountTransaction;

public class StagingChunkUpdater extends JdbcTemplate implements
        ItemWriteListener<AccountTransaction> {

    private String SQL = " set processed = true ";
    private String tableName;
    private String whereClause = "";

    public void beforeWrite(List<? extends AccountTransaction> items) {
    }

    public void afterWrite(List<? extends AccountTransaction> items) {
        for (AccountTransaction accountTransaction : items) {
            update("update " + tableName + SQL + whereClause,
                        new Object[] {accountTransaction.getId()});
        }
    }

    public void onWriteError(Exception exception,
            List<? extends AccountTransaction> items) {
    }

    public void setTableName(String tableName) {
        this.tableName = tableName;
```

```
    }

    public void setWhereClause(String whereClause) {
        this.whereClause = whereClause;
    }
}
```

As chunks are processed, regardless of the thread, StagingChunkUpdater updates the items to be flagged as processed. You still need to do two things. First, you need to update the configuration to use the new listeners; and second, you need to update the query used for this step's ItemReader to include jobId and the processed flag in its criteria. Listing 11-6 shows the updated configuration including the updated ItemReader, the new staging listeners, and the updated calculateTransactionFees step.

Listing 11-6. Configuration for the Multithreaded Step with Staging Listeners

```
...
<beans:bean id="transactionPricingItemReader"
  class="org.springframework.batch.item.database.JdbcCursorItemReader" scope="step">
  <beans:property name="dataSource" ref="dataSource"/>
  <beans:property name="sql" value="select a.id as accountId, a.accountNumber,
    t.id as transactionId, t.qty, tk.ticker, a.tier, t.executedTime, t.dollarAmount from
    account a inner join transaction t on a.id = t.account_id inner join ticker tk on
    t.tickerId = tk.id and t.processed = false and t.jobId = #{jobParameters[run.id]}
    order by t.executedTime"/>
  <beans:property name="rowMapper" ref="transactionPricingRowMapper"/>
</beans:bean>

<beans:bean id="transactionPricingRowMapper"
  class="com.apress.springbatch.statement.reader.AccountTransactionRowMapper"/>

<step id="calculateTransactionFees">
  <tasklet task-executor="taskExecutor">
    <chunk reader="transactionPricingItemReader" processor="feesItemProcessor"
      writer="applyFeeWriter" commit-interval="100"/>
    <listeners>
      <listener ref="stagingStepListener"/>
      <listener ref="stagingChunkUpdater"/>
    </listeners>
  </tasklet>
</step>

<beans:bean id="stagingStepListener"
  class="com.apress.springbatch.statement.listener.StagingStepListener" scope="step">
  <beans:property name="dataSource" ref="dataSource"/>
  <beans:property name="tableName" value="transaction"/>
  <beans:property name="whereClause"
    value="where jobId is null and processed is null"/>
  <beans:property name="jobId" value="#{jobParameters[run.id]}"/>
</beans:bean>

<beans:bean id="stagingChunkUpdater"
  class="com.apress.springbatch.statement.listener.StagingChunkUpdater" scope="step">
```

```
    <beans:property name="dataSource" ref="dataSource"/>
    <beans:property name="tableName" value="transaction"/>
    <beans:property name="whereClause" value="where id = ?"/>
</beans:bean>

<beans:bean id="taskExecutor"
  class="org.springframework.core.task.SimpleAsyncTaskExecutor">
    <beans:property name="concurrencyLimit" value="10"/>
</beans:bean>
...
```

By taking the staged-record approach, you allow Spring Batch to not worry about the state of the step because it's maintained separately. Unfortunately, this solution still isn't perfect because it's only practical when you're using input sources that can be managed this way (databases are the typical use case). Flat files can't be managed in a staged manner. In the end, however, most input situations can be addressed in a way that allows for multithreaded processing.

Parallel Steps

Multithreaded steps provide the ability to process chunks of items within the same step of a job in parallel, but sometimes it's also helpful to be able to execute entire steps in parallel. Take for example importing multiple files that have no relationship to each other. There is no reason for one import to need to wait for the other import to complete before it begins. Spring Batch's ability to execute steps and even flows (reusable groups of steps) in parallel allows you to improve overall throughput on a job. This section looks at how to use Spring Batch's parallel steps and flows to improve the overall performance of your jobs.

If you think about submitting an order online, a number of things need to happen before the item is put into the box and handed to the postman to be delivered to your door. You need to store the order. Payment needs to be confirmed. Inventory needs to be validated. Pick lists need to be generated for the item to be obtained from a warehouse and packed. But not all these pieces of work need to be performed in order. As an example of parallel processing, let's look at a job that receives an order, imports it into a database, and then in parallel verifies payment and inventory. If both are available, the order is processed. Figure 11-14 shows a diagram of the process flow for this sample job.

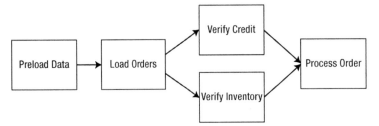

Figure 11-14. *Process flow for an order-processing job*

This is a four-step job. Step 1 prepopulates a JMS queue with data to be read in step 2.[1] Although you can use any number of input options, using JMS for order delivery is a realistic option for the real world; so, this example uses it. Step 2 reads from a JMS queue and saves the database so that if an issue occurs during future processing, you won't lose the order. From there, you execute two different steps in parallel. One step validates that funds are available for the purchase. The second verifies inventory with an inventory system. If both of those checks are successful, the order is processed and the pick slip for the warehouse is generated.

To begin working through this job, let's look at the object model. Specifically, there are three domain classes: Customer, Order, and OrderItem, as shown in Figure 11-15.

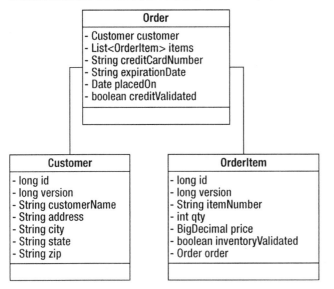

Figure 11-15. *Class diagram for a parallel processing job*

An Order, as shown in Figure 11-15, consists of a Customer, order-specific information (mostly payment information), and a list of OrderItems. Each item the customer is purchasing has an OrderItem entry in the list containing item-specific information including item number and quantity ordered.

To make this job work, you need to write a small amount of code. Specifically:

- OrderGenerator: ItemReader that generates the sample orders for your job

- CreditService/InventoryService: Services used as ItemProcessors to validate the user's credit and validate that you have the inventory to process the order

- PickListFormatter: Line aggregator that generates the format required for the picklists you generate

---

[1] This first step probably doesn't make much sense in the grand scheme of things. It obviously won't go into your production jobs. Instead, it's a great way to build test data prior to the execution of a job.

Since you can't do much without the orders you will process, Step 1 of your job is to generate orders for processing. The next section discusses the code and configuration required to make this happen.

Preloading Data for Processing

Without a storefront to sell things, you will need to build your own orders for processing. To do that, you will create an ItemReader implementation that generates random orders based upon hard coded data. While you wouldn't do this in production, it will allow you to setup the data required to test the rest of your job. In this section we will code and configure the components required to generate test data.

Let's start by looking at the OrderGenerator ItemReader implementation. To generate test files for most of the jobs in this book, I wrote Ruby scripts (included in the book's source code) to generate data much faster than I could do it by hand. This class isn't much more than a Java equivalent of those Ruby scripts. Listing 11-7 shows the code for the OrderGenerator.

Listing 11-7. OrderGenerator

```
package com.apress.springbatch.chapter11processor;

import java.math.BigDecimal;
import java.text.DateFormat;
import java.text.SimpleDateFormat;
import java.util.ArrayList;
import java.util.Date;
import java.util.List;
import java.util.Random;

import org.springframework.batch.item.ItemReader;

import com.apress.springbatch.chapter11.domain.Customer;
import com.apress.springbatch.chapter11.domain.Order;
import com.apress.springbatch.chapter11.domain.OrderItem;

public class OrderGenerator implements ItemReader<Order> {

    private static final String [] STREETS = {"Second", "Third", "Fourth", "Park", "Fifth"};
    private static final String[] CITIES = {"Franklin", "Clinton", "Springfield",
        "Greenville"};
    private static final String[] FIRST_NAME = {"Jacob", "Ethan", "Michael", "Alexander"};
    private static final String[] LAST_NAME = {"Smith", "Jones", "Thompson", "Williams"};
    private static final String[] STATES = {"AL", "AK", "AZ", "AR", "CA", "CO", "CT", "DE"};

    private Random generator = new Random();
    private DateFormat formatter = new SimpleDateFormat("MM/yy");
    private int counter = 0;

    public Order read() throws Exception {
        if(counter < 100) {
            Order curOrder = new Order();

            curOrder.setCreditCardNumber(String.valueOf(generator.nextLong()));
```

```
                    curOrder.setCustomer(buildCustomer());
                    curOrder.setExpirationDate(formatter.format(new Date()));
                    curOrder.setPlacedOn(new Date());
                    curOrder.setItems(buildItems(curOrder));

                    counter ++;

                    return curOrder;
                } else {
                    return null;
                }
            }

            private List<OrderItem> buildItems(Order order) {
                List<OrderItem> items = new ArrayList<OrderItem>();
                int total = 0;

                while(total <= 0) {
                    total = generator.nextInt(10);
                }

                for(int i = 0; i < total; i++) {
                    OrderItem item = new OrderItem();

                    item.setItemNumber(String.format("%09d", generator.nextLong()));
                    item.setPrice(BigDecimal.valueOf(generator.nextDouble()));
                    item.setQty(generator.nextInt(5));
                    item.setOrder(order);

                    items.add(item);
                }

                return items;
            }

            private Customer buildCustomer() {
                Customer customer = new Customer();

                customer.setAddress(generator.nextInt(999) + " " +
                                    STREETS[counter % STREETS.length]);
                customer.setCity(CITIES[counter % CITIES.length]);
                customer.setCustomerName(FIRST_NAME[counter % FIRST_NAME.length] + " " +
                                         LAST_NAME[counter % LAST_NAME.length]);
                customer.setState(STATES[counter % STATES.length]);
                customer.setZip(String.format("%05d", generator.nextInt(99999)));

                return customer;
            }
        }
```

The OrderGenerator code is pretty simple. You build an Order object, populate the Customer and generate a few OrderItems, and send it on its way. When you use Spring Batch to set up your data like this, you can easily run a variety of test scenarios.

To put this class to use, you need to begin building your job. Because the first step consists only of generating Orders using OrderGenerator and writing them to a JMS queue, you can wire all that up and test it without needing to go any further. Listing 11-8 shows the configuration of the job as a single-step job that generates data and puts it on the queue for future steps to pick up.

Listing 11-8. Parallel Job Configured in parallelJob.xml with the First Step Configured

```xml
<?xml version="1.0" encoding="UTF-8"?>
<beans:beans xmlns="http://www.springframework.org/schema/batch"
  xmlns:beans="http://www.springframework.org/schema/beans"
  xmlns:util="http://www.springframework.org/schema/beans"
  xmlns:xsi="http://www.w3.org/2001/XMLSchema-instance"
  xsi:schemaLocation="http://www.springframework.org/schema/beans
    http://www.springframework.org/schema/beans/spring-beans-3.0.xsd
    http://www.springframework.org/schema/util
    http://www.springframework.org/schema/util/spring-util.xsd
    http://www.springframework.org/schema/batch
    http://www.springframework.org/schema/batch/spring-batch-2.1.xsd">

  <beans:import resource="../launch-context.xml"/>

  <beans:bean id="jmsWriter" class="org.springframework.batch.item.jms.JmsItemWriter">
    <beans:property name="jmsTemplate" ref="jmsTemplate"/>
  </beans:bean>

  <beans:bean id="dataGenerator"
    class="com.apress.springbatch.chapter11.processor.OrderGenerator"/>

  <step id="preloadDataStep">
    <tasklet>
      <chunk reader="dataGenerator" writer="jmsWriter" commit-interval="10"/>
    </tasklet>
  </step>

  <job id="parallelJob">
    <step id="step1" parent="preloadDataStep"/>
  </job>
</beans:beans>
```

Although the job itself is now configured, you need to make a couple of small tweaks to launch-context.xml and your POM file for this job. Specifically, you need to configure JMS support and Hibernate support (you use Hibernate for this job to simplify storing the object hierarchy) in launch-context.xml and add the appropriate dependencies to your POM file.[2]

Let's update the POM file first. Listing 11-9 shows the additional dependencies for ActiveMQ and Spring's JMS support as well as the Hibernate dependencies and Spring's ORM supporting modules.

Listing 11-9. Updating the POM File to Support JMS and Hibernate

---

[2] See Chapters 7 and 9 to learn more about using Hibernate and JMS in your jobs.

```
...
<dependency>
  <groupId>org.springframework</groupId>
  <artifactId>spring-jms</artifactId>
  <version>${spring.framework.version}</version>
</dependency>
<dependency>
  <groupId>org.springframework</groupId>
  <artifactId>spring-orm</artifactId>
  <version>${spring.framework.version}</version>
</dependency>
<dependency>
  <groupId>org.hibernate</groupId>
  <artifactId>hibernate-core</artifactId>
  <version>3.3.0.SP1</version>
</dependency>
<dependency>
  <groupId>org.hibernate</groupId>
  <artifactId>hibernate-entitymanager</artifactId>
  <optional>true</optional>
  <version>3.3.2.GA</version>
</dependency>
<dependency>
  <groupId>org.hibernate</groupId>
  <artifactId>hibernate-annotations</artifactId>
  <optional>true</optional>
  <version>3.4.0.GA</version>
</dependency>
<dependency>
  <groupId>org.apache.activemq</groupId>
  <artifactId>activemq-core</artifactId>
  <version>5.4.2</version>
  <exclusions>
    <exclusion>
      <groupId>org.apache.activemq</groupId>
      <artifactId>activeio-core</artifactId>
    </exclusion>
  </exclusions>
</dependency>
    ...
```

With the POM file updated, you can update launch-context.xml. The updates required are the configuration of the JMS resources (connection factory, destination, and JmsTemplate) as well as the Hibernate resources (a SessionFactory and updated transaction manager). Listing 11-10 shows the launch-context.xml file for this job.

Listing 11-10. launch-context.xml

```xml
<?xml version="1.0" encoding="UTF-8"?>
<beans xmlns="http://www.springframework.org/schema/beans"
  xmlns:p="http://www.springframework.org/schema/p"
  xmlns:xsi="http://www.w3.org/2001/XMLSchema-instance"
```

```
    xsi:schemaLocation="http://www.springframework.org/schema/beans
      http://www.springframework.org/schema/beans/spring-beans-3.0.xsd">

  <bean id="jobOperator"
class="org.springframework.batch.core.launch.support.SimpleJobOperator"
    p:jobLauncher-ref="jobLauncher" p:jobExplorer-ref="jobExplorer"
    p:jobRepository-ref="jobRepository" p:jobRegistry-ref="jobRegistry" />

  <bean id="jobExplorer"
    class="org.springframework.batch.core.explore.support.JobExplorerFactoryBean"
    p:dataSource-ref="dataSource" />

  <bean id="jobRegistry"
     class="org.springframework.batch.core.configuration.support.MapJobRegistry" />

  <bean
class="org.springframework.batch.core.configuration.support.JobRegistryBeanPostProcessor">
    <property name="jobRegistry" ref="jobRegistry"/>
  </bean>

  <bean id="jobLauncher"
class="org.springframework.batch.core.launch.support.SimpleJobLauncher">
    <property name="jobRepository" ref="jobRepository" />
  </bean>

  <bean id="jobRepository"
    class="org.springframework.batch.core.repository.support.JobRepositoryFactoryBean"
    p:dataSource-ref="dataSource" p:transactionManager-ref="transactionManager" />

  <bean id="jmsConnectionFactory" class="org.apache.activemq.ActiveMQConnectionFactory">
    <property name="brokerURL" value="vm://localhost"/>
  </bean>

  <bean id="jmsTemplate" class="org.springframework.jms.core.JmsTemplate">
    <property name="connectionFactory" ref="jmsConnectionFactory"/>
    <property name="defaultDestination" ref="destination"/>
    <property name="receiveTimeout" value="5000"/>
  </bean>

  <bean id="destination" class="org.apache.activemq.command.ActiveMQQueue">
    <constructor-arg value="orderQueue"/>
  </bean>

  <bean id="dataSource" class="org.apache.commons.dbcp.BasicDataSource">
    <property name="driverClassName" value="${batch.jdbc.driver}" />
    <property name="url" value="${batch.jdbc.url}" />
    <property name="username" value="${batch.jdbc.user}" />
    <property name="password" value="${batch.jdbc.password}" />
  </bean>

  <bean id="sessionFactory"
class="org.springframework.orm.hibernate3.LocalSessionFactoryBean">
```

```
    <property name="dataSource" ref="dataSource" />
    <property name="configLocation">
      <value>classpath:hibernate.cfg.xml</value>
    </property>
    <property  name="configurationClass">
      <value>org.hibernate.cfg.AnnotationConfiguration</value>
    </property>
    <property name="hibernateProperties">
      <props>
        <prop key="hibernate.show_sql">false</prop>
        <prop key="hibernate.format_sql">false</prop>
        <prop key="hibernate.hbm2ddl.auto">update</prop>
        <prop key="hibernate.dialect">org.hibernate.dialect.MySQLDialect</prop>
      </props>
    </property>
  </bean>

  <bean id="transactionManager"
    class="org.springframework.orm.hibernate3.HibernateTransactionManager"
    lazy-init="true">
    <property name="sessionFactory" ref="sessionFactory" />
  </bean>

  <bean id="placeholderProperties"
    class="org.springframework.beans.factory.config.PropertyPlaceholderConfigurer">
    <property name="location" value="classpath:batch.properties" />
    <property name="systemPropertiesModeName"
      value="SYSTEM_PROPERTIES_MODE_OVERRIDE" />
    <property name="ignoreUnresolvablePlaceholders" value="true" />
    <property name="order" value="1" />
  </bean>
</beans>
```

As you can see, the vast majority of launch-context.xml is the default. The main changes are the addition of the JMS resources and Hibernate resources at the end. Note the TransactionManager configured by default has been replaced with the one you're using for this job.

The last piece of configuration that you need to do in order for the pieces of this job to work together is the hibernate.cfg.xml file. Because you're using annotations to do the mapping, the hibernate.cfg.xml file is nothing more than a list of classes that are mapped. Listing 11-11 contains the source of the file for this example.

Listing 11-11. hibernate.cfg.xml

```xml
<!DOCTYPE hibernate-configuration PUBLIC
  "-//Hibernate/Hibernate Configuration DTD 3.0//EN"
  "http://hibernate.sourceforge.net/hibernate-configuration-3.0.dtd">

<hibernate-configuration>
  <session-factory>
    <mapping class="com.apress.springbatch.chapter11.domain.Customer"/>
    <mapping class="com.apress.springbatch.chapter11.domain.Order"/>
    <mapping class="com.apress.springbatch.chapter11.domain.OrderItem"/>
  </session-factory>
</hibernate-configuration>
```

When you build and run the job as is, you can confirm that 100 items are read and 100 items are written (as specified in the OrderGenerator class) to your JMS queue using either the JobRepository directly or checking in Spring Batch Admin. In either case, you're ready to begin building the batch job that does the work.

Loading Orders Into the Database

The first step real step of the job (step 2 in actuality) reads orders from the JMS queue and stores them in your database for further processing. This step, like many before, consists only of XML configuration. You need to configure a JMSItemReader to obtain the orders from the queue and a HibernateItemWriter to store the objects in your database. However, before you look at the configuration for the ItemReader and ItemWriter, Listing 11-12 has the code for the Customer, Order, and OrderItem objects, showing their Hibernate mappings.

Listing 11-12. Hibernate Mappings for Customer, Order, and OrderItem

Customer

```java
package com.apress.springbatch.chapter11.domain;

import java.io.Serializable;

import javax.persistence.Entity;
import javax.persistence.GeneratedValue;
import javax.persistence.GenerationType;
import javax.persistence.Id;
import javax.persistence.Table;
import javax.persistence.Version;

@Entity
@Table(name="customers")
public class Customer implements Serializable{

    private static final long serialVersionUID = 1L;

    @Id
```

```java
    @GeneratedValue(strategy = GenerationType.IDENTITY)
    private long id;
    @Version
    private long version;
    private String customerName;
    private String address;
    private String city;
    private String state;
    private String zip;

    // Accessors go here
    ...
}
```

Order

```java
package com.apress.springbatch.chapter11.domain;

import java.io.Serializable;
import java.util.Date;
import java.util.List;

import javax.persistence.CascadeType;
import javax.persistence.Entity;
import javax.persistence.FetchType;
import javax.persistence.GeneratedValue;
import javax.persistence.GenerationType;
import javax.persistence.Id;
import javax.persistence.ManyToOne;
import javax.persistence.OneToMany;
import javax.persistence.Table;
import javax.persistence.Version;

@Entity
@Table(name="orders")
public class Order implements Serializable{

    private static final long serialVersionUID = 1L;

    @Id
    @GeneratedValue(strategy = GenerationType.IDENTITY)
    private long id;
    @Version
    private long version;

    @ManyToOne(cascade = CascadeType.ALL)
    private Customer customer;
    private String creditCardNumber;
    private String expirationDate;

    @OneToMany(cascade = CascadeType.ALL, mappedBy="order", fetch = FetchType.LAZY)
    private List<OrderItem> items;
```

```
    private Date placedOn;
    private Boolean creditValidated;

    // Accessors go here
    ...
}
```

OrderItem

```
package com.apress.springbatch.chapter11.domain;

import java.io.Serializable;
import java.math.BigDecimal;

import javax.persistence.Entity;
import javax.persistence.GeneratedValue;
import javax.persistence.GenerationType;
import javax.persistence.Id;
import javax.persistence.ManyToOne;
import javax.persistence.Table;
import javax.persistence.Version;

@Entity
@Table(name="orderItems")
public class OrderItem implements Serializable{

    private static final long serialVersionUID = 1L;

    @Id
    @GeneratedValue(strategy = GenerationType.IDENTITY)
    private long id;
    @Version
    private long version;
    private String itemNumber;
    private int qty;
    private BigDecimal price;
    private Boolean inventoryValidated;
    @ManyToOne
    private Order order;

    // Accessors go here
    ...
}
```

The annotations are the final piece of the baseline configuration of your JMS and database resources. Now you can configure step 2 of the job to read orders from the JMS queue and save them in your database. Listing 11-13 shows the configuration for step 2 of the parallel job.

Listing 11-13. Step 2 of ParallelJob

```
...
<beans:bean id="jmsReader" class="org.springframework.batch.item.jms.JmsItemReader">
  <beans:property name="jmsTemplate" ref="jmsTemplate"/>
</beans:bean>

<beans:bean id="orderWriter"
  class="org.springframework.batch.item.database.HibernateItemWriter">
  <beans:property name="sessionFactory" ref="sessionFactory"/>
</beans:bean>

<step id="batchOrderProcessingStep">
  <tasklet>
    <chunk reader="jmsReader" writer="orderWriter" commit-interval="10"/>
  </tasklet>
</step>

<job id="parallelJob">
  <step id="step1" parent="preloadDataStep" next="step2"/>
  <step id="step2" parent="batchOrderProcessingStep"/>
</job>
...
```

Next, you need to verify that the customer's credit card will go through and that you have the inventory to fulfill the order. Because these functions aren't directly related, you can do them in parallel to improve the overall throughput of the job. You'll look at how these steps are configured next.

Configuring the Parallel Steps

To execute steps in parallel, Spring Batch again uses Spring's TaskExecutor. In this case, each flow is executed in its own thread, allowing you to execute multiple flows in parallel. To configure this, you use Spring Batch's split tag. The split tag takes three required attributes:

- id: The id of the element.

- task-executor: A reference to the TaskExecutor implementation that Spring Batch uses to manage the threading used for your parallel processing.

- next: Tells Spring Batch what step to execute once all the flows complete successfully. A split tag wraps multiple steps into a single pseudostep; if any of the flows fails in its execution, the other steps running at the same time complete and then the job fails when parallel processing was to end.

It's important to note that the execution order of a job using split is similar to that of a regular job. In a regular job, a step doesn't complete until all the items are processed for the step and the next step doesn't begin until the previous one is completed. Using split, the step after the split isn't executed until all the flows configured within the split have been completed.

▓**Note** The step after a split isn't executed until all the flows within a split are completed.

In order to do the credit verification and inventory checking required in this job, you can develop a couple of high-tech services to perform the checking for you. You use each of these services as ItemProcessors in your steps. First let's look at CreditServiceImpl, which is responsible for verifying that the customer's credit card will go through. Listing 11-14 shows the code related to this process.

Listing 11-14. CreditServiceImpl

```
package com.apress.springbatch.chapter11.service.impl;

import com.apress.springbatch.chapter11.domain.Order;
import com.apress.springbatch.chapter11.service.CreditService;

public class CreditServiceImpl implements CreditService {

@Override
public Order validateCharge(Order order) {
        if(order.getId() % 3 == 0) {
            order.setCreditValidated(true);
        } else {
            order.setCreditValidated(false);
        }

        return order;
    }
}
```

Because you don't actually process orders here, it doesn't make much sense to validate that credit cards go through. Instead, the service approves a third of the orders. Because CreditServiceImpl has a simplistic approach to verifying funds, you can imagine that InventoryServiceImpl has a similar approach to making sure you have the product on hand to fulfill the order. Listing 11-15 shows the code to verify that you have the inventory for each OrderItem.

Listing 11-15. InventoryServiceImpl

```
package com.apress.springbatch.chapter11.service.impl;

import com.apress.springbatch.chapter11.domain.OrderItem;
import com.apress.springbatch.chapter11.service.InventoryService;

public class InventoryServiceImpl implements InventoryService {

    @Override
    public OrderItem validateInventory(OrderItem item) {
        if(item.getId() % 2 == 0) {
            item.setInventoryValidated(true);
        } else {
```

```
                item.setInventoryValidated(false);
        }

        return item;
    }
}
```

Now that the business processing is written, let's configure these two services to run in parallel. To do that, as mentioned earlier, you use Spring Batch's split tag along with the SimpleAsyncTaskExecutor provided with Spring to handle thread management. Listing 11-16 shows the configuration for the steps you run in parallel.

Listing 11-16. Configuration of Parallel Steps

```
...
<beans:bean id="taskExecutor"
  class="org.springframework.core.task.SimpleAsyncTaskExecutor"/>

<beans:bean id="orderItemReader"
  class="org.springframework.batch.item.database.HibernateCursorItemReader"
  scope="step">
  <beans:property name="sessionFactory" ref="sessionFactory"/>
  <beans:property name="queryString" value="from OrderItem where inventoryValidated is null"/>
</beans:bean>

<beans:bean id="orderReader"
  class="org.springframework.batch.item.database.HibernateCursorItemReader"
  scope="step">
  <beans:property name="sessionFactory" ref="sessionFactory"/>
  <beans:property name="queryString" value="from Order where creditValidated is null"/>
</beans:bean>

<beans:bean id="orderWriter"
  class="org.springframework.batch.item.database.HibernateItemWriter">
  <beans:property name="sessionFactory" ref="sessionFactory"/>
</beans:bean>

<beans:bean id="creditService"
  class="com.apress.springbatch.chapter11.service.impl.CreditServiceImpl"/>

<beans:bean id="creditVerificationProcessor"
  class="org.springframework.batch.item.adapter.ItemProcessorAdapter">
  <beans:property name="targetObject" ref="creditService"/>
  <beans:property name="targetMethod" value="validateCharge"/>
</beans:bean>

<beans:bean id="inventoryService"
  class="com.apress.springbatch.chapter11.service.impl.InventoryServiceImpl"/>

<beans:bean id="inventoryVerificationProcessor"
  class="org.springframework.batch.item.adapter.ItemProcessorAdapter">
  <beans:property name="targetObject" ref="inventoryService"/>
```

```
      <beans:property name="targetMethod" value="validateInventory"/>
  </beans:bean>

  <step id="creditVerificationStep">
    <tasklet>
      <chunk reader="orderReader" processor="creditVerificationProcessor"
        writer="orderWriter" commit-interval="10"/>
    </tasklet>
  </step>

  <step id="inventoryVerificationStep">
    <tasklet>
      <chunk reader="orderItemReader" processor="inventoryVerificationProcessor"
        writer="orderWriter" commit-interval="10"/>
    </tasklet>
  </step>

  <job id="parallelJob">
    <step id="step1" parent="preloadDataStep" next="step2"/>
    <step id="step2" parent="batchOrderProcessingStep" next="parallelProcessing"/>
    <split id="parallelProcessing" task-executor="taskExecutor">
      <flow>
        <step id="step3" parent="creditVerificationStep"/>
      </flow>
      <flow>
        <step id="step4" parent="inventoryVerificationStep"/>
      </flow>
    </split>
  </job>
  …
```

Listing 11-16 shows the configuration of the required ItemReaders and ItemWriters as you would expect as well as creditService and inventoryService. You use ItemProcessorAdapter to turn your services into ItemProcessors and finally wire up each of the steps. It's in the job itself that things get interesting for this example.

Within parallelJob, you begin with step 1, which points to step 2 (via the next attribute). However, step 2 doesn't point to a step in the next attribute. Instead, it points to the split tag. Within the split tag, you define two flows: one for the credit-card verification (using creditVerificationStep) and one for inventory verification (using inventoryVerificationStep). These two flows are executed at the same time. The parallelProcessing "step" is considered complete when both steps have completed.

That's it for the parallel processing aspect of the job. The final step, generation of the pick lists is executed once the split pseudostep is complete. In the next section you will look at the required code for the step and how that step is configured.

Building the Picklists

The final piece of the puzzle for this job is to write out picklists for the warehouse to pull the items. In this case, you generate one picklist for each order that passed the credit-verification step (creditValidated = true) and for which all the OrderItems in the order passed the inventory check (inventoryValidated = true). For this you have a HibernateCursorItemReader that reads only the appropriate orders and passes them to a MultiResourceItemWriter so that each picklist is contained within its own file. For this final step, you need to write a small amount of code in the LineAggregator for the writer because you need to loop over the OrderItems in the order. Listing 11-17 shows the code for the LineAggregator, PickListFormatter.

Listing 11-17. PickListFormatter

```
package com.apress.springbatch.chapter11.writer;

import org.springframework.batch.item.file.transform.LineAggregator;

import com.apress.springbatch.chapter11.domain.Order;
import com.apress.springbatch.chapter11.domain.OrderItem;

public class PickListFormatter implements LineAggregator<Order> {

    public String aggregate(Order order) {
        StringBuilder builder = new StringBuilder();

        builder.append("Items to pick\n");

        if(order.getItems() != null) {
            for (OrderItem item : order.getItems()) {
                builder.append(item.getItemNumber() + ":" + item.getQty() + "\n");
            }
        } else {
            builder.append("No items to pick");
        }

        return builder.toString();
    }
}
```

Because all you need to do is write a small header ("Items to pick") and then list the item numbers and the quantity to pick, this LineAggregator is very simple to code. The configuration for the final step consists of adding the new step to the job and pointing the split tag to the step after both flows have completed. Listing 11-18 shows the configuration of the final step and the completed job.

Listing 11-18. The Completed parallelJob Configuration

```
...
<beans:bean id="validatedOrderItemReader"
  class="org.springframework.batch.item.database.HibernateCursorItemReader"
  scope="step">
  <beans:property name="sessionFactory" ref="sessionFactory"/>
  <beans:property name="queryString"
    value="from Order as o where o.creditValidated = true and not exists
(from OrderItem oi where oi.order = o and oi.inventoryValidated = false)"/>
  <beans:property name="useStatelessSession" value="false"/>
</beans:bean>
```

```
<beans:bean id="outputFile" class="org.springframework.core.io.FileSystemResource"
  scope="step">
  <beans:constructor-arg value="#{jobParameters[outputFile]}"/>
</beans:bean>

<beans:bean id="pickListFormatter"
  class="com.apress.springbatch.chapter11.writer.PickListFormatter"/>

<beans:bean id="pickListOutputWriter"
  class="org.springframework.batch.item.file.FlatFileItemWriter">
  <beans:property name="lineAggregator" ref="pickListFormatter"/>
</beans:bean>

<beans:bean id="pickListWriter"
  class="org.springframework.batch.item.file.MultiResourceItemWriter">
  <beans:property name="resource" ref="outputFile"/>
  <beans:property name="delegate" ref="pickListOutputWriter"/>
  <beans:property name="itemCountLimitPerResource" value="1"/>
</beans:bean>

<step id="processOrderStep">
  <tasklet>
    <chunk reader="validatedOrderItemReader" writer="pickListWriter"
      commit-interval="1"/>
  </tasklet>
</step>

<job id="parallelJob">
  <step id="step1" parent="preloadDataStep" next="step2"/>
  <step id="step2" parent="batchOrderProcessingStep" next="parallelProcessing"/>
  <split id="parallelProcessing" task-executor="taskExecutor" next="step5">
    <flow>
      <step id="step3" parent="creditVerificationStep"/>
    </flow>
    <flow>
      <step id="step4" parent="inventoryVerificationStep"/>
    </flow>
  </split>
  <step id="step5" parent="processOrderStep"/>
</job>
...
```

Obviously, when you run this job, the output will vary given that the orders are randomly generated. However, for any given run, a couple of picklists are generated. Listing 11-19 shows the output of a picklist generated from the batch job.

Listing 11-19. Picklist Output

```
Items to pick
5837232417899987867:1
```

As you can see, developing jobs that use parallel processing using Spring Batch is typically as simple as updating some XML. However, these approaches have limits. Up to this point, you've used only a single JVM. Because of that, you're restricted to the CPU and memory available on the box on which you start the job. But what about more complex scenarios where things are computationally hard? And how can you take advantage of server clusters to improve throughput? The next two sections look at how to scale Spring Batch jobs past a single JVM.

Remote Chunking

Java's multithreading abilities allow very high-performance software to be developed. But there is a limit to what any single JVM can do. Let's begin to look at ways to spread out the processing of a given task to many computers. The largest example of this type of distributed computing is the SETI@home project. SETI (Search for Extraterrestrial Intelligence) takes signals it records from radio telescopes and divides them in to small chunks of work. To analyze the work, SETI offers a screensaver that anyone can download onto their computer. The screensaver analyzes the data downloaded from SETI and returns the results. As of the writing of this book, the SETI@home project has had more than 5.2 million participants providing over 2 million years of aggregate computing time. The only way to scale to numbers like this is to get more computers involved.

Although you probably won't need to scale to the levels of SETI@home, the fact remains that the amount of data you need to process will probably at least tax the limits of a single JVM and may be prohibitively large to process in the time window you have. This section looks at how to use Spring Batch's remote chunking functionality to extend processing past what a single JVM can do.

Spring Batch provides two ways to scale beyond a single JVM. *Remote chunking* reads data locally, sends it to a remote JVM for processing, and then receives the results back in the original JVM for writing. This type of scaling outside of a single JVM is useful only when item processing is the bottleneck in your process. If input or output is the bottleneck, this type of scaling only makes things worse. There are a couple things to consider before using remote chunking as your method for scaling batch processing:

- *Processing needs to be the bottleneck:* Because reading and writing are completed in the master JVM, in order for remote chunking to be of any benefit, the cost of sending data to the slaves for processing must be less than the benefit received from parallelizing the processing.

- *Guaranteed delivery is required:* Because Spring Batch doesn't maintain any type of information about who is processing what, if one of the slaves goes down during processing, Spring Batch has no way to know what data is in play. Thus a persisted form of communication (typically JMS) is required.

Remote chunking takes advantage of two additional Spring projects. The Spring Integration project is an extension of the Spring project that is intended to provide lightweight messaging in Spring applications as well as adapters for interacting with remote applications via messaging. In the case of remote chunking, you use its adapters to interact with slave nodes via JMS. The other project that remote chunking relies on is the Spring Batch Integration project. This subproject of the Spring Batch

Admin project contains classes to implement features including remote chunking and partitioning as well as other integration patterns that are still in development. Although Spring Batch Integration is currently a subproject of the Spring Batch Admin project, the long-term intent is to break it out once the community has grown enough.

To implement remote chunking in your jobs, you use the helper project contained in Spring Batch Admin called Spring Batch Integration. This project is still young and growing in the community. Once it's mature enough, it will be branched into its own independent project. Until then, it has a number of helpful resources for your scalability needs.

To configure a job using remote chunking, you begin with a normally configured job that contains a step that you want to execute remotely. Spring Batch allows you to add this functionality with no changes to the configuration of the job itself. Instead, you hijack the ItemProcessor of the step to be remotely processed and insert an instance of a ChunkHandler implementation (provided by Spring Batch Integration). The org.springframework.batch.integration.chunk.ChunkHandler interface has a single method, handleChunk, that works just like the ItemProcessor interface. However, instead of actually doing the work for a given item, the ChunkHandler implementation sends the item to be processed remotely and listens for the response. When the item returns, it's written normally by the local ItemWriter. Figure 11-16 shows the structure of a step that is using remote chunking.

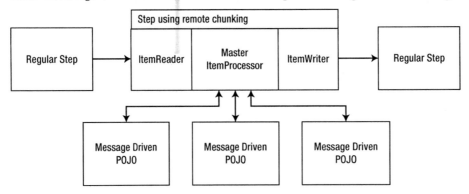

Figure 11-16. The structure of a step using remote chunking

As Figure 11-16 shows, any one of the steps in a job can be configured to do its processing via remote chunking. When you configure a given step, that step's ItemProcessor is replaced with a ChunkHandler, as mentioned previously. That ChunkHandler's implementation uses a special writer (org.springframework.batch.integration.chunk.ChunkMessageChannelItemWriter) to write the items to the queue. The slaves are nothing more than message-driven POJOs that execute your business logic. When the processing is completed, the output of the ItemProcessor is sent back to the ChunkHandler and passed on to the real ItemWriter.

For this example, you update a table of customer information with the longitude and latitude of the address each customer has on file. These coordinates are useful for using most mapping APIs on the Web to display a marker for a given point. To do obtain the geocoding for your customers, you call a web service, sending it the address information and receiving the customer's longitude and latitude to be saved.

The potential for a bottleneck exists when you call to a web service you don't control, so you use remote chunking to process this step. To begin, let's make a list of the items you need to address in this job:

1. *Write the Java for the job:* This job requires only a small amount of code. Specifically, you need to develop a domain object (Customer), a RowMapper implementation to map the customer data you retrieve as input from the database to your customer objects, an ItemProcessor to handle the web service call, and a class with a main method (discussed later).

2. *Configure the basic job:* The use of remote chunking doesn't require any change to the way you configure a job, so you should create a fully operational job before adding remote chunking to it.

3. *Update the POM file with integration dependencies:* Because remote chunking requires a couple of additional dependencies, you need to update your POM file to include them.

4. *Configure remote chunking:* Finally you configure the job to have remote workers to help process your customers.

Before you get to the code, let's review the data model for this example. The Customers table is the same as the one used in various other examples in this book. The only additions are the two new columns for the longitude and latitude. Figure 11-17 shows the updated table format.

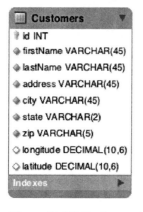

Figure 11-17. Customers table

With the data model defined, let's look at the Java code required. None of the code contains anything specific to remote chunking, and that is by design. Adding remote chunking is something you can do with no impact on the way your job is developed. The domain object for this project, Customer, contains all the fields you would expect; see Listing 11-20.

Listing 11-20. Customer.java

```java
package com.apress.springbatch.chapter11.domain;

import java.io.Serializable;

public class Customer implements Serializable{
```

```
        private static final long serialVersionUID = 1L;
        private long id;
        private String firstName;
        private String lastName;
        private String address;
        private String city;
        private String state;
        private String zip;
        private Double longitude;
        private Double latitude;

        // Accessors go here
        ...

        @Override
        public String toString() {
            return firstName + " " + lastName + " lives at " +
                    address + "," + city + " " + state + "," + zip;
        }
}
```

The two things to note about the Customer class are that it implements the java.io.Serializable interface so that it can be serialized and sent over the JMS queues you're using, and that you override the toString method with something useful so you can see who is processed by what slave nodes later.

The next object to code is the RowMapper implementation that maps the data from the Customers table in Figure 11-17 to the Customer object. Listing 11-21 shows the code for CustomerRowMapper.

Listing 11-21. CustomerRowMapper

```
package com.apress.springbatch.chapter11.jdbc;

import java.sql.ResultSet;
import java.sql.SQLException;

import org.springframework.jdbc.core.RowMapper;

import com.apress.springbatch.chapter11.domain.Customer;

public class CustomerRowMapper implements RowMapper<Customer> {

    public Customer mapRow(ResultSet rs, int arg1) throws SQLException {
        Customer cust = new Customer();

        cust.setAddress(rs.getString("address"));
        cust.setCity(rs.getString("city"));
        cust.setFirstName(rs.getString("firstName"));
        cust.setId(rs.getLong("id"));
        cust.setLastName(rs.getString("lastName"));
        cust.setState(rs.getString("state"));
        cust.setZip(rs.getString("zip"));
        cust.setLongitude(rs.getDouble("longitude"));
        cust.setLatitude(rs.getDouble("latitude"));
```

```
        return cust;
    }
}
```

Because the object and table are both straightforward, the RowMapper consists of nothing more than moving each column from the result set to its related customer attribute.

The final piece of the job is the ItemProcessor you use to call the web service and geocode customers' addresses. Most of this code matches the code you used in the statement job previously to obtain stock prices. Using HttpClient, you build a GET request and parse the comma-delimited results into the customer's latitude and longitude. Listing 11-22 shows the code for GeocodingItemProcessor.

Listing 11-22. GeocodingItemProcessor

```java
package com.apress.springbatch.chapter11.processor;

import java.net.URLEncoder;

import org.apache.commons.io.IOUtils;
import org.apache.commons.lang.StringUtils;
import org.apache.http.HttpEntity;
import org.apache.http.HttpResponse;
import org.apache.http.client.HttpClient;
import org.apache.http.client.methods.HttpGet;
import org.apache.http.impl.client.DefaultHttpClient;
import org.springframework.batch.item.ItemProcessor;

import com.apress.springbatch.chapter11.domain.Customer;

public class GeocodingItemProcessor implements ItemProcessor<Customer, Customer> {

    private static final String COMMA = ",";
    private static final String UTF_8 = "UTF-8";
    private String url;

    public Customer process(Customer customer) throws Exception {
        System.out.println("******** I'm going to process " + customer);
        HttpClient client = new DefaultHttpClient();

        String address = buildAddress(customer);

        if(address == null) {
            return null;
        }

        HttpGet get = new HttpGet(url + "?q=" + address);

        HttpResponse response = client.execute(get);

        HttpEntity entity = response.getEntity();

        String coordinantes = IOUtils.toString(entity.getContent());
```

425

```
            coordinantes = StringUtils.strip(coordinantes);

            if(coordinantes.length() > 0) {
                String [] values = coordinantes.split(COMMA);
                customer.setLongitude(Double.valueOf(values[0]));
                customer.setLatitude(Double.valueOf(values[1]));
            }

            return customer;
        }

    private String buildAddress(Customer customer) throws Exception {
        if(customer.getCity() == null && customer.getZip() == null) {
            return null;
        } else {
            StringBuilder address = new StringBuilder();

            address.append(
                StringUtils.defaultIfEmpty(
                    URLEncoder.encode(customer.getCity(), UTF_8) + COMMA, ""));
            address.append(
                StringUtils.defaultIfEmpty(
                    URLEncoder.encode(customer.getState(), UTF_8) + COMMA, ""));
            address.append(
                StringUtils.defaultIfEmpty(
                    URLEncoder.encode(customer.getZip(), UTF_8) + COMMA, ""));

            return address.substring(0, address.length() - 1);
        }
    }

    public void setUrl(String url) {
        this.url = url;
    }
}
```

Although GeocodingItemProcessor doesn't contain anything truly unusual that you haven't seen already, look at the first line of the process method. You call System.out.println on each customer so that when you run the job, you can see where each customer is processed. This way, you can see in the output of each console who processed what items.

The rest of the code consists of the construction of the HTTP GET request you send to obtain each customer's longitude and latitude. That's all the coding you need to do for the batch job. You need another class for the remote-chunking piece, but you look at that in a bit. For now, let's configure the job and make sure it works before you attempt to tackle the added complexity of remote chunking.

To configure the job, you start with a JdbcCursorItemReader that selects all customers that have null for either longitude or latitude. That reader requires a RowMapper, which is configured next. Then, you configure the ItemProcessor that does the heavy lifting of determining the customer's coordinates. The service you use to geocode the addresses is called TinyGeocoder. You provide the URL to the service as the ItemProcessor's only dependency. Next is the ItemWriter, a JdbcBatchItemWriter in this job. In this case, you update the customer records, setting the longitude and latitude for each item as required. The job configuration to assemble these elements wraps up the configuration. Listing 11-23 shows the configuration for this job.

Listing 11-23. Configuration for geocodingJob in geocodingJob.xml

```xml
<?xml version="1.0" encoding="UTF-8"?>
<beans:beans xmlns="http://www.springframework.org/schema/batch"
  xmlns:beans="http://www.springframework.org/schema/beans"
  xmlns:xsi="http://www.w3.org/2001/XMLSchema-instance"
  xsi:schemaLocation="http://www.springframework.org/schema/beans
    http://www.springframework.org/schema/beans/spring-beans-3.0.xsd
    http://www.springframework.org/schema/batch
    http://www.springframework.org/schema/batch/spring-batch-2.1.xsd">

  <beans:import resource="../launch-context.xml"/>

  <beans:bean id="customerReader"
    class="org.springframework.batch.item.database.JdbcCursorItemReader">
    <beans:property name="dataSource" ref="dataSource"/>
    <beans:property name="sql"
      value="select * from customers where longitude is null or latitude is null"/>
    <beans:property name="rowMapper" ref="customerRowMapper"/>
  </beans:bean>

  <beans:bean id="customerRowMapper"
    class="com.apress.springbatch.chapter11.jdbc.CustomerRowMapper"/>

  <beans:bean id="geocoder"
    class="com.apress.springbatch.chapter11.processor.GeocodingItemProcessor">
    <beans:property name="url" value="http://tinygeocoder.com/create-api.php"/>
  </beans:bean>

  <beans:bean id="customerImportWriter"
    class="org.springframework.batch.item.database.JdbcBatchItemWriter">
    <beans:property name="dataSource" ref="dataSource"/>
    <beans:property name="sql" value="update customers set longitude = :longitude,
latitude = :latitude where id = :id"/>
    <beans:property name="itemSqlParameterSourceProvider">
      <beans:bean class="org.springframework.batch.item.database.
BeanPropertyItemSqlParameterSourceProvider"/>
    </beans:property>
  </beans:bean>

  <job id="geocodingJob">
    <step id="step1">
      <tasklet>
        <chunk reader="customerReader" processor="geocoder" writer="customerImportWriter"
          commit-interval="1"/>
      </tasklet>
    </step>
  </job>
</beans:beans>
```

At this point, you can build and execute the job as you would any other job, and it works fine. However, because you want to add remote chunking to this job, you need to make a couple of additions to the project. As mentioned previously, you need to add dependencies to the POM file, write one more Java class, and configure the pieces required for remote chunking.

To start, let's add the new dependencies to your POM file. These dependencies are for the Spring Integration project (www.springsource.org/spring-integration); Spring Integration's JMS module; the Spring Batch Integration subproject (http://static.springsource.org/spring-batch/trunk/spring-batch-integration/); the Apache HttpClient project (http://hc.apache.org/httpcomponents-client-ga/) to handle your web service calls; and ActiveMQ, which serves as the JMS implementation for this job. Listing 11-24 shows the additional dependencies[3] added to the POM file.

Listing 11-24. Remote Chunking's Additional Dependencies

```
...
...
<dependency>
  <groupId>org.springframework.integration</groupId>
  <artifactId>spring-integration-core</artifactId>
  <version>${spring.integration.version}</version>
</dependency>
<dependency>
  <groupId>org.springframework.integration</groupId>
  <artifactId>spring-integration-jms</artifactId>
  <version>${spring.integration.version}</version>
</dependency>
<dependency>
  <groupId>org.springframework.batch</groupId>
  <artifactId>spring-batch-integration</artifactId>
  <version>${spring.batch-integration.version}</version>
</dependency>
<dependency>
  <groupId>org.apache.httpcomponents</groupId>
  <artifactId>httpclient</artifactId>
  <version>4.1</version>
</dependency>
<dependency>
  <groupId>org.apache.activemq</groupId>
  <artifactId>activemq-core</artifactId>
  <version>5.4.2</version>
  <exclusions>
    <exclusion>
      <groupId>org.apache.activemq</groupId>
      <artifactId>activeio-core</artifactId>
    </exclusion>
  </exclusions>
</dependency>
...
```

---

[3] For this example, you're using Spring 3.0.5.RELEASE, Spring Batch 2.1.7.RELEASE, Spring Batch Integration 1.2.0.RELEASE, and Spring Integration 2.0.3.RELEASE.

There is one additional thing you need to do. This project has two artifacts: the normal jar file from which you run jobs and a jar file that you launch for each of your slave JVMs. The only difference between the two is the main class you use. By default, your jar files are created with the CommandLineJobRunner defined as the main class, and this works fine for the jar file from which you execute the job. However, in the other JVMs, you don't want to execute the job; instead, you want to bootstrap Spring and register your listeners to be able to process any items that come their way. For this other jar file, you create a main class that bootstraps Spring for you and then blocks so that it doesn't shut down.

But what does this new jar file have to do with your POM file? Because the POM file specifies the main class that your jar file is configured to execute, you want to make it more versatile for you to generate the two jar files. To do this, you define two profiles: one for each of the two artifacts you generate. You use these profiles to define the main class that's configured for each of the jar files you generate. Creating these profiles consists of two steps: deleting the reference to the maven-jar-plugin in the build section of the POM file, and then adding your profiles. One is named *listener* and is used to build the jar file for your slave JVMs. The other is called *batch*, is the default profile, and configures the jar file to use CommandLineJobRunner as the jar file's main class. Listing 11-25 shows the new profile configurations.

Listing 11-25. Maven Profiles Used to Generate Both Required Artifacts

```
...
<profiles>
  <profile>
    <id>listener</id>
    <build>
      <finalName>remote-chunking-1.0-listener-SNAPSHOT</finalName>
      <plugins>
        <plugin>
          <groupId>org.apache.maven.plugins</groupId>
          <artifactId>maven-jar-plugin</artifactId>
          <configuration>
            <archive>
              <index>false</index>
              <manifest>
                <mainClass>com.apress.springbatch.chapter11.main.Geocoder</mainClass>
                <addClasspath>true</addClasspath>
                <classpathPrefix>lib/</classpathPrefix>
              </manifest>
              <manifestFile>${project.build.outputDirectory}/META-
INF/MANIFEST.MF</manifestFile>
            </archive>
          </configuration>
        </plugin>
      </plugins>
    </build>
  </profile>
  <profile>
    <id>batch</id>
    <activation>
      <activeByDefault>true</activeByDefault>
    </activation>
```

```
      <build>
        <plugins>
          <plugin>
            <groupId>org.apache.maven.plugins</groupId>
            <artifactId>maven-jar-plugin</artifactId>
            <configuration>
              <archive>
                <index>false</index>
                <manifest>
                  <mainClass>
                    org.springframework.batch.core.launch.support.CommandLineJobRunner
                  </mainClass>
                  <addClasspath>true</addClasspath>
                  <classpathPrefix>lib/</classpathPrefix>
                </manifest>
                <manifestFile>${project.build.outputDirectory}/META-
INF/MANIFEST.MF</manifestFile>
              </archive>
            </configuration>
          </plugin>
        </plugins>
      </build>
    </profile>
</profiles>
...
```

To build your artifacts, you use the standard mvn clean install command for the main jar file
because the batch profile has been configured to be active by default. To build the slave jar file, invoke
the listener profile using the mvn clean install -P listener command. In order for the listener profile
to work, however, you need to write the Geocoder class; see Listing 11-26.

Listing 11-26. Geocoder

```
package com.apress.springbatch.chapter11.main;

import org.springframework.context.support.ClassPathXmlApplicationContext;

public class Geocoder {

    /**
     * @param args
     */
    public static void main(String[] args) throws Exception {
        new ClassPathXmlApplicationContext("/jobs/geocodeJob.xml");
        System.in.read();
    }
}
```

As you can see in Listing 11-26, all the Geocoder class does is load your context and block by calling
System.in.read(). This keeps the application up and running until you decide to kill it. Because you can
build your two jar files at this point, let's look at what it takes to add remote chunking to the application.

The additional configuration consists of adding the following nine new beans to the geocodeJob.xml file:

- chunkHandler: This is a factory bean used to create the ChunkHandler that replaces the ItemProcessor in the step in question. It also does the replacement for you.

- chunkWriter: This bean is a special writer used to send items out to the listening slave nodes for processing. It also listens for the responses and takes them off the inbound queue for the ItemWriter to complete processing.

- messageGateway: This is the MessagingTemplate from Spring Integration that the chunkWriter uses to do the JMS calls.

- requests *and* incoming: These are the incoming and outgoing message channels for the chunkWriter.

- *A JMS outbound channel adapter*: This bean adapts your Spring Integration channel to the physical outbound request's JMS queue.

- headerExtractor: Because Spring Integration channels are in-memory concepts, you run the risk of losing messages if one of the end points goes down. Spring Integration addresses this by implementing a redelivery system. This header extractor extracts the related header and sets it on the org.springframework.batch.integration.chunk.ChunkResponse so that your job knows whether this was the original response.

- replies: This is the Spring Integration channel used to send the processed item back from the slave node to the master job.

- listenerContainer: This is the definition of the message listener that acts as the slave elements and processes each of the messages sent out by the master job.

As you can see, this example includes a number of moving parts. Although it looks like a long list, the configuration isn't that bad. Listing 11-27 shows the configuration for geocodingJob.

Listing 11-27. gecodingJob Configured with Remote Chunking

```xml
<?xml version="1.0" encoding="UTF-8"?>
<beans:beans xmlns="http://www.springframework.org/schema/batch"
  xmlns:beans="http://www.springframework.org/schema/beans"
  xmlns:int-jms="http://www.springframework.org/schema/integration/jms"
  xmlns:int="http://www.springframework.org/schema/integration"
  xmlns:jms="http://www.springframework.org/schema/jms"
  xmlns:xsi="http://www.w3.org/2001/XMLSchema-instance"
  xsi:schemaLocation="http://www.springframework.org/schema/beans
    http://www.springframework.org/schema/beans/spring-beans-3.0.xsd
    http://www.springframework.org/schema/integration/jms
    http://www.springframework.org/schema/integration/jms/spring-integration-jms.xsd
    http://www.springframework.org/schema/integration
    http://www.springframework.org/schema/integration/spring-integration-2.0.xsd
    http://www.springframework.org/schema/jms
    http://www.springframework.org/schema/jms/spring-jms-3.0.xsd
    http://www.springframework.org/schema/batch
```

```
      http://www.springframework.org/schema/batch/spring-batch-2.1.xsd">

      ...

  <beans:bean id="chunkHandler"
    class="org.springframework.batch.integration.chunk.RemoteChunkHandlerFactoryBean">
    <beans:property name="chunkWriter" ref="chunkWriter" />
    <beans:property name="step" ref="step1" />
  </beans:bean>

  <beans:bean id="chunkWriter"
    class="org.springframework.batch.integration.chunk.ChunkMessageChannelItemWriter"
    scope="step">
    <beans:property name="messagingOperations" ref="messagingGateway" />
    <beans:property name="replyChannel" ref="replies" />
    <beans:property name="maxWaitTimeouts" value="10"/>
</beans:bean>

  <beans:bean id="messagingGateway"
    class="org.springframework.integration.core.MessagingTemplate">
    <beans:property name="defaultChannel" ref="requests"/>
    <beans:property name="receiveTimeout" value="1000"/>
  </beans:bean>

  <int:channel id="requests" />
  <int:channel id="incoming" />
  <int-jms:outbound-channel-adapter connection-factory="connectionFactory"
    channel="requests" destination-name="requests" />

  <int:transformer input-channel="incoming" output-channel="replies"
    ref="headerExtractor" method="extract" />

  <beans:bean id="headerExtractor"
    class="org.springframework.batch.integration.chunk.JmsRedeliveredExtractor" />

  <int:channel id="replies">
    <int:queue />
    <int:interceptors>
      <beans:bean id="pollerInterceptor"
        class="org.springframework.batch.integration.chunk.MessageSourcePollerInterceptor">
        <beans:property name="messageSource">
          <beans:bean class="org.springframework.integration.jms.JmsDestinationPollingSource">
            <beans:constructor-arg>
              <beans:bean class="org.springframework.jms.core.JmsTemplate">
                <beans:property name="connectionFactory" ref="connectionFactory" />
                <beans:property name="defaultDestinationName" value="replies" />
                <beans:property name="receiveTimeout" value="1000" />
              </beans:bean>
            </beans:constructor-arg>
          </beans:bean>
        </beans:property>
        <beans:property name="channel" ref="incoming" />
```

```
      </beans:bean>
    </int:interceptors>
  </int:channel>

  <jms:listener-container connection-factory="connectionFactory"
    transaction-manager="transactionManager" acknowledge="transacted">
    <jms:listener destination="requests" ref="chunkHandler"
      response-destination="replies" method="handleChunk"/>
  </jms:listener-container>
</beans:beans>
```

The configuration for the remote-chunking piece of the example begins with the ChunkHandler. It's configured as an instance of org.springframework.batch.integration.chunk.RemoteChunkHandlerFactoryBean, which creates an instance of a ChunkHandler and injects it into the step you configure as its ItemProcessor. The other dependency the RemoteChunkHandler has is the ChunkWriter, which is the next bean configured.

The ChunkWriter, as you saw previously, is a specially created writer used to send the items out to the slave listeners to be processed and listen for the items to come back as processing completes. This class requires three dependencies: a reference to a MessageTemplate to perform the required JMS functions, the name of the reply channel (because the request channel is the default for the MessageTemplate), and the maximum timeout errors it can accept before considering the job a failure (10 in this case). If, during execution of the job, the number of timeouts you configure is reached, the step is marked as a failure.

The messageGateway bean is an instance of Spring Integration's org.springframework.integration.core.MessageTemplate and is used to do the heavy lifting with regard to JMS functions in remote chunking. You define the outgoing channel (requests) as defaultChannel and specify a timeout value for how long to wait when listening for replies.

The requests channel is an in-memory representation of a queue. Spring Integration uses channels to abstract the concept of messaging from an application to let you use either real JMS queues or lighter-weight in-memory messaging. In this case, you back this up with a real JMS queue later in the configuration. Just as the requests channel sends items from your job to the slave nodes, the incoming channel receives the results.

To back up the requests channel with a true JMS queue, you use Spring Integration's outbound channel adapter. This adapter takes all interactions done with the channel and persists them to the queue you configure. In order for it to work, you need to specify a connection factory for it to connect with your JMS queues, tell it what channel to get the items from, and specify the name of the queue to put it on.

As you process messages from remote servers, a number of things can happen, such as timeouts or various nodes going down. Because of this, an item is flagged as redelivered if it has been delivered more than once for any reason. What you do with it from there depends on a number of business conditions (whether this a restart, and so on). However, to obtain that redelivered flag, you use a Spring Integration *transformer*. This transformer takes the messages from one channel (incoming), applies some form of logic (the extract method of the headerExtractor bean, in this case), and places them on another channel (replies, in this case).

With all the communication configured as well as the components used in your job, the only thing left to configure are the slave workers. Each slave in this case is nothing more than a message-driven POJO, configured using Spring Integration's listener container and listener. The listener container is used to pull messages off of the queue and put replies back on it. For each message it receives, the listener itself is called.

That's it! The explanation may seem a bit overwhelming, but to run this example, you build the two artifacts discussed earlier: one for the slave JVMs and one for the job. To test all the pieces, you need to start at least three things:

- *ActiveMQ:* In order for your JVMs to communicate with each other, you need to run the ActiveMQ server. You can download it from http://apache.activemq.org. From ActiveMQ's bin directory, execute the activeMq script to launch the server.

- *Slave JVMs:* You can start as many of these as you wish. These are the JVMs that execute the ItemProcessor on each item the slave reads off of the queue. To start the slave JVMs, execute the command java -jar remote-chunking-0.0.1-listener-SNAPSHOT.jar for each of the slaves you wish to run.

- *The job:* The last step of launching this job is to execute the jar file that is configured to execute the job. You execute it like any other job, with the command java -jar remote-chunking-0.0.1-SNAPSHOT.jar jobs/geocodeJob.xml geocodingJob.

Spring Batch takes care of the rest!

But how do you know that your slaves did some of the work? The proof is in the output. The first place to look is the database, where the longitude and latitude for each customer should now be populated. Above and beyond that, each slave node as well as the JVM in which the job was run has output statements showing who was processed at each node. Listing 11-28 shows an example of the output from one of the slaves.

Listing 11-28. Results of geocodingJob

```
2011-04-11 21:49:31,668 DEBUG
org.springframework.jms.listener.DefaultMessageListenerContainer#0-1
[org.springframework.batch.integration.chunk.ChunkProcessorChunkHandler] - <Handling chunk:
ChunkRequest: jobId=8573, sequence=9, contribution=[StepContribution: read=0, written=0,
filtered=0, readSkips=0, writeSkips=0, processSkips=0, exitStatus=EXECUTING], item count=1>

("******** I'm going to process Merideth Gray lives at 303 W Comstock Street,Seattle
WA,98119

2011-04-11 21:49:31,971 DEBUG
org.springframework.jms.listener.DefaultMessageListenerContainer#0-1
[org.springframework.batch.item.database.JdbcBatchItemWriter] - <Executing batch with 1
items.>
```

You may notice that not only are the slave nodes processing your items, but the local JVM that is executing the job is also processing items. The reason is in your configuration. Because the job's configuration contains the information for the listener, the local JVM has a listener processing items just like any other slave. This is a good thing because there is rarely a reason to completely offload all the processing to other nodes, while the JVM executing your batch job sits doing nothing other than listening for results.

Remote chunking is a great way to spread the cost of processing items across multiple JVMs. It has the benefits of requiring no changes to your job configuration and using dumb workers (workers with no knowledge of Spring Batch or your job's database, and so on). But keep in mind that durable communication like JMS is required, and this approach can't provide any benefits for jobs where the bottleneck exists in the input or output phase of the step.

In situations where offloading just the ItemProcessor's work isn't enough (situations when I/O is the bottleneck, for example), Spring Batch has one other option up its sleeve: partitioning. You look at partitioning and how you can use it to scale your jobs in the next section.

Partitioning

Although remote chunking is useful when you're working with a process that has a bottleneck in the processing of items, most of the time the bottleneck exists in the input and output. Interacting with a database or reading files typically is where performance and scalability concerns come into play. To help with that, Spring Batch provides the ability for multiple workers to execute complete steps. The entire ItemReader, ItemProcessor, and ItemWriter interaction can be offloaded to slave workers. This section looks at what partitioning is and how to configure jobs to take advantage of this powerful Spring Batch feature.

Partitioning is a concept where a master step farms out work to any number of listening slave steps for processing. This may sound very similar to remote chunking (and it is), but there are some key differences. First, the slave nodes aren't message-driven POJOs as they are with remote chunking. The slaves in partitioning are Spring Batch steps, each complete with its own reader, processor, and writer. Because they're full Spring Batch steps, partitioning offers a couple of unique benefits over a remote-chunking implementation.

The first advantage of partitioning over remote chunking is that you don't need a guaranteed delivery system (JMS for example). Each step maintains its own state just like any other Spring Batch step. Currently, the Spring Batch Integration project uses Spring Integration's channels to abstract out the communication mechanism so you can use anything Spring Integration supports.

The second advantage is that you don't need to develop custom components. Because the slave is a regular Spring Batch step, there is almost nothing special you need to code (there is one extra class, a Partitioner implementation you see later).

But even with these advantages, you need to keep a couple of things in mind. First, remote steps need to be able to communicate with your job repository. Because each slave is a true Spring Batch step, it has its own StepExecution and maintains its state in the database like any other step. In addition, the input and output need to be accessible from all the slave nodes. With remote chunking, the master handles all input and output, so the data can be centralized. But with partitioning, slaves are responsible for their own input and output. Thus some forms of I/O lend themselves more toward partitioning than others (databases are typically easier than files, for example).

To see the structural difference between remote chunking and partitioning, Figure 11-18 shows how a job using partitioning is structured.

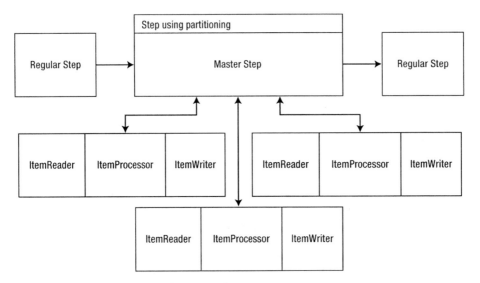

Figure 11-18. A partitioned job

As you can see, the master job step is responsible for dividing the work into partitions to be processed by each of the slaves. It then sends a message consisting of a StepExecution to be consumed by the slaves; this describes what to process. Unlike remote chunking, where the data is sent remotely, partitioning only *describes* the data to be processed by the slave. For example, the master step may determine a range of database ids to process for each partition and send that out. Once each slave has completed the work requested, it returns the StepExecution, updated with the results of the step for the master to interpret. When all the partitions have been successfully completed, the step is considered complete, and the job continues. If any of the partitions fail, the step is considered failed, and the job stops.

To look at how partitioning works in a job, let's reuse the geocoding job you used in the remote-chunking example, but refactor it to use partitioning. Its single step is now executed remotely in a number of JVMs. Because most of the code is the same, let's start by looking at the one new class that partitioning requires: an implementation of the Partitioner interface.

The org.springframework.batch.core.partition.support.Partitioner interface has a single method, partition(int gridSize), which returns a Map of partition names as the keys and a StepExecution as the value. Each of the StepExecutions in the Map contains the information the slave steps need in order to know what to do. In this case, you store two properties in the StepExecution for each slave: the start id for the customers to process and an end id. Listing 11-29 shows the code for ColumnRangePartitioner.

Listing 11-29. ColumnRangePartitioner

```
package com.apress.springbatch.chapter11.partition;

import java.util.HashMap;
import java.util.Map;

import org.springframework.batch.core.partition.support.Partitioner;
import org.springframework.batch.item.ExecutionContext;
```

```java
import org.springframework.jdbc.core.JdbcTemplate;

public class ColumnRangePartitioner extends JdbcTemplate implements Partitioner {

    private String column;
    private String table;
    private int gridSize;

    public Map<String, ExecutionContext> partition(int arg0) {
        int min = queryForInt("SELECT MIN(" + column + ") from "
                + table);
        int max = queryForInt("SELECT MAX(" + column + ") from "
                + table);
        int targetSize = (max - min) / gridSize;

        Map<String, ExecutionContext> result = new HashMap<String, ExecutionContext>();
        int number = 0;
        int start = min;
        int end = start + targetSize - 1;

        while (start <= max) {

            ExecutionContext value = new ExecutionContext();
            result.put("partition" + number, value);

            if (end >= max) {
                end = max;
            }
            value.putInt("minValue", start);
            value.putInt("maxValue", end);

            start += targetSize;
            end += targetSize;
            number++;
        }

        return result;
    }

    public void setColumn(String column) {
        this.column = column;
    }

    public void setTable(String table) {
        this.table = table;
    }

    public void setGridSize(int gridSize) {
        this.gridSize = gridSize;
    }
}
```

The partition method obtains the min and the max ids in the Customers table (you configure the table name and column name in the XML). From there, you divide that range based on the number of slaves you have and create a StepExecution with the min and max id to be processed. When all the StepExecutions are created and saved in the Map, you return the Map.

ColumnRangePartitioner is the only new class you need to write to use partitioning in your job. The other required changes are in the configuration. Before you look at the configuration, let's talk about how the flow of the messages occurs. Figure 11-19 shows how each message is processed.

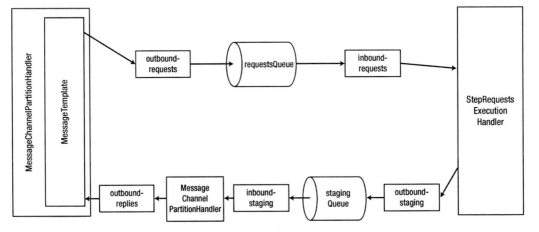

Figure 11-19. Message processing with a partitioned job

The job is configured with a new type of step. Up to this point, you've been using tasklet steps to execute your code. For a step to be partitioned, you use a *partition step*. This type of step, unlike a tasklet step that configures a chunk of processing, configures how to partition a step (via the Partitioner implementation) and a handler that is responsible for sending the messages to the slaves and receiving the responses.

■ **Note** Communication with remote workers in partitioned processing doesn't need to be transactional or have guaranteed delivery.

The Spring Batch Integration project provides an implementation of the PartitionHandler interface called MessageChannelPartitionHandler. This class uses Spring Integration channels as the form of communication to eliminate any dependencies on a particular type of communication. For this example, you use JMS. The communication consists of three queues: a request queue for the master step to send out the work requests, a staging queue on which the slave steps reply, and a reply queue to send the consolidated reply back to the master. There are two queues on the way back because each step replies with the StepExecution from that step. You use an aggregator to consolidate all the responses into a single list of StepExecutions so they can be processed at once.

Let's look at the configuration for geocodingJob using partitioning; see Listing 11-30.

Listing 11-30. geocodingJob Using Partitioning Configured in geocodeJob.xml

```xml
<?xml version="1.0" encoding="UTF-8"?>
<beans:beans xmlns="http://www.springframework.org/schema/batch"
  xmlns:beans="http://www.springframework.org/schema/beans"
  xmlns:int-jms="http://www.springframework.org/schema/integration/jms"
  xmlns:int="http://www.springframework.org/schema/integration"
  xmlns:jms="http://www.springframework.org/schema/jms"
  xmlns:xsi="http://www.w3.org/2001/XMLSchema-instance"
  xmlns:task="http://www.springframework.org/schema/task"
  xsi:schemaLocation="http://www.springframework.org/schema/beans
    http://www.springframework.org/schema/beans/spring-beans-3.0.xsd
    http://www.springframework.org/schema/integration/jms
    http://www.springframework.org/schema/integration/jms/spring-integration-jms-2.0.xsd
    http://www.springframework.org/schema/integration
    http://www.springframework.org/schema/integration/spring-integration-2.0.xsd
    http://www.springframework.org/schema/jms
    http://www.springframework.org/schema/jms/spring-jms-3.0.xsd
    http://www.springframework.org/schema/task
    http://www.springframework.org/schema/task/spring-task-3.0.xsd
    http://www.springframework.org/schema/batch
    http://www.springframework.org/schema/batch/spring-batch-2.1.xsd">

  <beans:import resource="../launch-context.xml"/>

  <job id="geocodingJob">
    <step id="step1.master">
      <partition partitioner="partitioner" handler="partitionHandler"/>
    </step>
  </job>

  <beans:bean id="partitioner"
    class="com.apress.springbatch.chapter11.partition.ColumnRangePartitioner">
    <beans:property name="dataSource" ref="dataSource"/>
    <beans:property name="column" value="id"/>
    <beans:property name="table" value="customers"/>
    <beans:property name="gridSize" value="3"/>
  </beans:bean>

  <step id="step1">
    <tasklet>
      <chunk reader="customerReader" processor="geocoder" writer="customerImportWriter"
        commit-interval="1"/>
    </tasklet>
  </step>

  <beans:bean id="customerReader"
    class="org.springframework.batch.item.database.JdbcCursorItemReader" scope="step">
    <beans:property name="dataSource" ref="dataSource"/>
    <beans:property name="sql">
      <beans:value><![CDATA[
```

```
          select * from customers where id >= ? and id <=  ?
      ]]></beans:value>
    </beans:property>
    <beans:property name="preparedStatementSetter">
      <beans:bean
        class="org.springframework.batch.core.resource.ListPreparedStatementSetter">
        <beans:property name="parameters">
          <beans:list>
            <beans:value>#{stepExecutionContext[minValue]}</beans:value>
            <beans:value>#{stepExecutionContext[maxValue]}</beans:value>
          </beans:list>
        </beans:property>
      </beans:bean>
    </beans:property>
    <beans:property name="rowMapper" ref="customerRowMapper"/>
  </beans:bean>

  <beans:bean id="customerRowMapper"
    class="com.apress.springbatch.chapter11.jdbc.CustomerRowMapper"/>

  <beans:bean id="geocoder"
    class="com.apress.springbatch.chapter11.processor.GeocodingItemProcessor">
    <beans:property name="url" value="http://tinygeocoder.com/create-api.php"/>
  </beans:bean>

  <beans:bean id="customerImportWriter"
    class="org.springframework.batch.item.database.JdbcBatchItemWriter">
    <beans:property name="dataSource" ref="dataSource"/>
    <beans:property name="sql"
      value="update customers set longitude = :longitude, latitude = :latitude where id =
:id"/>
    <beans:property name="itemSqlParameterSourceProvider">
      <beans:bean class="org.springframework.batch.item.database.
BeanPropertyItemSqlParameterSourceProvider"/>
    </beans:property>
  </beans:bean>

  <beans:bean id="partitionHandler" class="org.springframework.batch.integration.partition.
MessageChannelPartitionHandler">
    <beans:property name="stepName" value="step1"/>
    <beans:property name="gridSize" value="3"/>
    <beans:property name="replyChannel" ref="outbound-replies"/>
    <beans:property name="messagingOperations">
      <beans:bean class="org.springframework.integration.core.MessagingTemplate">
        <beans:property name="defaultChannel" ref="outbound-requests"/>
        <beans:property name="receiveTimeout" value="100000"/>
      </beans:bean>
    </beans:property>
  </beans:bean>

  <int:channel id="outbound-requests"/>
  <int-jms:outbound-channel-adapter connection-factory="connectionFactory"
```

```
      destination="requestsQueue" channel="outbound-requests"/>

  <int:channel id="inbound-requests"/>
  <int-jms:message-driven-channel-adapter connection-factory="connectionFactory"
    destination="requestsQueue" channel="inbound-requests"/>

  <beans:bean id="stepExecutionRequestHandler"
    class="org.springframework.batch.integration.partition.StepExecutionRequestHandler">
    <beans:property name="jobExplorer" ref="jobExplorer"/>
    <beans:property name="stepLocator" ref="stepLocator"/>
  </beans:bean>

  <int:service-activator ref="stepExecutionRequestHandler"
    input-channel="inbound-requests" output-channel="outbound-staging"/>

  <int:channel id="outbound-staging"/>
  <int-jms:outbound-channel-adapter connection-factory="connectionFactory"
    destination="stagingQueue" channel="outbound-staging"/>

  <int:channel id="inbound-staging"/>
  <int-jms:message-driven-channel-adapter connection-factory="connectionFactory"
    destination="stagingQueue" channel="inbound-staging"/>

  <int:aggregator ref="partitionHandler" input-channel="inbound-staging"
    output-channel="outbound-replies"/>

  <int:channel id="outbound-replies">
    <int:queue />
  </int:channel>
</beans:beans>
```

The configuration for the job begins with the job itself. Although the name and the step's name are the same here as they were in the remote-chunking example, what this step does is quite different. Step1.master serves as the master step, which doles out work to the slaves and aggregates the resulting statuses to determine whether the step was successful. The partition step for step1.master requires two dependencies: an implementation of the Partitioner interface to divide the work into partitions and a PartitionHandler to do the work of sending out the messages to the slaves and receiving the results.

ColumnRangePartitioner is the implementation of the Partitioner interface that you're using for this example. As you saw in Listing 11-29, ColumnRangePartitioner extends Spring's JdbcTemplate, so it depends on a DataSource implementation as well as the required table and column to use for partitioning and the number of slaves (gridSize) so you can divide the work appropriately.

The step that is configured after the partitioner is the exact same step used in the remote-chunking example. But this step is run as your slave worker as opposed to within the context of a job. Along with the configuration of the step, you configure its ItemReader and required RowMapper implementation (customerReader and customerRowMapper), an ItemProcessor (geocoder), and an ItemWriter (customerImportWriter).

Next, you move on to the configuration of the beans related to partitioning. Because the PartitionHandler is the center of the processing for a partitioned step, let's begin with it. org.springframework.batch.integration.partition.MessageChannelPartitionHandler requires four dependencies:

- stepName: The name of the step to be remotely executed by the slave processes. In this case, it's the step1 step.

- gridSize: The number of slaves involved in the processing of the partitioned step. You run three JVMs, so you have three slaves.

- replyChannel: Where MessageChannelPartitionHandler listens for incoming replies from the remotely executed steps.

- messagingOperations: A MessageTemplate configured with the requests queue as the default channel. MessageChannelPartitionHandler uses this to send outgoing messages to the slave JVMs as well as listen for incoming messages.

After MessageChannelPartitionHandler, you configure the channels you use for communication. Five channels are involved in this example: an inbound and an outbound channel on each of the two queues and a channel for the final aggregated message. Each outbound channel puts messages on the queues; the inbound channels receive messages from each queue. The following channels and adapters are configured for this job:

- outbound-requests: This channel puts the requests for each partition on the request queue. You use a JMS outbound channel adapter to take the messages from the Spring Integration channel and put them on the JMS queue.

- inbound-requests: This channel receives the messages put on the requests queue. A message-driven channel adapter pulls the messages off the JMS queue and puts them in this channel.

- outbound-staging: When a step has been processed, the response from an individual step is staged in this channel, which is then persisted to the staging queue. Again, a JMS outbound channel adapter persists the messages to the JMS staging queue.

- inbound-staging: Messages received from the staging queue are placed in this channel via a message-driven channel adapter, to be aggregated together into a single message for processing by MessageChannelPartitionHandler.

- outbound-replies: This is the single channel used to transport the aggregated step results back to MessageChannelPartitionHandler.

You're already putting messages onto the outbound-requests channel and receiving them with the outbound-replies channel with MessageChannelPartitionHandler. To execute the job when you receive a message, you use the next bean that is configured: StepExecutionRequestHandler.

StepExecutionRequestHandler takes the StepExecution you created in the ColumnRangePartitioner and executes the step you've requested with that StepExecution. Because it's a message-driven POJO, you use Spring Integration's service activator to execute it as messages are received. The two dependencies with which StepExecutionRequestHandler is configured are references to a JobExplorer and a StepLocator. Both are used to locate and execute the step.

The last thing to configure is a Spring Integration aggregator. You use this because MessageChannelPartitionHandler expects a single message containing a list of StepExecutions in return for sending out all the individual StepExecutions to worker JVMs. Because MessageChannelPartitionHandler requires the consolidated input, it's what provides the method to do the aggregation, as you can see in the configuration.

Before you consider the configuration finished, let's examine a couple of elements in the launch-context.xml file, shown in Listing 11-31.

Listing 11-31. launch-context.xml

```xml
<?xml version="1.0" encoding="UTF-8"?>
<beans xmlns="http://www.springframework.org/schema/beans"
  xmlns:p="http://www.springframework.org/schema/p"
  xmlns:xsi="http://www.w3.org/2001/XMLSchema-instance"
  xmlns:amq="http://activemq.apache.org/schema/core"
  xsi:schemaLocation="http://www.springframework.org/schema/beans
    http://www.springframework.org/schema/beans/spring-beans-3.0.xsd
    http://activemq.apache.org/schema/core
    http://activemq.apache.org/schema/core/activemq-core-5.4.2.xsd ">

  <bean id="jobOperator"
    class="org.springframework.batch.core.launch.support.SimpleJobOperator"
    p:jobLauncher-ref="jobLauncher" p:jobExplorer-ref="jobExplorer"
    p:jobRepository-ref="jobRepository" p:jobRegistry-ref="jobRegistry" />

  <bean id="jobExplorer"
    class="org.springframework.batch.core.explore.support.JobExplorerFactoryBean"
    p:dataSource-ref="dataSource" />

  <bean id="jobRegistry"
    class="org.springframework.batch.core.configuration.support.MapJobRegistry" />

  <bean
    class="org.springframework.batch.core.configuration.support.JobRegistryBeanPostProcessor">
    <property name="jobRegistry" ref="jobRegistry"/>
  </bean>

  <bean id="jobLauncher"
    class="org.springframework.batch.core.launch.support.SimpleJobLauncher">
    <property name="jobRepository" ref="jobRepository" />
  </bean>

  <bean id="stepLocator"
    class="org.springframework.batch.integration.partition.BeanFactoryStepLocator" />

  <bean id="jobRepository"
    class="org.springframework.batch.core.repository.support.JobRepositoryFactoryBean"
    p:dataSource-ref="dataSource" p:transactionManager-ref="transactionManager" />

  <bean id="jmsConnectionFactory" class="org.apache.activemq.ActiveMQConnectionFactory">
    <property name="brokerURL" value="vm://localhost"/>
  </bean>

  <bean id="jmsTemplate" class="org.springframework.jms.core.JmsTemplate">
    <property name="connectionFactory" ref="jmsConnectionFactory"/>
    <property name="defaultDestination" ref="destination"/>
    <property name="receiveTimeout" value="5000"/>
  </bean>
```

```xml
<bean id="destination" class="org.apache.activemq.command.ActiveMQQueue">
  <constructor-arg value="orderQueue"/>
</bean>

<bean id="dataSource" class="org.apache.commons.dbcp.BasicDataSource">
  <property name="driverClassName" value="${batch.jdbc.driver}" />
  <property name="url" value="${batch.jdbc.url}" />
  <property name="username" value="${batch.jdbc.user}" />
  <property name="password" value="${batch.jdbc.password}" />
</bean>

<bean id="sessionFactory"
  class="org.springframework.orm.hibernate3.LocalSessionFactoryBean">
  <property name="dataSource" ref="dataSource" />
  <property name="configLocation">
    <value>classpath:hibernate.cfg.xml</value>
  </property>
  <property  name="configurationClass">
    <value>org.hibernate.cfg.AnnotationConfiguration</value>
  </property>
  <property name="hibernateProperties">
    <props>
      <prop key="hibernate.show_sql">false</prop>
      <prop key="hibernate.format_sql">false</prop>
      <prop key="hibernate.hbm2ddl.auto">update</prop>
      <prop key="hibernate.dialect">org.hibernate.dialect.MySQLDialect</prop>
    </props>
  </property>
</bean>

<bean id="transactionManager"
  class="org.springframework.orm.hibernate3.HibernateTransactionManager"
  lazy-init="true">
  <property name="sessionFactory" ref="sessionFactory" />
</bean>

<amq:queue id="requestsQueue"
  physicalName="com.apress.springbatch.chapter11.partition.requests"/>
<amq:queue id="stagingQueue"
  physicalName="com.apress.springbatch.chapter11.partition.staging"/>
<amq:queue id="repliesQueue"
  physicalName="com.apress.springbatch.chapter11.partition.replies"/>

<bean id="placeholderProperties"
  class="org.springframework.beans.factory.config.PropertyPlaceholderConfigurer">
  <property name="location" value="classpath:batch.properties" />
  <property name="systemPropertiesModeName"
    value="SYSTEM_PROPERTIES_MODE_OVERRIDE" />
  <property name="ignoreUnresolvablePlaceholders" value="true" />
  <property name="order" value="1" />
</bean>
</beans>
```

Most of the launch-context.xml file should look familiar from other examples. However, let's call out a couple of beans specifically. The first is stepLocator. This instance of BeanFactoryStepLocator is used to query the current bean factory for any beans of type Step. For partitioning, Spring Batch uses it to find the remote step configurations located in remote Spring containers.

The other piece of the launch-context.xml file you need to look at is the configuration of the queues themselves. This example uses three ActiveMQ JMS queues. Fortunately, the ActiveMQ XSD makes it easy to configure them. All you need to do is configure the bean id and the physical name for each of the queues.

The configuration is now complete. Just as in the remote-chunking example, you use two Maven profiles to construct the two jar files required for this example. First, build using the mvn clean install -P listener command to create the jar file used by each of the worker JVMs. To build the jar file you use to execute the job, use the default profile via mvn clean install.

To execute the job, you need to execute three Java processes. The first two serve as the slave nodes for the job; execute them by running java -jar partitioning-0.0.1-listener-SNAPSHOT.jar using the jar you created with the -P listener option. With both of those nodes running, you can run the job with the command java -jar partitioning-0.0.1-SNAPSHOT.jar jobs/geocodeJob.xml geocodingJob. When the job completes, you can verify the results by looking at the Customers table in the database and verifying that everyone in the table has longitude and latitude values saved.

Using partitioning as a way to scale a Spring Batch job is a great way to take advantage of the computing power of multiple servers. This approach is different than remote chunking, but it provides its own set of benefits for remote processing.

Summary

One of the primary reasons for using Spring Batch is its ability to scale without having a large impact on your existing code base. Although you could write any of these features yourself, none of them are easy to implement well, and it doesn't make sense to reinvent the wheel. Spring Batch provides an excellent set of ways to scale jobs with a number of options.

This chapter looked at how to profile jobs to obtain information about where bottlenecks exist. You then worked through examples of each of the four options Spring Batch provides for scalability: parallel steps, multithreaded steps, remote chunking, and partitioning.

## CHAPTER 12

Testing Batch Processes

Testing: everyone's favorite part of programming. The funny thing is, like most things in life, once you get good at it, testing actually is fun. It allows you to be more productive. It provides a safety net for you to try new things. Programmatic tests also give you a test bed to try new technologies (most companies don't mind if you want to try something new in the tests but mind greatly if you try it in code that's going to production). You've spent the previous 10 chapters writing code without the ability to prove that any of it works. This chapter looks at how to exercise your code in a variety of ways so you can not only prove that it works as designed, but also provide a safety net for when you change it.

This chapter covers the following topics:

- *Unit tests with JUnit and Mockito*: You begin with a high-level overview of the JUnit and Mockito frameworks. Although you move past JUnit's base functionality in the later parts of the chapter, the concepts that Spring has incorporated into its testing apparatus are based in the JUnit conventions, so knowing them helps you understand what is going on in the more advanced tests. The chapter also covers how the mock object framework Mockito can help you unit-test the components you develop for your batch processes.

- *Integration testing with Spring's test framework*: Spring has done to testing what it's done to most other harder Java tasks: made it easy. It provides a collection of classes that allow you to easily test interactions with your various resources (databases, files, and so on) with minimal overhead. You learn how to use the Spring testing components to test various aspects of your Spring Batch jobs.

The most fundamental aspect of testing begins with unit testing, so the discussion begins there.

Unit Tests with JUnit and Mockito

Probably the easiest to write and perhaps the most valuable, unit tests are the most overlooked type of testing. Although the development done in this book hasn't taken a test-driven approach for a number of reasons, you're encouraged to do so in your own development. As a proven way to improve not only the quality of the software you produce but also the overall productivity of any individual developer and a team as a whole, the code encased in these tests is some of the most valuable you can produce. This section looks at how to use JUnit and Mockito to unit-test the components you develop for your batch processes.

What is a unit test? It's a test of a single, isolated component in a repeatable way. Let's break down that definition to understand how it applies to what you're trying to do:

- *A test of a single:* One. Unit tests are intended to test the smallest building blocks of your application. A single method is typically the scope of a unit test.

- *Isolated:* Dependencies can wreak havoc on the testing of a system. Yet all systems have dependencies. The goal of a unit test isn't to test your integration with each of these dependencies, but to instead test how your component works by itself.

- *In a repeatable way:* When you fire up a browser and click through your application, it isn't a repeatable exercise. You may enter different data each time. You may click the buttons in a slightly different order. Unit tests should be able to repeat the exact same scenario time and time again. This allows you to use them to regression-test as you make changes in your system.

The frameworks you use to execute the isolated testing of your components in a repeatable way are JUnit, Mockito, and the Spring framework. The first two are common, multipurpose frameworks that are useful for creating unit tests for your code. The Spring test utilities are helpful for testing more broad concerns including the integration of the different layers and even testing job execution from end to end (from a service or Spring Batch component to the database and back).

JUnit

Considered the gold standard for testing frameworks in Java,[1] JUnit is a simple framework that provides the ability to unit-test Java classes in a standard way. Whereas most frameworks you work with require add-ons to things like your IDE and build process, Maven and most Java IDEs have JUnit support built in with no additional configuration required. Entire books have been written on the topic of testing and using frameworks like JUnit, but it's important to quickly review these concepts. This section looks at JUnit and its most commonly used features.

The current version of JUnit as of the writing of this book is JUnit 4.8.2. Although each revision contains marginal improvements and bug fixes, the last major revision of the framework was the move from JUnit 3 to JUnit 4, which introduced annotations to configure test cases. Test cases? Let's step back a minute and go over how JUnit test are structured.

JUnit Lifecycle

JUnit tests are broken down into what are called *test cases*. Each test case is intended to test a particular piece of functionality, with the common divisor being at the class level. The common practice is to have at least one test case for each class. A test case is nothing more than a Java class configured with JUnit annotations to be executed by JUnit. In a test case exist both test methods and methods that are executed to set preconditions and clean up post conditions after each test or group of tests. Listing 12-1 shows a very basic JUnit test case.

Listing 12-1. A Basic JUnit Test Case

```
package com.apress.springbatch.chapter12;

import org.junit.Test;
import static org.junit.Assert.*;

public class StringTest {
```

---

[1] Or at least it won the Betamax versus VHS wars against frameworks like TestNG and others.

```
@Test

public void testStringEquals() {
    String michael = "Michael";
    String michael2 = michael;
    String michael3 = new String("Michael");
    String michael4 = "Michael";

    assertTrue(michael == michael2);
    assertFalse(michael == michael3);
    assertTrue(michael.equals(michael2));
    assertTrue(michael.equals(michael3));
    assertTrue(michael == michael4);
    assertTrue(michael.equals(michael4));
    }
}
```

There is nothing fancy about the unit test in Listing 12-1. All it does is prove that using == when comparing Strings isn't the same as using the .equals method. However, let's walk through the different pieces of the test. First, a JUnit test case a regular POJO. You aren't required to extend any particular class, and the only requirement that JUnit has for your class is that it have a no argument constructor.

In each test, you have one or more test methods (one in this case). Each test method is required to be public, to be void, and to take zero arguments. To indicate that a method is a test method to be executed by JUnit, you use the @Test annotation. JUnit executes each method annotated with the @Test annotation once during the execution of a given test.

The last piece of StringTest are the assert methods used in the test method. The test method has a simple flow. It begins by setting up the conditions required for this test, and then it executes the tests and validates the results at the same time using JUnit's assert methods. The methods of the org.junit.Assert class are used to validate the results of a given test scenario. In the case of StringTest in Listing 12-1, you're validating that calling the .equals method on a String object compares the contents of the string, whereas using == to compare two strings verifies that they're the same instance only.

Although this test is helpful, there are a couple other useful annotations that you should know about when using JUnit. The first two are related to the JUnit test lifecycle. JUnit allows you to configure methods to run before each test method and after each test method so that you can set up generic preconditions and do basic cleanup after each execution. To execute a method before each test method, you use the @Before annotation; @After indicates that the method should be executed after each test method.[2] Just like any test method, the @Before (setUp) and @After (tearDown) marked methods are required to be public, be void, and take no arguments. Typically, you create a new instance of an object to be tested in the method marked with @Before to prevent any residual effects from one test having an effect on another test. Figure 12-1 shows the lifecycle of a JUnit test case using the @Before, @Test, and @After annotations.

---

[2] These methods were called setUp and tearDown in previous versions of JUnit.

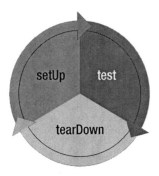

Figure 12-1. JUnit lifecycle

As Figure 12-1 shows, JUnit executes those three methods in sequence for each method identified with the @Test annotation until all the test methods in the test case have been executed. Listing 12-2 shows an example test case using all three of the discussed annotations.

Listing 12-2. Test of Foo

```
package com.apress.springbatch.chapter12;

import static org.junit.Assert.assertEquals;
import static org.junit.Assert.assertNotNull;

import org.junit.After;
import org.junit.Before;
import org.junit.Test;

public class FooTest {

    private Foo fooInstance;

    @Before
    public void setUp() {
        fooInstance = new Foo();
    }

    @Test
    public void testBar() {
        String results = fooInstance.bar();

        assertNotNull("Results were null", results);
        assertEquals("The test was not a success", "success", results);
    }

    @After
    public void tearDown() {
        fooInstance.close();
    }
}
```

JUnit provides a number of other variants on these features, including @BeforeClass to execute one-time setup for all the test methods in a given test class, @Ignore to indicate test methods and classes to skip, and @RunWith to indicate a class to run your test case other than the default used by JUnit. However, those are outside of the scope of this book. The goal of this section is to give you the tools required to be able to test your batch processes. Using just the @Before, @Test, and @After annotations along with the assert methods available on JUnit's Assert class, you can test the vast majority of scenarios required.

But there is a small catch. The earlier unit-test definition said that unit testing is the testing of components in isolation. How can you test a data access object (DAO) using JUnit when it depends on JDBC and a database? How about testing an ItemStream, which requires you to use Spring Batch components as some of its parameters? Mock objects fill this void, and you look at those next.

Mock Objects

It would be very easy to write software like the String object tested earlier, which has no dependencies. However, most systems are complex. Batch jobs can require dozens or more classes and depend on external systems including application servers, JMS middleware, and databases, just to name a few. All these moving parts can be difficult to manage and provide interactions that are outside the scope of a unit test. For example, when you want to test the business logic for one of your ItemProcessors, do you really need to test that Spring Batch is saving the context correctly to your database? That is outside the scope of a unit test. Don't get this wrong—that does need to be tested, and you look at it later in this chapter. However, to test your business logic, you don't need to exercise the various dependencies that your production system interacts with. You use mock objects to replace these dependencies in your testing environment and exercise your business logic without being effected by outside dependencies.

▓ **Note** Stubs are not mock objects. Stubs are hard coded implementations that are used in testing where mock objects are reusable constructs that allow the definition of the required behavior at run time.

Let's take a minute to call out that mock objects aren't stubs. *Stubs* are implementations that you write to replace various pieces of an application. Stubs contain hard-coded logic intended to mimic a particular behavior during execution. They aren't mock objects (no matter what they're named in your project)!

How do mock objects work? There are essentially two different approaches most mock object frameworks take: proxy based and class remapping. Because proxy-based mock objects are not only the most popular but the easiest to use, let's look at them first.

A *proxy object* is an object that is used to take the place of a real object. In the case of mock objects, a proxy object is used to imitate the real object your code is dependent on. You create a proxy object with the mocking framework and then set it on the object using either a setter or constructor. This points out an inherent issue with mocking using proxy objects: you have to be able to set up the dependency through an external means. In other words, you can't create the dependency by calling new MyObject() in your method, because there is no way to mock the object created by calling new MyObject().[3] This is

---

[3] This isn't 100% true. PowerMock lets you mock the new operator. You can find more information on PowerMock at http://code.google.com/p/powermock/.

one of the reasons Dependency Injection frameworks like Spring have taken off—they allow you to inject your proxy objects without modifying any code.

The second form of mocking is to remap the class file in the class loader. The mocking framework JMockit is the only framework I'm aware of that currently exploits this ability for mock objects. The concept is relatively new (because JDK 1.5 although JMockit supports JDK 1.4 thru other means as well) and is provided by the new java.lang.instrument.Insturmentation interface. You tell the classloader to remap the reference to the class file it loads. So, let's say you have a class MyDependency with the corresponding .class file MyDependency.class, and you want to mock it to use MyMock instead. By using this type of mock objects, you actually remap in the classloader the reference from MyDependency to MyMock.class. This allows you to mock objects that are created by using the new operator. Although this approach provides more power than the proxy-object approach because of its ability to inject literally any implementation into the classloader, it's also harder and more confusing to get going given the knowledge of classloaders you need in order to be able to use all its features.

Mockito is a popular proxy-based mock-object framework that provides a large amount of flexibility coupled with an expressive syntax. It allows you to create easy-to-understand unit tests with relative ease. Let's take a look.

Mockito

Around 2008, with EasyMock as the dominant mocking framework, a couple of guys took a look at the framework and asked some questions. EasyMock is a proxy-based mock-object framework that requires the model, record, play, and verify. First you record the behavior you need. Then you execute the functionality under test, and finally you verify all the executions that you previously recorded. However, why do you need to define all the possible interactions for an object to go through? And why do you need to confirm that all the interactions occurred? Mockito allows you to mock the behaviors you care about and verify only the behaviors that matter. In this section you look at some of the functionality available with Mockito and use it to test Spring Batch components.

Although JUnit is included by default any time you use Maven as your build system, for you to use Mockito, you need to add its dependency. Listing 12-3 shows the dependency required for Mockito.

Listing 12-3. Maven Dependency for Mocktio

```
...
<dependency>
    <groupId>org.mockito</groupId>
    <artifactId>mockito-all</artifactId>
    <version>1.8.5</version>
    <scope>test</scope>
</dependency>
...
```

To see how Mockito works, let's look at one of the classes you developed for the statement job in Chapter 10. The CustomerStatementReader you created to build the Statement object is a prime candidate to use mock objects, with its dependencies on an external ItemReader as well as a DAO. To refresh your memory, Listing 12-4 shows the code from that ItemReader.

Listing 12-4. CustomerStatementReader

```
package com.apress.springbatch.statement.reader;

import org.springframework.batch.item.ItemReader;
```

```
import org.springframework.batch.item.ParseException;
import org.springframework.batch.item.UnexpectedInputException;

import com.apress.springbatch.statement.dao.TickerDao;
import com.apress.springbatch.statement.domain.Customer;
import com.apress.springbatch.statement.domain.Statement;

public class CustomerStatementReader implements ItemReader<Statement> {

    private ItemReader<Customer> customerReader;
    private TickerDao tickerDao;

    public Statement read() throws Exception, UnexpectedInputException,
            ParseException {

        Customer customer = customerReader.read();

        if(customer == null) {
            return null;
        } else {
            Statement statement = new Statement();

            statement.setCustomer(customer);
            statement.setSecurityTotal(
                tickerDao.getTotalValueForCustomer(customer.getId()));
            statement.setStocks(tickerDao.getStocksForCustomer(customer.getId()));

            return statement;
        }
    }

    public void setCustomerReader(ItemReader<Customer> customerReader) {
        this.customerReader = customerReader;
    }

    public void setTickerDao(TickerDao tickerDao) {
        this.tickerDao = tickerDao;
    }
}
```

The method you're testing for this class is obviously read(). This method requires two external dependencies: an instance of an ItemReader (remember, you used a JdbcCursorItemReader in the actual job) and a reference to your TickerDao. To test this method, you have two test methods, one for each of the method's two execution branches (one for when the customer is null and one for when it isn't).

To start this test, let's create the test-case class and the @Before method so your objects are built for later use. Listing 12-5 shows the test case with the setup method identified with the @Before annotation and three class attributes.

Listing 12-5. CustomerStatementReaderTest

```
package com.apress.springbatch.statement.reader;
```

```
import static org.junit.Assert.assertEquals;
import static org.junit.Assert.assertNull;
import static org.mockito.Mockito.when;

import java.math.BigDecimal;
import java.util.ArrayList;

import org.junit.Before;
import org.junit.Test;
import org.mockito.Mock;
import org.mockito.MockitoAnnotations;
import org.springframework.batch.item.ItemReader;

import com.apress.springbatch.statement.dao.TickerDao;
import com.apress.springbatch.statement.domain.Customer;
import com.apress.springbatch.statement.domain.Statement;
import com.apress.springbatch.statement.domain.Transaction;

public class CustomerStatementReaderTest {

    private CustomerStatementReader reader;
    @Mock
    private TickerDao tickerDao;
    @Mock
    private ItemReader<Customer> customerReader;

    @Before
    public void setUp() {
        MockitoAnnotations.initMocks(this);

        reader = new CustomerStatementReader();
        reader.setCustomerReader(customerReader);
        reader.setTickerDao(tickerDao);
    }
    ...
}
```

The three attributes of the test class are the class under test (CustomerStatementReader) and the two dependencies (TickerDao and the ItemReader). By using the @Mock annotation, you tell Mockito that these attributes should be mocked for your test. When the test is executed, Mockito creates a proxy for each of these for your test to use.

In the setup method, you do two things. First you initialize the mocks with Mockito's MockitoAnnotations.initMocks method. This method initializes all the objects you previously indicated with a mock object for you to use. This is a quick and easy way to create the mock objects you need in the future.

The next thing you do in the setup method is create a new instance of the class to test. By creating this class here, you can be sure that each test method contains a clean instance of the class under test. This prevents any residual state in the test object from one method from having an impact on your other test methods. After you create CustomerStatementReader, you inject the mock objects the same way Spring would do it for you on bootstrapping the application.

Because you now have a new instance of the object under test and a fresh set of mock objects to satisfy your dependencies on the Spring Batch framework as well as the database, you can write your test methods. The first one, which tests when no customers are returned from the delegate, is very easy; see Listing 12-6.

Listing 12-6. testReadNoCustomers()

```
...
@Test
public void testReadNoCustomers() throws Exception {
       assertNull(reader.read());
    }
...
```

Wait, that's it? What happened? There is a lot more happening under the covers of this extremely simple test method than meets the eye. When you execute this method, CustomerStatementReader's read method is called. In there, Mockito returns null when the mock ItemReader's read method is called on line 40. By default, if you don't tell Mockito what to return when a method is called on a mock object, it returns a type-appropriate value (null for objects, false for booleans, -1 for ints, and so on). Because you want your mock object to return null for this test, you don't need to tell Mockito to do anything for you. Aftre Mockito returns null from the ItemReader you injected, the logic returns null as required. Your test verifies that the reader returns null with JUnit's Assert.assertNull method.

The second test method you need to write for the read method of CustomerStatementReader tests that the Statement object is being built correctly when a customer is returned. In this scenario, because you aren't working with a database, you need to tell Mockito what to return when tickerDao.getTotalValueForCustomer and tickerDao.getStocksForCustomer are called with the customer's id. Listing 12-7 shows the code for the testReadWithCustomer method.

Listing 12-7. testReadWtihCustomer

```
...
@SuppressWarnings("serial")
@Test
    public void testReadWithCustomer() throws Exception {
        Customer customer = new Customer();
        customer.setId(5l);

        when(customerReader.read()).thenReturn(customer);
        when(tickerDao.getTotalValueForCustomer(5l)).thenReturn(
                new BigDecimal("500.00"));
        when(tickerDao.getStocksForCustomer(5l)).thenReturn(
                new ArrayList<Transaction>() {
                    {
                        add(new Transaction());
                    }
                });

        Statement result = reader.read();

        assertEquals(customer, result.getCustomer());
        assertEquals(500.00, result.getSecurityTotal().doubleValue(), 0);
        assertEquals(1, result.getStocks().size());
    }
...
```

The testReadWithCustomer method is a good example of how to work with Mockito. You begin by creating any data you need. In this case, you create the Customer object that your mock objects returns. Then you tell Mockito what to return for each of the calls you care about: the call to customerReader.read() and the two calls to tickerDao. In the listing, you set the customer id to be 5 and tell Mockito to expect that 5 is the customer id passed to the two tickerDao calls. To tell this to Mockito, you use the Mockito.when method to record what method call you care about. Only when these scenarios occur does Mockito return what you specify in the thenReturn call.

With the mocks setup, you then execute the method you're testing (reader.read() in this case). With the results you receive from that method call, you can verify that your Statement object is built as you expect based on the data it received.

How does this provide you with a safety net? Simple. Let's say that you change CustomerStatementReader to pass the id of the account instead of the id of the customer to one of the tickerDao calls. The test fails if this occurs, indicating to you that a change that is incompatible with your expectations has occurred and needs to be addressed.

Unit tests are the foundation of a solid system. They not only provide the ability to make the changes you need without fear, but also force you to keep your code concise and serve as executable documentation for your system. However, you don't build a foundation just to look at it. You build on top of it. In the next section, you expand your testing capabilities.

Integration Tests with Spring Classes

The previous section discussed unit tests and their benefits. Unit tests, however useful they are, do have their limits. Integration testing takes your automated testing to the next level by bootstrapping your application and running it with the same dependencies you tried so hard to extract previously. This section looks at how to use Spring's integration test facilities to test interactions with various Spring beans, databases, and finally batch resources.

General Integration Testing with Spring

Integration testing is about testing different pieces talking to each other. Does the DAO get wired correctly, and is the Hibernate mapping correct so you can save the data you need? Does your service retrieve the correct beans from a given factory? These and other cases are tested when you write integration tests. But how do you do that without having to set up all the infrastructure and make sure that infrastructure is available everywhere you want to run these tests? Luckily, you don't have to.

The two primary use cases for integration testing with the core Spring integration-testing facilities are to test database interaction and to test Spring bean interaction (was a service wired up correctly, and so on). To test this, let's look at the TickerDao you mocked in the unit tests previously (CustomerStatementReader). However, this time, you let Spring wire up TickerDao itself, and you use an in-memory instance of HSQLDB[4] as your database so that you can execute the tests anywhere, anytime. HSQLDB is a 100% Java implemented database that is great for integration testing because it's lightweight to spool up an instance. To get started, let's look at how to configure your test environment.

---

[4] It's important to note that using JDBC and switching database types can be difficult due to differences in implemting SQL between databases. In this case, the only difference should be the create statements, for which you can use separate scripts.

Configuring the Testing Environment

To isolate your test execution from external resource requirements (specific database servers, and so on), you should configure a couple of things. Specifically, you should use a test configuration for your database that creates an instance of HSQLDB for you in memory. To do that, you need to do the following:

1. Update your POM file to include the HSQLDB database drivers.

2. Refactor the inclusion of Spring context files to allow for easier overriding of configurations for testing.

3. Configure test-specific properties.

Let's get started by adding the HSQLDB drivers to your POM file.[5] The specific dependency you need to add is shown in Listing 12-8.

Listing 12-8. HSQLDB's Database Driver Dependency

```
...
<dependency>
    <groupId>hsqldb</groupId>
    <artifactId>hsqldb</artifactId>
    <version>1.8.0.7</version>
</dependency>
...
```

The next step is to do a bit of refactoring. Up to this point, you've structured your Spring configuration files in a way that works great for batch jobs. You've put common components in the launch-context.xml file and had a job-specific XML file for each job after that. However, you run into an issue here: you currently have the properties hard-coded in launch-context.xml to be batch.properties, which is configured for MySQL.

To make this more flexible, you restructure the XML files so that there are three instead of two. The first is the normal launch-context.xml file without the placeholderProperties bean. The second is the normal statementJob.xml file without the import statement for the launch-context.xml file. The new file you create joins the three and configures the properties file location. Listing 12-9 shows the contents of the new configuration file, job-context.xml.

Listing 12-9. job-context.xml

```
<?xml version="1.0" encoding="UTF-8"?>
<beans xmlns="http://www.springframework.org/schema/beans"
  xmlns:xsi="http://www.w3.org/2001/XMLSchema-instance"
  xmlns:context="http://www.springframework.org/schema/context"
  xsi:schemaLocation="http://www.springframework.org/schema/beans
    http://www.springframework.org/schema/beans/spring-beans-3.0.xsd
    http://www.springframework.org/schema/context
```

---

[5] For the record, if you're using the POM file that comes with the Spring Batch CLI Archetype, you don't need to do this—the drivers are already included for Spring Batch's own testing. However, because you've used MySQL for all examples thus far, you may need to add them back.

```
        http://www.springframework.org/schema/context/spring-context-3.0.xsd">

    <import resource="classpath*:/launch-context.xml"/>
    <import resource="classpath*:/jobs/statementJob.xml"/>

    <bean id="placeholderProperties"
      class="org.springframework.beans.factory.config.PropertyPlaceholderConfigurer">
      <property name="location" value="classpath:batch.properties" />
      <property name="systemPropertiesModeName"
        value="SYSTEM_PROPERTIES_MODE_OVERRIDE" />
      <property name="ignoreUnresolvablePlaceholders" value="true" />
      <property name="order" value="1" />
    </bean>

    <bean id="dataSourceInitializer"
      class="org.springframework.jdbc.datasource.init.DataSourceInitializer">
      <property name="dataSource" ref="dataSource"/>
      <property name="enabled" value="true"/>
      <property name="databasePopulator">
        <bean class="org.springframework.jdbc.datasource.init.ResourceDatabasePopulator">
          <property name="continueOnError" value="false"/>
          <property name="ignoreFailedDrops" value="false"/>
          <property name="sqlScriptEncoding" value="UTF-8"/>
          <property name="scripts">
            <list>
              <value type="org.springframework.core.io.Resource">classpath:schema.sql</value>
            </list>
          </property>
        </bean>
      </property>
    </bean>
</beans>
```

The advantage of this configuration structure is that you can override it in test. The job-context.xml file is located in your <PROJECT>/src/main/resources directory. In <PROJECT>/src/test/resources, you create an identical file called test-context.xml. However, instead of referring to batch.properties for the location, you refer to test-batch.properties. The other addition to the test-context.xml file is the configuration of a utility that comes with Spring 3 that is a huge help in integration testing: DataSourceIntializer.

The test-batch.properties file mentioned earlier contains the required information for your HSQLDB instance and is located in the same directory as test-context.xml. Listing 12-10 shows the contents of test-batch.properties.

Listing 12-10. test-batch.properties

```
batch.jdbc.driver=org.hsqldb.jdbcDriver
batch.jdbc.url=jdbc:hsqldb:mem:testdb;sql.enforce_strict_size=true
batch.jdbc.user=sa
batch.jdbc.password=
batch.schema=
batch.schema.script=org/springframework/batch/core/schema-hsqldb.sql
```

The test-batch.properties file defines the information used by the datasource to connect to your database as well as a list of scripts to execute on startup. In this case, the HSQLDB connection information is very straightforward, and you have two scripts to run on startup: schema-hsqldb.sql creates the Spring Batch tables for you, and schema.sql creates the statement tables.

With the test environment configured, you can begin to write your first integration test. The next section looks at how to write an integration test for TickerDao.

Writing an Integration Test

Writing an integration test with Spring is very simple. You need to do three things:

1. Tell Spring the location from which to load your context.

2. Extend AbstractTransactionalJUnit4SpringContextTests (yes, that really is the name of the class) to get the transactional help that Spring provides.

3. Tell Spring what values to wire.

After you've done these three things, you can use your code just as if it was in your application. Let's start by telling Spring the location from which to load your context. To do this, you use Spring's @ContextConfiguration annotation at the class level. For your purposes, this annotation takes a single attribute, location, which tells Spring where to find the test-context.xml file.

One of the main advantages of using the Spring testing infrastructure is the transaction benefits it provides. It can be very helpful to be able to run a test in a transaction that rolls back after each test method is executed. This way, your database begins and ends each test case in the exact same state. By extending Spring's AbstractTransactionalJUnit4SpringContextTests class, you get that functionality with no further work. Listing 12-11 shows the shell of the integration test with the context location configured and the shell extending the correct class.

Listing 12-11. TickerDaoIntegrationTest Shell

```
package com.apress.springbatch.statement.dao;

import org.springframework.beans.factory.annotation.Autowired;
import org.springframework.test.context.ContextConfiguration;
import
  org.springframework.test.context.junit4.AbstractTransactionalJUnit4SpringContextTests;

@ContextConfiguration(locations = {"/test-context.xml"})
public class TickerDaoIntegrationTest extends
    AbstractTransactionalJUnit4SpringContextTests {

    ...
}
```

Now, because you're going to test TickerDao (the TickerDaoJdbc class, to be exact), you need Spring to wire it up and inject it into your test so it's available. To do this, you use Spring's @Autowired annotation to identify any class attribute that you want Spring to wire for you. Because all you need for this test is for TickerDao itself to be wired, that is all you need to indicate to Spring.

The rest of an integration test with Spring is the same as it would be if it was a unit test. You prepare any data required for the test, execute the code being tested, and finally use JUnit's assertions to validate what happened. The code in Listing 12-12 tests the saving and retrieving of a ticker using TickerDao.

Listing 12-12. Testing the Saving and Retrieving of a Ticker Using TickerDao

```java
package com.apress.springbatch.statement.dao;

import static org.junit.Assert.assertEquals;
import static org.junit.Assert.assertNotNull;
import static org.junit.Assert.assertTrue;

import java.math.BigDecimal;

import org.junit.Test;
import org.springframework.beans.factory.annotation.Autowired;
import org.springframework.test.context.ContextConfiguration;
import
  org.springframework.test.context.junit4.AbstractTransactionalJUnit4SpringContextTests;

import com.apress.springbatch.statement.domain.Ticker;

@ContextConfiguration(locations = {"/test-context.xml"})
public class TickerDaoIntegrationTest extends
    AbstractTransactionalJUnit4SpringContextTests {

    @Autowired
    private TickerDao tickerDao;

    @Test
    public void testTickerSaveRoundTrip() {
        Ticker ticker = new Ticker();
        ticker.setPrice(new BigDecimal("222.22"));
        ticker.setTicker("MTM");

        tickerDao.saveTicker(ticker);

        Ticker result = tickerDao.findTickerBySymbol("MTM");

        assertNotNull(result);
        assertEquals(222.22, result.getPrice().doubleValue(), 0);
        assertEquals("MTM", result.getTicker());
        assertTrue(result.getId() >= 0);
    }
}
```

The test shown in Listing 12-12 begins by creating a new Ticker object to be saved. You then use the tickerDao provided by Spring to save it and subsequently retrieve it. Finally, you validate that the data you saved matches the data that was retrieved and that the id was set, signifying that it truly was saved to the database.

When you execute this test, a new instance of HSQLDB is launched, the database schema is created, and your objects are bootstrapped and injected, all prior the execution of the test method. The test method is executed in its own transaction, which is rolled back at the end of the test, leaving the database pristine for the next test method to be executed.

Integration tests like testTickerSaveRoundTrip can be hugely valuable when you're developing a system. The ability to determine if things are being wired correctly, if SQL is correct, and even if the order of operations between components of a system is correct can provide considerable security when you're dealing with complex systems.

The final piece of testing with Spring Batch is testing the Spring Batch components themselves. ItemReaders, steps, and even entire jobs can be tested with the tools provided by Spring. The final section of this chapter looks at how to use those components and test pieces of your batch process.

Testing Spring Batch

Although the ability to test components like a DAO or a service is definitely needed when you're working with robust batch jobs, working with the Spring Batch framework introduces a collection of additional complexities into your code that need to be addressed in order to build a robust test suite. This section looks at how to handle testing Spring Batch–specific components, including elements that depend on custom scopes, Spring Batch steps, and even complete jobs.

Testing Step-Scoped Beans

As you've seen in many examples throughout this book, the step scope defined by Spring Batch for your Spring Beans is a very helpful tool. However, when you're writing integration tests for components that use the step scope, you run into an issue: if you're executing those components outside the scope of a step, how do those dependencies get resolved? In this section, you look at the two ways Spring Batch offers to simulate that a bean is being executed in the scope of a step.

You've seen in the past how using the step scope allows Spring Batch to inject runtime values from the job and/or step context into your beans. Previous examples include the injection of an input or output file name, or criteria for a particular database query. In each of those examples, Spring Batch obtains the values from the JobExecution or the StepExecution. If you aren't running the job in a step, you don't have either of those executions. Spring Batch provides two different ways to emulate the execution in a step so that those values can be injected. The first approach uses a TestExecutionListener.

TestExecutionListener is a Spring API that allows you to define things to occur before or after a test method. Unlike using JUnit's @Before and @After annotations, using Spring's TestExecutionListener allows you to inject behavior across all the methods in a test case in a more reusable way. Although Spring provides three useful implementations of the TestExecutionListener interface (DependencyInjectionTestExecutionListener, DirtiesContextTestExecutionListener, and TransactionalTestExecutionListener), Spring Batch provides one that handles what you're looking for: StepScopeTestExecutionListener.

StepScopeTestExecutionListener provides two features you need. First, it uses a factory method from your test case to obtain a StepExecution and uses the one returned as the context for the current test method. Second, it provides a StepContext for the life of each test method. Figure 12-2 shows the flow of a test being executed using StepScopeTestExecutionListener.

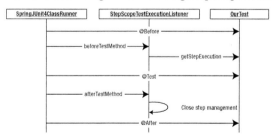

Figure 12-2. Test execution using StepScopeTestExecutionListener

As you can see, the factory method you create in the test case (getStepExecution) is called before each test method to obtain a new StepExecution. If there is no factory method, Spring Batch uses a default StepExecution.

To test this, you configure a FlatFileItemReader to obtain the location of the file to read from the jobParameters. First let's look at the configuration of the ItemReader to test and the resource you use (see Listing 12-13).

Listing 12-13. Car File's ItemReader Configuration

```
...
<beans:bean id="carFileReader"
  class="org.springframework.batch.item.file.FlatFileItemReader" scope="step">
  <beans:property name="resource" value="#{jobParameters[carFile]}"/>
  <beans:property name="lineMapper">
    <beans:bean
      class="org.springframework.batch.item.file.mapping.PassThroughLineMapper"/>
  </beans:property>
</beans:bean>
...
```

Listing 12-13 is a simple FlatFileItemReader that is configured to use the step scope so you can set the name of the input file at runtime via the job parameters. To test this ItemReader, you begin the same way you did with TickerDaoIntegrationTest by telling Spring the location of the context configuration using the @ContextConfiguration annotation. However, with this test, you expand the use of annotations to include the following:

- @TestExecutionListeners: Using DependencyInjectionTestExecutionListener eliminates the need to extend any specific class from Spring to obtain the ability to have your beans wired and injected via Spring. StepScopeTestExecutionListener calls getStepExecution to obtain a StepExecution complete with any parameters that Spring Batch would inject for you.

- @RunWith: The listeners in the previous item are a Spring concept unknown to JUnit. So, you need to use Spring's test runner instead of the standard JUnit one.

For this test to work, you need a test file for the ItemReader to read. For test purposes, it's a good idea to include any test files in the <PROJECT>/src/test/resources directory so they're available wherever the tests are run. In this case, you include a CSV file named carfile.csv in the directory <project_home>/src/test/resources/data. The contents of the file are shown in Listing 12-14.

Listing 12-14. carFile.csv

```
1987,Nissan,Sentra
1991,Plymouth,Laser
1995,Mercury,Cougar
2000,Infiniti,QX4
2001,Infiniti,QX4
```

With the environment configured using the same contexts you used in the previous example and the new ItemReader configured as well as a sample input file supplied for testing, you can put together the integration test. This integration test loops through the file, reading each line until the file is complete (five times, in this case). You verify that each record is returned until the final (sixth) call to the reader is null, indicating the input has been exhausted. Listing 12-15 shows the integration test.

Listing 12-15. CarFileReaderIntegrationTest

```java
package com.apress.springbatch.chapter12;

import static org.junit.Assert.assertEquals;
import static org.junit.Assert.assertNull;

import java.util.ArrayList;
import java.util.List;

import org.junit.Test;
import org.junit.runner.RunWith;
import org.springframework.batch.core.JobParameters;
import org.springframework.batch.core.JobParametersBuilder;
import org.springframework.batch.core.StepExecution;
import org.springframework.batch.item.ExecutionContext;
import org.springframework.batch.item.ItemReader;
import org.springframework.batch.item.ItemStream;
import org.springframework.batch.test.MetaDataInstanceFactory;
import org.springframework.batch.test.StepScopeTestExecutionListener;
import org.springframework.beans.factory.annotation.Autowired;
import org.springframework.test.context.ContextConfiguration;
import org.springframework.test.context.TestExecutionListeners;
import org.springframework.test.context.junit4.SpringJUnit4ClassRunner;
import org.springframework.test.context.support.DependencyInjectionTestExecutionListener;

@ContextConfiguration(locations = { "/test-context.xml" })
@TestExecutionListeners({ DependencyInjectionTestExecutionListener.class,
        StepScopeTestExecutionListener.class })
@RunWith(SpringJUnit4ClassRunner.class)
public class CarFileReaderIntegrationTest {

    @Autowired
    private ItemReader<String> carFileReader;

    @SuppressWarnings("serial")
    private List<String> records = new ArrayList<String>() {{
        add("1987,Nissan,Sentra");
        add("1991,Plymouth,Laser");
        add("1995,Mercury,Cougar");
        add("2000,Infiniti,QX4");
        add("2001,Infiniti,QX4");
    }};

    public StepExecution getStepExecution() {
        JobParameters jobParams = new JobParametersBuilder().addString(
                "carFile", "classpath:/data/carfile.txt").toJobParameters();

        return MetaDataInstanceFactory.createStepExecution(jobParams);
    }
```

```
@Test
public void testCarFileReader() throws Exception {
    ((ItemStream) carFileReader).open(new ExecutionContext());

    for(int i = 0; i < 5; i++) {
        assertEquals(carFileReader.read(), records.get(i));
    }

    assertNull(carFileReader.read());
}
}
```

CarFileReaderIntegrationTest uses a facility you haven't seen up to now. MetaDataInstanceFactory is a class provided by Spring Batch for creating mocks of the Spring Batch domain objects. Under most situations, I would strongly recommend using just Mockito to limit the coupling between your unit tests and Spring; but in this case, things are a bit different.

Spring Batch requires a StepExecution object. However, what it does with it is rather complex, and to mock that with Mockito would require you to have knowledge of the inner workings of Spring Batch. This type of situation isn't something you want to mock using Mockito, so you use Spring's MetaDataInstanceFactory to create the mock instead.

As mentioned earlier, there are two ways to test a Spring Batch component that is defined in the step scope. The first, being the listener approach you just saw, is non-invasive and lets you apply the step scope to all the test methods in your test case. But if you only need it for one or two of the test methods in your test case, Spring Batch provides a utility to wrap your execution in a step. Testing the same component, carFileReader, you can execute it in the scope of a step by using StepScopeTestUtils. Listing 12-16 shows the unit test updated to use StepScopeTestUtils instead of the listeners to simulate a step.

Listing 12-16. *Using StepScopeTestUtils*

```
package com.apress.springbatch.chapter12;

import static org.junit.Assert.assertEquals;

import java.util.concurrent.Callable;

import org.junit.Test;
import org.junit.runner.RunWith;
import org.springframework.batch.core.JobParameters;
import org.springframework.batch.core.JobParametersBuilder;
import org.springframework.batch.core.StepExecution;
import org.springframework.batch.item.ExecutionContext;
import org.springframework.batch.item.ItemReader;
import org.springframework.batch.item.ItemStream;
import org.springframework.batch.test.MetaDataInstanceFactory;
import org.springframework.batch.test.StepScopeTestUtils;
import org.springframework.beans.factory.annotation.Autowired;
import org.springframework.test.context.ContextConfiguration;
import org.springframework.test.context.TestExecutionListeners;
import org.springframework.test.context.junit4.SpringJUnit4ClassRunner;
import
  org.springframework.test.context.support.DependencyInjectionTestExecutionListener;
```

```
@ContextConfiguration(locations = { "/test-context.xml" })
@TestExecutionListeners({ DependencyInjectionTestExecutionListener.class })
@RunWith(SpringJUnit4ClassRunner.class)
public class CarFileReaderIntegrationTest {

    @Autowired
    private ItemReader<String> carFileReader;

    public StepExecution getStepExecution() {
        JobParameters jobParams = new JobParametersBuilder().addString(
                "carFile", "classpath:/data/carfile.txt").toJobParameters();

        return MetaDataInstanceFactory.createStepExecution(jobParams);
    }

    @Test
    public void testCarFileReader() throws Exception {
        StepExecution execution = getStepExecution();

        Integer readCount =
            StepScopeTestUtils.doInStepScope(execution, new Callable<Integer>() {

            @Override
            public Integer call() throws Exception {
                ((ItemStream) carFileReader).open(new ExecutionContext());

                int i = 0;

                while(carFileReader.read() != null) { i++; }

                return i;
            }
        });

        assertEquals(readCount.intValue(), 5);
    }
}
```

The StepScopeTestUtils object contains a single utility method called doInStepScope, as shown in Listing 12-16. This method accepts a StepExecution and a Callable implementation. When the test is executed, StepScopeTestUtils addresses the runtime injection, as Spring Batch normally would, and then executes the Callable implementation, returning the result. In this case, the Callable implementation counts the number of records in your test file and returns the number for you to validate that it's correct.

Integration tests of this nature can be very useful to test custom developed components such as custom ItemReaders and ItemWriters. However, as you can see, the value of testing Spring Batch's own components is minimal at best. Rest assured, it has test coverage for these very things. Instead, it may be more useful to test your batch jobs by executing an entire step. The next section looks at the tools Spring Batch provides to make that happen.

Testing a Step

Jobs are broken into steps. This book has established that. Each step is an independent piece of functionality that can be executed with minimal impact on other steps. Because of the inherent decoupling of steps with a batch job, steps become prime candidates for testing. In this section, you look at how to test a Spring Batch step in its entirety.

In the step scope–based examples in the previous section, you tested the ItemReader of a job that reads in a file and writes out the exact same file. This single-step job is the job you use now to demonstrate how to test the execution of a single step in Spring Batch. To begin, let's look at the configuration for the job; Listing 12-17 has the XML for the entire carJob.

Listing 12-17. carJob.xml

```xml
<?xml version="1.0" encoding="UTF-8"?>
<beans:beans xmlns="http://www.springframework.org/schema/batch"
  xmlns:beans="http://www.springframework.org/schema/beans"
  xmlns:util="http://www.springframework.org/schema/beans"
  xmlns:xsi="http://www.w3.org/2001/XMLSchema-instance"
  xsi:schemaLocation="http://www.springframework.org/schema/beans
    http://www.springframework.org/schema/beans/spring-beans-3.0.xsd
    http://www.springframework.org/schema/util
    http://www.springframework.org/schema/util/spring-util.xsd
    http://www.springframework.org/schema/batch
    http://www.springframework.org/schema/batch/spring-batch-2.1.xsd">

  <beans:bean id="carFileReader"
    class="org.springframework.batch.item.file.FlatFileItemReader" scope="step">
    <beans:property name="resource" value="#{jobParameters[carFile]}"/>
    <beans:property name="lineMapper">
      <beans:bean
        class="org.springframework.batch.item.file.mapping.PassThroughLineMapper"/>
    </beans:property>
  </beans:bean>

  <beans:bean id="carFileWriter"
    class="org.springframework.batch.item.file.FlatFileItemWriter" scope="step">
    <beans:property name="resource" value="#{jobParameters[outputFile]}"/>
    <beans:property name="lineAggregator">
      <beans:bean
        class="org.springframework.batch.item.file.transform.PassThroughLineAggregator"/>
    </beans:property>
  </beans:bean>

  <job id="carJob">
    <step id="carProcessingStep">
      <tasklet>
        <chunk reader="carFileReader" writer="carFileWriter" commit-interval="10"/>
      </tasklet>
    </step>
  </job>
</beans:beans>
```

carJob uses a FlatFileItemReader to read in a file whose location is passed in at runtime via the job parameters. It passes the input to a FlatFileItemWriter that writes the output to a file whose location is also provided at runtime via the job parameters. These two components are used in a single step to make up your job.

To execute this step via an integration test, the test is structured very much like CarFileReaderIntegrationTest shown in Listing 12-17. You use annotations to tell Spring where to find your context configuration files and what to inject, and you configure the test to be executed via SpringJUnit4ClassRunner. You even build your own JobParameters object to pass in to the job. But that is where the similarities end.

To execute a step, you use another utility provided by Spring Batch: JobLauncherTestUtils. This utility class provides a number of methods for launching both steps and jobs in a variety of ways (with parameters, without parameters, with an execution context, without, and so on). When you execute a step, you receive the JobExecution back, in which you can inspect what happened in the job. Listing 12-18 has the code to test carProcessingStep.

Listing 12-18. Testing carProcessingStep

```
package com.apress.springbatch.chapter12;

import static org.junit.Assert.assertEquals;
import static org.springframework.batch.test.AssertFile.assertFileEquals;

import org.junit.Test;
import org.junit.runner.RunWith;
import org.springframework.batch.core.BatchStatus;
import org.springframework.batch.core.ExitStatus;
import org.springframework.batch.core.JobExecution;
import org.springframework.batch.core.JobParameters;
import org.springframework.batch.core.JobParametersBuilder;
import org.springframework.batch.core.StepExecution;
import org.springframework.batch.test.JobLauncherTestUtils;
import org.springframework.beans.factory.annotation.Autowired;
import org.springframework.core.io.ClassPathResource;
import org.springframework.core.io.FileSystemResource;
import org.springframework.test.context.ContextConfiguration;
import org.springframework.test.context.TestExecutionListeners;
import org.springframework.test.context.junit4.SpringJUnit4ClassRunner;
import
   org.springframework.test.context.support.DependencyInjectionTestExecutionListener;

@ContextConfiguration(locations = { "/test-context.xml" })
@TestExecutionListeners({ DependencyInjectionTestExecutionListener.class })
@RunWith(SpringJUnit4ClassRunner.class)
public class CarProcessingStepIntegrationTest {

    private static final String OUTPUT_FILE = "/"
            + System.getProperty("java.io.tmpdir") + "carOutput.txt";
    private static final String INPUT_FILE = "/data/carfile.txt";
    @Autowired
    private JobLauncherTestUtils jobLauncherUtils;
```

```
@Test
public void testCarProcessingStep() throws Exception {
    assertEquals(BatchStatus.COMPLETED,
            jobLauncherUtils.launchStep("carProcessingStep", getParams())
                    .getStatus());

    assertFileEquals(new ClassPathResource(INPUT_FILE),
            new FileSystemResource(OUTPUT_FILE));
}

private JobParameters getParams() {
    return new JobParametersBuilder().addString("carFile", INPUT_FILE)
            .addString("outputFile", "file:/" + OUTPUT_FILE)
            .toJobParameters();
}
}
```

As mentioned, the structure of this test should be familiar. It's the same as you've used for the past few tests. However, a few aspects are interesting for this test. First is the bean jobLauncherUtils. This is the utility class mentioned earlier. Spring autowires it into your test and autowires its own dependencies to things like a datasource as well as a job launcher. Because of JobLauncherTestUtils' need to be autowired, you need to be sure to add it to your test-context.xml file. Listing 12-19 shows the contents of the test-context.xml file for this test.

Listing 12-19. test-context.xml

```xml
<?xml version="1.0" encoding="UTF-8"?>
<beans xmlns="http://www.springframework.org/schema/beans"
  xmlns:xsi="http://www.w3.org/2001/XMLSchema-instance"
  xmlns:context="http://www.springframework.org/schema/context"
  xmlns:util="http://www.springframework.org/schema/beans"
  xsi:schemaLocation="http://www.springframework.org/schema/beans
    http://www.springframework.org/schema/beans/spring-beans-3.0.xsd
    http://www.springframework.org/schema/util
    http://www.springframework.org/schema/util/spring-util.xsd
    http://www.springframework.org/schema/context
    http://www.springframework.org/schema/context/spring-context-2.5.xsd">

<import resource="launch-context.xml"/>
<import resource="jobs/carJob.xml"/>

<bean id="placeholderProperties"
  class="org.springframework.beans.factory.config.PropertyPlaceholderConfigurer">
  <property name="location" value="classpath:test-batch.properties" />
  <property name="systemPropertiesModeName"
    value="SYSTEM_PROPERTIES_MODE_OVERRIDE" />
  <property name="ignoreUnresolvablePlaceholders" value="true" />
  <property name="order" value="1" />
</bean>

<bean id="jobLauncherUtils" class="org.springframework.batch.test.JobLauncherTestUtils"/>
```

```
<bean id="dataSourceInitializer"
    class="org.springframework.jdbc.datasource.init.DataSourceInitializer">
    <property name="dataSource" ref="dataSource"/>
    <property name="enabled" value="true"/>
    <property name="databasePopulator">
        <bean class="org.springframework.jdbc.datasource.init.ResourceDatabasePopulator">
            <property name="continueOnError" value="false"/>
            <property name="ignoreFailedDrops" value="false"/>
            <property name="sqlScriptEncoding" value="UTF-8"/>
            <property name="scripts">
                <list>
                    <value type="org.springframework.core.io.Resource">
                        ${batch.schema.script}
                    </value>
                </list>
            </property>
        </bean>
    </property>
</bean>
</beans>
```

With `JobLauncherTestUtils` wired up, you use it to execute your step in the test's `testCarProcessingStep` method. On completion of executing the step, you verify two things: using the regular JUnit assertions, you verify that the step completed successfully; and you verify that the file that was created is the same as the one read in. Using JUnit to do something like this would be a very painful exercise; but because file manipulation is at the core of the Spring Batch framework, Spring Batch includes the ability to assert that two files are the same. The `AssertFile` utility class lets you compare two files in their entirety or just the line counts of two files. This is a very helpful tool in your testing arsenal.

The only thing left that you could possibly test is the entire job. In the next section, you move to true functional testing and test a batch job from end to end.

Testing a Job

Testing an entire job can be a daunting task. Some jobs, as you've seen, can be quite complex and require setup that isn't easy to do. However, the benefits of being able to automate the execution and result verification can't be ignored. Thus you're strongly encouraged to attempt to automate testing at this level whenever possible. This section looks at how to use `JobLauncherTestUtils` to execute an entire job for testing purposes.

In this example you use the same `carJob` as in the previous section, but this time you test the entire job instead of the encompassing step. To do so, the `JobLauncherTestUtils` class is again your friend and does all the hard work. Because you have only a single job configured in your context, all you need to do to execute the job is call `JobLauncherTestUtils`' `launchJob()` method. In this case, you call the variant that accepts a `JobParameters` object so you can pass in the locations of the input and output files you wish to process.

The `launchJob()` method returns a JobExecution object. This, as you know from Chapter 4, gives you access to just about everything that happened during the run of your job. You can check the `ExitStatus` of the job and each step, and you can verify the number of items read, processed, written, skipped, and so on by each step. The list goes on. The importance of being able to programmatically test jobs at this level with the ease that Spring Batch provides can't be overstated. Listing 12-20 shows the test method for testing `carJob` as a whole.

Listing 12-20. Testing carJob

...

```java
@Test
public void testCarJob() throws Exception {
    JobExecution execution = jobLauncherUtils.launchJob(getParams());

    assertEquals(ExitStatus.COMPLETED, execution.getExitStatus());

    StepExecution stepExecution =
            execution.getStepExecutions().iterator().next();
    assertEquals(ExitStatus.COMPLETED, stepExecution.getExitStatus());
    assertEquals(5, stepExecution.getReadCount());
    assertEquals(5, stepExecution.getWriteCount());

    assertFileEquals(new ClassPathResource(INPUT_FILE),
            new FileSystemResource(OUTPUT_FILE));
}

private JobParameters getParams() {
    return new JobParametersBuilder().addString("carFile", INPUT_FILE)
            .addString("outputFile", "file:/" + OUTPUT_FILE)
            .toJobParameters();
}
```

...

As Listing 12-20 shows, executing your job requires only a single line of code. From there, you're able to verify the ExitStatus of the job, any steps in the job, and the read and write count for those steps, and also assert that the results of the job match what you expected.

Summary

From unit-testing a single method in any component in your system all the way to executing batch jobs programmatically, you've covered the vast majority of testing scenarios you may encounter as a batch programmer. This chapter began with an overview of the JUnit test framework and the Mockito mock-object frameworks for unit testing. You then explored integration testing using the classes and annotations provided by Spring, including executing tests in transactions. Finally, you looked at Spring Batch–specific testing by executing components that are defined in the step scope, individual steps in jobs, and finally the entire job.

Index

■ P